A
WORLD OF
IDEAS

*ESSENTIAL READINGS
FOR COLLEGE WRITERS*

ALSO WRITTEN OR EDITED BY LEE A. JACOBUS

Improving College Reading, 1967, 1972, 1978, 1983
Aesthetics and the Arts, 1968
Issues and Response, 1968, 1972
Developing College Reading, 1970, 1979
Seventeen from Everywhere: Short Stories from around the World, 1971
Poems in Context (with William Moynihan), 1974
John Cleveland: A Critical Study, 1975
The Humanities through the Arts (with F. David Martin), 1975, 1978, 1982
The Sentence Book, 1976, 1980
The Paragraph and Essay Book, 1977
Sudden Apprehension: Aspects of Knowledge in Paradise Lost, 1976
Longman Anthology of American Drama, 1982
Humanities: The Evolution of Values, (forthcoming)

A
WORLD OF
IDEAS

ESSENTIAL READINGS
FOR COLLEGE WRITERS

EDITED BY
LEE A. JACOBUS
University of Connecticut

A Bedford Book
ST. MARTIN'S PRESS · NEW YORK

For information, write St. Martin's Press, Inc.
175 Fifth Avenue, New York, N.Y. 10010
Editorial offices, Bedford Books of St. Martin's Press
165 Marlborough Street, Boston, MA 02116

ISBN: 0-312-89219-5

Typography and cover design: Anna Post
Portraits: Anatoly Dverin

ACKNOWLEDGMENTS

Aristotle. "The Aim of Man." From *The Nichomachean Ethics*, trans. Martin
Ostwald, copyright © 1962 by the Bobbs-Merrill Company, Inc. Reprinted
by permission of the publisher.

*Acknowledgments and copyrights continue at the back of the book on page
613, which constitutes an extension of the copyright page.*

PREFACE

———— ❦ ————

This collection evolved from my twenty-one-year experience of helping freshman composition students develop their writing abilities. I soon found that students welcomed exposure to complex and influential ideas, like the ones I have included here. Furthermore, teaching students to write from such material proved not more difficult, but easier than teaching from more contemporary, popular sources. Serious ideas demanded students' response as well as their attention.

The twenty-eight essays collected here differ significantly from those in most anthologies for writers. Each essay was chosen for its importance, for its range of thought, and for its capacity to sustain discussion and stimulate writing. Discoursing on the general subjects of politics, psychology, science, philosophy, and art, the authors include Plato, Aristotle, Machiavelli, Rousseau, Jefferson, Marx, Darwin, Nietzsche, Freud, and Camus, among others. The essays are longer than those in most anthologies simply because developing a complex idea requires more than a few pages. Still, each essay has been calculated to represent a day's classwork—although most, of course, could command more attention.

Because this book is a text for writers, not just a stimulating collection of ideas, I have included copious aids to help students grasp the authors' thought and—more important—to help them become better writers. A general introduction, called "Writing about Ideas," provides students with guidance on understanding as they read, responding to ideas, and developing their own thoughts in writing. This chapter also introduces the rhetorical concepts and terms that will appear in later discussions of the essays: such basic terms as *definition* and *comparison;* such rhetorical structures as *narrative, exposition, encomium,* and *argument;* and such figurative language as *imagery, simile,* and *metaphor.*

Each subject, and thus each section, is introduced with an overview of its authors, their ideas, and their rhetorical strategies. Each essay also has its own lengthy introduction, providing background on the author and his or her ideas together with a specific analysis of the essay's rhetorical structure and strategies. All the essays offer useful models for writing, and the essay introductions show students how they can learn from Frederick Douglass, for instance, about constructing a narrative, or from Charles Darwin about using examples, or from Bertrand Russell about using imagery and metaphor.

Following each essay are both discussion questions and writing assignments. The discussion questions help students focus on the major issues of the essays and demonstrate their understanding of those issues. The assignments help students practice the rhetorical strategies illustrated in the selection in varied essays of their own, from brief personal statements to longer works requiring some research. And as the students' responses are guided by the discussion questions, they may also discover additional topics for writing.

The book ends with suggestions for additional readings about the authors and their ideas, and an index of the rhetorical terms used throughout. A separate, complimentary instructor's manual anticipates problems that may arise in teaching each essay, discusses the questions and writing assignments, and provides additional writing assignments, many of them linking one selection with another.

Although the writers collected in this book have shaped Western thought and still influence the way we think, few of them claimed their ideas to be original. What they could claim is a level of rhetorical skill that makes their thinking forceful. What they demonstrate repeatedly is that competent management of rhetorical strategies and techniques actually leads to more competent thinking. Effective writing fuses ideas and rhetoric.

I want to thank Charles Christensen for urging me on with this book; Joan Feinberg and Sylvan Barnet for thoughtful responses to the manuscript; Frank Kirk for his insightful and demanding copyediting; Timothy J. Kenslea for coordinating the production of the book; Jack

Davis for his encouragement; and Joanna Jacobus and Susan Gillgren for their help in gathering and ordering parts of the manuscript. I particularly want to thank Anatoly Dverin for his splendid portraits, which he made especially for this book. I wish to dedicate the book to the students and teachers who use it.

CONTENTS

———⌗———

WRITING ABOUT IDEAS: An Introduction to Rhetoric   **1**

PART ONE
THE POLITICAL AND
SOCIAL ORDER
– 35 –

NICCOLÒ MACHIAVELLI   The Qualities of the Prince   **39**

Discussing politics and behavior, Machiavelli raises important ethical issues about ends and means.

JEAN JACQUES ROUSSEAU   The Origin of Civil Society   **57**

In analyzing the relation between the governed and the governors, Rousseau speculates about the natural human state and stresses a revolutionary view: equality before the law.

THOMAS JEFFERSON   The Declaration of Independence   **79**

Jefferson's definition of the limits of power establishes the reasons for rebelling against improper authority.

ix

MARY WOLLSTONECRAFT   Pernicious Effects Which Arise
from the Unnatural Distinctions
Established in Society   89

In a seminal work protesting discrimination against women, Wollstonecraft raises issues of property rights, class, and law.

KARL MARX   The Communist Manifesto   107

Marx's responses to the general complaints against Communism provide a look at the theoretical politics of Communist nations.

HENRY DAVID THOREAU   A Plea for Captain John Brown   135

In pleading for the life of a violent abolitionist, Thoreau explores the morality of slavery and of protesting against immoral laws.

FREDERICK DOUGLASS   *from* The Narrative of the Life
of Frederick Douglass,
an American Slave   163

With acute self-awareness, Douglass tells of his escape from slavery and his emergence as an eloquent speaker for freedom.

MARTIN LUTHER KING, Jr.   Letter from Birmingham Jail   181

Comparing his mission with that of the early Christians, King provides a careful argument for nonviolent action on behalf of racial equality.

PART TWO

PSYCHOLOGY AND THE
NATURE OF HUMANKIND

– 203 –

FRIEDRICH NIETZSCHE   Apollonianism and Dionysianism   209

In a brilliant introduction to a lasting cultural dichotomy, Nietzsche contrasts the spirits of two Greek deities: the cool, intellectual Apollo, god of music, and the passionate, irrational Dionysos, god of wine.

WILLIAM JAMES   The Reality of the Unseen   229

James analyzes the sources of knowledge, considering the religious view that reliance on the senses is not the only way to know things.

SIGMUND FREUD   Infantile Sexuality   255

The controversial crux of Freud's sexual theories appears in this analysis of sexual development and its implications for the child's personality.

CARL JUNG   The Mother Archetype   277

Jung explains the mother archetype, an unconscious idea of the mother that finds universal expression in both individuals and cultures, and describes the psychological complexes that arise from failure to accept or understand the archetype.

B. F. SKINNER   What Is Man?   293

Expanding on his behaviorist view that we are largely the products of environmental conditioning, Skinner asserts that we must now forego personal freedoms in order to secure the general happiness of the community.

PART THREE

SCIENCE AND THE
CHANGING WORLD

– 321 –

FRANCIS BACON   The Four Idols   327

In a pioneering analysis, Bacon investigates the natural human prejudgments that impede learning and scientific discovery.

CHARLES DARWIN   Natural Selection   345

Drawing on observations of plants and animals, Darwin suggests that species undergo random, accidental, and useful changes because the fittest individuals mate and reproduce.

LINCOLN BARNETT   Einstein's Relativity   367

In a clear introduction to the work of the pioneering physicist, Barnett shows how both science and our sense of reality have been radically altered by Einstein's quantum theory and theory of relativity.

ALFRED NORTH WHITEHEAD   Religion and Science   391

While acknowledging that religion and science appear to be in conflict, Whitehead argues that their respective truths are actually quite separate.

THOMAS S. KUHN   The Essential Tension: Tradition and
Innovation in Scientific Research   **409**

In analyzing approaches to scientific research, Kuhn argues that most
creative scientists, paradoxically, are not eccentric thinkers but traditionalists in their training and in their acceptance of current scientific theories.

PART FOUR

PHILOSOPHY
ANCIENT AND MODERN
– 429 –

PLATO   The Allegory of the Cave   **435**

Plato's allegory compares unenlightened people, doomed to accept the
material world as the highest reality, to prisoners chained to the wall
of a cave, doomed to accept shadows on the wall as their reality.
Those who would be free must learn to value higher spiritual truths.

ARISTOTLE   The Aim of Man   **449**

In searching for the highest good, Aristotle proclaims, humans should
seek happiness. But the highest happiness is that of the community,
not just of the individual.

BERTRAND RUSSELL   A Free Man's Worship   **473**

Russell maintains that those who are unfree will worship power—
whether the natural power of the sun or the political power of people—
whereas the truly free will value the most human qualities of beauty
and spiritual goodness.

JOHN DEWEY   Some Historical Factors in
Philosophical Reconstruction   **487**

Considering Francis Bacon's aphorism that knowledge is power,
Dewey explores how scientific knowledge has given us power over our
world and how philosophy itself can be more scientific.

ALBERT CAMUS   The Myth of Sisyphus   507

*Using an allegory from classical mythology, Camus confronts the
meaninglessness of human existence and demonstrates the potential
for hope and dignity even in times of despair.*

PART FIVE

ARTS AND LETTERS
– 515 –

GEORGE SANTAYANA   The Nature of Beauty   521

*Maintaining that values are central to the arts, Santayana shows that
the connection between aesthetics and ethics is a connection between
a philosophy of preference—choosing the beautiful—and a philosophy
of avoidance—choosing not to behave badly.*

GYORGY KEPES   Comments on Art   547

*We have lost our capacity to see the world as a unified whole, Kepes
argues, but by contemplating the arts we can restore harmony to our
inner lives and unify our experiences.*

SUSANNE K. LANGER   Expressiveness   559

*Langer maintains that the arts are the educators of the emotions be-
cause they force us to confront emotion directly rather than through
the medium of language.*

A. C. BRADLEY   Poetry for Poetry's Sake   575

*In a masterful discussion of the age-old tension between subject and
form—is a poem great because of the subject or because of the treatment of the subject?—Bradley establishes their essential unity.*

T. S. ELIOT   Tradition and the Individual Talent   599

*Eliot's classic essay discusses how the modern poet, fully aware of the
culture's poetic tradition, can affect that tradition through his or her
own poetic achievement.*

SUGGESTIONS FOR FURTHER READING   615

INDEX OF RHETORICAL TERMS   633

A
WORLD OF
IDEAS

ESSENTIAL READINGS
FOR COLLEGE WRITERS

WRITING
ABOUT IDEAS

An Introduction
to Rhetoric

WRITING ABOUT IDEAS comprises both a thought process and a writing process, requiring study, analysis, and comprehension. When a written work confronts us with fresh or different ideas, we often have difficulty sorting them out and deciding whether to accept or to challenge them. Naturally we must expend energy and thought to determine the nature of important ideas—to be sure that we do indeed understand them—before we know whether, and to what extent, to accept or reject them. The act of writing in response to the works of such distinguished and influential figures as Thomas Jefferson, Karl Marx, and T. S. Eliot is complicated by the fact that we may or may not be predisposed to accept what they say. If we find that we do wish to accept their views, we may want to write a personal amplification of these ideas which would include corroboration of them based on our own perceptions and experiences. If we do not wish to accept them, we may choose to offer a counterproposal, a view or position that criticizes the ideas that we have read and discussed in the classroom. There will be more opportunities to examine the ideas expressed in the selections presented in this book through referring to the writing assignments, which permit us to offer certain modifications based upon our own analyses. Writers whose ideas are important and carefully developed will generate rather than stifle thought. Such thought is best expressed through the process of refinement we call writing.

READING FOR IDEAS

Knowing how to read carefully and attentively is essential. The writings in this collection are not simplified in any way, nor are they intended to be difficult. Each writer is concerned with communicating ideas to people who care about ideas, and each is skilled in the techniques of rhetoric which make thought both clear and persuasive. One consequence of such skill is that a writer may seem to have "said it all" in regard to his or her subject. Many readers are so overwhelmed by persuasive prose that they feel there is no room for their own thoughts. Careful use of reading techniques should help to solve two problems: (1) how to ensure a thorough understanding of what the author is saying and (2) how to develop ideas based on the author's work so that we will have something to say in response. This kind of reading is sometimes called studying; the following suggestions should increase the efficiency of studying these selections.

Yet, even the most efficient reading of these works is likely to produce a limited understanding because it will reflect only one individual's view. Classroom discussion is an indispensable aid to developing a thorough understanding of works of the kind presented in this book. Everyone has a slightly different point of view, a slightly different understanding. Frequently, another person's response to a complex work will help expand our own response by providing an intellectual context, a fresh attitude, or an unexpected connection that can make an otherwise obscure point clear and significant for us. Class discussion is a critical part of the study process; it becomes group analysis.

Annotating a Text

Annotations are your own notes made in response to reading. They can take many forms, but they usually consist of underlinings and comments in the margins (which is one reason there are generous margins in this book). By writing in the margins, we keep track of our thoughts as well as of the questions we may wish to raise during a class discussion. Annotations are a record of our responses as well as a stimulus to further response; they can be generated both by individual reading and by general discussion. Like other forms of writing, they record our thoughts.

One purpose of annotation is to keep track of the development of the author's thought; another is to record our own responses as we read. Annotating is not a passive act. It is also not an act that can be reduced to a formula. The thought processes of each one of us are complex, and because each of us has a unique background and temperament, our annotations will always be different from those of others. The importance of annotation cannot be overstressed. Most serious readers do not feel that they are reading at all unless they have a pen or pencil at hand to make notes with as they read. These notes act as a guide to ideas as they develop: they identify important ideas and locate them for ready reference when you are ready to write in response to them. Without annotations, one is reduced to having to skim vaguely through a piece looking for key points that were once clear and apparent but that, after a few moments, sink back again into the fabric of the prose and become virtually invisible. Annotation is the conquest of the invisible; it makes the most important ideas readily visible, and thus available.

Although annotation is not a process that everyone can carry out in the same fashion, there are certain fundamental and obvious rules that apply to clear annotation. Following are some of the most important rules:

1. Always read with a sharp pencil or a reliable pen in hand.
2. Begin by underlining the most important sentence or sentences in each paragraph.
3. Underline key words, which may appear with frequency.
4. Underline any words you may want to look up in a dictionary later.
5. Write in the margins: begin by making short notes that summarize what a paragraph says or what its main subject is.
6. Ask questions. Questions are of two kinds:
   a. Questions of understanding, such as, "What does this sentence really mean?"
   b. Questions of the material, such as, "Why doesn't Machiavelli take the concept of human decency into account here?" "How can Marx contradict what he just said in paragraph 4?"
7. Make statements. Talk to yourself and the author: "I think there's something wrong here." "Rousseau says this, too, but he means something else; look it up." "I agree—and there's even more to it

than she says." "This is important in psychology, not just politics." "My view is the opposite."

Since the task of annotation is different for everyone, the results will vary widely even when one applies these rules. They will vary not only because we are all different but also because we bring to the text different moods, attention spans, and demands. The following example demonstrates one way of going about this task, based on the first three paragraphs, and part of the fourth and eighth paragraphs, of a relatively demanding essay, Aristotle's "The Aim of Man," from his *Nichomachean Ethics*.

Definition of the Good

all things aim at the good.

Every art and every "scientific investigation," as well as every action and "purposive choice," appears to aim at some good; hence the good has rightly been declared to be that at which all things aim. A difference is observable, to be sure, among the several ends:

What does he mean by activities and products?

some of them are activities, while others are products over and above the activities that produce them. Wherever there are certain ends over and above the actions themselves, it is the nature of such products to be better than the activities.

Ends: health, victory, wealth.

As actions and arts and sciences are of many kinds, there must be a corresponding diversity of ends: health, for example, is the aim of medicine, ships of

Note military references

shipbuilding, victory of military strategy, and wealth of domestic economics. Where several such arts fall under some one faculty—as bridle-making and the other arts concerned with horses' equipment fall under horsemanship, while this in turn along with all other military matters falls under the head of strategy,

Aim of master art is most important.

and similarly in the case of other arts—the aim of the master art is always more choiceworthy than the aims of its subordinate arts, inasmuch as these are pursued for its sake. And this holds equally good whether the end in view is just the activity itself or something distinct from the activity, as in the case of the sciences above mentioned.

Primacy of Statecraft

What end do we wish on its own account?

If in all our conduct, then, <u>there is some end that we wish on its own</u> account, choosing everything else as a means to it; if, that is to say, we do not choose everything as a means to something else (for at that rate we should go on *ad infinitum*, and our desire would be left empty and vain); then clearly this one

What is the highest goal?

end must be the good—even, indeed, <u>the highest good.</u> Will not a knowledge of it, then, have an important influence on our lives? Will it not better enable us to hit the right mark, like archers who have a definite target to aim at? If so, we must try to comprehend, in outline at least, what that highest end is, and to which of the sciences or arts it belongs.

Statecraft is the master art.

Evidently the art or science in question must be the most absolute and most authoritative of all. <u>State-craft</u> answers best to this description. . . .

What is it that we declare to be the aim of state-craft; or, in other words, what is the highest of all realizable goods? As to its name there is pretty general agreement: the majority of men, as well as the cultured few, speak of it as happiness; and they would maintain that to live well and to do well are the same thing as to be happy.

No one reading these paragraphs for the first time is apt to feel that everything that Aristotle has said in them is clear. There are likely to be many questions in the margins, and some of these questions may not be cleared up even after the entire piece has been read. Those questions should be brought up in a general class discussion. Nevertheless, if we keep track of the observable important points that Aristotle makes—the fact that he thinks all things aim at the good, that the good can be an activity or a product of activity, that there are many kinds of activities with many different ends, that the highest good ought to be of greatest interest to us, and that the highest good must relate to statecraft (what we call politics)—we will be well prepared to understand the work.

Our annotations highlight the important points. They also record our own reactions, such as our surprise that Aristotle put so much stress on politics. Anyone who studies this piece is likely to record surprises, questions, and observations that differ from those of others.

One warning concerning annotation may be obvious but should be kept in mind: annotating can be overdone. If, on the one hand, it is useless to read most of the works presented here without annotation, it may be almost as useless to overannotate them. When there are so many underlinings, so many questions, and so many observations that the pages begin to look like an unweeded garden, the result is going to be confusion rather than enlightenment. Moderation—Aristotle's most famous advice—is the key. Annotate for the important, not the trivial. Remember what the end of annotation is: to retrieve the author's thoughts as well as your own thoughts, questions, responses, and observations when studying the passage.

Reading and Writing Summaries

Many of the writers in this collection pause every so often to provide a summary of what they have said so far. Generally, the summary appears toward the end of passages that are unusually difficult or that have covered a great deal of material. Not only does the summary explain what has been said; it sometimes also indicates the direction the essay will take or has been taking. Any effective summary makes our work of reading and studying easier because it provides us with a double check on our comprehension. For that reason, it is wise to highlight the summaries as one reads, making them visible for reference later on. Summaries are especially useful for quotation, since they present the substance of what has been said in a succinct manner.

Thus, we may consider that highlighting passages—sentences or paragraphs—that summarize a writer's points is a special kind of annotation. By studying them after the first reading of a piece, one can often clarify what could remain obscure.

In preparation for writing about any given selection, one of the most useful tasks we can perform is writing a summary of it as a whole or of that part of it which we wish to focus upon. Such a summary can often be developed from our annotations, since in many cases our responses will guide us to what the subject or point of any paragraph is. The way to produce the summary is to jot down the most important point or points made in each paragraph as one reads. Some may not find it useful to develop a summary from annotations. If that is the case, the best method is to use a notebook to record the substance of each paragraph, using short sentences and the author's key terms. It is important to remember that the summary should not include our own responses or opinions but simply focus on the essence of what the author is saying.

A summary of the first paragraphs of what Aristotle has said so far follows. It was produced from annotations and a rereading of the passage. It relies on Aristotle's terms and makes use of simple, short, and direct sentences.

> The good is what everything aims at. Some ends are activities and some are products, and sometimes the products are better than the activities. Any activity (art and science) will have several different ends, but the end of the master art -- the most important activity -- will be the most important end. Therefore, it is essential to begin by establishing what the most important art is. That way, we will know what the most important end is and therefore what the highest good is. Statecraft is the most authoritative art, so the highest good has to be related to it. The highest of all realizable goods is the aim of statecraft: happiness.

Another reader may summarize these paragraphs a bit differently, emphasizing other points or terms. But any person's summary will be an important guide for that person when he or she writes about these paragraphs. This summary points to the need to define the term "ends" with care. Since Aristotle does not do that, a topic for a brief essay has been discovered by means of working up a summary. Summarizing each paragraph is excessive, but summarizing logical groupings of paragraphs will often make the work of comprehension and retrieval much easier than it might otherwise be.

Apart from the summary's usefulness for our understanding of complex pieces, it is extremely useful to us when we write about those works. Just as our authors often pause at certain logical points to summarize what they have written, we too can seize the opportunity to provide an occasional summary. When writing a longer essay, it is particularly desirable to pause at appropriate points to summarize what one has established as aids to the reader's understanding. Writing a summary is a useful exercise even if it never actually appears in the composition!

Inventorying

Annotating and summarizing are important activities that prepare us to write about an essay or other work. Just as important is the act of inventorying, which is the process of going through an essay to look for relevant quotes or for information concerning the issue or subject that interests us. Some of the suggestions for essays following the selections ask for an inventory of a specific kind. With regard to the paragraphs quoted from Aristotle, it would be useful to inventory his military references. Such an inventory would consist of a list of each important reference. Doing such an inventory is essential both to making a clear analysis of, and to arriving at sound conclusions about, his concern with military matters in that it reveals to us the nature and the extent of his interest. Inventorying is the act of gathering from a work the basic evidence we will depend upon to build our own case. Writing, in this sense, is the process of gathering evidence and drawing inferences and conclusions. Inventorying is the first step in this process.

One way to inventory a work is to gather items that form a pattern or reveal a deep concern. Another is to list often used key terms, such as "the good," "ends," "activities," or "products." The fact is that as we read we are influenced by everything, even those things we are not fully conscious of at first. Inventorying key terms can be extremely helpful in enabling us to see patterns that might otherwise have escaped our attention.

There are other kinds of inventory. For instance, it would be very informative to list every instance of definition in Aristotle, or to consider how often he stops to define a term or concept. It would be very interesting to examine the kinds of terms Aristotle defines, just as it would be to consider those he does not define. The presence or absence of definitions might be a key to the care with which he approaches the task of making his thought clear. Writers who do not define their terms are often unable or unwilling to do so, either because they do not understand them themselves, or because they do not want their readers to realize how faulty their thought is.

One kind of inventory records the types of figurative language the writer uses. This kind of inventory is a way of revealing the pattern (or the lack of a pattern) formed by use of such language. Figurative language—imagery, simile, metaphor, symbolism, irony, and other types of figures of speech—is designed to have an emotional effect upon the reader. Imagery is the use of vivid word pictures that depend upon a concrete sensuous experience—something we can see, hear, smell, taste, or touch. A simile is an explicit comparison using the terms "like" or "as." A metaphor is a form of comparison in which one thing is identified with another, to a greater or lesser degree, without employing words such as "like" or "as." Metaphors are often expressed so subtly that only close study will reveal their presence. Symbolism is a form of comparison in which one thing is made to stand for another, as in Plato's cave, which stands for the human condition and implies the limits of human perception. Usually an author uses symbolism without telling us; like most figurative language, it works subliminally in our unconscious. In other words, it affects our emotions directly. Irony is saying one thing but meaning another. It is often expressed in the form of the antithesis—with the first part of the expression in a positive tone and the second part in a negative tone. Thoreau, for example, explains that most people are glad to go to church, just so long as they do not also have to behave like good Christians.

In the paragraphs quoted from Aristotle, the use of figurative language is not extensive because his appeal is not specifically emotional. But there are more references to military subjects than one might expect in a work entitled "The Aim of Man." His references to shipbuilding and to victory in paragraph 2 are flat statements, not figurative. Yet they are also comparisons (not similes or metaphors) which take on a special positive value because they are mentioned in the same context as health and wealth, two positive values that Aristotle's audience would naturally have approved. Then we note that bridle making and horsemanship also fall under the heading of military matters, which in turn falls under strategy. When one adds the simile (comparing us to military archers) in paragraph 3—which urges us to contemplate the highest end (statecraft) because it will "enable us to hit the right mark, like archers who have a definite target to aim at"—we begin to observe a preoccupation with military concepts. A simple inventory, a compilation of separate instances, reveals that to us.

Making sense out of what the inventory exemplifies for us is yet another matter, however, a matter of imagination and creativity. Once we have inventoried a list of items related to one another by some subject, use of language, and so forth, we have a body of evidence from which we must begin to draw inferences. Because that is a challenging task, it needs both the guidance of class discussion and the discipline gained by experience.

By way of summary, let us consider what the inventory can be:

1. A list of often repeated words or phrases.
2. A list of subjects often referred to.
3. A pattern of references, such as descriptions, definitions, or things of the same kind.

4. Frequent use of figurative language, such as imagery, irony, simile, metaphor, and symbolism.
5. Recurrent expressions or verbal techniques.

The study questions following each selection often ask that the selection be inventoried for such things as references to specific kinds of people, situations, ideas, or concerns. The most immediate value of the inventory is to make us conscious of patterns that are apparent only when their scattered elements are gathered together. The inventory is the intellectual instrument of gathering. It helps us get ready to write because it helps us gather our thoughts.

Developing Questions

Questions emerge from partial understanding, careful observations, and often from confusion as well. It is important to ask a question even when it may seem to be a dumb question. Socrates often played dumb with his students. He always asked them questions, some of which sounded fairly simpleminded. But he knew that knowledge arose from the process of asking and answering questions. Socrates said that the wisest person was the person who felt that he knew nothing. And if that observation still holds true, it means that none of us should fear asking any questions of the texts that appear in this book.

Questions of the Text. The first type of question ought to direct itself toward understanding the text itself. For instance, one of the first questions that should be asked of Aristotle's paragraphs is what he means by the term "art." It is obvious that he does not mean a fine art, such as painting. The context seems to mean something broader than that and something that requires skill in performance. The original Greek word for art was *techne,* which is the root of our words "technique," "technology," and the like. An art, then, is an activity demanding skill, such as shipbuilding or statecraft; the term also includes the sciences.

Another type of question explores the meaning of specific terms: "What is an end?" A trip to the dictionary—and most of us need to make the trip regularly—will help to clarify the fact that an end is a purpose or aim. Aristotle's examples of ends—health, victory, and wealth—help us understand this term. Eventually he will add "happiness" to this list, but it takes him a while to get there.

Questions of Inquiry. After questions of the text are dealt with, we may proceed to questions of inquiry. We want to inquire about Aristotle's purposes or perhaps about his anxieties. Our inventory revealed the fact that military references pervade this text. Why? That question may reveal something important to us. One answer is relatively simple: Aristotle lived in a period in which Athens was threatened by other, warlike states. In order to survive, Athens had to be particularly skillful in the art of war. Another answer is perhaps subtler. Since Aristotle's aim is to convince his readers that statecraft is the science or art to which the highest end belongs, he gives his argument a little extra "body English" by using metaphors that relate to statecraft. We well know that Athens could not have survived—that statecraft could not have survived—unless the Athenians had knowledge of the techniques of warfare. Thus, by inventorying these references, we can gain some insight into Aristotle's deepest concerns. Note, though, that Aristotle does not make war the science or art to which the highest end belongs; rather, warfare is subordinate to statecraft, just as bridle making is subordinate to military matters. As we make these observations, we make some progress toward understanding the aim of man, which must be, like everything else, directed "at some good."

The final question we ask as we read, then, will be: "At what does man aim?" Keeping that question in mind—and any other questions we develop as we go along—will help us generate our own ideas for writing in response to Aristotle's ideas as set forth in the paragraphs quoted. Ideas develop out of questions. That is why, like Socrates, some teachers put so much emphasis on them. They will even go so far as to say that the questions a student asks are more important than the answers the student gives to questions. That is true. Consider how many different essays on Aristotle might arise from just these basic questions of inquiry:

1. Does everything really aim at the good?
2. Are some products better than the activities that produce them?
3. Is statecraft the highest science or art?
4. Do we need to know the most important science or art to know the highest good?
5. Is one good higher than another?
6. Is there a highest good?
7. Do most people have a sense of what the highest good is?
8. Is happiness still considered to be the highest good?
9. Do the happiness of the individual and the "happiness" of the state conflict?

Innumerable questions may arise even from the few paragraphs quoted. The good writer will gather them in abundance in the acts of reading and studying.

WRITING ABOUT IDEAS

Writing about the ideas presented in these works, or about your own ideas as stimulated by them, demands careful preparation. The processes of annotating, summarizing, and inventorying are carried out prior to writing; if they are carried out well, the job of writing will be easier than it otherwise would be. Once these tasks have been carried out, we move to the writing itself. These tasks have to relate carefully to the work of writing, however; otherwise, much effort may result in little reward.

Again, limiting ourselves to the few paragraphs of Aristotle previously quoted, we can begin to illustrate some of the next stages of writing. Finding a workable subject is of first importance. The suggestions for essays following each selection supply such subjects, although other subjects may suggest themselves in the course of reading and thinking about a selection. Workable subjects for an essay based only on the paragraphs of Aristotle might be:

1. What kinds of activities are ends in themselves?
2. What products are more important than the activities that produce them?
3. What is the relationship between happiness and the art of state-craft?

These subjects for an essay have been posed as questions because one thing a brief essay does well is to answer a simple and direct question. These are very abstract subjects, however, and might present special difficulties in writing. To make an essay on one of these subjects effective, one would have to provide a considerable number of concrete examples.

Other, more concrete subjects for an essay might be:

1. Politics is neither the most authoritative nor the highest art.
2. Aristotle's frequent military references reveal an anxiety in his thinking about the aim of man.
3. The pursuit of happiness is the pursuit of the highest good.
4. Aristotle seems to value the state more highly than we do today.

Each of these statements involves several important things:

1. Identifying a limited subject that can be treated in a brief essay.
2. Deriving the subject from the essay itself.
3. Taking a stand on a specific issue.

Choosing a subject for writing involves a willingness to defend a view as well as the ability to inventory the work for evidence to support that view. The choices that follow each selection move the writer toward taking a position—there is room for many different personal views—and then finding evidence to support that position. Some suggestions for writing ask that a personal stand be taken on a controversial issue. Some ask for corroboration of the author's opinions or findings from personal experience. Some ask for an analysis of the author's approach to writing. Each suggestion, it must be stressed, should serve as a model for focusing one's thought and attention.

Stating the Thesis

The first stage in writing an essay is usually devoted to stating the thesis, which tells one's audience what one intends to accomplish. The workable subjects for an essay have sometimes been presented in a form that is close to a thesis statement and sometimes in the form of related questions. Some refinement is still needed, however. Consider these thesis statements (sometimes groups of statements) developed from the subjects listed above:

1. Politics may have been the most authoritative and highest art when Aristotle wrote, but because of the corruption of high officials and the deception of modern political leaders politics has lost its high position.
2. The many references to military matters in these paragraphs from *The Nichomachean Ethics* reveal a remarkable anxiety on Aristotle's part. Since in his time the fate of civilization depended on military skill, it is clear that even when considering ethical matters, his thinking is affected—and possibly distorted—by concerns about war.
3. Perhaps it was the same in Aristotle's time, but today it seems that the pursuit of happiness has become equivalent to the pursuit of the soft job; the big paycheck; the fancy car; the easy, mindless life; and the acquisition of useless objects. It is the pursuit of material goods.

4. Athens was a young city-state when Aristotle wrote. It was threatened by invaders and uncertain about the success of its own democratic ideals. But it was exciting and experimental, and Aristotle could express his enthusiasm for it more positively than people today can do about their own nations, which have possibly become a bit tired.

The thesis statement represents a job to be done in the essay. Each such statement focuses on a single job; by doing so, it brings the larger subject under better control. For instance, the first example will lead to an essay focusing on how modern politics has lost its positive value in comparison with Athenian politics. It will require some study of Athenian politics. The second example, on military matters, could focus on how the threats to Athens' security created considerable anxiety. The third example could concentrate on defining the pursuit of happiness totally in terms of materialistic values. The last example could focus on how it is possible for one to take an older, settled state for granted more than one would a new and experimental state.

The thesis, clearly stated, helps establish focus and unity. The temptation to be vague and fuzzy is always present. But, if the writer's focus is clear from the start, the writing ought to be clear. Any of the above suggestions should produce a brief essay that has both a reasonable focus and unity. Unity is achieved by the willingness to concentrate on one subject only, such as the significance of the military references.

Being Concrete in Abstract Situations: Using Examples

Most of the selections in this book have a high level of abstraction simply because ideas are by nature abstract. Aristotle himself is highly abstract in "The Aim of Man," and he praises abstract reasoning because it is so specifically human. Other animals cannot reason. It is our province alone, and therefore Aristotle believed that it was of the highest importance. That fact poses some serious problems both for him and for us, however.

Being too abstract is often a basic problem with many writers. Ideas such as the aim of statecraft, the highest good, the end of a given activity are very difficult to comprehend unless they are made less abstract. Aristotle offers us a lesson in this regard. His first paragraph is very abstract; but in his second paragraph, when he begins his discussion of ends, he immediately says, "health, for example, is the aim of medicine." He offers other examples as well, and although they are not so concrete as to be things that we can see, feel, or witness, they make it easier for us to understand what he means. He mentions bridle making as a way of helping us understand the relationship of activities to products. We are always grateful to any author who gives a concrete example of what is meant by a given abstract statement.

Thus, Aristotle provides us with a guide for our own writing: give good, meaningful examples when discussing complex ideas. Remember that the audience cannot be expected to have the same understanding you have of your subject and will welcome helpful cross-referencing and any details that will make your subject clearer.

Details, in the form of quotations, help as well when referring to a piece in order to comment on it. A careful quotation or group of quotations will usually make abstract points much clearer. For example, when we noted that Aristotle was preoccupied with military concepts, we inventoried his comments for observation. When we have an opinion concerning a text as complex as Aristotle's, it is extremely helpful to quote carefully and then to provide a thorough commentary on the quotation as a way of avoiding the kind of abstract thought that would leave a reader up in the air.

Thus, we can begin to specify some requirements for our own writing:

1. Provide examples from concrete experiences, instances, and references as a means of avoiding too much abstraction.
2. When commenting on a text, provide carefully chosen quotations to illustrate your point.
3. Provide commentary and analysis for the quotations you use. They represent concrete examples; your commentary makes use of them in a concrete fashion.
4. Rely on careful annotation and inventory to help provide specifics, examples, concrete details, and responses to make your writing less abstract.

Examining and Questioning Evidence

The views one may wish to defend regarding the selections in this book must be supported by reference to concrete evidence and reasoning drawn from the pieces themselves. We cannot expect our views to be accepted if they simply state our opinions. A reader expects to be convinced by evidence which is presented in a clear enough fashion so that it can be examined and evaluated.

Evidence comes in many shapes. One of them is a statement from an authority. Were we to find, for instance, that an authority on politics, such as Jean Jacques Rousseau, Jefferson, or Marx, agreed with Aristotle on the primacy of statecraft, a quotation would constitute usable evidence. It would not necessarily be totally conclusive, but it would be supportive. A contradictory view from such an authority would also constitute important evidence.

Facts are evidence, too. Any fact that supports Aristotle's belief that statecraft is of absolute primacy would be important to include in a defense of his belief. For instance, it might be proved that the freedoms which Americans enjoy depend upon the existence of the state as we know it. Further, it might be proved that community colleges, jazz, hoedown, and bluegrass music, abstract expressionist painting and pop art, as well as Rockefeller Center, skyscrapers, baseball, football, basketball, turkey shoots, hamburgers, hot dogs, Coca-Cola, Wheaties, and a great many more typically American phenomena would simply not exist if the state did not exist. If America had remained a British colony, would it have developed its present culture? If the North had lost the Civil War, would not American culture have developed differently? If the Axis powers had won World War II, would we have ever had rhythm and blues, gospel music, or rock 'n' roll? In the process of presenting such evidence, perhaps one would discover that Aristotle did not emphasize the military arts enough. Not only the individual's happiness but also the nature and shape of the culture depend upon the security of the state.

There is also evidence that appears in the form of reasoning. We take a point, examine it, deduce another point from it, and continue until we reach a conclusion. Doing this is a logical process, and it is important to test the logic of any statement that we must depend upon for evidence, or any statement we make ourselves. There is no exact method of conducting such a test, but there are some things we can do. For example, we can use a simple analytic process of treating each element of an argument separately and asking if, by itself, it seems to hold up under examination. We might ask, for instance, whether or not it is really necessary to determine what the master science or art is in order to discover the highest end. Aristotle eventually reasons that statecraft is the master science or art because it "employs all the other sciences, prescribing also what the citizens are to do and what they are to refrain from doing, its aim must embrace the aims of all the others; whence it follows that the aim of statecraft is man's proper good" (para. 4). He reasons that the aim of statecraft is the happiness of the people of the state. Thus, happiness is the greatest good.

We can question such reasoning. Does politics really come before all other arts? Before medicine? Before the practice of religion? Before the activities of scholarship? We might regard Aristotle's concepts with some suspicion, because our concepts of the state and of politics are much different from his. Does the state really make its people happy? Is it possible that people are happy in spite of the efforts of the state, as in Nazi Germany, Idi Amin's Uganda, or other totalitarian states?

Moreover, another interesting problem arises with Aristotle's reasoning in the passage quoted above. Later in paragraph 4 he says that "The securing of even one individual's good is cause for rejoicing, but to secure the good of a nation or of a city-state is nobler and more divine." Aristotle assumes that the interests of the state must supersede those of the individual. To what extent would we accept this statement as the premise of an argument? To what extent would we leave it unexamined? If we wish to test the conclusions of even a writer as important as Aristotle, we will be very skeptical about many assertions.

Some points to remember concerning evidence are:

1. Evidence can be authority, facts, events, personal experiences, concrete details, reasoning; it is never merely one's own opinion.
2. Evidence must be inventoried and presented for examination.
3. Reasoned conclusions in a text should be examined with particular care, just as one's own conclusions must be examined. Reasoned conclusions in a text are often quoted as evidence in an essay.

RHETORICAL ANALYSIS: THE COMMON TOPICS

All the writings in this collection are analyzed for their rhetorical methods. Before one can learn to emulate methods such as the common topics, one must learn to recognize and understand them. They represent five kinds of "arguments" or "approaches" that can be used to develop any subject or idea—on anything we can think about. They are called common because they can be used with any subject. The common topics are:

1. The Topic of Definition
2. The Topic of Comparison

3. The Topic of Relationship
4. The Topic of Circumstance
5. The Topic of Testimony

There is nothing that we wish to write about that cannot be developed by the use of one or more of these topics. All of them apply to everything we can think of. Moreover, each of these topics represents an aspect of natural thought. Even if we did not know of their existence, we would tend to use the topics at one time or another. Therefore, when we use one of these topics consciously we employ a natural intellectual force of great power to which our audience responds in an equally natural way.

The Topic of Definition

The topic of definition is of great value to any kind of prose writing. In our discussion of Aristotle we came back again and again to the fact that certain key terms needed full definition to enable us to comprehend what Aristotle means. Terms like "ends" and "activities" are clear up to a point, but they would be much clearer if there were a full definition of each of them. In our own writing we must keep in mind that our audience relishes good and complete definitions because they make the entire character of our prose clearer.

We must remember, too, that the topic of definition is not limited to dictionary definitions. After all, as a rhetorical technique it existed long before any dictionary existed—possibly thousands of years before! Therefore, it is rather naive to begin a passage which is meant to take advantage of the topic of definition with the worn-out statement, "According to the dictionary the word 'ends' . . ." True, we will sometimes consult a good dictionary, and we will sometimes simply define a term, but this procedure is subordinate to the topic of definition.

This topic, like the others, can be employed in any one of several ways. Its most basic use is defining a key term in the simplest fashion. Another, much broader use is writing a paragraph to explore the term by discussing what people have thought it means, what its functions are, what its purposes are, what it is like or unlike. Its component parts may be discussed and analyzed. Some ideas are very complex, and a paragraph may thus be hardly enough space in which to offer an adequate definition. A good example of definition is in Martin Luther King, Jr.'s, "Letter from Birmingham Jail":

> Let us consider a more concrete example of just and unjust laws. An unjust law is a code that a numerical or power majority group compels a minority group to obey but does not make binding on itself. This is *difference* made legal. By the same token, a just law is a code that a majority compels a minority to follow and that it is willing to follow itself. This is *sameness* made legal. (para. 17)

This is an adequate definition as far as it goes, but most serious ideas need more extensive definition than this passage gives us. And King does go further, providing what Aristotle does in his essay: examples and explanations. Every full definition will profit from the extension of understanding that an explanation and examples will provide. Consider paragraph 18:

> Let me give another explanation. A law is unjust if it is inflicted on a minority that, as a result of being denied the right to vote, had no part in enacting or devising the law. Who can say that the legislature of Alabama which set up that state's segregation laws was democratically elected? Throughout Alabama all sorts of devious methods are used to prevent Negroes from becoming registered voters, and there are some counties in which, even though Negroes constitute a majority of the population, not a single Negro is registered. Can any law enacted under such circumstances be considered democratically structured?

King illustrates the range of the definition here, and he makes us aware of an all-important fact: the topic of definition is not meant to be used simplemindedly. It is complex and capable of great subtlety. Moreover, it is useful not only for organizing a given paragraph—however important it is for us to remember that its usefulness in a paragraph is indeed very great—but also for ordering an entire essay. Aristotle's "The Aim of Man" is in effect an extensive definition of what that aim is.

Since some of the suggestions for essays ask you to use this topic in your own work, and since it is a natural way for any of us to write and think, it is essential to look closely at those who do it well. We can learn from them and, in the process, think more clearly about our subject.

When using the topic of definition, keep in mind that:

1. It can be used to develop a paragraph, a section, or an entire essay.
2. It can be as simple as a dictionary-style statement of meaning.
3. It considers questions of function, purpose, circumstance, and implications for different groups.
4. Explanations and examples make all definitions more complete and effective.

The Topic of Comparison

The topic of comparison is another completely natural operation of the mind. We rarely talk about anything without offering a comparison. We talk about our friends, our teachers, and our families in terms of comparison. We are fascinated by the ways in which our own circumstances compare with those of others. The topic of comparison is an aid when offering definitions because some things are better understood (defined) when they are seen in comparison with other things that resemble them, at least in some ways.

Like the topic of definition, comparison is useful for developing a paragraph, a segment, or an entire essay. Certain essays in part three, "Science and the Changing World," discuss the two theories of light, one of which describes it as particles, the other as waves. Both theories cannot be exclusively correct; light behaves like particles (photons) in some circumstances and like waves in other circumstances. The comparison of the theories is treated by Lincoln Barnett, Alfred North Whitehead, and Thomas S. Kuhn. Comparison is used by all the writers in this collection.

Some authors, of course, make comparison the center of their discussion. For instance, Friedrich Nietzsche in "Apollonianism and Dionysianism" devotes all his energies to comparing the cool, rational intellectualism of the Apollonian forces of ancient Greek culture with the intense, passionate intoxication of the Dionysian forces. He demonstrates that these forces are quite different, that they have different expressions, relate to different arts, demand different personal commitments from each of us—but then he shows us that, different though these forces are, the Greeks needed both of them to be able to be whole persons. Nietzsche's work has been interpreted as defining certain personality types, or certain aspects of personality we all possess, showing us that we may have to give each type of force its due to maintain our mental health. We recognize this best when we see these forces clarified in terms of comparison.

The topic of comparison usually has the following qualities:

1. A definition of two or more elements to be compared. Definition may be by example, explanation, description, or any combination of these.
2. Discussion of the qualities that the elements have in common.
3. Discussion of the qualities that the elements have in distinction from one another.
4. A clear reason for making the comparison or contrast.

The Topic of Relationship

The third common topic is the topic of relationship, which usually translates as a discussion of causes and effects, or of the antecedent and consequence (if this, then that) of specific events. This is a very subtle topic and is not as simple to employ as that of either definition or comparison. Yet it, too, is natural to our way of thinking and writing and is effective when used well. A marvelous example of this topic is in the following portion of paragraph 1 of the selection from Frederick Douglass's autobiography.

> I was quite disappointed at the general appearance of things in New Bedford. The impression which I had received respecting the character and condition of the people of the north, I found to be singularly erroneous. I had very strangely supposed, while in slavery, that few of the comforts, and scarcely any of the luxuries, of life were enjoyed at the north, compared with what were enjoyed by the slaveholders of the south. I probably came to this conclusion from the fact that northern people owned no slaves. I supposed that they were about upon a level with the non-slaveholding population of the south. I knew *they* were exceedingly poor, and I had been accustomed to regard their poverty as the necessary consequence of their being non-slaveholders. I had somehow imbibed the opinion that, in the absence of slaves, there could be no wealth, and very little refinement.

Douglass's conclusions were drawn from an analysis based on his experience in the South: people with slaves had wealth; those without had none. The antecedent (possessing slaves) naturally led in his mind to the consequence (being wealthy). Notice that Douglass is pointing out that his initial conclusion was wrong. We should all be warned that the use of antecedent and consequence, as well as the use of cause and effect—the topic of relationship in general—must be conducted with real attention to the terms and situations we write about. It is easy to be wrong. The nature of the relationships must be worked out thoughtfully.

In "The Essential Tension" Kuhn examines the question of creativity in the sciences. He knows that his audience assumes that free thinking, eccentric ideas—what he refers to here as "divergent thinking"—are essential to making discoveries of a creative sort in science. In other words, divergent thinking is antecedent to discovery. Well, Kuhn pops that bubble quickly. He demonstrates through careful argument—examining numerous instances of antecedent and consequence and cause and effect—that it is most often traditional thinking that produces discoveries. His essay is built around the topic of relationship, the relationship of traditional thought and divergent thought to making discoveries in science. It should be clear that he uses the topics of definition and of comparison in the process of using the topic of relationship. This is normal—for us as well as for a writer like Kuhn—and it only underscores the fact that a mastery of the topics implies an understanding of their subtlety as well as of their simplicity.

Mary Wollstonecraft, in "Pernicious Effects which arise from the Unnatural Distinctions Established in Society," is concerned with the relationship between the unequal treatment of women and their chances of success and happiness in her culture. Her analysis shows that unequal treatment produces unequal—and unhappy—people. Jefferson relies upon the topic of relationship in The Declaration of Independence. Even Plato, in "The Allegory of the Cave," speaks of the consequences of people being forced to interpret the world of experience entirely through watching shadows on a cave wall. The topic of relationship is a supple instrument for examining human experience, whether our own, our peers', or our culture's.

We can, then, make a few useful suggestions about using the topic of relationship:

1. Establish what is antecedent and what is consequent.
2. If using the cause-effect sequence, establish what is cause and what is effect.
3. Examine the relationship between antecedent and consequence or between cause and effect carefully enough to determine if the relationship is real or merely apparent.

The Topic of Circumstance

The topic of circumstance examines, as its name implies, the circumstances governing a given situation or an impending decision. It has two forms that are most common. The first is an examination of what is possible or impossible in a given situation. Usually the writer using this topic is trying to convince an audience that a given course of action should be taken because it is impossible to take another. Or the writer may be attempting to dissuade an audience from taking one course (which may seem inevitable) because another is possible. Thus, the second form of the topic of circumstance is an analysis of past fact and future possibility—what has been done and what might be done. In a sense, this form is a version of the first form, since what has been done was indeed once possible, and what might be done may also be possible.

Niccolò Machiavelli, whose "The Qualities of the Prince" is a study of the circumstances that accompany being a successful head of state, puts the topic of circumstance to work in a single paragraph:

> Therefore, it is not necessary for a prince to have all of the above-mentioned qualities, but it is very necessary for him to appear to have them. Furthermore, I shall be so bold as to assert this: that having them and practicing them at all times is harmful; and appearing to have them is useful; for instance, it is good to seem merciful, faithful, forthright, religious, humane, and to be so; but his mind should be disposed in such a way that should it become necessary not to be so, he will be able to change to the contrary. And it is essential to understand this: that a prince, and especially a new prince, cannot observe all those things by which men are considered good, for in order to maintain the state he is often obliged to act against his promise, against charity, against humanity, and against religion. And therefore, it is necessary that he have a mind ready to turn itself according to the way the winds of Fortune and the changeability of affairs require him; and, as I said above, as long as it is possible, he should not stray from the good, but he should know how to enter into evil when necessity commands. (para. 23)

In this paragraph Machiavelli, ever a "realist," projects a future situation in which the prince must behave badly in order to preserve the state; he is also concerned with what is possible. If it is possible to remain a good person, why, that's marvelous. But, if it is not possible, then one must do what one must do. His view, as generations of readers have well understood, is rather callous. Some people, it should be noted, believe that it is simply realistic. In any case, the prince's behavior is guided by circumstances, not by any ideal qualities.

Many of the writings in this collection are concerned with the topic of circumstance. For instance, The Declaration of Independence focuses almost entirely on issues of circumstance. The entire list of particulars against Great Britain is an outline of the circumstances (past time) that have obtained to cause the Colonies to determine their own future course as they have done. In the strictest sense, Jefferson is telling England that the Colonies find it impossible to continue with things as they have been. Henry David Thoreau's "A Plea for Captain John Brown" is based on a classical funeral oration, even though it is a plea for a living man—who raised a rebellion at Harpers Ferry, Virginia, to free a number of slaves. He reminds his audience that, even as he speaks, Brown may already have been executed for his crimes.

Thoreau's essay is guided by the topic of circumstance. He constantly asks his audience what would have been possible for a man with Brown's moral convictions when faced by lawful slavery. Slavery is immoral in the eyes of God: Would it have been possible for anyone who believed in a higher moral law not to have tried to overthrow the palpably immoral law of men? Of course, Thoreau does not take into consideration the alternate circumstances: Is it possible for a moral man to kill in the name of morality? Since John Brown knew that to conduct an uprising by force he would have to kill some slaveholders or soldiers in the process, he was himself in a circumstance worth detailed examination.

In a way, the whole of Rousseau's *The Social Contract* is guided by the topic of circumstance. He begins with one of the most famous first sentences in literature: "Man is born free, and everywhere he is in chains." The circumstances that have led to that fact are the subject of study in Rousseau's book. He examines past fact to the point of beginning with the origin of social structures in prehistory. The topic of circumstance is used by most writers at one time or another. Its flexibility, resilience, and usefulness for any discussion of action—any argument intended to move people to take a course of action or behavior which is desired—are considerable. It is, according to many rhetoricians, the chief topic to be used for trying to convince people to adopt a certain course of action.

When using the topic of circumstance, try to do the following things:

1. Clarify the question of possibility and impossibility.
2. Survey past action so that future action can be determined.
3. Conceive a course of action based on an analysis of possibility and past facts and future possibilities.
4. Clarify the circumstances that presently obtain, listing them if necessary. Be detailed and provide numerous examples. Concentrate on facts.

The Topic of Testimony

The final common topic to be considered is the topic of testimony. It is, quite simply, the judicious use of quotations from experts in a given field; comments from people, books, or other sources that express an interest in the subject at hand; and precedents or examples of similar kinds of issues and the way these issues were resolved. The topic of testimony can be used in conjunction with any of the topics previously discussed, or it can be used by itself. Today we tend to give statistics a special emphasis, and even though we are all warned that statistics can distort the truth, many arguments are won or lost on the basis of the accuracy with which people establish statistical evidence in a discussion. In classical writing aphorisms were often much more powerful than statistics. In an argument someone might point out that "A penny saved is a penny earned"; if the opponent did not have an effective contrary aphorism to offer, the argument would be over.

Machiavelli frequently uses aphorisms in his discussion of the prince. Surely there were few if any statistics to back up his views. But he also uses examples and precedents of princes who held on to their states by acting according to the principles Machiavelli advocates as well as of princes who lost their position by failing to act according to these principles. He gives an example:

> And that it be true that his other abilities would not have been sufficient can be seen from the example of Scipio, a most extraordinary man not only in his time but in all recorded history, whose armies in Spain rebelled against him; this came about from nothing other than his excessive compassion, which gave to his soldiers more liberty than military discipline allowed. For this he was censured in the senate by Fabius Maximus, who called him the corruptor of the Roman militia. The Locrians, having been ruined by one of Scipio's officers, were not avenged by him, nor was the arrogance of that officer corrected, all because of his tolerant nature; so that someone in the senate who tried to apologize for him said that there were many men who knew how not to err better than they knew how to correct errors. Such a nature would have, in time, damaged Scipio's fame and glory if he had maintained it during the empire; but living under the control of the senate, this harmful characteristic of his not only concealed itself but brought him fame. (para. 17)

Machiavelli uses this example from the life of Scipio to chasten anyone who thinks that "being a nice guy" will get the prince very far. Quite the contrary: the prince needs to be tough, disciplined, and firm. This testimonial from classical history—well known to all his readers—"proves" his point.

Many of the authors in this book depend on all the resources of the topic of testimony. William James's "The Reality of the Unseen" is almost entirely dominated by the testimonials of authority after authority who have seen, felt, or known something other than that which can be perceived. James's essay is replete with quotations from, and references to, those whose writings and statements corroborate his central thesis: that there are things about which we cannot know simply by relying on the five senses. Charles Darwin's "Natural Selection" is also filled with items and quotations from dozens of authorities. Darwin is almost like a magpie: he presents evidence from all kinds of sources to help establish that his views are incontrovertible. *The Origin of Species* contains a mountain of testimony from personal experience and experiment, examples from nature, and the writings of innumerable authorities. Its structure is guided by Darwin's desire to present testimony which is so plentiful as to make disagreement with his argument unthinkable. For us, as well as for writers that we regard as significant, it is clear that the topic of testimony is of utmost importance for making an essay strong, convincing, and authoritative.

Following are some of the main things to remember when using the topic of testimony:

1. Use recognized authorities and quote them accurately.
2. When using examples, look for some that will be familiar to your readers.
3. Interviews are a source of fresh testimonial and should be used with a wide sampling unless the persons interviewed are experts in the field discussed.
4. Examples are especially effective testimony.
5. Statistics must be double-checked and never deliberately distorted.
6. Aphorisms, precedents, and certain laws can be effective testimony.
7. Testimony is usually conclusive; examine it carefully; place it effectively in the essay.

Organization

The common topics are used by the writers in this collection as a guide to developing thought. What these writers have to say about the ideas they work with is determined, in part, by the topics they apply to them. In some cases an entire essay focuses on definition, comparison, circumstance, relationship, or even testimony. In such cases the organization of the essay is guided by considerations relevant to the topic so employed. There are other ways to organize an essay, however. The writers in this collection make use of most of the important ones, and they therefore offer us useful models for our own prose. We needn't be thinkers of the quality of these writers to be able to learn how to use their techniques.

In the most general sense, we might keep in mind the advice of the ancients regarding the organization of an essay: be sure that it has a beginning, a middle, and an end. In order to follow this advice, we need to study the models that are offered to us. The essays in this book are often chapters from books, but many of them are complete essays, which were written to be read as they are presented here. Thus, for advice on what the beginning, middle, and end ought to be in an essay, we would do well to examine the essays of King, James, Kuhn, Bertrand Russell, Gyorgy Kepes, A. C. Bradley, and Eliot.

Little specific advice needs to be given concerning how to begin an essay. There are, after all, a great many ways to begin an essay. But most competent beginnings will prepare the reader by suggesting what the essay is to be about. In the case of a difficult subject, some background may be provided, some significant questions raised, some curiosity concerning the subject piqued—and, of course, some sense of what the essay will attempt to achieve should be included in the beginning. The middle of the essay will contain the "hardware" of details and examples and the specific elements of an argument, discussion, or exposition.

James piques our interest by suggesting that there are some psychological peculiarities inherent in religion's commitment to a belief in "an unseen order." Because James's piece was originally delivered as one of a series of lectures, he was offering his thoughts to a group of interested listeners and so did not bother to stimulate them with any special "thrilling facts" or peculiarities. Instead, he begins with a relatively low-grade paradox: "material sensations actually present may have a weaker influence on our action than ideas of remoter facts." In a nutshell, he tells us that the immaterial world, the "unseen," affects us more than the seen world does. Once this point has been made, James is free to develop the idea by amassing his testimony from many diverse sources. In the middle of the essay James offers the testimony and examines it, considering it carefully for its support of the idea as well as for its possible contradictions. He ends his essay on a sober note, considering the power of religion, particularly as it has been expressed by the sword and the machine gun. Again, because this work was just one lecture in a series, his ending is not fully conclusive. Instead, he points to the subject of his next lectures, offering a guide to the interested listener.

It should be kept in mind, however, that in most endings certain functions must predominate. It is useful to remind the reader of the importance of the essay's main ideas and their development. It is also helpful to summarize briefly what those ideas and their development were and what they imply. Naturally, this must be done gracefully as well as effectively. In a sense, the conclusion of an essay provides an opportunity for one to remind a reader of what the essay has accomplished and what it implies for the reader in a future situation. Above all, the ending of an essay ought to be "conclusive": it should convey to the reader a sense of finality.

The final paragraph of Kuhn's "The Essential Tension" leaves his audience with something to think about:

> Is there a further conclusion to be drawn from all this? One speculative thought forces itself upon me. If I read the working papers [from the conference Kuhn is addressing] correctly, they suggest that most of you are really in search of the *inventive* personality, a sort of person who does emphasize divergent thinking but whom the United States has already produced in abundance. In the process you may be ignoring certain of the essential requisites of the basic scientist, a rather different sort of person, to whose ranks America's contributions have as yet been notoriously sparse. Since most of you are, in fact, Americans, this correlation may not be entirely coincidental.

Learning how to end an essay is made a bit easier by examining the way writers such as those in this book conclude their pieces. But it is also important to remember that conclusions are personal things. Probably the most important factor to keep in mind is that all essays' endings should be and sound conclusive. They will then give the reader his or her desired sense of closure and reinforce the writer's sense of having accomplished something.

On another level of organization, there are some special ways of structuring essays that are based on established categories: the narrative, the exposition, the encomium, the argument, and the letter are among those illustrated in this collection. These modes of organization are available to any writer, depending upon what the writer wishes to accomplish. And all of them, like the common topics, are natural ways of thinking about things.

NARRATIVE. The narrative is useful in almost any kind of writing. It presents a sequence of events to illustrate whatever the writer feels is significant. In some cases it may simply be a sequence for its own sake, as in the case of the piece by Douglass, who narrates a portion of his life for the benefit of those who may profit from knowing what he lived through, what he felt, and what he did. In Douglass's case the narrative is governed by time sequence, and is thus a chronological narrative. This is among the most natural types of writing that there is. For example, when telling someone about a personal experience, we naturally tend to relate the story in chronological order. In fact, when describing such an experience, many people correct themselves when they get an item out of sequence.

King narrates the sequence of events that led to his being jailed. Rousseau, in a sense, narrates a sequence of imaginary events leading up to the current political situation. Jefferson narrates, in a list of outrages, the circumstances that led to a revolution. Narrative is indispensable for the writer.

EXPOSITION. Exposition is also of immense importance to the writer: it is the ordering of an essay by means of explaining how something came to be, how it works, what its processes are, and what its significance may be. Barnett in "Einstein's Relativity" relies upon exposition in discussing Albert Einstein's theories of quantum mechanics and relativity. Sigmund Freud in "Infantile Sexuality" relies upon it as he tries to expose the mysteries of infantile sexuality. Bacon is expository when he details the qualities that relate to each of the Four Idols that imprison mankind's thought processes. Darwin's "Natural Selection" is an exposition of the main points of the theory that led him toward his description of evolution.

ENCOMIUM. The encomium is a special kind of essay that praises an individual. Thoreau uses the encomium in discussing the merits of John Brown. To a certain extent, Machiavelli makes use of the encomium as well, even though he does not name his prince. The encomium's prime work is to distinguish what is especially worthwhile about a person, describe it carefully, establish its value, and then remind us that the person in question indeed possesses (or possessed) such a quality. The encomium usually tends to understate the person's less worthy qualities by putting them in a perspective that makes them seem of secondary importance. Since Thoreau discusses a violent revolutionary, he works hard to do just this with John Brown.

ARGUMENT. By far the most common—and for most of us the most important—mode of organization used in this collection is the argument. There is no single structure for an argument, but there are some clear demands that must be met for the argument to be an effective and convincing one. For one thing, the terms of the argument must be established clearly, and accomplishing that task sometimes depends upon the use of definition and example. Whenever one defends a position or argues a case, it is essential to state the case so that the reader can understand it. Doing this is not always as simple as it sounds. For instance, Aristotle's ultimate aim is to establish the thesis that happiness is the greatest good and, as such, is the aim of man. In order to begin defending this thesis, Aristotle spends a considerable amount of time trying to determine what happiness is and what it has to do with statecraft and mankind.

Plato's thesis in "The Allegory of the Cave" is that the world of the five senses is actually an unreal world and that the only real world exists in a higher realm. He does not try to say this directly. Rather, he provides us with an allegory to contemplate, convinces us of the significance of the allegory and the situation of the people in it, then relies upon us to apply the situation of the allegory to our own circumstances. Albert Camus, in "The Myth of Sisyphus," uses a similar technique.

Most of the arguments in the writings presented in this collection work by means of reason or testimony. Machiavelli reasons that the prince who is not capable of being totally ruthless when need be will fail. He reasons that the end of achieving a well-run, well-ordered state is important enough to warrant the use of any means to attain it, including tyranny. King reasons that his behavior in breaking a human law to achieve a higher moral purpose is like the behavior of the Apostles of the early Christian Church, such as St. Paul. His argument is in the form of a letter, and a careful reader will see that it follows some features of the structure of the letters that St. Paul wrote to early Christians, and which now appear as books of the New Testament.

Arguments that focus on testimony—masses of evidence of various sorts—are perhaps more common than those based on reasoning. They have an interesting quality of usually appearing not to be arguments. If they do not state a thesis, they begin convincing us before we have time to put up our guard. Freud's case for the existence of infantile sexuality met with great resistance, but he proceeds as if he were simply giving the results of his research and had virtually no argumentative role in the essay at all. B. F. Skinner's "What Is Man?" is an argument for changing the way we think about our own personal worth. He is trying to convince us that it is essential to give up traditional views of personal freedom in order to preserve the greater good: the human race itself. Bacon's attack on the Four Idols constitutes an argument asking his readers to accept his view that no progress in science or thought will be possible until we rid ourselves of certain intellectual limitations. Kuhn argues that divergent thought does not produce scientists capable of achieving major breakthroughs but that quite the opposite is true.

In every case the pieces that constitute an argument defend a position with reason and evidence. They state an argument clearly, establish a position, respect the complexity of the issues, and refute the positions that oppose their own, which is, in fact, what all good argumentative essays—essays that take a stand on issues and ideas—usually do.

The writing assignments following the selections in this book make use of the organizational strategies of the authors. They give some direction and opportunity for each of us to try out some of the organizational modes ourselves.

A SAMPLE ESSAY

The following sample is based on the first few paragraphs of *The Nichomachean Ethics*, quoted in the first part of this introduction. In the essay the student uses the rhetorical principles discussed throughout this book. As the marginal notes point out, the student has relied on some of the common topics. The student has taken the subject from the annotations, which indicate the frequency of military references in the text. The thesis statement is that *"The Nichomachean Ethics* reveals a remarkable anxiety on Aristotle's part." The objective is to prove that military matters are prominent in Aristotle's thought and perhaps even distort it. Thus the student has organized the essay on the basis of that argument, and produced and discussed evidence from the text accordingly. In addition, by providing evidence taken from a brief study of Aristotle's biography, the student has established the climate of war that prevailed in Aristotle's time. The student has also introduced more evidence, from personal observation, experience, and reflection, which serves to make the texture of the essay concrete. The thesis statement has produced a focus and a unity which are maintained as the essay develops. The student has written a brief essay (about 700 words), stressing the most important points and omitting many minor ones.

Aristotle's Military Worries

Thesis statement

The Nichomachean Ethics reveals a remarkable anxiety on Aristotle's part. Since in his time the fate of Athens depended on military skill, it is clear that even when considering ethical matters, his thinking is affected -- and possibly distorted -- by concerns about war. His anxiety is revealed by an unusual number of military references within only a few paragraphs. His basic subject, "The Aim of Man," is eventually defined as happiness, "the highest of all realizable goods." The connection between happiness and the references to military affairs shows that Aristotle's concerns for, and worries about, the security of the Athenian state, while certainly justified, may have made him overemphasize statecraft and underemphasize the value of the individual.

Evidence to be developed

Topic of relationship (for later development)

Inventory of evidence: military references

At first glance the reader may not even notice the frequent military references in these paragraphs. Aristotle is talking about the nature of the "good" and about the "aims" or "ends" of certain kinds of activities. His examples -- the aims of "health," "ships," "victory," and "wealth" -- are actually all related to the art of war. Healthy soldiers, strong ships, and the wealth of the state are essential to any victory. Moreover, the reference to "bridle-making" is, Aristotle tells us, an admission of his preoccupation: "military matters." Even his simile comparing us in our search for the highest good to "archers" tends to make us accept his military emphasis unconsciously.

Examination of the evidence topic of relationship

Why does all this military emphasis invade a discussion of the search for happiness, the highest good? One reason is possibly that the frequency of wars in his time caused Aristotle to worry about the destruction of Athens and the consequent loss of happiness that would result in his being thrown into slavery or exile, which is what happened to citizens of city-states that lost wars. According to the Oxford Classical Dictionary,[1] Athens

[1] Oxford Classical Dictionary, 2nd ed. (Oxford: Oxford University Press, 1970), pp. 140 - 141.

Topic of testimony: evidence from an outside source

went through many changes of fortune during Aristotle's life (384 - 322 B.C.). Before Aristotle was born, Athens had been ruled by tyrants and was "a dependent of Sparta." But in 403 B.C. Athens rebuilt and restored its democracy. One of its leaders, Philip, restored military power and during most of Aristotle's life waged wars that kept Athens independent. Alexander the Great, Aristotle's own student, ultimately brought Athens under his control, however. When he died in 323 B.C. the Athenians were fighting the Lamian war, which they lost. By the year that Aristotle died, Athens had actually lost its independence. In short, Aristotle lived in troubled times and had good reason to worry.

Examining evidence

Aristotle's distortion, it seems to me, is in relating happiness, "the highest good," to statecraft. He seems to think that happiness cannot be pursued except within a state like Athens. If so, then it may be true that a strong state would be essential to happiness. Preoccupation with military matters would then be justified. But if a strong state is so important, the individual will have to consider his personal happiness as being subordinate to the general "happiness" of the state. Aristotle admits this later in his discussion.

Topic of circumstance: past and present time

In modern democratic nations the state exists to help an individual to be happy. For Aristotle it almost seems that the individual's responsibility is to secure the happiness of the state. After all, statecraft is the "most absolute and most authoritative" art of all. Today we seem to value the individual more and the state less, just as -- despite our own worries about war -- we are less concerned that our nation will cease to exist.

Conclusion

Even though Aristotle reveals his worries through what seem like casual references, his concern for the survival of the state and for maintaining military power may have an effect on his judgment of what the highest good is. Or, if his concerns do not affect what that good is, since he never defines happiness here, they may affect how one pursues that good. They will also affect the question of what conflicts might arise during its pursuit.

Today we would not put statecraft first as the highest art. If
we did, though, we might also fret about war and come to some
conclusions that would be similar to Aristotle's.

This is a very brief essay, and not every aspect of the subject can
be treated in 600 or 700 words. Yet, there is a useful review of the
evidence which produces a response on the part of the student who
wrote the essay. And the student has focused the essay well. We
should enjoy knowing more about the relationship of the individual to
the state, particularly when they are in conflict. A longer essay would
have been able to treat that point more fully. A longer essay would
also have been able to go more deeply into the rest of Aristotle's
discussion, since it is filled with much more material to stimulate
writing.

The selections that follow are useful for informing us of what has
been thought and said about important ideas. They are also useful for
stimulating us to write in response to them. There are no absolute
rules for how to do this. But observing how serious writers work and
how they apply rhetorical methods in their writing is one of the ways
to begin our own development as writers. The suggestions for essays
following each selection provide guides that can be useful for learning
from these writers, who encourage our learning and reward our study.

PART ONE

THE POLITICAL AND SOCIAL ORDER

Niccolò Machiavelli ··· *Jean Jacques Rousseau*
Thomas Jefferson ··· *Mary Wollstonecraft*
Karl Marx ··· *Henry David Thoreau*
Frederick Douglass ··· *Martin Luther King, Jr.*

INTRODUCTION

THE EIGHT SELECTIONS in this part include significant writings of a wide range of theorists and activists in political and social thought. Niccolò Machiavelli, Jean Jacques Rousseau, and Karl Marx are among the most influential of all writers in these areas. Mary Wollstonecraft and Frederick Douglass both stand as a nation's conscience directed at those who would oppress others and profit from that oppression. Three Americans—Thomas Jefferson, Henry David Thoreau, and Martin Luther King, Jr.—represent a fascinating range of social activism; each, in his way, is a revolutionary who contributed to major changes in the social and political thought of our nation.

Each of these works was conceived and written in an effort to explain a controversial position and to help others understand and, eventually, accept it. Jefferson's rhetoric is directed toward those who would know why the United States felt it necessary to break from its parent nation by force. *The Communist Manifesto* was designed to arouse the working class and to explain clearly what Communists stood for and why their critics misunderstood them and their cause. Rousseau examines the basic theories that underlie all states and the concept of the state, whereas Machiavelli's rhetorical approach to the exercise of political power concentrates on practice, not only on theory. The practicality stressed in *The Prince* has guided politicians since the sixteenth century. Frederick Douglass reveals the awakening of the free mind, the joy that accompanies liberty. His story of achieving his freedom from slavery is powerful and moving; rhetorically, its excitation of emotion helps convince us of the rightness of his illegal act. Much the same is achieved—but by totally different rhetorical means—by Thoreau in his plea for the life of John Brown, who tried to free a group of slaves by force and who was eventually executed for criminal acts. Again, to answer his critics, King constructed a carefully planned logical analysis of each complaint rendered against him. Logic has its place in rhetoric, particularly as a tool of analysis. And King's "Letter from Birmingham Jail" gives us a good sense of how logic can be used in modern writing.

The range of rhetorical skill demonstrated in these selections offers us wonderful schooling in how we, ourselves, can write. The fact that each writer is working with powerful ideas—ideas that have changed the world we live in—reinforces all the more the fact that great ideas need the support of thoughtful rhetorical strategies. We may not be inspired to utter great ideas. But we can model our own writing on the rhetorical achievements of those who have done so. And the fascinating thing is that, as we do, we discover that our own ideas can become more fully developed, more powerful, and more meaningful and useful even to ourselves.

The fact is that incompetent rhetoric usually leads to intellectual incompetence. Competent management of rhetorical tasks, such as those which are discussed in each of the following passages, actually leads to competent thought. The ideas of most of the following writers, despite their influence and fame, were hardly original with them. It would be difficult to point to even a single original idea in any of the passages presented. What makes them influential, and what makes them documents worth reading and pondering, is the way in which the ideas are expressed, explored, and related to each other.

The capacity of these ideas to change our thought inheres less in the ideas themselves than in the rhetorical forms in which they present themselves to us. Because of that fact, we too can participate in the exploration of these ideas to the extent to which we are willing to master the forms and structures in which they appear.

NICCOLÒ MACHIAVELLI

The Qualities of the Prince

NICCOLÒ MACHIAVELLI (1469–1527) *was an aristocrat whose fortunes wavered according to the shifts in power in Florence. Renaissance Italy was a collection of powerful city-states which were sometimes volatile and unstable. When Florence's famed Medici princes were returned to power in 1512 after eighteen years of banishment, Machiavelli did not fare well. He was suspected of crimes against the state and imprisoned. Even though he was not guilty, he had to learn to support himself as a writer instead of continuing his career in civil service.*

His works often contrast two forces: luck (one's fortune) and character (one's virtues). His own character outlasted his bad luck in regard to the Medicis, and he was returned to a position of responsibility. The Prince (1513), his most celebrated work, was a general treatise on the qualities the prince (i.e., a ruler) must have to maintain his power. In a more particular way, it was directed at the Medicis to encourage them to save Italy from the predatory incursions of France and Spain, whose troops were nibbling at the crumbling Italian principalities and who would, in time, control much of Italy.

From *The Prince*. Translated by Peter Bondanella and Mark Musa.

The chapters presented here contain the core of the philosophy Machiavelli became famous for. His instructions to the prince are curiously devoid of any high-sounding moralizing or any encouragement to be good as a matter of principle. Machiavelli recommends a very practical course of action for the prince: secure power; secure it by practical, simple, and effective means. It may be that Machiavelli fully expects that the prince will use his power for good ends—certainly he does not recommend tyranny. But he also supports questionable means that will achieve the final end of becoming and remaining the prince. Machiavelli believes that there is a conflict between the ends and the means used to achieve them, and he certainly does not fret over the possible problems that may accompany the use of "unpleasant" means, such as punishment of upstarts, and in general the use of repression, imprisonment, and torture.

Machiavelli's view of human nature has come under criticism for its cynicism. He suggests that a perfectly good person would not last long in any high office because that person would have to compete with the mass of people, who, he says, are basically bad. Machiavelli constantly tells us that he is describing the world as it really is, not as it should be. He implies that if the prince operated as if the world were as it ought to be, he would not last very long. Perhaps Machiavelli is correct, but people have long resented the way he approves of cunning, deceit, and outright lying as means of staying in power.

MACHIAVELLI'S RHETORIC

This selection is impressive for its brevity. Each chapter is terse and economical. Machiavelli announces his primary point clearly; he usually refers to a historical precedent (or several) to support his point; then he explains why his position is the best one by appealing to both common sense and historical experience. In those cases in which he suspects the reader will not share his view wholeheartedly, he suggests an alternate argument, then explains why it is wrong. This is a very forceful way of presenting one's views. It gives the appearance of fairness and thoroughness—and, as we learn from reading Machiavelli, he is very much concerned with appearances. His method also gives his work fullness, a quality which makes us forget how brief it really is.

One of his rhetorical methods is to discuss opposites, including both sides of an issue. From the first he makes a number of opposi-

tions—the art of war and the art of life, liberality and stinginess, cruelty and clemency, the fox and the lion. The method is simplicity itself, but it is important because it employs one of the basic techniques of rhetoric—the topic of comparison (see page 20), in which we perform one of the mind's favorite tasks, comparison and contrast. We may not have much to say about a subject, but somehow we can always think of something to say about how it relates to something else.

The aphorism is another of Machiavelli's rhetorical weapons. The aphorism is a saying—or a sentence that sounds like a saying—which has been accepted as true. Familiar examples are "A penny saved is a penny earned" and "There is no fool like an old fool." Machiavelli tells us: To be feared is much safer than to be loved; any man who tries to be good all the time is bound to come to ruin among the great number who are not good.

Such definite statements have several important qualities. One is that they are pithy—they seem to say a great deal in a few words. Another is that they appear to contain a great deal of wisdom, in part because they are delivered with such certainty, and in part because they sound like other aphorisms which we accept as true. Finally, because they sound like aphorisms, we tend to accept them much more readily than perhaps we should. Use of language which has the appearance of truth is much more likely to be accepted as conveying truth than any other use of language. This may be why the speeches of contemporary politicians (modern versions of the prince) are often sprinkled with such expressions. Machiavelli's rhetorical technique is still reliable, still effective, and still worth studying.

The Qualities of the Prince

A Prince's Duty Concerning Military Matters

A prince, therefore, must not have any other object nor any other 1
thought, nor must he take anything as his profession but war, its institutions, and its discipline; because that is the only profession which befits one who commands; and it is of such importance that not only

does it maintain those who were born princes, but many times it enables men of private station to rise to that position; and, on the other hand, it is evident that when princes have given more thought to personal luxuries than to arms, they have lost their state. And the first way to lose it is to neglect this art; and the way to acquire it is to be well versed in this art.

Francesco Sforza[1] became Duke of Milan from being a private citizen because he was armed; his sons, since they avoided the inconveniences of arms, became private citizens after having been dukes. For, among the other bad effects it causes, being disarmed makes you despised; this is one of those infamies a prince should guard himself against, as will be treated below: for between an armed and an unarmed man there is no comparison whatsoever, and it is not reasonable for an armed man to obey an unarmed man willingly, nor that an unarmed man should be safe among armed servants; since, when the former is suspicious and the latter are contemptuous, it is impossible for them to work well together. And therefore, a prince who does not understand military matters, besides the other misfortunes already noted, cannot be esteemed by his own soldiers, nor can he trust them.

He must, therefore, never raise his thought from this exercise of war, and in peacetime he must train himself more than in time of war; this can be done in two ways: one by action, the other by the mind. And as far as actions are concerned, besides keeping his soldiers well disciplined and trained, he must always be out hunting, and must accustom his body to hardships in this manner; and he must also learn the nature of the terrain, and know how mountains slope, how valleys open, how plains lie, and understand the nature of rivers and swamps; and he should devote much attention to such activities. Such knowledge is useful in two ways: first, one learns to know one's own country and can better understand how to defend it; second, with the knowledge and experience of the terrain, one can easily comprehend the characteristics of any other terrain that it is necessary to explore for the first time; for the hills, valleys, plains, rivers, and swamps of Tuscany,[2] for instance, have certain similarities to those of other provinces; so that by knowing the lay of the land in one province one can

---

[1]*Francesco Sforza (1401–1466)* Became duke of Milan in 1450. He was, like most of Machiavelli's examples, a skilled diplomat and soldier. His court was a model of Renaissance scholarship and gentility.

[2]*Tuscany* Florence is in the region known as Tuscany, which is noted for its beautiful hills.

easily understand it in others. And a prince who lacks this ability lacks the most important quality in a leader; because this skill teaches you to find the enemy, choose a campsite, lead troops, organize them for battle, and besiege towns to your own advantage.

Philopoemon, Prince of the Achaeans,[3] among the other praises   4
given to him by writers, is praised because in peacetime he thought of nothing except the means of waging war; and when he was out in the country with his friends, he often stopped and reasoned with them: "If the enemy were on that hilltop and we were here with our army, which of the two of us would have the advantage? How could we attack them without breaking formation? If we wanted to retreat, how could we do this? If they were to retreat, how could we pursue them?" And he proposed to them, as they rode along, all the contingencies that can occur in an army; he heard their opinions, expressed his own, and backed it up with arguments; so that, because of these continuous deliberations, when leading his troops no unforeseen incident could arise for which he did not have the remedy.

But as for the exercise of the mind, the prince must read histories   5
and in them study the deeds of great men; he must see how they conducted themselves in wars; he must examine the reasons for their victories and for their defeats in order to avoid the latter and to imitate the former; and above all else he must do as some distinguished man before him has done, who elected to imitate someone who had been praised and honored before him, and always keep in mind his deeds and actions; just as it is reported that Alexander the Great imitated Achilles; Caesar, Alexander; Scipio, Cyrus.[4] And anyone who reads the life of Cyrus written by Xenophon then realizes how important in the life of Scipio that imitation was to his glory and how much, in purity, goodness, humanity, and generosity, Scipio conformed to those characteristics of Cyrus that Xenophon had written about.

---

[3]***Philopoemon (253–184 B.C.), Prince of the Achaeans*** Philopoemon, from the city-state of Megalopolis, was a Greek general noted for skillful diplomacy. He led the Achaeans, a group of Greek states that formed the Achaean League, in several important expeditions, notably against Sparta. His cruelty in putting down a Spartan uprising caused him to be reprimanded by his superiors.

[4]***Cyrus (d. 529 B.C.)*** Persian emperor. Cyrus and the other figures featured in this sentence—Alexander the Great (356–323 B.C.); Achilles, hero of Homer's *Iliad*; Julius Caesar (102–44 B.C.); and Scipio Africanus, legendary Roman general—are all examples of politicians who were also great military geniuses. Xenophon (434?–?355 B.C.) was one of the earliest Greek historians; he chronicled the lives and military exploits of Cyrus and his son Darius.

Such methods as these a wise prince must follow, and never in   6
peaceful times must he be idle; but he must turn them diligently to
his advantage in order to be able to profit from them in times of ad-
versity, so that, when Fortune changes, she will find him prepared to
withstand such times.

On Those Things for Which Men, and Particularly Princes, Are Praised or Blamed

Now there remains to be examined what should be the methods   7
and procedures of a prince in dealing whith his subjects and friends.
And because I know that many have written about this, I am afraid
that by writing about it again I shall be thought of as presumptuous,
since in discussing this material I depart radically from the procedures
of others. But since my intention is to write something useful for anyone who understands it, it seemed more suitable to me to search after
the effectual truth of the matter rather than its imagined one. And
many writers have imagined for themselves republics and principalities that have never been seen nor known to exist in reality; for there
is such a gap between how one lives and how one ought to live that
anyone who abandons what is done for what ought to be done learns
his ruin rather than his preservation: for a man who wishes to make a
vocation of being good at all times will come to ruin among so many
who are not good. Hence it is necessary for a prince who wishes to
maintain his position to learn how not to be good, and to use this
knowledge or not to use it according to necessity.

Leaving aside, therefore, the imagined things concerning a prince,   8
and taking into account those that are true, I say that all men, when
they are spoken of, and particularly princes, since they are placed on a
higher level, are judged by some of these qualities which bring them
either blame or praise. And this is why one is considered generous,
another miserly (to use a Tuscan word, since "avaricious" in our language is still used to mean one who wishes to acquire by means of
theft; we call "miserly" one who excessively avoids using what he
has); one is considered a giver, the other rapacious; one cruel, another
merciful; one treacherous, another faithful; one effeminate and cowardly, another bold and courageous; one humane, another haughty; one
lascivious, another chaste; one trustworthy, another cunning; one
harsh, another lenient; one serious, another frivolous; one religious,
another unbelieving; and the like. And I know that everyone will ad-

mit that it would be a very praiseworthy thing to find in a prince, of the qualities mentioned above, those that are held to be good; but since it is neither possible to have them nor to observe them all completely, because human nature does not permit it, a prince must be prudent enough to know how to escape the bad reputation of those vices that would lose the state for him, and must protect himself from those that will not lose it for him, if this is possible; but if he cannot, he need not concern himself unduly if he ignores these less serious vices. And, moreover, he need not worry about incurring the bad reputation of those vices without which it would be difficult to hold his state; since, carefully taking everything into account, one will discover that something which appears to be a virtue, if pursued, will end in his destruction; while some other thing which seems to be a vice, if pursued, will result in his safety and his well-being.

On Generosity and Miserliness

Beginning, therefore, with the first of the above-mentioned qualities, I say that it would be good to be considered generous; nevertheless, genorosity used in such a manner as to give you a reputation for it will harm you; because if it is employed virtuously and as one should employ it, it will not be recognized and you will not avoid the reproach of its opposite. And so, if a prince wants to maintain his reputation for generosity among men, it is necessary for him not to neglect any possible means of lavish display; in so doing such a prince will always use up all his resources and he will be obliged, eventually, if he wishes to maintain his reputation for generosity, to burden the people with excessive taxes and to do everything possible to raise funds. This will begin to make him hateful to his subjects, and, becoming impoverished, he will not be much esteemed by anyone; so that, as a consequence of his generosity, having offended many and rewarded few, he will feel the effects of any slight unrest and will be ruined at the first sign of danger; recognizing this and wishing to alter his policies, he immediately runs the risk of being reproached as a miser. 9

A prince, therefore, unable to use this virtue of generosity in a manner which will not harm himself if he is known for it, should, if he is wise, not worry about being called a miser; for with time he will come to be considered more generous once it is evident that, as a result of his parsimony, his income is sufficient, he can defend himself from anyone who makes war against him, and he can undertake enterprises without overburdening his people, so that he comes to be gen- 10 erous with all those from whom he takes nothing, who are countless, and miserly with all those to whom he gives nothing, who are few. In our times we have not seen great deeds accomplished except by those who were considered miserly; all others were done away wi.h. Pope Julius II,[5] although he made use of his reputation for generosity in order to gain the papacy, then decided not to maintain it in order to be able to wage war; the present King of France[6] has waged many wars without imposing extra taxes on his subjects, only because his habitual parsimony has provided for the additional expenditures; the present King of Spain,[7] if he had been considered generous, would not have engaged in nor won so many campaigns.

Therefore, in order not to have to rob his subjects, to be able to defend himself, not to become poor and contemptible, and not to be forced to become rapacious, a prince must consider it of little importance if he incurs the name of miser, for this is one of those vices that permits him to rule. And if someone were to say: Caesar with his generosity came to rule the empire, and many others, because they were generous and known to be so, achieved very high positions; I reply: you are either already a prince or you are on the way to becoming one; in the first instance such generosity is damaging; in the second it is very necessary to be thought generous. And Caesar was one of those who wanted to gain the principality of Rome; but if, after obtaining this, he had lived and had not moderated his expenditures, he would have destroyed that empire. And if someone were to reply: there have existed many princes who have accomplished great deeds with their armies who have been reputed to be generous; I answer you: a prince either spends his own money and that of his subjects or that of others; in the first case he must be economical; in the second he must not restrain any part of his generosity. And for that prince who goes out with his soldiers and lives by looting, sacking, and ransoms, who controls the property of others, such generosity is necessary; otherwise he would not be followed by his troops. And with what does not belong to you or to your subjects you can be a more liberal giver, as were Cyrus, Caesar, and Alexander; for spending the wealth of oth-

[5]***Pope Julius II (1443–1513)*** Giuliano della Rovere, pope from 1503 to 1513. Like many of the popes of the day, Julius II was also a diplomat and a general.

[6]***present King of France*** Louis XII (1462–1515). He entered Italy on a successful military campaign in 1494.

[7]***present King of Spain*** Ferdinand V (1452–1516). A studied politician; he and Queen Isabella (1451–1504) financed Christopher Columbus's voyage to the New World in 1492.

ers does not lessen your reputation but adds to it; only the spending of your own is what harms you. And there is nothing that uses itself up faster than generosity, for as you employ it you lose the means of employing it, and you become either poor or despised or, in order to escape poverty, rapacious and hated. And above all other things a prince must guard himself against being despised and hated; and generosity leads you to both one and the other. So it is wiser to live with the reputation of a miser, which produces reproach without hatred, than to be forced to incur the reputation of rapacity, which produces reproach along with hatred, because you want to be considered as generous.

On Cruelty and Mercy
and Whether It Is Better to be Loved Than to be Feared
or the Contrary

Proceeding to the other qualities mentioned above, I say that every 12 prince must desire to be considered merciful and not cruel; nevertheless, he must take care not to misuse this mercy. Cesare Borgia[8] was considered cruel; nonetheless, his cruelty had brought order to Romagna,[9] united it, restored it to peace and obedience. If we examine this carefully, we shall see that he was more merciful than the Florentine people, who, in order to avoid being considered cruel, allowed the destruction of Pistoia.[10] Therefore, a prince must not worry about the reproach of cruelty when it is a matter of keeping his subjects united and loyal; for with a very few examples of cruelty he will be more compassionate than those who, out of excessive mercy, permit disorders to continue, from which arise murders and plundering; for these usually harm the community at large, while the executions that come from the prince harm one individual in particular. And the new prince, above all other princes, cannot escape the reputation of being called cruel, since new states are full of dangers. And Virgil, through Dido,

---

[8]*Cesare Borgia (1476–1507)* He was known for his brutality and lack of scruples, not to mention his exceptionally good luck. He was a firm ruler, son of Pope Alexander VI.

[9]*Romagna* Region northwest of Tuscany; includes the towns of Bologna, Ferrara, Ravenna, and Rimini. Borgia united it as his base of power in 1501.

[10]*Pistoia* A town near Florence, disturbed by a civil war in 1501 which could have been averted by strong repressive measures.

states: "My difficult condition and the newness of my rule make me act in such a manner, and to set guards over my land on all sides."[11]

Nevertheless, a prince must be cautious in believing and in acting, 13 nor should he be afraid of his own shadow; and he should proceed in such a manner, tempered by prudence and humanity, so that too much trust may not render him imprudent nor too much distrust render him intolerable.

From this arises an argument: whether it is better to be loved than 14 to be feared, or the contrary. I reply that one should like to be both one and the other; but since it is difficult to join them together, it is much safer to be feared than to be loved when one of the two must be lacking. For one can generally say this about men: that they are ungrateful, fickle, simulators and deceivers, avoiders of danger, greedy for gain; and while you work for their good they are completely yours, offering you their blood, their property, their lives, and their sons, as I said earlier, when danger is far away; but when it comes nearer to you they turn away. And that prince who bases his power entirely on their words, finding himself stripped of other preparations, comes to ruin; for friendships that are acquired by a price and not by greatness and nobility of character are purchased but are not owned, and at the proper moment they cannot be spent. And men are less hesitant about harming someone who makes himself loved than one who makes himself feared because love is held together by a chain of obligation which, since men are a sorry lot, is broken on every occasion in which their own self-interest is concerned; but fear is held together by a dread of punishment which will never abandon you.

A prince must nevertheless make himself feared in such a manner 15 that he will avoid hatred, even if he does not acquire love; since to be feared and not to be hated can very well be combined; and this will always be so when he keeps his hands off the property and the women of his citizens and his subjects. And if he must take someone's life, he should do so when there is proper justification and manifest cause; but, above all, he should avoid the property of others; for men forget more quickly the death of their father than the loss of their patrimony. Moreover, the reasons for seizing their property are never lacking; and he who begins to live by stealing always finds a reason for taking what belongs to others; on the contrary, reasons for taking a life are rarer and disappear sooner.

---

[11]The quotation is from the *Aeneid* (II. 563–564), the greatest Latin epic poem, written by Virgil (70–19 B.C.). Dido in the poem is a woman general who rules Carthage.

But when the prince is with his armies and has under his command 16
a multitude of troops, then it is absolutely necessary that he not worry
about being considered cruel; for without that reputation he will never
keep an army united or prepared for any combat. Among the praiseworthy deeds of Hannibal[12] is counted this: that, having a very large
army, made up of all kinds of men, which he commanded in foreign
lands, there never arose the slightest dissention, neither among themselves nor against their prince, both during his good and his bad fortune. This could not have arisen from anything other than his inhuman cruelty, which, along with his many other abilities, made him
always respected and terrifying in the eyes of his soldiers; and without
that, to attain the same effect, his other abilities would not have sufficed. And the writers of history, having considered this matter very
little, on the one hand admire these deeds of his and on the other
condemn the main cause of them.

And that it be true that his other abilities would not have been 17
sufficient can be seen from the example of Scipio, a most extraordinary
man not only in his time but in all recorded history, whose armies in
Spain rebelled against him; this came about from nothing other than
his excessive compassion, which gave to his soldiers more liberty than
military discipline allowed. For this he was censured in the senate by
Fabius Maximus,[13] who called him the corruptor of the Roman militia.
The Locrians,[14] having been ruined by one of Scipio's officers, were not
avenged by him, nor was the arrogance of that officer corrected, all
because of his tolerant nature; so that someone in the senate who tried
to apologize for him said that there were many men who knew how
not to err better than they knew how to correct errors. Such a nature
would have, in time, damaged Scipio's fame and glory if he had maintained it during the empire; but, living under the control of the senate,
this harmful characteristic of his not only concealed itself but brought
him fame.

I conclude, therefore, returning to the problem of being feared and 18
loved, that since men love at their own pleasure and fear at the pleasure of the prince, a wise prince should build his foundation upon that

---

[12]*Hannibal (247–183 B.C.)* An amazingly inventive military tactician who led
the Carthaginian armies against Rome for more than fifteen years. He crossed the Alps
from Gaul in order to surprise Rome. He was noted for use of the ambush and for "inhuman cruelty."

[13]*Fabius Maximus (?–203 B.C.)* Roman general who fought Hannibal. He was jealous
of the younger Roman general Scipio.

[14]*Locrians* Inhabitants of Locri, an Italian town settled by the Greeks in 683 B.C.

which belongs to him, not upon that which belongs to others: he must strive only to avoid hatred, as has been said.

How a Prince Should Keep His Word

How praiseworthy it is for a prince to keep his word and to live by integrity and not by deceit everyone knows; nevertheless, one sees from the experience of our times that the princes who have accomplished great deeds are those who have cared little for keeping their promises and who have known how to manipulate the minds of men by shrewdness; and in the end they have surpassed those who laid their foundations upon honesty. [19]

You must, therefore, know that there are two means of fighting: one according to the laws, the other with force; the first way is proper to man, the second to beasts; but because the first, in many cases, is not sufficient, it becomes necessary to have recourse to the second. Therefore, a prince must know how to use wisely the natures of the beast and the man. This policy was taught to princes allegorically by the ancient writers, who described how Achilles and many other ancient princes were given to Chiron[15] the Centaur to be raised and taught under his discipline. This can only mean that, having a half-beast and half-man as a teacher, a prince must know how to employ the nature of the one and the other; and the one without the other cannot endure. [20]

Since, then, a prince must know how to make good use of the nature of the beast, he should choose from among the beasts the fox and the lion; for the lion cannot defend itself from traps and the fox cannot protect itself from wolves. It is therefore necessary to be a fox in order to recognize the traps and a lion in order to frighten the wolves. Those who play only the part of the lion do not understand matters. A wise ruler, therefore, cannot and should not keep his word when such an observance of faith would be to his disadvantage and when the reasons which made him promise are removed. And if men were all good, this rule would not be good; but since men are a sorry lot and will not keep their promises to you, you likewise need not keep yours to them. A prince never lacks legitimate reasons to break his promises. Of this one could cite an endless number of modern ex-

---

[15]*Chiron*   A mythical figure, a centaur (half man, half horse). Unlike most centaurs, he was wise and benevolent; he was also a legendary physician.

amples to show how many pacts, how many promises have been made null and void because of the infidelity of princes; and he who has known best how to use the fox has come to a better end. But it is necessary to know how to disguise this nature well and to be a great hypocrite and a liar: and men are so simpleminded and so controlled by their present necessities that one who deceives will always find another who will allow himself to be deceived.

I do not wish to remain silent about one of these recent instances. 22 Alexander VI[16] did nothing else, he thought about nothing else, except to deceive men, and he always found the occasion to do this. And there never was a man who had more forcefulness in his oaths, who affirmed a thing with more promises, and who honored his word less; nevertheless, his tricks always succeeded perfectly since he was well acquainted with this aspect of the world.

Therefore, it is not necessary for a prince to have all of the above- 23 mentioned qualities, but it is very necessary for him to appear to have them. Furthermore, I shall be so bold as to assert this: that having them and practicing them at all times is harmful; and appearing to have them is useful; for instance, to seem merciful, faithful, humane, forthright, religious, and to be so; but his mind should be disposed in such a way that should it become necessary not to be so, he will be able and know how to change to the contrary. And it is essential to understand this: that a prince, and especially a new prince, cannot observe all those things by which men are considered good, for in order to maintain the state he is often obliged to act against his promise, against charity, against humanity, and against religion. And therefore, it is necessary that he have a mind ready to turn itself according to the way the winds of Fortune and the changeability of affairs require him; and, as I said above, as long as it is possible, he should not stray from the good, but he should know how to enter into evil when necessity commands.

A prince, therefore, must be very careful never to let anything slip 24 from his lips which is not full of the five qualities mentioned above: he should appear, upon seeing and hearing him, to be all mercy, all faithfulness, all integrity, all kindness, all religion. And there is nothing more necessary than to seem to possess this last quality. And men in general judge more by their eyes than their hands; for everyone can see but few can feel. Everyone sees what you seem to be, few perceive

---

[16]***Alexander VI (1431–1503)*** Roderigo Borgia, pope from 1492 to 1503. He was Cesare Borgia's father and a corrupt but immensely powerful pope.

what you are, and those few do not dare to contradict the opinion of the many who have the majesty of the state to defend them; and in the actions of all men, and especially of princes, where there is no impartial arbiter, one must consider the final result.[17] Let a prince therefore act to seize and to maintain the state; his methods will always be judged honorable and will be praised by all; for ordinary people are always deceived by appearances and by the outcome of a thing; and in the world there is nothing but ordinary people; and there is no room for the few, while the many have a place to lean on. A certain prince[18] of the present day, whom I shall refrain from naming, preaches nothing but peace and faith, and to both one and the other he is entirely opposed; and both, if he had put them into practice, would have cost him many times over either his reputation or his state.

On Avoiding Being Despised and Hated

But since, concerning the qualities mentioned above, I have spoken   25
about the most important, I should like to discuss the others briefly in this general manner: that the prince, as was noted above, should think about avoiding those things which make him hated and despised; and when he has avoided this, he will have carried out his duties and will find no danger whatsoever in other vices. As I have said, what makes him hated above all else is being rapacious and a usurper of the property and the women of his subjects; he must refrain from this; and in most cases, so long as you do not deprive them of either their property or their honor, the majority of men live happily; and you have only to deal with the ambition of a few, who can be restrained without difficulty and by many means. What makes him despised is being considered changeable, frivolous, effeminate, cowardly, irresolute; from these qualities a prince must guard himself as if from a reef, and he must strive to make everyone recognize in his actions greatness, spirit, dignity, and strength; and concerning the private affairs of his subjects, he must insist that his decision be irrevocable; and he should maintain himself in such a way that no man could imagine that he can deceive or cheat him.

That prince who projects such an opinion of himself is greatly es-   26
teemed; and it is difficult to conspire against a man with such a repu-

---

[17]The Italian original, *si guarda al fine*, has often been mistranslated as "the ends justify the means," something Machiavelli never wrote. [Translators' note]

[18]**A certain prince** Probably King Ferdinand V of Spain (1452–1516).

tation and difficult to attack him, provided that he is understood to be of great merit and revered by his subjects. For a prince must have two fears: one, internal, concerning his subjects; the other, external, concerning foreign powers. From the latter he can defend himself by his good troops and friends; and he will always have good friends if he has good troops; and internal affairs will always be stable when external affairs are stable, provided that they are not already disturbed by a conspiracy; and even if external conditions change, if he is properly organized and lives as I have said and does not lose control of himself, he will always be able to withstand every attack, just as I said that Nabis the Spartan[19] did. But concerning his subjects, when external affairs do not change, he has to fear that they may conspire secretly: the prince secures himself from this by avoiding being hated or despised and by keeping the people satisfied with him; this is a necessary matter, as was treated above at length. And one of the most powerful remedies a prince has against conspiracies is not to be hated by the masses; for a man who plans a conspiracy always believes that he will satisfy the people by killing the prince; but when he thinks he might anger them, he cannot work up the courage to undertake such a deed; for the problems on the side of the conspirators are countless. And experience demonstrates that conspiracies have been many but few have been concluded successfully; for anyone who conspires cannot be alone, nor can he find companions except from amongst those whom he believes to be dissatisfied; and as soon as you have uncovered your intent to one dissatisfied man, you give him the means to make himself happy, since he can have everything he desires by uncovering the plot; so much is this so that, seeing a sure gain on the one hand and one doubtful and full of danger on the other, if he is to maintain faith with you he has to be either an unusually good friend or a completely determined enemy of the prince. And to treat the matter briefly, I say that on the part of the conspirator there is nothing but fear, jealousy, and the thought of punishment that terrifies him; but on the part of the prince there is the majesty of the principality, the laws, the defenses of friends and the state to protect him; so that, with the good will of the people added to all these things, it is impossible for anyone to be so rash as to plot against him. For, where usually a conspirator has to be afraid before he executes his evil deed, in this case he must be afraid, having the people as an enemy, even after the crime is performed, nor can he hope to find any refuge because of this.

---

[19]*Nabis the Spartan (fl. 220 B.C.)* A Greek tyrant routed by Philopoemon and the Achaean League.

One could cite countless examples on this subject; but I want to   27
satisfy myself with only one which occurred during the time of our
fathers. Messer Annibale Bentivogli, prince of Bologna and grandfather
of the present Messer Annibale, was murdered by the Canneschi[20]
family, who conspired against him; he left behind no heir except Messer Giovanni,[21] then only a baby. As soon as this murder occurred, the
people rose up and killed all the Canneschi. This came about because
of the good will that the house of the Bentivogli enjoyed in those days;
this good will was so great that with Annibale dead, and there being
no one of that family left in the city who could rule Bologna, the Bolo-
gnese people, having heard that in Florence there was one of the Bentivogli blood who was believed until that time to be the son of a black-
smith, went to Florence to find him, and they gave him the control of
that city; it was ruled by him until Messer Giovanni became of age to
rule.

I conclude, therefore, that a prince must be little concerned with   28
conspiracies when the people are well disposed toward him; but when
the populace is hostile and regards him with hatred, he must fear
everything and everyone. And well-organized states and wise princes
have, with great diligence, taken care not to anger the nobles and to
satisfy the common people and keep them contented; for this is one
of the most important concerns that a prince has.

---

[20]*Canneschi*   Prominent family in Bologna.

[21]*Giovanni Bentivogli (1443–1508)*   Former tyrant of Bologna. In sequence he was
a conspirator against, then a conspirator with Cesare Borgia.

QUESTIONS

1. The usual criticism of Machiavelli is that he advises his prince to be un-
   scrupulous. Does this seem to be the case in this excerpt?
2. Is Machiavelli correct when he asserts that the great number of people are
   not good? Does our government assume that to be true, too?
3. Politicians—especially heads of state—are the contemporary counterparts
   of the prince. Should successful heads of state show skill in war to the
   same extent Machiavelli's prince does?
4. Clarify the advice Machiavelli gives concerning liberality and stinginess.
   Is this still good advice?
5. Are modern politicians likely to succeed by following all or most of
   Machiavelli's recommendations?

WRITING ASSIGNMENTS

1. In speaking of the prince's military duties, Machiavelli says, "being disarmed makes you despised." Take a stand on this issue. If possible, choose an example or instance to strengthen your argument. Is it possible that in modern society being defenseless is an advantage?

2. One of Machiavelli's most controversial statements is: "A man who wishes to make a vocation of being good at all times will come to ruin among so many who are not good." Defend or attack this view. As much as possible, use personal experiences to bolster your opinion.

3. Find evidence within this excerpt to demonstrate that Machiavelli's attitude toward human nature is accurate. Remember that the usual criticism of Machiavelli is that he is cynical—that he thinks the worst of people rather than the best. Inventory quotations from the excerpt that would support either or both of these views; then use them in an essay, with analysis, to clarify just what Machiavelli's views on human nature are.

4. By referring to current events and current leaders—either local, national, or international—decide whether or not Machiavelli's advice to the prince would be useful to the modern politician. Consider the question of whether the advice is completely useless, completely reliable, or whether its value depends upon specific conditions. Establish first exactly what the advice is; show how it is applicable or inapplicable for specific politicians; then critique its general usefulness.

5. Probably the chief ethical issue raised by *The Prince* is the question of whether or not the ends justify the means that need to be used to achieve them. Write an essay in which you take a stand on this question. Begin by defining the issue: What does the phrase "the ends justify the means" actually mean? What are the difficulties in accepting the fact that unworthy means may achieve worthy ends? If possible, use some historical or personal examples that will give your argument substance. Carefully analyze Machiavelli's references to circumstances in which questionable means have been (or should have been) used to achieve worthy ends. Is it possible for a politician to concern himself only with ends and ignore the means entirely?

JEAN JACQUES ROUSSEAU

───·◦∞◦·───

The Origin of Civil Society

JEAN JACQUES ROUSSEAU (1712–1794) was the son of a watch-maker and grew to be a man of letters, with a wide variety of accomplishments. Among other works, he wrote a novel, Émile; an opera, The Village Soothsayer; and an autobiography, The Confessions. The Social Contract, published in 1762, became a bible of the French Revolution. When Rousseau died, his body was given a place of honor in the Pantheon in Paris.

The Social Contract is notable for the way in which it establishes the relationship among the members of a body politic. By emphasizing the fact that each member of a society forfeits a certain amount of personal freedom for the greater good of the whole, and by emphasizing that the sovereign has immense responsibilities to the people, Rousseau conceived the structure of government in a novel way. Today we think of that way as basically democratic, since Rousseau constantly talks about certain types of equality which he expects to find in a well-ordered society. Equality before the law is probably the most important element of that society.

Equality before the law, a concept which we approve today, was

---

From *The Social Contract*. Translated by Gerard Hopkins.

a very revolutionary view for 1762. It implied that people who were born aristocrats would be equal before the law with those who were born commoners; it implied the same thing for the wealthy property holder and the pauper. Neither of these conditions obtained in any nation of the time, although Rousseau saw some hope for such equality in the achievements of English law. Rousseau is careful not to say more than was possible considering the times, but he implies that the body politic should be a commonwealth in which property would be much more widely distributed than it was in contemporary France.

He takes an interesting stance in proposing a time which he calls the natural state when men were not joined in social orders. Eventually they surrendered that natural state for a civil state; because there was a general willingness to subordinate individual rights, government came into being. The novelty of this idea for Rousseau's day was his emphasis on government as a product of the act of the people's will rather than as a product of the force of the sovereign. It introduced, as well, the concept of the responsibility of the sovereign to govern well, a concept the French monarch Louis XV (1710–1774) was not quick to accept or understand.

ROUSSEAU'S RHETORIC

Little of what Rousseau says here is original. His way of putting his points and of organizing and clarifying them is what makes the work effective. One important technique he uses is that of analogy. His most impressive use is the analogy of the family to the state. The technique of analogy always implies comparing a very familiar thing—the family—with something less familiar—the state. Then, Rousseau looks for the similarities between the two, such as the children as the people and the father as the sovereign. Such analogies can be enlightening or dangerous, depending on how far one is willing to push them.

The main rhetorical device Rousseau uses is analysis, particularly analysis of a logical type. He proposes a statement which seems, on the surface, to be reasonable; then he analyzes it part by part until he proves to the reader that it is either to be accepted or rejected. He is conspicuous in this application of logic in his section "Of Slavery," in which he proves that slavery is not defensible on any ground, including the widely held ground that prisoners of war may legitimately be made into slaves because they owe their lives to their captors.

During his passages of analysis, Rousseau occasionally pauses to provide definitions of terms or circumstances or concepts. It is usually during the process of defining that Rousseau clarifies his argument so that the truth can be recognized. The technique is both simple and effective and is therefore important for us to examine, since we may use it as easily as he does.

The reference to other authorities, a rhetorical technique called the topic of testimony, is sometimes overdone by writers of this period. But Rousseau depends on only a few authorities, notably Hugo Grotius, the Dutch legal authority, and Thomas Hobbes, the English social philosopher. They are most prominent in the early pages of the selection, and they provide only a few basic points that are indispensable for the argument. Again, this rhetorical technique is easy for most of us to use, and its effectiveness cannot be underestimated.

Finally, it should be pointed out that Rousseau is in the habit of posing a considerable number of rhetorical questions. He says, "Man is born free, and everywhere he is in chains. Many a man believes himself to be the master of others who is, no less than they, a slave. How did this change take place? I do not know. What can make it legitimate?" He tells us that for the second question he may have a few answers. The technique of posing serious questions and then attempting to answer them is effective because the clarity of the question-and-answer structure is immediately apparent to the reader. Naturally, the technique can be overworked, but a careful balancing of question and answer can help provide a clarity that might otherwise be missing.

Paradox, a rhetorical device designed to capture a reader's attention and to provoke serious thought, is one of Rousseau's strengths. Being born free, but being everywhere now in chains is one of the most arresting paradoxes in literature. It is so strong that it provokes us to share Rousseau's seriousness in searching out the reasons—even to the point of examining the birth of society itself.

The Origin of Civil Society

Note

It is my wish to inquire whether it be possible, within the civil 1
*order, to discover a legitimate and stable basis of Government. This
I shall do by considering human beings as they are and laws as they
might be. I shall attempt, throughout my investigations, to maintain
a constant connection between what right permits and interest demands, in order that no separation may be made between justice and
utility. I intend to begin without first proving the importance of my
subject. Am I, it will be asked, either prince or legislator that I take
it upon me to write of politics? My answer is—No; and it is for that
very reason that I have chosen politics as the matter of my book.
Were I either the one or the other I should not waste my time in
laying down what has to be done. I should do it, or else hold my
peace.*

I was born into a free state and am a member of its sovereign 2
*body. My influence on public affairs may be small, but because I
have a right to exercise my vote, it is my duty to learn their nature,
and it has been for me a matter of constant delight, while meditating
on problems of Government in general, to find ever fresh reasons for
regarding with true affection the way in which these things are ordered in my native land.*

The Subject of the First Book

Man is born free, and everywhere he is in chains. Many a man 3
believes himself to be the master of others who is, no less than they,
a slave. How did this change take place? I do not know. What can
make it legitimate? To this question I hope to be able to furnish an
answer.

Were I considering only force and the effects of force, I should say: 4
"So long as a People is constrained to obey, and does, in fact, obey, it
does well. So soon as it can shake off its yoke, and succeeds in doing
so, it does better. The fact that it has recovered its liberty by virtue of

60

that same right by which it was stolen, means either that it is entitled to resume it, or that its theft by others was, in the first place, without justification." But the social order is a sacred right which serves as a foundation for all other rights. This right, however, since it comes not by nature, must have been built upon conventions. To discover what these conventions are is the matter of our inquiry. But, before proceeding further, I must establish the truth of what I have so far advanced.

Of Primitive Societies

The oldest form of society—and the only natural one—is the family. Children remain bound to their father for only just so long as they feel the need of him for their self-preservation. Once that need ceases the natural bond is dissolved. From then on, the children, freed from the obedience which they formerly owed, and the father, cleared of his debt of responsibility to them, return to a condition of equal independence. If the bond remain operative it is no longer something imposed by nature, but has become a matter of deliberate choice. The family is a family still, but by reason of convention only. 5

This shared liberty is a consequence of man's nature. Its first law is that of self-preservation: its first concern is for what it owes itself. As soon as a man attains the age of reason he becomes his own master, because he alone can judge of what will best assure his continued existence. 6

We may, therefore, if we will, regard the family as the basic model of all political associations. The ruler is the father writ large: the people are, by analogy, his children, and all, ruler and people alike, alienate their freedom only so far as it is to their advantage to do so. The only difference is that, whereas in the family the father's love for his children is sufficient reward to him for the care he has lavished on them, in the State, the pleasure of commanding others takes its place, since the ruler is not in a relation of love to his people. 7

Grotius[1] denies that political power is ever exercised in the interests of the governed, and quotes the institution of slavery in support of his contention. His invariable method of arguing is to derive Right from Fact. It might be possible to adopt a more logical system of reasoning, but none which would be more favorable to tyrants. 8

---

[1] ***Hugo Grotius (1583–1645)*** A Dutch lawyer who spent some time in exile in Paris. His fame as a child prodigy was considerable; his book on the laws of war *(De jure belli)* was widely known in Europe.

According to Grotius, therefore, it is doubtful whether the term 9
"human race" belongs to only a few hundred men, or whether those
few hundred men belong to the human race. From the evidence of his
book it seems clear that he holds by the first of these alternatives, and
on this point Hobbes[2] is in agreement with him. If this is so, then
humanity is divided into herds of livestock, each with its "guardian"
who watches over his charges only that he may ultimately devour
them.

Just as the shepherd is superior in kind to his sheep, so, too, the 10
shepherds of men, or, in other words, their rulers, are superior in kind
to their peoples. This, according to Philo,[3] was the argument advanced
by Caligula,[4] the Emperor, who drew from the analogy the perfectly
true conclusion that either Kings are Gods or their subjects brute
beasts.

The reasoning of Caligula, of Hobbes, and of Grotius is fundamen- 11
tally the same. Far earlier, Aristotle, too, had maintained that men are
not by nature equal, but that some are born to be slaves, others to be
masters.

Aristotle[5] was right: but he mistook the effect for the cause. Noth- 12
ing is more certain than that a man born into a condition of slavery is
a slave by nature. A slave in fetters loses everything—even the desire
to be freed from them. He grows to love his slavery, as the companions
of Ulysses grew to love their state of brutish transformation.[6]

If some men are by nature slaves, the reason is that they have been 13
made slaves *against* nature. Force made the first slaves: cowardice has
perpetuated the species.

I have made no mention of King Adam or of the Emperor Noah, 14

---

[2]***Thomas Hobbes (1588–1679)*** Known as a materialist philosopher who did not
credit divine influence in politics. An Englishman, he became famous for *Leviathan*, a
study of politics that treated the state as if it were a monster (leviathan) with a life of its
own.

[3]***Philo (fl. c. 10 B.C.)*** A Jew who had absorbed Greek culture and who wrote
widely on many subjects. His studies on Mosaic Law were considered important.

[4]***Caligula (12–41 A.D.)*** Roman emperor of uncertain sanity. He loved his sister
Drusilla so much that he had her deified when she died. A military commander, he was
assassinated by an officer.

[5]***Aristotle (384–322 B.C.)*** A student of Plato; his philosophical method became the
dominant intellectual force in Western thought.

[6]***state of brutish transformation*** This sentence refers to the Circe episode in Homer's *Odyssey* (X–XII). Circe was a sorceress who, by means of drugs, enchanted men
and turned them into swine. Ulysses (Latin name of Odysseus), king of Ithaca, is the
central figure of the *Odyssey*.

the father of three great Monarchs[7] who divided up the universe between them, as did the children of Saturn,[8] whom some have been tempted to identify with them. I trust that I may be given credit for my moderation, since, being descended in a direct line from one of these Princes, and quite possibly belonging to the elder branch, I may, for all I know, were my claims supported in law, be even now the legitimate Sovereign of the Human Race.[9] However that may be, all will concur in the view that Adam was King of the World, as was Robinson Crusoe of his island, only so long as he was its only inhabitant, and that the great advantage of empire held on such terms was that the Monarch, firmly seated on his throne, had no need to fear rebellions, conspiracy, or war.

Of the Right of the Strongest

However strong a man, he is never strong enough to remain master   15
always, unless he transform his Might into Right, and Obedience into
Duty. Hence we have come to speak of the Right of the Strongest, a
right which, seemingly assumed in irony, has, in fact, become established in principle. But the meaning of the phrase has never been adequately explained. Strength is a physical attribute, and I fail to see how
any moral sanction can attach to its effects. To yield to the strong is
an act of necessity, not of will. At most it is the result of a dictate of
prudence. How, then, can it become a duty?

Let us assume for a moment that some such Right does really exist.   16
The only deduction from this premise is inexplicable gibberish. For to
admit that Might makes Right is to reverse the process of effect and
cause. The mighty man who defeats his rival becomes heir to his
Right. So soon as we can disobey with impunity, disobedience becomes legitimate. And, since the Mightiest is always right, it merely
remains for us to become possessed of Might. But what validity can
there be in a Right which ceases to exist when Might changes hands?
If a man be constrained by Might to obey, what need has he to obey

---

[7]***the father of three great Monarchs***   Adam in the Bible (Genesis 1:1–2:4) fathered
Cain, Abel, and Seth. Noah's sons, Shem, Ham, and Japhet, repopulated the world after
the Flood (Genesis 6:11–9:19).

[8]***children of Saturn***   Saturn is a mythic god associated with the golden age of Rome.
The reference to children is obscure, since Picus was his only son.

[9]***Sovereign of the Human Race***   Rousseau is being ironic, of course; like the rest of
us, he is descended from Adam.

by Duty? And if he is not constrained to obey, there is no further obligation on him to do so. It follows, therefore, that the word Right adds nothing to the idea of Might. It becomes, in this connection, completely meaningless.

Obey the Powers that be. If that means Yield to Force, the precept 17 is admirable but redundant. My reply to those who advance it is that no case will ever be found of its violation. All power comes from God. Certainly, but so do all ailments. Are we to conclude from such an argument that we are never to call in the doctor? If I am waylaid by a footpad at the corner of a wood, I am constrained by force to give him my purse. But if I can manage to keep it from him, is it my duty to hand it over? His pistol is also a symbol of Power. It must, then, be admitted that Might does not create Right, and that no man is under an obligation to obey any but the legitimate powers of the State. And so I continually come back to the question I first asked.

Of Slavery

Since no man has natural authority over his fellows, and since 18 Might can produce no Right, the only foundation left for legitimate authority in human societies is Agreement.

If a private citizen, says Grotius, can alienate his liberty and make 19 himself another man's slave, why should not a whole people do the same, and subject themselves to the will of a King? The argument contains a number of ambiguous words which stand in need of explanation. But let us confine our attention to one only—*alienate.* To alienate means to give or to sell. Now a man who becomes the slave of another does not give himself. He sells himself in return for bare subsistence, if for nothing more. But why should a whole people sell themselves? So far from furnishing subsistence to his subjects, a King draws his own from them, and from them alone. According to Rabelais,[10] it takes a lot to keep a King. Do we, then, maintain that a subject surrenders his person on condition that his property be taken too? It is difficult to see what he will have left.

It will be said that the despot guarantees civil peace to his subjects. 20 So be it. But how are they the gainers if the wars to which his ambition may expose them, his insatiable greed, and the vexatious demands of his Ministers cause them more loss than would any outbreak of

---

[10]***François Rabelais (1490–1553)*** French writer, author of *Gargantua* and *Pantagruel,* satires on politics and religion.

internal dissension? How do they benefit if that very condition of civil peace be one of the causes of their wretchedness? One can live peacefully enough in a dungeon, but such peace will hardly, of itself, ensure one's happiness. The Greeks imprisoned in the cave of Cyclops[11] lived peacefully while awaiting their turn to be devoured.

To say that a man gives himself for nothing is to commit oneself 21 to an absurd and inconceivable statement. Such an act of surrender is illegitimate, null, and void by the mere fact that he who makes it is not in his right mind. To say the same thing of a whole People is tantamount to admitting that the People in question are a nation of imbeciles. Imbecility does not produce Right.

Even if a man can alienate himself, he cannot alienate his children. 22 They are born free, their liberty belongs to them, and no one but themselves has a right to dispose of it. Before they have attained the age of reason their father may make, on their behalf, certain rules with a view to ensuring their preservation and well-being. But any such limitation of their freedom of choice must be regarded as neither irrevocable nor unconditional, for to alienate another's liberty is contrary to the natural order, and is an abuse of the father's rights. It follows that an arbitrary government can be legitimate only on condition that each successive generation of subjects is free either to accept or to reject it, and if this is so, then the government will no longer be arbitrary.

When a man renounces his liberty he renounces his essential man- 23 hood, his rights, and even his duty as a human being. There is no compensation possible for such complete renunciation. It is incompatible with man's nature, and to deprive him of his free will is to deprive his actions of all moral sanction. The convention, in short, which sets up on one side an absolute authority, and on the other an obligation to obey without question, is vain and meaningless. Is it not obvious that where we can demand everything we owe nothing? Where there is no mutual obligation, no interchange of duties, it must, surely, be clear that the actions of the commanded cease to have any moral value? For how can it be maintained that my slave has any "right" against me when everything that he has is my property? His right being *my* right, it is absurd to speak of it as ever operating to my disadvantage.

Grotius, and those who think like him, have found in the fact of 24 war another justification for the so-called "right" of slavery. They ar-

---

[11]***cave of Cyclops*** The cyclops is a one-eyed giant cannibal whose cave is the scene of one of Odysseus's triumphs in Homer's *Odyssey*.

gue that since the victor has a *right* to kill his defeated enemy, the latter may, if he so wish, ransom his life at the expense of his liberty, and that this compact is the more legitimate in that it benefits both parties.

But it is evident that this alleged *right* of a man to kill his enemies is not in any way a derivative of the state of war, if only because men, in their primitive condition of independence, are not bound to one another by any relationship sufficiently stable to produce a state either of war or of peace. They are not *naturally* enemies. It is the link between *things* rather than between *men* that constitutes war, and since a state of war cannot originate in simple personal relations, but only in relations between things, private hostility between man and man cannot obtain either in a state of nature where there is no generally accepted system of private property, or in a state of society where law is the supreme authority.   25

Single combats, duels, personal encounters are incidents which do not constitute a "state" of anything. As to those private wars which were authorized by the Ordinances of King Louis IX[12] and suspended by the Peace of God, they were merely an abuse of Feudalism—that most absurd of all systems of government, so contrary was it to the principles of Natural Right and of all good polity.   26

War, therefore, is something that occurs not between man and man, but between States. The individuals who become involved in it are enemies only by accident. They fight not as men or even as citizens, but as soldiers: not as members of this or that national group, but as its defenders. A State can have as its enemies only other States, not men at all, seeing that there can be no true relationship between things of a different nature.   27

This principle is in harmony with that of all periods, and with the constant practice of every civilized society. A declaration of war is a warning, not so much to Governments as to their subjects. The foreigner—whether king, private person, or nation as a whole—who steals, murders, or holds in durance the subjects of another country without first declaring war on that country's Prince, acts not as an enemy but as a brigand. Even when war has been joined, the just Prince, though he may seize all public property in enemy territory, yet respects the property and possessions of individuals, and, in so doing,   28

---

[12]***King Louis IX (1214–1270)*** King of France, also called St. Louis. He was looked upon as an ideal monarch.

shows his concern for those rights on which his own laws are based. The object of war being the destruction of the enemy State, a commander has a perfect right to kill its defenders so long as their arms are in their hands: but once they have laid them down and have submitted, they cease to be enemies, or instruments employed by an enemy, and revert to the condition of men, pure and simple, over whose lives no one can any longer exercise a rightful claim. Sometimes it is possible to destroy a State without killing any of its subjects, and nothing in war can be claimed as a right save what may be necessary for the accomplishment of the victor's end. These principles are not those of Grotius, nor are they based on the authority of poets, but derive from the Nature of Things, and are founded upon Reason.

The Right of Conquest finds its sole sanction in the Law of the   29 Strongest. If war does not give to the victor the right to massacre his defeated enemies, he cannot base upon a nonexistent right any claim to the further one of enslaving them. We have the right to kill our enemies only when we cannot enslave them. It follows, therefore, that the right to enslave cannot be deduced from the right to kill, and that we are guilty of enforcing an iniquitous exchange if we make a vanquished foeman purchase with his liberty that life over which we have no right. Is it not obvious that once we begin basing the right of life and death on the right to enslave, and the right to enslave on the right of life and death, we are caught in a vicious circle? Even if we assume the existence of this terrible right to kill all and sundry, I still maintain that a man enslaved, or a People conquered, in war is under no obligation to obey beyond the point at which force ceases to be operative. If the victor spares the life of his defeated opponent in return for an equivalent, he cannot be said to have shown him mercy. In either case he destroys him, but in the latter case he derives value from his act, while in the former he gains nothing. His authority, however, rests on no basis but that of force. There is still a state of war between the two men, and it conditions the whole relationship in which they stand to one another. The enjoyment of the Rights of War presupposes that there has been no treaty of Peace. Conqueror and conquered have, to be sure, entered into a compact, but such a compact, far from liquidating the state of war, assumes its continuance.

Thus, in whatever way we look at the matter, the "Right" to en-   30 slave has no existence, not only because it is without legal validity, but because the very term is absurd and meaningless. The words *Slavery* and *Right* are contradictory and mutually exclusive. Whether we be considering the relation of one man to another man, or of an indi-

vidual to a whole People, it is equally idiotic to say—"You and I have
made a compact which represents nothing but loss to you and gain to
me. I shall observe it so long as it pleases me to do so—and so shall
you, until I cease to find it convenient."

That We Must Always Go Back
to an Original Compact

Even were I to grant all that I have so far refuted, the champions of 31
despotism would not be one whit the better off. There will always be
a vast difference between subduing a mob and governing a social
group. No matter how many isolated individuals may submit to the
enforced control of a single conqueror, the resulting relationship will
ever be that of Master and Slave, never of People and Ruler. The body
of men so controlled may be an agglomeration; it is not an association.
It implies neither public welfare nor a body politic. An individual may
conquer half the world, but he is still only an individual. His interests,
wholly different from those of his subjects, are private to himself.
When he dies his empire is left scattered and disintegrated. He is like
an oak which crumbles and collapses in ashes so soon as the fire consumes it.

"A People," says Grotius, "may give themselves to a king." His 32
argument implies that the said People were already a People before
this act of surrender. The very act of gift was that of a political group
and presupposed public deliberation. Before, therefore, we consider the
act by which a People chooses their king, it were well if we considered
the act by which a People is constituted as such. For it necessarily
precedes the other, and is the true foundation on which all Societies
rest.

Had there been no original compact, why, unless the choice were 33
unanimous, should the minority ever have agreed to accept the decision of the majority? What right have the hundred who desire a master
to vote for the ten who do not? The institution of the franchise is, in
itself, a form of compact, and assumes that, at least once in its operation, complete unanimity existed.

Of the Social Pact

I assume, for the sake of argument, that a point was reached in the 34
history of mankind when the obstacles to continuing in a state of Na-

ture were stronger than the forces which each individual could employ to the end of continuing in it. The original state of Nature, therefore, could no longer endure, and the human race would have perished had it not changed its manner of existence.

Now, since men can by no means engender new powers, but can only unite and control those of which they are already possessed, there is no way in which they can maintain themselves save by coming together and pooling their strength in a way that will enable them to withstand any resistance exerted upon them from without. They must develop some sort of central direction and learn to act in concert.

Such a concentration of powers can be brought about only as the consequence of an agreement reached between individuals. But the self-preservation of each single man derives primarily from his own strength and from his own freedom. How, then, can he limit these without, at the same time, doing himself an injury and neglecting that care which it is his duty to devote to his own concerns? This difficulty, in so far as it is relevant to my subject, can be expressed as follows:

"Some form of association must be found as a result of which the whole strength of the community will be enlisted for the protection of the person and property of each constituent member, in such a way that each, when united to his fellows, renders obedience to his own will, and remains as free as he was before." That is the basic problem of which the Social Contract provides the solution.

The clauses of this Contract are determined by the Act of Association in such a way that the least modification must render them null and void. Even though they may never have been formally enunciated, they must be everywhere the same, and everywhere tacitly admitted and recognized. So completely must this be the case that, should the social compact be violated, each associated individual would at once resume all the rights which once were his, and regain his natural liberty, by the mere fact of losing the agreed liberty for which he renounced it.

It must be clearly understood that the clauses in question can be reduced, in the last analysis, to one only, to wit, the complete alienation by each associate member to the community of *all his rights.* For, in the first place, since each has made surrender of himself without reservation, the resultant conditions are the same for all: and, because they are the same for all, it is in the interest of none to make them onerous to his fellows.

Furthermore, this alienation having been made unreservedly, the union of individuals is as perfect as it well can be, none of the associated members having any claim against the community. For should there be any rights left to individuals, and no common authority be empowered to pronounce as between them and the public, then each, being in some things his own judge, would soon claim to be so in all. Were that so, a state of Nature would still remain in being, the conditions of association becoming either despotic or ineffective.

In short, whoso gives himself to all gives himself to none. And, since there is no member of the social group over whom we do not acquire precisely the same rights as those over ourselves which we have surrendered to him, it follows that we gain the exact equivalent of what we lose, as well as an added power to conserve what we already have.   41

If, then, we take from the social pact everything which is not essential to it, we shall find it to be reduced to the following terms: "each of us contributes to the group his person and the powers which he wields as a person under the supreme direction of the general will, and we receive into the body politic each individual as forming an indivisible part of the whole."   42

As soon as the act of association becomes a reality, it substitutes for the person of each of the contracting parties a moral and collective body made up of as many members as the constituting assembly has votes, which body receives from this very act of constitution its unity, its dispersed *self*, and its will. The public person thus formed by the union of individuals was known in the old days as a *City*, but now as the *Republic* or *Body Politic*. This, when it fulfils a passive role, is known by its members as *The State*, when an active one, as *The Sovereign People*, and, in contrast to other similar bodies, as a *Power*. In respect of the constituent associates, it enjoys the collective name of *The People*, the individuals who compose it being known as *Citizens* in so far as they share in the sovereign authority, as *Subjects* in so far as they owe obedience to the laws of the State. But these different terms frequently overlap, and are used indiscriminately one for the other. It is enough that we should realize the difference between them when they are employed in a precise sense.   43

Of the Sovereign

It is clear from the above formula that the act of association implies a mutual undertaking between the body politic and its constituent members. Each individual comprising the former contracts, so to speak, with himself and has a twofold function. As a member of the   44 sovereign people he owes a duty to each of his neighbors, and, as a Citizen, to the sovereign people as a whole. But we cannot here apply that maxim of Civil Law according to which no man can be held to an undertaking entered into with himself, because there is a great difference between a man's duty to himself and to a whole of which he forms a part.

Here it should be pointed out that a public decision which can enjoin obedience on all subjects to their Sovereign, by reason of the double aspect under which each is seen, cannot, on the contrary, bind the sovereign in his dealings with himself. Consequently, it is against the nature of the body politic that the sovereign should impose upon himself a law which he cannot infringe. For, since he can regard himself under one aspect only, he is in the position of an individual entering into a contract with himself. Whence it follows that there is not, nor can be, any fundamental law which is obligatory for the whole body of the People, not even the social contract itself. This does not mean that the body politic is unable to enter into engagements with some other Power, provided always that such engagements do not derogate from the nature of the Contract; for the relation of the body politic to a foreign Power is that of a simple individual. 45

But the body politic, or Sovereign, in that it derives its being simply and solely from the sanctity of the said Contract, can never bind itself, even in its relations with a foreign Power, by any decision which might derogate from the validity of the original act. It may not, for instance, alienate any portion of itself, nor make submission to any other sovereign. To violate the act by reason of which it exists would be tantamount to destroying itself, and that which is nothing can produce nothing. 46

As soon as a mob has become united into a body politic, any attack upon one of its members is an attack upon itself. Still more important is the fact that, should any offense be committed against the body politic as a whole, the effect must be felt by each of its members. Both duty and interest, therefore, oblige the two contracting parties to render one another mutual assistance. The same individuals should seek to unite under this double aspect all the advantages which flow from it. 47

Now, the Sovereign People, having no existence outside that of the individuals who compose it, has, and can have, no interest at variance with theirs. Consequently, the sovereign power need give no guarantee to its subjects, since it is impossible that the body should wish to injure all its members, nor, as we shall see later, can it injure any single individual. The Sovereign, by merely existing, is always what it should be. 48

But the same does not hold true of the relation of subject to sover- 49
eign. In spite of common interest, there can be no guarantee that the
subject will observe his duty to the sovereign unless means are found
to ensure his loyalty.

Each individual, indeed, may, as a man, exercise a will at variance 50
with, or different from, that general will to which, as citizen, he contributes. His personal interest may dictate a line of action quite other
than that demanded by the interest of all. The fact that his own existence as an individual has an absolute value, and that he is, by nature,
an independent being, may lead him to conclude that what he owes to
the common cause is something that he renders of his own free will;
and he may decide that by leaving the debt unpaid he does less harm
to his fellows than he would to himself should he make the necessary
surrender. Regarding the moral entity constituting the State as a rational abstraction because it is not a man, he might enjoy his rights as
a citizen without, at the same time, fulfilling his duties as a subject,
and the resultant injustice might grow until it brought ruin upon the
whole body politic.

In order, then, that the social compact may not be but a vain for- 51
mula, it must contain, though unexpressed, the single undertaking
which can alone give force to the whole, namely, that whoever shall
refuse to obey the general will must be constrained by the whole body
of his fellow citizens to do so: which is no more than to say that it
may be necessary to compel a man to be free—freedom being that condition which, by giving each citizen to his country, guarantees him
from all personal dependence and is the foundation upon which the
whole political machine rests, and supplies the power which works it.
Only the recognition by the individual of the rights of the community
can give legal force to undertakings entered into between citizens,
which, otherwise, would become absurd, tyrannical, and exposed to
vast abuses.

Of the Civil State

The passage from the state of nature to the civil state produces a 52
truly remarkable change in the individual. It substitutes justice for instinct in his behavior, and gives to his actions a moral basis which
formerly was lacking. Only when the voice of duty replaces physical
impulse and when right replaces the cravings of appetite does the man
who, till then, was concerned solely with himself, realize that he is
under compulsion to obey quite different principles, and that he must

now consult his reason and not merely respond to the promptings of desire. Although he may find himself deprived of many advantages which were his in a state of nature, he will recognize that he has gained others which are of far greater value. By dint of being exercised, his faculties will develop, his ideas take on a wider scope, his sentiments become ennobled, and his whole soul be so elevated, that, but for the fact that misuse of the new conditions still, at times, degrades him to a point below that from which he has emerged, he would unceasingly bless the day which freed him for ever from his ancient state, and turned him from a limited and stupid animal into an intelligent being and a Man.

Let us reduce all this to terms which can be easily compared. What 53 a man loses as a result of the Social Contract is his natural liberty and his unqualified right to lay hands on all that tempts him, provided only that he can compass its possession. What he gains is civil liberty and the ownership of what belongs to him. That we may labor under no illusion concerning these compensations, it is well that we distinguish between natural liberty which the individual enjoys so long as he is strong enough to maintain it, and civil liberty which is curtailed by the general will. Between possessions which derive from physical strength and the right of the first-comer, and ownership which can be based only on a positive title.

To the benefits conferred by the status of citizenship might be 54 added that of Moral Freedom, which alone makes a man his own master. For to be subject to appetite is to be a slave, while to obey the laws laid down by society is to be free. But I have already said enough on this point, and am not concerned here with the philosophical meaning of the word *liberty*.

Of Real Property

Each individual member of the Community gives himself to it at 55 the moment of its formation. What he gives is the whole man as he then is, with all his qualities of strength and power, and everything of which he stands possessed. Not that, as a result of this act of gift, such possessions, by changing hands and becoming the property of the Sovereign, change their nature. Just as the resources of strength upon which the City can draw are incomparably greater than those at the disposition of any single individual, so, too, is public possession when backed by a greater power. It is made more irrevocable, though not, so far, at least, as regards foreigners, more legitimate. For the State, by reason of the Social Contract which, within it, is the basis of all Rights, is the master of all its members' goods, though, in its dealings with other Powers, it is so only by virtue of its rights as first occupier, which come to it from the individuals who make it up.

The Right of "first occupancy," though more real than the "Right 56 of the strongest," becomes a genuine right only after the right of property has been established. All men have a natural right to what is necessary to them. But the positive act which establishes a man's claim to any particular item of property limits him to that and excludes him from all others. His share having been determined, he must confine himself to that, and no longer has any claim on the property of the community. That is why the right of "first occupancy," however weak it be in a state of nature, is guaranteed to every man enjoying the status of citizen. In so far as he benefits from this right, he withholds his claim, not so much from what is another's, as from what is not specifically his.

In order that the right of "first occupancy" may be legalized, the 57 following conditions must be present. (1) There must be no one already living on the land in question. (2) A man must occupy only so much of it as is necessary for his subsistence. (3) He must take possession of it, not by empty ceremony, but by virtue of his intention to work and to cultivate it, for that, in the absence of legal title, alone constitutes a claim which will be respected by others.

In effect, by according the right of "first occupancy" to a man's 58 needs and to his will to work, are we not stretching it as far as it will go? Should not some limits be set to this right? Has a man only to set foot on land belonging to the community to justify his claim to be its master? Just because he is strong enough, at one particular moment, to keep others off, can he demand that they shall never return? How can a man or a People take possession of vast territories, thereby excluding the rest of the world from their enjoyment, save by an act of criminal usurpation, since, as the result of such an act, the rest of humanity is deprived of the amenities of dwelling and subsistence which nature has provided for their common enjoyment? When Nuñez Balboa,[13] landing upon a strip of coast, claimed the Southern Sea and the whole of South America as the property of the crown of Castille, was he thereby justified in dispossessing its former inhabitants, and in excluding from it all the other princes of the earth? Grant that, and there will be no end to such vain ceremonies. It would be open to His

---

[13]**Nuñez Balboa (1475–1519)** Spanish explorer who discovered the Pacific Ocean.

Catholic Majesty[14] to claim from his Council Chamber possession of the whole Universe, only excepting those portions of it already in the ownership of other princes.

One can understand how the lands of individuals, separate but con- 59 tiguous, become public territory, and how the right of sovereignty, extending from men to the land they occupy, becomes at one real and personal—a fact which makes their owners more than ever dependent, and turns their very strength into a guarantee of their fidelity. This is an advantage which does not seem to have been considered by the monarchs of the ancient world, who, claiming to be no more than kings of the Persians, the Scythians, the Macedonians, seem to have regarded themselves rather as the rulers of men than as the masters of countries. Those of our day are cleverer, for they style themselves kings of France, of Spain, of England, and so forth. Thus, by controlling the land, they can be very sure of controlling its inhabitants.

The strange thing about this act of alienation is that, far from de- 60 priving its members of their property by accepting its surrender, the Community actually establishes their claim to its legitimate ownership, and changes what was formerly mere usurpation into a right, by virtue of which they may enjoy possession. As owners they are Trustees for the Commonwealth. Their rights are respected by their fellow citizens and are maintained by the united strength of the community against any outside attack. From ceding their property to the State— and thus, to themselves—they derive nothing but advantage, since they have, so to speak, acquired all that they have surrendered. This paradox is easily explained once we realize the distinction between the rights exercised by the Sovereign and by the Owner over the same piece of property, as will be seen later.

It may so happen that a number of men begin to group themselves 61 into a community before ever they own property at all, and that only later, when they have got possession of land sufficient to maintain them all, do they either enjoy it in common or parcel it between themselves in equal lots or in accordance with such scale of proportion as may be established by the sovereign. However this acquisition be made, the right exercised by each individual over his own particular share must always be subordinated to the overriding claim of the Community as such. Otherwise there would be no strength in the social bond, nor any real power in the exercise of sovereignty.

---

[14]***His Catholic Majesty*** A reference to the king of Spain, probably Ferdinand II of Aragon (1452–1516).

I will conclude this chapter, and the present Book, with a remark 62
which should serve as basis for every social system: that, so far from
destroying natural equality, the primitive compact substitutes for it a
moral and legal equality which compensates for all those physical in-
equalities from which men suffer. However unequal they may be in
bodily strength or in intellectual gifts, they become equal in the eyes
of the law, and as a result of the compact into which they have entered.

QUESTIONS

1. Rousseau says that the oldest and only natural form of society is the
   family. Is this true? Are there any other natural forms of society evident
   to you?
2. What is the meaning of the phrase "might makes right"?
3. Is political power ever exercised in the interest of the governed?
4. Rousseau describes a "body politic." What does he mean by the term?
   What does he mean by "Commonwealth" when he describes the social
   order by that term?
5. Rousseau emphasizes natural, moral, and legal equality. What does each
   kind of equality imply?

WRITING ASSIGNMENTS

1. The famous opening lines—"Man is born free, and everywhere he is in
   chains. Many a man believes himself to be the master of others who is, no
   less than they, a slave"—were greeted with extraordinary enthusiasm in
   Rousseau's time. Is it possible to apply these lines to the condition of people you know in your own community? In the nation at large? In what
   senses do people make slaves of themselves today? In what senses are they
   made slaves by others?
2. Define the difference between one's duty to oneself and one's duty to the
   whole of which one forms a part. Assume that the individual is yourself
   and that the "whole" is your social structure (locally, nationally, on cam-
   pus). Define each kind of duty, referring as much as possible to specific
   acts or responsibilities; then establish the differences and the ways in
   which they may come into conflict with one another.
3. One of the most controversial statements in this extract is: "All men have
   a natural right to what is necessary to them." Examine this statement
   carefully. What things or circumstances are necessary to people? Be specific and inclusive. Does Rousseau indicate what is necessary and what is
   not? Take a stand on whether or not Rousseau is correct in his statement.

If he is correct, who should provide the necessities to those who cannot provide for themselves? Does Rousseau take into account those who cannot provide for themselves? Should the necessities be provided for those who will not (as opposed to cannot) provide for themselves? If society will not provide necessities, does the individual have the right of revolution? What rights does the individual have?

4. Consider in some detail the appropriateness of the analogy between the family and the state. Is Rousseau correct in making the analogy in the first place? To what extent does he feel it is a reasonable comparison? By analyzing the details of the family as you know it, establish what the similarities and the differences are between the family and the government. Which responsibilities in one situation carry over to the other? In what sense may it be said that learning to live in a family is preparation for learning to live in a social state?

5. Rousseau contrasts natural liberty with civil liberty. Natural liberty is possible in a state of nature; civil liberty is possible in a civil state. Define each kind of liberty carefully, using a number of examples. What will the differences be between life in a state of nature and life in a civil state? Which state is preferable? What are the reasons for your views? Point to Rousseau's own arguments (he prefers the civil state) and analyze them carefully to support your views. Look for opportunities to use analogy in treating this issue.

THOMAS JEFFERSON

The Declaration of Independence

THOMAS JEFFERSON (1743–1826), an exceptionally accomplished and well-educated man, is probably best known for writing the Declaration of Independence, a work composed under the eyes of Benjamin Franklin, John Adams, and the Continental Congress, which spent two and a half days going over every word. The substance of the document was developed in committee, but Jefferson, because of the grace of his style, was chosen to do the actual writing. The result is one of the most memorable statements in American history.

Jefferson had a long and distinguished career. He received a classical education and went on to become a lawyer. By the time he took a seat in the House of Burgesses, which governed Virginia, that colony was already on a course toward revolution. His "A Summary View of the Rights of British America" (1774) first brought him to the attention of those who were agitating for independence.

Jefferson's services to Virginia were considerable. In addition to serving in the House of Burgesses, he became governor (1779) and founded the University of Virginia (1809). Many details of the design of the university's buildings reflect Jefferson's considerable skill as an architect. His one book, Notes on Virginia (1782), is sometimes personal, sometimes public, sometimes scientific, sometimes haphazard. He discusses slavery, racial differences, the effects of the environment on people, and some of his own feelings about revolution while describing his home state, its geography and its people.

Jefferson's services to the nation include being the first secretary of state (1789–1797), second vice-president (1797–1801), and third president (1801–1809). During his presidency he negotiated the Louisiana Purchase, buying 800,000 square miles of land west of the Mississippi from France for only $15 million. He was sympathetic to the efforts of the French to throw off their monarchy, but when Napoleon extended French influence into the rest of Europe by waging war, Jefferson was careful to keep the United States neutral.

Jefferson was a well-educated eighteenth-century gentleman. His training in the classics and his wide reading in modern authors helped him become a gifted stylist. His work has balance and eloquence as well as clarity. The Declaration of Independence says little that was not familiar or widely understood at the time, but what it does say, it says in a fashion that is memorable.

JEFFERSON'S RHETORIC

Jefferson is notable for a number of interesting techniques. One is the periodic sentence, which was very typical of the age. The first sentence of the Declaration is periodic, which means that it is long and carefully balanced, and the main point comes at the end. Such sentences are not popular today, although an occasional periodic sentence can be powerful in contemporary prose. That first sentence says (in paraphrase): When one nation must sever its relations with a parent nation . . . and stand as an independent nation itself . . . the causes ought to be explained. The entire paragraph is taken up by this one sentence. Moreover, the main body of the Declaration is devoted to listing the "causes," so we see that the most important element of the sentence comes at the end.

The periodic sentence demands certain qualities of balance and parallelism which all good writers ought to pay attention to. The first sentence in paragraph 2 demonstrates both qualities. The balance is achieved by making each part of the sentence about the same length. The parallelism is achieved by using certain key linking words in repetition (they are in roman type in the analysis below). Note how the "truths" mentioned in the first clause are enumerated in the succession of noun clauses beginning with "that"; "Rights" are enumerated in the final clause.

We hold these truths to be self-evident,
   that all men are created equal,
   that they are endowed by their Creator with certain
      unalienable Rights,
   that among these are Life, Liberty and the pursuit of Happiness.

Parallelism is one of the greatest stylistic techniques available to a writer sensitive to rhetoric. It is a natural technique—many untrained writers and speakers develop it on their own.

One result of using parallelism is that one tends to employ the very useful device of enumeration, or the list. Many writers use this technique very effectively by establishing from the first that: "There are three important issues I wish to address. . . ."; and then numbering them: "First, I want to say. . . . Secondly. . . ," and so on. Naturally, as with any technique, this can become tiresome. Used judiciously, it is exceptionally authoritative and powerful. Jefferson devotes paragraphs 3–29 to enumerating the "causes" he mentioned in paragraph 1. Each one constitutes a separate paragraph; thus, each has separate weight and importance. Each begins with "He" or "For" and is therefore in parallel structure. The technique is called anaphora, *repetition of the same words at the beginning of successive lines. Jefferson's use of anaphora here is one of the best-known and most effective in all literature. The "He" referred to is England's King George III (1738–1820), who is never mentioned by name. It is not a personality Congress is opposed to; it is the sovereign of a nation which is oppressing the United States and a tyrant who is not dignified by being named. The "For" introduces grievous acts the king has given his assent for; these are offenses against the colonies.*

None of the causes is developed in any detail. We do not have specific information about what trade was cut off by the British, what taxes were imposed without consent, how King George waged war or abdicated government in the colonies. Presumably, Jefferson's audience knew the details. What he did, in listing in twenty-seven paragraphs all the causes, was to point out how many there were. And all are so serious that one alone could cause a revolution. The effect of this enumeration is to illustrate the patience of the colonies up to this point. Jefferson is telling the world that the colonies have finally lost patience, as a result of the causes he lists. The Declaration of Independence projects the careful meditations and decisions of exceptionally calm, patient, and—above all—reasonable people. The periodicity of the sentences and the balance of their parallelism underscore thoughtfulness, grace, learning, and ultimately wisdom.

The Declaration of Independence

In Congress, July 4, 1776

**The Unanimous Declaration of the Thirteen
United States of America**

When in the Course of human events, it becomes necessary for one 1
people to dissolve the political bands which have connected them with
another, and to assume among the Powers of the earth, the separate
and equal station to which the Laws of Nature and of Nature's God
entitle them, a decent respect to the opinions of mankind requires that
they should declare the causes which impel them to the separation.

We hold these truths to be self-evident, that all men are created 2
equal, that they are endowed by their Creator with certain unalienable
Rights, that among these are Life, Liberty and the pursuit of Happiness. That to secure these rights, Governments are instituted among
Men, deriving their just powers from the consent of the governed. That
whenever any Form of Government becomes destructive of these ends,
it is the Right of the People to alter or to abolish it, and to institute a
new Government, laying its foundation on such principles and organizing its powers in such form, as to them shall seem most likely to
effect their Safety and Happiness. Prudence, indeed, will dictate that
Governments long established should not be changed for light and
transient causes; and accordingly all experience hath shown, that mankind are more disposed to suffer, while evils are sufferable, than to
right themselves by abolishing the forms to which they are accustomed. But when a long train of abuses and usurpations, pursuing invariably the same Object evinces a design to reduce them under absolute Despotism, it is their right, it is their duty, to throw off such
Government, and to provide new Guards for their future security.—
Such has been the patient sufferance of these Colonies; and such is
now the necessity which constrains them to alter their former Systems
of Government. The history of the present King of Great Britain is a
history of repeated injuries and usurpations, all having in direct object
the establishment of an absolute Tyranny over these States. To prove
this, let Facts be submitted to a candid world.

He has refused his Assent to Laws, the most wholesome and nec-   3
essary for the public good.

He has forbidden his Governors to pass Laws of immediate and   4
pressing importance, unless suspended in their operation till his Assent should be obtained; and when so suspended, he has utterly neglected to attend to them.

He has refused to pass other laws for the accommodation of large   5
districts of people, unless those people would relinquish the right of
Representation in the Legislature, a right inestimable to them and for-
midable to tyrants only.

He has called together legislative bodies at places unusual, uncom-   6
fortable, and distant from the depository of their Public Records, for
the sole purpose of fatiguing them into compliance with his measures.

He has dissolved Representative Houses repeatedly, for opposing   7
with manly firmness his invasions on the rights of the people.

He has refused for a long time, after such dissolutions, to cause   8
others to be elected; whereby the Legislative Powers, incapable of Annihilation, have returned to the People at large for their exercise; the
State remaining in the mean time exposed to all the dangers of invasion from without, and convulsions within.

He has endeavoured to prevent the population of these States;[1] for   9
that purpose obstructing the Laws for Naturalization of Foreigners; refusing to pass others to encourage their migration hither, and raising
the conditions of new Appropriations of Lands.

He has obstructed the Administration of Justice, by refusing his   10
Assent to Laws for establishing Judiciary Powers.

He has made Judges dependent on his Will alone, for the tenure of   11
their offices, and the amount and payment of their salaries.

He has erected a multitude of New Offices, and sent hither swarms   12
of Officers to harass our People, and eat out their substance.

He has kept among us, in times of peace, Standing Armies without   13
the Consent of our legislature.

He has affected to render the Military independent of and superior   14
to the Civil Power.

He has combined with others to subject us to a jurisdiction foreign   15
to our constitution, and unacknowledged by our laws; giving his Assent to their acts of pretended Legislation:

For quartering large bodies of armed troops among us: 16

---

[1]***prevent the population of these States*** This meant limiting emigration to the Colonies, thus controlling their growth.

For protecting them, by a mock Trial, from Punishment for any 17
Murders which they should commit on the Inhabitants of these States:

For cutting off our Trade with all parts of the world: 18

For imposing taxes on us without our Consent: 19

For depriving us in many cases, of the benefits of Trial by Jury: 20

For transporting us beyond Seas to be tried for pretended offences: 21

For abolishing the free System of English Laws in a neighbouring 22
Province, establishing therein an Arbitrary government, and enlarging
its Boundaries so as to render it at once an example and fit instrument
for introducing the same absolute rule into these Colonies:

For taking away our Charters, abolishing our most valuable Laws, 23
and altering fundamentally the Forms of our Governments:

For suspending our own Legislatures, and declaring themselves in- 24
vested with Power to legislate for us in all cases whatsoever.

He has abdicated Government here, by declaring us out of his Pro- 25
tection and waging War against us.

He has plundered our seas, ravaged our Coasts, burnt our towns, 26
and destroyed the lives of our people.

He is at this time transporting large armies of foreign mercenaries 27
to compleat the works of death, desolation and tyranny, already begun
with circumstances of Cruelty & perfidy scarcely paralleled in the
most barbarous ages, and totally unworthy the Head of a civilized nation.

He has constrained our fellow Citizens taken Captive on the High 28
Seas to bear Arms against their Country, to become the executioners
of their friends and Brethren, or to fall themselves by their Hands.

He has excited domestic insurrections amongst us, and has endeav- 29
oured to bring on the inhabitants of our frontiers, the merciless Indian
Savages, whose Known rule of warfare, is an undistinguished destruction of all ages, sexes and conditions.

In every stage of these Oppressions We have Petitioned for Redress 30
in the most humble terms: Our repeated Petitions have been answered
only by repeated injury. A Prince, whose character is thus marked by
every act which may define a Tyrant, is unfit to be the ruler of a free
People.

Nor have We been wanting in attention to our British brethren. We 31
have warned them from time to time of attempts by their legislature
to extend an unwarrantable jurisdiction over us. We have reminded
them of the circumstances of our emigration and settlement here. We
have appealed to their native justice and magnanimity, and we have
conjured them by the ties of our common kindred to disavow these
usurpations, which, would inevitably interrupt our connections and

correspondence. They too have been deaf to the voice of justice and of consanguinity. We must, therefore, acquiesce in the necessity, which denounces our Separation, and hold them, as we hold the rest of mankind, Enemies in War, in Peace Friends.

We, therefore, the Representatives of the united States of America, 32 in General Congress, Assembled, appealing to the Supreme Judge of the world for the rectitude of our intentions, do, in the Name, and by Authority of the good People of these Colonies, solemnly publish and declare, That these United Colonies are, and of Right ought to be Free and Independent States, that they are Absolved from all Allegiance to the British Crown, and that all political connection between them and the State of Great Britain, is and ought to be totally dissolved; and that as Free and Independent States, they have full Power to levy War, conclude Peace, contract Alliances, establish Commerce, and to do all other Acts and Things which Independent States may of right do. And for the support of this Declaration, with a firm reliance on the Protection of Divine Providence, we mutually pledge to each other our Lives, our Fortunes and our sacred Honor.

QUESTIONS

1. What are the laws of nature Jefferson refers to in paragraph 1? Is there evidence to indicate he had read Rousseau?
2. What do you think Jefferson feels is the function of government (para. 2)?
3. Find at least two examples of the periodic sentence in the Declaration.
4. Find at least one use of parallel structure in the Declaration. What key terms are repeated as a means of guaranteeing that structure?
5. Which of the causes listed in paragraphs 3–29 are the most serious? Is any one of them trivial? Is any one serious enough to cause a revolution?
6. Find the most graceful sentence in the entire Declaration. Where is it placed in the Declaration? Do you think it was put there consciously, as a means of attracting attention?

WRITING ASSIGNMENTS

1. Jefferson states that the unalienable rights of a citizen are "Life, Liberty and the pursuit of Happiness." Do you think these are indeed unalienable rights? In the course of answering this question—using careful parallelism of any sort you like—be certain that you define what each of these terms really means. Define them for yourself, for our time.
2. Write an essay with at least three periodic sentences (and underline them)

in which you discuss what you feel the function of government should be. You may want to establish first what you think Jefferson's conception of the function of government is, then compare or contrast it with your own.

3. Write a critique of Jefferson's style. What are the qualities you most value in it? Analyze a few words, expressions, sentences, or paragraphs for their stylistic achievement. Do you like or dislike his style?

4. Jefferson envisioned a government that made it possible for its citizens to have the rights of life, liberty, and the pursuit of happiness. Has Jefferson's revolutionary vision been achieved in America? Begin with a definition of your key terms: "life," "liberty," and "the pursuit of happiness." Then, taking each in turn and using any examples available—drawn from current events, your own experience, your general background in American history—take a clear and well-argued stand on whether our nation has achieved Jefferson's goal.

5. Slavery was legal in America in 1776, and Jefferson reluctantly owned slaves. He had a plan to grant gradual emancipation to the slaves, but it was never presented to Congress because he realized that Congress would never approve it. Jefferson and Franklin financed a plan to buy slaves and return them to Africa, where they founded the nation of Liberia. To what degree does the practice of slavery by the people who wrote it invalidate the Declaration of Independence? Does it invalidate it at all? Take a stand on these questions and defend it. You may wish to read the relevant chapters on Jefferson and slavery in Merrill D. Peterson's *Thomas Jefferson and the New Nation* (1970).

6. The Declaration of Independence establishes the right of the Colonies to mount a revolution against the British government. According to Jefferson, when can a government be abolished by a people? Be sure to use the technique of enumeration in qualifying the causes or conditions, in modern terms, and in reference to our own government, which would make you feel it necessary to abolish a government. As you do so, be certain to define very carefully what it means to abolish a government.

MARY WOLLSTONECRAFT

Pernicious Effects Which Arise from the Unnatural Distinctions Established in Society

Mary Wollstonecraft (1759–1797) *was born into relatively simple circumstances, with a father whose heavy drinking and spending eventually ruined the family and left her and her sisters to support themselves. She became a governess, a teacher, and eventually a writer. Her views were among the most enlightened of her day—particularly regarding women and women's rights. She is thought of in our time as a very forward-looking feminist.*

Her thinking, however, is comprehensive and is not to be limited to a single issue. She was known to the American patriot Thomas Paine; to Dr. Samuel Johnson; and to the English philosopher William Godwin (1756–1836), whom she eventually married. Her views on marriage were remarkable for her times; among other things, she felt it unnecessary to marry a man in order to live happily with him. Her first liaison, with an American, Gilbert Imlay, gave her the opportunity to travel and learn something about commerce and capitalism at first hand. Her second liaison, with Godwin, brought her into the intellectual circles of her day. She married Godwin when she was pregnant with Mary, who married the poet Percy Bysshe Shelley and

---

From A Vindication of the Rights of Women.

wrote the novel Frankenstein (1818). Mary Wollstonecraft died giving birth to this daughter.

The excitement generated by the French Revolution (1789–1799) caused her to react against the very conservative view put forward by the philosopher Edmund Burke. Her pamphlet, A Vindication of the Rights of Men (1790), was well received. She followed it with A Vindication of the Rights of Women (1792), which was translated into French.

She sees the feminist problem in political terms. The chapter reprinted here concentrates on questions of property, class, and law. As a person committed to the revolutionary principles of liberty, equality, and fraternity, Wollstonecraft links the present condition of women to the political and social structure of her society. Her aim is to point up the inequities in treatment of women—which her society simply did not perceive—and to attempt to rectify them.

WOLLSTONECRAFT'S RHETORIC

Stylistically, Mary Wollstonecraft is sometimes overblown and wordy. She was writing for an audience that did not necessarily appreciate brief, exact expression. Rather, they appreciated a more luxuriant and leisurely style than we do today. However, she is capable of handling imagery carefully and does so (especially in the first paragraph) without overburdening her prose. She uses an approach which she herself calls "episodical observations" (para. 12). These are anecdotes—personal stories—and apparently casual cataloguings of thoughts on a number of related issues. She was aware that her structure was not tight, that it did not develop a specific argument, and that it did not force the reader to accept or reject her position. This was a wise approach, since it was obvious to her that her audience was completely prejudiced against her view. To attempt to convince them of her views was to invite total defeat.

Instead, she simply puts forward several observations which stand by themselves as examples of the evils she condemns. Even those who stand against her will see that there is some validity to her claims; and they will not be so threatened by her argument as to become defensive before they have learned something new. Her appeal is always to the higher intellectual capacities of both men and women. Her complaints are directed, as well, against both men and women. This balance of opinion, coupled with a range of examples—

all of which are thought-provoking—makes her views seem sane, clear, and convincing.

The use of metaphor is also distinctive in this passage. A metaphor is an implied comparison, made without using "like" or "as." The second sentence of the first paragraph is particularly heavy with metaphor: "For it is in the most polished society that noisome reptiles and venomous serpents lurk under the rank herbage; and there is voluptuousness pampered by the still sultry air, which relaxes every good disposition before it ripens into virtue." The metaphor presents society as a garden in which the grass is decaying and dangerous serpents are lurking. Good disposition—character—is a plant that might ripen, but—continuing the metaphor—it ripens into virtue, not just a fruit. A favorite source of metaphors for Wollstonecraft is drapery (dressmaking). When she uses one of these metaphors she is usually reminding us that drapery gives a new shape to things, that it sometimes hides the truth, and that it ought not put a false appearance on what it covers.

One interesting technique she uses, and which we can easily use ourselves, is that of literary allusion. By alluding to important literary works and writers—such as William Shakespeare, Jean Jacques Rousseau, Dr. Johnson, and Greek mythology—she is not only demonstrating her learning but is also showing that she respects her audience, which she presumes shares her learning. She does not show off her learning by overquoting or by referring to very obscure writers. She balances it perfectly, even by transforming folk aphorisms into "homely proverbs" such as, "whoever the devil finds idle he will employ."

A very special area of allusion is to the art of dressmaking, something we associate with women. Her experiences with her difficult father gave her the further, unfortunate expertise in allusion to gambling tables and card games. She alludes further to personal experience shared by some of her audience when she talks about the degradation felt by a woman of some intelligence forced to act the governess—glorified servant—in a well-to-do family. Wollstonecraft makes excellent uses of these allusions, never overdoing them, always giving them just the right touch.

Pernicious Effects Which Arise from the Unnatural Distinctions Established in Society

From the respect paid to property flow, as from a poisoned fountain, most of the evils and vices which render this world such a dreary scene to the contemplative mind. For it is in the most polished society that noisome reptiles and venomous serpents lurk under the rank herbage; and there is voluptuousness pampered by the still sultry air, which relaxes every good disposition before it ripens into virtue.

One class presses on another; for all are aiming to procure respect on account of their property: and property, once gained, will procure the respect due only to talents and virtue. Men neglect the duties incumbent on man, yet are treated like demi-gods; religion is also separated from morality by a ceremonial veil, yet men wonder that the world is almost, literally speaking, a den of sharpers or oppressors.

There is a homely proverb, which speaks a shrewd truth, that whoever the devil finds idle he will employ. And what but habitual idleness can hereditary wealth and titles produce? For man is so constituted that he can only attain a proper use of his faculties by exercising them, and will not exercise them unless necessity of some kind first set the wheels in motion. Virtue likewise can only be acquired by the discharge of relative duties; but the importance of these sacred duties will scarcely be felt by the being who is cajoled out of his humanity by the flattery of sycophants.[1] There must be more equality established in society, or morality will never gain ground, and this virtuous equality will not rest firmly even when founded on a rock, if one half of mankind be chained to its bottom by fate, for they will be continually undermining it through ignorance or pride.

It is vain to expect virtue from women till they are in some degree independent of men; nay, it is vain to expect that strength of natural affection which would make them good wives and mothers. Whilst

---

[1]**sycophants** toadies or false flatterers.

they are absolutely dependent on their husbands they will be cunning, mean, and selfish, and the men who can be gratified by the fawning fondness of spaniel-like affection have not much delicacy, for love is not to be bought, in any sense of the words; its silken wings are instantly shrivelled up when anything beside a return in kind is sought. Yet whilst wealth enervates men, and women live, as it were, by their personal charms, how can we expect them to discharge those ennobling duties which equally require exertion and self-denial? Hereditary property sophisticates[2] the mind, and the unfortunate victims to it, if I may so express myself, swathed from their birth, seldom exert the locomotive faculty of body or mind; and, thus viewing everything through one medium, and that a false one, they are unable to discern in what true merit and happiness consist. False, indeed, must be the light when the drapery of situation hides the man, and makes him stalk in masquerade, dragging from one scene of dissipation to another the nerveless limbs that hang with stupid listlessness, and rolling round the vacant eye which plainly tells us that there is no mind at home.

I mean, therefore, to infer[3] that the society is not properly orga- 5 nized which does not compel men and women to discharge their respective duties, by making it the only way to acquire that countenance from their fellow-creatures which every human being wishes some way to attain. The respect, consequently, which is paid to wealth and mere personal charms, is a true north-east blast that blights the tender blossoms of affection and virtue. Nature has wisely attached affections to duties to sweeten toil, and to give that vigour to the exertions of reason which only the heart can give. But the affection which is put on merely because it is the appropriated insignia of a certain character, when its duties are not fulfilled, is one of the empty compliments which vice and folly are obliged to pay to virtue and the real nature of things.

To illustrate my opinion, I need only observe that when a woman 6 is admired for her beauty, and suffers herself to be so far intoxicated by the admiration she receives as to neglect to discharge the indispensable duty of a mother, she sins against herself by neglecting to cultivate an affection that would equally tend to make her useful and happy. True happiness, I mean all the contentment and virtuous satisfaction that can be snatched in this imperfect state, must arise from

---

[2]***sophisticates*** ruins or corrupts.
[3]***infer*** imply.

well regulated affections; and an affection includes a duty. Men are not aware of the misery they cause and the vicious weakness they cherish by only inciting women to render themselves pleasing; they do not consider that they thus make natural and artificial duties clash by sacrificing the comfort and respectability of a woman's life to voluptuous notions of beauty when in nature they all harmonize.

Cold would be the heart of a husband, were he not rendered unnatural by early debauchery, who did not feel more delight at seeing his child suckled by its mother, than the most artful wanton tricks could ever raise; yet this natural way of cementing the matrimonial tie and twisting esteem with fonder recollections, wealth leads women to spurn. To preserve their beauty and wear the flowery crown of the day, which gives them a kind of right to reign for a short time over the sex, they neglect to stamp impressions on their husbands' hearts that would be remembered with more tenderness when the snow on the head began to chill the bosom than even their virgin charms. The maternal solicitude of a reasonable affectionate woman is very interesting, and the chastened dignity with which a mother returns the caresses that she and her child receive from a father who has been fulfilling the serious duties of his station, is not only a respectable but a beautiful sight. So singular indeed are my feelings, and I have endeavoured not to catch factitious ones, that after having been fatigued with the sight of insipid grandeur and the slavish ceremonies that with cumbrous pomp supplied the place of domestic affections, I have turned to some other scene to relieve my eye by resting it on the refreshing green everywhere scattered by nature. I have then viewed with pleasure a woman nursing her children, and discharging the duties of her station with, perhaps, merely a servant maid to take off her hands the servile part of the household business. I have seen her prepare herself and children, with only the luxury of cleanliness, to receive her husband, who returning weary home in the evening found smiling babes and a clean hearth. My heart has loitered in the midst of the group, and has even throbbed with sympathetic emotion, when the scraping of the well known foot has raised a pleasing tumult. 7

Whilst my benevolence has been gratified by contemplating this artless picture, I have thought that a couple of this description, equally necessary and independent of each other, because each fulfilled the respective duties of their station, possessed all that life could give. Raised sufficiently above abject poverty not to be obliged to weigh the consequence of every farthing they spend, and having sufficient to prevent their attending to a frigid system of economy, which narrows 8 both heart and mind. I declare, so vulgar[4] are my conceptions, that I know not what is wanted to render this the happiest as well as the most respectable situation in the world, but a taste for literature, to throw a little variety and interest into social converse, and some superfluous money to give to the needy and to buy books. For it is not pleasant when the heart is opened by compassion and the head active in arranging plans of usefulness, to have a prim urchin continually twitching back the elbow to prevent the hand from drawing out an almost empty purse, whispering at the same time some prudential maxim about the priority of justice.

Destructive, however, as riches and inherited honours are to the human character, women are more debased and cramped, if possible, by them than men, because men may still, in some degree, unfold their faculties by becoming soldiers and statesmen. 9

As soldiers, I grant, they can now only gather, for the most part, vainglorious laurels, whilst they adjust to a hair the European balance, taking especial care that no bleak northern nook or sound incline the beam.[5] But the days of true heroism are over, when a citizen fought for his country like a Fabricius[6] or a Washington, and then returned to his farm to let his virtuous fervour run in a more placid, but not a less salutary, stream. No, our British heroes are oftener sent from the gaming table than from the plough[7] and their passions have been rather inflamed by hanging with dumb suspense on the turn of a die, than sublimated by panting after the adventurous march of virtue in the historic page. 10

The statesman, it is true, might with more propriety quit the faro bank, or card table, to guide the helm, for he has still but to shuffle and trick.[8] The whole system of British politics, if system it may cour- 11

---

[4]*vulgar* common.

[5]*incline the beam* The metaphor is of the balance—the scale that representations of blind justice hold up. Wollstonecraft's point is that in her time soldiers fought to prevent the slightest changes in a balance of power that grew ever more delicate, not in heroic wars with heroic consequences.

[6]*Fabricius (fl. 282 B.C.)* A worthy Roman general known for resistance to corruption.

[7]*from the plough* Worthy Roman heroes were humble farmers, not gamblers.

[8]*shuffle and trick* The upper class spent much of its time gambling: faro is a high-stakes card game. Wollstonecraft is ironic when she says the statesman has "still but to shuffle and trick," but she connects the "training" of faro with the practice of politics in a deft, sardonic fashion. She is punning on the multiple meanings of *shuffle*—to mix up a deck of cards and to move oneself or one's papers about slowly and aimlessly—and *trick*—to win one turn of a card game and to do a devious deed.

teously be called, consisting in multiplying dependents and contriving taxes which grind the poor to pamper the rich; thus a war, or any wild goose chase, is, as the vulgar use the phrase, a lucky turn-up of patronage for the minister, whose chief merit is the art of keeping himself in place. It is not necessary then that he should have bowels for[9] the poor, so he can secure for his family the odd trick. Or should some show of respect, for what is termed with ignorant ostentation an Englishman's birthright, be expedient to bubble the gruff mastiff[10] that he has to lead by the nose, he can make an empty show very safely by giving his single voice and suffering his light squadron to file off to the other side. And when a question of humanity is agitated he may dip a sop in the milk of human kindness to silence Cerberus,[11] and talk of the interest which his heart takes in an attempt to make the earth no longer cry for vengeance as it sucks in its children's blood, though his cold hand may at the very moment rivet their chains by sanctioning the abominable traffic. A minister is no longer a minister than while he can carry a point which he is determined to carry. Yet it is not necessary that a minister should feel like a man, when a bold push might shake his seat.

But, to have done with these episodical observations, let me return 12 to the more specious slavery which chains the very soul of woman, keeping her for ever under the bondage of ignorance.

The preposterous distinctions of rank, which render civilization a 13 curse by dividing the world between voluptuous tyrants and cunning envious dependents, corrupt, almost equally, every class of people, because respectability is not attached to the discharge of the relative duties of life, but to the station, and when the duties are not fulfilled the affections cannot gain sufficient strength to fortify the virtue of which they are the natural reward. Still there are some loopholes out of which a man may creep, and dare to think and act for himself; but for a woman it is a herculean task, because she has difficulties peculiar to her sex to overcome which require almost superhuman powers.

A truly benevolent legislator always endeavours to make it the in- 14 terest of each individual to be virtuous; and thus private virtue becoming the cement of public happiness, an orderly whole is consolidated by the tendency of all the parts towards a common centre. But, the private or public virtue of woman is very problematical; for Rousseau, and a numerous list of male writers, insist that she should all her life

---

[9]*bowels for*   feelings for; sense of pity.
[10]*to bubble the gruff mastiff*   This means to fool even a guard dog.
[11]*Cerberus*   The guard dog of Hades, the Greek hell or underworld.

be subjected to a severe restraint, that of propriety. Why subject her to propriety—blind propriety, if she be capable of acting from a nobler spring, if she be an heir of immortality? Is sugar always to be produced by vital blood? Is one half of the human species, like the poor African slaves, to be subject to prejudices that brutalize them, when principles would be a surer guard, only to sweeten the cup of man? Is not this indirectly to deny woman reason? for a gift is a mockery, if it be unfit for use.

Women are, in common with men, rendered weak and luxurious   15
by the relaxing pleasures which wealth procures; but added to this they are made slaves to their persons, and must render them alluring that man may lend them his reason to guide their tottering steps aright. Or should they be ambitious, they must govern their tyrants by sinister tricks, for without rights there cannot be any incumbent duties. The laws respecting woman, which I mean to discuss in a future part, make an absurd unit of a man and his wife;[12] and then, by the easy transition of only considering him as responsible, she is reduced to a mere cypher.

The being who discharges the duties of its station is independent;   16
and, speaking of women at large, their first duty is to themselves as rational creatures, and the next in point of importance, as citizens, is that which includes so many, of a mother. The rank in life which dispenses with their fulfilling this duty necessarily degrades them by making them mere dolls. Or, should they turn to something more important than merely fitting drapery upon a smooth block, their minds are only occupied by some soft platonic attachment; or, the actual management of an intrigue may keep their thoughts in motion; for when they neglect domestic duties, they have it not in their own power to take the field and march and counter-march like soldiers, or wrangle in the senate to keep their faculties from rusting.

I know that, as a proof of the inferiority of the sex, Rousseau has   17
exultingly exclaimed, How can they leave the nursery for the camp![13] And the camp has by some moralists been termed the school of the most heroic virtues; though, I think, it would puzzle a keen casuist[14] to prove the reasonableness of the greater number of wars that have dubbed heroes. I do not mean to consider this question critically; be-

---

[12]*absurd unit of a man and his wife*   In English law man and wife were legally one; the man spoke for both.

[13]*leave the nursery for the camp!*   Rousseau's Émile complains that women cannot leave a nursery to go to war.

[14]*casuist*   One who argues closely, persistently, and sometimes unfairly.

cause, having frequently viewed these freaks of ambition as the first natural mode of civilization, when the ground must be torn up, and the woods cleared by fire and sword, I do not choose to call them pests; but surely the present system of war has little connection with virtue of any denomination, being rather the school of *finesse* and effeminacy than of fortitude.

Yet if defensive war, the only justifiable war, in the present ad- 18 vanced state of society, where virtue can show its face and ripen amidst the rigours which purify the air on the mountain's top, were alone to be adopted as just and glorious, the true heroism of antiquity might again animate female bosoms. But fair and softly, gentle reader, male or female, do not alarm thyself, for though I have compared the character of a modern soldier with that of a civilized woman, I am not going to advise them to turn their distaff[15] into a musket, though I sincerely wish to see the bayonet converted into a pruning-hook. I only recreated an imagination, fatigued by contemplating the vices and follies which all proceed from a feculent[16] stream of wealth that has muddied the pure rills of natural affection, by supposing that society will some time or other be so constituted, that man must necessarily fulfill the duties of a citizen or be despised, and that while he was employed in any of the departments of civil life, his wife, also an active citizen, should be equally intent to manage her family, educate her children, and assist her neighbours.

But, to render her really virtuous and useful, she must not, if she 19 discharge her civil duties, want, individually, the protection of civil laws; she must not be dependent on her husband's bounty for her subsistence during his life or support after his death—for how can a being be generous who has nothing of its own? or virtuous, who is not free?

The wife, in the present state of things, who is faithful to her husband, and neither suckles nor educates her children, scarcely deserves the name of a wife, and has no right to that of a citizen. But take away natural rights, and duties become null.

Women then must be considered as only the wanton solace of men 20 when they become so weak in mind and body that they cannot exert themselves, unless to pursue some frothy pleasure or to invent some frivolous fashion. What can be a more melancholy sight to a thinking mind than to look into the numerous carriages that drive helter-skelter

---

[15]***distaff*** Instrument to wind wool in the act of spinning; notoriously a job only fit for women.

[16]***feculent*** filthy, polluted; related to *feces*.

about this metropolis in a morning full of pale-faced creatures who are flying from themselves. I have often wished, with Dr. Johnson,[17] to place some of them in a little shop with half a dozen children looking up to their languid countenances for support. I am much mistaken if some latent vigour would not soon give health and spirit to their eyes, and some lines drawn by the exercise of reason on the blank cheeks, which before were only undulated by dimples, might restore lost dignity to the character, or rather enable it to attain the true dignity of its nature. Virtue is not to be acquired even by speculation, much less by the negative supineness that wealth naturally generates.

Besides, when poverty is more disgraceful than even vice, is not morality cut to the quick? Still to avoid misconstruction, though I consider that women in the common walks of life are called to fulfill the duties of wives and mothers, by religion and reason, I cannot help lamenting that women of a superior cast have not a road open by which they can pursue more extensive plans of usefulness and independence. I may excite laughter by dropping a hint which I mean to pursue some future time, for I really think that women ought to have representatives, instead of being arbitrarily governed without having any direct share allowed them in the deliberations of government. 21

But, as the whole system of representation is now in this country only a convenient handle for despotism, they need not complain, for they are as well represented as a numerous class of hard-working mechanics, who pay for the support of royalty when they can scarcely stop their children's mouths with bread. How are they represented whose very sweat supports the splendid stud of an heir apparent, or varnishes the chariot of some female favourite who looks down on shame? Taxes on the very necessaries of life enable an endless tribe of idle princes and princesses to pass with stupid pomp before a gaping crowd, who almost worship the very parade which costs them so dear. This is mere gothic grandeur, something like the barbarous useless parade of having sentinels on horseback at Whitehall,[18] which I could never view without a mixture of contempt and indignation. 22

How strangely must the mind be sophisticated when this sort of state impresses it! But, till these monuments of folly are levelled by 23

---

[17]**Dr. Samuel Johnson (1709–1784)** The greatest lexicographer and one of the most respected authors of England's eighteenth century. He was known to Mary Wollstonecraft and to her sister, Eliza, a teacher. The reference is to an item published in his *Rambler,* essay 85.

[18]**sentinels on horseback at Whitehall** This is a reference to the expensive piece of showmanship which continues to our day: the changing of the guard at Whitehall.

virtue, similar follies will leaven the whole mass. For the same character, in some degree, will prevail in the aggregate of society; and the refinements of luxury, or the vicious repinings of envious poverty, will equally banish virtue from society, considered as the characteristic of that society, or only allow it to appear as one of the stripes of the harlequin coat worn by the civilized man.

In the superior ranks of life every duty is done by deputies, as if 24 duties could ever be waived, and the vain pleasures which consequent idleness forces the rich to pursue appear so enticing to the next rank that the numerous scramblers for wealth sacrifice everything to tread on their heels. The most sacred trusts are then considered as sinecures, because they were procured by interest, and only sought to enable a man to keep *good company*. Women, in particular, all want to be ladies. Which is simply to have nothing to do, but listlessly to go they scarcely care where, for they cannot tell what.

But what have women to do in society? I may be asked, but to 25 loiter with easy grace; surely you would not condemn them all to suckle fools and chronicle small beer![19] No. Women might certainly study the art of healing, and be physicians as well as nurses. And midwifery, decency seems to allot to them, though I am afraid the word midwife in our dictionaries will soon give place to *accoucheur*,[20] and one proof of the former delicacy of the sex be effaced from the language.

They might also study politics, and settle their benevolence on the 26 broadest basis; for the reading of history will scarcely be more useful than the perusal of romances, if read as mere biography; if the character of the times, the political improvements, arts, &c., be not observed. In short, if it be not considered as the history of man; and not of particular men, who filled a niche in the temple of fame, and dropped into the black rolling stream of time, that silently sweeps all before it, into the shapeless void called—eternity. For shape, can it be called, "that shape hath none"?[21]

Business of various kinds they might likewise pursue, if they were 27 educated in a more orderly manner, which might save many from common and legal prostitution. Women would not then marry for a

---

[19]*chronicle small beer!* *Othello* (II. i. 158). This means to keep the household accounts.

[20]**accoucheur** male version of the female midwife.

[21]*"that shape hath none"* The reference is to *Paradise Lost* (II. 667) by John Milton (1608–1674); it is an allusion to death.

support, as men accept of places under government, and neglect the implied duties; nor would an attempt to earn their own subsistence—a most laudable one!—sink them almost to the level of those poor abandoned creatures who live by prostitution. For are not milliners and mantua-makers[22] reckoned the next class? The few employments open to women, so far from being liberal, are menial; and when a superior education enables them to take charge of the education of children as governesses, they are not treated like the tutors of sons, though even clerical tutors are not always treated in a manner calculated to render them respectable in the eyes of their pupils, to say nothing of the private comfort of the individual. But as women educated like gentlewomen are never designed for the humiliating situation which necessity sometimes forces them to fill, these situations are considered in the light of a degradation; and they know little of the human heart, who need to be told that nothing so painfully sharpens sensibility as such a fall in life.

Some of these women might be restrained from marrying by a 28 proper spirit or delicacy, and others may not have had it in their power to escape in this pitiful way from servitude; is not that government then very defective, and very unmindful of the happiness of one half of its members, that does not provide for honest, independent women, by encouraging them to fill respectable stations? But in order to render their private virtue a public benefit, they must have a civil existence in the state, married or single; else we shall continually see some worthy woman, whose sensibility has been rendered painfully acute by undeserved contempt, droop like "the lily broken down by a plowshare."

It is a melancholy truth—yet such is the blessed effect of civiliza- 29 tion!—the most respectable women are the most oppressed; and, unless they have understandings far superior to the common run of understandings, taking in both sexes, they must, from being treated like contemptible beings, become contemptible. How many women thus waste life away the prey of discontent, who might have practised as physicians, regulated a farm, managed a shop, and stood erect, supported by their own industry, instead of hanging their heads surcharged with the dew of sensibility, that consumes the beauty to which it at first gave lustre; nay, I doubt whether pity and love are so

---

[22]***milliners and mantua-makers*** dressmakers, usually women (as tailors were usually men).

near akin as poets feign, for I have seldom seen much compassion excited by the helplessness of females, unless they were fair; then, perhaps pity was the soft handmaid of love, or the harbinger of lust.

How much more respectable is the woman who earns her own 30 bread by fulfilling any duty, than the most accomplished beauty!— beauty did I say?—so sensible am I of the beauty of moral loveliness, or the harmonious propriety that attunes the passions of a well-regulated mind, that I blush at making the comparison; yet I sigh to think how few women aim at attaining this respectability by withdrawing from the giddy whirl of pleasure, or the indolent calm that stupefies the good sort of women it sucks in.

Proud of their weakness, however, they must always be protected, 31 guarded from care, and all the rough toils that dignify the mind. If this be the fiat of fate, if they will make themselves insignificant and contemptible, sweetly to waste "life away," let them not expect to be valued when their beauty fades, for it is the fate of the fairest flowers to be admired and pulled to pieces by the careless hand that plucked them. In how many ways do I wish, from the purest benevolence, to impress this truth on my sex; yet I fear that they will not listen to a truth that dear-bought experience has brought home to many an agitated bosom, nor willingly resign the privileges of rank and sex for the privileges of humanity, to which those have no claim who do not discharge its duties.

Those writers are particularly useful, in my opinion, who make 32 man feel for man, independent of the station he fills, or the drapery of factitious sentiments. I then would fain[23] convince reasonable men of the importance of some of my remarks; and prevail on them to weigh dispassionately the whole tenor of my observations. I appeal to their understandings; and, as a fellow-creature, claim, in the name of my sex, some interest in their hearts. I entreat them to assist to emancipate their companion, to make her a *help meet* for them!

Would men but generously snap our chains, and be content with 33 rational fellowship instead of slavish obedience, they would find us more observant daughters, more affectionate sisters, more faithful wives, more reasonable mothers—in a word, better citizens. We should then love them with true affection, because we should learn to respect ourselves; and, the peace of mind of a worthy man would not be interrupted by the idle vanity of his wife, nor the babes sent to nestle in a strange bosom, having never found a home in their mother's.

---

[23]*fain* happily.

QUESTIONS

1. Who is the audience for Wollstonecraft's writing? Is she writing more for men than for women? Is it clear from what she says that there is an explicit audience with specific qualities?
2. Analyze paragraph 1 carefully for the use of imagery and metaphor. What are their actual effects? Are they overdone?
3. Wollstonecraft begins by attacking property, or the respect paid to it. What does she mean? Does she sustain that line of thought throughout the piece?
4. In paragraph 12, Wollstonecraft speaks of the "bondage of ignorance" in which women are held. Clarify what precisely she means by that expression.
5. In paragraph 29, Wollstonecraft says that people who are treated as if they were contemptible will become contemptible. Is this a political or a psychological judgment?
6. What is the substance of Wollstonecraft's complaint concerning women being admired for their beauty?

WRITING ASSIGNMENTS

1. Throughout the chapter Wollstonecraft attacks the unnatural distinctions made between men and women. Establish carefully what those unnatural distinctions are, why they are unnatural, and whether or not such distinctions persist to the present day. By contrast, establish what some natural distinctions between men and women are and whether or not Wollstonecraft has taken them into consideration.
2. References are made throughout the piece to prostitution and to the debaucheries of men. Paragraph 7 is specific in making reference to the "wanton tricks" of prostitutes. What is Wollstonecraft's attitude toward men in regard to sexuality and their attitudes toward women—both the loose women of the brothels and the women with whom they live? Find explicit passages in the piece which you can quote and analyze in an effort to clarify her views.
3. In paragraph 2, Wollstonecraft complains that "the respect due only to talents and virtue" is instead being given to people on account of their property. Further, she says in paragraph 9 that riches are "destructive . . . to the human character." Establish carefully, by means of reference to her passages and to analysis of those passages, just what Wollstonecraft means by such statements. Then, using your own anecdotes or "episodical observations," take a stand on whether these views are views you yourself can hold for our time. Are riches destructive to character? Is too much respect

paid to those who possess property? If it is possible to make use of metaphor, or of allusion—literary or personal—do so.

4. In paragraph 4, Wollstonecraft speaks of "men who can be gratified by the fawning fondness of spaniel-like affection" from their women. Search through the essay for other instances of similar views and analyze them carefully. Establish exactly what the men she describes want their women to be like. What do men today want their women to be like? Have today's men changed very much in their expectations? Why? Why not? Use personal observations where possible in answering this question.

5. The question of what roles women ought to have in society is addressed in paragraphs 25, 26, and 27. What are those roles? Why are they defined in terms of work? Do you agree that they are, indeed, the roles that women should assume? Are there more roles that you would include? Has our age improved with respect to giving women access to those roles? Consider the question of what women actually did in Wollstonecraft's time and what they do today.

KARL MARX

———— ⟨∞⟩ ————

The Communist Manifesto

*K*ARL MARX *(1818–1883) was born in Germany to Jewish parents who converted to Lutheranism. A very scholarly man, Marx studied literature and philosophy, ultimately earning a doctorate in philosophy at the University of Jena. He was denied a university position and was forced to begin making a livelihood from journalism.*

Soon after beginning his journalistic career, Marx came into conflict with Prussian authorities because of his radical social views, and after a period of exile in Paris he was forced to live in Brussels. After several more forced moves, Marx found his way to London, where he finally settled in absolute poverty. His friend Friedrich Engels (1820–1895) contributed money to prevent his and his family's starvation, and Marx wrote the books for which he is famous while at the same time writing for and editing newspapers. His contributions to the **New York Daily Herald** *number over three hundred items between the years 1852 and 1862.*

Marx is best known for his theories of socialism, best expressed in The Communist Manifesto *(1848)—which, like much of his im-*

Translated by Samuel Moore. Part III of *The Communist Manifesto,* "Socialist and Communist Literature," is omitted here.

portant work, was written with Engels's help—and in Das Kapital
(Capital), *published in 1867. In his own lifetime he was not well
known, nor were his ideas widely debated. Yet he was part of an
ongoing movement composed mainly of intellectuals. Vladimir Lenin
(1870–1924) was a disciple whose triumph in the Russian Revolution
of 1917 catapulted Marx to the forefront of world thought. Since 1917
Marx's thinking has been scrupulously analyzed, debated, and argued. Capitalist thinkers have found him illogical and uninformed,
whereas Communist thinkers have found him a prophet and keen an-
alyst of social structures.*

*In England, Marx's studies concentrated on economics. His
thought centered on the concept of an ongoing class struggle between
those who owned property—the bourgeois—and those who owned
nothing but whose work produced wealth—the proletariat. Marx was
concerned with the forces of history, and his view of history was that
it is progressive and, to an extent, inevitable. This view is very prominent in* The Communist Manifesto, *particularly in his review of the
overthrow of feudal forms of government by the bourgeoisie. He
thought that it was inevitable that the bourgeoisie and the proletariat
would engage in a class struggle from which the proletariat would
emerge victorious. In essence, Marx took a materialist position. He
denied the providence of God in the affairs of man and defended the
view that economic institutions evolve naturally and that, in their
evolution, they control the social order. Thus, communism was an
inevitable part of the process, and in the* Manifesto *he was concerned
to clarify the reasons why it was inevitable.*

M A R X ' S   R H E T O R I C

*The selection included here omits one section, the least important
for the modern reader. The first section has a relatively simple rhetorical structure that depends upon the topic of comparison. The title,
"Bourgeois and Proletarians," tells us right away that the section will
clarify the nature of each class and then go on to make some comparisons and contrasts. The concepts as such were by no means as widely
discussed or thought about in 1848 as they are today, so Marx is
careful to define his terms. At the same time, he establishes his theories regarding history by making further comparisons with class
struggles in earlier ages.*

Marx's style is simple and direct. He moves steadily from point to point, establishing his views on the nature of classes, on the nature of bourgeois society, on the questions of industrialism and its effects upon modern society. He considers questions of wealth, worth, nationality, production, agriculture, and machinery. Each point is dealt with in turn, usually in its own paragraph.

The organization of the next section, "Proletarians and Communists" (paras. 60–133), is not, despite its title, comparative in nature. Rather, with the proletariat defined as the class of the future, Marx tries to show that the Communist cause is the proletarian cause. In the process, Marx uses a fascinating rhetorical strategy. He assumes that he is addressed by an antagonist—presumably a bourgeois or a proletarian who is in sympathy with the bourgeois. He then proceeds to deal with each popular complaint against communism. He shows that it is not a party separate from other workers' parties (para. 61). He clarifies the question of abolition of existing property relations (paras. 68–93). He emphasizes the antagonism of capital and wage labor (para. 76); he discusses the disappearance of culture (para. 94); he clarifies the question of the family (para. 98) and of the exploitation of children (para. 101). The new system of public education is brought up (para. 102). The touchy issue of the "community of women" is raised (paras. 102–110), as well as the charge that Communists want to abolish nations (para. 111). Religion is brushed aside (para. 116), and when he is done with the complaints he gives us a rhetorical signal: "But let us have done with the bourgeois objections to Communism" (para. 126).

The rest of the second section contains a brief summary, and then Marx presents his ten-point program (para. 131). The structure is simple, direct, and effective. In the process of answering the charges against communism, Marx is able to clarify exactly what it is and what it promises. By contrast with his earlier arguments, the ten points of his Communist program seem clear, easy, and (again by contrast) almost acceptable. While the style is not dashing (despite a few memorable lines), the rhetorical structure is extraordinarily effective for the purposes at hand.

In the last section (paras. 135–146), in which Marx compares the Communists with other reform groups such as those agitating for redistribution of land and other agrarian reforms, he indicates that the Communists are everywhere fighting alongside existing groups for the rights of people who are oppressed by their societies. As Marx says, "In short, the Communists everywhere support every revolutionary movement against the existing social and political order of things." Nothing could be a more plain and direct declaration of sympathies.

The Communist Manifesto

A specter is haunting Europe—the specter of Communism. All the 1
Powers of old Europe have entered into a holy alliance to exorcise this
specter; Pope and Czar, Metternich[1] and Guizot,[2] French Radicals[3] and
German police-spies.

Where is the party in opposition that has not been decried as com- 2
munistic by its opponents in power? Where the Opposition that has
not hurled back the branding reproach of Communism against the
more advanced opposition parties, as well as against its reactionary
adversaries?

Two things result from this fact. 3

I. Communism is already acknowledged by all European Powers to 4
be itself a Power.

II. It is high time that Communists should openly, in the face of 5
the whole world, publish their views, their aims, their tendencies, and
meet this nursery tale of the specter of Communism with a Manifesto
of the party itself.

To this end, Communists of various nationalities have assembled 6
in London and sketched the following Manifesto, to be published in
the English, French, German, Italian, Flemish and Danish languages.

Bourgeois and Proletarians[4]

The history of all hitherto existing society is the history of class 7
struggles.

---

[1]***Prince Klemens von Metternich (1773–1859)*** An Austrian diplomat who had a
hand in establishing the peace after the final defeat in 1814 of Napoleon (1769–1821);
Metternich was highly influential in the crucial Vienna peace congress (1815).

[2]***François Pierre Guizot (1787–1874)*** Conservative French statesman, author,
and philosopher. Like Metternich, he was opposed to communism.

[3]***French Radicals*** Actually middle-class liberals who wanted a return to a republic
in 1848 after the eighteen-year reign of Louis Philippe (1773–1850), the "citizen king."

[4]By bourgeoisie is meant the class of modern Capitalists, owners of the means of
social production and employers of wage labor. By proletariat, the class of modern wage
laborers who, having no means of production of their own, are reduced to selling their
labor-power in order to live. [Marx's note]

Freeman and slave, patrician and plebeian, lord and serf, guild-mas- 8
ter and journeyman, in a word, oppressor and oppressed, stood in constant opposition to one another, carried on uninterrupted, now hidden,
now open fight, a fight that each time ended, either in a revolutionary
re-constitution of society at large, or in the common ruin of the con-
tending classes.

In the earlier epochs of history we find almost everywhere a com- 9
plicated arrangement of society into various orders, a manifold grada-
tion of social rank. In ancient Rome we have patricians, knights, ple-
beians, slaves; in the Middle Ages, feudal lords, vassals, guild-masters,
journeymen, apprentices, serfs; in almost all of these classes, again,
subordinate gradations.

The modern bourgeois society that has sprouted from the ruins of 10
feudal society, has not done away with class antagonisms. It has but
established new classes, new conditions of oppression, new forms of
struggle in place of the old ones.

Our epoch, the epoch of the bourgeoisie, possesses, however, this 11
distinctive feature; it has simplified the class antagonisms. Society as
a whole is more and more splitting up into two great hostile camps,
into two great classes directly facing each other: Bourgeoisie and Proletariat.

From the serfs of the Middle Ages sprang the chartered burghers of 12
the earliest towns. From these burgesses the first elements of the bourgeoisie were developed.

The discovery of America, the rounding of the Cape,[5] opened up 13
fresh ground for the rising bourgeoisie. The East Indian and Chinese
markets, the colonization of America, trade with the colonies, the increase in the means of exchange and in commodities generally, gave
to commerce, to navigation, to industry, an impulse never before
known, and thereby, to the revolutionary element in the tottering feudal society, a rapid development.

The feudal system of industry, under which industrial production 14
was monopolized by closed guilds, now no longer sufficed for the
growing wants of the new market. The manufacturing system took its
place. The guild-masters were pushed on one side by the manufacturing middle-class: division of labor between the different corporate
guilds vanished in the face of division of labor in each single workshop.

---

[5]***the Cape*** The Cape of Good Hope, at the southern tip of Africa. This was a main sea
route for trade with India and the Orient. Europe profited immensely from the opening
up of these new markets in the sixteenth century.

Meantime the markets kept ever growing, the demand ever rising. 15
Even manufacture no longer sufficed. Thereupon, steam and machinery revolutionized industrial production. The place of manufacture was taken by the giant, Modern Industry, the place of the industrial middle-class, by industrial millionaires, the leaders of whole
industrial armies, the modern bourgeois.

Modern industry has established the world market, for which the 16
discovery of America paved the way. This market has given an immense development to commerce, to navigation, to communication by
land. This development has, in its turn, reacted on the extension of
industry; and in proportion as industry, commerce, navigation, railways extended, in the same proportion the bourgeoisie developed, increased its capital, and pushed into the background every class handed
down from the Middle Ages.

We see, therefore, how the modern bourgeoisie is itself the product 17
of a long course of development, of a series of revolutions in the modes
of production and of exchange.

Each step in the development of the bourgeoisie was accompanied 18
by a corresponding political advance of that class. An oppressed class
under the sway of the feudal nobility, an armed and self-governing association in the medieval commune,[6] here independent urban republic
(as in Italy and Germany), there taxable "third estate"[7] of the monarchy (as in France), afterwards, in the period of manufacture proper,
serving either the semi-feudal or the absolute monarchy as a counter-
poise against nobility, and, in fact, corner stone of the great monarchies in general, the bourgeoisie has at last, since the establishment of
Modern Industry and of the world-market, conquered for itself, in the
modern representative State, exclusive political sway. The executive
of the modern State is but a committee for managing the common
affairs of the whole bourgeoisie.

The bourgeoisie, historically, has played a most revolutionary part. 19

The bourgeoisie, wherever it has got the upper hand, has put an 20
end to all feudal, patriarchal, idyllic relations. It has pitilessly torn
asunder the motley feudal ties that bound man to his "natural superiors," and has left no other nexus between man and man than naked
self-interest, than callous "cash payment." It has drowned the most

---

[6] *the medieval commune* Refers to the growth in the eleventh century of towns whose
economy was highly regulated by mutual interest and agreement.

[7] *"third estate"* The aristocracy was the first estate, the clergy the second estate, and
the bourgeoisie the third estate.

heavenly ecstasies of religious fervor,[8] of chivalrous enthusiasm, of Philistine sentimentalism, in the icy water of egotistical calculation. It has resolved personal worth into exchange value, and in place of the numberless indefeasible chartered freedoms, has set up that single, unconscionable freedom—Free Trade. In one word, for exploitation, veiled by religious and political illusions, it has substituted naked, shameless, direct, brutal exploitation.

The bourgeoisie has stripped of its halo every occupation hitherto   21 honored and looked up to with reverent awe. It has converted the physician, the lawyer, the priest, the poet, the man of science, into its paid wage laborers.

The bourgeoisie has torn away from the family its sentimental veil,   22 and has reduced the family relation to a mere money relation.

The bourgeoisie has disclosed how it came to pass that the brutal   23 display of vigor in the Middle Ages, which reactionists so much admire, found its fitting complement in the most slothful indolence. It has been the first to show what man's activity can bring about. It has accomplished wonders far surpassing Egyptian pyramids, Roman aqueducts and Gothic cathedrals; it has conducted expeditions that put in the shade all former Exoduses of nations and crusades.

The bourgeoisie cannot exist without constantly revolutionizing   24 the instruments of production, and thereby the relations of production, and with them the whole relations of society. Conservation of the old modes of production in unaltered form was, on the contrary, the first condition of existence for all earlier industrial classes. Constant revolutionizing of production, uninterrupted disturbance of all social conditions, everlasting uncertainty and agitation distinguish the bourgeois epoch from all earlier ones. All fixed, fast frozen relations, with their train of ancient and venerable prejudices and opinions, are swept away, all new formed ones become antiquated before they can ossify. All that is solid melts into the air, all that is holy is profaned, and man is at last compelled to face with sober senses, his real conditions of life, and his relations with his kind.

---

[8]***religious fervor*** This and other terms in this sentence contain a compressed historical observation. "Religious fervor" refers to the Middle Ages; "chivalrous enthusiasm" refers to the rise of the secular state and to the military power of knights; "Philistine sentimentalism" refers to the development of popular arts and literature in the sixteenth, seventeenth, and eighteenth centuries. The word "Philistine" meant those who were generally uncultured, that is, the general public. "Sentimentalism" was a code word for the encouragement of emotional response rather than rational thought.

The need of a constantly expanding market for its products chases   25
the bourgeoisie over the whole surface of the globe. It must nestle
everywhere, settle everywhere, establish connections everywhere.

The bourgeoisie has through its exploitation of the world-market   26
given a cosmopolitan character to production and consumption in
every country. To the great chagrin of reactionists, it has drawn from
under the feet of industry the national ground on which it stood. All
old-established national industries have been destroyed or are daily
being destroyed. They are dislodged by new industries, whose introduction becomes a life and death question for all civilized nations, by
industries that no longer work up indigenous raw material, but raw
material drawn from the remotest zones; industries whose products
are consumed, not only at home, but in every quarter of the globe. In
place of the old wants, satisfied by the productions of the country, we
find new wants, requiring for their satisfaction the products of distant
lands and climes. In place of the old local and national seclusion and
self-sufficiency, we have intercourse in every direction, universal interdependence of nations. And as in material, so also in intellectual
production. The intellectual creations of individual nations become
common property. National onesidedness and narrowmindedness become more and more impossible, and from the numerous national and
local literatures there arises a world-literature.

The bourgeoisie, by the rapid improvement of all instruments of   27
production, by the immensely facilitated means of communication,
draws all, even the most barbarian nations into civilization. The cheap
prices of its commodities are the heavy artillery with which it batters
down all Chinese walls, with which it forces the barbarians' intensely
obstinate hatred of foreigners to capitulate. It compels all nations, on
pain of extinction, to adopt the bourgeois mode of production; it compels them to introduce what it calls civilization into their midst, i.e.,
to become bourgeois themselves. In a word, it creates a world after its
own image.

The bourgeoisie has subjected the country to the rule of the towns.   28
It has created enormous cities, has greatly increased the urban population as compared with the rural and has thus rescued a considerable
part of the population from the idiocy of rural life. Just as it has made
the country dependent on the towns, so it has made barbarian and
semi-barbarian countries dependent on civilized ones, nations of peasants on nations of bourgeois, the East on the West.

The bourgeoisie keeps more and more doing away with the scat-   29
tered state of the population, of the means of production, and of property. It has agglomerated population, centralized means of production,

and has concentrated property in a few hands. The necessary consequence of this was political centralization. Independent, or but loosely
connected provinces, with separate interests, laws, governments, and
systems of taxation, became lumped together in one nation, with one
government, one code of laws, one national class interest, one frontier
and one customs tariff.

The bourgeoisie, during its rule of scarce one hundred years, has   30
created more massive and more colossal productive forces than have
all preceding generations together. Subjection of Nature's forces to
man, machinery, application of chemistry to industry and agriculture,
steam-navigation, railways, electric telegraphs, clearing of whole continents for cultivation, canalization of rivers, whole populations conjured out of the ground—what earlier century had even a presentiment
that such productive forces slumbered in the lap of social labor?

We see then: the means of production and of exchange on whose   31
foundation the bourgeoisie built itself up, were generated in feudal
society. At a certain stage in the development of these means of production and of exchange, the conditions under which feudal society
produced and exchanged, the feudal organization of agriculture and
manufacturing industry, in one word, the feudal relations of property
became no longer compatible with the already developed productive
forces; they became so many fetters. They had to burst asunder; they
were burst asunder.

Into their places stepped free competition, accompanied by social   32
and political constitution adapted to it, and by economical and political sway of the bourgeois class.

A similar movement is going on before our own eyes. Modern bour-   33
geois society with its relations of production, of exchange and of property, a society that has conjured up such gigantic means of production
and of exchange, is like the sorcerer, who is no longer able to control
the powers of the nether world whom he has called up by his spells.
For many a decade past, the history of industry and commerce is but
the history of the revolt of modern productive forces against modern
conditions of production, against the property relations that are the
conditions for the existence of the bourgeoisie and of its rule. It is
enough to mention the commercial crises that by their periodical return put on its trial, each time more threateningly, the existence of
the entire bourgeois society. In these crises a great part not only of the
existing products, but also of the previously created productive forces,
are periodically destroyed. In these crises there breaks out an epidemic
that, in all earlier epochs, would have seemed an absurdity—the epidemic of overproduction. Society suddenly finds itself put back into a

state of momentary barbarism; it appears as if a famine, a universal war of devastation, had cut off the supply of every means of subsistence; industry and commerce seem to be destroyed; and why? Because there is too much civilization, too much means of subsistence, too much industry, too much commerce. The productive forces at the disposal of society no longer tend to further the development of the conditions of the bourgeois property; on the contrary, they have become too powerful for these conditions by which they are fettered, and as soon as they overcome these fetters they bring disorder into the whole of bourgeois society, endanger the existence of bourgeois property. The conditions of bourgeois society are too narrow to comprise the wealth created by them. And how does the bourgeoisie get over these crises? On the one hand by enforced destruction of a mass of productive forces; on the other, by the conquest of new markets, and by the more thorough exploitation of the old ones. That is to say, by paving the way for more extensive and more destructive crises, and by diminishing the means whereby crises are prevented.

The weapons with which the bourgeoisie felled feudalism to the ground are now turned against the bourgeoisie itself. 34

But not only has the bourgeoisie forged the weapons that bring death to itself; it has also called into existence the men who are to wield those weapons—the modern working class—the proletarians. 35

In proportion as the bourgeoisie, i.e., capital, is developed, in the same proportion is the proletariat, the modern working class, developed, a class of laborers who live only so long as they find work, and who find work only so long as their labor increases capital. These laborers, who must sell themselves piecemeal, are a commodity, like every other article of commerce, and are consequently exposed to all the vicissitudes of competition, to all the fluctuations of the market. 36

Owing to the extensive use of machinery and to division of labor, the work of the proletarians has lost all individual character, and, consequently, all charm for the workman. He becomes an appendage of the machine, and it is only the most simple, most monotonous and most easily acquired knack that is required of him. Hence, the cost of production of a workman is restricted almost entirely to the means of subsistence that he requires for his maintenance, and for the propagation of his race. But the price of a commodity, and also of labor, is equal to its cost of production. In proportion, therefore, as the repulsiveness of the work increases the wage decreases. Nay more, in proportion as the use of machinery and division of labor increases, in the same proportion the burden of toil increases, whether by prolongation 37 of the working hours, by increase of the work enacted in a given time, or by increased speed of the machinery, etc.

Modern industry has converted the little workshop of the patriarchal master into the great factory of the industrial capitalist. Masses of laborers, crowded into factories, are organized like soldiers. As privates of the industrial army they are placed under the command of a perfect hierarchy of officers and sergeants. Not only are they the slaves of the bourgeois class and of the bourgeois state, they are daily and hourly enslaved by the machine, by the overlooker, and, above all, by the individual bourgeois manufacturer himself. The more openly this despotism proclaims gain to be its end and aim, the more petty, the more hateful and the more embittering it is. 38

The less the skill and exertion or strength implied in manual labor, in other words, the more modern industry becomes developed, the more is the labor of men superseded by that of women. Differences of age and sex have no longer any distinctive social validity for the working class. All are instruments of labor, more or less expensive to use, according to their age and sex. 39

No sooner is the exploitation of the laborer by the manufacturer, so far at an end, that he receives his wages in cash, than he is set upon by the other portions of the bourgeoisie, the landlord, the shopkeeper, the pawnbroker, etc. 40

The lower strata of the middle class—the small trades-people, shopkeepers and retired tradesmen generally, the handicraftsmen and peasants—all these sink gradually into the proletariat, partly because their diminutive capital does not suffice for the scale on which Modern Industry is carried on, and is swamped in the competition with the large capitalists, partly because their specialized skill is rendered worthless by new methods of production. Thus the proletariat is recruited from all classes of the population. 41

The proletariat goes through various stages of development. With its birth begins its struggle with the bourgeoisie. At first the contest is carried on by individual laborers, then by the workpeople of a factory, then by the operatives of one trade, in one locality, against the individual bourgeois who directly exploits them. They direct their attacks not against the bourgeois conditions of production, but against the instruments of production themselves; they destroy imported wares that compete with their labor, they smash to pieces machinery, they set factories ablaze, they seek to restore by force the vanished status of the workman of the Middle Ages. 42

At this stage the laborers still form an incoherent mass scattered 43 over the whole country, and broken up by their mutual competition. If anywhere they unite to form more compact bodies, this is not yet the consequence of their own active union, but of the union of the bourgeoisie, which class, in order to attain its own political ends, is compelled to set the whole proletariat in motion, and is moreover yet, for a time, able to do so. At this stage, therefore, the proletarians do not fight their enemies, but the enemies of their enemies, the remnants of absolute monarchy, the landowners, the non-industrial bourgeois, the petty bourgeoisie. Thus the whole historical movement is concentrated in the hands of the bourgeoisie, every victory so obtained is a victory for the bourgeoisie.

But with the development of industry the proletariat not only increases in number; it becomes concentrated in greater masses, its strength grows and it feels that strength more. The various interests and conditions of life within the ranks of the proletariat are more and more equalized, in proportion as machinery obliterates all distinctions of labor, and nearly everywhere reduces wages to the same low level. The growing competition among the bourgeois, and the resulting commercial crisis, make the wages of the workers even more fluctuating. The unceasing improvement of machinery, ever more rapidly developing, makes their livelihood more and more precarious; the collisions between individual workmen and individual bourgeois take more and more the character of collisions between two classes. Thereupon the workers begin to form combinations (Trades' Unions)[9] against the bourgeois; they club together in order to keep up the rate of wages; they found permanent associations in order to make provision beforehand for these occasional revolts. Here and there the contest breaks out into riots.

Now and then the workers are victorious, but only for a time. The real fruit of their battle lies not in the immediate result but in the ever-expanding union of workers. This union is helped on by the improved means of communication that are created by modern industry, and that places the workers of different localities in contact with one another. It was just this contact that was needed to centralize the numerous local struggles, all of the same character, into one national struggle between classes. But every class struggle is a political struggle. And that union, to attain which the burghers of the Middle Ages with

44

45

---

[9]*combinations (Trades' Unions)* The labor movement was only beginning in 1848. It consisted of Trades' Unions that started as social clubs but soon began agitating for labor reform. They represented an important step in the growth of socialism in Europe.

their miserable highways, required centuries, the modern proletarians, thanks to railways, achieve in a few years.

This organization of the proletarians into a class, and consequently into a political party, is continually being upset again by the competition between the workers themselves. But it ever rises up again, stronger, firmer, mightier. It compels legislative recognition of particular interests of the workers by taking advantage of the divisions among the bourgeoisie itself. Thus the ten hours' bill in England[10] was carried. 46

Altogether collisions between the classes of the old society further, in many ways, the course of development of the proletariat. The bourgeoisie finds itself involved in a constant battle. At first with the aristocracy; later on, with those portions of the bourgeoisie itself whose interests have become antagonistic to the progress of industry; at all times, with the bourgeoisie of foreign countries. In all these battles it sees itself compelled to appeal to the proletariat, to ask for its help, and thus, to drag it into the political arena. The bourgeoisie itself, therefore, supplies the proletariat with its own elements of political and general education; in other words, it furnishes the proletariat with weapons for fighting the bourgeoisie. 47

Further, as we have already seen, entire sections of the ruling classes are, by the advance of industry, precipitated into the proletariat, or are at least threatened in their conditions of existence. These also supply the proletariat with fresh elements of enlightenment and progress. 48

Finally, in times when the class-struggle nears the decisive hour, the process of dissolution going on within the ruling class—in fact, within the whole range of an old society—assumes such a violent, glaring character that a small section of the ruling class cuts itself adrift and joins the revolutionary class, the class that holds the future in its hands. Just as, therefore, at an earlier period, a section of the nobility went over to the bourgeoisie, so now a portion of the bourgeoisie goes over to the proletariat, and in particular, a portion of the bourgeois ideologists, who have raised themselves to the level of comprehending theoretically the historical movements as a whole. 49

Of all the classes that stand face to face with the bourgeoisie today the proletariat alone is a really revolutionary class. The other classes 50

---

[10]***the ten hours' bill in England*** This bill (1847) was an important innovation in labor reform. It limited the working day to only ten hours; at the time it was common for some people to work sixteen hours in a day. The bill's passage was a result of political division, not of benevolence on the part of the managers.

decay and finally disappear in the face of modern industry; the proletariat is its special and essential product.

The lower middle class, the small manufacturer, the shopkeeper, 51 the artisan, the peasant, all these fight against the bourgeoisie, to save from extinction their existence as fractions of the middle class. They are therefore not revolutionary, but conservative. Nay, more; they are reactionary, for they try to roll back the wheel of history. If by chance they are revolutionary, they are so only in view of their impending transfer into the proletariat; they thus defend not their present, but their future interests; they desert their own standpoint to place themselves at that of the proletariat.

The "dangerous class," the social scum, that passively rotting mass 52 thrown off by the lowest layers of old society, may, here and there, be swept into the movement by a proletarian revolution; its conditions of life, however, prepare it far more for the part of a bribed tool of reactionary intrigue.

In the conditions of the proletariat, those of the old society at large 53 are already virtually swamped. The proletarian is without property; his relation to his wife and children has no longer anything in common with the bourgeois family relations; modern industrial labor, modern subjection to capital, the same in England as in France, in America as in Germany, has stripped him of every trace of national character. Law, morality, religion, are to him so many bourgeois prejudices, behind which lurk in ambush just as many bourgeois interests.

All the preceding classes that got the upper hand sought to fortify 54 their already acquired status by subjecting society at large to their conditions of appropriation. The proletarians cannot become masters of the productive forces of society, except by abolishing their own previous mode of appropriation, and thereby also every other previous mode of appropriation. They have nothing of their own to secure and to fortify; their mission is to destroy all previous securities for and insurances of individual property.

All previous historical movements were movements of minorities, 55 or in the interest of minorities. The proletarian movement is the self-conscious, independent movement of the immense majority. The proletariat, the lowest stratum of our present society, cannot stir, cannot raise itself up without the whole superincumbent strata of official society being sprung into the air.

Though not in substance, yet in form, the struggle of the proletariat 56 with the bourgeoisie is at first a national struggle. The proletariat of each country must, of course, first of all settle matters with its own bourgeoisie.

In depicting the most general phases of the development of the pro- 57
letariat, we traced the more or less veiled civil war, raging within existing society, up to the point where that war breaks out into open
revolution, and where the violent overthrow of the bourgeoisie, lays
the foundations for the sway of the proletariat.

Hitherto every form of society has been based, as we have already 58
seen, on the antagonism of oppressing and oppressed classes. But in
order to oppress a class, certain conditions must be assured to it under
which it can, at least, continue its slavish existence. The serf, in the
period of serfdom, raised himself to membership in the commune, just
as the petty bourgeois, under the yoke of feudal absolutism managed
to develop into a bourgeois. The modern laborer, on the contrary, instead of rising with the progress of industry, sinks deeper and deepr
below the conditions of existence of his own class. He becomes a pauper, and pauperism develops more rapidly than population and wealth.
And here it becomes evident that the bourgeoisie is unfit any longer
to be the ruling class in society, and to impose its conditions of existence upon society as an over-riding law. It is unfit to rule, because it
is incompetent to assure an existence to its slave within his slavery,
because it cannot help letting him sink into such a state that it has to
feed him, instead of being fed by him. Society can no longer live under
this bourgeoisie; in other words, its existence is no longer compatible
with society.

The essential condition for the existence, and for the sway of the 59
bourgeois class, is the formation and augmentation of capital; the
condition for capital is wage labor. Wage labor rests exclusively on
competition between the laborers. The advance of industry, whose involuntary promoter is the bourgeoisie, replaces the isolation of the laborers, due to competition, by their involuntary combination, due to
association. The development of Modern Industry, therefore, cuts from
under its feet the very foundation on which the bourgeoisie produces
and appropriates products. What the bourgeoisie therefore produces,
above all, are its own grave diggers. Its fall and the victory of the proletariat are equally inevitable.

Proletarians and Communists

In what relation do the Communists stand to the proletarians as a 60
whole?

The Communists do not form a separate party opposed to other 61
working class parties.

They have no interests separate and apart from those of the prole- 62
tariat as a whole.

They do not set up any sectarian principles of their own, by which 63
to shape and mold the proletarian movement.

The Communists are distinguished from the other working class 64
parties by this only: 1. In the national struggles of the proletarians of
the different countries, they point out and bring to the front the common interests of the entire proletariat, independently of all nationality.
2. In the various stages of development which the struggle of the working class against the bourgeoisie has to pass through, they always and
everywhere represent the interests of the movement as a whole.

The Communists, therefore, are on the one hand practically the 65
most advanced and resolute section of the working class parties of
every country, that section which pushes forward all others; on the
other hand, theoretically, they have over the great mass of the proletariat the advantage of clearly understanding the line of march, the
conditions, and the ultimate general results of the proletarian movement.

The immediate aim of the Communists is the same as that of all 66
the other proletarian parties: formation of the proletariat into a class,
overthrow of the bourgeois of supremacy, conquest of political power
by the proletariat.

The theoretical conclusions of the Communists are in no way 67
based on ideas or principles that have been invented or discovered by
this or that would-be universal reformer.

They merely express, in general terms, actual relations springing 68
from an existing class struggle, from a historical movement going on
under our very eyes. The abolition of existing property relations is not
at all a distinctive feature of Communism.

All property relations in the past have continually been subject to 69
historical change consequent upon the change in historical conditions.

The French Revolution, for example, abolished feudal property in 70
favor of bourgeois property.

The distinguishing feature of Communism is not the abolition of 71
property generally, but the abolition of bourgeois property. But modern
bourgeois private property is the final and most complete expression
of the system of producing and appropriating products, that is based
on class antagonism, on the exploitation of the many by the few.

In this sense, the theory of the Communists may be summed up in 72
the single sentence: Abolition of private property.

We Communists have been reproached with the desire of abolish- 73 ing the right of personally acquiring property as the fruit of a man's own labor, which property is alleged to be the groundwork of all personal freedom, activity and independence.

Hard won, self-acquired, self-earned property! Do you mean the 74 property of the petty artisan and of the small peasant, a form of property that preceded the bourgeois form? There is no need to abolish that; the development of industry has to a great extent already destroyed it, and is still destroying it daily.

Or do you mean modern bourgeois private property? 75

But does wage labor create any property for the laborer? Not a bit. 76 It creates capital, i.e., that kind of property which exploits wage labor, and which cannot increase except upon condition of getting a new supply of wage labor for fresh exploitation. Property, in its present form, is based on the antagonism of capital and wage labor. Let us examine both sides of this antagonism.

To be a capitalist is to have not only a purely personal, but a social 77 status in production. Capital is a collective product, and only by the united action of many members, nay, in the last resort, only by the united action of all members of society, can it be set in motion.

Capital is therefore not a personal, it is a social power. 78

When, therefore, capital is converted into common property, into 79 the property of all members of society, personal property is not thereby transformed into social property. It is only the social character of the property that is changed. It loses its class character.

Let us now take wage labor. 80

The average price of wage labor is the minimum wage, i.e., that 81 quantum of the means of subsistence which is absolutely requisite to keep the laborer in bare existence as a laborer. What, therefore, the wage laborer appropriates by means of his labor, merely suffices to prolong and reproduce a bare existence. We by no means intend to abolish this personal appropriation of the products of labor, an appropriation that is made for the maintenance and reproduction of human life, and that leaves no surplus wherewith to command the labor of others. All that we want to do away with is the miserable character of this appropriation, under which the laborer lives merely to increase capital and is allowed to live only in so far as the interests of the ruling class require it.

In bourgeois society, living labor is but a means to increase accu- 82 mulated labor. In Communist society accumulated labor is but a means to widen, to enrich, to promote the existence of the laborer.

In bourgeois society, therefore, the past dominates the present; in 83

Communist society the present dominates the past. In bourgeois society, capital is independent and has individuality, while the living person is dependent and has no individuality.

And the abolition of this state of things is called by the bourgeois 84
abolition of individuality and freedom! And rightly so. The abolition
of bourgeois individuality, bourgeois independence and bourgeois freedom is undoubtedly aimed at.

By freedom is meant, under the present bourgeois conditions of 85
production, free trade, free selling and buying.

But if selling and buying disappears, free selling and buying disap- 86
pears also. This talk about free selling and buying, and all the other
"brave words" of our bourgeoisie about freedom in general have a
meaning, if any, only in contrast with restricted selling and buying,
with the fettered traders of the Middle Ages, but have no meaning
when opposed to the Communistic abolition of buying and selling, of
the bourgeois conditions of production, and of the bourgeoisie itself.

You are horrified at our intending to do away with private property. 87
But in your existing society private property is already done away with
for nine-tenths of the population; its existence for the few is solely
due to its non-existence in the hands of those nine-tenths. You reproach us, therefore, with intending to do away with a form of property, the necessary condition for whose existence is the non-existence
of any property for the immense majority of society.

In one word, you reproach us with intending to do away with your 88
property. Precisely so: that is just what we intend.

From the moment when labor can no longer be converted into capi- 89
tal, money, or rent, into a social power capable of being monopolized,
i.e., from the moment when individual property can no longer be
transformed into bourgeois property, into capital, from that moment,
you say, individuality vanishes.

You must, therefore, confess that by "individual" you mean no 90
other person than the bourgeois, than the middle-class owner of property. This person must, indeed, be swept out of the way and made
impossible.

Communism deprives no man of the power to appropriate the prod- 91
ucts of society: all that it does is to deprive him of the power to subjugate the labor of others by means of such appropriation.

It has been objected that upon the abolition of private property all 92
work will cease and universal laziness will overtake us.

According to this, bourgeois society ought long ago to have gone to 93
the dogs through sheer idleness; for those of its members who work
acquire nothing, and those who acquire anything do not work. The

whole of this objection is but another expression of the tautology: that there can no longer be any wage labor when there is no longer any capital.

All objections urged against the Communistic mode of producing and appropriating material products have, in the same way, been urged against the Communistic modes of producing and appropriating intellectual products. Just as, to the bourgeois, the disappearance of class property is the disappearance of production itself, so the disappearance of class culture is to him identical with the disappearance of all culture. 94

That culture, the loss of which he laments, is, for the enormous majority, a mere training to act as a machine. 95

But don't wrangle with us so long as you apply, to our intended abolition of bourgeois property, the standard of your bourgeois notions of freedom, culture, law, etc. Your very ideas are but the outgrowth of the conditions of your bourgeois production and bourgeois property, just as your jurisprudence is but the will of your class made into a law for all, a will whose essential character and direction are determined by the economical conditions of existence of your class. 96

The selfish misconception that induces you to transform into eternal laws of nature and of reason the social forms springing from your present mode of production and form of property—historical relations that rise and disappear in the progress of production—this misconception you share with every ruling class that has preceded you. What you see clearly in the case of ancient property, what you admit in the case of feudal property, you are of course forbidden to admit in the case of your own bourgeois form of property. 97

Abolition of the family! Even the most radical flare up at this infamous proposal of the Communists. 98

On what foundation is the present family, the bourgeois family, based? On capital, on private gain. In its completely developed form this family exists only among the bourgeoisie. But this state of things finds its complement in the practical absence of the family among the proletarians, and in public prostitution. 99

The bourgeois family will vanish as a matter of course when its complement vanishes, and both will vanish with the vanishing of capital. 100

Do you charge us with wanting to stop the exploitation of children by their parents? To this crime we plead guilty. 101

But, you will say, we destroy the most hallowed of relations when we replace home education by social. 102

And your education! Is not that also social, and determined by the 103 social conditions under which you educate; by the intervention, direct or indirect, of society by means of schools, etc.? The Communists have not invented the intervention of society in education; they do but seek to alter the character of that intervention, and to rescue education from the influence of the ruling class.

The bourgeois clap-trap about the family and education, about the 104 hallowed correlation of parent and child, become all the more disgusting, the more, by the action of Modern Industry, all family ties among the proletarians are torn asunder and their children transformed into simple articles of commerce and instruments of labor.

But you Communists would introduce community of women, 105 screams the whole bourgeoisie chorus.

The bourgeois sees in his wife a mere instrument of production. He 106 hears that the instruments of production are to be exploited in common, and, naturally, can come to no other conclusion, than that the lot of being common to all will likewise fall to the women.

He has not even a suspicion that the real point aimed at is to do 107 away with the status of women as mere instruments of production.

For the rest, nothing is more ridiculous than the virtuous indigna- 108 tion of our bourgeois at the community of women which, they pretend, is to be openly and officially establishd by the Communists. The Communists have no need to introduce community of women; it has existed almost from time immemorial.

Our bourgeois, not content with having the wives and daughters of 109 their proletarians at their disposal, not to speak of common prostitutes, take the greatest pleasure in seducing each others' wives.

Bourgeois marriage is in reality a system of wives in common, and 110 thus, at the most, what the Communists might possibly be reproached with, is that they desire to introduce, in substitution for a hypocritically concealed, an openly legalized community of women. For the rest, it is self-evident that the abolition of the present system of production must bring with it the abolition of the community of women springing from that system, i.e., of prostitution both public and private.

The Communists are further reproached with desiring to abolish 111 countries and nationalities.

The working men have no country. We cannot take from them 112 what they don't possess. Since the proletariat must first of all acquire political supremacy, must rise to be the leading class of the nation, must constitute itself the nation, it is, so far, itself national, though not in the bourgeois sense of the word.

National differences and antagonisms between peoples are daily 113 more and more vanishing, owing to the development of the bourgeoisie, to freedom of commerce, to the world-market, to uniformity in the mode of production and in the conditions of life corresponding thereto.

The supremacy of the proletariat will cause them to vanish still 114 faster. United action, of the leading civilized countries at least, is one of the first conditions for the emancipation of the proletariat.

In proportion as the exploitation of one individual by another is put 115 an end to, the exploitation of one nation by another will also be put an end to. In proportion as the antagonism between classes within the nation vanishes, the hostility of one nation to another will come to an end.

The charges against Communism made from a religious, a philo- 116 sophical, and generally, from an ideological standpoint, are not deserving of serious examination.

Does it require deep intuition to comprehend that man's ideas, 117 views and conceptions, in one word, man's consciousness, changes with every change in the conditions of his material existence, in his social relations and in his social life?

What else does the history of ideas prove than that intellectual pro- 118 duction changes in character in proportion as material production is changed? The ruling ideas of each age have ever been the ideas of its ruling class.

When people speak of ideas that revolutionize society they do but 119 express the fact that within the old society the elements of a new one have been created, and that the dissolution of the old ideas keeps even pace with the dissolution of the old conditions of existence.

When the ancient world was in its last throes the ancient religions 120 were overcome by Christianity. When Christian ideas succumbed in the 18th century to rationalist ideas, feudal society fought its death-battle with the then revolutionary bourgeoisie. The ideas of religious liberty and freedom of conscience merely gave expression to the sway of free competition within the domain of knowledge.

"Undoubtedly," it will be said, "religious, moral, philosophical and 121 judicial ideas have been modified in the course of historical development. But religion, morality, philosophy, political science, and law, constantly survived this change.

"There are, besides, eternal truths, such as Freedom, Justice, etc., 122 that are common to all states of society. But Communism abolishes eternal truths, it abolishes all religion and all morality, instead of constituting them on a new basis; it therefore acts in contradiction to all past historical experience."

What does this accusation reduce itself to? The history of all past 123
society has consisted in the development of class antagonisms, antagonisms that assumed different forms at different epochs.

But whatever form they may have taken, one fact is common to all 124
past ages, viz., the exploitation of one part of society by the other. No
wonder, then, that the social consciousness of past ages, despite all the
multiplicity and variety it displays, moves within certain common
forms, or general ideas, which cannot completely vanish except with
the total disappearance of class antagonisms.

The Communist revolution is the most radical rupture with tradi- 125
tional property relations; no wonder that its development involves the
most radical rupture with traditional ideas.

But let us have done with the bourgeois objections to Communism. 126

We have seen above that the first step in the revolution by the 127
working class is to raise the proletariat to the position of ruling class,
to win the battle of democracy.

The proletariat will use its political supremacy to wrest, by de- 128
grees, all capital from the bourgeoisie, to centralize all instruments of
production in the hands of the State, i.e., of the proletariat organized
as a ruling class; and to increase the total productive forces as rapidly
as possible.

Of course, in the beginning, this cannot be effected except by 129
means of despotic inroads on the rights of property, and on the conditions of bourgeois production; by means of measures, therefore, which
appear economically insufficient and untenable, but which in the
course of the movement outstrip themselves, necessitate further inroads upon the old social order, and are unavoidable as a means of
entirely revolutionizing the mode of production.

These measures will of course be different in different countries. 130

Nevertheless in the most advanced countries the following will be 131
pretty generally applicable:

1. Abolition of property in land and application of all rents of land to 132
   public purposes.
2. A heavy progressive or graduated income tax.
3. Abolition of all right of inheritance.
4. Confiscation of the property of all emigrants and rebels.
5. Centralization of credit in the hands of the State, by means of a
   national bank with State capital and an exclusive monopoly.
6. Centralization of the means of communication and transport in
   the hands of the State.
7. Extension of factories and instruments of production owned by the

State; the bringing into cultivation of waste lands, and the improvement of the soil generally in accordance with a common plan.

8. Equal liability of all to labor. Establishment of industrial armies, especially for agriculture.

9. Combination of agriculture with manufacturing industries; gradual abolition of the distinction between town and country by a more equable distribution of the population over the country.

10. Free education for all children in public schools. Abolition of children's factory labor in its present form. Combination of education with industrial production, etc., etc.

When, in the course of development, class distinctions have disap- 133
peared, and all production has been concentrated in the hands of a vast association of the whole nation, the public power will lose its political character. Political power, properly so called, is merely the organized power of one class for oppressing another. If the proletariat during its contest with the bourgeoisie is compelled, by the force of circumstances, to organize itself as a class, if, by means of a revolution, it makes itself the ruling class, and, as such, sweeps away by force the old conditions of production, then it will, along with these conditions, have swept away the conditions for the existence of class antagonism, and of classes generally, and will thereby have abolished its own supremacy as a class.

In place of the old bourgeois society, with its classes and class an- 134
tagonisms, we shall have an association in which the free development of each is the condition for the free development of all. . . .

Position of the Communists
in Relation to the Various Existing
Opposition Parties

[The preceding section] has made clear the relations of the Com- 135
munists to the existing working class parties, such as the Chartists in England and the Agrarian Reforms[11] in America.

---

[11]***Agrarian Reforms*** Agrarian reform was a very important issue in America after the Revolution. The Chartists were a radical English group established in 1838; they demanded reforms in land and labor. They were among the more violent revolutionaries of the day. Agrarian reform, redistribution of the land, was slow to come, and the issue often sparked violence between social classes.

The Communists fight for the attainment of the immediate aims, 136
for the enforcement of the momentary interests of the working class;
but in the movement of the present they also represent and take care
of the future of that movement. In France the Communists ally themselves with the Social-Democrats[12] against the conservative and radical bourgeoisie, reserving, however, the right to take up a critical position in regard to phrases and illusions traditionally handed down
from the great Revolution.

In Switzerland they support the Radicals,[13] without losing sight of 137
the fact that this party consists of antagonistic elements, partly of
Democratic Socialists, in the French sense, partly of radical bourgeois.

In Poland they support the party that insists on an agrarian revo- 138
lution, as the prime condition for national emancipation, that party
which fomented the insurrection of Cracow in 1846.[14]

In Germany they fight with the bourgeoisie whenever it acts in a 139
revolutionary way, against the absolute monarchy, the feudal squirear-
chy, and the petty bourgeoisie.

But they never cease for a single instant to instill into the working 140
class the clearest possible recognition of the hostile antagonism between bourgeoisie and proletariat, in order that the German workers
may straightway use, as so many weapons against the bourgeoisie, the
social and political conditions that the bourgeoisie must necessarily
introduce along with its supremacy, and in order that, after the fall of
the reactionary classes in Germany, the fight against the bourgeoisie
itself may immediately begin.

The Communists turn their attention chiefly to Germany, because 141
that country is on the eve of a bourgeois revolution,[15] that is bound to
be carried out under more advanced conditions of European civilization, and with a more developed proletariat, than that of England was

---

[12]***Social-Democrats*** In France in the 1840s, a group who proposed the ideal of labor
reform through the establishment of workshops supplied with government capital.

[13]***Radicals*** By 1848, European Radicals, taking their name from the violent revolutionaries of the French Revolution (1789–1799), were a nonviolent group content to wait
for change.

[14]***the insurrection of Cracow in 1846*** Cracow was an independent city in 1846.
The insurrection was designed to join Cracow with Poland and to further large-scale social reforms.

[15]***on the eve of a bourgeois revolution*** Ferdinand Lassalle (1825–1864) developed
the German labor movement and was in basic agreement with Marx, who was nevertheless convinced that Lassalle's approach was wrong. The environment in Germany seemed
appropriate for revolution, in part because of its fragmented political structure and in part
because no major revolutions had yet occurred there.

in the seventeenth and of France in the eighteenth century, and because the bourgeois revolution in Germany will be but the prelude to an immediately following proletarian revolution.

In short, the Communists everywhere support every revolutionary movement against the existing social and political order of things. 142

In all these movements they bring to the front, as the leading question in each, the property question, no matter what its degree of development at the time. 143

Finally, they labor everywhere for the union and agreement of the democratic parties of all countries. 144

The Communists disdain to conceal their views and aims. They openly declare that their ends can be attained only by the forcible overthrow of all existing social conditions. Let the ruling classes tremble at a Communistic revolution. The proletarians have nothing to lose but their chains. They have a world to win. 145

Working men of all countries, unite! 146

QUESTIONS

1. Begin by establishing your understanding of the terms "bourgeois" and "proletarian." Is the distinction Marx makes clear? Are such terms applicable to American society today? Do you feel that you can be properly associated with one or the other of these groups?
2. Marx makes the concept of social class fundamental to his theories. Can "social class" be easily defined? Are there social classes evident in our society? Are they engaged in a struggle of the sort Marx assumes?
3. What are Marx's views about the value of work in the society he describes?
4. Marx says that every class struggle is a political struggle. Is this true?
5. Examine the first part and total up the number of paragraphs devoted to the bourgeois and to the proletariat. Which class gets more paragraphs? Why?
6. Is the modern proletariat a revolutionary class?
7. Is Marx's analysis of history clear? Try to summarize his views on the progress of history.

WRITING ASSIGNMENTS

1. Defend or attack Marx's statement: "The executive of the modern State is but a committee for managing the common affairs of the whole bourgeoisie." Is this generally true? Take three "affairs of the whole bourgeoisie" and test each one in turn.

2. Inventory Marx's statements regarding women. Refer especially to paragraphs 39, 98, 105, and 110. Does he give evidence that his views are in conflict with his general society? After you have a list of his statements, see if you can establish exactly what he is recommending. Do you approve of his recommendations?

3. Marx's program of ten points is listed in paragraph 132. Using the technique that Marx himself uses—taking each point in its turn, clarifying the problems with the point, and finally deciding for or against the point—evaluate his program. Which points do you feel are most beneficial to society? Which are detrimental to society? What is your overall view of the general worth of the program? Do you think it would be possible to put such a program into effect?

4. All Marx's views are predicated on the present nature of property ownership and the changes that communism will institute. He says such things as, a rupture with property relations "involves the most radical rupture with traditional ideas" (para. 125). And he discusses in depth his proposal for the rupture of property relations (paras. 68–93). Clarify the traditional property relations—what can be owned and by whom—and then contrast with that the proposals Marx makes. Establish your own views as you go along, taking issue or expressing agreement (with your reasons) with Marx as you do so. What kinds of property relations do you see around you? What kinds are most desirable for a healthy society? Does Marx get you worried?

HENRY DAVID THOREAU

A Plea for
Captain John Brown

HENRY DAVID THOREAU (1817–1862) put principles before everything, including his personal comfort. He is best known for Walden
(1854), which recorded his experiences of living simply near Walden
Pond in Concord, Massachusetts. In that book he talks about the
deadening effects that property and ownership have upon the spirit.
Thoreau has been the conscience of generations of Americans, chastening us for giving in to materialism while neglecting our souls.

Thoreau was prominent among the group of thinkers and writers
who were styled the Transcendentalists. They derived their thinking
from the philosophy of Immanuel Kant (1724–1804) and the writings
of Samuel Taylor Coleridge (1772–1834) and Johann Wolfgang von
Goethe (1749–1832), among others, all of whom agreed that there
was a kind of knowledge—intuitive in human nature—that transcended the limits of the senses and experience. They were idealists:
they believed in the force of ideas and fought against the limits of
materialism. They were, for the most part, idealists in social action
as well. Thoreau's friend Ralph Waldo Emerson (1803–1882) was one
of the most eloquent spokesmen for the philosophy in America and
agreed with Thoreau that living close to nature was a worthwhile
ideal. Such communal social experiments as the utopian commune at
Brook Farm in West Roxbury, Massachusetts were one result of Tran-

scendentalist thought. Thoreau felt his defense of Brown was also
consistent with Transcendentalist views.

In the mid-1840s, Thoreau, like many northerners, became serious about wanting freedom for the slaves. Abolitionists like Capt.
John Brown (1800–1859) ran the Underground Railroad, a series of
homes that hid runaway slaves on their way to freedom in Canada.
Thoreau knew Brown and felt that he was an inspired man. Brown
held that no law that protected slaveholders and preserved the "peculiar institution" of slavery should be respected. He felt that freedom
for the slaves could be taken at the point of a gun if necessary. In
1859 he led a band of like-minded men, including his six sons, to
the U.S. Arsenal at Harpers Ferry in Virginia, to storm it, get at the
store of weapons, and arm slaves for an uprising that would gain
them their freedom. Brown achieved the first goal of his mission, but
government troops under the command of Robert E. Lee trapped him
in a railroad engine house. In a wildly disorganized battle, most of
Brown's band was killed and he was captured.

In this speech to his fellow citizens at Concord, given days after
the raid, Thoreau treats the question—not of slavery, since his audience agreed that it was evil—but of who John Brown was and what
he did. Moreover, he treats the question of what the government is
and what it ought to be. John Brown, as Thoreau fully expected, was
hanged by the government along with the other survivors of his band.
Ironically, it was only a matter of months later that the bloody Civil
War, which would end with the slaves being freed, would begin.

THOREAU'S RHETORIC

This is an impassioned speech, although Thoreau keeps it carefully under control. It is related to the great classical orations which
were designed to be spoken at the funeral of a great man. Today we
have few such speeches, but Thoreau's audience realized that they
were expected to make a connection between his speech and the most
famous speech of Greek funeral rhetoric: the Funeral Oration of Peri-
cles (495–429 B.C.), the great democratic statesman of Athens, delivered in 431 B.C. to honor the dead Athenians who had fought Sparta
in the Peloponnesian War. In other words, the form Thoreau chose
was known to his audience and was designed to elevate John Brown
to the level of heroes of classical Greece.

The strategy of the oration is simple enough on the surface. Thoreau begins with a discussion of Brown's forebears because, as the

Greeks said, from a bad crow come bad eggs. Well, Brown was a New Englander by birth, like Thoreau and his audience. His people were good people. Then Thoreau discusses Brown's personal qualities and declares that he is a good man (paras. 3–8). Once he has established Brown's personal worth—from observation, report, and the testimony even of his enemies—Thoreau goes on to examine the worth of the men he traveled to Harpers Ferry with. He does this because the classical orator always felt that a person is best known by the company he keeps. The company Brown keeps is worthy and good (paras. 9–10). Then Thoreau examines his ideas (para. 12); his tact and prudence (para. 13); his suffering (para. 14); and the failure of his enterprise at Harpers Ferry (paras. 15–16). He then goes on to examine Brown's motives, intentions, and sanity, and numerous other relevant subjects which have a bearing on how we evaluate what Brown did.

Thoreau's style is marked by considerable grace. He can be oratorical, as when he says, "These men, in teaching us how to die, have at the same time taught us how to live" (para. 62). His gift for irony is revealed when he says, "The modern Christian is a man who has consented to say all the prayers in the liturgy, provided you will let him go straight to bed and sleep quietly afterward" (para. 27). In both these sentences, irony is achieved by the rhetorical technique of antithesis, a figure of speech in which two parts—in this case two clauses—are strongly contrasted with one another. In the latter case, the first part has a strongly positive connotation while the second part has a strongly negative connotation. The technique is particularly effective in this form because the positive beginning does not prepare us for the surprise of the negative ending.

Thoreau's language is also rich in metaphor (an implied comparison) and other comparisons, such as simile (a comparison using "like" or "as"), and symbol (where one thing stands for another). Thoreau refers metaphorically to the Kansas Territory, where Brown campaigned against the introduction of slavery, as the "university of the West" (para. 7), because it was there Brown learned that violence was necessary to achieve his mission. A particularly powerful metaphor is contained in the observation: "Such do not know that like the seed is the fruit, and that, in the moral world, when good seed is planted, good fruit is inevitable, and does not depend on our watering and cultivating; that when you plant, or bury, a hero in his field, a crop of heroes is sure to spring up" (para. 22). The "hero" (Brown himself) is implicitly likened to the seed. In addition, this is an allusion to a New Testament parable spoken by Christ and recorded in

Matthew 13:3–23, known as "The Parable of the Sower." Parables are themselves metaphors that Christ used when imparting his teachings to his followers.

In paragraph 69, Thoreau works out one of his most complex comparisons: that of Brown to Christ. At times it seems that Christ's actions are used as a symbol of Brown's (as in the "saviour" reference in para. 67). The nature of the comparison is explained using the image of a chain: "Some eighteen hundred years ago Christ was crucified; this morning, perchance, Captain Brown was hung. These are the two ends of a chain which is not without its links. He is not Old Brown any longer; he is an angel of light." The Concord audience could not have missed the symbolic reference to Captain Brown as Christ, the savior of all mankind, who willingly sacrificed himself to free his people. Thoreau is using the symbolism to elevate Captain Brown to the status of an angel, almost a deity. It is a daring rhetorical device—almost an example of overreach.

A Plea for
Captain John Brown

I trust that you will pardon me for being here. I do not wish to force my thoughts upon you, but I feel forced myself. Little as I know of Captain Brown, I would fain do my part to correct the tone and the statements of the newspapers, and of my countrymen generally, respecting his character and actions. It costs us nothing to be just. We can at least express our sympathy with, and admiration of, him and his companions, and that is what I now propose to do. 1

First, as to his history. I will endeavor to omit, as much as possible, what you have already read. I need not describe his person to you, for probably most of you have seen and will not soon forget him. I am told that his grandfather, John Brown, was an officer in the Revolution; that he himself was born in Connecticut about the beginning of this century, but early went with his father to Ohio. I heard him say that his father was a contractor who furnished beef to the army there, in 2 the war of 1812; that he accompanied him to the camp, and assisted him in that employment, seeing a good deal of military life—more, perhaps, than if he had been a soldier; for he was often present at the councils of the officers. Especially, he learned by experience how armies are supplied and maintained in the field—a work which, he observed, requires at least as much experience and skill as to lead them in battle. He said that few persons had any conception of the cost, even the pecuniary cost,[1] of firing a single bullet in war. He saw enough, at any rate, to disgust him with a military life; indeed, to excite in him a great abhorrence of it; so much so, that though he was tempted by the offer of some petty office in the army, when he was about eighteen, he not only declined that, but he also refused to train when warned, and was fined for it. He then resolved that he would never have anything to do with any war, unless it were a war for liberty.

When the troubles in Kansas began, he sent several of his sons 3 thither to strengthen the party of the Free State men, fitting them out with such weapons as he had; telling them that if the troubles should increase, and there should be need of him, he would follow, to assist them with his hand and counsel. This, as you all know, he soon after did; and it was through his agency, far more than any other's, that Kansas was made free.

For a part of his life he was a surveyor, and at one time he was 4 engaged in wool-growing, and he went to Europe as an agent about that business. There, as everywhere, he had his eyes about him, and made many original observations. He said, for instance, that he saw why the soil of England was so rich, and that of Germany (I think it was) so poor, and he thought of writing to some of the crowned heads about it. It was because in England the peasantry live on the soil which they cultivate, but in Germany they are gathered into villages at night. It is a pity that he did not make a book of his observations.

I should say that he was an old-fashioned man in his respect for 5 the Constitution, and his faith in the permanence of this Union. Slavery he deemed to be wholly opposed to these, and he was its determined foe.

He was by descent and birth a New England farmer, a man of great 6 common sense, deliberate and practical as that class is, and tenfold more so. He was like the best of those who stood at Concord Bridge once, on Lexington Common, and on Bunker Hill, only he was firmer

---

[1]**pecuniary cost** cost in dollars and cents.

and higher principled[2] than any that I have chanced to hear of as there. It was no abolition lecturer that converted him. Ethan Allen and Stark,[3] with whom he may in some respects be compared, were rangers in a lower and less important field. They could bravely face their country's foes, but he had the courage to face his country herself when she was in the wrong. A Western writer says, to account for his escape from so many perils, that he was concealed under a "rural exterior"; as if, in that prairie land, a hero should, by good rights, wear a citizen's dress only.

He did not go to the college called Harvard, good old Alma Mater 7 as she is. He was not fed on the pap that is there furnished. As he phrased it, "I know no more of grammar than one of your calves." But he went to the great university of the West, where he sedulously pursued the study of Liberty, for which he had early betrayed a fondness, and having taken many degrees, he finally commenced the public practice of Humanity in Kansas, as you all know. Such were *his humanities*, and not any study of grammar. He would have left a Greek accent slanting the wrong way, and righted up a falling man.

He was one of that class of whom we hear a great deal, but, for 8 the most part, see nothing at all—the Puritans. It would be in vain to kill him. He died lately in the time of Cromwell,[4] but he reappeared here. Why should he not? Some of the Puritan stock are said to have come over and settled in New England. They were a class that did something else than celebrate their forefathers' day, and eat parched corn in remembrance of that time. They were neither Democrats nor Republicans, but men of simple habits, straightforward, prayerful; not thinking much of rulers who did not fear God, not making many compromises, nor seeking after available candidates.

"In his camp," as one has recently written, and as I have myself 9 heard him state, "he permitted no profanity; no man of loose morals was suffered to remain there, unless, indeed, as a prisoner of war. 'I would rather,' said he, 'have the small-pox, yellow fever, and cholera,

---

[2]*firmer and higher principled* Thoreau reminds his audience that our nation was made free by means of violence; the implication is that Brown may be thought of as a hero by future generations.

[3]*Ethan Allen (1738–1789) and John Stark (1728–1822)* Vermont generals who gained fame in the Revolutionary War in their battles with the British at Ticonderoga and on the way to Saratoga.

[4]*Oliver Cromwell (1599–1658)* The military leader of the English Puritans during the English Civil War in the 1640s. He became lord protector of the Commonwealth after the beheading of King Charles I (1600–1649). Thoreau reminds his audience that even the Puritans had blood on their hands.

all together in my camp, than a man without principle. . . . It is a mistake, sir, that our people make, when they think that bullies are the best fighters, or that they are the fit men to oppose these Southerners. Give me men of good principles—God-fearing men—men who respect themselves, and with a dozen of them I will oppose any hundred such men as these Buford[5] ruffians.' " He said that if one offered himself to be a soldier under him, who was forward to tell what he could or would do if he could only get sight of the enemy, he had but little confidence in him.

He was never able to find more than a score or so of recruits whom 10 he would accept, and only about a dozen, among them his sons, in whom he had perfect faith. When he was here some years ago, he showed to a few a little manuscript book—his "orderly book" I think he called it—containing the names of his company in Kansas, and the rules by which they bound themselves; and he stated that several of them had already sealed the contract with their blood. When some one remarked that, with the addition of a chaplain, it would have been a perfect Cromwellian troop, he observed that he would have been glad to add a chaplain to the list, if he could have found one who could fill that office worthily. It is easy enough to find one for the United States army. I believe that he had prayers in his camp morning and evening, nevertheless.

He was a man of Spartan habits, and at sixty was scrupulous about 11 his diet at your table excusing himself by saying that he must eat sparingly and fare hard, as became a soldier, or one who was fitting himself for difficult enterprises, a life of exposure.

A man of rare common sense and directness of speech, as of action; 12 a transcendentalist above all,[6] a man of ideas and principles—that was what distinguished him. Not yielding to a whim or transient impulse, but carrying out the purpose of a life. I noticed that he did not overstate anything, but spoke within bounds. I remember, particularly, how, in his speech here, he referred to what his family had suffered in Kansas, without ever giving the least vent to his pent-up fire. It was a volcano with an ordinary chimney-flue. Also referring to the deeds of certain Border Ruffians, he said, rapidly paring away his speech, like an experienced soldier, keeping a reserve of force and meaning, "They had a perfect right to be hung." He was not in the least a rhetorician,

---

[5]***Buford*** Possible reference to the army command of John Buford (1826–1863) of Kentucky.

[6]***transcendentalist above all*** Thoreau's highest compliment.

was not talking to Buncombe[7] or his constituents anywhere, had no need to invent anything but to tell the simple truth, and communicate his own resolution; therefore he appeared incomparably strong, and eloquence in Congress and elsewhere seemed to me at a discount. It was like the speeches of Cromwell compared with those of an ordinary king.

As for his tact and prudence, I will merely say, that at a time when   13
scarcely a man from the Free States was able to reach Kansas by any direct route, at least without having his arms taken from him, he, carrying what imperfect guns and other weapons he could collect, openly and slowly drove an ox-cart through Missouri, apparently in the capacity of a surveyor, with his surveying compass exposed in it, and so passed unsuspected, and had ample opportunity to learn the designs of the enemy. For some time after his arrival he still followed the same profession. When, for instance, he was a knot of the ruffians on the prairie, discussing, of course, the single topic[8] which then occupied their minds, he would, perhaps, take his compass and one of his sons, and proceed to run an imaginary line right through the very spot on which that conclave had assembled, and when he came up to them, he would naturally pause and have some talk with them, learning their news, and, at last, all their plans perfectly; and having thus completed his real survey he would resume his imaginary one, and run on his line till he was out of sight.

When I expressed surprise that he could live in Kansas at all, with   14
a price set upon his head, and so large a number, including the authorities, exasperated against him, he accounted for it by saying, "It is perfectly well understood that I will not be taken." Much of the time for some years he has had to skulk in swamps, suffering from poverty and from sickness, which was the consequence of exposure, befriended only by Indians and a few whites. But though it might be known that he was lurking in a particular swamp, his foes commonly did not care to go in after him. He could even come out into a town where there were more Border Ruffians than Free State men, and transact some business, without delaying long, and yet not be molested; for, said he, "no little handful of men were willing to undertake it, and a large body could not be got together in season."

As for his recent failure, we do not know the facts about it. It was   15

---

[7]*talking to Buncombe* Reference to politicians who address only their narrow self-interests; from a speech delivered in Buncombe County, North Carolina, in 1820.

[8]*single topic* Introducing slavery into the territory. The metaphor that follows here is well used; Thoreau was a surveyor at one time.

evidently far from being a wild and desperate attempt. His enemy, Mr. Vallandigham,[9] is compelled to say that "it was among the best planned and executed conspiracies that ever failed."

Not to mention his other successes, was it a failure, or did it show   16 a want of good management, to deliver from bondage a dozen human beings, and walk off with them by broad daylight, for weeks if not months, at a leisurely pace, through one State after another, for half the length of the North, conspicuous to all parties, with a price set upon his head, going into a courtroom on his way and telling what he had done, thus convincing Missouri that it was not profitable to try to hold slaves in his neighborhood?—and this, not because the government menials were lenient, but because they were afraid of him.

Yet he did not attribute his success, foolishly, to "his star," or to   17 any magic. He said, truly, that the reason why such greatly superior numbers quailed before him was, as one of his prisoners confessed, because they *lacked a cause*—a kind of armor which he and his party never lacked. When the time came, few men were found willing to lay down their lives in defense of what they knew to be wrong; they did not like that this should be their last act in this world.

But to make haste to *his* last act, and its effects.   18

The newspapers seem to ignore, or perhaps are really ignorant, of   19 the fact that there are at least as many as two or three individuals to a town throughout the North who think much as the present speaker does about him and his enterprise. I do not hesitate to say that they are an important and growing party. We aspire to be something more than stupid and timid chattels,[10] pretending to read history and our Bibles, but desecrating every house and every day we breathe in. Perhaps anxious politicians may prove that only seventeen white men and five negroes were concerned in the late enterprise; but their very anxiety to prove this might suggest to themselves that all is not told. Why do they still dodge the truth? They are so anxious because of a dim consciousness of the fact, which they do not distinctly face, that at least a million of the free inhabitants of the United States would have rejoiced if it had succeeded. They at most only criticize the tactics. Though we wear no crape,[11] the thought of that man's position

---

[9]*Clement Vallandigham (1820–1871)* A senator from Ohio who was sympathetic to the South.

[10]*stupid and timid chattels* cattle; followers.

[11]*crape* Mourning clothes; Thoreau speaks as if Brown were already dead but then reminds his audience that he may yet be alive; thus he reminds them that this is an unusual funeral oration.

and probable fate is spoiling many a man's day here at the North for other thinking. If any one who has seen him here can pursue success-fully any other train of thought, I do not know what he is made of. If there is any such who gets his usual allowance of sleep, I will warrant him to fatten easily under any circumstances which do not touch his body or purse. I put a piece of paper and a pencil under my pillow, and when I could not sleep I wrote in the dark.

On the whole, my respect for my fellow-men, except as one may   20 outweigh a million, is not being increased these days. I have noticed the cold-blooded way in which newspaper writers and men generally speak of this event, as if an ordinary malefactor, though one of unusual "pluck,"—as the Governor of Virginia is reported to have said, using the language of the cock-pit,[12] "the gamest man he ever saw,"—had been caught, and were about to be hung. He was not dreaming of his foes when the governor thought he looked so brave. It turns what sweetness I have to gall, to hear, or hear of, the remarks of some of my neighbors. When we heard at first that he was dead, one of my townsmen observed that "he died as the fool dieth"; which, pardon me, for an instant suggested a likeness in him dying to my neighbor living. Others, craven-hearted, said disparagingly, that "he threw his life away," because he resisted the government. Which way have they thrown *their* lives, pray?—such as would praise a man for attacking singly an ordinary band of thieves or murderers. I hear another ask, Yankee-like, "What will he gain by it?" as if he expected to fill his pockets by this enterprise. Such a one has no idea of gain but in this worldly sense. If it does not lead to a "surprise" party, if he does not get a new pair of boots, or a vote of thanks, it must be a failure. "But he won't gain anything by it."

Well, no, I don't suppose he could get four-and-sixpence a day for   21 being hung, take the year round; but then he stands a chance to save a considerable part of his soul—and *such* a soul!—when *you* do not. No doubt you can get more in your market for a quart of milk than for a quart of blood, but that is not the market that heroes carry their blood to.

Such do not know that like the seed is the fruit, and that, in the   22 moral world, when good seed is planted, good fruit is inevitable, and does not depend on our watering and cultivating; that when you plant, or bury, a hero in his field, a crop of heroes is sure to spring up. This

---

[12]*language of the cock-pit*   This expression refers to fights between roosters (game-cocks), held in pits, a "sport" then prevalent in many parts of the country.

is a seed of such force and vitality, that it does not ask our leave to germinate.

The momentary charge at Balaklava, in obedience to a blundering command, proving what a perfect machine the soldier is, has, properly enough, been celebrated by a poet laureate;[13] but the steady, and for the most part successful, charge of this man, for some years, against the legions of Slavery, in obedience to an infinitely higher command, is as much more memorable than that as an intelligent and conscientious man is superior to a machine. Do you think that that will go unsung? 23

"Served him right,"—"A dangerous man,"—"He is undoubtedly insane." So they proceed to live their sane, and wise, and altogether admirable lives, reading their Plutarch a little, but chiefly pausing at that feat of Putnam,[14] who was let down into a wolf's den; and in this wise they nourish themselves for brave and patriotic deeds some time or other. The Tract Society[15] could afford to print that story of Putnam. You might open the district schools with the reading of it, for there is nothing about Slavery or the Church in it; unless it occurs to the reader that some pastors are *wolves* in sheep's clothing. "The American Board of Commissioners for Foreign Missions,"[16] even, might dare to protest against *that* wolf. I have heard of boards, and of American boards, but it chances that I never heard of this particular lumber till lately. And yet I hear of Northern men, and women, and children, by families, buying a "life-membership" in societies as these. A life-membership in the grave! You can get buried cheaper than that. 24

Our foes are in our midst and all about us. There is hardly a house but is divided against itself, for our foe is the all but universal woodenness of both head and heart, the want of vitality in man, which is the effect of our vice; and hence are begotten fear, superstition, bigotry, persecution, and slavery of all kinds. We are mere figure-heads upon a hulk,[17] with livers in the place of hearts. The curse is the wor- 25

---

[13]*a poet laureate*   Alfred, Lord Tennyson (1809–1892), whose poem, "The Charge of the Light Brigade," was already famous. The charge at Balaklava occurred during the Crimean War (1855–1856), which pitted England and France against Russia. Of 700 cavalry who charged the cannon, only 190 returned.

[14]*Israel Putnam (1718–1790)*   A general during the Connecticut campaign in the Revolutionary War; the wolf was a symbol related to his bravery.

[15]*The Tract Society*   Formed in 1699 to print and distribute Protestant religious literature. Branches of this society, and related societies, flourished in Europe and America.

[16]*"The American Board of Commissioners for Foreign Missions"*   Protestant missionary organization formed in 1810 to convert Orientals to Christianity.

[17]*a hulk*   A heavy and clumsy ship or wreck of a ship.

ship of idols, which at length changes the worshiper into a stone image himself; and the New Englander is just as much as idolater as the Hindoo. This man was an exception, for he did not set up even a political graven image between him and his God.

A church that can never have done with excommunicating Christ   26
while it exists! Away with your broad and flat churches, and your narrow and tall churches! Take a step forward, and invent a new style of out-houses. Invent a salt that will save you, and defend our nostrils.

The modern Christian is a man who has consented to say all the   27
prayers in the liturgy, provided you will let him go straight to bed and sleep quietly afterward. All his prayers begin with "Now I lay me down to sleep," and he is forever looking forward to the time when he shall go to his *"long* rest." He has consented to perform certain old-established charities, too, after a fashion, but he does not wish to hear of any new-fangled ones; he doesn't wish to have any supplementary articles added to the contract, to fit it to the present time. He shows the whites of his eyes on the Sabbath, and the blacks all the rest of the week. The evil is not merely a stagnation of blood, but a stagnation of spirit. Many, no doubt, are well disposed, but sluggish by constitution and by habit, and they cannot conceive of a man who is actuated by higher motives than they are. Accordingly they pronounce this man insane, for they know that *they* could never act as he does, as long as they are themselves.

We dream of foreign countries, of other times and races of men,   28
placing them at a distance in history or space; but let some significant event like the present occur in our midst, and we discover, often, this distance and this strangeness between us and our nearest neighbors. *They* are our Austrias, and Chinas, and South Sea Islands. Our crowded society becomes well spaced all at once, clean and handsome to the eye—a city of magnificent distances. We discover why it was that we never got beyond compliments and surfaces with them before; we become aware of as many versts[18] between us and them as there are between a wandering Tartar and a Chinese town. The thoughtful man becomes a hermit in the thoroughfares of the market-place. Impassable seas suddenly find their level between us, or dumb steppes stretch themselves out there. It is the difference of constitution, of intelligence, and faith, and not streams and mountains, that make the

---

[18]**versts**   Russian measure of distance, about two-thirds of a mile. "A wandering Tartar" refers to the nomadic people who lived in what is now the northwestern part of China and the southwestern part of the Soviet Union—an enormous distance from any established "Chinese town."

true and impassable boundaries between individuals and between states. None but the like-minded can come plenipotentiary to our court.[19]

I read all the newspapers I could get within a week after this event, 29 and I do not remember in them a single expression of sympathy for these men. I have since seen one noble statement, in a Boston paper, not editorial. Some voluminous sheets decided not to print the full report of Brown's words to the exclusion of other matter. It was as if a publisher should reject the manuscript of the New Testament, and print Wilson's last speech. The same journal which contained this pregnant news was chiefly filled, in parallel columns, with the reports of the political conventions that were being held. But the descent to them was too steep. They should have been spared this contrast—been printed in an extra, at least. To turn from the voices and deeds of earnest men to the *cackling* of political conventions! Office-seekers and speech-makers, who do not so much as lay an honest egg, but wear their breasts bare upon an egg of chalk! Their great game is the game of straws, or rather that universal aboriginal game of the platter, at which the Indians cried *hub, bub!* Exclude the reports of religious and political conventions, and publish the words of a living man.

But I object not so much to what they have omitted as to what 30 they have inserted. Even the *Liberator*[20] called it "a misguided, wild, and apparently insane effort." As for the herd of newspapers and magazines, I do not chance to know an editor in the country who will deliberately print anything which he knows will ultimately and permanently reduce the number of his subscribers. They do not believe that it would be expedient. How then can they print truth? If we do not say pleasant things, they argue, nobody will attend to us. And so they do like some traveling auctioneers, who sing an obscene song, in order to draw a crowd around them. Republican editors, obliged to get their sentences ready for the morning edition, and accustomed to look at everything by the twilight of politics, express no admiration, nor true sorrow even, but call these men "deluded fanatics"—"mistaken men"—"insane," or "crazed." It suggests what a *sane* set of editors we are blessed with, *not* "mistaken men"; who know very well on which side their bread is buttered, at least.

---

[19]***our court*** Our own circle. In this sentence Thoreau means that we tolerate diversity elsewhere, but in our own circle those who have the fullest power ("plenipotentiary") are really those with whom we agree, those who are basically like us.

[20]**Liberator** Famous abolitionist newspaper edited by William Lloyd Garrison (1805–1879).

A man does a brave and humane deed, and at once, on all sides, we   31
hear people and parties declaring, "I didn't do it, nor countenance *him*
to do it, in any conceivable way. It can't be fairly inferred from my
past career." I, for one, am not interested to hear you define your position. I don't know that I ever was or ever shall be. I think it is mere
egotism, or impertinent at this time. Ye needn't take so much pains
to wash your skirts of him. No intelligent man will ever be convinced
that he was any creature of yours. He went and came, as he himself
informs us, "under the auspices of John Brown and nobody else." The
Republican party does not perceive how many his *failure* will make to
vote more correctly than they would have them. They have counted
the votes of Pennsylvania & Co.,[21] but they have not correctly counted
Captain Brown's vote. He has taken the wind out of their sails—the
little wind they had—and they may as well lie to and repair.

What though he did not belong to your clique! Though you may   32
not approve of his method or his principles, recognize his magnanimity. Would you not like to claim kindredship with him in that, though
in no other thing he is like, or likely, to you? Do you think that you
would lose your reputation so? What you lost at the spile, you would
gain at the bung.[22]

If they do not mean all this, then they do not speak the truth, and   33
say what they mean. They are simply at their old tricks still.

"It was always conceded to him," *says one who calls him crazy,*   34
"that he was a conscientious man, very modest in his demeanor, apparently inoffensive, until the subject of Slavery was introduced, when
he would exhibit a feeling of indignation unparalleled."

The slave-ship is on her way, crowded with its dying victims; new   35
cargoes are being added in mid-ocean; a small crew of slaveholders,
countenanced by a large body of passengers, is smothering four millions under the hatches, and yet the politician asserts that the only
proper way by which deliverance is to be obtained is by "the quiet
diffusion of the sentiments of humanity," without any "outbreak." As
if the sentiments of humanity were ever found unaccompanied by its
deeds, and you could disperse them, all finished to order, the pure article, as easily as water with a watering-pot, and so lay the dust. What
is that that I hear cast overboard? The bodies of the dead that have

---

[21]**Pennsylvania & Co.**   A reference to the railroad building in which Brown holed
up against the army assault.

[22]**spile . . . bung**   The reference is to barrels used in commerce. The spile is the
tap or faucet used to empty the barrel; the bung is the hole through which it is filled.

found deliverance. That is the way we are "diffusing" humanity, and its sentiments with it.

Prominent and influential editors, accustomed to deal with politi- 36 cians, men of an infinitely lower grade, say, in their ignorance, that he acted "on the principle of revenge." They do not know the man. They must enlarge themselves to conceive of him. I have no doubt that the time will come when they will begin to see him as he was. They have got to conceive of a man of faith and of religious principle, and not a politician or an Indian; of a man who did not wait till he was personally interfered with or thwarted in some harmless business before he gave his life to the cause of the oppressed.

If Walker[23] may be considered the representative of the South, I 37 wish I could say that Brown was the representative of the North. He was a superior man. He did not value his bodily life in comparison with ideal things. He did not recognize unjust human laws, but resisted them as he was bid. For once we are lifted out of the trivialness and dust of politics into the region of truth and manhood. No man in America has ever stood up so persistently and effectively for the dignity of human nature, knowing himself for a man, and the equal of any and all governments. In that sense he was the most American of us all. He needed no babbling lawyer, making false issues, to defend him. He was more than a match for all the judges that American voters, or office-holders of whatever grade, can create. He could not have been tried by a jury of his peers, because his peers did not exist. When a man stands up serenely against the condemnation and vengeance of mankind, rising above them literally *by a whole body*—even though he were of late the vilest murderer, who has settled that matter with himself—the spectacle is a sublime one—didn't ye know it, ye *Liberators*, ye *Tribunes*, ye *Republicans!*—and we become criminal in comparison. Do yourselves the honor to recognize him. He needs none of your respect.

As for the Democratic journals, they are not human enough to af- 38 fect me at all. I do not feel indignation at anything they may say.

I am aware that I anticipate a little—that he was still, at the last 39 accounts, alive in the hands of his foes; but that being the case, I have all along found myself thinking and speaking of him as physically dead.

---

[23]***Robert Walker (1801–1869)*** Prominent speculator and businessman who supported slave interests, the Mexican War, and other southern sectional concerns. He was governor of Kansas in 1857.

I do not believe in erecting statues to those who still live in our 40
hearts, whose bones have not yet crumbled in the earth around us, but
I would rather see the statue of Captain Brown in the Massachusetts
State-House yard than that of any other man whom I know. I rejoice
that I live in this age, that I am his contemporary.

What a contrast, when we turn to that political party which is so 41
anxiously shuffling him and his plot out of its way, and looking
around for some available slaveholder, perhaps, to be its candidate, at
least for one who will execute the Fugitive Slave Law[24] and all those
other unjust laws which he took up arms to annul!

Insane! A father and six sons, and one son-in-law, and several more 42
men besides—as many at least as twelve disciples—all struck with
insanity at once; while the sane tyrant holds with a firmer grip than
every his four millions of slaves, and a thousand sane editors, his abet-
tors, are saving their country and their bacon! Just as insane were his
efforts in Kansas. Ask the tyrant who is his most dangerous foe, the
sane man or the insane? Do the thousands who know him best, who
have rejoiced at his deeds in Kansas, and have afforded him material
aid there, think him insane? Such a use of this word is a mere trope[25]
with most who persist in using it, and I have no doubt that many of
the rest have already in silence retracted their words.

Read his admirable answers to Mason[26] and others. How they are 43
dwarfed and defeated by the contrast! On the one side, half-brutish,
half-timid questioning; on the other, truth, clear as lightning, crashing
into their obscene temples. They are made to stand with Pilate, and
Gessler,[27] and the Inquisition. How ineffectual their speech and action! and what a void their silence! They are but helpless tools in this
great work. It was no human power that gathered them about this
preacher.

What have Massachusetts and the North sent a few *sane* represen- 44
tatives to Congress for, of late years?—to declare with effect what kind

---

[24]*Fugitive Slave Law* The latest version of the Act (1850) provided stiff penalties for
those who harbored runaway slaves. In reaction to these laws, the Underground Railroad
worked more vigorously to help runaways escape to Canada.

[25]*mere trope* Trope means figure of speech; Thoreau is saying that calling Brown insane is unreasonable and has no substance in fact.

[26]*James Murray Mason (1798–1871)* United States senator from Virginia. He wrote
the Fugitive Slave Act of 1850 and was prominent in the government of the Confederacy.

[27]*Gessler* The legendary Swiss tyrant who ordered William Tell to shoot an apple
from his son's head with an arrow. Tell later killed Gessler. The story was especially
popular in the nineteenth century, and Friedrich von Schiller's dramatic version (*Wilhelm
Tell,* 1804) was widely performed.

of sentiments? All their speeches put together and boiled down—and probably they themselves will confess it—do not match for manly directness and force, and for simple truth, the few casual remarks of crazy John Brown on the floor of the Harper's Ferry engine-house—that man whom you are about to hang, to send to the other world, though not to represent *you* there. No, he was not our representative in any sense. He was too fair a specimen of a man to represent the like of us. Who, then, *were* his constituents? If you read his words understandingly you will find out. In his case there is no idle eloquence, no made, nor maiden speech, no compliments to the oppressor. Truth is his inspirer, and earnestness the polisher of his sentences. He could afford to lose his Sharps rifles,[28] while he retained his faculty of speech—a Sharps rifle of infinitely surer and longer range.

And the New York *Herald* reports the conversation *verbatim!* It 45 does not know of what undying words it is made the vehicle.

I have no respect for the penetration of any man who can read the 46 report of that conversation and still call the principal in it insane. It has the ring of a saner sanity than an ordinary discipline and habits of life, than an ordinary organization, secure. Take any sentence of it— "Any questions that I can honorably answer, I will; not otherwise. So far as I am myself concerned, I have told everything truthfully. I value my word, sir." The few who talk about his vindictive spirit, while they really admire his heroism, have no test by which to detect a noble man, no amalgam to combine with his pure gold. They mix their own dross with it.

It is a relief to turn from these slanders to the testimony of his 47 more truthful, but frightened jailers and hangmen. Governor Wise[29] speaks far more justly and appreciatingly of him than any Northern editor, or politician, or public personage, that I chance to have heard from. I know that you can afford to hear him again on this subject. He says: "They are themselves mistaken who take him to be a madman. . . . He is cool, collected, and indomitable, and it is but just to him to say that he was humane to his prisoners. . . . And he inspired me with great trust in his integrity as a man of truth. He is a fanatic, vain and garrulous" (I leave that part to Mr. Wise), "but firm, truthful, and intelligent. His men, too, who survive, are like him. . . . Colonel Washington says that he was the coolest and firmest man he ever saw

---

[28]***Sharps rifles*** Nineteenth-century American breech-loading (loading from the rear) rifles highly prized at the time.

[29]***Governor Henry Alexander Wise (1807–1876)*** Governor of Virginia, 1855–1860. He signed John Brown's death warrant.

in defying danger and death. With one son dead by his side, and another shot through, he felt the pulse of his dying son with one hand, and held his rifle with the other, and commanded his men with the utmost composure, encouraging them to be firm, and to sell their lives as dear as they could. Of the three white prisoners, Brown, Stevens, and Coppoc,[30] it was hard to say which was most firm."

Almost the first Northern men whom the slaveholder has learned 48
to respect!

The testimony of Mr. Vallandigham, though less valuable, is of the 49
same purport, that "it is vain to underrate either the man or his conspiracy. . . . He is the farthest possible removed from the ordinary ruffian, fanatic, or madman."

"All is quiet at Harper's Ferry," says the journals. What is the char- 50
acter of that calm which follows when the law and the slaveholder prevail? I regard this event as a touchstone designed to bring out, with glaring distinctness, the character of this government. We needed to be thus assisted to see it by the light of history. It needed to see itself. When a government puts forth its strength on the side of injustice, as ours to maintain slavery and kill the liberators of the slave, it reveals itself a merely brute force, or worse, a demoniacal force. It is the head of the Plug-Uglies.[31] It is more manifest than ever that tyranny rules. I see this government to be effectually allied with France and Austria in oppressing mankind. There sits a tyrant holding fettered four millions of slaves; here comes their heroic liberator. This most hypocritical and diabolical government looks up from its seat on the gasping four millions, and inquires with an assumption of innocence: "What do you assault me for? Am I not an honest man? Cease agitation on this subject, or I will make a slave of you, too, or else hang you."

We talk about a *representative* government; but what a monster of 51
a government is that where the noblest faculties of the mind, and the *whole* heart, are not *represented*. A semi-human tiger or ox, stalking over the earth, with its heart taken out and the top of its brain shot away. Heroes have fought well on their stumps when their legs were shot off, but I never heard of any good done by such a government as that.

The only government that I recognize—and it matters not how few 52

---

[30]***Stevens and Coppoc***   Ten of the thirteen whites were killed in the taking of the Engine House. Brown was wounded and was later hanged with the survivors, Stevens and Coppoc.

[31]***Plug-Uglies***   The term refers to New York gangs whose members wore plugs or plug hats—a slang term for top hats. Note the pun in the reference to "head."

are at the head of it, or how small its army—is that power that establishes justice in the land, never that which establishes injustice. What shall we think of a government to which all the truly brave and just men in the land are enemies, standing between it and those whom it oppresses? A government that pretends to be Christian and crucifies a million Christs every day!

Treason! Where does such treason take its rise? I cannot help 53 thinking of you as you deserve, ye governments. Can you dry up the fountains of thought? High treason, when it is resistance to tyranny here below, has its origin in, and is first committed by, the power that makes and forever recreates man. When you have caught and hung all these human rebels, you have accomplished nothing but your own guilt, for you have not struck at the fountainhead. You presume to contend with a foe against whom West Point cadets and rifled cannon *point* not. Can all the art of the cannon founder tempt matter to turn against its maker? Is the form in which the founder thinks he casts it more essential than the constitution of it and of himself?

The United States have a coffle[32] of four millions of slaves. They 54 are determined to keep them in this condition; and Massachusetts is one of the confederated overseers to prevent their escape. Such are not all the inhabitants of Massachusetts, but such are they who rule and are obeyed here. It was Massachusetts, as well as Virginia, that put down this insurrection at Harper's Ferry. She sent the marines there, and she will have *to pay the penalty of her sin.*

Suppose that there is a society in this State that out of its own 55 purse and magnanimity saves all the fugitive slaves that run to us, and protects our colored fellow-citizens, and leaves the other work to the government, so called. Is not that government fast losing its occupation, and becoming contemptible to mankind? If private men are obliged to perform the offices of government, to protect the weak and dispense justice, then the government becomes only a hired man, or clerk, to perform menial or indifferent services. Of course, that is but the shadow of a government whose existence necessitates a Vigilant Committee. What should we think of the Oriental Cadi[33] even, behind whom worked in secret a Vigilant Committee? But such is the character of our Northern States generally; each has its Vigilant Committee. And, to a certain extent, these crazy governments recognize and accept this relation. They say, virtually, "We'll be glad to work for you

---

[32]*coffle* Slaves (or animals) tied together and driven along in a group.

[33]*Oriental Cadi* Judge of canon law in an Islamic court. The power and severity of such judges was naturally intimidating to Thoreau's Christian audience.

on these terms, only don't make a noise about it." And thus the government, its salary being insured, withdraws into the back shop, taking the constitution with it, and bestows most of its labor on repairing that. When I hear it at work sometimes, as I go by, it reminds me, at best, of those farmers who in winter contrive to turn a penny by following the coopering business. And what kind of spirit is their barrel made to hold? They speculate in stocks, and bore holes in mountains, but they are not competent to lay out even a decent highway. The only *free* road, the Underground Railroad, is owned and managed by the Vigilant Committee. *They* have tunneled under the whole breadth of the land. Such a government is losing its power and respectability as surely as water runs out of a leaky vessel, and is held by one that can contain it.

I hear many condemn these men because they were so few. When 56 were the good and the brave ever in a majority? Would you have had him wait till that time came?—till you and I came over to him? The very fact that he had no rabble or troop of hirelings about him would alone distinguish him from ordinary heroes. His company was small indeed, because few could be found worthy to pass muster. Each one who there laid down his life for the poor and oppressed was a picked man, culled out of many thousands, if not millions; apparently a man of principle, of rare courage, and devoted humanity; ready to sacrifice his life at any moment for the benefit of his fellow-man. It may be doubted if there were as many more their equals in these respects in all the country—I speak of his followers only—for their leader, no doubt, scoured the land far and wide, seeking to swell his troop. These alone were ready to step between the oppressor and the oppressed. Surely they were the very best men you could select to be hung. That was the greatest compliment which this country could pay them. They were ripe for her gallows. She has tried a long time, she has hung a good many, but never found the right one before.

When I think of him, and his six sons, and his son-in-law, not to 57 enumerate the others, enlisted for this fight, proceeding coolly, reverently, humanely to work, for months if not years, sleeping and waking upon it, summering and wintering the thought, without expecting any reward but a good conscience, while almost all America stood ranked on the other side—I say again that it affects me as a sublime spectacle. If he had had any journal advocating *"his cause,"* any organ, as the phrase is, monotonously and wearisomely playing the same old tune, and then passing round the hat, it would have been fatal to his efficiency. If he had acted in any way so as to be let alone by the government, he might have been suspected. It was the fact that the tyrant must give place to him, or he to the tyrant, that distinguished him from all the reformers of the day that I know.

It was his peculiar doctrine that a man has a perfect right to inter- 58
fere by force with the slaveholder, in order to rescue the slave. I agree with him. They who are continually shocked by slavery have some right to be shocked by the violent death of the slaveholder, but no others. Such will be more shocked by his life than by his death. I shall not be forward to think him mistaken in his method who quickest succeeds to liberate the slave. I speak for the slave when I say that I prefer the philanthropy of Captain Brown to that philanthropy which neither shoots me nor liberates me. At any rate, I do not think it is quite sane for one to spend his whole life in talking or writing about this matter, unless he is continuously inspired, and I have not done so. A man may have other affairs to attend to. I do not wish to kill nor to be killed, but I can foresee circumstances in which both these things would be by me unavoidable. We preserve the so-called peace of our community by deeds of petty violence every day. Look at the policeman's billy and handcuffs! Look at the jail! Look at the gallows! Look at the chaplain of the regiment! We are hoping only to live safely on the outskirts of *this* provisional army. So we defend ourselves and our hen-roosts, and maintain slavery. I know that the mass of my countrymen think that the only righteous use that can be made of Sharps rifles and revolvers is to fight duels with them, when we are insulted by other nations, or to hunt Indians, or shoot fugitive slaves with them, or the like. I think that for once the Sharps rifles and the revolvers were employed in a righteous cause. The tools were in the hands of one who could use them.

The same indignation that is said to have cleared the temple once 59
will clear it again. The question is not about the weapon, but the spirit in which you use it. No man has appeared in America, as yet, who loved his fellow-man so well, and treated him so tenderly. He lived for him. He took up his life and he laid it down for him. What sort of violence is that which is encouraged, not by soldiers, but by peaceable citizens, not so much by laymen as by ministers of the Gospel, not so much by the fighting sects as by the Quakers, and not so much by Quaker men as by Quaker women?

This event advertises me[34] that there is such a fact as death—the 60
possibility of a man's dying. It seems as if no man had ever died in America before; for in order to die you must first have lived. I don't

---

[34]*advertises me* warns (or notifies) me.

believe in the hearses, and palls, and funerals that they have had. There was no death in the case, because there had been no life; they merely rotted or sloughed off, pretty much as they had rotted or sloughed along. No temple's veil was rent, only a hole dug somewhere. Let the dead bury their dead. The best of them fairly ran down like a clock. Franklin—Washington—they were let off without dying; they were merely missing one day. I hear a good many pretend that they are going to die; or that they have died, for aught that I know. Nonsense! I'll defy them to do it. They haven't got life enough in them. They'll deliquesce like fungi,[35] and keep a hundred eulogists mopping the spot where they left off. Only half a dozen or so have died since the world began. Do you think that you are going to die, sir? No! there's no hope of you. You haven't got your lesson yet. You've got to stay after school. We make a needless ado about capital punishment— taking lives, when there is no life to take. *Memento mori!*[36] We don't understand that sublime sentence which some worthy got sculptured on his gravestone once. We've interpreted it in a groveling and sniveling sense; we've wholly forgotten how to die.

But be sure you do die nevertheless. Do your work, and finish it. If 61 you know how to begin you will know when to end.

These men, in teaching us how to die, have at the same time taught 62 us how to live. If this man's acts and words do not create a revival, it will be the severest possible satire on the acts and words that do. It is the best news that America has ever heard. It has already quickened the feeble pulse of the North, and infused more and more generous blood into her veins and heart than any number of years of what is called commercial and political prosperity could. How many a man who was lately contemplating suicide has now something to live for!

One writer says that Brown's peculiar monomania made him to be 63 "dreaded by the Missourians as a supernatural being." Sure enough, a hero in the midst of us cowards is always so dreaded. He is just that thing. He shows himself superior to nature. He has a spark of divinity in him.

---

[35]*They'll deliquesce like fungi* Thoreau means that such people haven't any real substance, and so cannot be said to be truly alive; hence, they cannot truly die. Like fungi, they will deliquesce—branch out into many subdivisions—while lacking a main axis, or stem (one might say basic vital principle). This is one of the more powerful similes in this passage, because of the surprise value of comparing people with mushrooms.

[36]**Memento mori!** A reminder that we ourselves must die (literally, "Remember that you must die").

> Unless above himself he can
> Erect himself, how poor a thing is man![37]

Newspaper editors argue also that it is a proof of his *insanity* that 64
he thought he was appointed to do this work which he did—that he
did not suspect himself for a moment! They talk as if it were impossible that a man could be "divinely appointed" in these days to do any
work whatever; as if vows and religion were out of date as connected
with any man's daily work; as if the agent to abolish slavery could
only be somebody appointed by the President, or by some political
party. They talk as if a man's death were a failure, and his continued
life, be it of whatever character, were a success.

When I reflect to what a cause this man devoted himself, and how 65
religiously, and then reflect to what cause his judges and all who condemn him so angrily and fluently devote themselves, I see that they
are as far apart as the heavens and earth are asunder.

The amount of it is, our *"leading men"* are a harmless kind of folk, 66
and they know *well enough* that *they* were not divinely appointed, but
elected by the votes of their party.

Who is it whose safety requires that Captain Brown be hung? Is it 67
indispensable to any Northern man? Is there no resource but to cast
this man also to the Minotaur?[38] If you do not wish it, say so distinctly. While these things are being done, beauty stands veiled and
music is a screeching lie. Think of him—of his rare qualities!—such a
man as it takes ages to make, and ages to understand; no mock hero,
nor the representative of any party. A man such as the sun may not
rise upon again in this benighted land. To whose making went the
costliest material, the finest adamant;[39] sent to be the redeemer of
those in captivity; and the only use to which you can put him is to
hang him at the end of a rope! You who pretend to care for Christ
crucified, consider what you are about to do to him who offered himself to be the saviour of four millions of men.

Any man knows when he is justified, and all the wits in the world 68

---

[37]***how poor a thing is man!*** Samuel Daniel (1562–1619), from *Epistle to the
Countess of Cumberland*, stanza 12.

[38]***Minotaur*** In a Greek myth, seven Athenian youths and seven maidens were occasionally sacrificed to this monster—who was half-man and half-bull—until Theseus
killed it.

[39]***the finest adamant*** The finest stone (diamond), at one time thought to be unbreak-
able.

cannot enlighten him on that point. The murderer always knows that he is justly punished; but when a government takes the life of a man without the consent of his conscience, it is an audacious government, and is taking a step towards its own dissolution. Is it not possible that an individual may be right and a government wrong? Are laws to be enforced simply because they were made? or declared by any number of men to be good, if they are *not* good? Is there any necessity for a man's being a tool to perform a deed of which his better nature disapproves? Is it the intention of law-makers that *good* men shall be hung ever? Are judges to interpret the law according to the letter, and not the spirit? What right have *you* to enter into a compact with yourself that you *will* do thus or so, against the light within you? Is it for *you* to *make up* your mind—to form any resolution whatever—and not accept the convictions that are forced upon you, and which ever pass your understanding? I do not believe in lawyers, in that mode of attacking or defending a man, because you descend to meet the judge on his own ground, and, in cases of the highest importance, it is of no consequence whether a man breaks a human law or not. Let lawyers decide trivial cases. Business men may arrange that among themselves. If they were the interpreters of the everlasting laws which rightfully bind man, that would be another thing. A counterfeiting law-factory, standing half in a slave land and half in a free! What kind of laws for free men can you expect from that?

I am here to plead his cause with you. I plead not for his life, but 69 for his character—his immortal life; and so it becomes your cause wholly, and is not his in the least. Some eighteen hundred years ago Christ was crucified; this morning, perchance, Captain Brown was hung. These are the two ends of a chain which is not without its links. He is not Old Brown any longer; he is an angel of light.

I see now that it was necessary that the bravest and humanest man 70 in all the country should be hung. Perhaps he saw it himself. I *almost fear* that I may yet hear of his deliverance, doubting if a prolonged life, if *any* life, can do as much good as his death.

"Misguided!" "Garrulous!" "Insane!" "Vindictive!" So ye write in 71 your easy-chairs, and thus he wounded responds from the floor of the Armory, clear as a cloudless sky, true as the voice of nature is: "No man sent me here; it was my own prompting and that of my Maker. I acknowledge no master in human form."

And in what a sweet and noble strain he proceeds, addressing his 72 captors, who stand over him: "I think, my friends, you are guilty of a great wrong against God and humanity, and it would be perfectly right for any one to interfere with you so far as to free those you willfully and wickedly hold in bondage."

And, referring to his movement: "It is, in my opinion, the greatest 73 service a man can render to God."

"I pity the poor in bondage that have none to help them; that is 74 why I am here; not to gratify any personal animosity, revenge, or vindictive spirit. It is my sympathy with the oppressed and the wronged, that are as good as you, and as precious in the sight of God."

You don't know your testament when you see it. 75

"I want you to understand that I respect the rights of the poorest 76 and weakest of colored people, oppressed by the slave power, just as much as I do those of the most wealthy and powerful."

"I wish to say, furthermore, that you had better, all you people at 77 the South, prepare yourselves for a settlement of that question, that must come up for settlement sooner than you are prepared for it. The sooner you are prepared the better. You may dispose of me very easily. I am nearly disposed of now; but this question is still to be settled— this negro question, I mean; the end of that is not yet."

I foresee the time when the painter will paint that scene, no longer 78 going to Rome for a subject; the poet will sing it; the historian record it; and, with the Landing of the Pilgrims and the Declaration of Independence, it will be the ornament of some future national gallery, when at least the present form of slavery shall be no more here. We shall then be at liberty to weep for Captain Brown. Then, and not till then, we will take our revenge.

QUESTIONS

1. Look up John Brown in a full-sized encyclopedia or in a biographical resource such as *The McGraw-Hill Encyclopedia of World Biography.* Is Thoreau's description of him fair and complete?
2. Find at least three instances of Thoreau's use of irony. What is their effect? Would they insult an audience?
3. In paragraph 1 Thoreau says, "It costs us nothing to be just." What does he mean by this? What function does his speech have in relation to his desire to be just?
4. Do you feel that this speech is too long? That it is too short? Qualify your views on its length by careful reasoning.
5. What kind of a person does Thoreau seem to be? Can you tell much about his personality from this speech? Would you have enjoyed knowing him? What would you have talked about with him?

WRITING ASSIGNMENTS

1. Thoreau has a great deal to say about the government. Go through the speech and find the best quotes that characterize government. Refer to paragraphs 50–55 for Thoreau's complete discussion. What does Thoreau think of his government? How does he describe it? With what might it be compared? Has our government changed enough so that it would suit Thoreau?

2. Based on Thoreau's description and on whatever other biographical sources you can locate, offer a brief character sketch of John Brown. Try to portray him to a friend as either worthy or unworthy of Thoreau's praise. As an alternate project, look up Thoreau in a biographical resource and offer a brief character sketch of him. Adhere to the pattern of talking about forebears, the man himself, those who were his associates, and his ideas.

3. Go through the selection carefully to collect all the comparisons, metaphors, similes, and symbolic links Thoreau makes between Brown and other historical figures, between Brown's men and such figures, between governments here and abroad. Be sure to include the seed passage in paragraph 22, the comparison with the Puritans in paragraph 8, and the many comparisons with Jesus Christ. How effective are the techniques of comparison in this speech? Check The Parable of the Sower (Matthew 13:3–23). Is it effective? Does Thoreau use it effectively? What is the effect of Thoreau's comparisons? What are they meant to do, and what do they do?

4. The central issue in the speech is the question of whether it is right to take up arms against a law that is unjust. And it is not just any such law but a law such as the one that permitted slavery, a law that unfairly "imprisoned" four million people. Perhaps the center of the arguments he raises are in paragraph 68. What are your views on taking up arms against an unjust law? Is John Brown, for example, a greater hero because he had the courage not only to face his country's foes but his country when it was wrong (para. 6)? Do you expect your government to agree with your views? If you agree with Thoreau and Brown, then your views disagree with the law. Does this idea upset you?

5. From paragraph 42 to 55 Thoreau discusses the questions of Brown's sanity, the nature of tyranny, and the nature of government. Using material from this section (and elsewhere in the selection), construct an essay that establishes the connection between these issues. Why are they treated in the same section of the speech? What are Thoreau's views on these issues? Do you agree with his views? Take him to task where you can, or reinforce with your own experience the views he holds.

FREDERICK DOUGLASS

from
The Narrative of the Life of Frederick Douglass, an American Slave

FREDERICK DOUGLASS (1817–1895) was born into slavery in Maryland; he died not only a free man but a man who commanded the respect of his country, his government, and hosts of supporters. His owner's wife, Mrs. Auld, was a northerner and did not know about the slaveholders' practice of forbidding slaves to learn to read and write. This was a lucky accident, indeed: Mrs. Auld taught Douglass enough so that he could begin his own education—and escape to freedom.

The selection presented here describes how Douglass gained his victory. In his description—the Narrative was published in 1845— Douglass was careful to avoid mentioning details that would likely have hurt other slaves' chances of gaining their freedom. Douglass used the papers of a freed black sailor to impersonate him, and so he was able to sail from Baltimore to New York, where he gained his freedom. His method was dangerous but simple. He lived first in New York, then settled in New Bedford, Massachusetts.

The rest of the Narrative is filled with stories about his growing up as a slave. He had little connection with his family. His mother, Harriet Bailey, was not able to be close with him, nor was he ever to know who his father was. He records not only the beatings he witnessed as a slave but also the conditions under which he lived and the struggles he felt within himself to be a free man. He, himself, *survived brutal beatings and torture by a professional slave "breaker."*

This section of the Narrative is fascinating for its revelation of the observations of a freed slave concerning the world he entered. His concerns for work, economy, and justice are everywhere apparent in these pages. When they were published—apparently as a result of encouragement by Harvard students who had heard his powerful oratory—these pages made him one of the most sought-after speakers in the North. He became a lecturer for the Massachusetts Antislavery League. Yet, as a fugitive slave, he lived in constant fear of being kidnapped and returned to slavery.

After publication of an early version of his life, to avoid capture he spent a few years in England, then returned to the United States and became the editor of the North Star, an abolitionist paper in Rochester, New York. One of his chief concerns was for the welfare of the slaves who managed to secure their freedom. When John Brown invited him to participate in the raid at Harpers Ferry, Virginia, Douglass was famous throughout the North. He refused Brown's invitation because he believed that such an act would not benefit the antislavery cause. When the Civil War began, Douglass managed to get Lincoln's ear. Originally there were no plans to free the slaves, but Douglass helped convince Lincoln that it would help the war effort to free them, and in 1863 Lincoln delivered the Emancipation Proclamation.

The years after the war and Lincoln's death were not good for freed slaves. Terrorist groups in both the North and the South worked to keep them from enjoying freedom, and programs which might have been effective in training black ex-slaves were never fully instituted. During this time Douglass worked in various capacities for the government, both as an ambassador to foreign countries and as an official in Washington, D.C. He was the first black American to become a national figure and to have powerful influence with the government.

DOUGLASS'S RHETORIC

Douglass was essentially a self-taught man. He is said to have been a commanding speaker who could move people to agree with his views. His speeches were often full and somewhat high-flown in the fashion of the day. This excerpt from the Narrative, however, is remarkable for having none of the characteristics of the overdone rhetoric we find in the writing of the time. Instead, it is surprisingly direct, simple, and clear. The use of the first person is as simple as one could wish it to be, and yet the feelings that are projected are genuine and moving.

The structure Douglass employs in the **Narrative** is one of the most basic in all rhetoric: the chronological narrative. He begins his story at a given point in time, explaining what happened at that moment. He then progresses to the next sequence of events, always pushing the narrative closer to the present time. He even includes some key dates, so that one can measure the progress of the narrative. The structure is one that we all recognize and feel comfortable with. There are no interruptions such as flashbacks or ruminations on what might have been. Rather, after his introductory two paragraphs, he tells what happened as it happened.

Douglass's style is a bit formal by modern standards. His sentences are somewhat long, although they are carefully balanced by an occasional very brief sentence. His paragraphs are in general very long, indeed. He tends to take a given subject and work it out thoroughly before dropping it, and to begin a new subject in the next paragraph. Yet even now, 140 years later, the style appears easy and direct. No modern reader will have difficulty responding to what Frederick Douglass has to say. His views on justice, on liberty, and on the relationship between economy and government are as accessible now as they were when they were originally written.

---

from
The Narrative of the Life of Frederick Douglass, an American Slave

I now come to that part of my life during which I planned, and finally succeeded in making, my escape from slavery. But before narrating any of the peculiar circumstances, I deem it proper to make known my intention not to state all the facts connected with the transaction. My reasons for pursuing this course may be understood from the following: First, were I to give a minute statement of all the facts, it is not only possible, but quite probable, that others would thereby be involved in the most embarrassing difficulties. Secondly, such a statement would most undoubtedly induce greater vigilance on the part of slaveholders than has existed heretofore among them; which would, of course be the means of guarding a door whereby some dear brother bondman might escape his galling chains. I deeply regret the necessity that impels me to suppress any thing of importance connected with my experience in slavery. It would afford me great pleasure indeed, as well as materially add to the interest of my narrative, were I at liberty to gratify a curiosity, which I know exists in the minds of many, by an accurate statement of all the facts pertaining to my most fortunate escape. But I must deprive myself of this pleasure, and the curious of the gratification which such a statement would afford. I would allow myself to suffer under the greatest imputations which evil-minded men might suggest, rather than exculpate myself,[1] and thereby run the hazard of closing the slightest avenue by which a brother slave might clear himself of the chains and fetters of slavery.

I have never approved of the very public manner in which some of our western friends have conducted what they call the *underground railroad*,[2] but which, I think, by their open declarations, has been made most emphatically the *upperground railroad*. I honor those good men and women for their noble daring, and applaud them for willingly subjecting themselves to bloody persecution, by openly avowing their participation in the escape of slaves. I, however, can see very little good resulting from such a course, either to themselves or the slaves escaping; while, upon the other hand, I see and feel assured that those open declarations are a positive evil to the slaves remaining, who are seeking to escape. They do nothing towards enlightening the slave, whilst they do much towards enlightening the master. They stimulate him to greater watchfulness, and enhance his power to capture his slave. We owe something to the slaves south of the line as well as to those north of it; and in aiding the latter on their way to freedom, we should be careful to do nothing which would be likely to hinder the former from escaping from slavery. I would keep the merciless slave-

---

[1] ***exculpate myself*** This is a mild bit of irony; Douglass means that if he revealed his method of escape he would be innocent of the charge of not telling the whole truth.

[2] ***underground railroad*** An organization of "safe houses" to help escaped slaves find their way to freedom in Canada. The Fugitive Slave Act (1850) made the work of this abolitionist group a crime.

holder profoundly ignorant of the means of flight adopted by the slave. I would leave him to imagine himself surrounded by myriads of invisible tormentors, ever ready to snatch from his infernal grasp his trembling prey. Let him be left to feel his way in the dark; let darkness commensurate with his crime hover over him; and let him feel that at every step he takes, in pursuit of the flying bondman, he is running the frightful risk of having his hot brains dashed out by an invisible agency. Let us render the tyrant no aid; let us not hold the light by which he can trace the footprints of our flying brother. But enough of this. I will now proceed to the statement of those facts, connected with my escape, for which I am alone responsible, and for which no one can be made to suffer but myself.

In the early part of the year 1838, I became quite restless. I could ³ see no reason why I should, at the end of each week, pour the reward of my toil into the purse of my master. When I carried to him my weekly wages, he would, after counting the money, look me in the face with a robber-like fierceness, and ask, "Is this all?" He was satisfied with nothing less than the last cent. He would, however, when I made him six dollars, sometimes give me six cents, to encourage me. It had the opposite effect. I regarded it as a sort of admission of my right to the whole. The fact that he gave me any part of my wages was proof, to my mind, that he believed me entitled to the whole of them. I always felt worse for having received any thing; for I feared that the giving me a few cents would ease his conscience, and make him feel himself to be a pretty honorable sort of robber. My discontent grew upon me. I was ever on the look-out for means of escape; and, finding no direct means, I determined to try to hire my time, with a view of getting money with which to make my escape. In the spring of 1838, when Master Thomas³ came to Baltimore to purchase his spring goods, I got an opportunity, and applied to him to allow me to hire my time. He unhesitatingly refused my request, and told me this was another stratagem by which to escape.⁴ He told me I could go nowhere but that he could get me; and that, in the event of my running away, he should spare no pains in his efforts to catch me. He exhorted me to content myself, and be obedient. He told me, if I would be happy, I must lay out no plans for the future. He said, if I behaved myself properly, he would take care of me. Indeed, he advised me to complete thought-

---

³**Master Thomas** Thomas Lloyd, his owner, had lent Douglass to Hugh Auld of Baltimore. Auld's wife, a northerner, taught Douglass to read and write.

⁴**another stratagem by which to escape** He had escaped once before and was captured by a professional slave "breaker."

lessness of the future, and taught me to depend solely upon him for happiness. He seemed to see fully the pressing necessity of setting aside my intellectual nature, in order to contentment in slavery. But in spite of him, and even in spite of myself, I continued to think, and to think about the injustice of my enslavement, and the means of escape.

About two months after this, I applied to Master Hugh for the privilege of hiring my time. He was not acquainted with the fact that I had applied to Master Thomas, and had been refused. He too, at first, seemed disposed to refuse; but, after some reflection, he granted me the privilege, and proposed the following term: I was to be allowed all my time, make all contracts with those for whom I worked, and find my own employment; and, in return for this liberty, I was to pay him three dollars at the end of each week; find myself in[5] calking tools, and in board and clothing. My board was two dollars and a half per week. This, with the wear and tear of clothing and calking tools, made my regular expenses about six dollars per week. This amount I was compelled to make up, or relinquish the privilege of hiring my time. Rain or shine, work or no work, at the end of each week the money must be forthcoming, or I must give up my privilege. This arrangement, it will be perceived, was decidedly in my master's favor. It relieved him of all need of looking after me. His money was sure. He received all the benefits of slaveholding without its evils; while I endured all the evils of a slave, and suffered all the care and anxiety of a freeman. I found it a hard bargain. But, hard as it was, I thought it better than the old mode of getting along. It was a step towards freedom to be allowed to bear the responsibilities of a freeman, and I was determined to hold on upon it. I bent myself to the work of making money. I was ready to work at night as well as day, and by the most untiring perseverance and industry, I made enough to meet my expenses, and lay up a little money every week. I went on thus from May till August. Master Hugh then refused to allow me to hire my time longer. The ground for his refusal was a failure on my part, one Saturday night, to pay him for my week's time. This failure was occasioned by my attending a camp meeting about ten miles from Baltimore. During the week, I had entered into an engagement with a number of young friends to start from Baltimore to the camp ground early Saturday evening; and being detained by my employer, I was unable to

4

---

[5]*find myself in* Douglass means to provide himself with the means to equip himself with his tools and to pay for his board and clothing.

get down to Master Hugh's without disappointing the company. I knew that Master Hugh was in no special need of the money that night. I therefore decided to go to camp meeting, and upon my return pay him the three dollars. I staid at the camp meeting one day longer than I intended when I left. But as soon as I returned, I called upon him to pay him what he considered his due. I found him very angry; he could scarce restrain his wrath. He said he had a great mind to give me a severe whipping. He wished to know how I dared go out of the city without asking his permission. I told him I hired my time, and while I paid him the price which he asked for it, I did not know that I was bound to ask him when and where I should go. This reply troubled him; and, after reflecting a few moments, he turned to me, and said I should hire my time no longer; that the next thing he should know of, I would be running away. Upon the same plea, he told me to bring my tools and clothing home forthwith. I did so; but instead of seeking work, as I had been accustomed to do previously to hiring my time, I spent the whole week without the performance of a single stroke of work. I did this in retaliation. Saturday night, he called upon me as usual for my week's wages. I told him I had no wages; I had done no work that week. Here we were upon the point of coming to blows. He raved, and swore his determination to get hold of me. I did not allow myself a single word; but was resolved, if he laid the weight of his hand upon me, it should be blow for blow. He did not strike me, but told me that he would find me in constant employment in future. I thought the matter over during the next day, Sunday, and finally resolved upon the third day of September, as the day upon which I would make a second attempt to secure my freedom. I now had three weeks during which to prepare for my journey. Early on Monday morning, before Master Hugh had time to make any engagement for me, I went out and got employment of Mr. Butler, at his ship-yard near the drawbridge, upon what is called the City Block, thus making it unnecessary for him to seek employment for me. At the end of the week, I brought him between eight and nine dollars. He seemed very well pleased, and asked me why I did not do the same the week before. He little knew what my plans were. My object in working steadily was to remove any suspicion he might entertain of my intent to run away; and in this I succeeded admirably. I suppose he thought I was never better satisfied with my condition than at the very time during which I was planning my escape. The second week passed, and again I carried him my full wages; and so well pleased was he, that he gave me twenty-five cents (quite a large sum for a slaveholder to give a slave) and bade me to make a good use of it. I told him I would.

Things went on without very smoothly indeed, but within there 5
was trouble. It is impossible for me to describe my feelings as the time
of my contemplated start drew near. I had a number of warm-hearted
friends in Baltimore—friends that I loved almost as I did my life—and
the thought of being separated from them forever was painful beyond
expression. It is my opinion that thousands would escape from slavery,
who now remain, but for the strong cords of affection that bind them
to their friends. The thought of leaving my friends was decidedly the
most painful thought with which I had to contend. The love of them
was my tender point, and shook my decision more than all things else.
Besides the pain of separation, the dread and apprehension of a failure
exceeded what I had experienced at my first attempt. The appalling
defeat I then sustained returned to torment me. I felt assured that, if I
failed in this attempt, my case would be a hopeless one—it would seal
my fate as a slave forever. I could not hope to get off with any thing
less than the severest punishment, and being placed beyond the means
of escape. It required no very vivid imagination to depict the most
frightful scenes through which I should have to pass, in case I failed.
The wretchedness of slavery, and the blessedness of freedom, were perpetually before me. It was life and death with me. But I remained firm,
and, according to my resolution, on the third day of September, 1838,
I left my chains, and succeeded in reaching New York without the
slightest interruption of any kind. How I did so—what means I
adopted—what direction I travelled, and by what mode of convey-
ance—I must leave unexplained, for the reasons before mentioned.

I have been frequently asked how I felt when I found myself in a 6
free State. I have never been able to answer the question with any
satisfaction to myself. It was a moment of the highest excitement I
ever experienced. I suppose I felt as one may imagine the unarmed
mariner to feel when he is rescued by a friendly man-of-war from the
pursuit of a pirate. In writing to a dear friend, immediately after my
arrival at New York, I said I felt like one who had escaped a den of
hungry lions. This state of mind, however, very soon subsided; and I
was again seized with a feeling of great insecurity and loneliness. I was
yet liable to be taken back, and subjected to all the tortures of slavery.
This in itself was enough to damp the ardor of my enthusiasm. But
the loneliness overcame me. There I was in the midst of thousands,
and yet a perfect stranger; without home and without friends, in the
midst of thousands of my own brethren—children of a common Father, and yet I dared not to unfold to any one of them my sad condition. I was afraid to speak to any one for fear of speaking to the wrong
one, and thereby falling into the hands of money-loving kidnappers,

whose business it was to lie in wait for the panting fugitive, as the ferocious beasts of the forest lie in wait for their prey. The motto which I adopted when I started from slavery was this—"Trust no man!" I saw in every white man an enemy, and in almost every colored man cause for distrust. It was a most painful situation; and, to understand it, one must needs experience it, or imagine himself in similar circumstances. Let him be a fugitive slave in a strange land—a land given up to be the hunting-ground for slaveholders—whose inhabitants are legalized kidnappers—where he is every moment subjected to the terrible liability of being seized upon by his fellow-men, as the hideous crocodile seizes upon his prey!—I say, let him place himself in my situation—without home or friends—without money or credit—wanting shelter, and no one to give it—wanting bread, and no money to buy it—and at the same time let him feel that he is pursued by merciless men-hunters, and in total darkness as to what to do, where to go, or where to stay—perfectly helpless both as to the means of defense and means of escape—in the midst of plenty, yet suffering the terrible gnawings of hunger—in the midst of houses, yet having no home—among fellow-men, yet feeling as if in the midst of wild beasts, whose greediness to swallow up the trembling and half-famished fugitive is only equalled by that with which the monsters of the deep swallow up the helpless fish upon which they subsist—I say, let him be placed in this most trying situation—the situation in which I was placed—then, and not till then, will he fully appreciate the hardships of, and know how to sympathize with, the toil-worn and whip-scarred fugitive slave.

Thank Heaven, I remained but a short time in this distressed situation. I was relieved from it by the humane hand of Mr. David Ruggles, whose vigilance, kindness, and perseverance, I shall never forget. I am glad of an opportunity to express, as far as words can, the love and gratitude I bear him. Mr. Ruggles is now afflicted with blindness, and is himself in need of the same kind offices which he was once so forward in the performance of toward others. I had been in New York but a few days, when Mr. Ruggles sought me out, and very kindly took me to his boarding-house at the corner of Church and Lespenard Streets. Mr. Ruggles was then very deeply engaged in the memorable *Darg* case,[6] as well as attending to a number of other fugitive slaves, devising ways and means for their successful escape; and, though watched

7

---

[6]**Darg** *case* Mr. Ruggles tried to help a fugitive slave named Darg escape authorities who were compelled to return him to his owners.

and hemmed in on almost every side, he seemed to be more than a
match for his enemies.

Very soon after I went to Mr. Ruggles, he wished to know of me 8
where I wanted to go; as he deemed it unsafe for me to remain in New
York. I told him I was a calker, and should like to go where I could get
work. I thought of going to Canada; but he decided against it, and in
favor of my going to New Bedford, thinking I should be able to get
work there at my trade. At this time, Anna,[7] my intended wife, came
on; for I wrote to her immediately after my arrival at New York (notwithstanding my homeless, houseless, and helpless condition) informing her of my successful flight, and wishing her to come on forthwith.
In a few days after her arrival, Mr. Ruggles called in the Rev. J. W. C.
Pennington, who, in the presence of Mr. Ruggles, Mrs. Michaels, and
two or three others, performed the marriage ceremony, and gave us a
certificate, of which the following is an exact copy:

> THIS may certify, that I joined together in holy matrimony Freder-
> ick Johnson[8] and Anna Murray, as man and wife, in the presence of Mr.
> David Ruggles and Mrs. Michaels.
>
> JAMES W. C. PENNINGTON.
> *New York, Sept. 15, 1838.*

Upon receiving this certificate, and a five-dollar bill from Mr. Rug- 9
gles, I shouldered one part of our baggage, and Anna took up the other,
and we set out forthwith to take passage on board of the steamboat
John W. Richmond for Newport, on our way to New Bedford. Mr. Ruggles gave me a letter to a Mr. Shaw in Newport, and told me, in case
my money did not serve me to New Bedford, to stop in Newport and
obtain further assistance; but upon our arrival at Newport, we were so
anxious to get to a place of safety, that, notwithstanding we lacked the
necessary money to pay our fare, we decided to take seats in the stage,
and promise to pay when we got to New Bedford. We were encouraged
to do this by two excellent gentlemen, residents of New Bedford,
whose names I afterward ascertained to be Joseph Ricketson and William C. Taber. They seemed at once to understand our circumstances,
and gave us such assurance of their friendliness as put us fully at ease
in their presence. It was good indeed to meet with such friends, at such
a time. Upon reaching New Bedford, we were directed to the house of
Mr. Nathan Johnson, by whom we were kindly received, and hospita-
bly provided for. Both Mr. and Mrs. Johnson took a deep and lively

---

[7]She was free. [Douglass's note]

[8]I had changed my name from Frederick *Bailey* to that of *Johnson*. [Douglass's note]

interest in our welfare. They proved themselves quite worthy of the name of abolitionists. When the stage-driver found us unable to pay our fare, he held on upon our baggage as security for the debt. I had but to mention the fact to Mr. Johnson, and he forthwith advanced the money.

We now began to feel a degree of safety, and to prepare ourselves   10
for the duties and responsibilities of a life of freedom. On the morning after our arrival at New Bedford, while at the breakfast-table, the question arose as to what name I should be called by. The name given me by my mother was, "Frederick Augustus Washington Bailey." I, however, had dispensed with the two middle names long before I left Maryland so that I was generally known by the name of "Frederick Bailey." I started from Baltimore bearing the name of "Stanley." When I got to New York, I again changed my name to "Frederick Johnson," and thought that would be the last change. But when I got to New Bedford, I found it necessary again to change my name. The reason of this necessity was, that there were so many Johnsons in New Bedford, it was already quite difficult to distinguish between them. I gave Mr. Johnson the privilege of choosing me a name, but told him he must not take from me the name of "Frederick." I must hold on to that, to preserve a sense of my identity. Mr. Johnson had just been reading the "Lady of the Lake,"[9] and at once suggested that my name be "Douglass." From that time until now I have been called "Frederick Douglass"; and as I am more widely known by that name than by either of the others, I shall continue to use it as my own.

I was quite disappointed at the general appearance of things in New   11
Bedford. The impression which I had received respecting the character and condition of the people of the north, I found to be singularly erroneous. I had very strangely supposed, while in slavery, that few of the comforts, and scarcely any of the luxuries, of life were enjoyed at the north, compared with what were enjoyed by the slaveholders of the south. I probably came to this conclusion from the fact that northern people owned no slaves. I supposed that they were about upon a level with the non-slaveholding population of the south. I knew *they* were exceedingly poor, and I had been accustomed to regard their poverty as the necessary consequence of their being non-slaveholders. I had somehow imbibed the opinion that, in the absence of slaves, there could be no wealth, and very little refinement. And upon coming to the north,

---

[9]*"Lady of the Lake"*   A long narrative poem by Sir Walter Scott (1771–1832), published in 1810. The fugitive Lord James Douglas is a primary character.

I expected to meet with a rough, hard-handed, and uncultivated population, living in the most Spartan-like simplicity, knowing nothing of the ease, luxury, pomp, and grandeur of southern slaveholders. Such being my conjectures, any one acquainted with the appearance of New Bedford may very readily infer how palpably I must have seen my mistake.

In the afternoon of the day when I reached New Bedford, I visited   12 the wharves, to take a view of the shipping. Here I found myself surrounded with the strongest proofs of wealth. Lying at the wharves, and riding in the stream, I saw many ships of the finest model, in the best order, and of the largest size. Upon the right and left, I was walled in by granite warehouses of the widest dimensions, stowed to their utmost capacity with the necessaries and comforts of life. Added to this, almost every body seemed to be at work, but noiselessly so, compared with what I had been accustomed to in Baltimore. There were no loud songs heard from those engaged in loading and unloading ships. I heard no deep oaths or horrid curses on the laborer. I saw no whipping of men; but all seemed to go smoothly on. Every man appeared to understand his work, and went at it with a sober, yet cheerful earnestness, which betokened the deep interest which he felt in what he was doing, as well as a sense of his own dignity as a man. To me this looked exceedingly strange. From the wharves I strolled around and over the town, gazing with wonder and admiration at the splendid churches, beautiful dwellings, and finely-cultivated gardens; evincing an amount of wealth, comfort, taste, and refinement, such as I had never seen in any part of slaveholding Maryland.

Every thing looked clean, new and beautiful. I saw few or no dilapi-   13 dated houses, with poverty-stricken inmates; no half-naked children and barefooted women, such as I had been accustomed to see in Hillsborough, Easton, St. Michael's, and Baltimore. The people looked more able, stronger, healthier, and happier, than those of Maryland. I was for once made glad by a view of extreme wealth, without being saddened by seeing extreme poverty. But the most astonishing as well as the most interesting thing to me was the condition of the colored people, a great many of whom, like myself, had escaped thither as a refuge from the hunters of men. I found many, who had not been seven years out of their chains, living in finer houses, and evidently enjoying more of the comforts of life, than the average of slaveholders in Maryland. I will venture to assert that my friend Mr. Nathan Johnson (of whom I can say with a grateful heart, "I was hungry, and he gave me meat; I was thirsty, and he gave me drink; I was a stranger, and he took me in"] lived in a neater house; dined at a better table; took, paid for, and read, more newspapers; better understood the moral, religious, and political character of the nation—than nine tenths of the slaveholders in Talbot county, Maryland. Yet Mr. Johnson was a working man. His hands were hardened by toil, and not his alone, but those also of Mrs. Johnson. I found the colored people much more spirited than I had supposed they would be. I found among them a determination to protect each other from the blood-thirsty kidnapper, at all hazards. Soon after my arrival, I was told of a circumstance which illustrated their spirit. A colored man and a fugitive slave were on unfriendly terms. The former was heard to threaten the latter with informing his master of his whereabouts. Straightway a meeting was called among the colored people, under the stereotyped[10] notice, "Business of importance!" The betrayer was invited to attend. The people came at the appointed hour, and organized the meeting by appointing a very religious old gentleman as president, who, I believe, made a prayer, after which he addressed the meeting as follows: *"Friends, we have got him here, and I would recommend that you young men just take him outside the door, and kill him!"* With this, a number of them bolted at him; but they were intercepted by some more timid than themselves, and the betrayer escaped their vengeance, and has not been seen in New Bedford since. I believe there have been no more such threats, and should there be hereafter, I doubt not that death would be the consequence.

I found employment, the third day after my arrival, in stowing a   14
sloop with a load of oil. It was new, dirty, and hard work for me; but I went at it with a glad heart and a willing hand. I was now my own master. It was a happy moment, the rapture of which can be understood only by those who have been slaves. It was the first work, the reward of which was to be entirely my own. There was no Master Hugh standing ready, the moment I earned the money, to rob me of it. I worked that day with a pleasure I had never before experienced. I was at work for myself and newly-married wife. It was to me the starting-point of a new existence. When I got through with that job, I went in pursuit of a job of calking; but such was the strength of prejudice against color, among the white calkers, that they refused to work with me, and of course I could get no employment.[11] Finding my trade of

---

[10]***stereotyped*** He means printed. Stereotyping is one of several methods of printing and is used to print both newspapers and books.

[11]I am told that colored persons can now get employment at calking in New Bedford—a result of anti-slavery effort. [Douglass's note]

no immediate benefit, I threw off my calking habiliments, and prepared myself to do any kind of work I could get to do. Mr. Johnson kindly let me have his wood-horse and saw, and I very soon found myself a plenty of work. There was no work too hard—none too dirty. I was ready to saw wood, shovel coal, carry the hod, sweep the chimney, or roll oil casks—all of which I did for nearly three years in New Bedford, before I became known to the anti-slavery world.

In about four months after I went to New Bedford, there came a   15
young man to me, and inquired if I did not wish to take the "Liberator."[12] I told him I did; but, just having made my escape from slavery, I remarked that I was unable to pay for it then. I, however, finally became a subscriber to it. The paper came, and I read it from week to week with such feelings as it would be quite idle for me to attempt to describe. The paper became my meat and my drink. My soul was set all on fire. Its sympathy for my brethren in bonds—its scathing denunciations of slaveholders—its faithful exposures of slavery—and its powerful attacks upon the upholders of the institution—sent a thrill of joy through my soul, such as I had never felt before!

I had not long been a reader of the "Liberator," before I got a pretty   16
correct idea of the principles, measures and spirit of the anti-slavery reform. I took right hold of the cause. I could do but little; but what I could, I did with a joyful heart, and never felt happier than when in an anti-slavery meeting. I seldom had much to say at the meetings, because what I wanted to say was said so much better by others. But, while attending an anti-slavery convention at Nantucket, on the 11th of August, 1841, I felt strongly moved to speak, and was at the same time much urged to do so by Mr. William C. Coffin, a gentleman who had heard me speak in the colored people's meeting at New Bedford. It was a severe cross, and I took it up reluctantly. The truth was, I felt myself a slave, and the idea of speaking to white people weighed me down. I spoke but a few moments, when I felt a degree of freedom, and said what I desired with considerable ease. From that time until now, I have been engaged in pleading the cause of my brethren—with what success, and with what devotion, I leave those acquainted with my labors to decide.

---

[12]*the "Liberator"* The celebrated abolitionist newspaper edited by William Lloyd Garrison (1805–1879).

QUESTIONS

1. If you find Douglass's story engrossing, try to explain what it is about his rhetorical approach to his subject that makes it so. If you find it dull, explain why. What aspects of Douglass's style are effective? What aspects are not effective?
2. What is the significance of Douglass's concerns with the future, as expressed in paragraph 3? Can you see a psychological validity in the slaveowner's insistence on his forgetting the future entirely? Does that idea have implications for your own life?
3. What did it mean for Douglass to hire himself out? Does the practice surprise you?
4. How much freedom did Douglass have as a slave? What was the nature of that freedom?
5. Find three passages that best reveal racial awareness on the part of Douglass or others mentioned in the narrative.
6. Why was Douglass fearful of being kidnapped?

WRITING ASSIGNMENTS

1. Establish what you feel is the real importance of the "six-cents episode" in paragraph 3. Consider its implications for the value of work, the meaning of money, the relationship between slave and slaveowner, and any other related issue you feel it brings into play. How effective is this episode for revealing the most serious issues that concern Douglass?
2. In paragraph 10, Douglass discusses his name changes and alludes to the issue of his own identity. Using that passage as a starting point, take a stand on the issue of whether or not a person's name is closely connected—or connected at all—with that person's sense of his or her identity. What does Douglass reveal about his own sense of identity? Can you detect any changes he reveals in his sense of himself when he was a slave compared with when he was free?
3. Tell a story in the first person of any injustice you feel has been done to you. Use Douglass's technique of chronological narrative; his clear description of scenes; and his reference to, and description of, people and the inclusion of their names. As much as possible use his approach to tell your story.
4. In paragraph 6, Douglass says firmly that once he had gained his freedom he was determined to be wary of strangers and careful not to be kidnapped by those who would get a reward for his return. To that end he declares that he will "Trust no man!" Examine this selection carefully and, by inventorying relevant events and useful quotes, decide whether or not he held to this advice. If you feel that he did not do so, why would he include

his statement? Do you think that Douglass reveals himself to be a trusting man at heart? If so (or if not), what does that mean? What is Douglass's deepest feeling about the goodness or the badness of mankind?

5. When he goes to New Bedford, Massachusetts, he reveals a considerable degree of surprise. In paragraph 11 and several following paragraphs, he gives us his reaction and his thinking. He actually is giving forth an economic theory regarding slaveholding and the production (or maintenance) of wealth. Establish carefully just what surprises him, what conclusions he had drawn while in the South, and what new conclusions he must draw in New Bedford. What genuine conclusions do you feel must be drawn as a result of his observations? What is the economic consequence of slavery for southern society (not just for southern slaveholders)? Use the selection to gather quotations and references that will make your conclusions clearer and more forceful. Consider, too, Douglass's observations on the way blacks and whites lived and worked in New Bedford. At this time, incidentally, New Bedford was a thriving whaling town with a considerable industry and numerous economic opportunities.

MARTIN LUTHER KING, Jr.

Letter from
Birmingham Jail

MARTIN LUTHER KING, JR. (1929–1968) was the most influential leader for black civil rights in America for a little more than fifteen years. He was an ordained minister with a doctorate in theology from Boston University. He worked primarily in the South, where he worked steadily to overthrow laws that promoted segregation and to increase the number of black voters registered in southern communities.

The period from 1958 to 1968 was the most active in American history for demonstrations and activities that resulted in opening up opportunities for black Americans. Many laws existed prohibiting blacks from sitting in certain sections of buses, from using facilities such as water fountains in bus stations, and from sitting at luncheon counters with whites. Such laws—patently unfair and insulting, not to mention unconstitutional—were not challenged by local authorities. Martin Luther King, Jr., who had become famous for supporting a program to integrate buses in Montgomery, Alabama, was asked by the Southern Christian Leadership Conference to assist in the fight for civil rights in Birmingham, Alabama, where the SCLC meeting was to be held.

King was arrested as the result of a program of sit-ins at luncheon counters and wrote the letter printed here to a number of Christian ministers who had criticized his position. King had been arrested before and would be arrested again—resembling Thoreau somewhat in his attitude toward laws that did not constitute moral justice.

Eventually, the causes King had promoted were victorious. His efforts helped not only to change attitudes in the South but also to spur legislation that has benefited Americans all over the country. His views concerning nonviolence were spread throughout the world and were the basis of his successful efforts to change the character of life in America. By the early 1960s he had become a world-famous man, a man who stood for human rights and human dignity virtually everywhere. He won the Nobel Peace Prize in 1964.

King himself was nonviolent, but his program left both King and his followers open to the threat of violence. The sit-ins and voter registration programs spurred countless acts of violence, bombings, threats, and murders on the part of the white community. His life was often threatened, his home bombed, his followers harassed. He was assassinated at the Lorraine Motel in Memphis, Tennessee, on April 4, 1968. But before he died he saw—largely through his own efforts, influence, and example—the face of America change.

KING'S RHETORIC

The most obvious rhetorical tradition King assumes in this important work is that of the books of the Bible which were originally letters, such as Paul's Epistle to the Ephesians and his several letters to the Corinthians. Many of Paul's letters were written while he was in prison in Rome. In each of those instances, Paul was establishing a moral position which was far in advance of that of the citizens who received the letters, and at the same time Paul was doing the most important work of the early Christian Church: spreading the Word to those who wished to be Christians but who needed clarification and encouragement.

It is not clear that the churchmen who received the letter fully understood the rhetorical tradition King assumed—but since they were men who preached from the Bible they certainly should have understood. The general public, which is less acquainted or concerned with the Bible, may have needed some reminding, and the text itself alludes to the mission of Paul and to his communications to his people. King assumes this rhetorical tradition, not only because it is effective, but because it connects him with the deepest *aspect of his calling: spreading the gospel of Christ. Brotherhood was his message.*

King's tone is one of utmost patience with his critics. He seems bent on winning them over to his point of view, just as he seems confident that—because they are, like him, clergymen—their goodwill should help them see the justice of his views.

His method is that of careful reasoning, centering on the substance of their criticism, particularly focusing on their complaints that his actions were "unwise and untimely." Each of those charges is taken in turn, with a careful analysis. of the arguments against his position; then follows a statement, in the clearest possible terms, of his own views and why he feels they are worth adhering to. The "Letter from Birmingham Jail" is a model of careful and reasonable analysis of a very complex situation. It succeeds largely because it remains concrete, treating one issue carefully after another, refusing to be caught up in passion or posturing. King remains grounded in logic. He is convinced that his statement of his views will convince his audience.

Letter from Birmingham Jail

April 16, 1963

MY DEAR FELLOW CLERGYMEN:[1]

    While confined here in the Birmingham city jail, I came across your recent statement calling my present activities "unwise and untimely." 1

---

[1]This response to a published statement by eight fellow clergymen from Alabama (Bishop C. C. J. Carpenter, Bishop Joseph A. Durick, Rabbi Hilton L. Grafman, Bishop Paul Hardin, Bishop Holan B. Harmon, the Reverend George M. Murray, the Reverend Edward V. Ramage and the Reverend Earl Stallings) was composed under somewhat constricting circumstances. Begun on the margins of the newspaper in which the statement appeared while I was in jail, the letter was continued on scraps of writing paper supplied by a friendly Negro trusty, and concluded on a pad my attorneys were eventually permitted to leave me. Although the text remains in substance unaltered, I have indulged in the author's prerogative of polishing it for publication. [King's note]

Seldom do I pause to answer criticism of my work and ideas. If I sought to answer all the criticisms that cross my desk, my secretaries would have little time for anything other than such correspondence in the course of the day, and I would have no time for constructive work. But since I feel that you are men of genuine good will and that your criticisms are sincerely set forth, I want to try to answer your statement in what I hope will be patient and reasonable terms.

I think I should indicate why I am here in Birmingham, since you   2
have been influenced by the view which argues against "outsiders coming in." I have the honor of serving as president of the Southern Christian Leadership Conference, an organization operating in every southern state, with headquarters in Atlanta, Georgia. We have some eighty-five affiliated organizations across the South, and one of them is the Alabama Christian Movement for Human Rights. Frequently we share staff, educational, and financial resources with our affiliates. Several months ago the affiliate here in Birmingham asked us to be on call to engage in a nonviolent direct-action program if such were deemed necessary. We readily consented, and when the hour came we lived up to our promise. So I, along with several members of my staff, am here because I was invited here. I am here because I have organizational ties here.

But more basically, I am in Birmingham because injustice is here.   3
Just as the prophets of the eighth century B.C. left their villages and carried their "thus saith the Lord" far beyond the boundaries of their home towns, and just as the Apostle Paul left his village of Tarsus[2] and carried the gospel of Jesus Christ to the far corners of the Greco-Roman world, so am I compelled to carry the gospel of freedom beyond my own home town. Like Paul, I must constantly respond to the Macedonian call for aid.[3]

Moreover, I am cognizant of the interrelatedness of all communi-   4
ties and states. I cannot sit idly by in Atlanta and not be concerned about what happens in Birmingham. Injustice anywhere is a threat to justice everywhere. We are caught in an inescapable network of mutuality, tied in a single garment of destiny. Whatever affects one directly, affects all indirectly. Never again can we afford to live with the

---

[2]*village of Tarsus* Birthplace of St. Paul (?–67A.D.), in Asia Minor, present-day Turkey, close to Syria.

[3]*the Macedonian call for aid* The citizens of Philippi, in Macedonia (northern Greece) were among the staunchest Christians. Paul went to their aid frequently; he also had to resolve occasional bitter disputes within the Christian community there (see Philippians 2:2–14).

narrow, provincial, "outside agitator" idea. Anyone who lives inside the United States can never be considered an outsider anywhere within its bounds.

You deplore the demonstrations taking place in Birmingham. But 5 your statement, I am sorry to say, fails to express a similar concern for the conditions that brought about the demonstrations. I am sure that none of you would want to rest content with the superficial kind of social analysis that deals merely with effects and does not grapple with underlying causes. It is unfortunate that demonstrations are taking place in Birmingham, but it is even more unfortunate that the city's white power structure left the Negro community with no alternative.

In any nonviolent campaign there are four basic steps: collection of 6 the facts to determine whether injustices exist; negotiation; self-purification; and direct action. We have gone through all these steps in Birmingham. There can be no gainsaying the fact that racial injustice engulfs this community. Birmingham is probably the most thoroughly segregated city in the United States. Its ugly record of brutality is widely known. Negroes have experienced grossly unjust treatment in the courts. There have been more unsolved bombings of Negro homes and churches in Birmingham than in any other city in the nation. These are the hard brutal facts of the case. On the basis of these conditions, Negro leaders sought to negotiate with the city fathers. But the latter consistently refused to engage in good-faith negotiation.

Then, last September, came the opportunity to talk with leaders of 7 Birmingham's economic community. In the course of the negotiations, certain promises were made by the merchants—for example, to remove the stores' humiliating racial signs. On the basis of these promises, the Reverend Fred Shuttlesworth and the leaders of the Alabama Christian Movement for Human Rights agreed to a moratorium on all demonstrations. As the weeks and months went by, we realized that we were the victims of a broken promise. A few signs, briefly removed, returned; the others remained.

As in so many past experiences, our hopes had been blasted, and 8 the shadow of deep disappointment settled upon us. We had no alternative except to prepare for direct action, whereby we would present our very bodies as a means of laying our case before the conscience of the local and the national community. Mindful of the difficulties involved, we decided to undertake a process of self-purification. We began a series of workshops on nonviolence, and we repeatedly asked ourselves: "Are you able to accept blows without retaliating?" "Are you able to endure the ordeal of jail?" We decided to schedule our direct-action program for the Easter season, realizing that except for

Christmas, this is the main shopping period of the year. Knowing that a strong economic-withdrawal program would be the by-product of direct action, we felt that this would be the best time to bring pressure to bear on the merchants for the needed change.

Then it occurred to us that Birmingham's mayoral election was   9
coming up in March, and we speedily decided to postpone action until after election day. When we discovered that the Commissioner of Public Safety, Eugene "Bull" Connor, had piled up enough votes to be in the run-off, we decided again to postpone action until the day after the run-off so that the demonstrations could not be used to cloud the issues. Like many others, we waited to see Mr. Connor defeated, and to this end we endured postponement after postponement. Having aided in this community need, we felt that our direct-action program could be delayed no longer.

You may well ask, "Why direct action? Why sit-ins, marches, and   10
so forth? Isn't negotiation a better path?" You are quite right in calling for negotiation. Indeed, this is the very purpose of direct action. Nonviolent direct action seeks to create such a crisis and foster such a tension that a community which has constantly refused to negotiate is forced to confront the issue. It seeks so to dramatize the issue that it can no longer be ignored. My citing the creation of tension as part of the work of the nonviolent resister may sound rather shocking. But I must confess that I am not afraid of the word "tension." I have earnestly opposed violent tension, but there is a type of constructive, nonviolent tension which is necessary for growth. Just as Socrates[4] felt that it was necessary to create a tension in the mind so that individuals could rise from the bondage of myths and half truths to the unfettered realm of creative analysis and objective appraisal, so must we see the need for nonviolent gadflies to create the kind of tension in society that will help men rise from the dark depths of prejudice and racism to the majestic heights of understanding and brotherhood.

The purpose of our direct-action program is to create a situation so   11
crisis-packed that it will inevitably open the door to negotiation. I therefore concur with you in your call for negotiation. Too long has our beloved Southland been bogged down in a tragic effort to live in monologue rather than dialogue.

---

[4]*Socrates (470?–399 B.C.)* The tension in the mind King refers to is created by the question-answer technique known as the Socratic method. By posing questions in the beginning of the paragraph, King shows his willingness to share Socrates' rhetorical techniques. Socrates was imprisoned and killed for his civil disobedience (see paragraph 21). He was the greatest of Greek philosophers.

One of the basic points in your statement is that the action that I 12
and my associates have taken in Birmingham is untimely. Some have
asked: "Why didn't you give the new city administration time to act?"
The only answer that I can give to this query is that the new Birmingham administration must be prodded about as much as the outgoing
one, before it will act. We are sadly mistaken if we feel that the election of Albert Boutwell as mayor will bring the millennium[5] to Birmingham. While Mr. Boutwell is a much more gentle person than Mr.
Connor, they are both segregationists, dedicated to maintenance of the
status quo. I have hoped that Mr. Boutwell will be reasonable enough
to see the futility of massive resistance to desegregation. But he will
not see this without pressure from devotees of civil rights. My friends,
I must say to you that we have not made a single gain in civil rights
without determined legal and nonviolent pressure. Lamentably, it is
an historical fact that privileged groups seldom give up their privileges
voluntarily. Individuals may see the moral light and voluntarily give
up their unjust posture; but, as Reinhold Niebuhr[6] has reminded us,
groups tend to be more immoral than individuals.

We know through painful experience that freedom is never volun- 13
tarily given by the oppressor; it must be demanded by the oppressed.
Frankly, I have yet to engage in a direct-action campaign that was
"well timed" in the view of those who have not suffered unduly from
the disease of segregation. For years now I have heard the word "Wait!"
It rings in the ear of every Negro with piercing familiarity. This "Wait"
has almost always meant "Never." We must come to see, with one of
our distinguished jurists, that "justice too long delayed is justice denied."[7]

We have waited for more than 340 years for our constitutional and 14
God-given rights. The nations of Asia and Africa are moving with jet-
like speed toward gaining political independence, but we still creep at
horse-and-buggy pace toward gaining a cup of coffee at a lunch

[5]*the millennium* A reference to Revelation 20, according to which the Second
Coming of Christ will be followed by 1,000 years of peace, when the devil will be inca-
pacitated. After this will come a final battle between good and evil, followed by the Last
Judgment.

[6]*Reinhold Niebuhr (1892–1971)* Protestant American philosopher who urged
church members to put their beliefs into action against social injustice. He urged Protestantism to develop and practice a code of social ethics, and wrote in *Moral Man and
Immoral Society* (1932) of the point King mentions here.

[7]*"justice too long delayed is justice denied"* Chief Justice Earl Warren's expression in 1954 was adapted from English writer Walter Savage Landor's phrase, "Justice
delayed is justice denied."

counter. Perhaps it is easy for those who have never felt the stinging darts of segregation to say, "Wait." But when you have seen vicious mobs lynch your mothers and fathers at will and drown your sisters and brothers at whim; when you have seen hate-filled policemen curse, kick, and even kill your black brothers and sisters; when you see the vast majority of your twenty million Negro brothers smothering in an airtight cage of poverty in the midst of an affluent society; when you suddenly find your tongue twisted and your speech stammering as you seek to explain to your six-year-old daughter why she can't go to the public amusement park that has just been advertised on television, and see tears welling up in her eyes when she is told that Funtown is closed to colored children, and see ominous clouds of inferiority beginning to form in her little mental sky, and see her beginning to distort her personality by developing an unconscious bitterness toward white people; when you have to concoct an answer for a five-year-old son who is asking, "Daddy, why do white people treat colored people so mean?"; when you take a cross-country drive and find it necessary to sleep night after night in the uncomfortable corners of your automobile because no motel will accept you; when you are humiliated day in and day out by nagging signs reading "white" and "colored"; when your first name becomes "nigger," your middle name becomes "boy" (however old you are) and your last name becomes "John," and your wife and mother are never given the respected title "Mrs."; when you are harried by day and haunted by night by the fact that you are a Negro, living constantly at tiptoe stance, never quite knowing what to expect next, and are plagued with inner fears and outer resentments; when you are forever fighting a degenerating sense of "nobodiness"—then you will understand why we find it difficult to wait. There comes a time when the cup of endurance runs over, and men are no longer willing to be plunged into the abyss of despair. I hope, sirs, you can understand our legitimate and unavoidable impatience.

You express a great deal of anxiety over our willingness to break   15 laws. This is certainly a legitimate concern. Since we so diligently urge people to obey the Supreme Court's decision of 1954 outlawing segregation in the public schools, at first glance it may seem rather paradoxical for us consciously to break laws. One may well ask: "How can you advocate breaking some laws and obeying others?" The answer lies in the fact that there are two types of laws: just and unjust. I would be the first to advocate obeying just laws. One has not only a legal but a moral responsibility to obey just laws. Conversely, one has a moral responsibility to disobey unjust laws. I would agree with St. Augustine[8] that "an unjust law is no law at all."

Now, what is the difference between the two? How does one deter- 16 mine whether a law is just or unjust? A just law is a man-made code that squares with the moral law or the law of God. An unjust law is a code that is out of harmony with the moral law. To put it in the terms of St. Thomas Aquinas:[9] An unjust law is a human law that is not rooted in eternal law and natural law. Any law that uplifts human personality is just. Any law that degrades human personality is unjust. All segregation statutes are unjust because segregation distorts the soul and damages the personality. It gives the segregator a false sense of superiority and the segregated a false sense of inferiority. Segregation, to use the terminology of the Jewish philosopher Martin Buber,[10] substitutes an "I-it" relationship for an "I-thou" relationship and ends up relegating persons to the status of things. Hence segregation is not only politically, economically, and sociologically unsound, it is morally wrong and sinful. Paul Tillich[11] has said that sin is separation. Is not segregation an existential expression of man's tragic separation, his awful estrangement, his terrible sinfulness? Thus it is that I can urge men to obey the 1954 decision of the Supreme Court, for it is morally right; and I can urge them to disobey segregation ordinances, for they are morally wrong.

Let us consider a more concrete example of just and unjust laws. 17 An unjust law is a code that a numerical or power majority group compels a minority group to obey but does not make binding on itself. This is *difference* made legal. By the same token, a just law is a code that a majority compels a minority to follow and that it is willing to follow itself. This is *sameness* made legal.

Let me give another explanation. A law is unjust if it is inflicted 18

---

[8]*St. Augustine (354–430)* Early bishop of the Christian church; great church authority who deeply influenced the spirit of Christianity for many centuries.

[9]*St. Thomas Aquinas (1225–1274)* The greatest of the medieval Christian philosophers and one of the greatest church authorities.

[10]*Martin Buber (1878–1965)* Jewish theologian; *I and Thou* (1923) is his most famous book.

[11]*Paul Tillich (1886–1965)* An important twentieth-century Protestant theologian who held that Christianity was reasonable and effective in modern life. Tillich saw sin as an expression of man's separation from God, from himself, and from his fellow man. King sees the separation of the races as a further manifestation of man's sinfulness. Tillich, who was himself driven out of Germany by the Nazis, stresses the need for activism and the importance of action in determining moral vitality, just as does King.

on a minority that, as a result of being denied the right to vote, had no part in enacting or devising the law. Who can say that the legislature of Alabama which set up that state's segregation laws was democratically elected? Throughout Alabama all sorts of devious methods are used to prevent Negroes from becoming registered voters, and there are some counties in which, even though Negroes constitute a majority of the population, not a single Negro is registered. Can any law enacted under such circumstances be considered democratically structured?

Sometimes a law is just on its face and unjust in its application. 19 For instance, I have been arrested on a charge of parading without a permit. Now, there is nothing wrong in having an ordinance which requires a permit for a parade. But such an ordinance becomes unjust when it is used to maintain segregation and to deny citizens the First Amendment privilege of peaceful assembly and protest.

I hope you are able to see the distinction I am trying to point out. 20 In no sense do I advocate evading or defying the law, as would the rabid segregationist. That would lead to anarchy. One who breaks an unjust law must do so openly, lovingly, and with a willingness to accept the penalty. I submit that an individual who breaks a law that conscience tells him is unjust, and who willingly accepts the penalty of imprisonment in order to arouse the conscience of the community over its injustice, is in reality expressing the highest respect for law.

Of course, there is nothing new about this kind of civil disobedience. 21 It was evidenced sublimely in the refusal of Shadrach, Meshach, and Abednego to obey the laws of Nebuchadnezzar,[12] on the ground that a higher moral law was at stake. It was practiced superbly by the early Christians, who were willing to face hungry lions and the excruciating pain of chopping blocks rather than submit to certain unjust laws of the Roman Empire. To a degree, academic freedom is a reality today because Socrates practiced civil disobedience. In our own nation, the Boston Tea Party represented a massive act of civil disobedience.

We should never forget that everything Adolf Hitler did in Germany was "legal" and everything the Hungarian freedom fighters[13] did in Hungary was "illegal." It was "illegal" to aid and comfort a Jew in 22

---

[12]***Nebuchadnezzar* (c. 630–562 B.C.)** Chaldean king who twice attacked Jerusalem. He ordered Shadrach, Meshach, and Abedniego to worship a golden image. They refused, were cast into a roaring furnace, and were saved by God (see Daniel 1:7–3:30).

[13]***Hungarian freedom fighters*** The Hungarians rose in revolt against Soviet rule in 1956. Russian tanks put down the uprising with great force that shocked the world. Many freedom fighters died, and many others escaped to the West.

Hitler's Germany. Even so, I am sure that, had I lived in Germany at the time, I would have aided and comforted my Jewish brothers. If today I lived in a Communist country where certain principles dear to the Christian faith are suppressed, I would openly advocate disobeying that country's antireligious laws.

I must make two honest confessions to you, my Christian and Jewish brothers. First, I must confess that over the past few years I have been gravely disappointed with the white moderate. I have almost reached the regrettable conclusion that the Negro's great stumbling block in his stride toward freedom is not the White Citizen's Counciler[14] or the Ku Klux Klanner, but the white moderate, who is more devoted to "order" than to justice; who prefers a negative peace which is the absence of tension to a positive peace which is the presence of justice; who constantly says, "I agree with you in the goal you seek, but I cannot agree with your methods of direct action"; who paternalistically believes he can set the timetable for another man's freedom; who lives by a mythical concept of time and who constantly advises the Negro to wait for a "more convenient season." Shallow understanding from people of good will is more frustrating than absolute misunderstanding from people of ill will. Lukewarm acceptance is much more bewildering than outright rejection. 23

I had hoped that the white moderate would understand that law and order exist for the purpose of establishing justice and that when they fail in this purpose they become the dangerously structured dams that block the flow of social progress. I had hoped that the white moderate would understand that the present tension in the South is a necessary phase of the transition from an obnoxious negative peace, in which the Negro passively accepted his unjust plight, to a substantive and positive peace, in which all men will respect the dignity and worth of human personality. Actually, we who engage in nonviolent direct action are not the creators of tension. We merely bring to the surface the hidden tension that is already alive. We bring it out in the open, where it can be seen and dealt with. Like a boil that can never be cured so long as it is covered up but must be opened with all its ugliness to the natural medicines of air and light, injustice must be exposed, with all the tension its exposure creates, to the light of human conscience and the air of national opinion, before it can be cured. 24

In your statement you assert that our actions, even though peace- 25

---

[14]***White Citizen's Counciler*** White Citizen's Councils organized in Southern states in 1954 to fight school desegregation as ordered by the Supreme Court in May 1954. The councils were not as secret or violent as the Klan; they were also ineffective.

ful, must be condemned because they precipitate violence. But is this a logical assertion? Isn't this like condemning a robbed man because his possession of money precipitated the evil act of robbery? Isn't this like condemning Socrates because his unswerving commitment to truth and his philosophical inquiries precipitated the act by the misguided populace in which they made him drink hemlock? Isn't this like condemning Jesus because his unique God-consciousness and never-ceasing devotion to God's will precipitated the evil act of crucifixion? We must come to see that, as the federal courts have consistently affirmed, it is wrong to urge an individual to cease his efforts to gain his basic constitutional rights because the quest may precipitate violence. Society must protect the robbed and punish the robber.

I had also hoped that the white moderate would reject the myth 26 concerning time in relation to the struggle for freedom. I have just received a letter from a white brother in Texas. He writes: "All Christians know that the colored people will receive equal rights eventually, but it is possible that you are in too great a religious hurry. It has taken Christianity almost two thousand years to accomplish what it has. The teachings of Christ take time to come to earth." Such an attitude stems from a tragic misconception of time, from the strangely irrational notion that there is something in the very flow of time that will inevitably cure all ills. Actually, time itself is neutral; it can be used either destructively or constructively. More and more I feel that the people of ill will have used time much more effectively than have the people of good will. We will have to repent in this generation not merely for the hateful words and actions of the bad people, but for the appalling silence of the good people. Human progress never rolls in on wheels of inevitability; it comes through the tireless efforts of men willing to be co-workers with God, and without this hard work, time itself becomes an ally of the forces of social stagnation. We must use time creatively, in the knowledge that the time is always ripe to do right. Now is the time to make real the promise of democracy and transform our pending national elegy into a creative psalm of brotherhood. Now is the time to lift our national policy from the quicksand of racial injustice to the solid rock of human dignity.

You speak of our activity in Birmingham as extreme. At first I was 27 rather disappointed that fellow clergymen would see my nonviolent efforts as those of an extremist. I began thinking about the fact that I stand in the middle of two opposing forces in the Negro community. One is a force of complacency, made up in part of Negroes who, as a result of long years of oppression, are so drained of self-respect and a sense of "somebodiness" that they have adjusted to segregation; and in part of a few middle-class Negroes who, because of a degree of academic and economic security and because in some ways they profit by segregation, have become insensitive to the problems of the masses. The other force is one of bitterness and hatred, and it comes perilously close to advocating violence. It is expressed in the various black nationalist groups that are springing up across the nation, the largest and best known being Elijah Muhammad's Muslim movement.[15] Nourished by the Negro's frustration over the continued existence of racial discrimination, this movement is made up of people who have lost faith in America, who have absolutely repudiated Christianity, and who have concluded that the white man is an incorrigible "devil."

28   I have tried to stand between these two forces, saying that we need emulate neither the "do-nothingism" of the complacent nor the hatred and despair of the black nationalist. For there is the more excellent way of love and nonviolent protest. I am grateful to God that, through the influence of the Negro church, the way of nonviolence became an integral part of our struggle.

29   If this philosophy had not emerged, by now many streets of the South would, I am convinced, be flowing with blood. And I am further convinced that if our white brothers dismiss as "rabble-rousers" and "outside agitators" those of us who employ nonviolent direct action, and if they refuse to support our nonviolent efforts, millions of Negroes will, out of frustration and despair, seek solace and security in black nationalist ideologies—a development that would inevitably lead to a frightening racial nightmare.[16]

30   Oppressed people cannot remain oppressed forever. The yearning for freedom eventually manifests itself, and that is what has happened to the American Negro. Something within has reminded him of his birthright of freedom, and something without has reminded him that it can be gained. Consciously or unconsciously, he has been caught up by the *Zeitgeist*,[17] and with his black brothers of Africa and his brown and yellow brothers of Asia, South America, and the Caribbean, the

---

[15]***Elijah Muhammad's Muslim movement*** The Black Muslim movement, which began in the 1920s but flourished in the 1960s under its leader, Elijah Muhammad (1897–1975). Among notable figures who became Black Muslims were the poet Imamu Amiri Baraka (b. 1934), the world championship prizefighter Muhammad Ali (b. 1942), and the controversial reformer and religious leader Malcolm X (1925–1965). King saw their rejection of white society (and consequently brotherhood) as a threat.

[16]***a frightening racial nightmare*** The black uprisings of the 1960s in all major American cities, and the conditions that led to them, were indeed a racial nightmare. King's prophecy was quick to come true.

[17]**Zeitgeist** German word for the intellectual, moral, and cultural spirit of the times.

United States Negro is moving with a sense of great urgency toward the promised land of racial justice. If one recognizes this vital urge that has engulfed the Negro community, one should readily understand why public demonstrations are taking place. The Negro has many pent-up resentments and latent frustrations, and he must release them. So let him march; let him make prayer pilgrimages to the city hall; let him go on freedom rides[18]—and try to understand why he must do so. If his repressed emotions are not released in nonviolent ways, they will seek expression through violence; this is not a threat but a fact of history. So I have not said to my people, "Get rid of your discontent." Rather, I have tried to say that this normal and healthy discontent can be channeled into the creative outlet of nonviolent direct action. And now this approach is being termed extremist.

But though I was initially disappointed at being categorized as an extremist, as I continued to think about the matter I gradually gained a measure of satisfaction from the label. Was not Jesus an extremist for love: "Love your enemies, bless them that curse you, do good to them that hate you, and pray for them which despitefully use you, and persecute you." Was not Amos an extremist for justice: "Let justice roll down like waters and righteousness like an ever-flowing stream." Was not Paul an extremist for the Christian gospel: "I bear in my body the marks of the Lord Jesus." Was not Martin Luther an extremist: "Here I stand; I cannot do otherwise, so help me God." And John Bunyan: "I will stay in jail to the end of my days before I make a butchery of my conscience." And Abraham Lincoln: "This nation cannot survive half slave and half free." And Thomas Jefferson:[19] "We hold these truths to be self-evident, that all men are created equal. . . ." So the question is not whether we will be extremists, but what kind of extremists we will be. Will we be extremists for hate or for love? Will we be extremists for the preservation of injustice or for the extension of justice? In that dramatic scene on Calvary's hill three men were

31

---

[18]*freedom rides* In 1961 the Congress of Racial Equality (CORE) organized rides of whites and blacks to test segregation in southern buses and bus terminals with interstate passengers. More than 600 federal marshalls were needed to protect the riders, most of whom were arrested.

[19]*Amos, Old Testament prophet (8th century B.C.); Paul (?–67 A.D.); Martin Luther (1483–1546); John Bunyan (1628–1688); Abraham Lincoln (1809–1865); and Thomas Jefferson (1743–1826)* These figures are all noted for religious, moral, or political innovations that changed the world. Amos was a prophet who favored social justice; Paul argued against Roman law; Luther began the Reformation of the Christian Church; Bunyan was imprisoned for preaching the gospel according to his own understanding; Jefferson drafted the Declaration of Independence.

crucified. We must never forget that all three were crucified for the same crime—the crime of extremism. Two were extremists for immorality, and thus fell below their environment. The other, Jesus Christ, was an extremist for love, truth, and goodness, and thereby rose above his environment. Perhaps the South, the nation, and the world are in dire need of creative extremists.

I had hoped that the white moderate would see this need. Perhaps   32
I was too optimistic; perhaps I expected too much. I suppose I should have realized that few members of the oppressor race can understand the deep groans and passionate yearnings of the oppressed race, and still fewer have the vision to see that injustice must be rooted out by strong, persistent, and determined action. I am thankful, however, that some of our white brothers in the South have grasped the meaning of this social revolution and committed themselves to it. They are still all too few in quantity, but they are big in quality. Some—such as Ralph McGill, Lillian Smith, Harry Golden, James McBride Dabbs, Ann Braden, and Sarah Patton Boyle—have written about our struggle[20] in eloquent and prophetic terms. Others have marched with us down nameless streets of the South. They have languished in filthy, roach-infested jails, suffering the abuse and brutality of policemen who view them as "dirty nigger-lovers." Unlike so many of their moderate brothers and sisters, they have recognized the urgency of the moment and sensed the need for powerful "action" antidotes to combat the disease of segregation.

Let me take note of my other major disappointment. I have been   33
so greatly disappointed with the white church and its leadership. Of course, there are some notable exceptions. I am not unmindful of the fact that each of you has taken some significant stands on this issue. I commend you, Reverend Stallings, for your Christian stand on this past Sunday, in welcoming Negroes to your worship service on a non-segregated basis. I commend the Catholic leaders of this state for integrating Spring Hill College several years ago.

But despite these notable exceptions, I must honestly reiterate that   34
I have been disappointed with the church. I do not say this as one of those negative critics who can always find something wrong with the church. I say this as a minister of the gospel, who loves the church; who was nurtured in its bosom; who has been sustained by its spiri-

---

[20]***written about our struggle***   These are all prominent southern writers who expressed their feelings regarding segregation in the South. Some of them, like Smith and Golden, wrote very popular books with a wide influence. Some, like McGill and Smith, were severely rebuked by white southerners.

tual blessings and who will remain true to it as long as the cord of life shall lengthen.

When I was suddenly catapulted into the leadership of the bus pro- 35 test in Montgomery, Alabama, a few years ago, I felt we would be supported by the white church. I felt that the white ministers, priests, and rabbis of the South would be among our strongest allies. Instead, some have been outright opponents, refusing to understand the freedom movement and misrepresenting its leaders; all too many others have been more cautious than courageous and have remained silent behind the anesthetizing security of stained-glass windows.

In spite of my shattered dreams, I came to Birmingham with the 36 hope that the white religious leadership of this community would see the justice of our cause and, with deep moral concern, would serve as the channel through which our just grievances could reach the power structure. I had hoped that each of you would understand. But again I have been disappointed. . . .

There was a time when the church was very powerful—in the time 37 when the early Christians rejoiced at being deemed worthy to suffer for what they believed. In those days the church was not merely a thermometer that recorded the ideas and principles of popular opinion; it was a thermostat that transformed the mores of society. Whenever the early Christians entered a town, the people in power became disturbed and immediately sought to convict the Christians for being "disturbers of the peace" and "outside agitators." But the Christians pressed on, in the conviction that they were "a colony of heaven," called to obey God rather than man. Small in number, they were big in commitment. They were too God intoxicated to be "astronomically intimidated." By their effort and example they brought an end to such ancient evils as infanticide and gladiatorial contests.

Things are different now. So often the contemporary church is a 38 weak, ineffectual voice with an uncertain sound. So often it is an arch-defender of the status quo. Far from being disturbed by the presence of the church, the power structure of the average community is consoled by the church's silent—and often even vocal—sanction of things as they are.

But the judgment of God is upon the church as never before. If 39 today's church does not recapture the sacrificial spirit of the early church, it will lose its authenticity, forfeit the loyalty of millions, and be dismissed as an irrelevant social club with no meaning for the twentieth century. Every day I meet young people whose disappointment with the church has turned into outright disgust.

Perhaps I have once again been too optimistic. Is organized religion 40 too inextricably bound to the status quo to save our nation and the world? Perhaps I must turn my faith to the inner spiritual church, the church within the church, as the true *ekklesia*[21] and the hope of the world. But again I am thankful to God that some noble souls from the ranks of organized religion have broken loose from the paralyzing chains of conformity and joined us as active partners in the struggle for freedom. They have left their secure congregations and walked the streets of Albany, Georgia, with us. They have gone down the highways of the South on torturous rides for freedom. Yes, they have gone to jail with us. Some have been dismissed from their churches, have lost the support of their bishops and fellow ministers. But they have acted in the faith that right defeated is stronger than evil triumphant. Their witness has been the spiritual salt that has preserved the true meaning of the gospel in these troubled times. They have carved a tunnel of hope through the dark mountain of disappointment.

I hope the church as a whole will meet the challenge of this deci- 41 sive hour. But even if the church does not come to the aid of justice, I have no despair about the future. I have no fear about the outcome of our struggle in Birmingham, even if our motives are at present misunderstood. We will reach the goal of freedom in Birmingham and all over the nation, because the goal of America is freedom. Abused and scorned though we may be, our destiny is tied up with America's destiny. Before the pilgrims landed at Plymouth, we were here. Before the pen of Jefferson etched the majestic words of the Declaration of Independence across the pages of history, we were here. For more than two centuries our forebears labored in this country without wages; they made cotton king; they built the homes of their masters while suffering gross injustice and shameful humiliation—and yet out of a bottomless vitality they continued to thrive and develop. If the inexpressible cruelties of slavery could not stop us, the opposition we now face will surely fail. We will win our freedom because the sacred heritage of our nation and the eternal will of God are embodied in our echoing demands.

Before closing I feel impelled to mention one other point in your 42 statement that has troubled me profoundly. You warmly commended the Birmingham police force for keeping "order" and "preventing violence." I doubt that you would have so warmly commended the police force if you had seen its dogs sinking their teeth into unarmed, non-

---

[21]**ekklesia** Greek word for church; it means not just the institution but the spirit of the church.

violent Negroes. I doubt that you would so quickly commend the policemen if you were to observe their ugly and inhumane treatment of Negroes here in the city jail; if you were to watch them push and curse old Negro women and young Negro girls; if you were to see them slap and kick old Negro men and young boys; if you were to observe them, as they did on two occasions, refuse to give us food because we wanted to sing our grace together. I cannot join you in your praise of the Birmingham police department.

It is true that the police have exercised a degree of discipline in 43 handling the demonstrators. In this sense they have conducted themselves rather "nonviolently" in public. But for what purpose? To preserve the evil system of segregation. Over the past few years I have consistently preached that nonviolence demands that the means we use must be as pure as the ends we seek. I have tried to make clear that it is wrong to use immoral means to attain moral ends. But now I must affirm that it is just as wrong, or perhaps even more so, to use moral means to preserve immoral ends. Perhaps Mr. Connor and his policemen have been rather nonviolent in public, as was Chief Pritchett in Albany, Georgia, but they have used the moral means of nonviolence to maintain the immoral end of racial injustice. As T. S. Eliot[22] has said, "The last temptation is the greatest treason: To do the right deed for the wrong reason."

I wish you had commended the Negro sit-inners and demonstrators 44 of Birmingham for their sublime courage, their willingness to suffer, and their amazing discipline in the midst of great provocation. One day the South will recognize its real heroes. They will be the James Merediths,[23] with the noble sense of purpose that enables them to face jeering and hostile mobs, and with the agonizing loneliness that characterizes the life of the pioneer. They will be old, oppressed, battered

---

[22]*Thomas Stearns Eliot (1888–1965)* One of the first great twentieth-century poets writing in English. Eliot was born in the United States but in 1927 became a British citizen and a member of the Church of England. Many of his poems focused on religious and moral themes. These lines are from Eliot's play *Murder in the Cathedral*, about Saint Thomas à Becket (1118–1170), the archbishop of Canterbury, who was martyred for his opposition to King Henry II.

[23]*the James Merediths* James Meredith (b. 1933) was the first black to become a student at the University of Mississippi. His admission in 1961 created the first important confrontation between federal and state authorities, when Governor Ross Barnett personally blocked Meredith's entry to the university. Meredith graduated in 1963 and went on to study law at Columbia University.

Negro women, symbolized in a seventy-two-year-old woman in Mont-gomery, Alabama, who rose up with a sense of dignity and with her people decided not to ride segregated buses, and who responded with ungrammatical profundity to one who inquired about her weariness: "My feets is tired, but my soul is at rest." They will be the young high school and college students, the young ministers of the gospel and a host of their elders, courageously and nonviolently sitting in at lunch counters and willingly going to jail for conscience' sake. One day the South will know that when these disinherited children of God sat down at lunch counters, they were in reality standing up for what is best in the American dream and for the most sacred values in our Judaeo-Christian heritage, thereby bringing our nation back to those great wells of democracy which were dug deep by the founding fathers in their formulation of the Constitution and the Declaration of Inde-pendence.

Never before have I written so long a letter. I'm afraid it is much 45 too long to take your precious time. I can assure you that it would have been much shorter if I had been writing from a comfortable desk, but what else can one do when he is alone in a narrow jail cell, other than write long letters, think long thoughts, and pray long prayers?

If I have said anything in this letter that overstates the truth and 46 indicates an unreasonable impatience, I beg you to forgive me. If I have said anything that understates the truth and indicates my having a patience that allows me to settle for anything less than brotherhood, I beg God to forgive me.

I hope this letter finds you strong in the faith. I also hope that 47 circumstances will soon make it possible for me to meet each of you, not as an integrationist or a civil rights leader but as a fellow clergy-man and a Christian brother. Let us all hope that the dark clouds of racial prejudice will soon pass away and the deep fog of misunder-standing will be lifted from our fear-drenched communities, and in some not too distant tomorrow the radiant stars of love and brother-hood will shine over our great nation with all their scintillating beauty.

> Yours in the cause of
> Peace and Brotherhood,
>
> MARTIN LUTHER KING, JR.

QUESTIONS

1. What is the definition of "nonviolent direct action"? In what areas of human life is it best directed? Is politics its best area of application? What are the four steps in a nonviolent campaign?
2. Is King optimistic about the future of race relations in America? What evidence in the letter points in the direction of optimism or pessimism?
3. Which paragraphs in the letter are the most persuasive? Why? Did any part of the letter actually change your thinking on an important issue? Which part? Why was your thinking changed?
4. If you had to select the best-written paragraph in the essay, which would it be? Why?
5. King cites "tension" in paragraph 10 and elsewhere as a beneficial force. Is it beneficial? What kind of tension does he mean?
6. Was King an extremist (paras. 30–31)?

WRITING ASSIGNMENTS

1. In paragraph 43 King says, "I have consistently preached that nonviolence demands that the means we use must be as pure as the ends we seek." What, exactly, does he mean by this? Define the ends he seeks; define the means he approves. Do you agree with him on this point? If you have read the selection from Machiavelli, could you contrast their respective views? Which view seems more reasonable to you?
2. Write a brief letter protesting an injustice that you feel may not be entirely understood by people you respect. Clarify the nature of the injustice, the reasons that people will hold to an unjust view, and the reasons why your views should be accepted. Consult King's letter and consciously use his techniques.
3. The first part of the letter is a defense of King's having come to Birmingham as a Christian to help his fellows gain their rights. He challenges the view that he is an outsider, using such expressions as "network of mutuality" and "garment of destiny." How effective is the argument that he raises? Are you convinced by it? Inventory the letter for expressions such as those just quoted that justify King's intervention on behalf of his brothers and sisters. If the logic of his position holds, what other social areas could be justifiably "intervened" into? In what area of life might you endeavor to exert your own views on behalf of mankind? Would you expect your endeavors to be welcomed? Are there any areas in which you might consider it wrong to intervene?
4. In paragraphs 15–22, King discusses two kinds of laws, those which are morally right and those which are morally wrong. Analyze his argument carefully, establishing what you feel his views are. For King, which laws are morally right? Name several such laws that you know about. Which

laws are morally wrong, according to King? Name some laws, if possible, that you have personal knowledge of. Take a stand on one or two current laws that you feel are morally wrong. Be sure to be fair in describing the laws. Establish their nature and then explain why they are morally wrong. Would you feel justified in breaking these laws? Would you feel prepared, as King was, to pay the penalties demanded of one who breaks the law?

5. Make a comparison of King's letter with sections of Paul's letters to the faithful in the New Testament. Either choose a single letter, such as the Epistle to the Romans, or select passages from Romans, the two letters to the Corinthians, the Galatians, the Ephesians, the Thessalonians, or the Philippians. What positions have Paul and King held in common or in distinction concerning brotherly love, the mission of Christ, the mission of the church, concern for the law, and the duties of the faithful? Inventory the New Testament and the letter carefully for concrete evidence of similar or contrary positions.

PART TWO

PSYCHOLOGY AND THE NATURE OF HUMANKIND

———∽∾———

Friedrich Nietzsche
William James ··· *Sigmund Freud*
Carl Jung ··· *B. F. Skinner*

Some of the most exciting intellectual advances of our time have been made in the area of psychology, a science which, until the nineteenth century, remained in its infancy. Traditional concerns in psychology—the nature of personality, cultural patterns, what can be known—dominated the field until William James began speculating, in the 1880s, on the nature of the unconscious mind. Then, in the early part of the twentieth century, Sigmund Freud began the extraordinary exploratory studies that mapped out the relationship between the mind we seem to be aware of, our conscious mind, and the storehouse that lies beneath it, the unconscious. One of the most recent avenues of research has taken us into behaviorism, as B. F. Skinner informs us, showing that the behavior of humans, like that of all animals, is modified by the environment—in the case of humans, particularly by cultural systems of rewards and punishments.

Friedrich Nietzsche did not intend to write about psychology when he began his discussion of the Apollonian and Dionysian personality traits that he observed in ancient Greek culture. Instead, he meant to write about music and the works of the great German composer Richard Wagner (1813–1883). But, since music—particularly Wagner's—excites the emotions, it was perhaps inevitable that Nietzsche would find himself in deep psychological waters. What he observed was that in Greek society there were two approaches to music, and thus to art, and that these approaches grew from a deep psychological commitment representing profound forces deep in the Greek psyche. Since the word "psyche" in Greek means soul, by studying the psyche he was studying the soul of Greek culture.

His discovery was that the austere, rational, calm, and dispassionate Apollonian intellectualism of Greek high culture actually needed the dark, passionate, irrational forces of the god of intoxication, Dionysius. Nietzsche maps out two very distinct personality traits that are as recognizable in our society as they are in Greek society. They are forces that, as Nietzsche describes them, seem to be an inherent part of human nature. At one time the individualizing force of Apollonianism will dominate; at another, the crowd-loving force of Dionysius will surface. Nietzsche realizes, however, that the human being is a fusion of both forces and thus must find ways in which both can function in the same psyche.

William James concerns himself with ways of knowing that go beyond the logic of rationality. In his "The Reality of the Unseen," he explores evidence of perception that does not depend upon immediate sensory awareness. In this chapter, his contribution is to the psychology of religion, and it is an effort to give psychological credibility to beliefs founded upon feeling.

What Sigmund Freud has to say in his essay on infantile sexuality seems fairly tame and perhaps even a bit obvious to us today. But it was a bombshell in its own day. People had always thought that children had no psychosexual awareness or drives until after puberty. Freud demonstrated that the sexual drive, which he had predicated as the strongest of psychic drives, was present even in the infant. His study was a pioneering effort that changed the nature of psychology entirely.

Carl Jung's study of the mother archetype is only one of his efforts to locate archetypal patterns that exist in the human psyche. From his study of myths, finding that basic patterns persisted throughout human history in widely divergent communities, he reasoned that their similarity stemmed from patterns that were already present and common in the human psychology. The myths, he felt, were a kind of collective unconscious, a storehouse for symbols created by this unconscious to deal with psychological issues. Thus, the mother archetype, one of the most powerful, expresses itself in the psychology of those who do not know their mother as well as in the psychology of those who do.

The controversial theories of B. F. Skinner are called theories of behavioral psychology. Skinner observes that we are, like all animals, a product of the interaction of our psychology and our environment. Our behavior can be modified by rewards and by punishments. Moreover, he points out that the price we pay in our society for the freedom to do as we are able to do may be too great. He believes that we have reached the point at which we will have to forgo freedom in order to achieve stability and greater happiness. Skinner's views have not been popular with traditional humanists, because he professes a "scientific" view of humankind that sees us as much more closely related to the animal world than we have been willing to admit.

The range of rhetoric in these essays is considerable. Since all these writers are basically philosophers and scientists, we do not expect their prose to be dashing or stylistically innovative. They are experts speaking to generally well-informed readers, doing their best to make complex thoughts as clear as they can be made. James relies upon the topic of testimony, gathering as much evidence from other sources as possible, placing them in a context, then offering an analysis of what they say. Nietzsche, of course, in talking about two diverse character traits, relies upon the tried-and-true topic of comparison and contrast.

Freud's rhetorical method is the process of evidence and inference. He breaks up his essay into a number of sections, presents evidence for his beliefs in each section, then analyzes the evidence for its implications. His inferences are then further tested as he proceeds. Freud is also the master of the memorable phrase or term, such as "psychoanalysis," "the Oedipus complex," and "the castration complex." Carl Jung is equally simple in his rhetoric, depending upon exposition: establishing that there is a mother archetype, then showing its nature and its effects on the psyche.

Skinner begins with another time-honored technique, the rhetorical question: What is man? Like most of the other psychologists here, Skinner moves quickly to an examination of evidence that leads to certain conclusions regarding human psychology. Since he knows that his conclusions are likely to be unpopular, he is very careful to go slowly and to persuade us of the correctness of his views as completely as possible before he goes on to draw his conclusions. And his conclusions, concerning the extent to which we are self-directed individuals, are indeed difficult for most of us to accept. The answer to the question—What is man?—is not at all what we might have hoped for.

FRIEDRICH NIETZSCHE

Apollonianism and
Dionysianism

*F*RIEDRICH NIETZSCHE *(1844–1900) was one of the most influential thinkers of nineteenth-century Germany. He was particularly fearful that changes in attitudes toward religion and science would result in a loss of a sense of purpose in human life. The result of that would be loss of energy, of direction, and ultimately of civilization itself. His works are largely an effort to construct a meaningfulness based upon a deep psychological self-understanding. His sometimes misunderstood major work,* Thus Spake Zarathustra *(1883–1892), makes the point that the greatest joy comes from self-understanding, self-domination, and self-control. The resultant creativity which springs from the "superman" who can achieve such a state is so overwhelming as to be godlike. For Nietzsche, attainment of this state was reason enough to live.*

His own personal life was rather difficult. He was the son of a minister, but his father died when he was four, and Nietzsche was raised by a gathering of family women. There is an antifemale tone to certain of the writings, and some critics have felt that it is a result

---

From *The Birth of Tragedy from the Spirit of Music.* Translated by Francis Golffing.

of his upbringing. It may also be related to the fact that, when a young man, he contracted syphilis from a prostitute in Leipzig.

He was a brilliant student, particularly of the classics, and became a professor at the University of Basel at a very young age. His first book, **The Birth of Tragedy** (1872), is the result of an effort to clarify certain aspects of the music of Richard Wagner, the contemporary composer of the Ring Cycle of operas based on Celtic mythology as interpreted by Wagner. Nietzsche eventually broke with Wagner on philosophical matters, but his regard for Wagner's music remained strong. The insight on which the work rests, presented in the selection, attempts to clarify the two basic psychological forces in humankind: Apollonian intellectuality and Dionysian passion. Both forces were present in ancient Greek society, which Nietzsche seems to take as a standard of high civilization, particularly in its Doric phase—a phase of clear, calm, beautiful works exemplified by the Parthenon in Athens. Although the Apollonian is opposed to the Dionysian, Nietzsche points out that the Greeks discovered that both forces need to be present together in a culture. The tragedy, he says, was the ground on which these forces were able to meet in ancient Greece. In Nietzsche's time—as he points out in a section not included here—they meet in the music of Richard Wagner.

Nietzsche relies on art to help him clarify the psychological types represented by each of these Greek gods. Apollo dominates intellectually. He demands clarity, order, reason, and calm. He is also the god of the individual. Dionysius, on the other hand, is the god of ecstasy and passion. Obscurity, disorder, irrational behavior, even hysteria are encouraged by Dionysius. He is the god of throngs and mobs. After reading this excerpt, we realize that most of us have both capacities within us and that one of the challenges of life is learning how to balance them.

NIETZSCHE'S RHETORIC

The most obvious rhetorical device Nietzsche uses is comparison and contrast. The Apollonian contrasts with the Dionysian; the Greek with the barbarian; the dream with the illusion; gods with people; the individual with the group; the one with the many; even life with death. In this sense, the subject at hand has governed the basic shape of the work.

Nietzsche's task was to explain the different polarities, how they express themselves, and what their effect is. Since these were terms which were quite new to most readers when he wrote this work, it took him some time to clarify the nature of the Apollonian and the Dionysian. In a sense, the first paragraphs are spent in the task of definition. Some of the paragraphs explore the topic of circumstance, a survey of past time, particularly in regard to Greek society. Once each polarity is defined, Nietzsche goes on to explain its sphere of influence, what we can expect of it, and what its implications are. Insofar as those qualities are present in the rhetoric, the essay is itself Apollonian.

There is a surprise in Nietzsche's use of rhetoric here, however. He also illustrates, through rhetorical techniques, some aspects of the Dionysian nature. There are passages in the selection, such as paragraph 5 when he is speaking of Dionysius, which can best be described as ecstatic, poetic—and, if not irrational, certainly obscure and difficult to grasp. The Dionysian aspects of the passage are based on feeling. We all know that there are poems we read which we cannot break down into other words—or even explain to others. What we get from such poems is not an understanding but a feeling or an impression. The same is true of the passages which we confront in this essay. They challenge us because we know that the general character of any essay must be Apollonian. When we are greeted by Dionysian verbal excursions, we are a bit thrown off. Yet, that is part of Nietzsche's point: verbal artifacts (such as Greek tragedy) can combine both forces.

In fact, it may be that Nietzsche's most important point is that both forces yearn to be joined in some kind of artifact. For the ancients it was in the work of the Greek tragedians. For the Elizabethans it was in Shakespeare. For people of his own day it was in the Ring Cycle of Wagner. The ultimate effect of using the rhetorical device of comparison and contrast is to emphasize the fact that these two forces must be unified in the highest cultures. Diversity is everywhere in nature, as Nietzsche implies throughout, but that diversity has one deep longing: to be One with the One. As he says (para. 14), the eternal goal of the original Oneness is its redemption through illusion. Illusion is art, not just dream. The great psychologists who built twentieth-century theories understood both dream and illusion; they are projections of mental states and give access to the inner nature of humankind.

Apollonianism and
Dionysianism

Much will have been gained for esthetics once we have succeeded 1
in apprehending directly—rather than merely *ascertaining*—that art
owes its continuous evolution to the Apollonian-Dionysiac duality,
even as the propagation of the species depends on the duality of the
sexes, their constant conflicts and periodic acts of reconciliation. I
have borrowed my adjectives from the Greeks, who developed their
mystical doctrines of art through plausible *embodiments*, not through
purely conceptual means. It is by those two art-sponsoring deities,
Apollo and Dionysos,[1] that we are made to recognize the tremendous
split, as regards both origins and objectives, between the plastic, Apollonian arts and the non-visual art of music inspired by Dionysos. The
two creative tendencies developed alongside one another, usually in
fierce opposition, each by its taunts forcing the other to more energetic
production, both perpetuating in a discordant concord that agon[2]
which the term *art* but feebly denominates: until at last, by the
thaumaturgy[3] of an Hellenic act of will, the pair accepted the yoke of
marriage and, in this condition, begot Attic tragedy,[4] which exhibits
the salient features of both parents.

To reach a closer understanding of both these tendencies, let us 2
begin by viewing them as the separate art realms of *dream* and *intoxication*, two physiological phenomena standing toward one another in
much the same relationship as the Apollonian and Dionysiac. It was
in a dream, according to Lucretius,[5] that the marvelous gods and goddesses first presented themselves to the minds of men. That great

---

[1]***Apollo and Dionysos (Dionysius)***   Apollo is the god of music and is also regarded
as the god of light. Dionysius is the god of wine and drunkenness.

[2]***agon***   a contest or opposition of forces.

[3]***thaumaturgy***   a magical change. Nietzsche means that a powerful transformation was
needed for Apollo and Dionysius to be able to join together.

[4]***Attic tragedy***   Greek tragedy performed in Athens, in the Greek region of Attica,
sixth century–fourth century B.C.

[5]***Lucretius (96?–!55 B.C.)***   A Roman philosopher whose book on natural science
was standard for more than a millennium.

sculptor, Phidias,[6] beheld in a dream the entrancing bodies of more-than-human beings, and likewise, if anyone had asked the Greek poets about the mystery of poetic creation, they too would have referred him to dreams and instructed him much as Hans Sachs[7] instructs us in *Die Meistersinger:*

> My friend, it is the poet's work
> Dreams to interpret and to mark.
> Believe me that man's true conceit
> In a dream becomes complete:
> All poetry we ever read
> Is but true dreams interpreted.

The fair illusion of the dream sphere, in the production of which every man proves himself an accomplished artist, is a precondition not only of all plastic art, but even, as we shall see presently, of a wide range of poetry. Here we enjoy an immediate apprehension of form, all shapes speak to us directly, nothing seems indifferent or redundant. Despite the high intensity with which these dream realities exist for us, we still have a residual sensation that they are illusions; at least such has been my experience—and the frequency, not to say normality, of the experience is borne out in many passages of the poets. Men of philosophical disposition are known for their constant premonition that our everyday reality, too, is an illusion, hiding another, totally different kind of reality. It was Schopenhauer[8] who considered the ability to view at certain times all men and things as mere phantoms or dream images to be the true mark of philosophic talent. The person who is responsive to the stimuli of art behaves toward the reality of dream much the way the philosopher behaves toward the reality of existence: he observes exactly and enjoys his observations, for it is by these images that he interprets life, by these processes that he rehearses it. Nor is it by pleasant images only that such plausible connections are made: the whole divine comedy of life, including its somber aspects, its sudden balkings, impish accidents, anxious expectations, moves past him, not quite like a shadow play—for it is he himself, after all, who lives and suffers through these scenes—yet never

3

---

[6]***Phidias (fl. 430 B.C.)*** Greek sculptor who carved the figures of the gods and goddesses on the Parthenon.

[7]***Hans Sachs*** The legendary singer-hero of Richard Wagner's opera, *The Master-Singer;* the lines quoted are from that opera.

[8]***Arthur Schopenhauer (1788–1860)*** German philosopher who influenced Nietzsche. His books, *The World as Will and Idea* (1883–1886) and *On the Will and Nature* (1889), emphasized the power of free will as a chief force in the world.

without giving a fleeting sense of illusion; and I imagine that many persons have reassured themselves amidst the perils of dream by calling out, "It is a dream! I want it to go on." I have even heard of people spinning out the causality of one and the same dream over three or more successive nights. All these facts clearly bear witness that our innermost being, the common substratum of humanity, experiences dreams with deep delight and a sense of real necessity. This deep and happy sense of the necessity of dream experiences was expressed by the Greeks in the image of Apollo. Apollo is at once the god of all plastic powers and the soothsaying god. He who is etymologically the "lucent" one, the god of light, reigns also over the fair illusion of our inner world of fantasy. The perfection of these conditions in contrast to our imperfectly understood waking reality, as well as our profound awareness of nature's healing powers during the interval of sleep and dream, furnishes a symbolic analogue to the soothsaying faculty and quite generally to the arts, which make life possible and worth living. But the image of Apollo must incorporate that thin line which the dream image may not cross, under penalty of becoming pathological, of imposing itself on us as crass reality: a discreet limitation, a freedom from all extravagant urges, the sapient tranquillity of the plastic god. His eye must be sunlike, in keeping with his origin. Even at those moments when he is angry and ill-tempered there lies upon him the consecration of fair illusion. In an eccentric way one might say of Apollo what Schopenhauer says, in the first part of *The World as Will and Idea*, of man caught in the veil of Maya:[9] "Even as on an immense, raging sea, assailed by huge wave crests, a man sits in a little rowboat trusting his frail craft, so, amidst the furious torments of this world, the individual sits tranquilly, supported by the *principium individuationis*[10] and relying on it." One might say that the unshakable confidence in that principle has received its most magnificent expression in Apollo, and that Apollo himself may be regarded as the marvelous divine image of the *principium individuationis*, whose looks and gestures radiate the full delight, wisdom, and beauty of "illusion."

In the same context Schopenhauer has described for us the tremendous awe which seizes man when he suddenly begins to doubt the cognitive modes of experience, in other words, when in a given in-

4

---

[9]*Maya* A Hindu term for the material world of the senses. The veil of Maya is the illusion hiding the reality that lies beneath material surfaces.

[10]**principium individuationis** The principle of the individual, as apart from the crowd.

stance the law of causation seems to suspend itself. If we add to this awe the glorious transport which arises in man, even from the very depths of nature, at the shattering of the *principium individuationis*, then we are in a position to apprehend the essence of Dionysiac rapture, whose closest analogy is furnished by physical intoxication. Dionysiac stirrings arise either through the influence of those narcotic potions of which all primitive races speak in their hymns, or through the powerful approach of spring, which penetrates with joy the whole frame of nature. So stirred, the individual forgets himself completely. It is the same Dionysiac power which in medieval Germany drove ever increasing crowds of people singing and dancing from place to place; we recognize in these St. John's and St. Vitus' dancers the bacchic choruses[11] of the Greeks, who had their precursors in Asia Minor and as far back as Babylon and the orgiastic Sacaea.[12] There are people who, either from lack of experience or out of sheer stupidity, turn away from such phenomena, and, strong in the sense of their own sanity, label them either mockingly or pityingly "endemic diseases." These benighted souls have no idea how cadaverous and ghostly their "sanity" appears as the intense throng of Dionysiac revelers sweeps past them.

Not only does the bond between man and man come to be forged once more by the magic of the Dionysiac rite, but nature itself, long alienated or subjugated, rises again to celebrate the reconciliation with her prodigal son, man. The earth offers its gifts voluntarily, and the savage beasts of mountain and desert approach in peace. The chariot of Dionysos is bedecked with flowers and garlands; panthers and tigers stride beneath his yoke. If one were to convert Beethoven's "Paean to Joy"[13] into a painting, and refuse to curb the imagination when that multitude prostrates itself reverently in the dust, one might form some apprehension of Dionysiac ritual. Now the slave emerges as a freeman; all the rigid, hostile walls which either necessity or despotism has erected between men are shattered. Now that the gospel of universal harmony is sounded, each individual becomes not only reconciled to

5

---

[11]*bacchic choruses* Bacchus was the god of wine (a variant of Dionysius); thus, this term means drunken choruses. The St. John's and St. Vitus' dancers were ecstatic Christian dancers of the Middle Ages. Their dance was a mania which spread to a number of major religious centers.

[12]*Sacaea* A Babylonian summer festival for the god Ishtar. The point is that such religious orgies are ancient.

[13]*"Paean to Joy"* This is Friedrich von Schiller's (1759–1805) poem, *Ode to Joy*, which Ludwig van Beethoven (1770–1827) set to music in the last movement of his Symphony no. 9, the Choral symphony.

his fellow but actually at one with him—as though the veil of Maya had been torn apart and there remained only shreds floating before the vision of mystical Oneness. Man now expresses himself through song and dance as the member of a higher community; he has forgotten how to walk, how to speak, and is on the brink of taking wing as he dances. Each of his gestures betokens enchantment; through him sounds a supernatural power, the same power which makes the animals speak and the earth render up milk and honey. He feels himself to be godlike and strides with the same elation and ecstasy as the gods he has seen in his dreams. No longer the *artist*, he has himself become a *work of art:* the productive power of the whole universe is now manifest in his transport, to the glorious satisfaction of the primordial One. The finest clay, the most precious marble—man—is here kneaded and hewn, and the chisel blows of the Dionysiac world artist are accompanied by the cry of the Eleusinian mystagogues:[14] "Do you fall on your knees, multitudes, do you divine your creator?"

So far we have examined the Apollonian and Dionysiac states as the product of formative forces arising directly from nature without the mediation of the human artist. At this stage artistic urges are satisfied directly, on the one hand through the imagery of dreams, whose perfection is quite independent of the intellectual rank, the artistic development of the individual; on the other hand, through an ecstatic reality which once again takes no account of the individual and may even destroy him, or else redeem him through a mystical experience of the collective. In relation to these immediate creative conditions of nature every artist must appear as "imitator," either as the Apollonian dream artist or the Dionysiac ecstatic artist, or, finally (as in Greek tragedy, for example) as dream and ecstatic artist in one. We might picture to ourselves how the last of these, in a state of Dionysiac intoxication and mystical self-abrogation,[15] wandering apart from the reveling throng, sinks upon the ground, and how there is then revealed to him his own condition—complete oneness with the essence of the universe—in a dream similitude. 6

Having set down these general premises and distinctions, we now turn to the Greeks in order to realize to what degree the formative forces of nature were developed in them. Such an inquiry will enable us to assess properly the relation of the Greek artist to his prototypes 7

---

[14]*Eleusinian mystagogues* Those who participate in the ancient Greek Eleusinian secret ceremonies celebrating life after death.

[15]*self-abrogation* The reveler "loses" his self, his sense of being an individual apart from the throng.

or, to use Aristotle's expression, his "imitation of nature."[16] Of the dreams the Greeks dreamed it is not possible to speak with any certainty, despite the extant dream literature and the large number of dream anecdotes. But considering the incredible accuracy of their eyes, their keen and unabashed delight in colors, one can hardly be wrong in assuming that their dreams too showed a strict consequence of lines and contours, hues and groupings, a progression of scenes similar to their best bas-reliefs.[17] The perfection of these dream scenes might almost tempt us to consider the dreaming Greek as a Homer and Homer as a dreaming Greek; which would be as though the modern man were to compare himself in his dreaming to Shakespeare.

Yet there is another point about which we do not have to conjecture at all: I mean the profound gap separating the Dionysiac Greeks from the Dionysiac barbarians. Throughout the range of ancient civilization (leaving the newer civilizations out of account for the moment) we find evidence of Dionysiac celebrations which stand to the Greek type in much the same relation as the bearded satyr,[18] whose name and attributes are derived from the he-goat, stands to the god Dionysos. The central concern of such celebrations was, almost universally, a complete sexual promiscuity overriding every form of established tribal law; all the savage urges of the mind were unleashed on those occasions until they reached that paroxysm of lust and cruelty which has always struck me as the "witches' cauldron" *par excellence.* It would appear that the Greeks were for a while quite immune from these feverish excesses which must have reached them by every known land or sea route. What kept Greece safe was the proud, imposing image of Apollo, who in holding up the head of the Gorgon[19] to those brutal and grotesque Dionysiac forces subdued them. Doric art has immortalized Apollo's majestic rejection of all license. But resistance became difficult, even impossible, as soon as similar urges began to break forth from the deep substratum of Hellenism itself. Soon the

8

---

[16]***"imitation of nature"*** A key term in Aristotle's theory of *mimesis*, the doctrine that art imitates nature and that the artist must observe nature carefully. Nietzsche emphasizes dreams as a part of nature and something to be closely observed by the artist.

[17]***bas-reliefs*** Sculptures projecting only slightly from a flat surface; they usually tell a story in a series of scenes.

[18]***satyr*** Greek god, half man, half goat; a symbol of lechery.

[19]***Gorgon*** Powerful monster in Greek mythology with serpents for hair. There were three Gorgons, all sisters, but only Medusa was not immortal. With the help of the goddess Athena, Perseus beheaded Medusa, whose very glance was supposed to turn men to stone. Later Perseus vanquished his enemies by exposing the head to them and turning them to stone.

function of the Delphic god[20] developed into something quite different and much more limited: all he could hope to accomplish now was to wrest the destructive weapon, by a timely gesture of pacification, from his opponent's hand. That act of pacification represents the most important event in the history of Greek ritual; every department of life now shows symptoms of a revolutionary change. The two great antagonists have been reconciled. Each feels obliged henceforth to keep to his bounds, each will honor the other by the bestowal of periodic gifts, while the cleavage remains fundamentally the same. And yet, if we examine what happened to the Dionysiac powers under the pressure of that treaty we notice a great difference: in the place of the Babylonian Sacaea, with their throwback of men to the condition of apes and tigers, we now see entirely new rites celebrated: rites of universal redemption, of glorious transfiguration. Only now has it become possible to speak of nature's celebrating an *esthetic* triumph; only now has the abrogation of the *principium individuationis* become an esthetic event. That terrible witches' brew concocted of lust and cruelty has lost all power under the new conditions. Yet the peculiar blending of emotions in the heart of the Dionysiac reveler—his ambiguity if you will—seems still to hark back (as the medicinal drug harks back to the deadly poison) to the days when the infliction of pain was experienced as joy while a sense of supreme triumph elicited cries of anguish from the heart. For now in every exuberant joy there is heard an undertone of terror, or else a wistful lament over an irrecoverable loss. It is as though in these Greek festivals a sentimental trait of nature were coming to the fore, as though nature were bemoaning the fact of her fragmentation, her decomposition into separate individuals. The chants and gestures of these revelers, so ambiguous in their motivation, represented an absolute *novum*[21] in the world of the Homeric Greeks; their Dionysiac music, in especial, spread abroad terror and a deep shudder. It is true: music had long been familiar to the Greeks as an Apollonian art, as a regular beat like that of waves lapping the shore, a plastic rhythm[22] expressly developed for the portrayal of Apollonian conditions. Apollo's music was a Doric architecture of sound—of

---

[20]*Delphic god* Apollo. The oracle at the temple to Apollo at Delphi, in Greece, was for more than 1,000 years a source of prophecies of the future. It was among the most sacred places in Greece.

[21]*an absolute* novum a genuine novelty.

[22]*plastic rhythm* Plastic in this sense means capable of being shaped, responsive to slight changes—not rigid.

barely hinted sounds such as are proper to the cithara.[23] Those very elements which characterize Dionysiac music and, after it, music quite generally: the heart-shaking power of tone, the uniform stream of melody, the incomparable resources of harmony—all those elements had been carefully kept at a distance as being inconsonant with the Apollonian norm. In the Dionysiac dithyramb[24] man is incited to strain his symbolic faculties to the utmost; something quite unheard of is now clamoring to be heard: the desire to tear asunder the veil of Maya, to sink back into the original oneness of nature; the desire to express the very essence of nature symbolically. Thus an entirely new set of symbols springs into being. First, all the symbols pertaining to physical features: mouth, face, the spoken word, the dance movement which coordinates the limbs and bends them to its rhythm. Then suddenly all the rest of the symbolic forces—music and rhythm as such, dynamics, harmony—assert themselves with great energy. In order to comprehend this total emancipation of all the symbolic powers one must have reached the same measure of inner freedom those powers themselves were making manifest; which is to say that the votary of Dionysos[25] could not be understood except by his own kind. It is not difficult to imagine the awed surprise with which the Apollonian Greek must have looked on him. And that surprise would be further increased as the latter realized, with a shudder, that all this was not so alien to him after all, that his Apollonian consciousness was but a thin veil hiding from him the whole Dionysiac realm.

In order to comprehend this we must take down the elaborate edifice of Apollonian culture stone by stone until we discover its foundations. At first the eye is struck by the marvelous shapes of the Olympian gods who stand upon its pediments, and whose exploits, in shining bas-relief, adorn its friezes. The fact that among them we find Apollo as one god among many, making no claim to a privileged position, should not mislead us. The same drive that found its most complete representation in Apollo generated the whole Olympian world, and in this sense we may consider Apollo the father of that world. But what was the radical need out of which that illustrious society of Olympian beings sprang?

9

---

[23]*cithara* An ancient stringed instrument, the lyre, used to accompany songs and recitations.

[24]*Dionysiac dithyramb* A passionate hymn to Dionysius, usually delivered by a chorus.

[25]*votary of Dionysos* A follower of Dionysius; one devoted to Dionysian ecstasy.

Whoever approaches the Olympians with a different religion in his   10
heart, seeking moral elevation, sanctity, spirituality, loving-kindness,
will presently be forced to turn away from them in ill-humored disappointment. Nothing in these deities reminds us of asceticism, high
intellect, or duty: we are confronted by luxuriant, triumphant *existence*, which deifies the good and the bad indifferently. And the beholder may find himself dismayed in the presence of such overflowing
life and ask himself what potion these heady people must have drunk
in order to behold, in whatever direction they looked, Helen[26] laughing
back at them, the beguiling image of their own existence. But we shall
call out to this beholder, who has already turned his back: Don't go!
Listen first to what the Greeks themselves have to say of this life,
which spreads itself before you with such puzzling serenity. An old
legend has it that King Midas[27] hunted a long time in the woods for
the wise Silenus, companion of Dionysos, without being able to catch
him. When he had finally caught him the king asked him what he
considered man's greatest good. The daemon remained sullen and un-
communicative until finally, forced by the king, he broke into a shrill
laugh and spoke: "Ephemeral wretch, begotten by accident and toil,
why do you force me to tell you what it would be your greatest boon
not to hear? What would be best for you is quite beyond your reach:
not to have been born, not to *be*, to be *nothing*. But the second best
is to die soon."

What is the relation of the Olympian gods to this popular wisdom?   11
It is that of the entranced vision of the martyr to his torment.

Now the Olympian magic mountain opens itself before us, show-   12
ing us its very roots. The Greeks were keenly aware of the terrors and
horrors of existence; in order to be able to live at all they had to place
before them the shining fantasy of the Olympians. Their tremendous
distrust of the titanic forces of nature: *Moira*,[28] mercilessly enthroned
beyond the knowable world; the vulture which fed upon the great phi-
lanthropist Prometheus;[29] the terrible lot drawn by wise Oedipus; the

---

[26]**Helen**   The runaway wife of Menelaus, immortalized in Homer's *Iliad* as the cause
of the ten-year Trojan War. She was not "good" or ascetic, but her intensity of living
secured her a permanent place in history and myth.

[27]**King Midas**   Midas was a foolish king who kidnapped Silenus, a satyr (half man,
half goat) who was a companion of Dionysius. Silenus, a daemon or spirit, granted Midas
his wish to have everything he touched turn to gold. Because his food turned to gold, he
almost died. Dionysius eventually saved him by bathing him in a sacred river.

[28]**Moira**   Fate personified; the figure who gives each person his fate.

[29]**Prometheus**   The god who gave men fire—thus, his generosity is philanthropy, the
love of man. He was punished by the gods.

curse on the house of Atreus which brought Orestes to the murder of his mother: that whole Panic philosophy,[30] in short, with its mythic examples, by which the gloomy Etruscans perished, the Greeks conquered—or at least hid from view—again and again by means of this artificial Olympus. In order to live at all the Greeks had to construct these deities. The Apollonian need for beauty had to develop the Olympian hierarchy of joy by slow degrees from the original titanic hierarchy of terror, as roses are seen to break from a thorny thicket. How else could life have been borne by a race so hypersensitive, so emotionally intense, so equipped for suffering? The same drive which called art into being as a completion and consummation of existence, and as a guarantee of further existence, gave rise also to that Olympian realm which acted as a transfiguring mirror to the Hellenic will. The gods justified human life by living it themselves—the only satisfactory theodicy[31] ever invented. To exist in the clear sunlight of such deities was now felt to be the highest good, and the only real grief suffered by Homeric man was inspired by the thought of leaving that sunlight, especially when the departure seemed imminent. Now it became possible to stand the wisdom of Silenus on its head and proclaim that it was the worst evil for man to die soon, and second worst for him to die at all. Such laments as arise now arise over short-lived Achilles,[32] over the generations ephemeral as leaves, the decline of the heroic age. It is not unbecoming to even the greatest hero to yearn for an afterlife, though it be as a day laborer. So impetuously, during the Apollonian phase, does man's will desire to remain on earth, so identified does he become with existence, that even his lament turns to a song of praise.

It should have become apparent by now that the harmony with 13 nature which we late-comers regard with such nostalgia, and for which Schiller has coined the cant term *naïve*,[33] is by no means a simple and

---

[30]**Panic philosophy** Belief in fate. Oedipus's fate was to murder his father and marry his mother. He tried to escape it, but could not. Orestes murdered his mother, Clytemnestra, because she had murdered his father Agamemnon. All of these were members of the cursed house of Atreus and examples of how fate works.

[31]**theodicy** Examination of the question whether the gods are just. Because the gods shared human life, they ennobled it; they suffered evil as well.

[32]**short-lived Achilles** Achilles' fate was to lead the Greeks to victory at Troy, but to die by an arrow shot by Paris, who had taken Helen to Troy. Apollo guided the arrow so that it hit Achilles in the heel, his one vulnerable spot. Achilles, like many heroes, lived a brief but intense life.

[33]**naïve** Schiller's *On the Naïve and the Sentimental in Poetry* (1795–1796) contrasted the Classic (naïve) with the Romantic (sentimental) in art. It is not the same as Nietzsche's distinction, but it is similar. Nietzsche uses "naïve" to refer to a kind of classical purity and temper.

inevitable condition to be found at the gateway to every culture, a kind of paradise. Such a belief could have been endorsed only by a period for which Rousseau's Emile was an artist and Homer just such an artist nurtured in the bosom of nature. Whenever we encounter "naïveté" in art, we are face to face with the ripest fruit of Apollonian culture—which must always triumph first over titans, kill monsters, and overcome the somber contemplation of actuality, the intense susceptibility to suffering, by means of illusions strenuously and zestfully entertained. But how rare are the instances of true naïveté, of that complete identification with the beauty of appearance! It is this achievement which makes Homer so magnificent—Homer, who, as a single individual, stood to Apollonian popular culture in the same relation as the individual dream artist to the oneiric[34] capacity of a race and of nature generally. The naïveté of Homer must be viewed as a complete victory of Apollonian illusion. Nature often uses illusions of this sort in order to accomplish its secret purposes. The true goal is covered over by a phantasm. We stretch out our hands to the latter, while nature, aided by our deception, attains the former. In the case of the Greeks it was the will wishing to behold itself in the work of art, in the transcendence of genius; but in order so to behold itself its creatures had first to view themselves as glorious, to transpose themselves to a higher sphere, without having that sphere of pure contemplation either challenge them or upbraid them with insufficiency. It was in that sphere of beauty that the Greeks saw the Olympians as their mirror images; it was by means of that esthetic mirror that the Greek will opposed suffering and the somber wisdom of suffering which always accompanies artistic talent. As a monument to its victory stands Homer, the naïve artist.

We can learn something about that naïve artist through the analogy of dream. We can imagine the dreamer as he calls out to himself, still caught in the illusion of his dream and without disturbing it, "This is a dream, and I want to go on dreaming," and we can infer, on the one hand, that he takes deep delight in the contemplation of his dream, and, on the other, that he must have forgotten the day, with its horrible importunity, so to enjoy his dream. Apollo, the interpreter of dreams, will furnish the clue to what is happening here. Although of the two halves of life—the waking and the dreaming—the former is generally considered not only the more important but the only one

14

---

[34]**oneiric** pertaining to dreams.

which is truly lived, I would, at the risk of sounding paradoxical, propose the opposite view. The more I have come to realize in nature those omnipotent formative tendencies and, with them, an intense longing for illusion, the more I feel inclined to the hypothesis that the original Oneness, the ground of Being, ever-suffering and contradictory, time and again has need of rapt vision and delightful illusion to redeem itself. Since we ourselves are the very stuff of such illusions, we must view ourselves as the truly non-existent, that is to say, as a perpetual unfolding in time, space, and causality—what we label "empiric reality."[35] But if, for the moment, we abstract from our own reality, viewing our empiric existence, as well as the existence of the world at large, as the *idea* of the original Oneness, produced anew each instant, then our dreams will appear to us as illusions of illusions, hence as a still higher form of satisfaction of the original desire for illusion. It is for this reason that the very core of nature takes such a deep delight in the naïve artist and the naïve work of art, which likewise is merely the illusion of an illusion. Raphael,[36] himself one of those immortal "naïve" artists, in a symbolic canvas has illustrated that reduction of illusion to further illusion which is the original act of the naïve artist and at the same time of all Apollonian culture. In the lower half of his "Transfiguration," through the figures of the possessed boy, the despairing bearers, the helpless, terrified disciples, we see a reflection of original pain, the sole ground of being: "illusion" here is a reflection of eternal contradiction, begetter of all things. From this illusion there rises, like the fragrance of ambrosia, a new illusory world, invisible to those enmeshed in the first: a radiant vision of pure delight, a rapt seeing through wide-open eyes. Here we have, in a great symbol of art, both the fair world of Apollo and its substratum, the terrible wisdom of Silenus, and we can comprehend intuitively how they mutually require one another. But Apollo appears to us once again as the apotheosis[37] of the *principium individuationis*, in whom the eternal goal of the original Oneness, namely its redemption through illusion, accomplishes itself. With august gesture the god

---

[35]*"empiric reality"* The reality we can test by experience.

[36]*Raphael (1483–1520)* A Renaissance artist. Raphael was influenced by Classical forms, but his work became progressively more humanistic, in some cases tending to Schiller's "sentimental." *Transfiguration* (1517–1520), his last painting, points to the new age of Baroque painting: an intense, emotional, ecstatic style.

[37]*apotheosis* Godlike embodiment. Nietzsche is saying that Apollo is the god in whom the concept of the individual is best expressed.

shows us how there is need for a whole world of torment in order for the individual to produce the redemptive vision and to sit quietly in his rocking rowboat in mid-sea, absorbed in contemplation.

If this apotheosis of individuation is to be read in normative terms, 15 we may infer that there is one norm only: the individual—or, more precisely, the observance of the limits of the individual: *sophrosyne*.[38] As a moral deity Apollo demands self-control from his people and, in order to observe such self-control, a knowledge of self. And so we find that the esthetic necessity of beauty is accompanied by the imperatives, "Know thyself," and "Nothing too much." Conversely, excess and *hubris*[39] come to be regarded as the hostile spirits of the non-Apollonian sphere, hence as properties of the pre-Apollonian era—the age of Titans[40]—and the extra-Apollonian world, that is to say the world of the barbarians. It was because of his Titanic love of man that Prometheus had to be devoured by vultures; it was because of his extravagant wisdom which succeeded in solving the riddle of the Sphinx[41] that Oedipus had to be cast into a whirlpool of crime: in this fashion does the Delphic god interpret the Greek past.

The effects of the Dionysiac spirit struck the Apollonian Greeks as 16 titanic and barbaric; yet they could not disguise from themselves the fact that they were essentially akin to those deposed Titans and heroes. They felt more than that: their whole existence, with its temperate beauty, rested upon a base of suffering and *knowledge* which had been hidden from them until the reinstatement of Dionysos uncovered it once more. And lo and behold! Apollo found it impossible to live without Dionysos. The elements of titanism and barbarism turned out to be quite as fundamental as the Apollonian element. And now let us imagine how the ecstatic sounds of the Dionysiac rites penetrated ever more enticingly into that artificially restrained and discreet world of

---

[38]**sophrosyne**   Greek word for wisdom.

[39]**hubris**   Greek word for pride, especially dangerous, defiant pride.

[40]**age of Titans**   A reference to the gods who reigned before Zeus; an unenlightened age.

[41]**riddle of the Sphinx**   The sphinx, half man and half lion, waited outside Thebes for years, killing all who passed by and could not solve its riddle. Oedipus (see note 30) answered the riddle: "What walks on four legs in the morning, two legs in the day, and three legs in the evening?" The answer: man, who crawls in infancy, walks upright in his prime, and uses a cane in old age. The solution freed Thebes from its bondage to the Sphinx, but it brought Oedipus closer to his awful fate.

illusion, how this clamor expressed the whole outrageous gamut of nature—delight, grief, knowledge—even to the most piercing cry; and then let us imagine how the Apollonian artist with his thin, monotonous harp music must have sounded beside the demoniac chant of the multitude! The muses presiding over the illusory arts paled before an art which enthusiastically told the truth, and the wisdom of Silenus cried "Woe!" against the serene Olympians. The individual, with his limits and moderations, forgot himself in the Dionysiac vortex and became oblivious to the laws of Apollo. Indiscreet extravagance revealed itself as truth, and contradiction, a delight born of pain, spoke out of the bosom of nature. Wherever the Dionysiac voice was heard, the Apollonian norm seemed suspended or destroyed. Yet it is equally true that, in those places where the first assault was withstood, the prestige and majesty of the Delphic god appeared more rigid and threatening than before. The only way I am able to view Doric art and the Doric[42] state is as a perpetual military encampment of the Apollonian forces. An art so defiantly austere, so ringed about with fortifications—an education so military and exacting—a polity so ruthlessly cruel—could endure only in a continual state of resistance against the titanic and barbaric menace of Dionysos.

Up to this point I have developed at some length a theme which was sounded at the beginning of this essay: how the Dionysiac and Apollonian elements, in a continuous chain of creations, each enhancing the other, dominated the Hellenic mind: how from the Iron Age,[43] with its battles of Titans and its austere popular philosophy, there developed under the aegis of Apollo the Homeric world of beauty; how this "naïve" splendor was then absorbed once more by the Dionysiac torrent, and how, face to face with this new power, the Apollonian code rigidified into the majesty of Doric art and contemplation. If the earlier phase of Greek history may justly be broken down into four major artistic epochs dramatizing the battle between the two hostile principles, then we must inquire further (lest Doric art appear to us as the acme and final goal of all these striving tendencies) what was the true end toward which that evolution moved. And our eyes will come to rest on the sublime and much lauded achievement of the dramatic

17

---

[42]**Doric** The Doric styles were unadorned, clear, intellectual rather than sensual. They represent purity and uprightness.

[43]**Iron Age** An earlier age, ruled by sterner, less humane gods, the Titans.

dithyramb and Attic tragedy, as the common goal of both urges; whose mysterious marriage, after long discord, ennobled itself with such a child, at once Antigone and Cassandra.[44]

---

[44]***Antigone and Cassandra*** Children in Greek tragedies; Antigone, daughter of Oedipus, defied the authorities in *Antigone* by Sophocles (496?–406 B.C.), and suffered; Cassandra, daughter of Priam, king of Troy, appears in Homer's *Iliad* and several tragedies by Aeschylus (525–456 B.C.) and Euripides (480?–?406 B.C.). She had the gift of prophecy, but was doomed never to be believed. She foresaw the destruction of Troy, and after its fall she was taken prisoner by Agamemnon. She and Antigone were both heroic in their suffering.

QUESTIONS

1. Begin by defining "Apollonianism" and "Dionysianism." What kind of behavior does each word stand for?
2. What are the important distinctions between the self and the mob? Dream and illusion?
3. In paragraph 6, Nietzsche speaks of the "mystical experience of the collective." What does he mean by this phrase? Is there such a thing?
4. Which paragraphs in the selection are most obscure and difficult to understand? Do they seem to show Dionysian qualities?
5. Do you feel that any contemporary art unifies the Apollonian and the Dionysian? Would Nietzsche have thought a modern film could do so?
6. Are the distinctions Nietzsche makes useful for contemporary psychology? Do they give you useful insights into behavior?

WRITING ASSIGNMENTS

1. Examine paragraph 6 carefully. How valid are Nietzsche's insights concerning the self and the "reveling throng"? Drawing on personal experience, contrast the behavior of yourself or a friend—first as an individual, then as a member of a large gathering of people. Are you (or your friend) "possessed" when a member of such an assemblage? Be as specific as possible in writing about this contrast.
2. What are the psychological implications of Nietzsche's views on the divergence of Apollonianism and Dionysianism? Have you observed these distinctions in people? Do you feel both qualities in yourself? Discuss these implications with others who may know this work. How many people are aware of these forces within themselves? What kinds of language are used to describe them? Finally, do you feel that Nietzsche gives you insight into your own nature?

3. Music is the inspiration for this essay. Choose a piece of music that is very important to you. Consider it as an artifact and describe the qualities it has that you feel are Apollonian and those that are Dionysian. Is the range of the music—in terms of exciting or sustaining emotional response—narrow or great? Describe your emotional and intellectual reactions to the music and ask others about their responses to the same music. Is music an appropriate source for finding the conjunction of these two forces?

4. Examine aspects of our culture. Do they reveal our culture to be basically Apollonian or basically Dionysian? Be sure to consider political life; education; entertainment of various kinds, including literature, music, and sports; and any aspects of personal life in your immediate environment. In considering these features of our culture, you have an opportunity to use Nietzsche's technique of comparison and contrast. For instance, you may find the Apollonian and Dionysian sides of, say, football as interesting contrasts, just as you may wish to contrast the games of chess and rugby, rock music and Muzak, or any other related pairs.

5. Inventory the selection for references to dreams and illusion. As best you can, make sense of what Nietzsche has to say about these manifestations of psychology. Remember that contemporary psychologists feel that dreams reveal our inner state, our "unconscious," and that Freud, among others, referred to literature (one of art's illusions) as a repository of psychological fantasies that help us give shape to our own psychology. What is Nietzsche's opinion concerning the nature of the dreams and illusions we have, their value to us in daily life, and our need of them? Use quotations and analyze them in your effort to clarify Nietzsche's thought.

WILLIAM JAMES

The Reality of the Unseen

WILLIAM JAMES (1842–1910), trained as a medical doctor, was both a philosopher and a psychologist. He taught psychology as a science at Harvard University and made some important contributions to the connections between psychology and philosophy and between psychology and religion. His work, from its beginnings, was brilliant and caught the attention of the most demanding minds of his generation. His family was among the most remarkable of modern times, being as it was distinguished in many fields of thought. His younger brother, Henry, was the most distinguished American novelist of his times.

Principles of Psychology (1890) was a landmark book, particularly for its examinations of patterns of habit, stream of consciousness, and the nature of emotion and will. It was among the clearest formulations of thought on those issues in psychology up to that time. His views were picked up and developed by a number of important writers who became famous in the early part of the twentieth century. Possibly the most influential of his books is Varieties of Religious Experience, composed of series of lectures he delivered at the University

From Varieties of Religious Experience.

of Edinburgh in 1901 and 1902, and published in 1902. The excerpt which appears here is his third lecture, dealing with the experiences of people who have sensed "otherness" with no explicit sensory information before them.

James begins by connecting such experience with Plato, who felt that the world of sensory knowledge was transitory and unreliable. Ideas, Plato thought, were permanent, unchangeable, and of paramount importance. The kinds of experience that are recorded in this lecture are connected with Plato's thought because they are not excited by sensory experience of any ordinary sort. They are products of abstraction—which is to say, they are not specific (like the perception of a red motorcycle) but abstract (like the concept of red or the concept of motorcycle). Thus, James's experiences are psychological: they are ideas, thoughts, and feelings that reside within the subject who describes them. He is talking about the psychology of religion—or, at least, an aspect of it.

The distinction he makes between the kinds of knowledge available to us is of utmost importance because his age was given to absolute confidence in science, which was thought to be a product of careful sensory observation and the hypotheses drawn from that observation. The idea that there is a total world of experience—thought, feeling, understanding (aspects of psychology)—and that it is of utmost importance to matters of religion was perhaps his most important point.

James was fascinated by unexplained phenomena and alternative states of consciousness. He experimented with mind-altering drugs and came to think that our "ordinary" state of consciousness was only one of many possibilities. However, he was also a hard-minded scientist and avoided merely impressionistic ways of working. He was, for example, a champion of Charles Darwin's theories of evolution and believed that they were totally compatible with his concepts of psychology and of religion.

JAMES'S RHETORIC

Even though this selection is a lecture, there is little in James's rhetoric that could be called emotive, flashy, or designed to be catchy. The basic rhetorical technique he uses is the topic of testimony, mentioned earlier in the introduction to Rousseau. The entire lecture is a commentary on a selection of almost twenty statements by "informants" who described experiences which are connected with religion and the perception of the "unseen." These informants have provided the testimony which his rhetorical method depends upon.

James's rhetorical structure is also simple enough. The first eleven paragraphs establish a most important truth: many eminent philosophers, from the ancient Plato to post-Renaissance philosophers such as Ralph Waldo Emerson (1803–1882) and Immanuel Kant (1724–1804), have emphasized the importance of the unseen world. Ideas, he explains, have universal value, and this truth has been recognized by important thinkers for ages. This technique—referring to important recognized authorities—is, of course, also the topic of testimony, although James does not burden us with quotations of statements of each philosopher referred to.

The body of the lecture is devoted to a presentation of statements made by relatively modern persons, most of whom are as anonymous as those sitting in James's audience. At paragraph 33, James begins his conclusion, drawing the inferences he feels are reasonable from a review of the testimony he and others have gathered.

Rhetorically, the strategy is as simple as one could wish. The opening paragraphs establish James's authority by connecting him with past and present thinkers; the body of the essay seems almost a casual gathering of statements and "witnesses" to testify to the truths which he has already committed himself to; and the conclusion leaves the listener with a real conclusion: that in matters of religion, rationality based on concrete sensory experience (a la science) is not likely to be as important as the kinds of psychological experiences and feelings he has brought forth for our examination.

The Reality of the Unseen

Were one asked to characterize the life of religion in the broadest and most general terms possible, one might say that it consists of the belief that there is an unseen order, and that our supreme good lies in harmoniously adjusting ourselves thereto. This belief and this adjustment are the religious attitude in the soul. I wish during this hour to call your attention to some of the psychological pecularities of such an attitude as this, or belief in an object which we cannot see. All our attitudes, moral, practical, or emotional, as well as religious, are due to the "objects" of our consciousness, the things which we believe to exist, whether really or ideally, along with ourselves. Such objects may be present to our senses, or they may be present only to our thought. In either case they elicit from us a *reaction;* and the reaction due to things of thought is notoriously in many cases as strong as that due to sensible presences. It may be even stronger. The memory of an insult may make us angrier than the insult did when we received it. We are frequently more ashamed of our blunders afterwards than we were at the moment of making them; and in general our whole higher prudential and moral life is based on the fact that material sensations actually present may have a weaker influence on our action than ideas of remoter facts.

The more concrete objects of most men's religion, the deities whom they worship, are known to them only in idea. It has been vouchsafed, for example, to very few Christian believers to have had a sensible vision of their Saviour; though enough appearances of this sort are on record, by way of miraculous exception, to merit our attention later. The whole force of the Christian religion, therefore, so far as belief in the divine personages determines the prevalent attitude of the believer, is in general exerted by the instrumentality[1] of pure ideas, of which nothing in the individual's past experience directly serves as a model.

But in addition to these ideas of the more concrete religious objects, religion is full of abstract objects which prove to have an equal power. God's attributes as such, his holiness, his justice, his mercy, his absoluteness, his infinity, his omniscience, his tri-unity, the various mysteries of the redemptive process, the operation of the sacraments, etc., have proved fertile wells of inspiring meditation for Christian believers.[2] We shall see later that the absence of definite sensible images is positively insisted on by the mystical authorities in all religions as the *sine qua non*[3] of a successful orison, or contemplation of

---

[1]*instrumentality* James means that Christianity has, as its instruments of instruction and dissemination, only the force of ideas.

[2]Example: "I have had much comfort lately in meditating on the passages which show the personality of the Holy Ghost, and his distinctness from the Father and the Son. It is a subject that requires searching into to find out, but, when realized, gives one so much more true and lively a sense of the fullness of the Godhead, and its work in us and to us, than when only thinking of the Spirit in its effect on us." Augustus Hare, *Memorials,* i. 244, Maria Hare to Lucy H. Hare. [James's note]

[3]*sine qua non* Latin phrase meaning the most important element (lit., the thing without which nothing is possible). An *orison* is a prayer.

the higher divine truths. Such contemplations are expected (and abundantly verify the expectation, as we shall also see) to influence the believer's subsequent attitude very powerfully for good.

Immanuel Kant[4] held a curious doctrine about such objects of belief as God, the design of creation, the soul, its freedom, and the life hereafter. These things, he said, are properly not objects of knowledge at all. Our conceptions always require a sense-content to work with, and as the words "soul," "God," "immortality," cover no distinctive sense-content whatever, it follows that theoretically speaking they are words devoid of any significance. Yet strangely enough they have a definite meaning *for our practice*. We can act *as if* there were a God; feel *as if* we were free; consider Nature *as if* she were full of special designs; lay plans *as if* we were to be immortal; and we find then that these words do make a genuine difference in our moral life. Our faith *that* these unintelligible objects actually exist proves thus to be a full equivalent in *praktischer Hinsicht*,[5] as Kant calls it, or from the point of view of our action, for a knowledge of *what* they might be, in case we were permitted positively to conceive them. So we have the strange phenomenon, as Kant assures us, of a mind believing with all its strength in the real presence of a set of things of no one of which it can form any notion whatsoever.

My object in thus recalling Kant's doctrine to your mind is not to express any opinion as to the accuracy of this particularly uncouth part of his philosophy, but only to illustrate the characteristic of human nature which we are considering, by an example so classical in its exaggeration. The sentiment of reality can indeed attach itself so strongly to our object of belief that our whole life is polarized through and through, so to speak, by its sense of the existence of the thing believed in, and yet that thing, for purpose of definite description, can hardly be said to be present to our mind at all. It is as if a bar of iron, without touch or sight, with no representative faculty whatever, might nevertheless be strongly endowed with an inner capacity for magnetic feeling; and as if, through the various arousals of its magnetism by magnets coming and going in its neighborhood, it might be consciously determined to different attitudes and tendencies. Such a bar

4

5

---

[4]***Immanuel Kant (1724–1804)*** Important German philosopher. His influential idealist philosophy insisted that there was a world of observable things *(phenomena)* to be known, but that there was also a world of ideas *(noumena)* which were no less real and cannot be known. The things James mentions are, according to Kant, unknowable because they cannot be sensed.

[5]**praktischer Hinsicht** German term meaning in a practical sense.

of iron could never give you an outward description of the agencies that had the power of stirring it so strongly; yet of their presence, and of their significance for its life, it would be intensely aware through every fiber of its being.

It is not only the Ideas of pure Reason[6] as Kant styled them, that have this power of making us vitally feel presences that we are impotent articulately to describe. All sorts of higher abstractions bring with them the same kind of impalpable appeal. Remember those passages from Emerson[7] which I read at my last lecture. The whole universe of concrete objects, as we know them, swims, not only for such a transcendentalist writer, but for all of us, in a wider and higher universe of abstract ideas, that lend it its significance. As time, space, and the ether soak through all things so (we feel) do abstract and essential goodness, beauty, strength, significance, justice, soak through all things good, strong, significant, and just.

Such ideas, and others equally abstract, form the background for all our facts, the fountain-head of all the possibilities we conceive of. They give its "nature," as we call it, to every special thing. Everything we know is "what" it is by sharing in the nature of one of these abstractions. We can never look directly at them, for they are bodiless and featureless and footless, but we grasp all other things by their means, and in handling the real world we should be stricken with helplessness in just so far forth as we might lose these mental objects, these adjectives and adverbs and predicates and heads of classification and conception.

This absolute determinability of our mind by abstractions is one of the cardinal facts in our human constitution. Polarizing and magnetizing us as they do, we turn towards them and from them, we seek them, hold them, hate them, bless them, just as if they were so many concrete beings. And beings they are, beings as real in the realm which they inhabit as the changing things of sense are in the realm of space.

Plato gave so brilliant and impressive a defense of this common human feeling, that the doctrine of the reality of abstract objects has been known as the platonic theory of ideas ever since. Abstract Beauty, for example, is for Plato a perfectly definite individual being, of which

6

7

8

9

---

[6]***Ideas of pure Reason***   Kant's *Critique of Pure Reason* (1781) was an idealist and transcendentalist work, focusing on the nature of reason itself as a proper study for philosophy.

[7]***Ralph Waldo Emerson (1803–1882)***   An American philosopher who gave credence to spiritual values. He was a Transcendentalist, a leader in that nineteenth-century movement, which believed that there was a reality that transcended sensory knowledge.

the intellect is aware as of something additional to all the perishing beauties of the earth. "The true order of going," he says, in the often quoted passage in his "Banquet,"[8] "is to use the beauties of earth as steps along which one mounts upwards for the sake of that other Beauty, going from one to two, and from two to all fair forms, and from fair forms to fair actions, and from fair actions to fair notions, until from fair notions, he arrives at the notion of absolute Beauty, and at last knows what the essence of Beauty is."[9] In our last lecture we had a glimpse of the way in which a platonizing writer like Emerson may treat the abstract divineness of things, the moral structure of the universe, as a fact worthy of worship. In those various churches without a God which today are spreading through the world under the name of ethical societies, we have a similar worship of the abstract divine, the moral law believed in as an ultimate object. "Science" in many minds is genuinely taking the place of a religion. Where this is so, the scientist treats the "Laws of Nature" as objective facts to be revered. A brilliant school of interpretation of Greek mythology would have it that in their origin the Greek gods were only half-metaphoric personifications of those great spheres of abstract law and order into which the natural world falls apart—the sky-sphere, the ocean-sphere, the earth-sphere, and the like; just as even now we may speak of the smile of the morning, the kiss of the breeze, or the bite of the cold, without really meaning that these phenomena of nature actually wear a human face.[10]

As regards the origin of the Greek gods, we need not at present seek an opinion. But the whole array of our instances leads to a conclusion something like this: It is as if there were in the human consciousness a *sense of reality, a feeling of objective presence, a perception* of what we may call "something there," more deep and more general than any of the special and particular "senses" by which the current psychology supposes existent realities to be originally revealed. If this were so, we might suppose the senses to waken our attitudes and conduct as they so habitually do, by first exciting this sense of reality; but anything else, any idea, for example, that might similarly excite it,

10

---

[8]*"Banquet"* This is *Symposium,* a dialogue portraying an older Socrates discoursing on the way the beautiful leads to the good. This idea was popular with the Transcendentalists.

[9]*Symposium,* Jowett, 1871, i. 527. [James's note]

[10]Example: "Nature is always so interesting, under whatever aspect she shows herself, that when it rains, I seem to see a beautiful woman weeping. She appears the more beautiful, the more afflicted she is." B. de St. Pierre. [James's note]

would have that same prerogative of appearing real which objects of sense normally possess. So far as religious conceptions were able to touch this reality-feeling, they would be believed in in spite of criticism, even though they might be so vague and remote as to be almost unimaginable, even though they might be such non-entities in point of *whatness*, as Kant makes the objects of his moral theology to be.

The most curious proofs of the existence of such an undifferen- 11 tiated sense of reality as this are found in experiences of hallucination. It often happens that an hallucination is imperfectly developed: the person affected will feel a "presence" in the room, definitely localized, facing in one particular way, real in the most emphatic sense of the word, often coming suddenly, and as suddenly gone; and yet neither seen, heard, touched, nor cognized in any of the usual "sensible" ways. Let me give you an example of this, before I pass to the objects with whose presence religion is more peculiarly concerned.

An intimate friend of mine, one of the keenest intellects I know, 12 has had several experiences of this sort. He writes as follows in response to my inquiries:

> I have several times within the past few years felt the so-called "consciousness of a presence." The experiences which I have in mind are clearly distinguishable from another kind of experience which I have had very frequently, and which I fancy many persons would also call the "consciousness of a presence." But the difference for me between the two sets of experience is as great as the difference between feeling a slight warmth originating I know not where, and standing in the midst of a conflagration with all the ordinary senses alert.
>
> It was about September, 1884, when I had the first experience. On the previous night I had had, after getting into bed at my rooms in College, a vivid tactile hallucination of being grasped by the arm, which made me get up and search the room for an intruder; but the sense of presence properly so called came on the next night. After I had got into bed and blown out the candle, I lay awake awhile thinking on the previous night's experience, when suddenly I *felt* something come into the room and stay close to my bed. It remained only a minute or two. I did not recognize it by any ordinary sense, and yet there was a horribly unpleasant "sensation" connected with it. It stirred something more at the roots of my being than any ordinary perception. The feeling had something of the quality of a very large tearing vital pain spreading chiefly over the chest, but within the organism—and yet the feeling was not *pain* so much as *abhorrence*. At all events, something was present with me, and I knew its presence far more surely than I have ever known the presence of any fleshly living creature. I was conscious

of its departure as of its coming: an almost instantaneously swift going through the door, and the "horrible sensation" disappeared.

On the third night when I retired my mind was absorbed in some lectures which I was preparing, and I was still absorbed in these when I became aware of the actual presence (though not of the *coming*) of the thing that was there the night before, and of the "horrible sensation." I then mentally concentrated all my effort to charge this "thing," if it was evil, to depart, if it was *not* evil, to tell me who or what it was, and if it could not explain itself, to go, and that I would compel it to go. It went as on the previous night, and my body quickly recovered its normal state.

On two other occasions in my life I have had precisely the same "horrible sensation." Once it lasted a full quarter of an hour. In all three instances the certainty that there in outward space there stood *something* was indescribably *stronger* than the ordinary certainty of companionship when we are in the close presence of ordinary living people. The something seemed close to me, and intensely more real than any ordinary perception. Although I felt it to be like unto myself, so to speak, or finite, small, and distressful, as it were, I didn't recognize it as any individual being or person.

Of course such an experience as this does not connect itself with 13 the religious sphere. Yet it may upon occasion do so; and the same correspondent informs me that at more than one other conjuncture he had the sense of presence developed with equal intensity and abruptness, only then it was filled with a quality of joy.

There was not a mere consciousness of something there, but fused in the central happiness of it, a startling awareness of some ineffable good. Not vague either, not like the emotional effect of some poem, or scene, or blossom, or music, but the sure knowledge of the close presence of a sort of mighty person, and after it went, the memory persisted as the one perception of reality. Everything else might be a dream, but not that.

My friend, as it oddly happens, does not interpret these latter ex- 14 periences theistically, as signifying the presence of God. But it would clearly not have been unnatural to interpret them as a revelation of the deity's existence. When we reach the subject of mysticism, we shall have much more to say upon this head.

Lest the oddity of these phenomena should disconcert you, I will 15 venture to read you a couple of similar narratives, much shorter, merely to show that we are dealing with a well-marked natural kind of fact. In the first case, which I take from the *Journal of the Society for Psychical Research,* the sense of presence developed in a few moments into a distinctly visualized hallucination—but I leave that part of the story out.

> "I had read," the narrator says, "some twenty minutes or so, was thoroughly absorbed in the book, my mind was perfectly quiet, and for the time being my friends were quite forgotten, when suddenly without a moment's warning my whole being seemed roused to the highest state of tension or aliveness, and I was aware, with an intenseness not easily imagined by those who had never experienced it, that another being or presence was not only in the room, but quite close to me. I put my book down, and although my excitement was great, I felt quite collected, and not conscious of any sense of fear. Without changing my position, and looking straight at the fire, I knew somehow that my friend A. H. was standing at my left elbow, but so far behind me as to be hidden by the armchair in which I was leaning back. Moving my eyes round slightly without otherwise changing my position, the lower portion of one leg became visible, and I instantly recognized the gray-blue material of trousers he often wore, but the stuff appeared semi-transparent, reminding me of tobacco smoke in consistency"[11]—and hereupon the visual hallucination came.

Another informant writes: 16

> Quite early in the night I was awakened. . . . I felt as if I had been aroused intentionally, and at first thought some one was breaking into the house. . . . I then turned on my side to go to sleep again, and immediately felt a consciousness of a presence in the room, and singular to state, it was not the consciousness of a live person, but of a spiritual presence. This may provoke a smile, but I can only tell you the facts as they occurred to me. I do not know how to better describe my sensations than by simply stating that I felt a consciousness of a spiritual presence. . . . I felt also at the same time a strong feeling of superstitious dread, as if something strange and fearful were about to happen.[12]

Professor Flournoy[13] of Geneva gives me the following testimony   17
of a friend of his, a lady, who has the gift of automatic or involuntary
writing:

---

[11]*Journal of the S.P.R.*, February, 1895, p. 26. [James's note] The Society for Psychical Research, based in London and New York, was devoted to the study of spirits, ghosts, and psychic phenomena.

[12]E. Gurney: *Phantasms of the Living,* i. 384. [James's note]

[13]**Theodore Flournoy**   A contemporary student of automatic writing and seances. His writings were well known in James's time.

Whenever I practice automatic writing, what makes me feel that it is not due to a subconscious self is the feeling I always have of a foreign presence, external to my body. It is sometimes so definitely characterized that I could point to its exact position. This impression of presence is impossible to describe. It varies in intensity and clearness according to the personality from whom the writing professes to come. If it is some one whom I love, I feel it immediately, before any writing has come. My heart seems to recognize it.

In an earlier book of mine I have cited at full length a curious case 18 of presence felt by a blind man. The presence was that of the figure of a gray-bearded man dressed in a pepper and salt suit, squeezing himself under the crack of the door and moving across the floor of the room towards a sofa. The blind subject of this quasi-hallucination is an exceptionally intelligent reporter. He is entirely without internal visual imagery and cannot represent light or colors to himself, and is positive that his other senses, hearing, etc., were not involved in this false perception. It seems to have been an abstract conception rather, with the feelings of reality and spatial outwardness directly attached to it—in other words, a fully objectified and exteriorized *idea.*

Such cases, taken along with others which would be too tedious for 19 quotation, seem sufficiently to prove the existence in our mental machinery of a sense of present reality more diffused and general than that which our special senses yield. For the psychologists the tracing of the organic seat of such a feeling would form a pretty problem— nothing could be more natural than to connect it with the muscular sense, with the feeling that our muscles were innervating themselves for action. Whatsoever thus innervated our activity, or "made our flesh creep"—our senses are what do so oftenest—might then appear real and present, even though it were but an abstract idea. But with such vague conjectures we have no concern at present, for our interest lies with the faculty rather than with its organic seat.

Like all positive affections of consciousness, the sense of reality 20 has its negative counterpart in the shape of a feeling of unreality by which persons may be haunted, and of which one sometimes hears complaint:

> "When I reflect on the fact that I have made my appearance by accident upon a globe itself whirled through space as the sport of the catastrophes of the heavens," says Madame Ackermann; "when I see myself surrounded by beings as ephemeral and incomprehensible as I am myself, and all excitedly pursuing pure chimeras,[14] I experience a

---

[14]***chimeras*** illusions.

strange feeling of being in a dream. It seems to me as if I have loved and suffered and that erelong I shall die, in a dream. My last word will be, 'I have been dreaming.' "[15]

In another lecture we shall see how in morbid melancholy this sense of the unreality of things may become a carking[16] pain, and even lead to suicide. 21

We may now lay it down as certain that in the distinctively religious sphere of experience, many persons (how many we cannot tell) possess the objects of their belief, not in the form of mere conceptions which their intellect accepts as true, but rather in the form of quasi-sensible realities directly apprehended. As his sense of the real presence of these objects fluctuates, so the believer alternates between warmth and coldness in his faith. Other examples will bring this home to one better than abstract description, so I proceed immediately to cite some. The first example is a negative one, deploring the loss of the sense in question. I have extracted it from an account given me by a scientific man of my acquaintance, of his religious life. It seems to me to show clearly that the feeling of reality may be something more like a sensation than an intellectual operation properly so-called. 22

> Between twenty and thirty I gradually became more and more agnostic and irreligious, yet I cannot say that I ever lost that "indefinite consciousness" which Herbert Spencer[17] describes so well, of an Absolute Reality behind phenomena. For me this Reality was not the pure Unknowable of Spencer's philosophy, for although I had ceased my childish prayers to God, and never prayed to *It* in a formal manner, yet my more recent experience shows me to have been in a relation to *It* which practically was the same thing as prayer. Whenever I had any trouble, especially when I had conflict with other people, either domestically or in the way of business, or when I was depressed in spirits or anxious about affairs, I now recognize that I used to fall back for support upon this curious relation I felt myself to be in to this fundamental cosmical *It*. It was on my side, or I was on Its side, however you please to term it, in the particular trouble, and it always strengthened me and seemed to give me endless vitality to feel its underlying and supporting presence. In fact, it was an unfailing fountain of living justice, truth, and strength, to which I instinctively turned at times of

---

[15]*Pensées d'un Solitaire,* p. 66. [James's note]

[16]**carking** distressing.

[17]**Herbert Spencer (1820–1903)** English philosopher who tried to systematize the sciences. The "pure Unknowable" is a term for God.

weakness, and it always brought me out. I know now that it was a personal relation I was in to it, because of late years the power of communicating with it has left me, and I am conscious of a perfectly definite loss. I used never to fail to find it when I turned to it. Then came a set of years when sometimes I found it, and then again I would be wholly unable to make connection with it. I remember many occasions on which at night in bed, I would be unable to get to sleep on account of worry. I turned this way and that in the darkness, and groped mentally for the familiar sense of that higher mind of my mind which had always seemed to be close at hand as it were, closing the passage, and yielding support, but there was no electric current. A blank was there instead of *It:* I couldn't find anything. Now, at the age of nearly fifty, my power of getting into connection with it has entirely left me; and I have to confess that a great help has gone out of my life. Life has become curiously dead and indifferent; and I can now see that my old experience was probably exactly the same thing as the prayers of the orthodox, only I did not call them by that name. What I have spoken of as "It" was practically not Spencer's Unknowable, but just my own instinctive and individual God, whom I relied upon for higher sympathy, but whom somehow I have lost.

Nothing is more common in the pages of religious biography than 23 the way in which seasons of lively and of difficult faith are described as alternating. Probably every religious person has the recollection of particular crisis in which a directer vision of the truth, a direct perception, perhaps, of a living God's existence, swept in and overwhelmed the languor of the more ordinary belief. In James Russell Lowell's correspondence there is a brief memorandum of an experience of this kind:

> I had a revelation last Friday evening. I was at Mary's, and happening to say something of the presence of spirits (of whom, I said, I was often dimly aware), Mr. Putnam entered into an argument with me on spiritual matters. As I was speaking, the whole system rose up before me like a vague destiny looming from the Abyss. I never before so clearly felt the Spirit of God in me and around me. The whole room seemed to me full of God. The air seemed to waver to and fro with the presence of Something I knew not what. I spoke with the calmness and clearness of a prophet. I cannot tell you what this revelation was; I have not yet studied it enough. But I shall perfect it one day, and then you shall hear it and acknowledge its grandeur.[18]

---

[18]*Letters of Lowell,* i. 75. [James's note] James Russell Lowell (1819–1891) was an important American writer. He was also the first editor of *The Atlantic Monthly.*

Here is a longer and more developed experience from a manuscript 24
communication by a clergyman—I take it from Starbuck's[19] manuscript collection:

> I remember the night, and almost the very spot on the hilltop,
> where my soul opened out, as it were, into the Infinite, and there was
> a rushing together of the two worlds, the inner and the outer. It was
> deep calling unto deep—the deep that my own struggle had opened up
> within being answered by the unfathomable deep without, reaching be-
> yond the stars. I stood alone with Him who had made me, and all the
> beauty of the world, and love, and sorrow, and even temptation. I did
> not seek Him, but felt the perfect unison of my spirit with His. The
> ordinary sense of things around me faded. For the moment nothing but
> an ineffable joy and exultation remained. It is impossible fully to de-
> scribe the experience. It was like the effect of some great orchestra
> when all the separate notes have melted into one swelling harmony
> that leaves the listener conscious of nothing save that his soul is being
> wafted upwards, and almost bursting with its own emotion. The perfect
> stillness of the night was thrilled by a more solemn silence. The dark-
> ness held a presence that was all the more felt because it was not seen.
> I could not any more have doubted that *He* was there than that I was.
> Indeed, I felt myself to be, if possible, the less real of the two.
>
> My highest faith in God and truest idea of him were then born in
> me. I have stood upon the Mount of Vision since, and felt the Eternal
> round about me. But never since has there come quite the same stirring
> of the heart. Then, if ever, I believe, I stood face to face with God, and
> was born anew of his spirit. There was, as I recall it, no sudden change
> of thought or of belief, except that my early crude conception, had, as
> it were, burst into flower. There was no destruction of the old, but a
> rapid, wonderful unfolding. Since that time no discussion that I have
> heard of the proofs of God's existence has been able to shake my faith.
> Having once felt the presence of God's spirit, I have never lost it again
> for long. My most assuring evidence of his existence is deeply rooted
> in that hour of vision, in the memory of that supreme experience, and
> in the conviction, gained from reading and reflection, that something
> the same has come to all who have found God. I am aware that it may
> justly be called mystical. I am not enough acquainted with philosophy
> to defend it from that or any other charge. I feel that in writing of it I
> have overlaid it with words rather than put it clearly to your thought.
> But, such as it is, I have described it as carefully as I now am able
> to do.

---

[19]***Edwin D. Starbuck (1866–1947)*** Leading researcher into the psychology of religious experience. Starbuck concentrated his studies on the experience of adolescents.
James wrote a preface to his major work, *The Psychology of Religion* (1901).

Here is another document, even more definite in character, which, 25
the writer being a Swiss, I translate from the French original.[20]

> I was in perfect health: we were on our sixth day of tramping, and
> in good training. We had come the day before from Sixt to Trient by
> Buet.[21] I felt neither fatigue, hunger, nor thirst, and my state of mind
> was equally healthy. I had had at Forlaz good news from home; I was
> subject to no anxiety, either near or remote, for we had a good guide,
> and there was not a shadow of uncertainty about the road we should
> follow. I can best describe the condition in which I was by calling it a
> state of equilibrium. When all at once I experienced a feeling of being
> raised above myself, I felt the presence of God—I tell of the thing just
> as I was conscious of it—as if his goodness and his power were pene-
> trating me altogether. The throb of emotion was so violent that I could
> barely tell the boys to pass on and not wait for me. I then sat down on
> a stone, unable to stand any longer, and my eyes overflowed with tears.
> I thanked God that in the course of my life he had taught me to know
> him, that he sustained my life and took pity both on the insignificant
> creature and on the sinner that I was. I begged him ardently that my
> life might be consecrated to the doing of his will. I felt his reply, which
> was that I should do his will from day to day, in humility and poverty,
> leaving him, the Almighty God, to be judge of whether I should some
> time be called to bear witness more conspicuously. Then, slowly, the
> ecstasy left my heart; that is, I felt that God had withdrawn the com-
> munion which he had granted, and I was able to walk on, but very
> slowly, so strongly was I still possessed by the interior emotion. Be-
> sides, I had wept uninterruptedly for several minutes, my eyes were
> swollen, and I did not wish my companions to see me. The state of
> ecstasy may have lasted four or five minutes, although it seemed at the
> time to last much longer. My comrades waited for me ten minutes at
> the cross of Barine, but I took about twenty-five or thirty minutes to
> join them, for as well as I can remember, they said that I had kept them
> back for about half an hour. The impression had been so profound that
> in climbing slowly the slope I asked myself if it were possible that
> Moses on Sinai[22] could have had a more intimate communication with
> God. I think it well to add that in this ecstasy of mine God had neither
> form, color, odor, nor taste; moreover, that the feeling of his presence
> was accompanied with no determinate localization. It was rather as if
> my personality had been transformed by the presence of a *spiritual*

---

[20]I borrow it, with Professor Flournoy's permission, from his rich collection of psychological documents. [James's note]

[21]*Sixt to Trient by Buet* Tiny Swiss towns, as is Forlaz in the sentences that follow.

[22]*Moses on Sinai* Moses spoke to God and received the commandments on
Mount Sinai. (See Exodus 19:20–25, 24:15–31:18.)

spirit. But the more I seek words to express this intimate intercourse, the more I feel the impossibility of describing the thing by any of our usual images. At bottom the expression most apt to render what I felt is this: God was present, though invisible; he fell under no one of my senses, yet my consciousness perceived him.

The adjective "mystical" is technically applied, most often, to 26 states that are of brief duration. Of course such hours of rapture as the last two persons describe are mystical experiences, of which in a later lecture I shall have much to say. Meanwhile here is the abridged record of another mystical or semi-mystical experience, in a mind evidently framed by nature for ardent piety. I owe it to Starbuck's collection. The lady who gives the account is the daughter of a man well known in his time as a writer against Christianity. The suddenness of her conversion shows well how native the sense of God's presence must be to certain minds. She relates that she was brought up in entire ignorance of Christian doctrine, but, when in Germany, after being talked to by Christian friends, she read the Bible and prayed, and finally the plan of salvation flashed upon her like a stream of light.

"To this day," she writes, "I cannot understand dallying with religion and the commands of God. The very instant I heard my Father's cry calling unto me, my heart bounded in recognition. I ran, I stretched forth my arms, I cried aloud, 'Here, here I am, my Father.' Oh, happy child, what should I do? 'Love me,' answered my God. 'I do, I do,' I cried passionately. 'Come unto me,' called my Father. 'I will,' my heart panted. Did I stop to ask a single question? Not one. It never occurred to me to ask whether I was good enough, or to hesitate over my unfitness, or to find out what I thought of his church, or . . . to wait until I should be satisfied. Satisfied! I was satisfied. Had I not found my God and my Father? Did he not love me? Had he not called me? Was there not a Church into which I might enter? . . . Since then I have had direct answers to prayer—so significant as to be almost like talking with God and hearing his answer. The idea of God's reality has never left me for one moment."

Here is still another case, the writer being a man aged twenty- 27 seven, in which the experience, probably almost as characteristic, is less vividly described:

I have on a number of occasions felt that I had enjoyed a period of intimate communion with the divine. These meetings came unasked and unexpected, and seemed to consist merely in the temporary obliteration of the conventionalities which usually surround and cover my life. . . . Once it was when from the summit of a high mountain I looked over a gashed and corrugated landscape extending to a long convex of ocean that ascended to the horizon, and again from the same point when I could see nothing beneath me but a boundless expanse of white cloud, on the blown surface of which a few high peaks, including the one I was on, seemed plunging about as if they were dragging their anchors. What I felt on these occasions was a temporary loss of my own identity, accompanied by an illumination which revealed to me a deeper significance than I had been wont to attach to life. It is in this that I find my justification for saying that I have enjoyed communication with God. Of course the absence of such a being as this would be chaos. I cannot conceive of life without its presence.

Of the more habitual and so to speak chronic sense of God's pres- 28 ence the following sample from Professor Starbuck's manuscript collection may serve to give an idea. It is from a man aged forty-nine— probably thousands of unpretending Christians would write an almost identical account.

> God is more real to me than any thought or thing or person. I feel his presence positively, and the more as I live in closer harmony with his laws as written in my body and mind. I feel him in the sunshine or rain; and awe mingled with a delicious restfulness most nearly describes my feelings. I talk to him as to a companion in prayer and praise, and our communion is delightful. He answers me again and again, often in words so clearly spoken that it seems my outer ear must have carried the tone, but generally in strong mental impressions. Usually a text of Scripture, unfolding some new view of him and his love for me, and care for my safety. I could give hundreds of instances, in school matters, social problems, financial difficulties, etc. That he is mine and I am his never leaves me, it is an abiding joy. Without it life would be a blank, a desert, a shoreless, trackless waste.

I subjoin[23] some more examples from writers of different ages and 29 sexes. They are also from Professor Starbuck's collection, and their number might be greatly multiplied. The first is from a man twenty-seven years old:

> God is quite real to me. I talk to him and often get answers. Thoughts sudden and distinct from any I have been entertaining come to my mind after asking God for his direction. Something over a year ago I was for some weeks in the direst perplexity. When the trouble first appeared before me I was dazed, but before long (two or three hours) I could hear distinctly a passage of Scripture: "My grace is sufficient for thee." Every time my thoughts turned to the trouble I could hear this quotation. I don't think I ever doubted the existence of God,

---

[23]***subjoin*** add below.

or had him drop out of my consciousness. God has frequently stepped into my affairs very perceptibly, and I feel that he directs many little details all the time. But on two or three occasions he has ordered ways for me very contrary to my ambitions and plans.

Another statement (none the less valuable psychologically for 30 being so decidedly childish) is that of a boy of seventeen:

> Sometimes as I go to church, I sit down, join in the service, and before I go out I feel as if God was with me, right side of me, singing and reading the Psalms with me. . . . And then again I feel as if I could sit beside him, and put my arms around him, kiss him, etc. When I am taking Holy Communion at the altar, I try to get with him and generally feel his presence.

I let a few other cases follow at random: 31

> God surrounds me like the physical atmosphere. He is closer to me than my own breath. In him literally I live and move and have my being.—
> There are times when I seem to stand in his very presence, to talk with him. Answers to prayer have come, sometimes direct and overwhelming in their revelation of his presence and powers. There are times when God seems far off, but this is always my own fault.—
> I have the sense of a presence, strong, and at the same time soothing, which hovers over me. Sometimes it seems to enwrap me with sustaining arms.

Such is the human ontological[24] imagination, and such is the con- 32 vincingness of what it brings to birth. Unpicturable beings are realized, and realized with an intensity almost like that of an hallucination. They determine our vital attitude as decisively as the vital attitude of lovers is determined by the habitual sense, by which each is haunted, of the other being in the world. A lover has notoriously this sense of the continuous being of his idol, even when his attention is addressed to other matters and he no longer represents her features. He cannot forget her; she uninterruptedly affects him through and through.

I spoke of the convincingness of these feelings of reality, and I must 33 dwell a moment longer on that point. They are as convincing to those who have them as any direct sensible experiences can be, and they are, as a rule, much more convincing than results established by mere logic ever are. One may indeed be entirely without them; probably more

---

[24]**ontological** Pertaining to a theory of being or reality; sense of existence.

than one of you here present is without them in any marked degree; but if you do have them, and have them at all strongly, the probability is that you cannot help regarding them as genuine perceptions of truth, as revelations of a kind of reality which no adverse argument, however unanswerable by you in words, can expel from your belief. The opinion opposed to mysticism in philosophy is sometimes spoken of as *rationalism*. Rationalism[25] insists that all our beliefs ought ultimately to find for themselves articulate grounds. Such grounds, for rationalism, must consist of four things: (1) definitely statable abstract principles; (2) definite facts of sensation; (3) definite hypotheses based on such facts; and (4) definite inferences logically drawn. Vague impressions of something indefinable have no place in the rationalistic system, which on its positive side is surely a splendid intellectual tendency, for not only are all our philosophies fruits of it, but physical science (among other good things) is its result.

Nevertheless, if we look on man's whole mental life as it exists, on the life of men that lies in them apart from their learning and science, and that they inwardly and privately follow, we have to confess that the part of it of which rationalism can give an account is relatively superficial. It is the part that has the *prestige* undoubtedly, for it has the loquacity,[26] it can challenge you for proofs, and chop logic, and put you down with words. But it will fail to convince or convert you all the same, if your dumb intuitions are opposed to its conclusions. If you have intuitions at all, they come from a deeper level of your nature than the loquacious level which rationalism inhabits. Your whole subconscious life, your impulses, your faiths, your needs, your divinations, have prepared the premises, of which your consciousness now feels the weight of the result; and something in you absolutely *knows* that that result must be truer than any logic-chopping rationalistic talk, however clever, that may contradict it. This inferiority of the rationalistic level in founding belief is just as manifest when rationalism argues for religion as when it argues against it. That vast literature of proofs of God's existence drawn from the order of nature, which a century ago seemed so overwhelmingly convincing, today does little more than gather dust in libraries, for the simple reason that our generation has ceased to believe in the kind of God it argued for. Whatever sort of a being God may be, we *know* today that he is nevermore that

34

---

[25]***Rationalism*** philosophy that emphasizes logic and reason; it is generally opposed to James's views.

[26]***loquacity*** verbal ease; talkativeness.

mere external inventor of "contrivances"[27] intended to make manifest his "glory" in which our great-grandfathers took such satisfaction, though just how we know this we cannot possibly make clear by words either to others or to ourselves. I defy any of you here fully to account for your persuasion that if a God exist he must be a more cosmic and tragic personage than that Being.

The truth is that in the metaphysical and religious sphere, articu- 35 late reasons are cogent for us only when our inarticulate feelings of reality have already been impressed in favor of the same conclusion. Then, indeed, our intuitions and our reason work together, and great world-ruling systems, like that of the Buddhist or of the Catholic philosophy, may grow up. Our impulsive belief is here always what sets up the original body of truth, and our articulately verbalized philosophy is but its showy translation into formulas. The unreasoned and immediate assurance is the deep thing in us, the reasoned argument is but a surface exhibition. Instinct leads, intelligence does but follow. If a person feels the presence of a living God after the fashion shown by my quotations, your critical arguments, be they never so superior, will vainly set themselves to change his faith.

Please observe, however, that I do not yet say that it is *better* that 36 the subconscious and non-rational should thus hold primacy in the religious realm. I confine myself to simply pointing out that they do so hold it as a matter of fact.

So much for our sense of the reality of the religious objects. Let me 37 now say a brief word more about the attitudes they characteristically awaken.

We have already agreed that they are *solemn;* and we have seen 38 reason to think that the most distinctive of them is the sort of joy which may result in extreme cases from absolute self-surrender. The sense of the kind of object to which the surrender is made has much to do with determining the precise complexion of the joy; and the whole phenomenon is more complex than any simple formula allows. In the literature of the subject, sadness and gladness have each been emphasized in turn. The ancient saying that the first maker of the Gods was fear receives voluminous corroboration from every age of religious history; but none the less does religious history show the part

---

[27]**contrivances** James belittles the Puritan views that God works various "schemes" to permit his people to magnify his glory. His implication is that God is within rather than without us.

which joy has evermore tended to play. Sometimes the joy has been primary; sometimes secondary, being the gladness of deliverance from the fear. This latter state of things, being the more complex, is also the more complete; and as we proceed, I think we shall have abundant reason for refusing to leave out either the sadness or the gladness, if we look at religion with the breadth of view which it demands. Stated in the completest possible terms, a man's religion involves both moods of contraction and moods of expansion of his being. But the quantitative mixture and order of these moods vary so much from one age of the world, from one system of thought, and from one individual to another, that you may insist either on the dread and the submission, or on the peace and the freedom as the essence of the matter, and still remain materially within the limits of the truth. The constitutionally somber and the constitutionally sanguine onlooker are bound to emphasize opposite aspects of what lies before their eyes.

The constitutionally somber religious person makes even of his religious peace a very sober thing. Danger still hovers in the air about it. Flexion and contraction are not wholly checked. It were sparrowlike and childish after our deliverance to explode into twittering laughter and caper-cutting, and utterly to forget the imminent hawk on bough. Lie low, rather, lie low; for you are in the hands of a living God. In the Book of Job,[28] for example, the impotence of man and the omnipotence of God is the exclusive burden of its author's mind. "It is as high as heaven; what canst thou do?—deeper than hell; what canst thou know?" There is an astringent relish about the truth of this conviction which some men can feel, and which for them is as near an approach as can be made to the feeling of religious joy.

> "In Job," says that coldly truthful writer, the author of Mark Rutherford, "God reminds us that man is not the measure of his creation. The world is immense, constructed on no plan or theory which the intellect of man can grasp. It is *transcendent* everywhere. This is the burden of every verse, and is the secret, if there be one, of the poem. Sufficient or insufficient, there is nothing more. . . . God is great, we know not his ways. He takes from us all we have, but yet if we possess our souls in patience, we *may* pass the valley of the shadow, and come out in sunlight again. We may or we may not! . . . What more have

---

[28]*the Book of Job* Biblical book in which God allows Job, "a perfect and an upright man," to suffer Satan's torments—he loses his property, his children die, he is "afflicted with sore boils." Against the urgings of his wife and his friends, Job refuses to accuse God of injustice. At the end, God appears, asserts his awesome power, and restores Job.

39

we to say now than God said from the whirlwind over two thousand five hundred years ago?"[29]

If we turn to the sanguine onlooker, on the other hand, we find [40] that deliverance is felt as incomplete unless the burden be altogether overcome and the danger forgotten. Such onlookers give us definitions that seem to the somber minds of whom we have just been speaking to leave out all the solemnity that makes religious peace so different from merely animal joys. In the opinion of some writers an attitude might be called religious, though no touch were left in it of sacrifice or submission, no tendency to flexion, no bowing of the head. Any "habitual and regulated admiration," says Professor J. R. Seeley,[30] "is worthy to be called a religion"; and accordingly he thinks that our Music, our Science, and our so-called "Civilization," as these things are now organized and admiringly believed in, form the more genuine religions of our time. Certainly the unhesitating and unreasoning way in which we feel that we must inflict our civilization upon "lower" races, by means of Hotchkiss guns,[31] etc., reminds one of nothing so much as of the early spirit of Islam[32] spreading its religion by the sword.

In my last lecture I quoted to you the ultra-radical opinion of Mr. [41] Havelock Ellis,[33] that laughter of any sort may be considered a religious exercise, for it bears witness to the soul's emancipation. I quoted this opinion in order to deny its adequacy. But we must now settle our scores more carefully with this whole optimistic way of thinking. It is far too complex to be decided off-hand. I propose accordingly that we make of religious optimism the theme of the next two lectures.

---

[29]*Mark Rutherford's Deliverance*, London, 1885, pp. 196, 198. [James's note] One of three novels written by William Hale White under the pen name of Mark Rutherford. White had intended to be a congregational minister.

[30]In his book (too little read, I fear), *Natural Religion*, 3d edition, Boston, 1886, pp. 91, 122. [James's note]

[31]**Hotchkiss guns** Automatic guns. The point is that Europeans forced their civilization on others.

[32]**Islam** In the seventh century Mohammed spread his religion by conquest and war.

[33]**Havelock Ellis (1859–1939)** English psychologist and author.

QUESTIONS

1. How does James make the connection between psychology and religion? Is this lecture more about one than the other?

2. James defines religion: "one might say that it consists of the belief that there is an unseen order, and that our supreme good lies in harmoniously adjusting ourselves thereto" (para. 1). What does he mean by this statement? Do you agree with him? Is it a good definition?

3. Which item of "testimony" do you find least effective in James's lecture? Which is most effective? What qualities make them most or least effective?

4. What are the strengths and the weaknesses of the topic of testimony?

5. Do you agree with the conclusions James reaches in paragraph 33 concerning the limits of rationalism?

6. Has James established the reality of the unseen in this lecture? If so, how? If not, why not?

WRITING ASSIGNMENTS

1. Establish the validity (or the inaccuracy) of James's statement: "All our attitudes, moral, practical, or emotional, as well as religious, are due to the 'objects' of our consciousness, the things which we believe to exist, whether really or ideally, along with ourselves" (para. 1). In the process, explain what " 'objects' of our consciousness" are and make the distinction between the real and ideal ways in which things can exist.

2. The psychology of religion usually contains concepts of good and bad. Are there, in the testimonies that James presents, evidences of good and/or bad forces or feelings associated with the experiences described? Do these forces or feelings have any implications for concepts of goodness or badness as applied to the psychology of religion in James's terms? Judging from James's samples, are concepts of good and bad essential to the religious experience?

3. If you or someone you know has had an experience of one or more of the kinds James mentions, try to fit it into the pattern of experiences he describes. Where would he fit the experience you and your acquaintance had? In your essay, describe the experience in a manner similar to the way James describes his items of testimony, then draw what conclusions you can from the experience and its relationship to James's lecture. Does your experience add to or weaken the meaning of the testimonies he has collected?

4. Use the topic of testimony yourself. Gather experiences from at least four people concerning their sense of the reality of the unseen. Ask them whether they have had awarenesses of presences of people or things that

they could not actually see. Ask them to tell you about those experiences. Write them down carefully so that you can include them in an essay. Then draw a conclusion: Do the experiences you collected now correlate with the experiences James was able to collect almost a hundred years ago? Point out the consistencies or inconsistencies between James's and your evidence as you go along.

5. Has James's argument convinced you of the importance of the unseen? If you found yourself skeptical as you approached this lecture, but then realized that James had conquered your skepticism, write an essay explaining how he was able to "convert" you to his way of thinking. You may want to clarify distinctions between your thought and his, but concentrate on an analysis of his argument and his testimonies in order to show how he was able to convince you of his position. In the process, consider the question of how important his first ten paragraphs are for helping to overcome the resistance of a skeptic.

6. Analyze the content of paragraph 34. Judging from your experience and the experience of others, is James correct about the limits of rationalism in our lives? Consider comments in paragraph 35 such as, "Instinct leads, intelligence does but follow." Is this statement true? What are the dangers of accepting this kind of thinking? What are its implications for education? Does this section of the conclusion really help explain the power of religion in the lives of many people? In what other areas of life might the power of the intuition or "unreason" have sway?

SIGMUND FREUD

Infantile Sexuality

SIGMUND FREUD (1856–1939) is, in the minds of many, the father of modern psychology. He developed the psychoanalytic method,
the examination of the mind using methods of dream analysis, the
analysis of the unconscious through free association, and the correlation of findings with attitudes toward sexuality and sexual development. His theories changed the way people treated neurosis and
most other mental disorders. Today his theories are spread all over
the world.

Freud was born in Freiberg, Moravia (now in Czechoslovakia),
and moved to Vienna, Austria, when he was four. He lived and
worked in Vienna until he was put under house arrest by the Nazis.
He was released in 1938 and moved to London. The psychoanalytic
movement of the twentieth century has often been described as a Viennese movement, or at least as a movement closely tied to the prosperity of the Viennese middle-class intellectuals of the time.

As a movement, psychoanalysis shocked most of the world by
postulating a superego, which establishes high standards of behavior;

From *Three Essays on the Theory of Sexuality*. Translated by A. A. Brill.

an ego, which corresponds to the apparent personality; an id, which includes the deepest primitive forces of life; and an unconscious into which thoughts and memories we cannot face are "repressed" or "sublimated." The origin of much mental illness, the theory presumes, is in the inability of the mind to find a way to sublimate—express in harmless and often creative ways—the painful thoughts which have been repressed. Dreams and unconscious actions sometimes act as "releases" or harmless expressions of these thoughts and memories.

Difficult as some of these ideas were to accept, they did not cause quite the furor of the present excerpt, from a book that was hotly debated and sometimes violently rejected: Three Essays on the Theory of Sexuality *(1905). At that time, Freud had become convinced by his work with neurotic patients that much of what disturbed them was connected with their sexuality. That led him to review the research on infantile sexuality and add to it with his own findings. It was also natural to his way of thinking to produce a theory of behavior built upon his researches.*

What infuriated people so much was the suggestion that tiny children, even infants, had a sexual life. That it should also figure in the psychological health of the adult was almost as serious. Most people rejected the idea out of hand because it did not square with what they already believed or with what they felt they observed. The typical Freudian habit of seeing psychoanalytic "meaning" in otherwise innocent gestures, such as thumbsucking and bed-wetting, was brought into play in his observations on the sexuality of infants. Freud had a gift for interpretation—analysis—of apparently meaningless events. His capacity to find meaning in such events is still resented by many readers, but that is in part because they do not accept Freud's view that the psychological being—the person— makes every word, gesture, and act "meaningful" to his whole being. For Freud there are no accidents; there are psychological intentions. When we understand those intentions, we begin to understand ourselves.

Freud knew that sexuality was perhaps the most powerful force in the psyche. He knew that middle-class propriety would be revolted by having to contemplate the concepts he presents in this piece. It is doubtful that he expected the middle class to accept his views. Yet he was rightly convinced that his views were too important to be swept aside in fear that society might be offended.

FREUD'S RHETORIC

Because this treatise is not aimed at a general public, Freud is left free to address a general scientific community. He spares them no details regarding bodily functions; he adds little color to an already graceful style. His rhetorical technique is quite simple: he establishes a theory, reviews the evidence which he and others have gathered, then derives certain conclusions from his process.

One would not think of this piece as having a beginning, a middle, and a conclusion. It has rather independent sections that treat specific problems and observations. All of the sections come under the general heading of infantile sexuality, and all relate to the general theory that Freud develops: that there is a connection between infantile sexuality and mature sexuality and that it is revealed in the common amnesia—the forgetting or repressing from conscious memory—of experiences related to sexual awareness in both the infant and the hysteric patient.

If one had to give a name to his rhetorical approach, it might best be called the process of evidence and inference. In this sense, it is similar to the accepted methods of science in most fields. Evidence points to an inference, which then must be tested by analysis. We observe the process as we read Freud's work.

This method sounds very straightforward and artless. Freud's writing is generally marked by those qualities. But there is one rhetorical technique which he is the master of: the memorable phrase. For example, the term "psychoanalysis," which we take so much for granted, was invented by Freud when he was thirty-nine; it is now universally used. The term "Oedipus complex," describing the condition of wishing your same-sex parent dead so that you will be left to "marry" your opposite-sex parent, is also universal now. "Penis envy," used in this selection, is known worldwide, as is the "castration complex." Freud changed both our language and our world.

Infantile Sexuality

The Neglect of the Infantile. It is a part of popular belief about the   1
sexual instinct that it is absent in childhood and that it first appears
in the period of life known as puberty. This, though a common error,
is serious in its consequences and is chiefly due to our ignorance of
the fundamental principles of the sexual life. A comprehensive study
of the sexual manifestations of childhood would probably reveal to us
the essential features of the sexual instinct and would show us its
development and its composition from various sources.

It is quite remarkable that those writers who endeavor to explain   2
the qualities and reactions of the adult individual have given so much
more attention to the ancestral period than to the period of the individual's own existence—that is, they have attributed more influence
to heredity than to childhood. As a matter of fact, it might well be
supposed that the influence of the latter period would be easier to understand, and that it would be entitled to more consideration than heredity. To be sure, one occasionally finds in medical literature notes
on the premature sexual activities of small children, about erections
and masturbation and even reactions resembling coitus, but these are
referred to merely as exceptional occurrences, as curiosities, or as
deterring[1] examples of premature perversity. No author has, to my
knowledge, recognized the normality of the sexual instinct in childhood, and in the numerous writings on the development of the child
the chapter on "Sexual Development" is usually passed over.

Infantile Amnesia. The reason for this remarkable negligence I seek   3
partly in conventional considerations, which influence writers because
of their own bringing up, and partly to a psychic phenomenon which
thus far has remained unexplained. I refer to the peculiar amnesia
which veils from most people (not from all) the first years of their
childhood, usually the first six or eight years. So far, it has not occurred to us that this amnesia should surprise us, though we have good
reasons for it. For we are informed that during those years which have
left nothing except a few incomprehensible memory fragments, we

---

[1]*deterring* frightening.

258

have vividly reacted to impressions, that we have manifested human pain and pleasure and that we have expressed love, jealousy and other passions as they then affected us. Indeed, we are told that we have uttered remarks which proved to grown-ups that we possessed understanding and a budding power of judgment. Still we know nothing of all this when we become older. Why does our memory lag behind all our other psychic activities? We really have reason to believe that at no time of life are we more capable of impressions and reproductions[2] than during the years of childhood.

On the other hand we must assume, or we may convince ourselves   4 through psychological observations on others, that the very impressions which we have forgotten have nevertheless left the deepest traces in our psychic life, and acted as determinants for our whole future development. We conclude therefore that we do not deal with a real forgetting of infantile impressions but rather with an amnesia similar to that observed in neurotics for later experiences, the nature of which consists in their being kept away from consciousness (repression). But what forces bring about this repression of the infantile impressions? He who can solve this riddle will also explain hysterical amnesia.[3]

We shall not, however, hesitate to assert that the existence of the   5 infantile amnesia gives us a new point of comparison between the psychic states of the child and those of the psychoneurotic. We have already encountered another point of comparison when confronted by the fact that the sexuality of the psychoneurotic preserves the infantile character or has returned to it. May there not be an ultimate connection between the infantile and the hysterical amnesias?

The connection between infantile and hysterical amnesias is really   6 more than a mere play of wit. Hysterical amnesia which serves the repression can only be explained by the fact that the individual already possesses a sum of memories which were withdrawn from conscious disposal and which by associative connection now seize that which is acted upon by the repelling forces of the repression emanating from consciousness. We may say that without infantile amnesia there would be no hysterical amnesia.

I therefore believe that the infantile amnesia which causes the in-   7 dividual to look upon his childhood as if it were a *prehistoric* time and

---

[2]***reproductions*** imitations, such as mimicry.

[3]***hysterical amnesia*** The forgetfulness induced by psychological shock; Freud sees a connection between it and the fact that we forget most of our earliest experience, even though it is of crucial importance to our growth.

conceals from him the beginning of his own sexual life—that this amnesia, is responsible for the fact that one does not usually attribute any value to the infantile period in the development of the sexual life. One single observer cannot fill the gap which has been thus produced in our knowledge. As early as 1896, I had already emphasized the significance of childhood for the origin of certain important phenomena connected with the sexual life, and since then I have not ceased to put into the foreground the importance of the infantile factor for sexuality.

The Sexual Latency Period
of Childhood and Its Interruptions

The extraordinary frequent discoveries of apparently abnormal and exceptional sexual manifestations in childhood, as well as the discovery of infantile reminiscences in neurotics, which were hitherto unconscious, allow us to sketch the following picture of the sexual behavior of childhood. It seems certain that the newborn child brings with it the germs of sexual feelings which continue to develop for some time and then succumb to a progressive suppression, which may in turn be broken through by the regular advances of the sexual development or may be checked by individual idiosyncrasies. Nothing is known concerning the laws and periodicity of this oscillating course of development. It seems, however, that the sexual life of the child mostly manifests itself in the third or fourth year in some form accessible to observation. 8

Sexual Inhibition. It is during this period of total or at least partial latency[4] that the psychic forces develop which later act as inhibitions on the sexual life, and narrow its direction like dams. These psychic forces are loathing, shame, and moral and esthetic ideal demands. We may gain the impression that the erection of these dams in the civilized child is the work of education; and surely education contributes much to it. In reality, however, this development is organically determined and can occasionally be produced without the help of education. Indeed education remains properly within its assigned domain if 9

---

[4]*latency*   period when sexual interests are not evident, as before puberty.

it strictly follows the path laid out by the organic,[5] and only imprints it somewhat cleaner and deeper.

Reaction Formation and Sublimation. What are the means that ac- 10 complish these very important constructions so important for the later personal culture and normality? They are probably brought about at the cost of the infantile sexuality itself. The influx of this sexuality does not stop even in this latency period, but its energy is deflected either wholly or partially from sexual utilization and conducted to other aims. The historians of civilization seem to be unanimous in the opinion that such deflection of sexual motive powers from sexual aims to new aims, a process which merits the name of *sublimation*,[6] has furnished powerful components for all cultural accomplishments. We will, therefore, add that the same process acts in the development of every individual, and that it begins to act in the sexual latency period.

We can also venture an opinion about the mechanisms of such sub- 11 limation. The sexual feelings of these infantile years would on the one hand be unusable, since the procreating functions are postponed—this is the chief character of the latency period; on the other hand, they would as such be perverse, as they would emanate from erogenous zones and from impulses which in the individual's course of development could only evoke a feeling of displeasure. They, therefore, awaken psychic counterforces (feelings of reaction), which build up the already mentioned psychical dams of disgust, shame and morality.

The Interruptions of the Latency Period. Without deluding ourselves 12 as to the hypothetical nature and deficient clearness of our understanding regarding the infantile period of latency and delay, we will return to reality and state that such a utilization of the infantile sexuality represents an ideal bringing up from which the development of the individual usually deviates in some measure, often very considerably. A part of the sexual manifestation which has withdrawn from sublimation occasionally breaks through, or a sexual activity remains throughout the whole duration of the latency period until the rein-

---

[5]**the organic** Freud means that the organism—the person—comes to certain understandings as a factor of growth and development. Education must respect organic growth and try not to get "out of order" with it.

[6]**sublimation** A psychological process whereby drives, such as the sexual drive, are transformed into different expressions, such as transforming a powerful sexual drive into a drive to make money or to excel in a given field.

forced breaking through of the sexual instinct in puberty. In so far as they have paid any attention to infantile sexuality, the educators behave as if they shared our views concerning the formation of the moral defense forces at the cost of sexuality. They seem to know that sexual activity makes the child uneducable, for they consider all sexual manifestations of the child as an "evil" in the face of which little can be accomplished. We have, however, every reason for directing our attention to those phenomena so much feared by the educators, for we expect to find in them the solution of the primary structure of the sexual instinct.

The Manifestations of
Infantile Sexuality

Thumbsucking. For reasons which we shall discuss later, we will take 13 as a model of the infantile sexual manifestations thumbsucking, to which the Hungarian pediatrist, Lindner, has devoted an excellent essay.

Thumbsucking, which manifests itself in the nursing baby and 14 which may be continued till maturity or throughout life, consists in a rhythmic repetition of sucking contact with the mouth (the lips), wherein the purpose of taking nourishment is excluded. A part of the lip itself, the tongue, which is another preferable skin region within reach, and even the big toe—may be taken as objects for sucking. Simultaneously, there is also a desire to grasp things, which manifests itself in a rhythmical pulling of the ear lobe and which may cause the child to grasp a part of another person (generally the ear) for the same purpose. The pleasure-sucking is connected with a full absorption of attention and leads to sleep or even to a motor reaction in the form of an orgasm. Pleasure-sucking is often combined with a rubbing contact with certain sensitive parts of the body, such as the breast and external genitals. It is by this path that many children go from thumbsucking to masturbation.

Lindner himself clearly recognized the sexual nature of this activ- 15 ity and openly emphasized it. In the nursery, thumbsucking is often treated in the same way as any other sexual "naughtiness" of the child. A very strong objection was raised against this view by many pediatrists and neurologists, which in part is certainly due to the confusion between the terms "sexual" and "genital." This contradiction raises the difficult question, which cannot be avoided, namely, in what general traits do we wish to recognize the sexual expression of the child.

I believe that the association of the manifestations into which we have gained an insight through psychoanalytic investigation justifies us in claiming thumbsucking as a sexual activity. Through thumbsucking we can study directly the essential features of infantile sexual activities.

Autoerotism. It is our duty here to devote more time to this manifestation. Let us emphasize the most striking character of this sexual activity which is, that the impulse is not directed to other persons but that the child gratifies himself on his own body; to use the happy term invented by Havelock Ellis, we will say that he is *autoerotic.*[7]   16

It is, moreover, clear that the action of the thumbsucking child is   17 determined by the fact that he seeks a pleasure which he has already experienced and now remembers. Through the rhythmic sucking on a portion of the skin or mucous membrane, he finds gratification in the simplest way. It is also easy to conjecture on what occasions the child first experienced this pleasure which he now strives to renew. The first and most important activity in the child's life, the sucking from the mother's breast (or its substitute), must have acquainted him with this pleasure. We would say that the child's lips behaved like an *erogenous zone,* and that the stimulus from the warm stream of milk was really the cause of the pleasurable sensation. To be sure, the gratification of the erogenous zone was at first united with the gratification of the need for nourishment. The sexual activity leans first on one of the self-preservative functions and only later makes itself independent of it. He who sees a satiated child sink back from the mother's breast and fall asleep with reddened cheeks and blissful smile, will have to admit that this picture remains as typical of the expression of sexual gratification in later life. But the desire for repetition of sexual gratification is then separated from the desire for taking nourishment; a separation which becomes unavoidable with the appearance of teeth when the nourishment is no longer sucked but chewed. The child does not make use of a strange object for sucking but prefers his own skin, because it is more convenient, because it thus makes himself independent of the outer world which he cannot control, and because in this way he creates for himself, as it were, a second, even if an inferior, erogenous zone. This inferiority of this second region urges him later to seek the same parts, the lips of another person. ("It is a pity that I cannot kiss myself," might be attributed to him.)

---

[7] **autoerotic** English psychologist Havelock Ellis (1859–1939) used the term to refer to masturbatory behavior.

Not all children suck their thumbs. It may be assumed that it is 18 found only in children in whom the erogenous significance of the lip-zone is constitutionally reinforced. If the latter is retained in some children, they develop into kissing epicures with a tendency to perverse kissing, or as men, they show a strong desire for drinking and smoking. But should repression come into play, they then show disgust for eating and evince hysterical vomiting. By virtue of the community of the lip-zone, the repression encroaches upon the instinct of nourishment. Many of my female patients showing disturbances in eating, such as *hysterical globus*,[8] choking sensations and vomiting have been energetic thumbsuckers in infancy.

In thumbsucking or pleasure-sucking, we are already able to observe the three essential characters of an infantile sexual manifestation. It has its origin in an *anaclitic*[9] relation to a physical function which is very important for life; it does not yet know any sexual object, that is, it is *autoerotic*, and its sexual aim is under the control of an *erogenous zone*. Let us assume for the present that these characteristics also hold true for most of the other activities of the infantile sexual instinct.

The Sexual Aim of the Infantile Sexuality

Characteristic Erogenous Zones. From the example of thumbsucking, 20 we may gather a great many points useful for distinguishing an erogenous zone. It is a portion of skin or mucous membrane in which stimuli produce a feeling of pleasure of definite quality. There is no doubt that the pleasure-producing stimuli are governed by special conditions; as yet we do not know them. The rhythmic characters must play some part and this strongly suggests an analogy to tickling. It does not, however, appear so certain whether the character of the pleasurable feeling evoked by the stimulus can be designated as "peculiar," and in what part of this peculiarity the sexual factor consists. Psychology is still groping in the dark when it concerns matters of pleasure and pain, and the most cautious assumption is therefore the most advisable. We may perhaps later come upon reasons which seem to support the peculiar quality of the sensation of pleasure.

---

[8]**hysterical globus** abnormal reaction to putting things in the mouth.
[9]**anaclitic** characterized by a strong emotional—but not sexual—dependence.

The erogenous quality may adhere most notably to definite regions 21
of the body. As is shown by the example of thumbsucking, there are
predestined erogenous zones. But the same example also shows that
any other region of skin or mucous membrane may assume the function of an erogenous zone, hence it must bring along a certain adapt-
ability for it. The production of the sensation of pleasure therefore depends more on the quality of the stimulus than on the nature of the
bodily region. The thumbsucking child looks around on his body and
selects any portion of it for pleasure-sucking, and becoming accustomed to this particular part, he then prefers it. If he accidentally
strikes upon a predestined region, such as breast, nipple or genitals, it
naturally gets the preference. A very analogous tendency to displacement is again found in the symptomatology of hysteria. In this neurosis, the repression mostly affects the genital zones proper, and they
in turn transmit their excitability to the other zones which are usually
dormant in adult life, but then behave exactly like genitals. But besides this, just as in thumbsucking, any other region of the body may
become endowed with the excitation of the genitals and raised to an
erogenous zone. Erogenous and hysterogenous zones show the same
characters.[10]

The Infantile Sexual Aim. The sexual aim of the infantile impulse 22
consists in the production of gratification through the proper excitation of this or that selected erogenous zone. To have a desire for its
repetition, this gratification must have been previously experienced,
and we may be sure that nature has devised definite means so as not
to leave this experience of gratification to mere chance. The arrangement which has fulfilled this purpose for the lip-zone, we have already
discussed; it is the simultaneous connection of this part of the body
with the taking of nourishment. We shall also meet other similar
mechanisms as sources of sexuality. The state of desire for repetition
of gratification can be recognized through a peculiar feeling of tension
which in itself is rather of a painful character, and through a *centrally-
conditioned* feeling of itching or sensitiveness which is projected into
the peripheral erogenous zone. The sexual aim may therefore be formulated by stating that the main object is to substitute for the projected feeling of sensitiveness in the erogenous zone that outer stimulus which removes the feeling of sensitiveness by evoking the feeling

---

[10]Further reflection and evaluation of other observations lead me to attribute the
quality of erotism to all parts of the body and inner organs. [Freud's note]

of gratification. This external stimulus consists usually in a manipulation which is analogous to sucking.

It is in full accord with our physiological knowledge, if the need 23 happens to be awakened also peripherally, through an actual change in the erogenous zone. The action is puzzling only to some extent, as one stimulus seems to want another applied to the same place for its own abrogation.

The Masturbatic
Sexual Manifestations

It is a matter of great satisfaction to know that there is nothing 24 further of great importance to learn about the sexual activity of the child, after the impulse of one erogenous zone has become comprehensible to us. The most pronounced differences are found in the action necessary for the gratification, which consists in sucking for the lip-zone, and which must be replaced by other muscular actions in the other zones, depending on their situation and nature.

The Activity of the Anal Zone. Like the lip-zone, the anal zone is, 25 through its position, adapted to produce an anaclisis of sexuality to other functions of the body. It should be assumed that the erogenous significance of this region of the body was originally very strong. Through psychoanalysis, one finds, not without surprise, the many transformations that normally take place in the sexual excitations emanating from here, and that this zone often retains for life a considerable fragment of genital irritability. The intestinal catarrhs[11] which occur quite frequently during infancy, produce sensitive irritations in this zone, and we often hear it said that intestinal catarrh at this delicate age causes "nervousness." In later neurotic diseases, they exert a definite influence on the symptomatic expression of the neurosis, placing at its disposal the whole sum of intestinal disturbances. Considering the erogenous significance of the anal zone which has been retained at least in transformation, one should not laugh at the hemorrhoidal influences to which the old medical literature attached so much weight in the explanation of neurotic states.

Children utilizing the erogenous sensitiveness of the anal zone, can 26 be recognized by their holding back of fecal masses until through ac-

---

[11]*catarrhs* inflammation of the membrane.

cumulation there result violent muscular contractions; the passage of these masses through the anus is apt to produce a marked irritation of the mucous membrane. Besides the pain, this must also produce a sensation of pleasure. One of the surest premonitions of later eccentricity or nervousness is when an infant obstinately refuses to empty his bowel when placed on the chamber by the nurse, and controls this function at his own pleasure. It naturally does not concern him that he will soil his bed; all he cares for is not to lose the subsidiary pleasure in defecating. Educators have again shown the right inkling when they designate children who withhold these functions as naughty.

27 The content of the bowel which acts as a stimulus to the sexually sensitive surface of mucous membrane, behaves like the precursor of another organ which does not become active until after the phase of childhood. In addition, it has other important meanings to the nursling. It is evidently treated as an additional part of the body; it represents the first "donation," the disposal of which expresses the pliability while the retention of it can express the spite of the little being towards his environment. From the idea of "donation," he later derives the meaning of the "babe," which according to one of the infantile sexual theories, is supposed to be acquired through eating, and born through the bowel.

28 The retention of fecal masses, which is at first intentional in order to utilize them, as it were, for masturbatic excitation of the anal zone, is at least one of the roots of constipation so frequent in neurotics. The whole significance of the anal zone is mirrored in the fact that there are but few neurotics who have not their special scatologic[12] customs, ceremonies, etc., which they retain with cautious secrecy.

29 Real masturbatic irritation of the anal zone by means of the fingers, evoked through either centrally or peripherally supported itching, is not at all rare in older children.

The Activity of the Genital Zone. 30 Among the erogenous zones of the child's body, there is one which certainly does not play the first role, and which cannot be the carrier of the earliest sexual feeling, which, however, is destined for great things in later life. In both male and female, it is connected with the voiding of urine (penis, clitoris), and in the former, it is enclosed in a sack of mucous membrane, probably in order not to miss the irritations caused by the secretions which may arouse sexual excitement at an early age. The sexual activities of this

---

[12]*scatologic*   pertaining to excrement, waste, or feces.

erogenous zone, which belongs to the real genitals, are the beginning of the later "normal" sexual life.

Owing to the anatomical position, the overflowing of secretions, 31 the washing and rubbing of the body, and to certain accidental excitements (the wandering of intestinal worms in the girl), it happens that the pleasurable feeling which these parts of the body are capable of producing makes itself noticeable to the child, even during the sucking age, and thus awakens a desire for repetition. When we consider the sum of all these arrangements and bear in mind that the measures for cleanliness hardly produce a different result than uncleanliness, we can scarcely ignore the fact that the infantile masturbation from which hardly anyone escapes, forms the foundation for the future primacy of this erogenous zone for sexual activity. The action of removing the stimulus and setting free the gratification consists in a rubbing contiguity with the hand or in a certain previously-formed pressure reflex, effected by the closure of the thighs. The latter procedure seems to be the more common in girls. The preference for the hand in boys already indicates what an important part of the male sexual activity will be accomplished in the future by the mastery impulse.

I can only make it clearer if I state that the infantile masturbation 32 should be divided into three phases. The first phase belongs to the nursing period, the second to the short flourishing period of sexual activity at about the fourth year, and only the third corresponds to the one which is often considered exclusively as masturbation of puberty.

Second Phase of Childhood Masturbation. Infantile masturbation 33 seems to disappear after a brief time, but it may continue uninterruptedly till puberty and thus represent the first marked deviation from that development which is desirable for civilized man. At some time during childhood after the nursing period, the sexual instinct of the genitals re-awakens and continues active for some time until it is again suppressed, or it may continue without interruption. The possible relations are very diverse and can only be elucidated through a more precise analysis of individual cases. The details, however, of this *second* infantile sexual activity leave behind the profoundest (unconscious) impressions in the person's memory; if the individual remains healthy they determine his character and if he becomes sick after puberty, they determine the symptomatology of his neurosis. In the latter case, it is found that this sexual period is forgotten and the conscious reminiscences pointing to it are displaced; I have already mentioned that I would like to connect the normal infantile amnesia with this infantile sexual activity. By psychoanalytic investigation, it is possible to bring to consciousness the forgotten material and thereby to remove a compulsion which emanates from the unconscious psychic material.

The Return of Infantile Masturbation. The sexual excitation of the 34 nursing period returns during the designated years of childhood as a centrally determined tickling sensation demanding masturbatic gratification, or as a pollution-like process which, analogous to the pollution of maturity, may attain gratification without the aid of any action. The latter case is more frequent in girls and in the second half of childhood; its determinants are not well understood, but it often, though not regularly, seems to have as a basis a period of early active masturbation. The symptomatology of this sexual manifestation is poor; the genital apparatus is still undeveloped and all signs are therefore displayed by the urinary apparatus which is, so to say, the guardian of the genital apparatus. Most of the so-called bladder disturbances of this period are of a sexual nature; whenever the *enuresis nocturna*[13] does not represent an epileptic attack, it corresponds to a pollution.

The return of the sexual activity is determined by inner and outer 35 causes, which can be conjectured from the formation of the neurotic symptoms and can be definitely revealed by psychoanalytic investigations. The internal causes will be discussed later; the accidental outer causes attain at this time a great and permanent importance. As the first outer cause, there is the influence of seduction which prematurely treats the child as a sexual object; under conditions favoring impressions, this teaches the child the gratification of the genital zones and thus, usually forces it to repeat this gratification in masturbation. Such influences can come from adults or other children. I cannot admit that I overestimated its frequency or its significance in my contributions to the etiology[14] of hysteria, though I did not know then that normal individuals may have the same experiences in their childhood, and hence placed a higher value on seductions than on the factors found in the sexual constitution and development. It is quite obvious that no seduction is necessary to awaken the sexual life of the child, that such an awakening may come on spontaneously from inner sources.

Polymorphous-Perverse Disposition. It is instructive to know that un- 36 der the influence of seduction, the child may become polymorphous-

---

[13]**enuresis nocturna**   nighttime bed-wetting.
[14]*etiology*   the source or cause of something, especially of a disease.

perverse[15] and may be misled into all sorts of transgressions. This goes to show that the child carries along the adaptation for them in his disposition. The formation of such perversions meets but slight resistance because the psychic dams against sexual transgressions, such as shame, loathing and morality—which depend on the age of the child— are not yet erected or are only in the process of formation. In this respect, the child perhaps does not behave differently from the average uncultured woman in whom the same polymorphous-perverse disposition exists. Such a woman may remain sexually normal under usual conditions, but under the guidance of a clever seducer, she will find pleasure in every perversion and will retain it as her sexual activity. The same polymorphous or infantile disposition fits the prostitute for her professional activity, still it is absolutely impossible not to recognize in the uniform disposition to all perversions, as shown by an enormous number of prostitutes and by many women who do not necessarily follow this calling, a universal and primitive human tendency.

Partial Impulses. For the rest, the influence of seduction does not aid us in unravelling the original relations of the sexual instinct, but rather confuses our understanding of the same, inasmuch as it prematurely supplies the child with a sexual object at a time when the infantile sexual instinct does not yet evince any desire for it. We must admit, however, that the infantile sexual life, though mainly under the control of erogenous zones, also shows components which from the very beginning point to other persons as sexual objects. Among these, we may mention the impulses for looking, showing off, and for cruelty, which manifest themselves somewhat independently of the erogenous zones and only later enter into intimate relationship with the sexual life; but along with the erogenous sexual activity they are noticeable even in the infantile years, as separate and independent strivings. The little child is, above all, shameless, and during his early years, he evinces definite pleasure in displaying his body and especially his sex organs. A counterpart to this perverse desire, the curiosity to see other persons' genitals, probably appears first in the later years of childhood when the hindrance of the feeling of shame has already reached a certain development. Under the influence of seduction, the looking perversion may attain great importance for the sexual life of the child. Still, from my investigations of the childhood years

---

[15]***polymorphous-perverse*** Freud's term for a person whose sexual expression is oral, anal, and genital rather than the usual adult expression, essentially genital.

of normal and neurotic patients, I must conclude that the impulse for looking can appear in the child as a spontaneous sexual manifestation. Small children, whose attention has once been directed to their own genitals—usually by masturbation—are wont to progress in this direction without outside interference and to develop a vivid interest in the genitals of their playmates. As the occasion for the gratification of such curiosity is generally afforded during the gratification of both excrementitious needs, such children become *voyeurs*[16] and are zealous spectators at the voiding of urine and feces of others. After this tendency has been repressed, the curiosity to see the genitals of others (one's own or those of the other sex) remains as a tormenting desire which in some neurotic cases, furnishes the strongest motive-power for the formation of symptoms.

The cruelty component of the sexual instinct develops in the child 38 with still greater independence of those sexual activities which are connected with erogenous zones. Cruelty is intimately related to the childish character, since the inhibition which restrains the mastery impulse before it causes pain to others—that is, the capacity for sympathy—develops comparatively late. As we know that a thorough psychological analysis of this impulse has not as yet been successfully done, we may assume that the feelings of cruelty emanate from the mastery impulse and appear at a period in the sexual life before the genitals have taken on their later role. This feeling then dominates a phase of the sexual life which we shall later describe as the pregenital organization. Children who are distinguished for evincing especial cruelty to animals and playmates may be justly suspected of an intensive and a premature sexual activity which emanates from the erogenous zones. But in a simultaneous prematurity of all sexual impulses, the erogenous sexual activity surely seems to be primary. The absence of the barrier of sympathy carries with it the danger that a connection formed in childhood between cruelty and the erogenous impulses will not be broken in later life.

An erogenous source of the passive impulse for cruelty (masoch- 39 ism) is found in the painful irritation of the gluteal region,[17] which is familiar to all educators since the confessions of J. J. Rousseau. This has justly caused them to demand that physical punishment, which is usually directed to this part of the body, should be withheld from all

---

[16]**voyeurs** those who get special pleasure from looking on, especially at something secret or private.

[17]***gluteal region*** the buttocks, where children are spanked. Rousseau in his *Confessions* (1782) admits a certain pleasure in corporal punishment.

children in whom the libido might be forced into collateral roads by the later demands of cultural education.

Study of Infantile
Sexual Investigation

Inquisitiveness. About the same time as the sexual life of the child 40 reaches its first rich development, from the age of three to the age of five, there appear the beginnings of that activity which are ascribed to the impulse for knowledge and investigation. The desire for knowledge can neither be reckoned among the elementary instinctive components, nor can it be altogether subsumed under sexuality. Its activity corresponds, on the one hand, to a sublimated form of acquisition, and on the other hand, the energy with which it works comes from the looking impulse. Its relation to the sexual life, however, is of particular importance, for we have learned from psychoanalysis that the inquisitiveness of children is directed to sexual problems unusually early and in an unexpectedly intensive manner; indeed, curiosity may perhaps first be awakened by sexual problems.

The Riddle of the Sphinx. It is not theoretical but practical interests, 41 which start the work of the child's investigation activity. The menace to the conditions of his existence through the actual or expected arrival of a new child, the fear of losing the care and love which is connected with this event, cause the child to become thoughtful and sagacious.[18] Corresponding with the history of this awakening, the first problem with which he occupies himself is not the question as to the difference between the sexes, but the riddle: Where do children come from? In a distorted form which can easily be unravelled, this is the same riddle which was proposed by the Theban Sphinx.[19] The fact of the two sexes is usually first accepted by the child without struggle and hesitation. It is quite natural for the male child to presuppose in all persons he knows a genital like his own, and to find it impossible to harmonize the lack of it with his conception of others.

The Castration Complex and Penis Envy. This conviction is energet- 42 ically adhered to by the boy and stubbornly defended against the con-

---

[18]*sagacious* shrewd, cunning.
[19]*Theban Sphinx* See n. 41 in the Nietzsche selection, p. 224.

tradictions which soon result, and is only given up after severe internal struggles (castration complex). The substitute formations of this lost penis on the part of the woman play a great role in the formation of many perversions.[20]

The assumption of the same (male) genital in all persons is the first 43 of the remarkable and consequential infantile sexual theories. It is of little help to the child when biological science agrees with his preconceptions and recognizes the feminine clitoris as the real substitute for the penis. The little girl does not react with similar rejections when she sees the differently formed genital of the boy. She is immediately prepared to recognize it and soon becomes envious of the penis; this envy reaches its highest point in the consequentially important wish that she also should be a boy.

Birth Theories. Many people can remember distinctly how intensely 44 they interested themselves, in the prepubescent period, in the question of where children came from. The anatomical solutions at that time read very differently; the children come out of the breast or are cut out of the body, or the navel opens itself to let them out. Outside of analysis, one only seldom remembers this investigation from early childhood years, for it had long since merged into repression; its results, however, are thoroughly uniform. One gets children by eating something special (as in the fairy tale) or they are born through the bowel, like a passage. These infantile theories recall the structures in the animal kingdom, especially the *cloaca*[21] of those animals which are on a lower scale than mammals.

Sadistic Conception of the Sexual Act. If children at so tender an age 45 witness the sexual act between adults, for which an occasion is furnished by the conviction of the adults that little children cannot understand anything sexual, they cannot help conceiving the sexual act as a kind of maltreating or overpowering; that is, it impresses them in a sadistic sense. Psychoanalysis teaches us also that such an early childhood impression contributes much to the disposition for a later sadistic displacement of the sexual aim. Besides this, children also oc-

---

[20]One has the right to speak also of a castration complex in women. Male and female children form the theory that originally the woman, too, had a penis, which has been lost through castration. The conviction finally won (that the woman has no penis) often produces in the male a lasting depreciation of the other sex. [Freud's note]

[21]**cloaca** all-purpose anal opening (as in a frog). The Latin word literally means a sewer.

cupy themselves with the problem of what the sexual act consists, or, as they grasp it, of what marriage consists, and seek the solution to the mystery usually in an intimacy carried on through the functions of urination and defecation.

The Typical Failure of the Infantile Sexual Investigation. It can be   46
stated in general about infantile sexual theories that they are models of the child's own sexual constitution, and that despite their grotesque mistakes, they show more understanding of the sexual processes than is credited to their creators. Children also notice the pregnancy of their mother and know how to interpret it correctly. The stork fable is very often related before auditors who respond with a deep, but mostly mute suspicion. Inasmuch as two elements remain unknown to infantile sexual investigation, namely, the role of the fructifying semen and the existence of the female genital opening—precisely the same points in which the infantile organization is still backward—the effort of the infantile mind regularly remains fruitless and ends in a rejection, which not infrequently leaves a lasting injury to the desire for knowledge. The sexual investigation of these early childhood years is always conducted alone; it signifies the first step towards an independent orientation of the world, and causes a marked estrangement between the child and the persons of his environment who formerly enjoyed his full confidence.

QUESTIONS

1. Freud begins with the question of the neglect of the infantile, the fact that most people paid little attention to the individual child's development (paras. 1–7). Explain what he means in these first seven paragraphs.
2. Children are said to go through a period of sexual latency. Clarify Freud's views on this question.
3. What kinds of sexual instincts are described in this selection? Are they recognizably sexual? Instinctual?
4. What are erogenous zones? Consult paragraph 20 and following.
5. Referring to paragraphs 42–43, clarify what Freud means by "castration complex" and "penis envy." What is their bearing on infantile sexuality?
6. What kind of audience would have found this work interesting and provocative? What kind would have found it repulsive? What kind would have found it unbelievable? Does Freud feel he must convince an unfriendly audience?

WRITING ASSIGNMENTS

1. Freud's complaint concerning the neglect of research and investigation into infantile behavior was written in 1905. Have things changed since then? What makes you feel that there is as much, less, or more neglect now than at that time? Do you feel that most people accept Freud's views on infantile sexuality now? Do you yourself accept his views?

2. Even the general educated public of 1905 found the theories expressed in this work utterly unacceptable. They were revolted both by Freud's views and by his methods of research. What would be distressing, alarming, or revolting about this piece? What could possibly cause people to react violently to Freud's views? Are there still people who would have such a reaction?

3. Take an aspect of Freud's theories with which you disagree and present your own argument. You may resort to your own childhood memories or those of friends. Refer directly to the aspects of Freud's thinking that seem least convincing to you and explore your reasons for rejecting them.

4. In paragraph 18, Freud refers to "kissing epicures." Establish just what is meant by that term, then clarify such persons' behavior. Do such epicures exist today? What is their current behavior? Have you known any? You may wish to supplement your personal knowledge by conducting two or three interviews with people who do know them. Be sure to try to connect your information with Freud's thoughts.

5. You may wish to offer your own theories concerning infantile sexuality. If so, you may use Freud's subject headings (where relevant to your theories) and rewrite the sections using your own thinking, your own evidence, and your own theories. Choose those subject headings that you feel are most important to your ideas. Headings such as "The Sexual Latency Period of Childhood and Its Interruptions," "Sexual Inhibition," and "The Sexual Aim of the Infantile Sexuality" may be of use to you. Naturally, you may make up your own headings if you wish.

6. The concepts of the castration complex and penis envy are both quite controversial. After establishing what Freud means by the terms, examine them to find out whether they are reasonable theories of behavior or whether they are not fully tenable. Moreover, consider the effect of holding such theories on matters related to social behavior—controversies related to feminism, for instance. Gather reactions from your friends. Do their views support Freud's theories or not? Do their views matter to you?

CARL JUNG

------- ✦ -------

The Mother Archetype

CARL JUNG *(1875–1961), probably the most famous disciple of Freud, was a Swiss psychiatrist who collaborated with Freud between 1907 and 1913, breaking from him finally on important doctrinal issues. The basis of their dispute was over the question of the "archetypes" which, for Jung, arise from the "collective unconscious." Both terms need explanation. Jung noticed in his analysis of patients that their dreams were patterned after myths and mythologies that the patients themselves could have had no knowledge of. Furthermore, a study of myths revealed a repository of dreamlike symbols that Jung took to be expressions of psychological elements of the unconscious. The myths, in other words, represented a collective unconscious for a given cultural group and arose from the psychological pressures within the culture.*

Once armed with that view, Jung observed that certain patterns repeated themselves in the myths of a specific culture and, often, in myths of different cultures. The most basic patterns he could discover he called archetypes, which means basic type or pattern. The archetypes he found were, he thought, basic to human psychology and,

---

From *The Archetypes and the Collective Unconscious.* Translated by R. F. C. Hull.

when not adapted to properly, could be the source of psychological disorder. The disorders which arose from a misunderstanding of archetypes he called "complexes," and that term, quickly adopted by Freud and others, has stayed with us as a general expression of disorder.

Jung believed that one of the modern world's problems is that humankind has disregarded its archetypal nature and, through its constructs of logic and reason, lost touch with an important part of itself. Children's stories and myths represent the culture's efforts to stay in touch, and by analyzing the archetypes Jung hoped to reveal one of the sources of modern neurosis.

The mother archetype is basic to all people, just as it is basic to myths of all people. It is a difficult concept offering highly controversial reading of a basic organic, human experience. Freud believed that Jung was on the wrong track in his work; he gave, Freud said, far too much importance to nonrational thought. Freud himself relied on myth occasionally, as in his discussion of the Oedipus complex. But he did not see the source of neurosis as something that is expressed in myth or in anything resembling a collective unconscious. For Freud, the unconscious was a personal repository.

Jung's thinking, however, has been extremely appealing. His followers gathered at the Jung Institute in Zurich, Switzerland, to further his work. The concept of the archetype, with examples in literature abundant everywhere, has been particularly fruitful, and Jungian analysis is thriving at this time. The archetype is a difficult concept, and not necessarily one that we must accept whole. Yet, it offers certain understandings that may not be available otherwise.

JUNG'S RHETORIC

The basis of the selection presented here is simply exposition. Jung establishes that there is such a thing as a mother archetype, describes its nature, points to its manifestation in myth and literature, clarifies its character as both positive and negative (like all archetypes), then proceeds to give us some insight into its effects on both sons and daughters. He establishes the range of symbols which stand for the mother—the cornucopia, the plowed field, a garden, the magic mandala—so that we can see the mode of the unconscious mind, which expresses everything in terms of symbols of the sort that appear in dreams and in literature. Then Jung continues by establishing patterns of behavior in those who identify with the mother and those who resist such identification.

In the process of establishing the nature of the archetype and exposing its qualities and functions, Jung uses the rhetorical device of allusion, often referring to esoteric Eastern writings. One of the richest sources of his allusion, though, is Greek and Roman mythology, the kind that is sometimes taught in grade schools and sometimes learned at a mother's knee. This point is very important, because it establishes a link between the mother and her archetype as expressed in literature and conveyed to the child.

As he discusses the mother archetype, Jung alludes, too, to another of his concepts: the anima (and animus). According to Jung—and apparent to some degree in our biology—there is a psychologically feminine side to each man (anima) and a masculine side to each woman (animus). Learning to live well with these "opposites" in ourselves is essential for psychological harmony. Likewise, learning to live with and to understand archetypes and their extraordinary psychological power is essential for psychological health and growth. Jung's views may seem unusual at first, but they are clearly fascinating and suggestive.

⋅⋅◦∞◦⋅⋅

The Mother Archetype

Like any other archetype, the mother archetype[1] appears under an almost infinite variety of aspects. I mention here only some of the more characteristic. First in importance are the personal mother and grandmother, stepmother and mother-in-law; then any woman with whom a relationship exists—for example, a nurse or governess or perhaps a remote ancestress. Then there are what might be termed mothers in a figurative sense. To this category belongs the goddess, and especially the Mother of God, the Virgin, and Sophia.[2] Mythology of-

1

---

[1] **mother archetype** An archetype is a psychological pattern basic to most or all people. The mother archetype is related to the genuine mother but expresses itself in terms of the symbols Jung discusses. Since the culture supplies the specific symbols, one is responsive to the mother archetype even if one does not know one's own mother.

[2] **Sophia** Greek goddess of wisdom.

fers many variations of the mother archetype, as for instance the mother who reappears as the maiden in the myth of Demeter and Kore;[3] or the mother who is also the beloved, as in the Cybele-Attis myth. Other symbols of the mother in a figurative sense appear in things representing the goal of our longing for redemption, such as Paradise, the Kingdom of God, the Heavenly Jerusalem.[4] Many things arousing devotion or feelings of awe, as for instance the Church, university, city or country, heaven, earth, the woods, the sea or any still waters, matter even, the underworld and the moon, can be mother symbols. The archetype is often associated with things and places standing for fertility and fruitfulness: the cornucopia, a ploughed field, a garden. It can be attached to a rock, a cave, a tree, a spring, a deep well, or to various vessels such as the baptismal font, or to vessel-shaped flowers like the rose or the lotus. Because of the protection it implies, the magic circle or mandala[5] can be a form of mother archetype. Hollow objects such as ovens and cooking vessels are associated with the mother archetype, and, of course, the uterus, yoni,[6] and anything of a like shape. Added to this list there are many animals, such as the cow, hare, and helpful animals in general.

All these symbols can have a positive, favorable meaning or a negative, evil meaning. An ambivalent aspect is seen in the goddesses of fate (Moira, Graeae, Norns).[7] Evil symbols are the witch, the dragon (or any devouring and entwining animal, such as a large fish or a serpent), the grave, the sarcophagus, deep water, death, nightmares and bogies (Empusa, Lilith, etc.).[8] This list is not, of course, complete; it presents only the most important features of the mother archetype.

The qualities associated with it are maternal solicitude and sympathy; the magic authority of the female; the wisdom and spiritual

---

[3]**Demeter and Kore** Demeter was the Greek goddess of the earth and its fertility. Her daughter Kore (the name means "maiden"), also known as Persephone, was abducted by Hades and taken to the underworld. Cybele was a Phrygian mother-goddess; Attis was her son. When he did not return her love, she drove him mad, and he castrated and killed himself.

[4]**Heavenly Jerusalem** Early Christian view of the heavenly city, usually portrayed as walled and circular.

[5]**mandala** circular oriental symbol representing the universe.

[6]**yoni** Indian word for vagina.

[7]**Moira, Graeae, Norns** Moira is the term for any of the many Greek goddesses of fate. The Graeae in Greek mythology were two ancient sisters who lived in a cave and shared one eye and one tooth, passing them back and forth. The Norns were the Norse goddesses of fate.

[8]**Empusa, Lilith** Greek and Hebrew female demons who appear in nightmares.

exaltation that transcend reason; any helpful instinct or impulse; all that is benign, all that cherishes and sustains, that fosters growth and fertility. The place of magic transformation and rebirth, together with the underworld and its inhabitants, are presided over by the mother. On the negative side the mother archetype may connote anything secret, hidden, dark; the abyss, the world of the dead, anything that devours, seduces, and poisons, that is terrifying and inescapable like fate. All these attributes of the mother archetype have been fully described and documented in my book *Symbols of Transformation.* There I formulated the ambivalence of these attributes as "the loving and the terrible mother." Perhaps the historical example of the dual nature of the mother most familiar to us is the Virgin Mary, who is not only the Lord's mother, but also, according to the medieval allegories, his cross. In India, "the loving and terrible mother" is the paradoxical Kali.[9] Sankhya philosophy has elaborated the mother archetype into the concept of *prakṛti* (matter) and assigned to it the three *gunas* or fundamental attributes: *sattva, rajas, tamas:* goodness, passion, and darkness. These are three essential aspects of the mother: her cherishing and nourishing goodness, her orgiastic emotionality, and her Stygian[10] depths. The special feature of the philosophical myth, which shows Prakṛti dancing before Purusha[11] in order to remind him of "discriminating knowledge," does not belong to the mother archetype but to the archetype of the anima,[12] which in a man's psychology invariably appears, at first, mingled with the mother image.

Although the figure of the mother as it appears in folklore is more or less universal, this image changes markedly when it appears in the individual psyche. In treating patients one is at first impressed, and indeed arrested, by the apparent significance of the personal mother. This figure of the personal mother looms so large in all personalistic psychologies that, as we know, they never got beyond it, even in theory, to other important etiological factors.[13] My own view differs from that of other medico-psychological theories principally in that I attribute to the personal mother only a limited etiological significance.

4

---

[9]*Kali* Indian, a divine she-ogre.

[10]*Stygian* Referring to River Styx in Hades; dark and unfathomable.

[11]*Prakṛti dancing before Purusha* In Hindu philosophy and mythology, Purusha is objectless consciousness, the soul. When Prakṛti, material nature, gets its attention, Purusha identifies with Prakṛti and starts the material world evolving. Purusha is seen as a male force, and Prakṛti as female.

[12]*anima* Jung's term for the feminine side of the masculine psyche.

[13]*etiological factors* factors concerning causes or origins.

That is to say, all those influences which the literature describes as being exerted on the children do not come from the mother herself, but rather from the archetype projected upon her, which gives her a mythological background and invests her with authority and numinosity.[14] The etiological and traumatic effects produced by the mother must be divided into two groups: (1) those corresponding to traits of character or attitudes actually present in the mother, and (2) those referring to traits which the mother only seems to possess, the reality being composed of more or less fantastic (i.e., archetypal) projections on the part of the child. Freud himself had already seen that the real etiology of neuroses does not lie in traumatic effects, as he at first suspected, but in a peculiar development of infantile fantasy. This is not to deny that such a development can be traced back to disturbing influences emanating from the mother. I myself make it a rule to look first for the cause of infantile neuroses in the mother, as I know from experience that a child is much more likely to develop normally than neurotically, and that in the great majority of cases definite causes of disturbances can be found in the parents, especially in the mother. The contents of the child's abnormal fantasies can be referred to the personal mother only in part, since they often contain clear and unmistakable allusions which could not possibly have reference to human beings. This is especially true where definitely mythological products are concerned, as is frequently the case in infantile phobias where the mother may appear as a wild beast, a witch, a specter, an ogre, a hermaphrodite, and so on. It must be borne in mind, however, that such fantasies are not always of unmistakably mythological origin, and even if they are, they may not always be rooted in the unconscious archetype but may have been occasioned by fairytales or accidental remarks. A thorough investigation is therefore indicated in each case. For practical reasons, such an investigation cannot be made so readily with children as with adults, who almost invariably transfer their fantasies to the physician during treatment—or, to be more precise, the fantasies are projected upon him automatically.

When that happens, nothing is gained by brushing them aside as   5
ridiculous, for archetypes are among the inalienable assets of every psyche. They form the "treasure in the realm of shadowy thoughts" of

---

[14]**numinosity** Literally, this word means a glow, like a halo; Jung uses it to mean a sense of holiness.

which Kant[15] spoke, and of which we have ample evidence in the countless treasure motifs of mythology. An archetype is in no sense just an annoying prejudice; it becomes so only when it is in the wrong place. In themselves, archetypal images are among the highest values of the human psyche; they have peopled the heavens of all races from time immemorial. To discard them as valueless would be a distinct loss. Our task is not, therefore, to deny the archetype, but to dissolve the projections, in order to restore their contents to the individual who has involuntarily lost them by projecting them outside himself.

The mother archetype forms the foundation of the so-called mother   6
complex. It is an open question whether a mother complex can develop without the mother having taken part in its formation as a demonstrable causal factor. My own experience leads me to believe that the mother always plays an active part in the origin of the disturbance, especially in infantile neuroses or in neuroses whose etiology undoubtedly dates back to early childhood. In any event, the child's instincts are disturbed, and this constellates archetypes which, in their turn, produce fantasies that come between the child and its mother as an alien and often frightening element. Thus, if the children of an overanxious mother regularly dream that she is a terrifying animal or a witch, these experiences point to a split in the child's psyche that predisposes it to a neurosis.

The Mother Complex of the Son

The effects of the mother complex differ according to whether it   7
appears in a son or a daughter. Typical effects on the son are homosexuality and Don Juanism,[16] and sometimes also impotence.[17] In homosexuality, the son's entire heterosexuality is tied to the mother in an unconscious form; in Don Juanism, he unconsciously seeks his mother in every woman he meets. The effects of a mother complex on the son may be seen in the ideology of the Cybele and Attis type: self-castration, madness, and early death. Because of the difference in sex,

---

[15]***Immanuel Kant (1724–1804)*** German idealist philosopher; see n. 4 in the James selection, p. 233. Jung is making an effort to expand Kant's idealism and belief in ideas by suggesting they are perceptions of the archetype.

[16]**Don Juanism** The practice of some males of seducing as many women as possible.

[17]But the father complex also plays a considerable part here. [Jung's note]

a son's mother complex does not appear in pure form. This is the reason why in every masculine mother complex, side by side with the mother archetype, a significant role is played by the image of the man's sexual counterpart, the anima. The mother is the first feminine being with whom the man-to-be comes in contact, and she cannot help playing, overtly or covertly, consciously or unconsciously, upon the son's masculinity, just as the son in his turn grows increasingly aware of his mother's femininity, or unconsciously responds to it by instinct. In the case of the son, therefore, the simple relationships of identity or of resistance and differentiation are continually cut across by erotic attraction or repulsion, which complicates matters very considerably. I do not mean to say that for this reason the mother complex of a son ought to be regarded as more serious than that of a daughter. The investigation of these complex psychic phenomena is still in the pioneer stage. Comparisons will not become feasible until we have some statistics at our disposal, and of these, so far, there is no sign.

Only in the daughter is the mother complex clear and uncompli- 8
cated. Here we have to do either with an overdevelopment of feminine instincts indirectly caused by the mother, or with a weakening of them to the point of complete extinction. In the first case, the preponderance of instinct makes the daughter unconscious of her own personality; in the latter, the instincts are projected upon the mother. For the present we must content ourselves with the statement that in the daughter a mother complex either unduly stimulates or else inhibits the feminine instinct, and that in the son it injures the masculine instinct through an unnatural sexualization.

Since a "mother complex" is a concept borrowed from psychopath- 9
ology, it is always associated with the idea of injury and illness. But if we take the concept out of its narrow psychopathological setting and give it a wider connotation, we can see that it has positive effects as well. Thus a man with a mother complex may have a finely differentiated Eros[18] instead of, or in addition to, homosexuality. (Something of this sort is suggested by Plato in his *Symposium*.)[19] This gives him a great capacity for friendship, which often creates ties of astonishing tenderness between men and may even rescue friendship between the sexes from the limbo of the impossible. He may have good taste and

---

[18]**Eros** Instinct directed toward achieving pleasure, especially sexual pleasure. Eros, in Greek mythology, is the son of Aphrodite, the goddess of love, and the equivalent of Cupid in Roman and other mythology.

[19]**Symposium** Plato's dialogue in which Socrates shows how an appreciation of the beautiful can lead to an understanding of the good.

an aesthetic sense which are fostered by the presence of a feminine streak. Then he may be supremely gifted as a teacher because of his almost feminine insight and tact. He is likely to have a feeling for history, and to be conservative in the best sense and cherish the values of the past. Often he is endowed with a wealth of religious feelings, which help to bring the *ecclesia spiritualis*[20] into reality; and a spiritual receptivity which makes him responsive to revelation.

In the same way, what in its negative aspect is Don Juanism can [10] appear positively as bold and resolute manliness; ambitious striving after the highest goals; opposition to all stupidity, narrow-mindedness, injustice, and laziness; willingness to make sacrifices for what is regarded as right, sometimes bordering on heroism; perseverance, inflexibility and toughness of will; a curiosity that does not shrink even from the riddles of the universe; and finally, a revolutionary spirit which strives to put a new face upon the world.

All these possibilities are reflected in the mythological motifs [11] enumerated earlier as different aspects of the mother archetype. As I have already dealt with the mother complex of the son, including the anima complication, elsewhere, and my present theme is the archetype of the mother, in the following discussion I shall relegate masculine psychology to the background.

The Mother Complex of the Daughter[21]

Hypertrophy of the Maternal Element. We have noted that in the [12] daughter the mother complex leads either to a hypertrophy of the feminine side or to its atrophy.[22] The exaggeration of the feminine side means an intensification of all female instincts, above all the maternal instinct. The negative aspect is seen in the woman whose only goal is childbirth. To her the husband is obviously of secondary importance; he is first and foremost the instrument of procreation, and she regards

---

[20]**ecclesia spiritualis** church of the spirit.

[21]In the present section I propose to present a series of different "types" of mother complex; in formulating them, I am drawing on my own therapeutic experiences. "Types" are not individual cases, neither are they freely invented schemata into which all individual cases have to be fitted. "Types" are ideal instances, or pictures of the average run of experience, with which no single individual can be identified. People whose experience is confined to books or psychological laboratories can form no proper idea of the cumulative experience of a practicing psychologist. [Jung's note]

[22]**hypertrophy . . . atrophy** Hypertrophy is an exaggeration or overdevelopment; atrophy is a withering away or underdevelopment.

him merely as an object to be looked after, along with children, poor relations, cats, dogs, and household furniture. Even her own personality is of secondary importance; she often remains entirely unconscious of it, for her life is lived in and through others, in more or less complete identification with all the objects of her care. First she gives birth to the children, and from then on she clings to them, for without them she has no existence whatsoever. Like Demeter, she compels the gods by her stubborn persistence to grant her the right of possession over her daughter. Her Eros develops exclusively as a maternal relationship while remaining unconscious as a personal one. An unconscious Eros always expresses itself as will to power.[23] Women of this type, though continually "living for others," are, as a matter of fact, unable to make any real sacrifice. Driven by ruthless will to power and a fanatical insistence on their own maternal rights, they often succeed in annihilating not only their own personality but also the personal lives of their children. The less conscious such a mother is of her own personality, the greater and the more violent is her unconscious will to power. For many such women Baubo[24] rather than Demeter would be the appropriate symbol. The mind is not cultivated for its own sake but usually remains in its original condition, altogether primitive, unrelated, and ruthless, but also as true, and sometimes as profound, as Nature herself. She herself does not know this and is therefore unable to appreciate the wittiness of her mind or to marvel philosophically at its profundity; like as not she will immediately forget what she has said.

Overdevelopment of Eros. It by no means follows that the complex 13 induced in a daughter by such a mother must necessarily result in hypertrophy of the maternal instinct. Quite the contrary, this instinct may be wiped out altogether. As a substitute, an overdeveloped Eros results, and this almost invariably leads to an unconscious incestuous relationship with the father.[25] The intensified Eros places an abnormal emphasis on the personality of others. Jealousy of the mother and the desire to outdo her become the leitmotifs[26] of subsequent undertak-

---

[23]This statement is based on the repeated experience that, where love is lacking, power fills the vacuum. [Jung's note]

[24]**Baubo** A goddess who made an obscene gesture when Demeter refused her drink. In Jung's sense, Baubo is a profane deity with a will to power.

[25]Here the initiative comes from the daughter. In other cases the father's psychology is responsible; his projection of the anima arouses an incestuous fixation in the daughter. [Jung's note]

[26]*leitmotifs* themes or patterns that repeat themselves.

ings, which are often disastrous. A woman of this type loves romantic and sensational episodes for their own sake, and is interested in married men, less for themselves than for the fact that they are married and so give her an opportunity to wreck a marriage, that being the whole point of her maneuver. Once the goal is attained, her interest evaporates for lack of any maternal instinct, and then it will be someone else's turn.[27] This type is noted for its remarkable unconsciousness. Such women really seem to be utterly blind to what they are doing,[28] which is anything but advantageous either for themselves or for their victims. I need hardly point out that for men with a passive Eros this type offers an excellent hook for anima projections.

Identity with the Mother. If a mother complex in a woman does not   14
produce an overdeveloped Eros, it leads to identification with the mother and to paralysis of the daughter's feminine initiative. A complete projection of her personality on to the mother then takes place, owing to the fact that she is unconscious both of her maternal instinct and of her Eros. Everything which reminds her of motherhood, responsibility, personal relationships, and erotic demands arouses feelings of inferiority and compels her to run away—to her mother, naturally, who lives to perfection everything that seems unattainable to her daughter. As a sort of superwoman (admired involuntarily by the daughter), the mother lives out for her beforehand all that the girl might have lived for herself. She is content to cling to her mother in selfless devotion, while at the same time unconsciously striving, almost against her will, to tyrannize over her, naturally under the mask of complete loyalty and devotion. The daughter leads a shadow existence, often visibly sucked dry by her mother, and she prolongs her mother's life by a sort of continuous blood transfusion. These bloodless maidens are by no means immune to marriage. On the contrary, despite their shadowiness and passivity, they command a high price on the marriage market. First, they are so empty that a man is free to impute to them anything he fancies. In addition, they are so unconscious that the unconscious puts out countless invisible feelers, veritable octopus tentacles, that suck up all masculine projections; and this pleases men enormously. All that feminine indefiniteness is the longed-for counterpart of male decisiveness and single-mindedness,

---

[27]Herein lies the difference between this type of complex and the feminine father complex related to it, where the "father" is mothered and coddled. [Jung's note]

[28]This does not mean that they are unconscious of the *facts*. It is only their *meaning* that escapes them. [Jung's note]

which can be satisfactorily achieved only if a man can get rid of everything doubtful, ambiguous, vague, and muddled by projecting it upon some charming example of feminine innocence.[29] Because of the woman's characteristic passivity, and the feelings of inferiority which make her continually play the injured innocent, the man finds himself cast in an attractive role: he has the privilege of putting up with the familiar feminine foibles with real superiority, and yet with forbearance, like a true knight. (Fortunately, he remains ignorant of the fact that these deficiencies consist largely of his own projections.) The girl's notorious helplessness is a special attraction. She is so much an appendage of her mother that she can only flutter confusedly when a man approaches. She just doesn't know a thing. She is so inexperienced, so terribly in need of help, that even the gentlest swain becomes a daring abductor who brutally robs a loving mother of her daughter. Such a marvellous opportunity to pass himself off as a gay Lothario does not occur every day and therefore acts as a strong incentive. This was how Pluto abducted Persephone[30] from the inconsolable Demeter. But, by a decree of the gods, he had to surrender his wife every year to his mother-in-law for the summer season. (The attentive reader will note that such legends do not come about by chance!)

Resistance to the Mother. These three extreme types are linked together by many intermediate stages, of which I shall mention only one important example. In the particular intermediate type I have in mind, the problem is less an overdevelopment or an inhibition of the feminine instincts than an overwhelming resistance to maternal supremacy, often to the exclusion of all else. It is the supreme example of the negative mother complex. The motto of this type is: Anything, so long as it is not like Mother! On one hand we have a fascination which never reaches the point of identification; on the other, an intensification of Eros which exhausts itself in jealous resistance. This kind of daughter knows what she does *not* want, but is usually completely at sea as to what she would choose as her own fate. All her instincts are concentrated on the mother in the negative form of resistance and are therefore of no use to her in building her own life. Should she get as far as marrying, either the marriage will be used for the sole purpose

15

---

[29]This type of woman has an oddly disarming effect on her husband, but only until he discovers that the person he has married and who shares his nuptial bed is his mother-in-law. [Jung's note]

[30]***Pluto abducted Persephone*** This is a version of the Demeter–Kore myth. Pluto is another name for Hades, god of the underworld.

of escaping from her mother, or else a diabolical fate will present her with a husband who shares all the essential traits of her mother's character. All instinctive processes meet with unexpected difficulties; either sexuality does not function properly, or the children are unwanted, or maternal duties seem unbearable, or the demands of marital life are responded to with impatience and irritation. This is quite natural, since none of it has anything to do with the realities of life when stubborn resistance to the power of the mother in every form has come to be life's dominating aim. In such cases one can often see the attributes of the mother archetype demonstrated in every detail. For example, the mother as representative of the family (or clan) causes either violent resistances or complete indifference to anything that comes under the head of family, community, society, convention, and the like. Resistance to the mother as *uterus* often manifests itself in menstrual disturbances, failure of conception, abhorrence of pregnancy, hemorrhages and excessive vomiting during pregnancy, miscarriages, and so on. The mother as *materia*, "matter," may be at the back of these women's impatience with objects, their clumsy handling of tools and crockery and bad taste in clothes.

Again, resistance to the mother can sometimes result in a sponta- 16
neous development of intellect for the purpose of creating a sphere of interest in which the mother has no place. This development springs from the daughter's own needs and not at all for the sake of a man whom she would like to impress or dazzle by a semblance of intellectual comradeship. Its real purpose is to break the mother's power by intellectual criticism and superior knowledge, so as to enumerate to her all her stupidities, mistakes in logic, and educational shortcomings. Intellectual development is often accompanied by the emergence of masculine traits in general.

QUESTIONS

1. What is an archetype? What is the mother archetype? What are Jung's symbols for the mother? Can you add to them?
2. Who is Jung addressing in this selection? What kind of background does he assume of his audience? Can he communicate with people whose background is not as rich as he assumes it to be?
3. In paragraph 4, Jung makes a distinction between the personal mother of an individual and the "archetype projected upon her." Clarify that distinction. Does it seem reasonable to you? Do you think that Jung's emphasis is where it should be?

4. What are the characteristics of the mother complex for males? For females? How do they relate to the mother archetype?
5. The term "Eros" is used in paragraphs 9, 12, and 13. Establish the meaning of the term in its contexts. How useful is it in a discussion of the mother archetype?

WRITING ASSIGNMENTS

1. In paragraph 1 Jung says, "the mother archetype appears under an almost infinite variety of aspects." Inventory this essay and establish which are the most important aspects Jung himself uses to reveal the archetype. Add to those aspects from your own experience.
2. What personal experience have you had that could either add to, or detract from, Jung's theories regarding the mother complex? Be specific in detailing your experience and relate it carefully to the passages in Jung which you feel you are addressing.
3. One of the first manifestations of the mother archetype Jung mentions is that of the Madonna, the Virgin Mary. If you have the appropriate background or are willing to interview those who do have such background, establish the connection or lack of it between the Virgin and Jung's concept of the archetype. Consider particularly the visual representations of the Madonna and Child and the symbolic significance they bear. If possible, read the Book of Matthew in the New Testament. Is there any sense in which a mother complex might relate to the Madonna as a mother archetype? Is the Madonna the mother archetype?
4. Consider the mothers who appear in the literature you read or heard as a child—including mother types, such as the witch in *Hansel and Gretel*, the older sisters in *Cinderella*, and the stepmother in "Mirror, mirror on the wall." Inventory for yourself—consulting with others, if need be—the main characters you can recall. Include books you read as a child or books you know of that are intended for children. You may select some books from the children's section in your library. Does your research bear out the widespread presence of the mother archetype in children's stories?
5. Inventory the selection for the positive and the negative meanings of the mother archetype. Does Jung present a biased portrait of the effect of the mother archetype? Is there any sense in which you could say that Jung himself reveals traces of a mother complex? Be sure to gather your evidence in the form of quotations which can be analyzed carefully.

B. F. SKINNER

⸻⟰⸻

What Is Man?

*B*URRHUS FREDERICK SKINNER *(b. 1904) is an experimental psychologist known for his theories of behaviorism. Behavioral psychology focuses on the ways animals and people behave in response to the myriad complexities of their physical and psychological environment. Skinner's thought has moved in interesting directions, particularly in dealing with the questions of freedom. To some extent, he holds, freedom is not entirely desirable in modern society. It is something that we can outgrow.*

Skinner's emphasis is on the reaction of the individual to the world in which he is placed, and to some extent Skinner sees the individual as a function of that world, as a person whose behavior is essentially created by reinforcement. Reinforcement may be aversive: punishment, such as a spanking, loss of a job, imprisonment. It may be positive: praise, a new job, greater privileges. The "contingencies of reinforcement," an expression he uses often in the present selection, can be aversive, positive, or both. Whatever form they take, they will create the personal behavior of most (if not all) individuals. In posing the question "What is man?" Skinner consciously raises

---

From *Beyond Freedom and Dignity.*

questions that have been addressed throughout the ages, from ancient Greek philosophers to modern theologians. In answering the question, he is trying to point the way to a new vision.

He calls his vision a scientific view of mankind. By calling it that he includes in his thinking the results of a considerable body of research into the behavior of lower animals as well as of human beings. He has studied the contingencies of reinforcement that have produced learning, which has, in turn, produced behavior of various sorts. To some extent, Skinner's scientific approach has postulated a view of the individual as not being the autonomous agent one would ordinarily assume. The "autonomous agent"—another of Skinner's key terms in this selection—feels able to do anything that free will dictates. The autonomous agent seems to be free and independent. But Skinner points out that such freedom and independence are to some extent illusions. The culture, the family, the peer group, even the prejudices and ignorances of the individual—all combine as contingencies of reinforcement not only to reduce but actually to erase the autonomy of the individual. "Autonomy," in this sense, refers to the individual, personally controlled behavior that each person (as well as each squirrel, rat, and lower animal) feels he or she has.

Naturally, Skinner's views are not wholeheartedly endorsed by most people who adhere to a more traditional view of humankind. Skinner seems heartless and, perhaps, merely scientific. Yet, Skinner's claims suggest that he is most interested in pulling aside the veil of illusion that makes us feel we are free and makes us accept the unconsciously imposed limits on freedom that most of us do. As he points out, cultures have long agreed to maintain certain fictions in order to explain something about the forces that act on people. The Greeks concerned themselves with the gods and with fate. The Christian view focuses on Jesus and God's providence. The eighteenth-century philosophers thought of the world in terms of a machine and believed that there was an ascertainable range of causes and effects that controls people's behavior. Skinner's view is different. He sees people as learning to adapt to an environment without even realizing that they do so. The invisible or unconscious aspects of this process of adaptation are the things that Skinner hopes we will begin to understand.

SKINNER'S RHETORIC

The most obvious rhetorical device Skinner uses is the rhetorical question: What is man? The rest of the essay is, quite logically, an *answer to that question. In the first sentences of the first paragraph, Skinner shifts the ground of the discussion by establishing that the question must be answered, not by looking mainly at the person, but by looking at the environment in which the person thrives. However, used to criticism of the simplified environmentalism that dominated nineteenth-century thought, he begins to clarify the entire nature of environment by examining the ways in which it begins to take over the function of direction, which had been thought to be the preserve only of the individual. He then goes on to examine traits of character, which are generally thought to reside only within the individual, and to show how they, too, are dependent upon the environment.*

Even the extent to which the world can be known is brought into question by Skinner (paras. 8–18), and the issues concerning words and the way they work to affect our sense of knowledge are clarified. From there, Skinner addresses the question of thinking, which he calls "the last stronghold of autonomous man." Thinking is something people share with other beings, as Skinner shows, and certain kinds of misunderstanding, shown to be buried in the "metaphor of storage" (paras. 23–29) in which it is assumed that a person can "possess" knowledge, his or her past, culture, even his or her character. This thinking leads to a consideration of the self (paras. 32–38) and to a rejection of low-grade views of man as a machine (paras. 39–41). In four paragraphs, Skinner discusses the question of direction and purpose in life (paras. 42–45), and then he springs an interesting trap. The chapter to that point had been clearly predicting the doom of autonomous man, with whom the reader has been led to identify. But in the beginning of paragraph 46 he says, "It is only autonomous man who has reached a dead end. Man himself may be controlled by his environment, but it is an environment which is almost wholly of his own making."

The point Skinner wishes to make in answering the question he poses is that until we realize the truth of what it means for autonomous man to be given up as a worn-out fiction, we will misunderstand our own nature. When Socrates insisted that we must know ourselves in order to function in the world, he raised the same issues Skinner has raised. But Skinner's answers to the most basic question—What is man?—are somewhat different from any we have heard before.

What Is Man?

As a science of behavior adopts the strategy of physics and biology, 1
the autonomous agent[1] to which behavior has traditionally been attributed is replaced by the environment—the environment in which the
species evolved and in which the behavior of the individual is shaped
and maintained. The vicissitudes of "environmentalism" show how
difficult it has been to make this change. That a man's behavior owes
something to antecedent events and that the environment is a more
promising point of attack than man himself has long been recognized.
As Crane Brinton observed, "a program to change things not just to
convert people" was a significant part of the English, French, and Russian revolutions.[2] It was Robert Owen,[3] according to Trevelyan, who
first "clearly grasped and taught that environment makes character and
that environment is under human control" or, as Gilbert Seldes[4]
wrote, "that man is a creature of circumstance, that if you changed the
environments of thirty little Hottentots and thirty little aristocratic
English children, the aristocrats would become Hottentots, for all
practical purposes, and the Hottentots little conservatives."

The evidence for a crude environmentalism is clear enough. People 2
are extraordinarily different in different places, and possibly just because of the places. The nomad on horseback in Outer Mongolia and
the astronaut in outer space are different people, but, as far as we
know, if they had been exchanged at birth, they would have taken each
other's place. (The expression "change places" shows how closely we

---

[1]*autonomous agent* Skinner's term for the individual who feels he is a free agent
directed by his own will and basically undirected by outside forces.

[2]*revolutions* The English "Glorious Revolution" of 1688 introduced a constitutional
monarchy; the French Revolution, 1789, created a republic (for a time); the Russian Revolution, 1917, introduced a communist government.

[3]*Robert Owen (1771–1858)* A Welsh industrialist and reformer who brought better living conditions and education to workers at his cotton mills in New Lanark, England, agitated for improved working conditions throughout England, and supported the
new labor union movement. Owen's social thought can be seen in his *A New View of
Society* (1813). In 1825 he founded a utopian community in the United States, at New
Harmony, Indiana, but it failed, and he lost most of his fortune.

[4]*. . . Gilbert Seldes* Crane Brinton, G. M. Trevelyan, and Seldes are all writers
on history, behavior, and thought.

identify a person's behavior with the environment in which it occurs.) But we need to know a great deal more before that fact becomes useful. What is it about the environment that produces a Hottentot? And what would need to be changed to produce an English conservative instead?

Both the enthusiasm of the environmentalist and his usually ig- 3 nominious failure are illustrated by Owen's utopian experiment at New Harmony. A long history of environmental reform—in education, penology, industry, and family life, not to mention government and religion—has shown the same pattern. Environments are constructed on the model of environments in which good behavior has been observed, but the behavior fails to appear. Two hundred years of this kind of environmentalism has very little to show for itself, and for a simple reason. We must know how the environment works before we can change it to change behavior. A mere shift in emphasis from man to environment means very little.

Let us consider some examples in which the environment takes 4 over the function and role of autonomous man. The first, often said to involve human nature, is *aggression*. Men often act in such a way that they harm others, and they often seem to be reinforced by signs of damage to others. The ethologists[5] have emphasized contingencies of survival which would contribute these features to the genetic endowment of the species, but the contingencies of reinforcement in the lifetime of the individual are also significant, since anyone who acts aggressively to harm others is likely to be reinforced in other ways—for example, by taking possession of goods. The contingencies explain the behavior quite apart from any state or feeling of aggression or any initiating act by autonomous man.

Another example involving a so-called "trait of character" is *indus-* 5 *try.* Some people are industrious in the sense that they work energetically for long periods of time, while others are lazy and idle in the sense that they do not. "Industry" and "laziness" are among thousands of so-called "traits." The behavior they refer to can be explained in other ways. Some of it may be attributed to genetic idiosyncrasies (and subject to change only through genetic measures), and the rest to environmental contingencies, which are much more important than is usually realized. Regardless of any normal genetic endowment, an organism will range between vigorous activity and complete quiescence

---

[5]*ethologists* those who study the formation and evolution of the human *ethos,* that is, the moral nature or guiding principles of a human group.

depending upon the schedules on which it has been reinforced. The explanation shifts from a trait of character to an environmental history of reinforcement.

A third example, a "cognitive" activity, is *attention*. A person responds only to a small part of the stimuli impinging upon him. The traditional view is that he himself determines which stimuli are to be effective by "paying attention" to them. Some kind of inner gatekeeper is said to allow some stimuli to enter and to keep all others out. A sudden or strong stimulus may break through and "attract" attention, but the person himself seems otherwise to be in control. An analysis of the environmental circumstances reverses the relation. The kinds of stimuli which break through by "attracting attention" do so because they have been associated in the evolutionary history of the species or the personal history of the individual with important—e.g., dangerous—things. Less forceful stimuli attract attention only to the extent that they have figured in contingencies of reinforcement. We can arrange contingencies which ensure that an organism—even such a "simple" organism as a pigeon—will attend to one object and not to another, or to one property of an object, such as its color, and not to another, such as its shape. The inner gatekeeper is replaced by the contingencies to which the organism has been exposed and which select the stimuli to which it reacts.

In the traditional view a person perceives the world around him and acts upon it to make it known to him. In a sense he reaches out and grasps it. He "takes it in" and possesses it. He "knows" it in the Biblical sense in which a man knows a woman. It has even been argued that the world would not exist if no one perceived it. The action is exactly reversed in an environmental analysis. There would, of course, be no perception if there were no world to be perceived, but an existing world would not be perceived if there were no appropriate contingencies. We say that a baby perceives his mother's face and knows it. Our evidence is that the baby responds in one way to his mother's face and in other ways to other faces or other things. He makes this distinction not through some mental act of perception but because of prior contingencies. Some of these may be contingencies of survival. Physical features of a species are particularly stable parts of the environment in which a species evolves. (That is why courtship and sex and relations between parent and offspring are given such a prominent place by ethologists.) The face and facial expressions of the human mother have been associated with security, warmth, food, and other important things, during both the evolution of the species and the life of the child.

We learn to perceive in the sense that we learn to respond to things 8
in particular ways because of the contingencies of which they are a
part. We may perceive the sun, for example, simply because it is an
extremely powerful stimulus, but it has been a permanent part of the
environment of the species throughout its evolution and more specific
behavior with respect to it could have been selected by contingencies
of survival (as it has been in many other species). The sun also figures
in many current contingencies of reinforcement: we move into or out
of sunlight depending on the temperature; we wait for the sun to rise
or set to take practical action; we talk about the sun and its effects;
and we eventually study the sun with the instruments and methods of
science. Our perception of the sun depends on what we do with respect
to it. Whatever we do, and hence however we perceive it, the fact remains that it is the environment which acts upon the perceiving person, not the perceiving person who acts upon the environment.

The perceiving and knowing which arise from verbal contingencies 9
are even more obviously products of the environment. We react to an
object in many practical ways because of its color; thus, we pick and
eat red apples of a particular variety but not green. It is clear that we
can "tell the difference" between red and green, but something more
is involved when we say that we *know* that one apple is red and the
other green. It is tempting to say that knowing is a cognitive process
altogether divorced from action, but the contingencies provide a more
useful distinction. When someone asks about the color of an object
which he cannot see, and we tell him that it is red, *we* do nothing
about the object in any other way. It is the person who has questioned
us and heard our answer who makes a practical response which depends on color. Only under verbal contingencies can a speaker respond
to an isolated property to which a nonverbal response cannot be made.
A response made to the property of an object without responding to
the object in any other way is called *abstract*. Abstract thinking is the
product of a particular kind of environment, not of a cognitive faculty.

As listeners we acquire a kind of knowledge from the verbal behav- 10
ior of others which may be extremely valuable in permitting us to
avoid direct exposure to contingencies. We learn from the experience
of others by responding to what they say about contingencies. When
we are warned against doing something or are advised to do something,
there may be no point in speaking of knowledge, but when we learn
more durable kinds of warnings and advice in the form of maxims or
rules, we may be said to have a special kind of knowledge about the
contingencies to which they apply. The laws of science are descriptions of contingencies of reinforcement, and one who knows a scien-

tific law may behave effectively without being exposed to the contingencies it describes. (He will, of course, have very different feelings about the contingencies, depending on whether he is following a rule or has been directly exposed to them. Scientific knowledge is "cold," but the behavior to which it gives rise is as effective as the "warm" knowledge which comes from personal experience.)

Isaiah Berlin has referred to a particular sense of knowing, said to 11 have been discovered by Giambattista Vico.[6] It is "the sense in which I know what it is to be poor, to fight for a cause, belong to a nation, to join or abandon a church or a party, to feel nostalgia, terror, the omnipresence of a god, to understand a gesture, a work of art, a joke, a man's character, that one is transformed or lying to oneself." These are the kinds of things one is likely to learn through direct contact with contingencies rather than from the verbal behavior of others, and special kinds of feelings are no doubt associated with them, but, even so, the knowledge is not somehow directly given. A person can know what it is to fight for a cause only after a long history during which he has learned to perceive and to know that state of affairs called fighting for a cause.

The role of the environment is particularly subtle when what is 12 known is the knower himself. If there is no external world to initiate knowing, must we not then say that the knower himself acts first? This is, of course, the field of consciousness, or awareness, a field which a scientific analysis of behavior is often accused of ignoring. The charge is a serious one and should be taken seriously. Man is said to differ from the other animals mainly because he is "aware of his own existence." He knows what he is doing; he knows that he has had a past and will have a future; he "reflects on his own nature"; he alone follows the classical injunction "Know thyself." Any analysis of human behavior which neglected these facts would be defective indeed. And some analyses do. What is called "methodological behaviorism" limits itself to what can be publicly observed; mental processes may exist, but they are ruled out of scientific consideration by their nature. The "behavioralists" in political science and many logical positivists[7] in philosophy have followed a similar line. But self-observation can be studied, and it must be included in any reasonably complete account

---

[6]**Giovanni Battista Vico (1668–1724)** Italian philosopher whose theories of history involve cycles of repetition of behavior. Sir Isaiah Berlin (b. 1909) is a British historian of ideas and philosopher.

[7]**logical positivists** Twentieth-century thinkers who felt human knowledge was limited to only those things that could be known from observation.

of human behavior. Rather than ignore consciousness, an experimental analysis of behavior has stressed certain crucial issues. The question is not whether a man can know himself but what he knows when he does so.

The problem arises in part from the indisputable fact of privacy: a 13 small part of the universe is enclosed within a human skin. It would be foolish to deny the existence of that private world, but it is also foolish to assert that because it is private it is of a different nature from the world outside. The difference is not in the stuff of which the private world is composed, but in its accessibility. There is an exclusive intimacy about a headache, or heartache, or a silent soliloquy. The intimacy is sometimes distressing (one cannot shut one's eyes to a headache), but it need not be, and it has seemed to support the doctrine that knowing is a kind of possession.

The difficulty is that although privacy may bring the knower closer 14 to what he knows, it interferes with the process through which he comes to know anything. As we saw in [an earlier chapter], the contingencies under which a child learns to describe his feelings are necessarily defective; the verbal community cannot use the procedures with which it teaches a child to describe objects. There are, of course, natural contingencies under which we learn to respond to private stimuli, and they generate behavior of great precision; we could not jump or walk or turn a handspring if we were not being stimulated by parts of our own body. But very little awareness is associated with this kind of behavior and, in fact, we behave in these ways most of the time without being aware of the stimuli to which we are responding. We do not attribute awareness to other species which obviously use similar private stimuli. To "know" private stimuli is more than to respond to them.

The verbal community specializes in self-descriptive contingen- 15 cies. It asks such questions as: What did you do yesterday? What are you doing now? What will you do tomorrow? Why did you do that? Do you really want to do that? How do you feel about that? The answers help people to adjust to each other effectively. And it is because such questions are asked that a person responds to himself and his behavior in the special way called knowing or being aware. Without the help of a verbal community all behavior would be unconscious. Consciousness is a social product. It is not only *not* the special field of autonomous man, it is *not* within range of a solitary man.

And it is not within the range of accuracy of anyone. The privacy 16 which seems to confer intimacy upon self-knowledge makes it impossible for the verbal community to maintain precise contingencies. In-

trospective vocabularies are by nature inaccurate, and that is one reason why they have varied so widely among schools of philosophy and
psychology. Even a carefully trained observer runs into trouble when
new private stimuli are studied. (Independent evidence of privaⱡe stimulation—for example, through physiological measures—would make it
possible to sharpen the contingencies which generate self-observation
and would, incidentally, confirm the present interpretation. Such evidence would not, as we noted in [an earlier chapter], offer any support
for a theory which attributed human behavior to an observable inner
agent.)

Theories of psychotherapy which emphasize awareness assign a 17
role to autonomous man which is properly, and much more effectively, reserved for contingencies of reinforcement. Awareness may
help if the problem is in part a lack of awareness, and "insight" into
one's condition may help if one then takes remedial action, but awareness or insight alone is not always enough, and it may be too much.
One need not be aware of one's behavior or the conditions controlling
it in order to behave effectively—or ineffectively. On the contrary, as
the toad's inquiry of the centipede demonstrates, constant self-observation may be a handicap. The accomplished pianist would perform
badly if he were as clearly aware of his behavior as the student who is
just learning to play.

Cultures are often judged by the extent to which they encourage 18
self-observation. Some cultures are said to breed unthinking men, and
Socrates[8] has been admired for inducing men to inquire into their own
nature, but self-observation is only a preliminary to action. The extent
to which a man *should* be aware of himself depends upon the importance of self-observation for effective behavior. Self-knowledge is valuable only to the extent that it helps to meet the contingencies under
which it has arisen.

Perhaps the last stronghold of autonomous man is that complex 19
"cognitive" activity called thinking. Because it is complex, it has
yielded only slowly to explanation in terms of contingencies of reinforcement. When we say that a person *discriminates* between red and
orange, we imply that discrimination is a kind of mental act. The

---

[8]*Socrates (469?–399 B.C.)* Greek philosopher. Socrates insisted upon rigorous
self-examination no matter what the cost. He was put to death for "corrupting the youth"
of Athens, which may indicate the problems inherent in promoting individualism in certain societies.

person himself does not seem to be doing anything; he responds in different ways to red and orange stimuli, but this is the result of discrimination rather than the act. Similarly, we say that a person *generalizes*—say, from his own limited experience to the world at large— but all we see is that he responds to the world at large as he has learned to respond to his own small world. We say that a person *forms a concept or an abstraction*, but all we see is that certain kinds of contingencies of reinforcement have brought a response under the control of a single property of a stimulus. We say that a person *recalls* or *remembers* what he has seen or heard, but all we see is that the present occasion evokes a response, possibly in weakened or altered form, acquired on another occasion. We say that a person *associates* one word with another, but all we observe is that one verbal stimulus evokes the response previously made to another. Rather than suppose that it is therefore autonomous man who discriminates, generalizes, forms concepts or abstractions, recalls or remembers, and associates, we can put matters in good order simply by noting that these terms do not refer to forms of behavior.

A person may take explicit action, however, when he solves a problem. In putting a jigsaw puzzle together he may move the pieces around to improve his chances of finding a fit. In solving an equation he may transpose, clear fractions, and extract roots to improve his chances of finding a form of the equation he has already learned how to solve. The creative artist may manipulate a medium until something of interest turns up. Much of this can be done covertly, and it is then likely to be assigned to a different dimensional system, but it can always be done overtly, perhaps more slowly but also often more effectively, and with rare exceptions it must have been learned in overt form. The culture promotes thinking by constructing special contingencies. It teaches a person to make fine discriminations by making differential reinforcement more precise. It teaches techniques to be used in solving problems. It provides rules which make it unnecessary to be exposed to the contingencies from which the rules are derived, and it provides rules for finding rules. 20

Self-control, or self-management, is a special kind of problem solving which, like self-knowledge, raises all the issues associated with privacy. We have discussed some techniques in connection with aversive control in [an earlier chapter]. It is always the environment which builds the behavior with which problems are solved, even when the problems are to be found in the private world inside the skin. None of this has been investigated in a very productive way, but the inadequacy of our analysis is no reason to fall back on a miracle-working 21 mind. If our understanding of contingencies of reinforcement is not yet sufficient to explain all kinds of thinking, we must remember that the appeal to mind explains nothing at all.

In shifting control from autonomous man to the observable envi- 22 ronment we do not leave an empty organism. A great deal goes on inside the skin, and physiology will eventually tell us more about it. It will explain why behavior is indeed related to the antecedent events of which it can be shown to be a function. The assignment is not always correctly understood. Many physiologists regard themselves as looking for the "physiological correlates" of mental events. Physiological research is regarded as simply a more scientific version of introspection. But physiological techniques are not, of course, designed to detect or measure personalities, ideas, attitudes, feelings, impulses, thoughts, or purposes. (If they were, we should have to answer a third question in addition to those raised in [an earlier chapter]: How can a personality, idea, feeling, or purpose affect the instruments of the physiologist?) At the moment neither introspection nor physiology supplies very adequate information about what is going on inside a man as he behaves, and since they are both directed inward, they have the same effect of diverting attention from the external environment.

Much of the misunderstanding about an inner man comes from the 23 metaphor of storage. Evolutionary and environmental histories change an organism, but they are not stored within it. Thus, we observe that babies suck their mothers' breasts, and we can easily imagine that a strong tendency to do so has survival value, but much more is implied by a "sucking instinct" regarded as something a baby possesses which enables it to suck. The concept of "human nature" or "genetic endowment" is dangerous when taken in that sense. We are closer to human nature in a baby than in an adult, or in a primitive culture than in an advanced, in the sense that environmental contingencies are less likely to have obscured the genetic endowment, and it is tempting to dramatize that endowment by implying that earlier stages have survived in concealed form: man is a naked ape, and "the paleolithic bull which survives in man's inner self still paws the earth whenever a threatening gesture is made on the social scene." But anatomists and physiologists will not find an ape, or a bull, or for that matter instincts. They will find anatomical and physiological features which are the product of an evolutionary history.

The personal history of the individual is also often said to be stored 24 within him. For "instinct" read "habit." The cigarette habit is presumably something more than the behavior said to show that a person possesses it; but the only other information we have concerns the reinforcers and the schedules of reinforcement which make a person smoke a great deal. The contingencies are not stored; they have simply left a changed person.

The environment is often said to be stored in the form of memories: to recall something we search for a copy of it, which can then be seen as the original thing was seen. As far as we know, however, there are no copies of the environment in the individual *at any time*, even when a thing is present and being observed. The products of more complex contingencies are also said to be stored; the repertoire acquired as a person learns to speak French is called a "knowledge of French." 25

Traits of character, whether derived from contingencies of survival or contingencies of reinforcement, are also said to be stored. A curious example occurs in Follett's *Modern American Usage:* "We say *He faced these adversities bravely,* aware without thought that the bravery is a property of the man, not of the facing; a brave act is poetic shorthand for the act of a person who shows bravery by performing it." But we call a man brave because of his acts, and he behaves bravely when environmental circumstances induce him to do so. The circumstances have changed his behavior; they have not implanted a trait or virtue. 26

Philosophies are also spoken of as things possessed. A man is said to speak or act in certain ways because he has a particular philosophy—such as idealism, dialectical materialism, or Calvinism.[9] Terms of this kind summarize the effect of environmental conditions which it would now be hard to trace, but the conditions must have existed and should not be ignored. A person who possesses a "philosophy of freedom" is one who has been changed in certain ways by the literatue of freedom. 27

The issue has had a curious place in theology. Does man sin because he is sinful, or is he sinful because he sins? Neither question points to anything very useful. To say that a man is sinful because he sins is to give an operational definition of sin. To say that he sins because he is sinful is to trace his behavior to a supposed inner trait. But whether or not a person engages in the kind of behavior called 28

---

[9]*idealism,* ***dialectical materialism,*** *or* ***Calvinism*** *Idealism* is the belief that reality is found in ideas rather than objects themselves; *dialectical materialism* is a Marxian belief in the conflict and resolution of powerful forces as well as a belief in material values and their reality; *Calvinism* is a strict Protestant religion which insists that people are totally depraved and only a few will be saved by the grace of God. All these philosophies have strong adherents today.

sinful depends upon circumstances which are not mentioned in either question. The sin assigned as an inner possession (the sin a person "knows") is to be found in a history of reinforcement. (The expression "God-fearing" suggests such a history, but piety, virtue, the immanence of God, a moral sense, or morality does not. As we have seen, man is not a moral animal in the sense of possessing a special trait or virtue; he has built a kind of social environment which induces him to behave in moral ways.)

These distinctions have practical implications. A recent survey of white Americans is said to have shown that "more than half blamed the inferior educational and economic status of blacks on 'something about Negroes themselves.'" The "something" was further identified as "lack of motivation," which was to be distinguished from *both* genetic and environmental factors. Significantly, motivation was said to be associated with "free will." To neglect the role of the environment in this way is to discourage any inquiry into the defective contingencies responsible for a "lack of motivation." 29

It is in the nature of an experimental analysis of human behavior that it should strip away the functions previously assigned to autonomous man and transfer them one by one to the controlling environment. The analysis leaves less and less for autonomous man to do. But what about man himself? Is there not something about a person which is more than a living body? Unless something called a self survives, how can we speak of self-knowledge or self-control? To whom is the injunction "Know thyself" addressed? 30

It is an important part of the contingencies to which a young child is exposed that his own body is the only part of his environment which remains the same *(idem)* from moment to moment and day to day. We say that he discovers his *identity* as he learns to distinguish between his body and the rest of the world. He does this long before the community teaches him to call things by name and to distinguish "me" from "it" or "you." 31

A self is a repertoire of behavior appropriate to a given set of contingencies. A substantial part of the conditions to which a person is exposed may play a dominant role, and under other conditions a person may report, "I'm not myself today," or, "I couldn't have done what you said I did, because that's not like me." The identity conferred upon a self arises from the contingencies responsible for the behavior. Two or more repertoires generated by different sets of contingencies compose two or more selves. A person possesses one repertoire appropriate to his life with his friends and another appropriate to his life 32 with his family, and a friend may find him a very different person if he sees him with his family or his family if they see him with his friends. The problem of identity arises when situations are intermingled, as when a person finds himself with both his family and his friends at the same time.

Self-knowledge and self-control imply two selves in this sense. The 33 self-knower is almost always a product of social contingencies, but the self that is known may come from other sources. The controlling self (the conscience or superego) is of social origin, but the controlled self is more likely to be the product of genetic susceptibilities to reinforcement (the id, or the Old Adam). The controlling self generally represents the interests of others, the controlled self the interests of the individual.

The picture which emerges from a scientific analysis *is* not of a 34 body with a person inside, but of a body which *is* a person in the sense that it displays a complex repertoire of behavior. The picture is, of course, unfamiliar. The man thus portrayed is a stranger, and from the traditional point of view he may not seem to be a man at all. "For at least one hundred years," said Joseph Wood Krutch,[10] "we have been prejudiced in every theory, including economic determinism, mechanistic behaviorism, and relativism, that reduces the stature of man until he ceases to be man at all in any sense that the humanists of an earlier generation would recognize." Matson has argued that "the empirical behavioral scientist . . . denies, if only by implication, that a unique being, called Man, exists." "What is now under attack," said Maslow, "is the 'being' of man." C. S. Lewis[11] put it quite bluntly: Man is being abolished.

There is clearly some difficulty in identifying the man to whom 35 these expressions refer. Lewis cannot have meant the human species, for not only is it not being abolished, it is filling the earth. (As a result it may eventually abolish itself through disease, famine, pollution, or a nuclear holocaust, but that is not what Lewis meant.) Nor are individual men growing less effective or productive. We are told that what

---

[10] ***Joseph Wood Krutch (1893–1970)*** American critic and writer whose books and essays on nature were famed. His most famous book is *The Measure of Man* (1954). He also wrote *Henry David Thoreau* (1948), a highly regarded biography and appreciation.

[11] ***Abraham Maslow (1908–1970) and C. S. Lewis (1898–1963)*** Widely known as writers on human values. Maslow, an American psychologist, based his thinking on a hierarchy of human needs, from survival at the bottom to self-actualization at the top. Lewis, an English critic and novelist, was one of the foremost twentieth-century spokesmen for orthodox Christian belief.

is threatened is "man *qua*[12] man" or "man in his humanity," or "man as Thou not It," or "man as a person not a thing." These are not very helpful expressions, but they supply a clue. What is being abolished is autonomous man—the inner man, the homunculus,[13] the possessing demon, the man defended by the literatures of freedom and dignity.

His abolition has long been overdue. Autonomous man is a device 36 used to explain what we cannot explain in any other way. He has been constructed from our ignorance, and as our understanding increases, the very stuff of which he is composed vanishes. Science does not dehumanize man, it de-homunculizes him, and it must do so if it is to prevent the abolition of the human species. To man *qua* man we readily say good riddance. Only by dispossessing him can we turn to the real causes of human behavior. Only then can we turn from the inferred to the observed, from the miraculous to the natural, from the inaccessible to the manipulable.

It is often said that in doing so we must treat the man who survives 37 as a mere animal. "Animal" is a pejorative term, but only because "man" has been made spuriously honorific. Krutch has argued that whereas the traditional view supports Hamlet's exclamation, "How like a god!," Pavlov,[14] the behavioral scientist, emphasized "How like a dog!" But that was a step forward. A god is the archetypal pattern of an explanatory fiction, of a miracle-working mind, of the metaphysical. Man is much more than a dog, but like a dog he is within range of a scientific analysis.

It is true that much of the experimental analysis of behavior has 38 been concerned with lower organisms. Genetic differences are minimized by using special strains; environmental histories can be controlled, perhaps from birth; strict regimens can be maintained during long experiments; and very little of this is possible with human subjects. Moreover, in working with lower animals the scientist is less likely to put his own responses to the experimental conditions among his data, or to design contingencies with an eye to their effect on him rather than on the experimental organism he is studying. No one is disturbed when physiologists study respiration, reproduction, nutrition, or endocrine systems in animals; they do so to take advantage of very great similarities. Comparable similarities in behavior are being

---

[12]*qua*   as.

[13]*homunculus*   A tiny man; in Goethe's *Faust,* a kind of possessing spirit.

[14]*Ivan Pavlov (1849–1936)*   Russian psychologist who conditioned a dog to salivate upon the ringing of a bell. Much behaviorist psychology is based upon his experiments.

discovered. There is, of course, always the danger that methods designed for the study of lower animals will emphasize only those characteristics which they have in common with men, but we cannot discover what is "essentially" human until we have investigated nonhuman subjects. Traditional theories of autonomous man have exaggerated species differences. Some of the complex contingencies of reinforcement now under investigation generate behavior in lower organisms which, if the subjects were human, would traditionally be said to involve higher mental processes.

Man is not made into a machine by analyzing his behavior in mechanical terms. Early theories of behavior, as we have seen, represented man as a push-pull automaton, close to the nineteenth-century notion of a machine, but progress has been made. Man is a machine in the sense that he is a complex system behaving in lawful ways, but the complexity is extraordinary. His capacity to adjust to contingencies of reinforcement will perhaps be eventually simulated by machines, but this has not yet been done, and the living system thus simulated will remain unique in other ways. 39

Nor is man made into a machine by inducing him to use machines. Some machines call for behavior which is repetitious and monotonous, and we escape from them when we can, but others enormously extend our effectiveness in dealing with the world around us. A person may respond to very small things with the help of an electron microscope and to very large things with radiotelescopes, and in doing so he may seem quite inhuman to those who use only their unaided senses. A person may act upon the environment with the delicate precision of a micromanipulator or with the range and power of a space rocket, and his behavior may seen inhuman to those who rely only on muscular contractions. (It has been argued that the apparatus used in the operant laboratory misrepresents natural behavior because it introduces an external source of power, but men use external sources when they fly kites, sail boats, or shoot bows and arrows. They would have to abandon all but a small fraction of their achievements if they used only the power of their muscles.) People record their behavior in books and other media, and the use they make of the records may seem quite inhuman to those who can use only what they remember. People describe complex contingencies in the form of rules, and rules for manipulating rules, and they introduce them into electronic systems which "think" with a speed that seems quite inhuman to the unaided thinker. Human beings do all this with machines, and they would be less than human if they did not. What we now regard as machine-like behavior was, in fact, much commoner before the invention of these 40 devices. The slave in the cotton field, the bookkeeper on his high stool, the student being drilled by a teacher—these were the machine-like men.

Machines replace people when they do what people have done, and the social consequences may be serious. As technology advances, machines will take over more and more of the functions of men, but only up to a point. We build machines which reduce some of the aversive features of our environment (grueling labor, for example) and which produce more positive reinforcers. We build them precisely because they do so. We have no reason to build machines to be reinforced by these consequences, and to do so would be to deprive ourselves of reinforcement. If the machines man makes eventually make him wholly expendable, it will be by accident, not design. 41

An important role of autonomous man has been to give human behavior direction, and it is often said that in dispossessing an inner agent we leave man himself without a purpose. As one writer has put it, "Since a scientific psychology must regard human behavior objectively, as determined by necessary laws, it must represent human behavior as unintentional." But "necessary laws" would have this effect only if they referred exclusively to antecedent conditions. Intention and purpose refer to selective consequences, the effects of which can be formulated in "necessary laws." Has life, in all the forms in which it exists on the surface of the earth, a purpose, and is this evidence of intentional design? The primate hand evolved *in order that* things might be more successfully manipulated, but its purpose is to be found not in a prior design but rather in the process of selection. Similarly, in operant conditioning the purpose of a skilled movement of the hand is to be found in the consequences which follow it. A pianist neither acquires nor executes the behavior of playing a scale smoothly because of a prior intention of doing so. Smoothly played scales are reinforcing for many reasons, and they select skilled movements. In neither the evolution of the human hand nor in the acquired use of the hand is any prior intention or purpose at issue. 42

The argument for purpose seems to be strengthened by moving back into the darker recesses of mutation. Jacques Barzun[15] has argued that Darwin and Marx both neglected not only human purpose but the creative purpose responsible for the variations upon which natural se- 43

---

[15]*Jacques Barzun (b. 1907)* A noted American scholar; Skinner is referring to his book, *Darwin, Marx, and Wagner.*

lection plays. It may prove to be the case, as some geneticists have argued, that mutations are not entirely random, but nonrandomness is not necessarily the proof of a creative mind. Mutations will not be random when geneticists explicitly design them in order that an organism will meet specific conditions of selection more successfully, and geneticists will then seem to be playing the role of the creative Mind in pre-evolutionary theory, but the purpose they display will have to be sought in their culture, in the social environment which has induced them to make genetic changes appropriate to contingencies of survival.

There is a difference between biological and individual purpose in 44 that the latter can be felt. No one could have felt the purpose in the development of the human hand, whereas a person can in a sense feel the purpose with which he plays a smooth scale. But he does not play a smooth scale *because* he feels the purpose of doing so; what he feels is a by-product of his behavior in relation to its consequences. The relation of the human hand to the contingencies of survival under which it evolved is, of course, out of reach of personal observation; the relation of the behavior to contingencies of reinforcement which have generated it is not.

A scientific analysis of behavior dispossesses autonomous man and 45 turns the control he has been said to exert over to the environment. The individual may then seem particularly vulnerable. He is henceforth to be controlled by the world around him, and in large part by other men. Is he not then simply a victim? Certainly men have been victims, as they have been victimizers, but the word is too strong. It implies despoliation, which is by no means an essential consequence of interpersonal control. But even under benevolent control is the individual not at best a spectator who may watch what happens but is helpless to do anything about it? Is he not "at a dead end in his long struggle to control his own destiny"?

It is only autonomous man who has reached a dead end. Man him- 46 self may be controlled by his environment, but it is an environment which is almost wholly of his own making. The physical environment of most people is largely man-made. The surfaces a person walks on, the walls which shelter him, the clothing he wears, many of the foods he eats, the tools he uses, the vehicles he moves about in, most of the things he listens to and looks at are human products. The social environment is obviously man-made—it generates the language a person speaks, the customs he follows, and the behavior he exhibits with respect to the ethical, religious, governmental, economic, educational, and psychotherapeutic institutions which control him. The evolution of a culture is in fact a kind of gigantic exercise in self-control. As the individual controls himself by manipulating the world in which he lives, so the human species has constructed an environment in which its members behave in a highly effective way. Mistakes have been made, and we have no assurance that the environment man has constructed will continue to provide gains which outstrip the losses, but man as we know him, for better or for worse, is what man has made of man.

This will not satisfy those who cry "Victim!" C. S. Lewis protested: "... the power of man to make himself what he pleases . . . means . . . the power of some men to make other men what they please." This is inevitable in the nature of cultural evolution. The controlling *self* must be distinguished from the controlled self, even when they are both inside the same skin, and when control is exercised through the design of an external environment, the selves are, with minor exceptions, distinct. The person who unintentionally or intentionally introduces a new cultural practice is only one among possibly billions who will be affected by it. If this does not seem like an act of self-control, it is only because we have misunderstood the nature of self-control in the individual. 47

When a person changes his physical or social environment "intentionally"—that is, in order to change human behavior, possibly including his own—he plays two roles: one as a controller, as the designer of a controlling culture, and another as the controlled, as the product of a culture. There is nothing inconsistent about this; it follows from the nature of the evolution of a culture, with or without intentional design. 48

The human species has probably not undergone much genetic change in recorded time. We have only to go back a thousand generations to reach the artists of the caves of Lascaux.[16] Features which bear directly on survival (such as resistance to disease) change substantially in a thousand generations, but the child of one of the Lascaux artists transplanted to the world of today might be almost indistinguishable from a modern child. It is possible that he would learn more slowly than his modern counterpart, that he could maintain only a smaller repertoire without confusion, or that he would forget more quickly; 49

---

[16]*caves of Lascaux* Lascaux is in southwest France. The caves discovered there were painted with bison, elk, and other figures some 15,000 to 20,000 years ago. Other such caves have been found in Spain and elsewhere in France.

we cannot be sure. But we can be sure that a twentieth-century child transplanted to the civilization of Lascaux would not be very different from the children he met there, for we have seen what happens when a modern child is raised in an impoverished environment.

Man has greatly changed himself as a person in the same period of time by changing the world in which he lives. Something of the order of a hundred generations will cover the development of modern religious practices, and something of the same order of magnitude modern government and law. Perhaps no more than twenty generations will account for modern industrial practices, and possibly no more than four or five for education and psychotherapy. The physical and biological technologies which have increased man's sensitivity to the world around him and his power to change that world have taken no more than four or five generations. 50

Man has "controlled his own destiny," if that expression means anything at all. The man that man has made is the product of the culture man has devised. He has emerged from two quite different processes of evolution: the biological evolution responsible for the human species and the cultural evolution carried out by that species. Both of these processes of evolution may now accelerate because they are both subject to intentional design. Men have already changed their genetic endowment by breeding selectively and by changing contingencies of survival, and they may now begin to introduce mutations directly related to survival. For a long time men have introduced new practices which serve as cultural mutations, and they have changed the conditions under which practices are selected. They may now begin to do both with a clearer eye to the consequences. 51

Man will presumably continue to change, but we cannot say in what direction. No one could have predicted the evolution of the human species at any point in its early history, and the direction of intentional genetic design will depend upon the evolution of a culture which is itself unpredictable for similar reasons. "The limits of perfection of the human species," said Étienne Cabet[17] in *Voyage en Icarie*, "are as yet unknown." But, of course, there are no limits. The human species will never reach a final state of perfection before it is exterminated—"some say in fire, some in ice," and some in radiation. 52

---

[17]*Étienne Cabet (1788–1856)* A French communist whose *Voyage en Icarie* (1840) offers a plan for a utopia which Cabet in 1848 tried to put into practice. He purchased land in the Red River in Texas, then sent 1,500 settlers there. The experiment failed. He later took his "Icarians" to Nauvoo, Illinois, a former Mormon settlement, where he remained their leader until his death.

The individual occupies a place in a culture not unlike his place in 53
the species, and in early evolutionary theory that place was hotly debated. Was the species simply a type of individual, and if so, in what
sense could it evolve? Darwin himself declared species "to be purely
subjective inventions of the taxonomist." A species has no existence
except as a collection of individuals, nor has a family, tribe, race, nation, or class. A culture has no existence apart from the behavior of
the individuals who maintain its practices. It is always an individual
who behaves, who acts upon the environment and is changed by the
consequences of his action, and who maintains the social contingencies which *are* a culture. The individual is the carrier of both his
species and his culture. Cultural practices, like genetic traits, are
transmitted from individual to individual. A new practice, like a new
genetic trait, appears first in an individual and tends to be transmitted
if it contributes to his survival as an individual.

Yet, the individual is at best a locus in which many lines of devel- 54
opment come together in a unique set. His individuality is unques-
tioned. Every cell in his body is a unique genetic product, as unique as
that classic mark of individuality, the fingerprint. And even within the
most regimented culture every personal history is unique. No intentional culture can destroy that uniqueness, and, as we have seen, any
effort to do so would be bad design. But the individual nevertheless
remains merely a stage in a process which began long before he came
into existence and will long outlast him. He has no ultimate responsibility for a species trait or a cultural practice, even though it was he
who underwent the mutation or introduced the practice which became
part of the species or culture. Even if Lamarck[18] had been right in supposing that the individual could change his genetic structure through
personal effort, we should have to point to the environmental circumstances responsible for the effort, as we shall have to do when geneticists begin to change the human endowment. And when an individual
engages in the intentional design of a cultural practice, we must turn
to the culture which induces him to do so and supplies the art or science he uses.

One of the great problems of individualism, seldom recognized as 55
such, is death—the inescapable fate of the individual, the final assault
on freedom and dignity. Death is one of those remote events which
are brought to bear on behavior only with the aid of cultural practices.

---

[18]*Jean Baptiste Lamarck (1744–1829)* French scientist who thought that it was
possible to inherit acquired characteristics genetically.

What we see is the death of others, as in Pascal's[19] famous metaphor: "Imagine a number of men in chains, all under sentence of death, some of whom are each day butchered in the sight of the others; those remaining see their own condition in that of their fellows, and looking at each other with grief and despair await their turn. This is an image of the human condition." Some religions have made death more important by picturing a future existence in heaven or hell, but the individualist has a special reason to fear death, engineered not by a religion but by the literatures of freedom and dignity. It is the prospect of personal annihilation. The individualist can find no solace in reflecting upon any contribution which will survive him. He has refused to act for the good of others and is therefore not reinforced by the fact that others whom he has helped will outlive him. He has refused to be concerned for the survival of his culture and is not reinforced by the fact that the culture will long survive him. In the defense of his own freedom and dignity he has denied the contributions of the past and must therefore relinquish all claim upon the future.

Science has probably never demanded a more sweeping change in a 56 traditional way of thinking about a subject, nor has there ever been a more important subject. In the traditional picture a person perceives the world around him, selects features to be perceived, discriminates among them, judges them good or bad, changes them to make them better (or, if he is careless, worse), and may be held responsible for his action and justly rewarded or punished for its consequences. In the scientific picture a person is a member of a species shaped by evolutionary contingencies of survival, displaying behavioral processes which bring him under the control of the environment in which he lives, and largely under the control of a social environment which he and millions of others like him have constructed and maintained during the evolution of a culture. The direction of the controlling relation is reversed: a person does not act upon the world, the world acts upon him.

It is difficult to accept such a change simply on intellectual 57 grounds and nearly impossible to accept its implications. The reaction of the traditionalist is usually described in terms of feelings. One of these, to which the Freudians have appealed in explaining the resistance to psychoanalysis, is wounded vanity. Freud himself expounded,

---

[19]***Blaise Pascal (1623–1662)*** French philosopher and scientist. He was generally enigmatic in his thought, particularly in his *Pensées* (1658), in which he begins to call all knowledge into doubt. Pascal was a devout Catholic, but the religious orthodoxy of his work is subject to debate.

as Ernest Jones[20] has said, "the three heavy blows which narcissism or self-love of mankind had suffered at the hands of science. The first was cosmological and was dealt by Copernicus;[21] the second was biological and was dealt by Darwin; the third was psychological and was dealt by Freud." (The blow was suffered by the belief that something at the center of man knows all that goes on within him and that an instrument called will power exercises command and control over the rest of one's personality.) But what are the signs or symptoms of wounded vanity, and how shall we explain them? What people *do* about such a scientific picture of man is call it wrong, demeaning, and dangerous, argue against it, and attack those who propose or defend it. They do so not out of wounded vanity but because the scientific formulation has destroyed accustomed reinforcers. If a person can no longer take credit or be admired for what he does, then he seems to suffer a loss of dignity or worth, and behavior previously reinforced by credit or admiration will undergo extinction. Extinction often leads to aggressive attack.

Another effect of the scientific picture has been described as a loss 58 of faith or "nerve," as a sense of doubt or powerlessness, or as discouragement, depression, or despondency. A person is said to feel that he can do nothing about his own destiny. But what he feels is a weakening of old responses which are no longer reinforced. People are indeed "powerless" when long-established verbal repertoires prove useless. For example, one historian has complained that if the deeds of men are "to be dismissed as simply the product of material and psychological conditioning," there is nothing to write about; "change must be at least partially the result of conscious mental activity."

Another effect is a kind of nostalgia. Old repertoires break through, 59 as similarities between present and past are seized upon and exaggerated. Old days are called the good old days, when the inherent dignity of man and the importance of spiritual values were recognized. Such fragments of outmoded behavior tend to be "wistful"—that is, they have the character of increasingly unsuccessful behavior.

These reactions to a scientific conception of man are certainly un- 60 fortunate. They immobilize men of good will, and anyone concerned with the future of his culture will do what he can to correct them. No

---

[20]***Ernest Jones (1879–1958)*** A follower of Freud. His book *Hamlet and Oedipus* (1949) applies Freud's theory to a literary classic, Shakespeare's *Hamlet*.
[21]***Nicolaus Copernicus (1473–1543)*** Polish astronomer who theorized that the earth revolved around the sun. His theory revolutionized astronomy and shook the foundations of Western thought.

theory changes what it is a theory about. Nothing is changed because we look at it, talk about it, or analyze it in a new way. Keats drank confusion to Newton[22] for analyzing the rainbow, but the rainbow remained as beautiful as ever and became for many even more beautiful. Man has not changed because we look at him, talk about him, and analyze him scientifically. His achievements in science, government, religion, art, and literature remain as they have always been, to be admired as one admires a storm at sea or autumn foliage or a mountain peak, quite apart from their origins and untouched by a scientific analysis. What does change is our chance of doing something about the subject of a theory. Newton's analysis of the light in a rainbow was a step in the directin of the laser.[23]

The traditional conception of man is flattering; it confers reinforc-   61
ing privileges. It is therefore easily defended and can be changed only with difficulty. It was designed to build up the individual as an instrument of countercontrol, and it did so effectively but in such a way as to limit progress. We have seen how the literatures of freedom and dignity, with their concern for autonomous man, have perpetuated the use of punishment and condoned the use of only weak nonpunitive techniques, and it is not difficult to demonstrate a connection between the unlimited right of the individual to pursue happiness and the catastrophes threatened by unchecked breeding, the unrestrained affluence which exhausts resources and pollutes the environment, and the imminence of nuclear war.

Physical and biological technologies have alleviated pestilence and   62
famine and many painful, dangerous, and exhausting features of daily life, and behavioral technology can begin to alleviate other kinds of ills. In the analysis of human behavior it is just possible that we are slightly beyond Newton's position in the analysis of light, for we are beginning to make technological applications. There are wonderful possibilities—and all the more wonderful because traditional approaches have been so ineffective. It is hard to imagine a world in which people live together without quarreling, maintain themselves

---

[22]*Sir Isaac Newton (1642–1727)* English scientist who invented differential and integral calculus and established the theory of gravity. His theories gave rise to a mechanical explanation of the universe in which all phenomena could be treated in terms of cause and effect. The English poet John Keats (1795–1821) reacted against Newton's analysis of the rainbow because he felt science was removing the romance and mystery from nature.

[23]*laser* A highly focused beam of electrons; a form of light. (The word is an acronym for *l*ight *a*mplification by *s*timulated *e*mission of *r*adiation.)

by producing the food, shelter, and clothing they need, enjoy themselves and contribute to the enjoyment of others in art, music, literature, and games, consume only a reasonable part of the resources of the world and add as little as possible to its pollution, bear no more children than can be raised decently, continue to explore the world around them and discover better ways of dealing with it, and come to know themselves accurately and, therefore, manage themselves effectively. Yet all this is possible, and even the slightest sign of progress should bring a kind of change which in traditional terms would be said to assuage wounded vanity, offset a sense of hopelessness or nostalgia, correct the impression that "we neither can nor need to do anything for ourselves," and promote a "sense of freedom and dignity" by building "a sense of confidence and worth." In other words, it should abundantly reinforce those who have been induced by their culture to work for its survival.

An experimental analysis shifts the determination of behavior from 63 autonomous man to the environment—an environment responsible both for the evolution of the species and for the repertoire acquired by each member. Early versions of environmentalism were inadequate because they could not explain how the environment worked, and much seemed to be left for autonomous man to do. But environmental contingencies now take over functions once attributed to autonomous man, and certain questions arise. Is man then "abolished"? Certainly not as a species or as an individual achiever. It is the autonomous inner man who is abolished, and that is a step forward. But does man not then become merely a victim or passive observer of what is happening to him? He is indeed controlled by his environment, but we must remember that it is an environment largely of his own making. The evolution of a culture is a gigantic exercise in self-control. It is often said that a scientific view of man leads to wounded vanity, a sense of hopelessness, and nostalgia. But no theory changes what it is a theory about; man remains what he has always been. And a new theory may change what can be done with its subject matter. A scientific view of man offers exciting possibilities. We have not yet seen what man can make of man.

QUESTIONS

1. Define the key terms of the chapter: "autonomous man," "contingencies of reinforcement," "environment," "the individual." Are there other key terms that need definition?

2. Skinner has not provided much of the scientific data on which his views are based because he wishes to address a general audience, one that can profit from the results, rather than the process, of scientific research. Should he have provided more scientific data? Is his audience a general audience? Would you like more data, more experimental information?
3. What are the most important ideas set forth in this piece? How do they relate to the area of psychology?
4. What kinds of different environments does Skinner take into account in the chapter? He mentions physical and social environments in paragraph 48. Are those the only ones there are?
5. Skinner believes that his view is scientific. Is he correct?

WRITING ASSIGNMENTS

1. One of the chief issues in the selection is concerned with the nature of the self. In an essay which uses Skinner's technique of the rhetorical question, answer the following question as carefully as he answers his: What is a self? Refer to paragraphs 32–34. Try to clarify what Skinner thinks the self is and offer, as you do so, your own views.
2. Inventory the selection for reference to character traits. By referring to specific quotations, and by analyzing them carefully in relation to one another, explain what Skinner means by "character traits." Is his analysis of this term reasonable? Is he convincing in suggesting that character traits may not be "permanent" or "basic" as we had thought?
3. Look around you for examples of contingencies of reinforcement. What kind of person does your environment seem to encourage you to be? What kinds of reinforcement are available in your immediate environment? Be as specific as possible in answering these questions.
4. Answer the question: Am I an autonomous agent? Use Skinner's strategy of examining first the environment in which you live, giving special attention to the contingencies of reinforcement which you are aware of. Then proceed to examine your own inner nature—insofar as that is possible—to see what that will contribute to your autonomy. Consider, as you answer this question, the issues of identity that are raised in the selection in paragraph 32 and thereafter. Does the process of answering this question help you to a better insight into your own identity?
5. Answer the question: Are my friends autonomous agents? Using Skinner's theories of contingencies of reinforcement, examine the behavior of two or three of your friends (or one in depth). Do they feel that they are free to do as they wish? Do you believe that they are aware of the limits on their freedom or of the degree to which they react to the reinforcements in their environment? To what extent is their behavior predictable by an outside observer?

6. In this selection, Skinner is basically predicting the death knell of the concept of the individual as an autonomous agent. What does he see as the alternative to this concept? Analyze closely the section of the piece beginning with paragraph 45 and ending with paragraph 55. What exactly is Skinner saying in these paragraphs? What will replace the concept of man as an autonomous agent? Is Skinner's view acceptable to you? How would you describe his vision of the future? Inventory the passage carefully to establish just what his thinking is on the nature of the individual in the future.

PART THREE

SCIENCE AND THE CHANGING WORLD

Francis Bacon · · · Charles Darwin
Lincoln Barnett · · · Alfred North Whitehead
Thomas S. Kuhn

SCIENCE EMERGED as a force to change the world in the seventeenth century, when Francis Bacon was in his maturity. Great writers such as the English poet John Donne (1572–1631) showed signs of worry and concern when they began to realize, as Donne said, that science "brings all into doubt." Since the seventeenth century, there have been extraordinary discoveries that have indeed brought much of ordinary belief into doubt. There have been advances that have clarified the nature of the universe, informing us about the moon, the sun, the planets, the stars, galaxies, and previously undreamed-of phenomena. We have begun to learn about the nature of the earth and its history, the relationship between animals and their development, the mysteries of quantum physics and relativity, the interiority of our genes, and the makeup of the brain itself. Science has called all into doubt, and it has offered answers to questions that, only a comparatively short time ago, never could have been asked.

We owe a great deal to Francis Bacon's pioneering efforts, which cleared the way for accurate thought in the age which was to begin the advance of science. Bacon realized that the human mind was so muddled with a variety of prejudices and illusions that it could not begin to undertake the gigantic task of reforming humankind's vision of the world until it faced and dealt with its own limitations. His four idols (illusions) are habits of thought that are so thoroughly ingrained that most people are not aware of them. In a series of brilliant analyses and observations, Bacon made people aware of limitations that they did not know they had. Even now, these limitations are at work, retarding progress in thought. Before Bacon, however, few people knew that they were at work.

Charles Darwin, despite his credentials as a trained minister in the Church of England, caused a remarkable stir in the middle of the nineteenth century when he developed his ideas concerning evolution. In "Natural Selection," Darwin explains how alterations in species can be selected by nature for survival, much the way people select desirable changes in breeds of cattle, horses, and dogs. Variations in a given species may appear naturally, he explains, but even more important is the fact that the fittest of the variations will soon dominate the rest. Survival, Darwin implies, is what nature is most interested in. It selects for the fittest individuals and so guarantees the fitness of the stock. Darwin's theories have caused traditionalists—those who believe in the biblical version of man's creation—a great deal of pain, but the scientific community has generally embraced them as accurate.

In the selection on Albert Einstein, Lincoln Barnett tells us about Einstein's early work on quantum physics, dealing with the baffling fact that in one sense light acts as if it were a series of particles, whereas in another sense it acts as if it were composed of waves. As we read about Einstein, we realize that it is not his thinking on the wave–particle controversy, nor even his celebrated theory of relativity, that makes him so important for us. From one perspective, his significance for us is attributable to his prominence as a physicist who described the world in terms of mathematics rather than in terms of perception. By doing so he shifted the ground of scientific research. He also made it almost impossible for the layman to immediately understand the new science. Bacon believed that the future of science lay in refining the instruments of perception. For his time he was quite accurate. Today, however, it lies in the refining of mathematical speculation.

Alfred North Whitehead addresses a more general problem: the relationship between science and religion. He acknowledges that they have been at odds in the past, and he examines some of the reasons for that fact. One important point he makes is that each has a province of its own and that it is appropriate to remember that each must respect the other's province. By doing so, Whitehead establishes that each can profit from refusing to claim too much. In an important essay, Thomas Kuhn reminds us that making scientific discoveries may not depend upon what he refers to as divergent thinking that is often prized by those who wish to be creative. Kuhn shows us that traditional thinking spawns scientific revolutions. It is a novel thought—but one that we must take seriously if there is to be progress in science.

The rhetorical strategies of these writers tend to the tried and true. They are each under an obligation to make difficult ideas clear to a general reader. Some naturally assume that their audience is more knowledgeable than others do, but each author is notable for clarity and straightforwardness. Each respects his readers and makes important contributions to his readers' education.

Bacon's use of enumeration—setting forth his ideas as being (in this case) four in number—is a simple, direct way of clarifying from the start just what he plans to do. Once having told us that he will treat four issues, he proceeds to do so, one after the other. Darwin emphasizes the topic of testimony, calling forth witness after witness to add to the strength of his argument; he also makes frequent use of the topic of definition. Lincoln Barnett, too, uses enumeration, testimony, and definition to clarify the very difficult concepts that constitute twentieth-century physics. Whitehead, in talking of religion and science, most naturally uses the topic of comparison. Because he is almost equally knowledgeable about both areas, his comparison is fascinating. Thomas Kuhn's use of enumeration and verbal signposts telling what comes next is quite impressive. All these writers depend on the topic of definition, because they are introducing new ideas or because they are determined to use every resource possible to be understood. Such dependence on basic rhetorical devices is one way to ensure clarity.

FRANCIS BACON

The Four Idols

FRANCIS BACON, Lord Verulam (1561–1626), lived during some of the most exciting times in history. Among his contemporaries were the essayist Michel de Montaigne; the playwrights Christopher Marlowe and William Shakespeare; the adventurer Sir Francis Drake; and Queen Elizabeth I, in whose reign he held several high offices. He became lord high chancellor of England in 1618, but fell from power in 1621 through a complicated series of actions, among which was his complicity in a bribery scheme. Yet his so-called crimes were minor, despite the fact he paid dearly for them. His book of Essays *(1597) was exceptionally popular during his lifetime, and when he found himself without a proper job, he devoted himself to what he declared to be his own true work, writing about philosophy and science.*

His purposes in Novum Organum *(The New Organon), published in 1620, were to replace the old organon, or instrument of thought, Aristotle's treatises on logic and thought. Despite the absolute stranglehold Aristotle held on sixteenth- and seventeenth-century minds through the fact that Aristotle's texts were used everywhere in schools*

From *Novum Organum.*

and colleges, Bacon thought that his logic would produce error. In Novum Organum he tried to set the stage for a new attitude toward logic and scientific inquiry. He proposed a system of reasoning usually referred to as induction. It is a quasi-scientific method involving the collecting and inventorying of a great mass of observations from nature. Once this mass of observations was gathered and organized, Bacon believed, the truth about what is observed would leap out at one.

Bacon is often credited with having invented the scientific method, but this notion is not accurate. He was on the right track with respect to collecting and observing. What he was wrong about was the result of that gathering. After all, one could watch an infinite number of apples (and oranges, too) fall to the ground without having the slightest sense of why they do so. What Bacon failed to realize— and he died before he could get close enough to scientific observation to realize it—is the creative function of the scientist as expressed in the hypothesis. The hypothesis—a shrewd guess about why something happens—is then tested by the kinds of observations Bacon approved.

Nonetheless, "The Four Idols" is a brilliant work. It does establish the requirements for the kind of observation that produces true scientific knowledge. Bacon despaired of any science in his own day, in part because no one paid any attention to the ways in which the idols strangled thought, observation, and imagination. He realized that the would-be scientist was foiled even before he began. Bacon was a farsighted man. He was correct about the failures of science in his time; and he was correct, moreover, about the fact that scientific advance would depend on sensory perception and on aids to perception, such as microscopes and telescopes. The really brilliant aspect of "The Four Idols" is the fact that Bacon focuses, not on what is observed, but on the instrument of observation, the human mind. Only when the instrument is freed of error can its observations be relied upon.

BACON'S RHETORIC

Bacon was trained during the great age of English rhetoric, and his prose (even though it is translated from Latin) shows the clarity, balance, and organization that naturally characterize the prose writing of seventeenth-century England. The most basic device Bacon uses is enumeration: stating clearly that there are four idols and implying that he will treat each one in turn.

Enumeration is one of the most common and most reliable rhetorical devices. The listener hears a speaker say, "I have only three things I want to say today. . . ." And the listener is alerted to listen for all three, while being secretly grateful that there are only three. The reader, when encountering complex material, is always happy to have such "road signs" as, "The second aspect of this question is . . . ."

"The Four Idols" begins, after a three-paragraph introduction, with a single paragraph devoted to each idol, so that we have an early definition of each idol and a sense of what to look for. Paragraphs 8–16 cover only the issues related to the Idols of the Tribe: the problems all people have simply because they are people. Paragraphs 17–22 consider the Idols of the Cave, those particular fixations individuals have because of their special backgrounds or limitations. Paragraphs 23–26 treat of the questions related to Idols of the Marketplace, particularly those that deal with the way people misuse words and abuse definitions. The remainder of the selection treats of the Idols of the Theater, which relate entirely to philosophic systems and preconceptions—all of which tend to narrow the scope of research and understanding.

Enumeration works within each of these groups of paragraphs as well. Bacon often begins a paragraph with such statements as, "There is one principal . . . distinction between different minds" (para. 19). Or he says, "The idols imposed by words on the understanding are of two kinds" (para. 24). The effect is to ensure clarity where confusion could easily reign.

As an added means of achieving clarity, Bacon sets aside a single paragraph—the last—as a summary of the main points that have been made, and in the order in which they were made.

Within any section of this selection, Bacon depends upon observation, example, and reason to make his points. When he speaks of a given idol, he defines it, gives several examples to make it clearer, discusses its effects on thought, then dismisses it as dangerous. He then goes on to the next idol. In some cases, and where appropriate, he names those who are victims of a specific idol. In each case he tries to be thorough, explanatory, and convincing.

Not only is this work a landmark in thought; it is also, because of its absolute clarity, a beacon. We can still profit from its light.

The Four Idols

The idols[1] and false notions which are now in possession of the human understanding, and have taken deep root therein, not only so beset men's minds that truth can hardly find entrance, but even after entrance obtained, they will again in the very instauration[2] of the sciences meet and trouble us, unless men being forewarned of the danger fortify themselves as far as may be against their assaults.

There are four classes of idols which beset men's minds. To these for distinction's sake I have assigned names—calling the first class *Idols of the Tribe*; the second, *Idols of the Cave*; the third, *Idols of the Marketplace*; the fourth, *Idols of the Theater*.

The formation of ideas and axioms by true induction[3] is no doubt the proper remedy to be applied for the keeping off and clearing away of idols. To point them out, however, is of great use; for the doctrine of idols is to the interpretation of nature what the doctrine of the refutation of sophisms[4] is to common logic.

The *Idols of the Tribe* have their foundation in human nature itself, and in the tribe or race of men. For it is a false assertion that the sense of man is the measure of things. On the contrary, all perceptions as well of the sense as of the mind are according to the measure of the individual and not according to the measure of the universe. And the human understanding is like a false mirror, which, receiving rays irregularly, distorts and discolors the nature of things by mingling its own nature with it.

The *Idols of the Cave* are the idols of the individual man. For ev-

---

[1]*idols* By this term Bacon means phantoms or illusions (see note 21). The Greek philosopher Democritus spoke of *eidola,* tiny representations of things that impressed themselves on the mind.

[2]*instauration* renewal; renovation.

[3]*induction* Bacon championed induction as the method by which new knowledge is developed. As he saw it, induction involved a patient gathering, inventorying, and categorizing of facts in the hope that a large number of them would point to the truth. As a process of gathering evidence from which inferences are drawn, induction is contrasted with Aristotle's method, *deduction,* according to which a theory is established and the truth deduced. Deduction places the stress on the authority of the expert; induction places the stress on the facts themselves.

[4]*sophisms* Apparently intelligent statements that are wrong; false wisdom.

eryone (besides the errors common to human nature in general) has a cave or den of his own, which refracts[5] and discolors the light of nature; owing either to his own proper and peculiar nature; or to his education and conversation with others; or to the reading of books, and the authority of those whom he esteems and admires; or to the differences of impressions, accordingly as they take place in a mind preoccupied and predisposed or in a mind indifferent and settled; or the like. So that the spirit of man (according as it is meted out to different individuals) is in fact a thing variable and full of perturbation,[6] and governed as it were by chance. Whence it was well observed by Heraclitus[7] that men look for sciences in their own lesser worlds, and not in the greater or common world.

There are also idols formed by the intercourse and association of men with each other, which I call *Idols of the Marketplace*, on account of the commerce and consort of men there. For it is by discourse that men associate; and words are imposed according to the apprehension of the vulgar.[8] And therefore the ill and unfit choice of words wonderfully obstructs the understanding. Nor do the definitions or explanations wherewith in some things learned men are wont[9] to guard and defend themselves, by any means set the matter right. But words plainly force and overrule the understanding, and throw all into confusion and lead men away into numberless empty controversies and idle fancies.

Lastly, there are idols which have immigrated into men's minds from the various dogmas of philosophies, and also from wrong laws of demonstration.[10] These I call *Idols of the Theater*; because in my judgment all the received systems[11] are but so many stage-plays, representing worlds of their own creation after an unreal and scenic fashion. Nor is it only of the systems now in vogue, or only of the ancient sects and philosophies, that I speak; for many more plays of the same kind may yet be composed and in like artificial manner set forth; seeing

---

[5]***refracts*** deflects, bends back, alters.

[6]***perturbation*** Uncertainty, disturbance. In astronomy, the motion caused by the gravity of nearby planets.

[7]***Heraclitus (535?–?475 B.C.)*** Greek philosopher who believed that there was no reality except in change; all else was illusion. He also believed that fire was the basis of all the world and that everything we see is a transformation of it.

[8]***vulgar*** common people.

[9]***wont*** accustomed.

[10]***laws of demonstration*** Bacon may be referring to Aristotle's logical system of syllogism and deduction.

[11]***received systems*** official or authorized views of scientific truth.

that errors the most widely different have nevertheless causes for the most part alike. Neither again do I mean this only of entire systems, but also of many principles and axioms in science, which by tradition, credulity, and negligence, have come to be received.

But of these several kinds of idols I must speak more largely and exactly, that the understanding may be duly cautioned. 8

The human understanding is of its own nature prone to suppose the existence of more order and regularity in the world than it finds. And though there be many things in nature which are singular and unmatched, yet it devises for them parallels and conjugates and relatives[12] which do not exist. Hence the fiction that all celestial bodies move in perfect circles; spirals and dragons being (except in name) utterly rejected. Hence too the element of fire with its orb is brought in, to make up the square with the other three which the sense perceives. Hence also the ratio of density[13] of the so-called elements is arbitrarily fixed at ten to one. And so on of other dreams. And these fancies affect not dogmas only, but simple notions also. 9

The human understanding when it has once adopted an opinion (either as being the received opinion or as being agreeable to itself) draws all things else to support and agree with it. And though there be a greater number and weight of instances to be found on the other side, yet these it either neglects and despises, or else by some distinction sets aside and rejects; in order that by this great and pernicious predetermination the authority of its former conclusions may remain inviolate. And therefore it was a good answer that was made by one who when they showed him hanging in a temple a picture of those who had paid their vows as having escaped shipwreck, and would have him say whether he did not now acknowledge the power of the gods— "Ay," asked he again, "but where are they painted that were drowned after their vows?" And such is the way of all superstition, whether in astrology, dreams, omens, divine judgments, or the like; wherein men having a delight in such vanities, mark the events where they are fulfilled, but where they fail, though this happen much oftener, neglect and pass them by. But with far more subtlety does this mischief insinuate itself into philosophy and the sciences; in which the first conclu- 10

---

[12]*parallels and conjugates and relatives*   A reference to the habit of assuming that phenomena are regular and ordered, consisting of squares, triangles, circles, and other regular shapes.

[13]*ratio of density*   The false assumption that the relationship of mass or weight to volume was ten to one. This is another example of Bacon's complaint, establishing a convenient regular "relative" or relationship.

sion colors and brings into conformity with itself all that come after, though far sounder and better. Besides, independently of that delight and vanity which I have described, it is the peculiar and perpetual error of the human intellect to be more moved and excited by affirmatives than by negatives; whereas it ought properly to hold itself indifferently disposed towards both alike. Indeed, in the establishment of any true axiom, the negative instance is the more forcible of the two.

The human understanding is moved by those things most which 11 strike and enter the mind simultaneously and suddenly, and so fill the imagination; and then it feigns and supposes all other things to be somehow, though it cannot see how, similar to those few things by which it is surrounded. But for that going to and fro to remote and heterogeneous instances, by which axioms are tried as in the fire,[14] the intellect is altogether slow and unfit, unless it be forced thereto by severe laws and overruling authority.

The human understanding is unquiet; it cannot stop or rest, and 12 still presses onward, but in vain. Therefore it is that we cannot conceive of any end or limit to the world, but always as of necessity it occurs to us that there is something beyond. Neither again can it be conceived how eternity has flowed down to the present day; for that distinction which is commonly received of infinity in time past and in time to come can by no means hold; for it would thence follow that one infinity is greater than another, and that infinity is wasting away and tending to become finite. The like subtlety arises touching the infinite divisibility of lines,[15] from the same inability of thought to stop. But this inability interferes more mischievously in the discovery of causes:[16] for although the most general principles in nature ought

---

[14]***tried as in the fire*** Trial by fire is a figure of speech representing thorough, rigorous testing even to the point of risking what is tested. An axiom is a statement of apparent truth that has not yet been put to the test of examination and investigation.

[15]***infinite divisibility of lines*** This gave rise to the paradox of Zeno, the Greek philosopher of the fifth century B.C. who showed that it was impossible to get from one point to another because one had to pass the midpoint of the line determined by the two original points, and then the midpoint of the remaining distance, and then of that remaining distance, down to an infinite number of points. By using accepted truths to "prove" an absurdity about motion, Zeno actually hoped to prove that motion itself did not exist. This is the "subtlety" or confusion Bacon says is produced by the "inability of thought to stop."

[16]***discovery of causes*** Knowledge of the world was based on four causes: efficient (who made it?); material (what is it made of?); formal (what is its shape?); and final (what is its purpose?). The scholastics concentrated their thinking on the first and last, while the "middle causes," related to matter and shape, were the proper subject matter of science because they alone yielded to observation. (See paragraph 33.)

to be held merely positive, as they are discovered, and cannot with truth be referred to a cause; nevertheless, the human understanding being unable to rest still seeks something prior in the order of nature. And then it is that in struggling towards that which is further off, it falls back upon that which is more nigh at hand; namely, on final causes: which have relation clearly to the nature of man rather than to the nature of the universe, and from this source have strangely defiled philosophy. But he is no less an unskilled and shallow philosopher who seeks causes of that which is most general, than he who in things subordinate and subaltern[17] omits to do so.

The human understanding is no dry light, but receives an infusion   13 from the will and affections;[18] whence proceed sciences which may be called "sciences as one would." For what a man had rather were true he more readily believes. Therefore he rejects difficult things from impatience of research; sober things, because they narrow hope; the deeper things of nature, from superstition; the light of experience, from arrogance and pride, lest his mind should seem to be occupied with things mean and transitory; things not commonly believed, out of deference to the opinion of the vulgar. Numberless in short are the ways, and sometimes imperceptible, in which the affections color and infect the understanding.

But by far the greatest hindrance and aberration of the human un-   14 derstanding proceeds from the dullness, incompetency, and deceptions of the senses; in that things which strike the sense outweigh things which do not immediately strike it, though they be more important. Hence it is that speculation commonly ceases where sight ceases; insomuch that of things invisible there is little or no observation. Hence all the working of the spirits[19] enclosed in tangible bodies lies hid and unobserved of men. So also all the more subtle changes of form in the parts of coarser substances (which they commonly call alteration, though it is in truth local motion through exceedingly small spaces) is in like manner unobserved. And yet unless these two things just mentioned be searched out and brought to light, nothing great can be achieved in nature, as far as the production of works is concerned. So again the essential nature of our common air, and of all bodies less dense than air (which are very many) is almost unknown. For the sense by itself is a thing infirm and erring; neither can instruments for en-

---

[17]**subaltern**   lower in status.
[18]**will and affections**   human free will and emotional needs and responses.
[19]**spirits**   the soul or animating force.

larging or sharpening the senses do much; but all the truer kind of interpretation of nature is effected by instances and experiments fit and apposite;[20] wherein the sense decides touching the experiment only, and the experiment touching the point in nature and the thing itself.

The human understanding is of its own nature prone to abstractions and gives a substance and reality to things which are fleeting. But to resolve nature into abstractions is less to our purpose than to dissect her into parts; as did the school of Democritus,[21] which went further into nature than the rest. Matter rather than forms should be the object of our attention, its configurations and changes of configuration, and simple action, and law of action or motion; for forms are figments of the human mind, unless you will call those laws of action forms.

Such then are the idols which I call *Idols of the Tribe;* and which take their rise either from the homogeneity of the substance of the human spirit,[22] or from its preoccupation, or from its narrowness, or from its restless motion, or from an infusion of the affections, or from the incompetency of the senses, or from the mode of impression.

The *Idols of the Cave* take their rise in the peculiar constitution, mental or bodily, of each individual; and also in education, habit, and accident. Of this kind there is a great number and variety; but I will instance those the pointing out of which contains the most important caution, and which have most effect in disturbing the clearness of the understanding.

Men become attached to certain particular sciences and speculations, either because they fancy themselves the authors and inventors thereof, or because they have bestowed the greatest pains upon them and become most habituated to them. But men of this kind, if they betake themselves to philosophy and contemplations of a general character, distort and color them in obedience to their former fancies; a thing especially to be noticed in Aristotle,[23] who made his natural

---

[20]*apposite* appropriate; well related.

[21]*Democritus (460?–?370 b.c.)* Greek philosopher who thought the world was composed of atoms. Bacon felt such "dissection" to be useless because it was impractical. Yet Democritus's concept of the *eidola,* the mind's impressions of things, may have contributed to Bacon's idea of "the idol."

[22]*human spirit* human nature.

[23]*Aristotle (384–322 b.c.)* Greek philosopher whose *Organon* (system of logic) dominated the thought of Bacon's time. Bacon sought to overthrow Aristotle's hold on science and thought.

philosophy[24] a mere bondservant to his logic, thereby rendering it contentious and well nigh useless. The race of chemists[25] again out of a few experiments of the furnace have built up a fantastic philosophy, framed with reference to a few things; and Gilbert[26] also, after he had employed himself most laboriously in the study and observation of the loadstone, proceeded at once to construct an entire system in accordance with his favorite subject.

There is one principal and, as it were, radical distinction between 19 different minds, in respect of philosophy and the sciences, which is this: that some minds are stronger and apter to mark the differences of things, others to mark their resemblances. The steady and acute mind can fix its contemplations and dwell and fasten on the subtlest distinctions: the lofty and discursive mind recognizes and puts together the finest and most general resemblances. Both kinds however easily err in excess, by catching the one at gradations, the other at shadows.

There are found some minds given to an extreme admiration of 20 antiquity, others to an extreme love and appetite for novelty; but few so duly tempered that they can hold the mean, neither carping at what has been well laid down by the ancients, nor despising what is well introduced by the moderns. This however turns to the great injury of the sciences and philosophy; since these affectations of antiquity and novelty are the humors[27] of partisans rather than judgments; and truth is to be sought for not in the felicity of any age, which is an unstable thing, but in the light of nature and experience, which is eternal. These factions therefore must be abjured,[28] and care must be taken that the intellect be not hurried by them into assent.

Contemplations of nature and of bodies in their simple form break 21 up and distract the understanding, while contemplations of nature and bodies in their composition and configuration overpower and dissolve the understanding: a distinction well seen in the school of Leucippus[29]

---

[24]**natural philosophy** The scientific study of nature in general—biology, zoology, geology, etc.

[25]**chemists** Alchemists had developed a "fantastic philosophy" from their experimental attempts to transmute lead into gold.

[26]**William Gilbert (1540–1603)** An English scientist who studied magnetism and codified many laws related to magnetic fields. He was particularly ridiculed by Bacon for being too narrow in his researches.

[27]**humors** used in a medical sense to mean a distortion caused by imbalance.

[28]**abjured** renounced, sworn off, repudiated.

[29]**Leucippus (fifth century B.C.)** Greek philosopher; teacher of Democritus and inventor of the atomistic theory. His works survive only in fragments.

and Democritus as compared with the other philosophies. For that school is so busied with the particles that it hardly attends to the structure; while the others are so lost in admiration of the structure that they do not penetrate to the simplicity of nature. These kinds of contemplation should therefore be alternated and taken by turns; that so the understanding may be rendered at once penetrating and comprehensive, and the inconveniences above mentioned, with the idols which proceed from them, may be avoided.

Let such then be our provision and contemplative prudence for 22 keeping off and dislodging the *Idols of the Cave*, which grow for the most part either out of the predominance of a favorite subject, or out of an excessive tendency to compare or to distinguish, or out of partiality for particular ages, or out of the largeness or minuteness of the objects contemplated. And generally let every student of nature take this as a rule—that whatever his mind seizes and dwells upon with peculiar satisfaction is to be held in suspicion, and that so much the more care is to be taken in dealing with such questions to keep the understanding even and clear.

But the *Idols of the Marketplace* are the most troublesome of all: 23 idols which have crept into the understanding through the alliances of words and names. For men believe that their reason governs words; but it is also true that words react on the understanding; and this it is that has rendered philosophy and the sciences sophistical and inactive. Now words, being commonly framed and applied according to the capacity of the vulgar, follow those lines of division which are most obvious to the vulgar understanding. And whenever an understanding of greater acuteness or a more diligent observation would alter those lines to suit the true divisions of nature, words stand in the way and resist the change. Whence it comes to pass that the high and formal discussions of learned men end oftentimes in disputes about words and names; with which (according to the use and wisdom of the mathematicians) it would be more prudent to begin, and so by means of definitions reduce them to order. Yet even definitions cannot cure this evil in dealing with natural and material things; since the definitions themselves consist of words, and those words beget others: so that it is necessary to recur to individual instances, and those in due series and order; as I shall say presently when I come to the method and scheme for the formation of notions and axioms.[30]

The idols imposed by words on the understanding are of two kinds. 24

---

[30]***notions and axioms*** conceptions and definitive statements of truth.

They are either names of things which do not exist (for as there are things left unnamed through lack of observation, so likewise are there names which result from fantastic suppositions and to which nothing in reality responds), or they are names of things which exist, but yet confused and ill-defined, and hastily and irregularly derived from realities. Of the former kind are Fortune, the Prime Mover, Planetary Orbits, Element of Fire, and like fictions which owe their origin to false and idle theories.[31] And this class of idols is more easily expelled, because to get rid of them it is only necessary that all theories should be steadily rejected and dismissed as obsolete.

But the other class, which springs out of a faulty and unskillful abstraction, is intricate and deeply rooted. Let us take for example such a word as *humid;* and see how far the several things which the word is used to signify agree with each other; and we shall find the word *humid* to be nothing else than a mark loosely and confusedly applied to denote a variety of actions which will not bear to be reduced to any constant meaning. For it both signifies that which easily spreads itself round any other body; and that which in itself is indeterminate and cannot solidize; and that which readily yields in every direction; and that which easily divides and scatters itself; and that which easily unites and collects itself; and that which readily flows and is put in motion; and that which readily clings to another body and wets it; and that which is easily reduced to a liquid, or being solid easily melts. Accordingly when you come to apply the word—if you take it in one sense, flame is humid; if in another, air is not humid; if in another, fine dust is humid; if in another, glass is humid. So that it is easy to see that the notion is taken by abstraction only from water and common and ordinary liquids, without any due verification. 25

There are however in words certain degrees of distortion and error. One of the least faulty kinds is that of names of substances, especially of lowest species and well-deduced (for the notion of *chalk* and of *mud* is good, of *earth* bad);[32] a more faulty kind is that of actions, as *to generate, to corrupt, to alter;* the most faulty is of qualities (except such as are the immediate objects of the sense), as *heavy, light, rare, dense,* and the like. Yet in all these cases some notions are of neces- 26

---

[31]*idle theories* These are things that cannot be observed and thus do not exist. Fortune is fate; the Prime Mover is God or some "first" force; the notion that planets orbited the sun was considered as "fantastic" as these others, or as the idea that everything was made up of fire and its many permutations.

[32]**earth bad** Chalk and mud were useful in manufacture; hence they were terms of approval. *Earth* is used here in the sense we use *dirt,* as in "digging in the dirt."

sity a little better than others, in proportion to the greater variety of subjects that fall within the range of the human sense.

But the *Idols of the Theater* are not innate, nor do they steal into 27 the understanding secretly, but are plainly impressed and received into the mind from the play-books of philosophical systems and the perverted rules of demonstration.[33] To attempt refutations in this case would be merely inconsistent with what I have already said: for since we agree neither upon principles nor upon demonstrations, there is no place for argument. And this is so far well, inasmuch as it leaves the honor of the ancients untouched. For they are no wise disparaged—the question between them and me being only as to the way. For as the saying is, the lame man who keeps the right road outstrips the runner who takes a wrong one. Nay, it is obvious that when a man runs the wrong way, the more active and swift he is the further he will go astray.

But the course I propose for the discovery of sciences is such as 28 leaves but little to the acuteness and strength of wits, but places all wits[34] and understandings nearly on a level. For as in the drawing of a straight line or perfect circle, much depends on the steadiness and practice of the hand, if it be done by aim of hand only, but if with the aid of rule or compass, little or nothing; so is it exactly with my plan. But though particular confutations[35] would be of no avail, yet touching the sects and general divisions of such systems I must say something; something also touching the external signs which show that they are unsound; and finally something touching the causes of such great infelicity and of such lasting and general agreement in error; that so the access to truth may be made less difficult, and the human understanding may the more willingly submit to its purgation and dismiss its idols.

Idols of the Theater, or of systems, are many, and there can be and 29 perhaps will be yet many more. For were it not that now for many ages men's minds have been busied with religion and theology; and were it not that civil governments, especially monarchies, have been averse to such novelties, even in matters speculative; so that men labor therein to the peril and harming of their fortunes—not only unrewarded, but exposed also to contempt and envy; doubtless there would

---

[33]***perverted rules of demonstration*** Another complaint against Aristotle's logic as misapplied in Bacon's day.

[34]***wits*** intelligence, reasoning powers.

[35]***confutations*** Specific counterarguments. Bacon means that he cannot offer particular arguments against each scientific sect; thus he offers a general warning.

have arisen many other philosophical sects like to those which in great variety flourished once among the Greeks. For as on the phenomena of the heavens many hypotheses may be constructed, so likewise (and more also) many various dogmas may be set up and established on the phenomena of philosophy. And in the plays of this philosophical theater you may observe the same thing which is found in the theater of the poets, that stories invented for the stage are more compact and elegant, and more as one would wish them to be, than true stories out of history.

In general, however, there is taken for the material of philosophy 30 either a great deal out of a few things, or a very little out of many things; so that on both sides philosophy is based on too narrow a foundation of experiment and natural history, and decides on the authority of too few cases. For the rational school of philosophers[36] snatches from experience a variety of common instances, neither duly ascertained nor diligently examined and weighed, and leaves all the rest to meditation and agitation of wit.

There is also another class of philosophers,[37] who having bestowed 31 much diligent and careful labor on a few experiments, have thence made bold to educe and construct systems; wresting all other facts in a strange fashion to conformity therewith.

And there is yet a third class,[38] consisting of those who out of faith 32 and veneration mix their philosophy with theology and traditions; among whom the vanity of some has gone so far aside as to seek the origin of sciences among spirits and genii.[39] So that this parent stock of errors—this false philosophy—is of three kinds; the sophistical, the empirical, and the superstitious. . . .

But the corruption of philosophy by superstition and an admixture 33 of theology is far more widely spread, and does the greatest harm,

---

[36]*rational school of philosophers* Platonists who felt that human reason alone could discover the truth and that experiment was unnecessary. Their observation of experience produced only a "variety of common instances" from which they reasoned.

[37]*another class of philosophers* William Gilbert (1540–1603) experimented tirelessly with magnetism, from which he derived numerous odd theories. Though Gilbert was a true scientist, Bacon thought of him as limited and on the wrong track.

[38]*a third class* Pythagoras (d. 497? B.C.) was a Greek philosopher who experimented rigorously with mathematics and a tuned string. He is said to have developed the musical scale. His theory of reincarnation, or the transmigration of souls, was somehow based on his travels in India and his work with scales. The superstitious belief in the movement of souls is what Bacon complains of.

[39]*genii* Oriental demons or spirits; a slap at Pythagoras, who traveled in the Orient.

whether to entire systems or to their parts. For the human understanding is obnoxious to the influence of the imagination no less than to the influence of common notions. For the contentious and sophistical kind of philosophy ensnares the understanding; but this kind, being fanciful and tumid[40] and half poetical, misleads it more by flattery. For there is in man an ambition of the understanding, no less than of the will, especially in high and lofty spirits.

Of this kind we have among the Greeks a striking example in 34 Pythagoras, though he united with it a coarser and more cumbrous superstition; another in Plato and his school,[41] more dangerous and subtle. It shows itself likewise in parts of other philosophies, in the introduction of abstract forms and final causes and first causes, with the omission in most cases of causes intermediate, and the like. Upon this point the greatest caution should be used. For nothing is so mischievous as the apotheosis of error; and it is a very plague of the understanding for vanity to become the object of veneration. Yet in this vanity some of the moderns have with extreme levity indulged so far as to attempt to found a system of natural philosophy on the first chapter of Genesis, on the book of Job, and other parts of the sacred writings; seeking for the dead among the living: which also makes the inhibition and repression of it the more important, because from this unwholesome mixture of things human and divine there arises not only a fantastic philosophy but also an heretical religion. Very meet it is therefore that we be sober-minded, and give to faith that only which is faith's. . . .

So much concerning the several classes of Idols, and their equipage: 35 all of which must be renounced and put away with a fixed and solemn determination, and the understanding thoroughly freed and cleansed; the entrance into the kingdom of man, founded on the sciences, being not much other than the entrance into the kingdom of heaven, whereinto none may enter except as a little child.

---

[40]***tumid*** overblown, swollen.

[41]***Plato and his school*** Plato's religious bent was further developed by Plotinus (205–270 A.D.) in his *Enneads*. Although Plotinus was not a Christian, his Neo-Platonism was welcomed as a philosophy compatible with Christianity.

QUESTIONS

1. Which of Bacon's idols is the most difficult to understand? Do your best to define it.
2. Which of these idols do we still need to worry about? Why? What dangers does it present?
3. What does Bacon mean by saying that our senses are weak (para. 14)? Is he correct in making that statement?
4. Occasionally Bacon says something in such a way that it seems a bit like an aphorism (see the introduction to Machiavelli). Find at least one such expression in this selection. Upon examination, does the expression have as much meaning as it seems to have?
5. What kind of readers did Bacon expect for this piece? What clues does his way of communicating provide regarding the nature of his anticipated readers?

WRITING ASSIGNMENTS

1. What special background—hobbies, skills, work experience, interests, intellectual commitments—do you have that you feel are special? Name at least three specific things in which you are involved. Using Bacon's technique of enumeration, show how each can affect your examination of, say, the best way to learn; the best way to use spare time; the best way to stay healthy; the best way to entertain a boyfriend or a girlfriend (choose one of these subjects or choose your own subject).
2. Which of Bacon's idols most seriously applies to you as a person? Using enumeration, put the idols in order of importance as you see them affecting your own judgment. If you prefer, you may write about which idol you believe is most important in impeding scientific investigation today.
3. Is it true, as Bacon says in paragraph 10, that people are in general more excited by affirmation than by negation? Do we really stress the positive and deemphasize the negative in the conduct of our general affairs? Find at least three instances in which people seem to gravitate toward the positive or the negative in a series of situations in daily life. Try to establish whether or not Bacon has, in fact, described what is a habit of mind.
4. In paragraph 13, Bacon states that the "will and affections" enter into matters of thought. By this he means that our understanding of what we observe is conditioned by what we want and what we feel. Thus, when he says, "For what a man had rather were true he more readily believes," he tells us that people tend to believe what they want to believe. Test this statement by means of observation. Find out, for example, how many older people are convinced that the world is deteriorating, how many younger people feel that there is a plot on the part of older people to hold them

back, how many women feel that men consciously oppress women, and how many men feel that feminists are not as feminine as they should be. What other beliefs can you discover that seem to have their origin in what people want to believe rather than in what is true?

5. Establish the extent to which the Idols of the Marketplace are relevant to issues in modern life. In particular, study the language used in the newspapers (and important magazines) to discuss nuclear warfare. To what extent are official words (those uttered by governments) designed to obscure issues? In what sense are they misleading? Consult the discussion in paragraph 23 and following paragraphs to answer this question. In what sense do "words stand in the way and resist . . . change" in regard to debate on nuclear war. If you wish to substitute another major issue (e.g., abortion, improving secondary schools, social welfare services, taxation, prayer in the schools), feel free to do so.

6. Bacon's views on religion have always been questionable. He grew up in a very religious time, but his writings rarely discuss religion positively. In this work he talks about giving "to faith only that which is faith's." He seems to feel that scientific investigation is something quite separate from religion. Examine this work carefully to establish what you think Bacon's view on this question is. Then take a stand on the issue of the relationship between religion and science. Should science be totally independent of religious concerns? Should religious issues control scientific experimentation? What does Bacon mean when he complains about the vanity of founding "a system of natural philosophy on the first chapter of Genesis, on the book of Job, and other parts of the sacred writings" (para. 34)? "Natural philosophy" means biology, chemistry, physics, and science in general. Are Bacon's complaints justified? Would his complaints be relevant today?

CHARLES DARWIN

Natural Selection

*CHARLES DARWIN (1809–1882) was trained as a minister in the
Church of England, but he was also the grandson of one of England's
greatest horticulturists, Erasmus Darwin. Partly as a way of putting
off taking orders in the church, and partly because of his natural curiosity and scientific enterprise, Darwin managed to find himself performing the functions of a naturalist on the H.M.S. Beagle, which was
engaged in scientific explorations around South America during the
years 1831–1836. Darwin's fascinating book, Voyage of the Beagle
(1839), details the experiences he had and offers us some views of his
self-education as a naturalist.*

*His experiences on the Beagle led him to take note of variations in
species of animals he found in various separate locales, particularly
between remote islands and the mainland. Varieties—his term for
any visible (or invisible) differences in markings, coloration, size or
shape of appendages, organs, or bodies—were of some peculiar use,
he believed, for the animals in the environments in which he found
them. He was not certain of what kind of use these varieties might
be, and he did not know whether the changes that created the vari-*

From *The Origin of Species on the Basis of Natural Selection.*

eties resulted from the environment or from some chance operation of nature. Ultimately, he concluded that varieties in nature were caused by three forces: (1) natural selection, in which varieties occur spontaneously by chance but are then "selected" for because they are aids to survival; (2) direct action of the environment, in which non-adaptive varieties do not survive because of climate, food conditions, or the like; and (3) the effects of use or disuse of a variation (somewhat like the short beak of a bird in paragraph 11 in the extract). Sexual selection, which figures prominently in this work, was later thought to be less significant by Darwin.

The idea of evolution—the gradual change of species through some kind of modification of varieties—had been in the air for many years when Darwin began his work. The English scientists C. W. Wells in 1813 and Patrick Matthew in 1831 had both proposed theories of natural selection, although Darwin was unaware of their work. Alfred Russell Wallace (1823–1913), a younger English scientist, revealed in 1858 that he was about to propose the same theory of evolution as was Darwin. They joined and published their theories (in sketchy form) together, and the next year Darwin rushed his Origin of Species to press.

Darwin does not mention human beings as part of the evolutionary process in the selection. Because he was particularly concerned with the likelihood of adverse reactions on the part of theologians, he merely promised later discussion of that subject. It came in The Descent of Man (1871), the companion to The Origin of Species.

When Darwin returned to England after completing his researches on the Beagle, he supplemented his knowledge with information gathered from breeders of pigeons, livestock, dogs, and horses. This research, it must be noted, was rather limited, involving relatively few samples, and was conducted according to comparatively unscientific practices. Yet, it corresponded with his observations of nature. The fact was that man could cause changes in species; it was Darwin's task to show that nature—through the process of natural selection—could do the same thing.

Naturally, The Descent of Man stirred up a great deal of controversy between the church and Darwin's supporters. Not since the Roman Catholic Church denied the fact that the earth went around the sun, as Galileo had proved scientifically in 1632 (and was banished for his pains), had there been a more serious confrontation of science and religion. Darwin was ridiculed by ministers and doubted by older scientists; but he was stoutly defended by younger scientists, many of whom had arrived at conclusions similar to Darwin's. In the end,

Darwin's views were accepted by the Church of England, and when he died in 1882 he was lionized and buried at Westminster Abbey in London. Only recently, controversy concerning his work has arisen again.

DARWIN'S RHETORIC

Darwin's writing is fluent, smooth, and stylistically sophisticated. Yet, his material is burdensome, detailed, and in general not appealing. Despite these drawbacks, he manages to keep the reader engaged. His rhetorical method depends entirely upon the yoking of thesis and demonstration. He uses the topic of definition frequently, but he most frequently uses the topic of testimony, as he gathers information and instances, both real and imaginary, from many different sources.

Interestingly enough, Darwin said that he used Francis Bacon's method of induction in his researches. That means the gathering of evidence of many instances of a given phenomenon, from which the truth—or a natural law—will emerge. The fact is that Darwin did not quite follow this path. He did, as most modern scientists do, establish a hypothesis after a period of observation; then he looked for evidence that would confirm or disconfirm the hypothesis. He was careful to include examples that argued against his view, but like most scientists, he emphasized the importance of the positive samples.

Induction plays a part in the rhetoric of this selection in that the selection is dominated by examples. There are examples taken from the breeding of birds, from the condition of birds in nature, from domestic farm animals and their breeding; and there are many, many examples taken from botany, including the breeding of plants and the interdependence between certain insects and certain plants. Erasmus Darwin was famous for his work with plants, and it is natural that such observations would play an important part in his grandson's thinking.

The process of natural selection is carefully discussed, particularly in paragraph 8 and thereafter. Darwin emphasizes its positive nature and its differences from selection by human breeders. The topic of comparison, which appears frequently in the selection, is most conspicuous in these paragraphs. He postulates a nature in which the fittest survive because they are best adapted for survival, but he does not dwell on the fate of those who are unfit individuals. Later writers, often misapplying his theories, were to do that.

Natural Selection

How will the struggle for existence . . . act in regard to variation?
Can the principle of selection, which we have seen is so potent in the
hands of man, apply under nature? I think we shall see that it can act
most efficiently. Let the endless number of slight variations and individual differences occurring in our domestic productions, and, in a
lesser degree, in those under nature, be borne in mind; as well as the
strength of the hereditary tendency. Under domestication, it may truly
be said that the whole organization becomes in some degree plastic.[1]
But the variability, which we almost universally meet with in our domestic productions, is not directly produced, as Hooker and Asa Gray[2]
have well remarked, by man; he can neither originate varieties nor
prevent their occurrence; he can only preserve and accumulate such as
do occur. Unintentionally he exposes organic beings to new and changing conditions of life, and variability ensues; but similar changes of
conditions might and do occur under nature. Let it also be borne in
mind how infinitely complex and close-fitting are the mutual relations
of all organic beings to each other and to their physical conditions of
life; and consequently what infinitely varied diversities of structure
might be of use to each being under changing conditions of life. Can it
then be thought improbable, seeing that variations useful to man have
undoubtedly occurred, that other variations useful in some way to
each being in the great and complex battle of life, should occur in the
course of many successive generations? If such do occur, can we doubt
(remembering that many more individuals are born than can possibly
survive) that individuals having any advantage, however slight, over
others, would have the best chance of surviving and procreating their
kind? On the other hand, we may feel sure that any variation in the
least degree injurious would be rigidly destroyed. This preservation of
favorable individual differences and variations, and the destruction of

---

[1]*plastic* capable of being shaped and changed.

[2]*Sir Joseph Dalton Hooker (1817–1911) and Asa Gray (1810–1888)* Hooker
was son of Sir William Jackson Hooker (1785–1865); both were great English botanists.
Joseph was a supporter of Darwin. Asa Gray was the greatest American botanist of his
time.

those which are injurious, I have called Natural Selection, or the Survival of the Fittest. Variations neither useful nor injurious would not be affected by natural selection, and would be left either a fluctuating element, as perhaps we see in certain polymorphic species,[3] or would ultimately become fixed, owing to the nature of the organism and the nature of the conditions.

Several writers have misapprehended or objected to the term Natural Selection. Some have even imagined that natural selection induces variability, whereas it implies only the preservation of such variations as arise and are beneficial to the being under its conditions of life. No one objects to agriculturists speaking of the potent effects of man's selection; and in this case the individual differences given by nature, which man for some object selects, must of necessity first occur. Others have objected that the term selection implies conscious choice in the animals which become modified; and it has even been urged, that, as plants have no volition, natural selection is not applicable to them! In the literal sense of the word, no doubt, natural selection is a false term; but who ever objected to chemists speaking of the elective affinities[4] of the various elements?—and yet an acid cannot strictly be said to elect the base with which it in preference combines. It has been said that I speak of natural selection as an active power or Deity; but who objects to an author speaking of the attraction of gravity as ruling the movements of the planets? Everyone knows what is meant and is implied by such metaphorical expressions; and they are almost necessary for brevity. So again it is difficult to avoid personifying the word Nature; but I mean by nature, only the aggregate action and product of many natural laws, and by laws the sequence of events as ascertained by us. With a little familiarity such superficial objections will be forgotten.

We shall best understand the probable course of natural selection by taking the case of a country undergoing some slight physical change, for instance, of climate. The proportional numbers of its inhabitants will almost immediately undergo a change, and some species will probably become extinct. We may conclude, from what we have seen of the intimate and complex manner in which the inhabitants of each country are bound together, that any change in the numerical proportions of the inhabitants, independently of the change of climate

---

[3]*polymorphic species* Species that have more than one form over the course of their lives, such as butterflies.

[4]*elective affinities* Defined and preferential chemical behavior, such as the combination of sodium and chloride into common table salt.

itself, would seriously affect the others. If the country were open on its borders, new forms would certainly immigrate, and this would likewise seriously disturb the relations of some of the former inhabitants. Let it be remembered how powerful the influence of a single introduced tree or mammal has been shown to be. But in the case of an island, or of a country partly surrounded by barriers, into which new and better adapted forms could not freely enter, we should then have places in the economy of nature which would assuredly be better filled up if some of the original inhabitants were in some manner modified; for, had the area been open to immigration, these same places would have been seized on by intruders. In such cases, slight modifications, which in any way favored the individuals of any species, by better adapting them to their altered conditions, would tend to be preserved; and natural selection would have free scope for the work of improvement.

We have good reason to believe . . . that changes in the conditions of life give a tendency to increased variability; and in the foregoing cases the conditions have changed, and this would manifestly be favorable to natural selection, by affording a better chance of the occurrence of profitable variations. Unless such occur, natural selection can do nothing. Under the term of "variations," it must never be forgotten that mere individual differences are included. As man can produce a great result with his domestic animals and plants by adding up in any given direction individual differences, so could natural selection, but far more easily from having incomparably longer time for action. Nor do I believe that any great physical change, as of climate, or any unusual degree of isolation, to check immigration, is necessary in order that new and unoccupied places should be left for natural selection to fill up by improving some of the varying inhabitants. For as all the inhabitants of each country are struggling together with nicely balanced forces, extremely slight modifications in the structure or habits of one species would often give it an advantage over others; and still further modifications of the same kind would often still further increase the advantage, as long as the species continued under the same conditions of life and profited by similar means of subsistence and defence. No country can be named in which all the native inhabitants are now so perfectly adapted to each other and to the physical conditions under which they live, that none of them could be still better adapted or improved; for in all countries the natives have been so far conquered by naturalized productions that they have allowed some foreigners to take firm possession of the land. And as foreigners have thus in every country beaten some of the natives, we may safely conclude that the natives might have been modified with advantage, so as to have better resisted the intruders.

As man can produce, and certainly has produced, a great result by his methodical and unconscious means of selection, what may not natural selection effect? Man can act only on external and visible characters; Nature, if I may be allowed to personify the natural preservation or survival of the fittest, cares nothing for appearances, except in so far as they are useful to any being. She can act on every internal organ, on every shade of constitutional difference, on the whole machinery of life. Man selects only for his own good; Nature, only for that of the being which she tends. Every selected character is fully exercised by her, as is implied by the fact of their selection. Man keeps the natives of many climates in the same country. He seldom exercises each selected character in some peculiar and fitting manner; he feeds a long and a short-beaked pigeon on the same food; he does not exercise a long-backed or long-legged quadruped in any peculiar manner; he exposes sheep with long and short wool to the same climate; does not allow the most vigorous males to struggle for the females; he does not rigidly destroy all inferior animals, but protects during each varying season, as far as lies in his power, all his productions. He often begins his selection by some half-monstrous form, or at least by some modification prominent enough to catch the eye or to be plainly useful to him. Under nature, the slightest differences of structure or constitution may well turn the nicely balanced scale in the struggle for life, and so be preserved. How fleeting are the wishes and efforts of man! How short his time, and consequently how poor will be his results, compared with those accumulated by Nature during whole geological periods! Can we wonder, then, that Nature's productions should be far "truer" in character than man's productions; that they should be infinitely better adapted to the most complex conditions of life, and should plainly bear the stamp of far higher workmanship?

It may metaphorically be said that natural selection is daily and hourly scrutinizing, throughout the world, the slightest variations; rejecting those that are bad, preserving and adding up all that are good; silently and insensibly working, *whenever and wherever opportunity offers*, at the improvement of each organic being in relation to its organic and inorganic conditions of life. We see nothing of these slow changes in progress, until the hand of time has marked the lapse of ages, and then so imperfect is our view into long-past geological ages that we see only that the forms of life are now different from what they formerly were.

In order that any great amount of modification should be effected in a species, a variety, when once formed, must again, perhaps after a long interval of time, vary or present individual differences of the same favorable nature as before; and these must again be preserved, and so onward, step by step. Seeing that individual differences of the same kind perpetually recur, this can hardly be considered as an unwarrantable assumption. But whether it is true, we can judge only by seeing how far the hypothesis accords with and explains the general phenomena of nature. On the other hand, the ordinary belief that the amount of possible variation is a strictly limited quantity, is likewise a simple assumption.

Although natural selection can act only through and for the good of each being, yet characters and structures, which we are apt to consider as of very trifling importance, may thus be acted on. When we see leaf-eating insects green, and bark-feeders mottled-gray; the alpine ptarmigan white in winter, the red grouse the color of heather, we must believe that these tints are of service to these birds and insects in preserving them from danger. Grouse, if not destroyed at some period of their lives, would increase in countless numbers; they are known to suffer largely from birds of prey; and hawks are guided by eyesight to their prey—so much so that on parts of the Continent[5] persons are warned not to keep white pigeons, as being the most liable to destruction. Hence natural selection might be effective in giving the proper color to each kind of grouse, and in keeping that color, when once acquired, true and constant. Nor ought we to think that the occasional destruction of an animal of any particular color would produce little effect; we should remember how essential it is in a flock of white sheep to destroy a lamb with the faintest trace of black. We have seen how the color of hogs, which feed on the "paint-root"[6] in Virginia, determines whether they shall live or die. In plants, the down on the fruit and the color of the flesh are considered by botanists as characters of the most trifling importance; yet we hear from an excellent horticulturist, Downing,[7] that in the United States the smooth-skinned fruits suffer far more from a beetle, a Curculio,[8] than those with down; that purple plums suffer far more from a certain disease than yellow plums; whereas another disease attacks yellow-fleshed peaches far

8

---

[5]**Continent** European continent (the contiguous land mass of Europe, excluding the British isles).

[6]**paint-root** an herb with sword-shaped leaves, also called redroot or bloodroot.

[7]**Andrew Jackson Downing (1815–1852)** American horticulturist, specialist in fruit and fruit trees.

[8]**Curculio** a weevil.

more than those with other colored flesh. If, with all the aids of art, these slight differences make a great difference in cultivating the several varieties, assuredly, in a state of nature, where the trees would have to struggle with other trees and with a host of enemies, such differences would effectually settle which variety, whether a smooth or downy, a yellow or a purple fleshed fruit, should succeed.

In looking at many small points of difference between species, 9 which, as far as our ignorance permits us to judge, seem quite unimportant, we must not forget that climate, food, etc., have no doubt produced some direct effect. It is also necessary to bear in mind, that, owing to the law of correlation,[9] when one part varies and the variations are accumulated through natural selection, other modifications, often of the most unexpected nature, will ensue.

As we see that those variations which, under domestication, appear 10 at any particular period of life, tend to reappear in the offspring at the same period; for instance, in the shape, size, and flavor of the seeds of the many varieties of our culinary and agricultural plants; in the caterpillar and cocoon stages of the varieties of the silkworm; in the eggs of poultry, and in the color of the down of their chickens; in the horns of our sheep and cattle when nearly adult; so in a state of nature natural selection will be enabled to act on and modify organic beings at any age, by the accumulation of variations profitable at that age, and by their inheritance at a corresponding age. If it profit a plant to have its seeds more and more widely disseminated by the wind, I can see no greater difficulty in this being effected through natural selection, than in the cotton-planter increasing and improving by selection the down in the pods on his cotton-trees. Natural selection may modify and adapt the larva of an insect to a score of contingencies, wholly different from those which concern the mature insect; and these modifications may affect, through correlation, the structure of the adult. So, conversely, modifications in the adult may affect the structure of the larva; but in all cases natural selection will insure that they shall not be injurious: for if they were so, the species would become extinct.

Natural selection will modify the structure of the young in relation 11 to the parent, and of the parent in relation to the young. In social animals it will adapt the structure of each individual for the benefit of the whole community; if the community profits by the selected change. What natural selection cannot do, is to modify the structure

---

[9]*law of correlation*   In certain plants and animals one condition relates to another, as in the case of blue-eyed white cats, which are always deaf; the reasons are not clear.

of one species, without giving it any advantage, for the good of another species; and though statements to this effect may be found in works of natural history, I cannot find one case which will bear investigation. A structure used only once in an animal's life, if of high importance to it, might be modified to any extent by natural selection; for instance, the great jaws possessed by certain insects, used exclusively for opening the cocoon—or the hard tip to the beak of unhatched birds, used for breaking the eggs. It has been asserted, that of the best short-beaked tumbler-pigeons a greater number perish in the egg than are able to get out of it; so that fanciers[10] assist in the act of hatching. Now, if nature had to make the beak of a full-grown pigeon very short for the bird's own advantage, the process of modification would be very slow, and there would be simultaneously the most rigorous selection of all the young birds within the egg, which had the most powerful and hardest beaks, for all with weak beaks would inevitably perish; or, more delicate and more easily broken shells might be selected, the thickness of the shell being known to vary like every other structure.

It may be well here to remark that with all beings there must be much fortuitous[11] destruction, which can have little or no influence on the course of natural selection. For instance, a vast number of eggs or seeds are annually devoured, and these could be modified through natural selection only if they varied in some manner which protected them from their enemies. Yet many of these eggs or seeds would perhaps, if not destroyed, have yielded individuals better adapted to their conditions of life than any of those which happened to survive. So again a vast number of mature animals and plants, whether or not they be the best adapted to their conditions, must be annually destroyed by accidental causes, which would not be in the least degree mitigated by certain changes of structure or constitution which would in other ways be beneficial to the species. But let the destruction of the adults be ever so heavy, if the number which can exist in any district be not wholly kept down by such causes—or again let the destruction of eggs or seeds be so great that only a hundredth or a thousandth part are developed—yet of those which do survive, the best adapted individuals, supposing that there is any variability in a favorable direction, will tend to propagate their kind in larger numbers than the less well adapted. If the numbers be wholly kept down by the causes just indicated, as will often have been the case, natural selection will be pow-

12

---

[10]*fanciers* amateurs who raise and race pigeons.
[11]*fortuitous* chance, arbitrary.

erless in certain beneficial directions; but this is no valid objection to its efficiency at other times and in other ways; for we are far from having any reason to suppose that many species ever undergo modification and improvement at the same time in the same area.

Sexual Selection

Inasmuch as peculiarities often appear under domestication in one sex and become hereditarily attached to that sex, so no doubt it will be under nature. Thus it is rendered possible for the two sexes to be modified through natural selection in relation to different habits of life, as is sometimes the case; or for one sex to be modified in relation to the other sex, as commonly occurs. This leads me to say a few words on what I have called sexual selection. This form of selection depends, not on a struggle for existence in relation to other organic beings or to external conditions, but on a struggle between the individuals of one sex, generally the males, for the possession of the other sex. The result is not death to the unsuccessful competitor, but few or no offspring. Sexual selection is, therefore, less rigorous than natural selection. Generally, the most vigorous males, those which are best fitted for their places in nature, will leave most progeny. But in many cases victory depends not so much on general vigor, as on having special weapons, confined to the male sex. A hornless stag or spurless cock would have a poor chance of leaving numerous offspring. Sexual selection, by always allowing the victor to breed, might surely give indomitable courage, length of spur, and strength to the wing to strike in the spurred leg, in nearly the same manner as does the brutal cockfighter[12] by the careful selection of his best cocks. How low in the scale of nature the law of battle descends, I know not; male alligators have been described as fighting, bellowing, and whirling round, like Indians in a war-dance, for the possession of the females; male salmons have been observed fighting all day long; male stag beetles sometimes bear wounds from the huge mandibles[13] of other males; the males of certain hymenopterous insects[14] have been frequently seen by that inimitable observer M. Fabre, fighting for a particular female

---

[12]**brutal cockfighter** Cockfights were a popular spectator sport in England, especially for gamblers; but many considered them a form of horrible brutality.

[13]**mandibles** jaws.

[14]**hymenopterous insects** Insects that cluster in large colonies, such as wasps, bees, and ants. Jean Henri Fabre (1823–1915) was a prominent French entomologist.

who sits by, an apparently unconcerned beholder of the struggle, and then retires with the conqueror. The war is, perhaps, severest between the males of polygamous animals,[15] and these seem oftenest provided with special weapons. The males of carnivorous animals are already well armed; though to them and to others, special means of defence may be given through means of sexual selection, as the mane of the lion, and the hooked jaw to the male salmon; for the shield may be as important for victory as the sword or spear.

Among birds, the contest is often of a more peaceful character. All those who have attended to the subject, believe that there is the severest rivalry between the males of many species to attract, by singing, the females. The rock thrush of Guiana,[16] birds of paradise, and some others, congregate, and successive males display with the most elaborate care, and show off in the best manner, their gorgeous plumage; they likewise perform strange antics before the females, which, standing by as spectators, at last choose the most attractive partner. Those who have closely attended to birds in confinement well know that they often take individual preferences and dislikes: thus Sir R. Heron[17] has described how a pied peacock was eminently attractive to all his hen birds. I cannot here enter on the necessary details; but if man can in a short time give beauty and an elegant carriage to his bantams,[18] according to his standard of beauty, I can see no good reason to doubt that female birds, by selecting, during thousands of generations, the most melodious or beautiful males, according to their standard of beauty, might produce a marked effect. Some well-known laws, with respect to the plumage of male and female birds, in comparison with the plumage of the young, can partly be explained through the action of sexual selection on variations occurring at different ages, and transmitted to the males alone or to both sexes at corresponding ages; but I have not space here to enter on this subject.

Thus it is, as I believe, that when the males and females of any animal have the same general habits of life, but differ in structure, color, or ornament, such differences have been mainly caused by sexual selection: that is, by individual males having had, in successive generations, some slight advantage over other males, in their weapons, means of defence, or charms, which they have transmitted to their

14

15

---

[15]*polygamous animals* Animals that typically have more than one mate.

[16]*Guiana* British Guiana, on the east coast of South America.

[17]*Sir Robert Heron (1765–1854)* English politician who maintained a "menagerie" of animals.

[18]*bantams* cocks bred for fighting.

male offspring alone. Yet I would not wish to attribute all sexual differences to this agency: for we see in our domestic animals peculiarities arising and becoming attached to the male sex, which apparently have not been augmented through selection by man. The tuft of hair on the breast of the wild turkey-cock cannot be of any use, and it is doubtful whether it can be ornamental in the eyes of the female bird; indeed, had the tuft appeared under domestication it would have been called a monstrosity.

Illustrations of the Action of Natural Selection, or the Survival of the Fittest

In order to make it clear how, as I believe, natural selection acts, I 16 must beg permission to give one or two imaginary illustrations. Let us take the case of a wolf which preys on various animals, securing some by craft, some by strength, and some by fleetness; and let us suppose that the fleetest prey, a deer for instance, had from any change in the country increased in numbers, or that other prey had decreased in numbers, during that season of the year when the wolf was hardest pressed for food. Under such circumstances the swiftest and slimmest wolves have the best chance of surviving, and so being preserved or selected, provided always that they retain strength to master their prey at this or some other period of the year, when they were compelled to prey on other animals. I can see no more reason to doubt that this would be the result, than that man should be able to improve the fleetness of his greyhounds by careful and methodical selection, or by that kind of unconscious selection which follows from each man trying to keep the best dogs without any thought of modifying the breed. I may add that, according to Mr. Pierce, there are two varieties of the wolf inhabiting the Catskill Mountains, in the United States, one with a light greyhound-like form, which pursues deer, and the other more bulky, with shorter legs, which more frequently attacks the shepherd's flocks.

It should be observed that in the above illustration, I speak of the 17 slimmest individual wolves, and not of any single strongly marked variation having been preserved. In former editions of this work I sometimes spoke as if this latter alternative had frequently occurred. I saw the great importance of individual differences, and this led me fully to discuss the results of unconscious selection by man, which depends on the preservation of all the more or less valuable individuals, and on the destruction of the worst. I saw, also, that the preservation in a state of nature of any occasional deviation of structure, such as a monstrosity, would be a rare event; and that, if at first preserved, it would generally be lost by subsequent intercrossing[19] with ordinary individuals. Nevertheless, until reading an able and valuable article in the *North British Review*[20] (1867), I did not appreciate how rarely single variations, whether slight or strongly marked, could be perpetuated. The author takes the case of a pair of animals, producing during their lifetime two hundred offspring, of which, from various causes of destruction, only two on an average survive to procreate their kind. This is rather an extreme estimate for most of the higher animals, but by no means so for many of the lower organisms. He then shows that if a single individual were born, which varied in some manner, giving it twice as good a chance of life as that of the other individuals, yet the chances would be strongly against its survival. Supposing it to survive and to breed, and that half its young inherited the favorable variation; still, as the reviewer goes on to show, the young would have only a slightly better chance of surviving and breeding; and this chance would go on decreasing in the succeeding generations. The justice of these remarks cannot, I think, be disputed. If, for instance, a bird of some kind could procure its food more easily by having its beak curved, and if one were born with its beak strongly curved, and which consequently flourished, nevertheless there would be a very poor chance of this one individual perpetuating its kind to the exclusion of the common form; but there can hardly be a doubt, judging by what we see taking place under domestication, that this result would follow from the preservation during many generations of a large number of individuals with more or less strongly curved beaks, and from the destruction of a still larger number with the straightest beaks.

It should not, however, be overlooked, that certain rather strongly marked variations, which no one would rank as mere individual differences, frequently recur owing to a similar organization being similarly acted on—of which fact numerous instances could be given with our domestic productions. In such cases, if the varying individual did not actually transmit to its offspring its newly acquired character, it would undoubtedly transmit to them, as long as the existing conditions remained the same, a still stronger tendency to vary in the same manner. There can also be little doubt that the tendency to vary in the same

18

---

[19]*intercrossing* breeding.

[20]**North British Review** A Scots Free Church journal that had begun to support liberal views regarding politics and the church.

manner has often been so strong that all the individuals of the same species have been similarly modified without the aid of any form of selection. Or only a third, fifth, or tenth part of the individuals may have been thus affected, of which fact several instances could be given. Thus Graba estimates that about one-fifth of the guillemots[21] in the Faroe Islands consist of a variety so well marked, that it was formerly ranked as a distinct species under the name of Uria lacrymans. In cases of this kind, if the variation were of a beneficial nature, the original form would soon be supplanted by the modified form, through the survival of the fittest.

To the effects of intercrossing in eliminating variations of all kinds, I shall have to recur: but it may be here remarked that most animals and plants keep to their proper homes, and do not needlessly wander about; we see this even with migratory birds, which almost always return to the same spot. Consequently each newly-formed variety would generally be at first local, as seems to be the common rule with varieties in a state of nature; so that similarly modified individuals would soon exist in a small body together, and would often breed together. If the new variety were successful in its battle for life, it would slowly spread from a central district, competing with and conquering the unchanged individuals on the margins of an ever-increasing circle. 19

It may be worth while to give another and more complex illustration of the action of natural selection. Certain plants excrete sweet juice, apparently for the sake of eliminating something injurious from the sap: this is effected, for instance, by glands at the base of the stipules[22] in some Leguminosae, and at the backs of the leaves of the common laurel. This juice, though small in quantity, is greedily sought by insects; but their visits do not in any way benefit the plant. Now, let us suppose that the juice or nectar was excreted from the inside of the flowers of a certain number of plants of any species. Insects in seeking the nectar would get dusted with pollen, and would often transport it from one flower to another. The flowers of two distinct individuals of the same species would thus get crossed; and the act of crossing, as can be fully proved, gives rise to vigorous seedlings, which consequently would have the best chance of flourishing and surviving. The plants which produced flowers with the largest glands or nectaries, excreting most nectar, would oftenest be visited by insects, and would oftenest be crossed; and so in the long run would gain 20

---

[21]*guillemots* A diving bird. The Faroe Islands are in the North Atlantic, near Iceland.

[22]*stipules* spines at the base of a leaf.

the upper hand and form a local variety. The flowers also, which had their stamens and pistils[23] placed, in relation to the size and habits of the particular insect which visited them, so as to favor in any degree the transportal of the pollen, would likewise be favored. We might have taken the case of insects visiting flowers for the sake of collecting pollen instead of nectar; and as pollen is formed for the sole purpose of fertilization, its destruction appears to be a simple loss to the plant; yet if a little pollen were carried, at first occasionally and then habitually, by the pollen-devouring insects from flower to flower, and a cross thus effected, although nine-tenths of the pollen were destroyed it might still be a great gain to the plant to be thus robbed; and the individuals which produced more and more pollen, and had larger anthers,[24] would be selected.

When our plant, by the above process long continued, had been 21 rendered highly attractive to insects, they would, unintentionally on their part, regularly carry pollen from flower to flower: and that they do this effectually I could easily show by many striking facts. I will give only one, as likewise illustrating one step in the separation of the sexes of plants. Some holly-trees bear only male flowers, which have four stamens producing a rather small quantity of pollen, and a rudimentary pistil; other holly-trees bear only female flowers; these have a full-sized pistil, and four stamens with shrivelled anthers, in which not a grain of pollen can be detected. Having found a female tree exactly sixty yards from a male tree, I put the stigmas[25] of twenty flowers, taken from different branches, under the microscope, and on all, without exception, there were a few pollen-grains, and on some a profusion. As the wind had set for several days from the female to the male tree, the pollen could not thus have been carried. The weather had been cold and boisterous and therefore not favorable to bees, nevertheless every female flower which I examined had been effectually fertilized by the bees, which had flown from tree to tree in search of nectar. But to return to our imaginary case; as soon as the plant had been rendered so highly attractive to insects that pollen was regularly carried from flower to flower, another process might commence. No naturalist doubts the advantage of what has been called the "physiological division of labor"; hence we may believe that it would be advantageous to a plant to produce stamens alone in one flower or on

---

[23]*stamens and pistils* Sexual organs of plants. The male and female organs appear together in the same flower.

[24]*anthers* An anther is that part of the stamen that contains pollen.

[25]*stigmas* where the plant's pollen develops.

one whole plant, and pistils alone in another flower or on another plant. In plants under culture and placed under new conditions of life, sometimes the male organs and sometimes the female organs become more or less impotent; now if we suppose this to occur in ever so slight a degree under nature, then, as pollen is already carried regularly from flower to flower, and as a more complete separation of the sexes of our plant would be advantageous on the principle of the division of labor, individuals with this tendency more and more increased would be continually favored or selected, until at last a complete separation of the sexes might be effected. It would take up too much space to show the various steps, through dimorphism[26] and other means, by which the separation of the sexes in plants of various kinds is apparently now in progress; but I may add that some of the species of holly in North America are, according to Asa Gray, in an exactly intermediate condition, or, as he expresses it, are more or less dioeciously polygamous.[27]

Let us now turn to the nectar-feeding insects; we may suppose the plant, of which we have been slowly increasing the nectar by continued selection, to be a common plant; and that certain insects depended in main part on its nectar for food. I could give many facts showing how anxious bees are to save time: for instance, their habit of cutting holes and sucking the nectar at the bases of certain flowers, which with a very little more trouble they can enter by the mouth. Bearing such facts in mind, it may be believed that under certain circumstances individual differences in the curvature or length of the proboscis,[28] etc., too slight to be appreciated by us, might profit a bee or other insect, so that certain individuals would be able to obtain their food more quickly than others; and thus the communities to which they belonged would flourish and throw off many swarms inheriting the same peculiarities. The tubes of the corolla[29] of the common red or incarnate clovers (Trifolium pratense and incarnatum) do not on a hasty glance appear to differ in length; yet the hive-bee can easily suck the nectar out of the incarnate clover, but not out of the common red clover, which is visited by humble-bees[30] alone, so that whole fields of

22

---

[26]***dimorphism*** having two forms.

[27]***dioeciously polygamous*** The word "dioeciously" refers to a type of plant in which the reproductive organs of each sex are found only on separate individuals; i.e., each plant has either male or female organs but not both. Such plants would consequently be dioeciously polygamous.

[28]***proboscis*** snout.

[29]***corolla*** inner set of floral petals.

[30]***humble-bees*** bumblebees.

the red clover offer in vain an abundant supply of precious nectar to the hive-bee. That this nectar is much liked by the hive-bee is certain; for I have repeatedly seen, but only in the autumn, many hive-bees sucking the flowers through holes bitten in the base of the tube by humble-bees. The difference in the length of the corolla in the two kinds of clover, which determines the visits of the hive-bee, must be very trifling; for I have been assured that when red clover has been mown, the flowers of the second crop are somewhat smaller, and that these are visited by many hive-bees. I do not know whether this statement is accurate; nor whether another published statement can be trusted, namely, that the Ligurian bee, which is generally considered a mere variety of the common hive-bee, and which freely crosses with it, is able to reach and suck the nectar of the red clover. Thus, in a country where this kind of clover abounded, it might be a great advantage to the hive-bee to have a slightly longer or differently constructed proboscis. On the other hand, as the fertility of this clover absolutely depends on bees visiting the flowers, if humble-bees were to become rare in any country, it might be a great advantage to the plant to have a shorter or more deeply divided corolla, so that the hive-bees should be enabled to suck its flowers. Thus I can understand how a flower and a bee might slowly become, either simultaneously or one after the other, modified and adapted to each other in the most perfect manner, by the continued preservation of all the individuals which presented slight deviations of structure mutually favorable to each other.

I am well aware that this doctrine of natural selection, exemplified in the above imaginary instances, is open to the same objections which were first urged against Sir Charles Lyell's noble views[31] on "the modern changes of the earth, as illustrative of geology"; but we now seldom hear the agencies which we see still at work, spoken of as trifling or insignificant, when used in explaining the excavation of the deepest valleys or the formation of long lines of inland cliffs. Natural selection acts only by the preservation and accumulation of small inherited modifications, each profitable to the preserved being; and as modern geology has almost banished such views as the excavation of a great 23

---

[31]***Sir Charles Lyell's noble views***   Lyell (1797–1879) was an English geologist whose landmark work, *Principles of Geology* (1830–1833), Darwin read while on the *Beagle*. The book inspired Darwin, and the two scientists became friends. Lyell was shown portions of *The Origin of Species* while Darwin was writing it.

valley by a single diluvial[32] wave, so will natural selection banish the belief of the continued creation of new organic beings, or of any great and sudden modification in their structure.

---

[32]*diluvial* pertaining to a flood. Darwin means that geological changes, such as those which caused the Grand Canyon, were no longer thought of as being created instantly by flood (or other catastrophes), but were considered to have developed over a long period of time, as he imagines happened in the evolution of species.

QUESTIONS

1. Darwin uses the metaphor of the "battle for life" (para. 1) several times in this chapter of his *Origin of Species*. What is the value of this metaphor for understanding the substance of his ideas?
2. What are the differences between natural selection and selection by humans? Why would it be easier to believe in the force of one but not of the other?
3. Does Darwin hold that natural selection is a positive force?
4. Why doesn't Darwin discuss varieties and selection with reference to people in this work?
5. What did Darwin assume about his audience? Did he expect a sympathetic, hostile, or indifferent audience?

WRITING ASSIGNMENTS

1. In paragraph 16, Darwin uses imaginary examples. Compare the value of his genuine examples and these imaginary ones. How effective is the use of imaginary examples in an argument? What requirements would an imaginary example have to have in order to be forceful in an argument? Do you find Darwin's imaginary examples to be strong or weak?
2. From paragraph 17 onward, Darwin discusses the process of modification of a species through its beginning in the modification of an individual. Explain, insofar as you understand the concept, just how a species could be modified by a variation which would occur in just one individual. In your explanation, use Darwin's rhetorical technique of the imaginary example.
3. Write an essay which takes as its thesis statement the following sentence from paragraph 23: "Natural selection acts only by the preservation and accumulation of small inherited modifications, each profitable to the preserved being." Be sure to inventory the work carefully to find other state-

ments by Darwin that will give added strength, clarity, and meaning to this one. You may also employ the Darwinian device of presenting "imaginary instances" in your essay.

4. A controversy exists concerning the Darwinian theory of evolution. Explore the *Reader's Guide to Periodical Literature* for up-to-date information on the Creationist-Evolutionist conflict in schools. Look up either term or both to see what articles you can find. Establish the nature of the controversy and attempt to defend one side. Use your knowledge of natural selection gained from this piece. Remember, too, that Darwin was trained as a minister of the church and was very concerned about religious opinion.

5. When Darwin wrote this piece, he believed that sexual selection was of great importance in evolutionary changes in species. Assuming that this belief is true, establish the similarities between sexual selection in plants and animals with sexual selection, as you have observed it, in people. Paragraphs 13–15 discuss this issue. Darwin does not discuss people, but it is clear that physical and stylistic distinctions between the sexes have some bearing on selection. Assuming that to be true, what qualities in people (physical and mental) are likely to survive? Why?

6. In the Middle Ages and earlier the official view of the church was that the world was flat. Columbus proved that the world was round, and the church agreed not to argue with him. The official view of the church was that the sun went around the earth. When Galileo proved otherwise, he was forced to deny his own observations and then he was banished. Only later, in the face of overwhelming evidence, did the church back down. Regarding Darwin, the church held that all species were created on a specially appointed day; evolution was impossible. The Church of England and the Roman Catholic Church, after some struggle, seem to have accepted Darwin's views. Why is it still difficult for some religious organizations to accept Darwin's views? In order to deal with this question, you may have to interview some people connected with a church that holds that Darwin's views are inaccurate. You may also find some religious literature attacking Darwin. If so, establish what the concern of some churches and other religious organizations may be. Make as clear an argument for such organizations' point of view as you can.

LINCOLN BARNETT

---···◦◦◦···---

Einstein's Relativity

ALBERT EINSTEIN (1879–1955) read the book by Lincoln Barnett
(b.1909) from which the following selection is taken and, in the Introduction to the book, expressed his approval of it. Einstein's own
writings are difficult to understand for those whose mathematics is
limited, and he recognized the need for an accessible version of what
he had discovered and of the implications of the modern theories of
physics.

Einstein was raised in Munich, Germany, and was educated in
Zurich, Switzerland, where he had some difficulty in school. It has
often delighted people to recall that Einstein—a genius whose thinking changed the world as few have ever done—could not speak
fluently until he was nine years old, that he had great difficulty in
secondary school because he found everything but mathematics bor-
ing, and that he failed the entrance examination required by the college of his choice: the Federal Institute of Technology in Zurich.

After a second examination, he was finally accepted at the institute and secured his diploma, but one of his professors barred him
from teaching there; and, after spending several years in a civil ser-

---

From *The Universe and Doctor Einstein.*

vice position at the Swiss Patent Office, he wrote the first of his most important technical papers in the field of physics. They achieved instant notice from professional physicists, and he was eventually made full professor, first at the University of Zurich, and then at the Federal Institute of Technology. In 1913 he became professor of physics and director of the Kaiser Wilhelm Institute at the University of Berlin. He became the victim of slander and acts of malice in Germany after he traveled on behalf of Zionism with Chaim Weizmann, later the first president of the then nonexistent State of Israel. Even after having won the Nobel Prize for Physics in 1921, Einstein was accused of practicing a "Jewish physics," and he was eventually hounded out of Europe. In 1933 he settled in the United States, where he taught at the Institute for Advanced Study in Princeton, New Jersey.

His work was instrumental in the conception and development of many modern devices such as television; the laser beam; and, as most people well know, the atomic bomb. As Barnett points out, one of Einstein's most important contributions—and it is really the contribution of modern physics—was changing the ground rules of scientific investigation. Instead of concentrating on what we can perceive or how we can perceive it, modern physics concentrates on mathematics and the models of the world that mathematical descriptions offer us. It was because Einstein concentrated on mathematics rather than on perception and words that he was able to develop his refinements of quantum theory and atomic theory and then was able to conceive the theory of relativity. Perception and words would have blocked him in all these areas, because "common sense" would have argued against almost everything he discovered. Working mathematically freed him. He had only to establish the validity of his equations in order to know what he had discovered.

As Barnett points out in the beginning of the chapter of his book presented here, the basis of the older science is perception and squaring that perception with what is already known. Likewise, the emphasis on perception forces emphasis on problems of causality: when we perceive something happen we assume it is caused, and so we search for its cause. Likewise, determination—knowing what will happen when a "cause" is applied in a given circumstance—is equally emphasized in a world in which only perception dominates thought. In Einstein's physics, neither cause nor determination is what we might think it to be (see para. 26). Consequently, to understand modern physics we need to think somewhat differently from the way we do with regard to everyday experience.

BARNETT'S RHETORIC

Barnett has the problem of explaining a highly complex system of mathematical physics to people who have little or no knowledge of mathematics and who are thus unfamiliar with the basic subject. Therefore, he is careful to take everything step by step and to use the simplest approach possible. Thus, his rhetoric is workmanlike and simple. He uses enumeration where possible, as when he guides us to an understanding of the concepts of the interior of the atom—which is dominated by his consequent discussion of particle and wave theory in relation to the concepts of quantum mechanics—and then to an understanding of the concepts pertaining to galaxies. He then brings us to a discussion of the theory of relativity and the concepts of mass and energy.

Because it is difficult to understand Einstein without understanding where he began his thought, Barnett takes considerable pains to bring us up to date historically. This is the application of the topic of relationship, focusing on past time, giving us historical perspective. This accomplished, Barnett concentrates on the exposition of the theories Einstein is famous for. He explains what we have learned by starting with the limits of perception (paras. 3–6), showing us how mathematics frees us from those limits. He explores the questions of subjective and objective reality, describes "sense-imprisoned man" (para. 11), and explores the quantum theory to show how thought based on sense impressions is baffled by a duality (wave and particle) of the sort that the universe is filled with (paras. 18–19).

Gradually, Barnett reveals that what he is tampering with is our own sense of reality, which, as we do not always realize, is based upon commonsense aspects of perception. Contemporary physicists, he points out, have had to do away with the notion of "really" (para. 23). Interestingly, Barnett shows that Einstein had to hypothesize mathematically in terms of imaginary examples (somewhat like Darwin). But he had to do this simply because total and definitive experimental evidence, particularly regarding the behavior of a single electron, is impossible to secure. And lest we begin to think that Einstein's mathematics is a figment of the imagination, Barnett reminds us that Einstein's description of the world works when his theories are applied in practice. We have the photoelectric theory at work in television, the laser, and light meters; we have the atomic theory at work in electricity plants. Relativity may be baffling, but it is everywhere around us. It is a fact of the most difficult kind of accept: one we cannot test with our own senses.

Einstein's Relativity

The factors that first led physicists to distrust their faith in a   1
smoothly functioning mechanical universe loomed on the inner and
outer horizons of knowledge—in the unseen realm of the atom and in
the fathomless depths of intergalactic space. To describe these phenomena quantitatively, two great theoretical systems were developed
between 1900 and 1927. One was the Quantum Theory, dealing with
the fundamental units of matter and energy. The other was Relativity,
dealing with space, time, and the structure of the universe as a whole.

Both are now accepted pillars of modern physical thought. Both   2
describe phenomena in their fields in terms of consistent, mathematical relationships. They do not answer the Newtonian "how" any more
than Newton's laws answered the Aristotelian "why."[1] They provide
equations, for example, that define with great accuracy the laws governing the radiation and propagation of light. But the actual mechanism by which the atom radiates light and by which light is propa-
gated through space remains one of nature's supreme mysteries. Similarly the laws governing the phenomenon of radioactivity enable scientists to predict that in a given quantity of uranium a certain number
of atoms will disintegrate in a certain length of time. But just which
atoms will decay and how they are selected for doom are questions
that man cannot yet answer.

In accepting a mathematical description of nature, physicists have   3
been forced to abandon the ordinary world of our experience, the world
of sense perceptions. To understand the significance of this retreat it
is necessary to step across the thin line that divides physics from metaphysics.[2] Questions involving the relationship between observer and
reality, subject and object, have haunted philosophical thinkers since
the dawn of reason. Twenty-three centuries ago the Greek philosopher
Democritus[3] wrote: "Sweet and bitter, cold and warm as well as all

---

[1]*Newton's laws*   Isaac Newton (1642–1727) formulated the laws of gravity and motion and invented differential calculus. His laws gave rise to a mechanical model of the
universe, which was imagined to be a rational system of causes and effects.

[2]*metaphysics*   Philosophy concerned with determining the real nature of things.

[3]*Democritus (460–370 B.C.)*   Greek philosopher who taught that the world was
constructed of atoms.

the colors, all these things exist but in opinion and not in reality; what really exists are unchangeable particles, atoms, and their motions in empty space." Galileo[4] also was aware of the purely subjective character of sense qualities like color, taste, smell, and sound and pointed out that "they can no more be ascribed to the external objects than can the tickling or the pain caused sometimes by touching such objects."

The English philosopher John Locke[5] tried to penetrate to the "real 4 essence of substances" by drawing a distinction between what he termed the primary and secondary qualities of matter. Thus he considered that shape, motion, solidity, and all geometrical properties were real or primary qualities, inherent in the object itself; while secondary qualities, like colors, sounds, tastes, were simply projections upon the organs of sense. The artificiality of this distinction was obvious to later thinkers.

"I am able to prove," wrote the great German mathematician, Leib- 5 nitz,[6] "that not only light, color, heat, and the like, but motion, shape, and extension too are mere apparent qualities." Just as our visual sense, for example, tells us that a golf ball is white, so vision abetted by our sense of touch tells us that it is also round, smooth, and small—qualities that have no more reality, independent of our senses, than the quality which we define by convention as white.

Thus gradually philosophers and scientists arrived at the startling 6 conclusion that since every object is simply the sum of its qualities, and since qualities exist only in the mind, the whole objective universe of matter and energy, atoms and stars, does not exist except as a construction of the consciousness, an edifice of conventional symbols shaped by the senses of man. As Berkeley,[7] the archenemy of materialism, phrased it: "All the choir of heaven and furniture of earth, in a word all those bodies which compose the mighty frame of the world, have not any substance without the mind. . . . So long as they are not actually perceived by me, or do not exist in my mind, or that of

---

[4]*Galileo Galilei (1564–1642)* Galileo proved that the earth rotated around the sun. His telescope extended the visual sense deep into space.

[5]*John Locke (1632–1704)* English empirical philosopher very much concerned with sense perception.

[6]*Gottfried Wilhelm von Leibnitz (1646–1716)* German philosopher and mathematician. Invented infinitesimal calculus independently of Newton. He was a rationalist who tried to make logic and reasoning dependent upon algebra and mathematics.

[7]*George Berkeley (1685–1753)* Irish bishop and philosopher. He proposed that nothing existed unless it was perceived. A tree falling in a forest with no one to hear it makes no sound, Berkeley insisted; that we know it does make a sound must mean we postulate the existence of God, who perceives all.

any other created spirit, they must either have no existence at all, or else subsist in the mind of some Eternal Spirit." Einstein carried this train of logic to its ultimate limits by showing that even space and time are forms of intuition, which can no more be divorced from consciousness than can our concepts of color, shape, or size. Space has no objective reality except as an order or arrangement of the objects we perceive in it, and time has no independent existence apart from the order of events by which we measure it.

These philosophical subtleties have a profound bearing on modern science. For along with the philosophers' reduction of all objective reality to a shadow-world of perceptions, scientists became aware of the alarming limitations of man's senses. Anyone who has ever thrust a glass prism into a sunbeam and seen the rainbow colors of the solar spectrum refracted on a screen has looked upon the whole range of visible light. For the human eye is sensitive only to the narrow band of radiation that falls between the red and the violet. A difference of a few one hundred thousandths of a centimeter in wave length makes the difference between visibility and invisibility. The wave length of red light is .00007 cm. and that of violet light .00004 cm. 7

But the sun also emits other kinds of radiation. Infrared rays,[8] for example, with a wave length of .00008 to .032 cm. are just a little too long to excite the retina to an impression of light, though the skin detects their impact as heat. Similarly ultraviolet rays[9] with a wave length of .00003 to .000001 cm. are too short for the eye to perceive but can be recorded on a photographic plate. Photographs can also be made by the "light" of X-rays which are even shorter than ultraviolet rays. And there are other electromagnetic waves of lesser and greater frequency—the gamma rays[10] of radium, radio waves, cosmic rays— which can be detected in various ways and differ from light only in wave length. It is evident, therefore, that the human eye suppresses most of the "lights" in the world, and that what man can perceive of the reality around him is distorted and enfeebled by the limitations of 8

---

[8]*infrared rays* The visible spectrum ends at red; these are rays whose wavelength is shorter than red. See caption with the chart of wavelengths, page 373.

[9]*ultraviolet rays* At the other end of the visible spectrum from red, these rays are detectable by special instruments.

[10]*gamma rays* Particles emitted spontaneously by a radioactive substance. See chart of wavelengths.

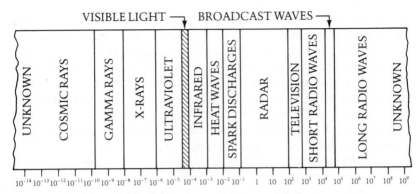

The electromagnetic spectrum reveals the narrow range of radiation visible to man's eye. From the standpoint of physics, the only difference between radio waves, visible light, and such high-frequency forms of radiation as X-rays and gamma rays lies in their wave length. But out of this vast range of electromagnetic radiation, extending from cosmic rays with wave lengths of only one trillionth of a centimeter up to infinitely long radio waves, the human eye selects only the narrow band indicated on the chart. Man's perceptions of the universe in which he dwells are thus restricted by the limitations of his visual sense. Wave lengths are indicated on the chart by the denary system: i.e. 10^3 centimeters equals $10 \times 10 \times 10$ equals $1,000;$ and 10^{-3} equals $1/10 \times 1/10 \times 1/10$ equals $1/1,000.$

his organ of vision. The world would appear far different to him if his eye were sensitive, for example, to X-rays.

Realization that our whole knowledge of the universe is simply a   9
residue of impressions clouded by our imperfect senses makes the quest for reality seem hopeless. If nothing has existence save in its being perceived, the world should dissolve into an anarchy of individual perceptions. But a curious order runs through our perceptions, as if indeed there might be an underlayer of objective reality which our senses translate. Although no man can ever know whether his sensation of red or of Middle C is the same as another man's it is nevertheless possible to act on the assumption that everyone sees colors and hears tones more or less alike.

This functional harmony of nature Berkeley, Descartes, and Spi-   10 noza attributed to God.[11] Modern physicists who prefer to solve their problems without recourse to God (although this seems to become more difficult all the time) emphasize that nature mysteriously operates on mathematical principles. It is the mathematical orthodoxy of the universe that enables theorists like Einstein to predict and discover natural laws simply by the solution of equations. But the paradox of physics today is that with every improvement in its mathematical apparatus the gulf between man the observer and the objective world of scientific description becomes more profound.

It is perhaps significant that in terms of simple magnitude man is the mean between macrocosm and microcosm.[12] Stated crudely this means that a supergiant red star (the largest material body in the universe) is just as much bigger than man as an electron (tiniest of physical entities) is smaller. It is not surprising, therefore, that the prime mysteries of nature dwell in those realms farthest removed from sense-imprisoned man, nor that science, unable to describe the extremes of reality in the homely metaphors of classical physics, should content itself with noting such mathematical relationships as may be revealed. 11

The first step in science's retreat from mechanical explanation toward mathematical abstraction was taken in 1900, when Max Planck[13] put forth his Quantum Theory to meet certain problems that had arisen in studies of radiation. It is common knowledge that when heated bodies become incandescent[14] they emit a red glow that turns to orange, then yellow, then white as the temperature increases. Painstaking efforts were made during the past century to formulate a law stating how the amount of radiant energy given off by such heated bodies varied with wave length and temperature. All attempts failed until Planck found by mathematical means an equation that satisfied the results of experiment. The extraordinary feature of his equation 12

---

[11]***attributed to God*** George Berkeley (1685–1753), René Descartes (1596–1650), and Baruch Spinoza (1632–1677) are influential philosophers who all postulated the existence of God.

[12]***macrocosm and microcosm*** The belief was long held that the largest things in the universe were mirrored or repeated in the smallest things. People, because they could conceive of both, stand somewhere between these two extremes of the galaxy *(macrocosm)* and the electron *(microcosm)*.

[13]***Max Planck (1858–1947)*** German physicist. He conducted extensive research into radiation, which led him to theorize that energy exists in measurable quanta—multiples of a tiny inexorable (inflexible; unavoidable) single quantity, Planck's Constant.

[14]***incandescent*** glowing, hot.

was that it rested on the assumption that radiant energy is emitted not in an unbroken stream but in discontinous bits or portions which he termed *quanta*.

Planck had no evidence for such an assumption, for no one knew anything (then or now) of the actual mechanism of radiation. But on purely theoretical grounds he concluded that each quantum carries an amount of energy given by the equation, $E = hv$, where v is the frequency of the radiation and h is Planck's Constant, a small but inexorable number (roughly .00000000000000000000000006624) which has since proved to be one of the most fundamental constants in nature. In any process of radiation the amount of emitted energy divided by the frequency is always equal to h. Although Planck's Constant has dominated the computations of atomic physics for half a century, its magnitude cannot be explained any more than the magnitude of the speed of light can be explained. Like other universal constants it is simply a mathematical fact for which no explanation can be given. Sir Arthur Eddington[15] once observed that any true law of nature is likely to seem irrational to rational man; hence Planck's quantum principle, he thought, is one of the few real natural laws science has revealed.

The far-reaching implications of Planck's conjecture did not become apparent till 1905, when Einstein, who almost alone among contemporary physicists appreciated its significance, carried the Quantum Theory into a new domain. Planck had believed he was simply patching up the equations of radiation. But Einstein postulated that all forms of radiant energy—light, heat, X-rays—actually travel through space in separate and discontinuous quanta. Thus the sensation of warmth we experience when sitting in front of a fire results from the bombardment of our skin by innumerable quanta of radiant heat. Similarly sensations of color arise from the bombardment of our optic nerves by light quanta which differ from each other just as the frequency v varies in the equation $E = hv$.

Einstein substantiated this idea by working out a law accurately defining a puzzling phenomenon known as the photoelectric effect. Physicists had been at a loss to explain the fact that when a beam of pure violet light is allowed to shine upon a metal plate the plate ejects

13

14

15

---

[15] *Sir Arthur Eddington (1882–1944)* English astronomer and astrophysicist. In 1930 he postulated that since matter curves space, the total number of atoms it would take to make space curve into hyperspace, or a hypersphere of more than three dimensions, is a finite number: 10^{79}.

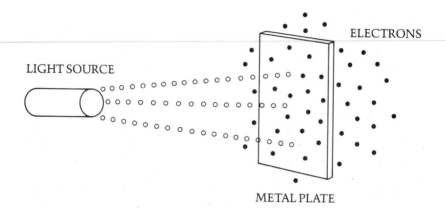

LIGHT SOURCE

ELECTRONS

METAL PLATE

The photoelectric effect was interpreted by Einstein in 1905. When light falls on a metal plate, the plate ejects a shower of electrons. This phenomenon cannot be explained by the classic wave theory of light. Einstein deduced that light is not a continuous stream of energy but is composed of individual particles or bundles of energy which he called *photons*. When a photon strikes an electron the resulting action is analogous to the impact of billiard balls, as shown in this simplified conception.

a shower of electrons. If light of lower frequency, say yellow or red, falls on the plate, electrons will again be ejected but at reduced velocities. The vehemence with which the electrons are torn from the metal depends only on the color of the light and not at all on its intensity. If the light source is removed to a considerable distance and dimmed to a faint glow the electrons that pop forth are fewer in number but their velocity is undiminished. The action is instantaneous even when the light fades to imperceptibility.

Einstein decided that these peculiar effects could be explained only by supposing that all light is composed of individual particles or grains of energy which he called *photons*, and that when one of them hits an electron the resulting action is comparable to the impact of two billiard balls. He reasoned further that photons of violet, ultraviolet, and other forms of high frequency radiation pack more energy than red and infrared photons, and that the velocity with which each electron flies from the metal plate is proportional to the energy content of the photon that strikes it. He expressed these principles in a series of historic equations which won him the Nobel Prize and profoundly influenced later work in quantum physics and spectroscopy.[16] Television and other applications of the photoelectric cell owe their existence to Einstein's Photoelectric Law.

In thus adducing an important new physical principle Einstein un-   17
covered at the same time one of the deepest and most troubling enigmas of nature. No one doubts today that all matter is made up of atoms which in turn are composed of even smaller building blocks called electrons, neutrons, and protons.[17] But Einstein's notion that light too may consist of discontinuous particles clashed with a far more venerable theory that light is made up of waves.

There are indeed certain phenomena involving light that can only   18
be explained by the wave theory. For example the shadows of ordinary objects like buildings, trees and telegraph poles appear sharply defined; but when a very fine wire or hair is held between a light source and a screen it casts no distinct shadow whatsoever, suggesting that light rays have bent around it just as waves of water bend around a small rock. Similarly a beam of light passing through a round aperture projects a sharply-defined disk upon a screen; but if the aperture is reduced to the size of a pinhole, then the disk becomes ribbed with alternating concentric bands of light and darkness, somewhat like those of a conventional target. This phenomenon is known as diffraction and has been compared with the tendency of ocean waves to bend and diverge on passing through the narrow mouth of a harbor. If instead of one pinhole, two pinholes are employed very close together and side by side, the diffraction patterns merge in a series of parallel stripes. Just as two wave systems meeting in a swimming pool will reinforce each other when crest coincides with crest and annul each other when the crest of one wave meets the trough of another, so in the case of the adjacent pinholes the bright stripes occur where two light waves reinforce each other and the dark stripes where two waves have interfered. These phenomena—diffraction and interference—are strictly wave characteristics and would not occur if light were made up of individual corpuscles.[18] More than two centuries of experiment and theory assert that light *must* consist of waves. Yet Einstein's photoelectric Law shows that light *must* consist of photons.

---

[16]*spectroscopy* The spectroscope analyzes light for its wavelength emissions, producing a spectrum analysis similar to that shown in the wavelength chart on page 373.

[17]*electrons, neutrons, and protons* Basic particles of the atom. Electrons are negatively charged; neutrons are uncharged; protons are positively charged.

[18]*corpuscles* minute, elementary particles.

This fundamental question—is light waves or is it particles?—has [19] never been answered. The dual character of light is, however, only one aspect of a deeper and more remarkable duality which pervades all nature.

The first hint of this strange dualism came in 1925, when a young [20] French physicist named Louis de Broglie[19] suggested that phenomena involving the interplay of matter and radiation could best be understood by regarding electrons not as individual particles but as systems of waves. This audacious concept flouted two decades of quantum research in which physicists had built up rather specific ideas about the elementary particles of matter. The atom had come to be pictured as a kind of miniature solar system composed of a central nucleus surrounded by varying numbers of electrons (1 for hydrogen, 92 for uranium) revolving in circular or elliptical orbits.[20] The electron was less vivid. Experiments showed that all electrons had exactly the same mass and the same electrical charge, so it was natural to regard them as the ultimate foundation stones of the universe. It also seemed logical at first to picture them simply as hard elastic spheres. But little by little, as investigation progressed, they became more capricious, defiant of observation and measurement. In many ways their behavior appeared too complex for any material particle. "The hard sphere," declared the British physicist, Sir James Jeans,[21] "has always a definite position in space; the electron apparently has not. A hard sphere takes up a very definite amount of room; an electron—well it is probably as meaningless to discuss how much room an electron takes up as it is to discuss how much room a fear, an anxiety, or an uncertainty takes up."

Shortly after de Broglie had his vision of "matter waves" a Viennese [21] physicist named Schrödinger[22] developed the same idea in coherent mathematical form, evolving a system that explained quantum phenomena by attributing specific wave functions to protons and elec-

---

[19]*Louis de Broglie (b. 1892)* When it was discovered that waves exhibited particle behavior, Broglie theorized that particles would exhibit wave behavior, thus adding to theories of quantum mechanics.

[20]*elliptical orbits* Compressed, noncircular orbits, like those of the planets; this is an example of macrocosm being a model for the microcosm (see note 12).

[21]*Sir James Jeans (1877–1946)* Jeans developed a theory that matter is continuously created throughout the universe.

[22]*Erwin Schrödinger (1887–1961)* Austrian physicist who won the Nobel Prize for Physics in 1933 for developing the Schrödinger equation, used in describing wave mechanics.

trons. This system, known as "wave mechanics," was corroborated in 1927 when two American scientists, Davisson and Germer,[23] proved by experiment that electrons actually do exhibit wave characteristics. They directed a beam of electrons upon a metal crystal and obtained diffraction patterns analogous to those produced when light is passed through a pinhole.[24] Their measurements indicated, moreover, that the wave length of an electron is of the precise magnitude predicted by de Broglie's equation, $\lambda = h/mv'$ where v is the velocity of the electron, m is its mass, and h is Planck's Constant. But further surprises were in store. For subsequent experiments showed that not only electrons but whole atoms and even molecules produce wave patterns when diffracted by a crystal surface, and that their wave lengths are exactly what de Broglie and Schrödinger forecast. And so all the basic units of matter—what J. Clerk Maxwell[25] called "the imperishable foundation stones of the universe"—gradually shed their substance. The old-fashioned spherical electron was reduced to an undulating charge of electrical energy, the atom to a system of superimposed waves. One could only conclude that all matter is made of waves and we live in a world of waves.

The paradox presented by waves of matter on the one hand and particles of light on the other was resolved by several developments in the decade before World War II. The German physicists, Heisenberg[26] and Born,[27] bridged the gap by developing a new mathematical apparatus that permitted accurate description of quantum phenomena either in terms of waves *or* in terms of particles as one wished. The idea behind their system had a profound influence on the philosophy of science. They maintained it is pointless of a physicist to worry about

22

---

[23]*Clinton Davisson (1881–1958) and Lester Germer (1896–1971)* Davisson won the Nobel Prize for Physics in 1937 for confirming Louis de Broglie's theory of particle behavior. Germer and Davisson discovered that crystals diffracted electrons. They worked at the Bell Laboratories in New Jersey.

[24]A crystal, because of the even and orderly arrangement of its component atoms and the closeness of their spacing, serves as a diffraction grating for very short wave lengths, such as those of X-rays. [Barnett's note]

[25]*J. Clerk Maxwell (1831–1879)* Influential Scots mathematician and physicist. He was notable for establishing the basic similarity between light waves and the electromagnetic field, demonstrating that a change in one field would have an effect on the other field.

[26]*Werner Karl Heisenberg (1901–1976)* Pioneer in quantum theory. He postulated the Heisenberg principle: that nothing in physics can be observed without the act of observation affecting its behavior.

[27]*Max Born (1882–1970)* Born's research on crystal lattices was influential in solid state physics.

the properties of a single electron; in the laboratory he works with beams or showers of electrons, each containing billions of individual particles (or waves); he is concerned therefore only with mass behavior, with statistics and the laws of probability and chance. So it makes no practical difference whether individual electrons are particles or systems of waves—in aggregate they can be pictured either way. For example, if two physicists are at the seashore one may analyze an ocean wave by saying, "Its properties and intensity are clearly indicated by the positions of its crest and its trough"; while the other may observe with equal accuracy, "The section which you term a crest is significant simply because it contains more molecules of water than the area you call a trough." Analogously Born took the mathematical expression used by Schrödinger in his equations to denote wave function and interpreted it as a "probability" in a statistical sense. That is to say he regarded the intensity of any part of a wave as a measure of the probable distribution of particles at that point. Thus he dealt with the phenomena of diffraction, which hitherto only the wave theory could explain, in terms of the probability of certain corpuscles—light quanta or electrons—following certain paths and arriving at certain places. And so "waves of matter" were reduced to "waves of probability." It no longer matters how we visualize an electron or an atom or a probability wave. The equations of Heisenberg and Born fit any picture. And we can, if we choose, imagine ourselves living in a universe of waves, a universe of particles, or as one facetious scientist has phrased it, a universe of "waveicles."

While quantum physics thus defines with great accuracy the mathematical relationships governing the basic units of radiation and matter, it further obscures the true nature of both. Most modern physicists, however, consider it rather naïve to speculate about the true nature of anything. They are "positivists"—or "logical empiricists"—who contend that a scientist can do no more than report his observations. And so if he performs two experiments with different instruments and one seems to reveal that light is made up of particles and the other that light is made up of waves, he must accept both results, regarding them not as contradictory but as complementary. By itself neither concept suffices to explain light, but together they do. Both are necessary to describe reality and it is meaningless to ask which is really true. For in the abstract lexicon of quantum physics there is no such word as "really."

It is futile, moreover, to hope that the invention of more delicate tools may enable man to penetrate much farther into the microcosm.

There is an indeterminacy about all the events of the atomic universe which refinements of measurement and observation can never dispel. The element of caprice in atomic behavior cannot be blamed on man's coarse-grained implements. It stems from the very nature of things, as shown by Heisenberg in 1927 in a famous statement of physical law known as the "Principle of Uncertainty." To illustrate his thesis Heisenberg pictured an imaginary experiment in which a physicist attempts to observe the position and velocity[28] of a moving electron by using an immensely powerful supermicroscope. Now, as has already been suggested, an individual electron appears to have no definite position or velocity. A physicist can define electron behavior accurately enough so long as he is dealing with great numbers of them. But when he tries to locate a particular electron in space the best he can say is that a certain point in the complex superimposed wave motions of the electron group represents the *probable* position of the electron in question. The individual electron is a blur—as indeterminate as the wind or a sound wave in the night—and the fewer the electrons with which the physicist deals, the more indeterminate his findings. To prove that this indeterminacy is a symptom not of man's immature science but of an ultimate barrier of nature, Heisenberg presupposed that the imaginary microscope used by his imaginary physicist is optically capable of magnifying by a hundred billion diameters—i.e., enough to bring an object the size of an electron within range of human visibility. But now a further difficulty is encountered. For inasmuch as an electron is smaller than a light wave, the physicist can "illuminate" his subject only by using radiation of shorter wave length. Even X-rays are useless. The electron can be rendered visible only by the high-frequency gamma rays of radium. But the photoelectric effect, it will be recalled, showed that photons of ordinary light exert a violent force on electrons; and X-rays knock them about even more roughly. Hence the impact of a still more potent gamma ray would prove disastrous.

The Principle of Uncertainty asserts therefore that it is absolutely and forever impossible to determine the position and the velocity of an electron at the same time—to state confidently that an electron is "right here at this spot" and is moving at "such and such a speed." For by the very act of observing its position, its velocity is changed; and, conversely, the more accurately its velocity is determined, the more indefinite its position becomes. And when the physicist computes the mathematical margin of uncertainty in his measurements of an elec-

25

---

[28]In physics the term "velocity" connotes direction as well as speed. [Barnett's note]

tron's position and velocity he finds it is always a function of that mysterious quantity—Planck's Constant, h.

Quantum physics thus demolishes two pillars of the old science, 26 causality and determination. For by dealing in terms of statistics and probabilities it abandons all idea that nature exhibits an inexorable sequence of cause and effect. And by its admission of margins of uncertainty it yields up the ancient hope that science, given the present state and velocity of every material body in the universe, can forecast the history of the universe for all time. One by-product of this surrender is a new argument for the existence of free will. For if physical events are indeterminate and the future is unpredictable, then perhaps the unknown quantity called "mind" may yet guide man's destiny among the infinite uncertainties of a capricious universe. But this notion invades a realm of thought with which the physicist is not concerned. Another conclusion of greater scientific importance is that in the evolution of quantum physics the barrier between man, peering dimly through the clouded windows of his senses, and whatever objective reality may exist has been rendered almost impassable. For whenever he attempts to penetrate and spy on the "real" objective world, he changes and distorts its workings by the very process of his observations. And when he tries to divorce this "real" world from his sense perceptions he is left with nothing but a mathematical scheme. He is indeed somewhat in the position of a blind man trying to discern the shape and texture of a snowflake. As soon as it touches his fingers or his tongue it dissolves. A wave electron, a photon, a wave of probability, cannot be visualized; they are simply symbols useful in expressing the mathematical relationship of the microcosm.

To the question, why does modern physics employ such esoteric 27 methods of description, the physicist answers: because the equations of quantum physics define more accurately than any mechanical model the fundamental phenomena beyond the range of vision. In short, *they work*, as the calculations which hatched the atomic bomb spectacularly proved. The aim of the practical physicist, therefore, is to enunciate the laws of nature in ever more precise mathematical terms. Where the nineteenth century physicist envisaged electricity as a fluid and, with this metaphor in mind, evolved the laws that generated our present electrical age, the twentieth century physicist tends to avoid metaphors. He knows that electricity is not a fluid, and he knows that such pictorial concepts as "waves" and "particles," while serving as guideposts to new discovery, must not be accepted as accurate representations of reality. In the abstract language of mathematics he can describe how things behave though he does not know—or need to know—what they are.

Yet there are present-day physicists to whom the void between science and reality presents a challenge. Einstein has more than once expressed the hope that the statistical method of quantum physics would prove a temporary expedient. "I cannot believe," he says, "that God plays dice with the world." He repudiates the positivist doctrine that science can only report and correlate the results of observation. He believes in a universe of order and harmony. And he believes that questing man may yet attain a knowledge of physical reality. To this end he has looked not within the atom, but outward to the stars, and beyond them to the vast drowned depths of empty space and time. . . . 28

In order to describe the mechanics of the physical universe, three quantities are required: time, distance, and mass. Since time and distance are relative quantities one might guess that the mass of a body also varies with its state of motion. And indeed the most important practical results of Relativity have arisen from this principle—the relativity of mass. 29

In its popular sense, "mass" is just another word for "weight." But as used by the physicist, it denotes a rather different and more fundamental property of matter: namely, resistance to a change of motion. A greater force is necessary to move a freight car than a velocipede;[29] the freight car resists motion more stubbornly than the velocipede because it has greater mass. In classical physics the mass of any body is a fixed and unchanging property. Thus the mass of a freight car should remain the same whether it is at rest on a siding, rolling across country at 60 miles an hour, or hurtling through outer space at 60,000 miles a second. But Relativity asserts that the mass of a moving body is by no means constant, but increases with its velocity. The old physics failed to discover this fact simply because man's senses and instruments are too crude to note the infinitesimal increases of mass produced by the feeble accelerations of ordinary experience. They become perceptible only when bodies attain velocities close to that of light. (This phenomenon, incidentally, does not conflict with the relativistic contraction of length. One is tempted to ask: how can an object become smaller and at the same time get heavier? The contraction, it should be noted, is only in the direction of motion; width and breadth 30

---

[29]*velocipede*   A three-wheeled railway inspection car used to check tracks and railbed.

are unaffected. Moreover mass is not "heaviness" but resistance to motion.)

Einstein's equation giving the increase of mass with velocity is similar in form to the other equations of Relativity but vastly more important in its consequences:

$$m = \frac{m_0}{\sqrt{1 - (v^2/c^2)}}$$

Here m stands for the mass of a body moving with velocity v, m_0 for its mass when at rest, and c for the velocity of light. Anyone who has ever studied elementary algebra can readily see that if v is small, as are all the velocities of ordinary experience, then the difference between m_0 and m is practically zero. But when v approaches the value of c then the increase of mass becomes very great, reaching infinity when the velocity of the moving body reaches the velocity of light. Since a body of infinite mass would offer infinite resistance to motion the conclusion is once again reached that no material body can travel with the speed of light.

Of all aspects of Relativity the principle of increase of mass has been most often verified and most fruitfully applied by experimental physicists. Electrons moving in powerful electrical fields and beta particles[30] ejected from the nuclei of radioactive substances attain velocities ranging up to 99 per cent that of light. For atomic physicists concerned with these great speeds, the increase of mass predicted by Relativity is no arguable theory but an empirical fact their calculations cannot ignore. In fact the mechanics of the proton-synchrotron[31] and other new super-energy machines are designed to allow for the increasing mass of particles as their speed approaches the velocity of light.

By further deduction from his principle of Relativity of mass, Einstein arrived at a conclusion of incalculable importance to the world. His train of reasoning ran somewhat as follows: since the mass of a moving body increases as its motion increases, and since motion is a form of energy (kinetic energy),[32] then the increased mass of a moving body comes from its increased energy. In short, energy has mass! By a few comparatively simple mathematical steps, Einstein found

31

32

33

---

[30]*beta particles* Electrons or neutrons issuing from the nucleus of an atom during radioactive decay.

[31]*proton-synchrotron* A synchrotron imparts high speeds to particles such as protons by means of alternate electric and magnetic field charges.

[32]*kinetic energy* Energy associated with motion. The concept that energy has mass is totally revolutionary and gave rise to Einstein's famous equation.

the value of the equivalent mass m in any unit of energy E and expressed it by the equation $m = E/c^2$. Given this relation a high school freshman can take the remaining algebraic step necessary to write the most important and certainly the most famous equation in history: $E = mc^2$.

The part played by this equation in the development of the atomic 34 bomb is familiar to most newspaper readers. It states in the shorthand of physics that the energy contained in any particle of matter is equal to the mass of that body (in grams) multiplied by the square of the velocity of light (in centimeters per second). This extraordinary relationship becomes more vivid when its terms are translated into concrete values: i.e., one kilogram of coal (about two pounds), if converted *entirely* into energy, would yield 25 billion kilowatt hours of electricity or as much as all the power plants in the U.S. could generate by running steadily for two months.

$E = mc^2$ provides the answer to many of the long-standing myster- 35 ies of physics. It explains how radioactive substances like radium and uranium are able to eject particles at enormous velocities and to go on doing so for millions of years. It explains how the sun and all the stars can go on radiating light and heat for billions of years, for if our sun were being consumed by ordinary processes of combustion, the earth would have died in frozen darkness eons ago. It reveals the magnitude of the energy that slumbers in the nuclei of atoms, and forecasts how many grams of uranium must go into a bomb in order to destroy a city. Finally it discloses some fundamental truths about physical reality. Prior to Relativity scientists had pictured the universe as a vessel containing two distinct elements, matter and energy—the former inert, tangible, and characterized by a property called mass, and the latter active, invisible, and without mass. But Einstein showed that mass and energy are equivalent: the property called mass is simply concentrated energy. In other words matter is energy and energy is matter, and the distinction is simply one of temporary state.

In the light of this broad principle many puzzles of nature are re- 36 solved. The baffling interplay of matter and radiation which appears sometimes to be a concourse of particles and sometimes a meeting of waves, becomes more understandable. The dual role of the electron as a unit of matter and a unit of electricity, the wave electron, the photon, waves of matter, waves of probability, a universe of waves—all these seem less paradoxical. For all these concepts simply describe different manifestations of the same underlying reality, and it no longer makes sense to ask what any one of them "really" is. Matter and energy are interchangeable. If matter sheds its mass and travels with the speed of light we call it radiation or energy. And conversely if energy congeals and becomes inert and we can ascertain its mass we call it matter. Heretofore science could only note their ephemeral properties and relations as they touched the perceptions of earthbound man. But since July 16, 1945, man has been able to transform one into the other. For on that night at Alamogordo, New Mexico,[33] man for the first time transmuted a substantial quantity of matter into the light, heat, sound, and motion which we call energy.

Yet the fundamental mystery remains. The whole march of science 37 toward the unification of concepts—the reduction of all matter to elements and then to a few types of particles, the reduction of "forces" to the single concept "energy," and then the reduction of matter *and* energy to a single basic quantity—leads still to the unknown. The many questions merge into one, to which there may never be an answer: what is the essence of this mass-energy substance, what is the underlying stratum of physical reality which science seeks to explore?

Thus Relativity, like the Quantum Theory, draws man's intellect 38 still farther away from the Newtonian universe, firmly rooted in space and time and functioning like some great, unerring, and manageable machine. Einstein's laws of motion, his basic principles of the relativity of distance, time, and mass, and his deductions from these principles comprise what is known as the Special Theory of Relativity. In the decade following the publication of this original work, he expanded his scientific and philosophical system into the General Theory of Relativity, through which he examined the mysterious force that guides the whirling of the stars, comets, meteors, and galaxies, and all the moving systems of iron, stone, vapor, and flame in the immense inscrutable void. Newton called this force "universal gravitation." From his own concept of gravitation Einstein attained a view of the vast architecture and anatomy of the universe as a whole.

QUESTIONS

1. What are the inner and outer horizons of knowledge mentioned in the first paragraph of this selection? What have they in common regarding the way we know things?
2. What are some of the still unsolvable questions in physics?
3. What is subjective reality? What is objective reality? How do we accom-

---

[33]*Alamogordo, New Mexico* The test site of the first nuclear explosion.

modate their differences? Are these separate realities problematic in everyday life?

4. What seem to have been the difficulties in resolving the problems caused by the difference between the particle theory and the wave theory of light? Are these problems still difficult for you to understand?

5. Define the following terms: "perception," "atom," "electron," "mass," the symbol "*c*," "energy," "functional harmony of nature." What other terms in this piece need exact definition?

6. How has mathematics brought about the abandonment of sense perception in modern physics (para. 3)?

WRITING ASSIGNMENTS

1. Offer a critique of this chapter of Barnett's book, evaluating its success at communicating a complex theory to the lay person. In what areas does he succeed well? In what areas does he not succeed well? Which concepts do you understand more fully after reading the passage? Which concepts are still vague to you?

2. Describe, as clearly as possible, the problems that arose as a result of the conflict between the particle and wave theories of light. How does Einstein resolve the two theories? Can the difficulties concerning particle and wave theory apply to any other phenomena besides light? Could wave and particle theory apply to crowds of people?

3. In paragraph 27, Barnett points out that science has to do away with metaphors such as "wave" and "particle" but then goes on to use several metaphors himself. Explain why such metaphors are useful and why they are also dangerous. Is it possible that the metaphor offers us a way of knowing something that would otherwise be impossible or difficult for us to know? Is it possible that the metaphor gives us false knowledge?

4. Enormously important and interesting considerations are raised in paragraph 9 concerning what we can hope to know of the world around us. Barnett says: "Realization that our whole knowledge of the universe is simply a residue of impressions clouded by our imperfect senses makes the quest for reality seem hopeless." Is this quest really hopeless? Take a stand on this question, using this passage and any other relevant background information you may have or that you may acquire through reading. Establish the impediments to knowing reality, and likewise establish the facts that might point to the hope of achieving a clearer knowledge of reality.

5. In paragraph 24, Barnett talks about the "element of caprice" in atomic particles. (Caprice may be translated as "chance" or "luck.") If it is true that atoms or particles of atoms behave in erratic or capricious ways, is it then true, as Barnett asserts, that the role of human free will plays a larger part in human life than has been thought? If chance governs the universe on an atomic level (even if it governs only a segment of atomic activity),

does that mean that the universe itself is governed by chance? What does it mean to say that chance "governs" anything? If chance and human free will were in some sense equal, which would have the greater effect upon our world?

6. The Heisenberg uncertainty principle demonstrates that an electron cannot be observed without affecting its position and/or velocity. Scientists have pointed out that, if that is true, nothing can be observed without being affected by the act of observation. What could this mean for all of our observations of the natural world? What would it mean for our observations of people? Can we observe anything without affecting it?

7. Explain the theories of quantum mechanics and relativity to your grandparents (or other older acquaintances) in a brief but complete essay. Try to imagine which aspects of these theories would be most difficult and which would be easiest for them to understand. Try also to explore with them some of the implications of these theories that you believe are most important for us to accept. Which problems associated with these theories would be most intriguing to them? Which ones would be least significant for them? Try to be most persuasive in asking them to accept those aspects of these theories that they would be most likely to discount.

ALFRED NORTH WHITEHEAD

―――――✦―――――

Religion and Science

ALFRED NORTH WHITEHEAD (1861–1947), one of the most important mathematicians of the twentieth century, was born in Rams-
gate, England, and was educated at Trinity College, Cambridge,
where he eventually taught mathematics. He and his student, Bertrand Russell (1872–1970), collaborated on one of the most important
modern works on mathematics, the three-volume Principia Mathematica (1910–1913). It was a work that demonstrated the connection
between mathematics and formal logic.

After leaving Cambridge, Whitehead became professor at London's Imperial College of Science and Technology. Later, in 1924,
Whitehead accepted a professorship in philosophy at Harvard University. The Lowell Lectures, which he delivered in 1925, were published as Science and the Modern World, one of the most influential
books of its time. It demonstrated that his interests and insights had
successfully encompassed, not just science and mathematics, but religion and the humanities as well.

Much of Whitehead's work is highly technical and thus is available only to those with special training. But most of his later philo-

―――――――――――――――――――――――――――――――――

From Science and the Modern World.

sophical work was written with an eye toward affecting a somewhat more general—although still reasonably well educated—reader.

"Religion and Science" discusses a controversy that was particularly apparent in society since the publication of Darwin's Origin of Species *in 1859. The issue was relevant in the 1920s because of the celebrated Scopes "Monkey Trial" in Dayton, Tennessee, which took place in 1925, testing whether or not a science teacher could teach the theory of evolution in a public school in that state. But, of course, the conflict between religion and science has a way of erupting age after age; and as Whitehead points out, the disagreements became serious as early as the seventeenth century. In the book from which the following selection is taken, Whitehead seems to be making a genuine effort to find a means of putting the conflict into perspective and of softening the disagreements.*

WHITEHEAD'S RHETORIC

The most obvious rhetorical device Whitehead relies upon is the topic of comparison, making a clear relationship between religion and science. Generally, he tries to establish a point relating to religion and then moves on to examine science for the same point.

As Whitehead approaches the comparative aspects of his subject, he also uses the topic of definition (paras. 1 and 27) and the topic of relationship (paras. 4, 5, 7, 9, and many others); in addition, he uses instances and examples at virtually every opportunity. The result is, as one might assume, an extraordinary degree of clarity, all the more remarkable considering the complexities of the subject—which he points out in paragraph 6.

Whitehead concentrates on showing us the areas in which religion and science are somewhat alike, as in paragraphs 7 and 8, and then on showing the ways in which they are quite distinct, as in paragraph 13. He cautions us against assuming that science is always right in any debate between religion and science. Too, he cautions religion against ignoring the changes in modern psychology that make "brute fear" an ineffective instrument of faith. He also cautions that when religion is unnecessarily on the defensive, it can overreact and create conflict where there is actually none (para. 20).

As one reads the following selection, it becomes quite obvious that Whitehead is not simply a scientist. In fact, if one did not know his reputation, one might not realize his eminence as a scientist. It is true that he speaks authoritatively of such things as the discovery of the element argon; that he understands the problems inherent in the wave and particle (corpuscular) theories of light; and that he is extraordinarily knowledgeable about the history of science, including its subtleties. But, by the same token, he speaks authoritatively about religion, referring to obscure Church Fathers as well as such great religious figures as St. Augustine and St. Francis of Assisi.

Whitehead's ultimate view is that much work must be done by our society to avoid harsh clashes between the forces of science and religion. And both forces must learn to recognize that a "clash of doctrines is no disaster," but that valuable change can emerge from them. His assurance is essentially optimistic. He asserts, finally, that progress for science implies progress for religion.

Religion and Science

The difficulty in approaching the question of the relations between   1
Religion and Science is, that its elucidation requires that we have in our minds some clear idea of what we mean by either of the terms, "religion" and "science." Also I wish to speak in the most general way possible, and to keep in the background any comparison of particular creeds, scientific or religious. We have got to understand the type of connection which exists between the two spheres, and then to draw some definite conclusions respecting the existing situation which at present confronts the world.

The *conflict* between religion and science is what naturally occurs   2
to our minds when we think of this subject. It seems as though, during the last half-century, the results of science and the beliefs of religion had come into a position of frank disagreement, from which there can be no escape, except by abandoning either the clear teaching of science, or the clear teaching of religion. This conclusion has been urged by controversialists on either side. Not by all controversialists, of course, but by those trenchant intellects which every controversy calls out into the open.

The distress of sensitive minds, and the zeal for truth, and the   3
sense of the importance of the issues, must command our sincerest sympathy. When we consider what religion is for mankind, and what

science is, it is no exaggeration to say that the future course of history depends upon the decision of this generation as to the relations between them. We have here the two strongest general forces (apart from the mere impulse of the various senses) which influence men, and they seem to be set one against the other—the force of our religious intuitions, and the force of our impulse to accurate observation and logical deduction.

A great English statesman once advised his countrymen to use large-scale maps, as a preservative against alarms, panics, and general misunderstanding of the true relations between nations. In the same way in dealing with the clash between permanent elements of human nature, it is well to map our history on a large scale, and to disengage ourselves from our immediate absorption in the present conflicts. When we do this, we immediately discover two great facts. In the first place, there has always been a conflict between religion and science; and in the second place, both religion and science have always been in a state of continual development. In the early days of Christianity, there was a general belief among Christians that the world was coming to an end in the lifetime of people then living. We can make only indirect inferences as to how far this belief was authoritatively proclaimed; but it is certain that it was widely held, and that it formed an impressive part of the popular religious doctrine. The belief proved itself to be mistaken, and Christian doctrine adjusted itself to the change. Again in the early Church individual theologians very confidently deduced from the Bible opinions concerning the nature of the physical universe. In the year A.D. 535, a monk named Cosmas[1] wrote a book which he entitled, *Christian Topography.* He was a travelled man who had visited India and Ethiopia; and finally he lived in a monastery at Alexandria,[2] which was then a great center of culture. In this book, basing himself upon the direct meaning of Biblical texts as construed by him in a literal fashion, he denied the existence of the antipodes,[3] and asserted that the world is a flat parallelogram whose length is double its breadth.

In the seventeenth century the doctrine of the motion of the earth[4] 5

---

[1]*Cf.* [William] Lecky's *The Rise and Influence of Rationalism in Europe,* Ch. III. [Whitehead's note]

[2]**Alexandria** City in Egypt; the center of Christianity's Coptic church.

[3]**antipodes** Whitehead means the north and south poles; antipodes generally means any two places on the earth that are opposite each other.

[4]**motion of the earth** The church taught that the earth was stationary and the sun and moon revolved about it. In 1632 Galileo proved otherwise and was condemned (see note 7).

was condemned by a Catholic tribunal. A hundred years ago the extension of time[5] demanded by geological science distressed religious people, Protestant and Catholic. And today the doctrine of evolution is an equal stumbling block. These are only a few instances illustrating a general fact.

But all our ideas will be in a wrong perspective if we think that this recurring perplexity was confined to contradictions between religion and science; and that in these controversies religion was always wrong, and that science was always right. The true facts of the case are very much more complex, and refuse to be summarized in these simple terms.

Theology itself exhibits exactly the same character of gradual development, arising from an aspect of conflict between its own proper ideas. This fact is a commonplace to theologians, but is often obscured in the stress of controversy. I do not wish to overstate my case; so I will confine myself to Roman Catholic writers. In the seventeenth century a learned Jesuit, Father Petavius, showed that the theologians of the first three centuries of Christianity made use of phrases and statements which since the fifth century would be condemned as heretical. Also Cardinal Newman[6] devoted a treatise to the discussion of the development of doctrine. He wrote it before he became a great Roman Catholic ecclesiastic; but throughout his life, it was never retracted and continually reissued.

Science is even more changeable than theology. No man of science could subscribe without qualification to Galileo's beliefs,[7] or to Newton's beliefs,[8] or to all his own scientific beliefs of ten years ago.

In both regions of thought, additions, distinctions, and modifications have been introduced. So that now, even when the same asser-

---

[5]***extension of time*** Calculating from biblical records and genealogies, Archbishop James Usher (1581–1656) established the date of creation as 4004 B.C. Geological science points to a date hundreds of millions of years earlier. Many religions still hold to Usher's dating.

[6]***John Henry Newman (1801–1890)*** *Lectures on the Prophetical Office of the Church* (1843) was published before Newman, an Englishman, converted from Anglicanism to Roman Catholicism (1845). He became a priest, and was made a cardinal in 1879. One of his most famous books is *The Idea of a University* (1852).

[7]***Galileo's beliefs*** Galileo Galilei (1564–1642), Italian astronomer who proved the Copernican theory, that the earth moves around the sun. The Roman Catholic church, which still officially held otherwise, forced him to recant.

[8]***Newton's beliefs*** Isaac Newton (1642–1727). English physicist; discovered the law of gravity; invented calculus. His laws of motion, fluids, and optics are still accurate and applicable in modern physics.

tion is made today as was made a thousand, or fifteen hundred years ago, it is made subject to limitations or expansions of meaning, which were not contemplated at the earlier epoch. We are told by logicians that a proposition must be either true or false, and that there is no middle term. But in practice, we may know that a proposition expresses an important truth, but that it is subject to limitations and qualifications which at present remain undiscovered. It is a general feature of our knowledge, that we are insistently aware of important truth; and yet that the only formulations of these truths which we are able to make presuppose a general standpoint of conceptions which may have to be modified. I will give you two illustrations, both from science: Galileo said that the earth moves and that the sun is fixed; the Inquisition said that the earth is fixed and the sun moves; and Newtonian astronomers, adopting an absolute theory of space, said that both the sun and the earth move. But now we say that any one of these three statements is equally true, provided that you have fixed your sense of "rest" and "motion" in the way required by the statement adopted. At the date of Galileo's controversy with the Inquisition, Galileo's way of stating the facts was, beyond question, the fruitful procedure for the sake of scientific research. But in itself it was not more true than the formulation of the Inquisition. But at that time the modern concepts of relative motion were in nobody's mind; so that the statements were made in ignorance of the qualifications required for their more perfect truth. Yet this question of the motions of the earth and the sun expresses a real fact in the universe; and all sides had got hold of important truths concerning it. But with the knowledge of those times, the truths appeared to be inconsistent.

Again I will give you another example taken from the state of modern physical science. Since the time of Newton and Huyghens[9] in the seventeenth century there have been two theories as to the physical nature of light. Newton's theory was that a beam of light consists of a stream of very minute particles, or corpuscles, and that we have the sensation of light when these corpuscles strike the retinas of our eyes. Huyghens' theory was that light consists of very minute waves of trembling in an all-pervading ether, and that these waves are travelling along a beam of light. The two theories are contradictory. In the eighteenth century Newton's theory was believed, in the nineteenth century Huyghens' theory was believed. Today there is one large group of   10

---

[9]*Christian Huyghens (1629–1695)* Dutch mathematician and astronomer. He founded the wave theory, discovered the rings of Saturn, invented the pendulum clock, and discovered the laws of centrifugal force. He was an extremely well known figure.

phenomena which can be explained only on the wave theory, and another large group which can be explained only on the corpuscular theory. Scientists have to leave it at that, and wait for the future, in the hope of attaining some wider vision which reconciles both.

We should apply these same principles to the questions in which there is a variance between science and religion. We would believe nothing in either sphere of thought which does not appear to us to be certified by solid reasons based upon the critical research either of ourselves or of competent authorities. But granting that we have honestly taken this precaution, a clash between the two on points of detail where they overlap should not lead us hastily to abandon doctrines for which we have solid evidence. It may be that we are more interested in one set of doctrines than in the other. But, if we have any sense of perspective and of the history of thought, we shall wait and refrain from mutual anathemas.[10]   11

We should wait: but we should not wait passively, or in despair. The clash is a sign that there are wider truths and finer perspectives within which a reconciliation of a deeper religion and a more subtle science will be found.   12

In one sense, therefore, the conflict between science and religion is a slight matter which has been unduly emphasized. A mere logical contradiction cannot in itself point to more than the necessity of some readjustments, possibly of a very minor character on both sides. Remember the widely different aspects of events which are dealt with in science and in religion respectively. Science is concerned with the general conditions which are observed to regulate physical phenomena; whereas religion is wholly wrapped up in the contemplation of moral and aesthetic values. On the one side there is the law of gravitation, and on the other the contemplation of the beauty of holiness. What one side sees, the other misses; and vice versa.   13

Consider, for example, the lives of John Wesley[11] and of Saint Francis of Assisi.[12] For physical science you have in these lives merely ordinary examples of the operation of the principles of physiological chemistry, and of the dynamics of nervous reactions: for religion you   14

---

[10]*anathemas*   denunciations; in religion, official anathema involved excommunication.

[11]*John Wesley (1703–1791)*   English clergyman, founder of the Methodist church, leading the religious revival in the eighteenth century.

[12]*Saint Francis of Assisi (1181–1226)*   Italian monk, founder of the Franciscan order of monks; like Wesley, he was a powerfully charismatic person who drew many followers. He preached good works, poverty, and charity.

have lives of the most profound significance in the history of the world. Can you be surprised that, in the absence of a perfect and complete phrasing of the principles of science and of the principles of religion which apply to these specific cases, the accounts of these lives from these divergent standpoints should involve discrepancies? It would be a miracle if it were not so.

It would, however, be missing the point to think that we need not trouble ourselves about the conflict between science and religion. In an intellectual age there can be no active interest which puts aside all hope of a vision of the harmony of truth. To acquiesce in discrepancy is destructive of candor, and of moral cleanliness. It belongs to the self-respect of intellect to pursue every tangle of thought to its final unravelment. If you check that impulse, you will get no religion and no science from an awakened thoughtfulness. The important question is, In what spirit are we going to face the issue? There we come to something absolutely vital.   15

A clash of doctrines is not a disaster—it is an opportunity. I will explain my meaning by some illustrations from science. The weight of an atom of nitrogen was well known. Also it was an established scientific doctrine that the average weight of such atoms in any considerable mass will be always the same. Two experimenters, the late Lord Rayleigh and the late Sir William Ramsay,[13] found that if they obtained nitrogen by two different methods, each equally effective for that purpose, they always observed a persistent slight difference between the average weights of the atoms in the two cases. Now I ask you, would it have been rational of these men to have despaired because of this conflict between chemical theory and scientific observation? Suppose that for some reason the chemical doctrine had been highly prized throughout some district as the foundation of its social order: would it have been wise, would it have been candid, would it have been moral, to forbid the disclosure of the fact that the experiments produced discordant results? Or, on the other hand, should Sir William Ramsay and Lord Rayleigh have proclaimed that chemical theory was now a detected delusion? We see at once that either of these ways would have been a method of facing the issue in an entirely wrong spirit. What Rayleigh and Ramsay did was this: They at once   16

---

[13]*John William Strutt, Lord Rayleigh (1844–1919) and Sir William Ramsay (1852–1916)* They shared the Nobel Prize for Physics in 1904; Ramsay discovered and worked with inert gases—helium (with Rayleigh); argon (with Travers, another scientist). Together they studied the density of nitrogen produced from air and ammonia, finding the figures persistently different.

perceived that they had hit upon a line of investigation which would disclose some subtlety of chemical theory that had hitherto eluded observation. The discrepancy was not a disaster: it was an opportunity to increase the sweep of chemical knowledge. You all know the end of the story: finally argon was discovered, a new chemical element which had lurked undetected, mixed with the nitrogen. But the story has a sequel which forms my second illustration. This discovery drew attention to the importance of observing accurately minute differences in chemical substances as obtained by different methods. Further researches of the most careful accuracy were undertaken. Finally another physicist, F. W. Aston, working in the Cavendish Laboratory at Cambridge in England, discovered that even the same element might assume two or more distinct forms, termed *isotopes*,[14] and that the law of the constancy of average atomic weight holds for each of these forms, but as between the different isotopes differs slightly. The research has effected a great stride in the power of chemical theory, far transcending in importance the discovery of argon from which it originated. The moral of these stories lies on the surface, and I will leave to you their application to the case of religion and science.

In formal logic, a contradiction is the signal of a defeat: but in the evolution of real knowledge it marks the first step in progress towards a victory. This is one great reason for the utmost toleration of variety of opinion. Once and forever, this duty of toleration has been summed up in the words, "Let both grow together until the harvest."[15] The failure of Christians to act up to this precept, of the highest authority, is one of the curiosities of religious history. But we have not yet exhausted the discussion of the moral temper required for the pursuit of truth. There are short cuts leading merely to an illusory success. It is easy enough to find a theory, logically harmonious and with important applications in the region of fact, provided that you are content to disregard half your evidence. Every age produces people with clear logical intellects, and with the most praiseworthy grasp of the importance of some sphere of human experience, who have elaborated, or inherited, a scheme of thought which exactly fits those experiences which claim their interest. Such people are apt resolutely to ignore, or to explain

17

---

[14]**isotopes** Molecules of the same element but having different molecular weights and detectable differences of behavior. Francis William Aston (1877–1945) established the existence of isotopes as a basic phenomenon of nature. The Cavendish Laboratories were founded at Cambridge University by J. C. Maxwell. (See note 25 in Barnett, p. 379.)

[15]The quotation is from Matthew 13:30, an argument against premature "weeding out" of things that might prove useful.

away, all evidence which confuses their scheme with contradictory instances; what they cannot fit in is for them nonsense. An unflinching determination to take the whole evidence into account is the only method of preservation against the fluctuating extremes of fashionable opinion. This advice seems so easy, and is in fact so difficult to follow.

One reason for this difficulty is that we cannot think first and act 18 afterwards. From the moment of birth we are immersed in action, and can only fitfully guide it by taking thought. We have, therefore, in various spheres of experience to adopt those ideas which seem to work within those spheres. It is absolutely necessary to trust to ideas which are generally adequate, even though we know that there are subtleties and distinctions beyond our ken. Also apart from the necessities of action, we cannot even keep before our minds the whole evidence except under the guise of doctrines which are incompletely harmonized. We cannot think in terms of an indefinite multiplicity of detail; our evidence can acquire its proper importance only if it comes before us marshalled by general ideas. These ideas we inherit—they form the tradition of our civilization. Such traditional ideas are never static. They are either fading into meaningless formulae, or are gaining power by the new lights thrown by a more delicate apprehension. They are transformed by the urge of critical reason, by the vivid evidence of emotional experience, and by the cold certainties of scientific perception. One fact is certain, you cannot keep them still. No generation can merely reproduce its ancestors. You may preserve the life in a flux of form, or preserve the form amid an ebb of life. But you cannot permanently enclose the same life in the same mold.

The present state of religion among the European races illustrates 19 the statements which I have been making. The phenomena are mixed. There have been reactions and revivals. But on the whole, during many generations, there has been a gradual decay of religious influence in European civilization. Each revival touches a lower peak than its predecessor, and each period of slackness a lower depth. The average curve marks a steady fall in religious tone. In some countries the interest in religion is higher than in others. But in those countries where the interest is relatively high, it still falls as the generations pass. Religion is tending to degenerate into a decent formula wherewith to embellish a comfortable life. A great historical movement on this scale results from the convergence of many causes. I wish to suggest two of them which lie within the scope of this chapter for consideration.

In the first place for over two centuries religion has been on the 20 defensive, and on a weak defensive. The period has been one of unprecedented intellectual progress. In this way a series of novel situations have been produced for thought. Each such occasion has found the religious thinkers unprepared. Something, which has been proclaimed to be vital, has finally, after struggle, distress, and anathema, been modified and otherwise interpreted. The next generation of religious apologists then congratulates the religious world on the deeper insight which has been gained. The result of the continued repetition of this undignified retreat, during many generations, has at last almost entirely destroyed the intellectual authority of religious thinkers. Consider this contrast: when Darwin or Einstein proclaim theories which modify our ideas, it is a triumph for science. We do not go about saying that there is another defeat for science, because its old ideas have been abandoned. We know that another step of scientific insight has been gained.

Religion will not regain its old power until it can face change in 21 the same spirit as does science. Its principles may be eternal, but the expression of those principles requires continual development. This evolution of religion is in the main a disengagement of its own proper ideas from the adventitious[16] notions which have crept into it by reason of the expression of its own ideas in terms of the imaginative picture of the world entertained in previous ages. Such a release of religion from the bonds of imperfect science is all to the good. It stresses its own genuine message. The great point to be kept in mind is that normally an advance in science will show that statements of various religious beliefs require some sort of modification. It may be that they have to be expanded or explained, or indeed entirely restated. If the religion is a sound expression of truth, this modification will only exhibit more adequately the exact point which is of importance. This process is a gain. In so far, therefore, as any religion has any contact with physical facts, it is to be expected that the point of view of those facts must be continually modified as scientific knowledge advances. In this way, the exact relevance of these facts for religious thought will grow more and more clear. The progress of science must result in the unceasing codification of religious thought, to the great advantage of religion.

The religious controversies of the sixteenth and seventeenth cen- 22 turies put theologians into a most unfortunate state of mind. They were always attacking and defending. They pictured themselves as the garrison of a fort surrounded by hostile forces. All such pictures express half-truths. That is why they are so popular. But they are danger-

---

[16]***adventitious*** borrowed, not original; not essential to something.

ous. This particular picture fostered a pugnacious party spirit which really expresses an ultimate lack of faith. They dared not modify, because they shirked the task of disengaging their spiritual message from the associations of a particular imagery.

Let me explain myself by an example. In the early medieval times, 23 Heaven was in the sky, and Hell was underground; volcanoes were the jaws of Hell. I do not assert that these beliefs entered into the official formulations: but they did enter into the popular understanding of the general doctrines of Heaven and Hell. These notions were what everyone thought to be implied by the doctrine of the future state. They entered into the explanations of the influential exponents of Christian belief. For example, they occur in the *Dialogues* of Pope Gregory,[17] the Great, a man whose high official position is surpassed only by the magnitude of his services to humanity. I am not saying what we ought to believe about the future state. But whatever be the right doctrine, in this instance the clash between religion and science, which has relegated the earth to the position of a second-rate planet attached to a second-rate sun, has been greatly to the benefit of the spirituality of religion by dispersing these medieval fancies.

Another way of looking at this question of the evolution of reli- 24 gious thought is to note that any verbal form of statement which has been before the world for some time discloses ambiguities; and that often such ambiguities strike at the very heart of the meaning. The effective sense in which a doctrine has been held in the past cannot be determined by the mere logical analysis of verbal statements, made in ignorance of the logical trap.[18] You have to take into account the whole reaction of human nature to the scheme of thought. This reaction is of a mixed character, including elements of emotion derived from our lower natures. It is here that the impersonal criticism of science and of philosophy comes to the aid of religious evolution. Example after example can be given of this motive force in development. For example, the logical difficulties inherent in the doctrine of the moral cleansing of human nature by the power of religion rent Chris-

---

[17]*Cf.* Gregorovius' *History of Rome in the Middle Ages,* Book III, Ch. III, Vol. II, English trans. [Whitehead's note] Pope Gregory I (540–604) established the model for the medieval papacy. He used the power of the church to relieve the misery of many people.

[18]**logical trap** A reference to the limits of verbal logic. See Aristotle's cautions in the opening of *The Nichomachean Ethics* on the limits of precision possible in certain inquiries. Matters of faith are not always susceptible to logic.

tianity in the days of Pelagius and Augustine[19]—that is to say, at the beginning of the fifth century. Echoes of that controversy still linger in theology.

So far, my point has been this: that religion is the expression of 25 one type of fundamental experiences of mankind: that religious thought develops into an increasing accuracy of expression, disengaged from adventitious imagery: that the interaction between religion and science is one great factor in promoting this development.

I now come to my second reason for the modern fading of interest 26 in religion. This involves the ultimate question which I stated in my opening sentences. We have to know what we mean by religion. The churches, in their presentation of their answers to this query, have put forward aspects of religion which are expressed in terms either suited to the emotional reactions of bygone times or directed to excite modern emotional interests of nonreligious character. What I mean under the first heading is that religious appeal is directed partly to excite that instinctive fear of the wrath of a tyrant which was inbred in the unhappy populations of the arbitrary empires of the ancient world, and in particular to excite that fear of an all-powerful arbitrary tyrant behind the unknown forces of nature. This appeal to the ready instinct of brute fear is losing its force. It lacks any directness of response, because modern science and modern conditions of life have taught us to meet occasions of apprehension by a critical analysis of their causes and conditions. Religion is the reaction of human nature to its search for God. The presentation of God under the aspect of power awakens every modern instinct of critical reaction. This is fatal; for religion collapses unless its main positions command immediacy of assent. In this respect the old phraseology is at variance with the psychology of modern civilizations. This change in psychology is largely due to science, and is one of the chief ways in which the advance of science has weakened the hold of the old religious forms of expression. The nonreligious motive which has entered into modern religious thought is the desire for a comfortable organization of modern society. Religion has been presented as valuable for the ordering of life. Its claims have been rested upon its function as a sanction to right conduct. Also the

---

[19]*Pelagius (360?–420) and Saint Augustine (354–430)* Their argument was over the issue of original sin. Pelagius said it was not visited on mankind; Augustine said that it was. The Roman Catholic church accepts Augustine's view.

purpose of right conduct quickly degenerates into the formation of pleasing social relations. We have here a subtle degradation of religious ideas, following upon their gradual purification under the influence of keener ethical intuitions. Conduct is a by-product of religion—an inevitable by-product, but not the main point. Every great religious teacher has revolted against the presentation of religion as a mere sanction of rules of conduct. Saint Paul[20] denounced the Law, and Puritan divines[21] spoke of the filthy rags of righteousness. The insistence upon rules of conduct marks the ebb of religious fervor. Above and beyond all things, the religious life is not a research after comfort. I must now state, in all diffidence, what I conceive to be the essential character of the religious spirit.

Religion is the vision of something which stands beyond, behind, and within, the passing flux of immediate things; something which is real, and yet waiting to be realized; something which is a remote possibility, and yet the greatest of present facts; something that gives meaning to all that passes, and yet eludes apprehension; something whose possession is the final good, and yet is beyond all reach; something which is the ultimate ideal, and the hopeless quest. 27

The immediate reaction of human nature to the religious vision is worship. Religion has emerged into human experience mixed with the crudest fancies of barbaric imagination. Gradually, slowly, steadily the vision recurs in history under nobler form and with clearer expression. It is the one element in human experience which persistently shows an upward trend. It fades and then recurs. But when it renews its force, it recurs with an added richness and purity of content. The fact of the religious vision, and its history of persistent expansion, is our one ground for optimism. Apart from it, human life is a flash of occasional enjoyments lighting up a mass of pain and misery, a bagatelle[22] of transient experience. 28

The vision claims nothing but worship; and worship is a surrender to the claim for assimilation, urged with the motive force of mutual love. The vision never overrules. It is always there, and it has the 29

---

[20]***Saint Paul (d. 64?–67 A.D.)*** The Apostle Paul wrote several letters denouncing morally indefensible Roman laws permitting persecution of Christians. He also repudiated Moses' Law, which he felt was superseded by Christianity.

[21]***Puritan divines*** Puritans in England and America in the early seventeenth century insisted that one must follow one's moral conscience even when it directs one to break the law. English Puritans opposed King Charles I (1600–1649), and had him beheaded after they seized power in a bloody Civil War.

[22]***bagatelle*** Something slight and amusing; a game similar to pool.

power of love presenting the one purpose whose fulfilment is eternal harmony. Such order as we find in nature is never force—it presents itself as the one harmonious adjustment of complex detail. Evil is the brute motive force of fragmentary purpose, disregarding the eternal vision. Evil is overruling, retarding, hurting. The power of God is the worship He inspires. That religion is strong which in its ritual and its modes of thought evokes an apprehension of the commanding vision. The worship of God is not a rule of safety—it is an adventure of the spirit, a flight after the unattainable. The death of religion comes with the repression of the high hope of adventure.

QUESTIONS

1. Review Whitehead's definitions of religion and science.
2. Whitehead uses the technique of enumeration at the end of paragraph 19. How effective is it? What, precisely, is he enumerating?
3. Is Whitehead clearer regarding religion or regarding science? When is he least clear?
4. This chapter was first delivered as a lecture at Harvard University. Most of Whitehead's listeners would have been students. Do you think most of them were science students? Humanities students? Can you tell from the chapter who he was trying hardest to reach?
5. Do you feel that Whitehead treats religion fairly in this piece?

WRITING ASSIGNMENTS

1. Using the material provided in the selection along with whatever background knowledge you have, establish exactly what the conflict has been between religion and science. Do you think that there have been adequate grounds for the conflict, or has it simply been a product of misunderstanding? Is the conflict inevitable? Do you believe that it will continue in your lifetime, or do you think that there is some end in sight?
2. Write a critique of Whitehead's handling of the topic of comparison or the topic of past time. Inventory the piece to see how often and where he uses these devices, then qualify their success. Consider how clearly each topic is used, how fully it is developed, and how effective it is for the argument that is being made.
3. In paragraph 15, Whitehead says, "It belongs to the self-respect of intellect to pursue every tangle of thought to its final unravelment." Clarify what he means by this statement and then decide if he is right. You may use genuine or imaginary instances in arguing your case. You may also refer to examples in Whitehead or any of the essays you have read in this book.

4. In paragraph 15, Whitehead describes the seriousness of the conflict be-tween religion and science, insisting that seekers of wisdom have a diffi-cult time giving up "a vision of the harmony of truth." Then, in paragraph 16, he recites a number of instances in which disputed research produced some interesting results. He tells us several stories and ends that paragraph by saying, "The moral of these stories lies on the surface, and I will leave to you their application to the case of religion and science." Follow his advice and apply the moral of the stories to the conflict between religion and science in your essay.

5. In paragraphs 21–23, Whitehead seems to be chastening religion for its approach to change. Clarify exactly what his complaint is and whether or not he is right in saying that religion should "face change in the same spirit as does science." Then analyze his argument in the succeeding paragraphs, where he asserts that one problem religion has lies in the imagery it uses to express its truths. Define his concept regarding that imagery. What, ex-actly, is he referring to? Would a change in imagery really entail a change in the conflict between religion and science?

6. Throughout the selection, Whitehead speaks of the fading of religion in modern life. He is most direct in paragraph 26, but he also refers to the withering of religion to a "decent formula" in paragraph 19. He also says, "Insistence upon rules of conduct marks the ebb of religious fervor." Does his view of the fading of religion from modern life square with your own observation of religion's role in life? Or has there been a renewal of reli-gious force in our time? If so, has science hindered or helped to bring about such a renewal? Argue that religion is or is not in decline in our time.

THOMAS S. KUHN

————◦∞◦————

The Essential Tension: Tradition and Innovation in Scientific Research

THOMAS KUHN (b. 1922) began as a physicist but soon switched from research to the study of the history of science. His contributions in that field have been so striking as to represent a revolution in thought. His first book, The Structure of Scientific Revolutions *(1962; 1970; 3rd ed. 1982), was a landmark in the history of science. He followed that work with a book on the effects of the Copernican revolution on thought as well as a book of essays,* The Essential Tension *(1976), from which the selection presented here, a lecture first delivered in 1959, is taken.*

Kuhn is an educator and a scholar, and has taught the history of science at Harvard University, the University of California at Berkeley, and Princeton University. He has been associated with the Institute for Advanced Study. Currently he teaches at the Massachusetts Institute of Technology (MIT). The talk which follows was delivered to a group of teachers and scholars at the University of Utah at a conference dedicated to discovering scientific talent in young people. As such, the conference was composed of people who were interested in creativity, imagination, and the intellectual problems involved with becoming a scientist.

Kuhn has an interesting concept buried deep within this talk, one that concerns the basic personality type that makes a good scientist.

This is not his focus, to be sure, nor does it directly enter into his thesis statement, but it underlies most of what he is saying. His conclusion is that the best scientist is that person who is most capable of working within the existing traditions of science. In fact, his conclusion is that in the long run such a person will be the most creative kind of scientist. Because this view is not quite what his audience expected to hear, it is buried rather than featured in his talk.

KUHN'S RHETORIC

Because Kuhn's presentation was given as a talk—and was only slightly altered for inclusion in his book—it has many of the typical rhetorical ingredients of a talk. One is the "signpost"—the statement of direction the speaker is taking. In paragraph 6 he points to time limitations which prevent him from giving a wide range of historical examples. He tells us in paragraph 7 that he will now "try briefly to epitomize the nature of education in the natural sciences." In paragraph 10 he tells us, "I shall shortly inquire about . . . ." In paragraph 18 he says, "and this is the point"; in paragraph 21, "What I have said so far. . ."; and in paragraph 26, "As first planned, my paper was to have ended at this point." All these signposts are set up to alert us to his direction, the moments of change of direction, the moments of summation, and the conclusion. Kuhn naturally refers to himself as "I," as most speakers do. Such a relaxed mode of address puts his listeners at ease and makes it simpler for him to explain what he is doing as he does it.

Kuhn also uses an age-old technique typical of a spoken address on a serious subject. He divides the talk into recognizable parts:

Introduction, in which he explains who he is and what he is going to talk about (paras. 1 and 2). His central thesis is stated at the end of paragraph 1.

Body, in which several subsections deal with separate issues:

1. A clarification of the tension between divergent and convergent thinking, with an emphasis on convergent thought (paras. 3–14). Paragraph 14 has a clear sense of a conclusion.

2. A discussion of the nature of education of scientists with an eye toward discovering what kind of personality the scientist should have (paras. 15–24), ending in another conclusion.

Conclusion, in which Kuhn adds a postscript, which is the final conclusion, summarizing his main argument (paras. 26–30).

Kuhn carefully considers theories that are contrary to his own, and while he does not use as many examples as, say, Darwin does, he offers a few key examples to help bolster his argument, as in his discussion of the wave–particle theories of light (para. 11), of science before Isaac Newton (para. 12), and his final discussion of Thomas Edison (1847–1931) in paragraph 29. All the while what he is doing is illustrating the essential tension between two kinds of thinking—the divergent thinking that his audience has already defined as necessary to creativity and the convergent thinking which he has deduced is essential to scientific progress. There must be a tension between these two kinds of thinking in the mind of the scientist who wishes to make creative discoveries. The topic of comparison is used implicitly throughout the essay.

Because his point is somewhat irregular—proposing that creativity comes directly out of the most complete commitment to tradition— Kuhn is careful to prepare his audience carefully for his conclusions. He realizes that what he is saying is a bit paradoxical, and he is cautious to make it clear that he is aware of the complexities of his position. What he wants most is to make his audience aware of the fact that looking only for examples of divergent thinking in prospective scientists is a mistake. Those whose thinking is essentially divergent in nature must accept the essential tension.

The Essential Tension:
Tradition and Innovation in
Scientific Research

I am grateful for the invitation to participate in this important con- 1
ference,[1] and I interpret it as evidence that students of creativity themselves possess the sensitivity to divergent approaches that they seek to
identify in others. But I am not altogether sanguine[2] about the outcome of your experiment with me. As most of you already know, I am
no psychologist, but rather an ex-physicist now working in the history
of science. Probably my concern is no less with creativity than your
own, but my goals, my techniques, and my sources of evidence are so
very different from yours that I am far from sure how much we do, or
even *should*, have to say to each other. These reservations imply no
apology: rather they hint at my central thesis. In the sciences, as I
shall suggest below, it is often better to do one's best with the tools at
hand than to pause for contemplation of divergent approaches.

If a person of my background and interests has anything relevant 2
to suggest to this conference, it will not be about your central concerns, the creative personality and its early identification. But implicit
in the numerous working papers distributed to participants in this
conference is an image of the scientific process and of the scientist;
that image almost certainly conditions many of the experiments you
try as well as the conclusions you draw; and about it the physicist-
historian may well have something to say. I shall restrict my attention
to one aspect of this image—an aspect epitomized as follows in one of
the working papers: The basic scientist "must lack prejudice to a degree where he can look at the most 'self-evident' facts or concepts
without necessarily accepting them, and, conversely, allow his imagination to play with the most unlikely possibilities.". . . In the more
technical language supplied by other working papers, ... this aspect

---

[1] ***this important conference*** It was a conference on the identification of scientific
talent held at the University of Utah in 1959.

[2] ***sanguine*** hopeful or optimistic.

of the image recurs as an emphasis upon "divergent thinking, . . . the freedom to go off in different directions, . . . rejecting the old solution and striking out in some new direction."

I do not at all doubt that this description of "divergent thinking" and the concomitant search for those able to do it are entirely proper. Some divergence characterizes all scientific work, and gigantic divergences lie at the core of the most significant episodes in scientific development. But both my own experience in scientific research and my reading of the history of sciences lead me to wonder whether flexibility and open-mindedness have not been too exclusively emphasized as the characteristics requisite for basic research. I shall therefore suggest below that something like "convergent thinking" is just as essential to scientific advance as is divergent. Since these two modes of thought are inevitably in conflict, it will follow that the ability to support a tension that can occasionally become almost unbearable is one of the prime requisites for the very best sort of scientific research.

I am elsewhere studying these points more historically, with emphasis on the importance to scientific development of "revolutions."[3] These are episodes—exemplified in their most extreme and readily recognized form by the advent of Copernicanism, Darwinism, or Einsteinianism—in which a scientific community abandons one time-honored way of regarding the world and of pursuing science in favor of some other, usually incompatible, approach to its discipline. I have argued in the draft that the historian constantly encounters many far smaller but structurally similar revolutionary episodes and that they are central to scientific advance. Contrary to a prevalent impression, most new discoveries and theories in the sciences are not merely additions to the existing stockpile of scientific knowledge. To assimilate them the scientist must usually rearrange the intellectual and manipulative equipment he has previously relied upon, discarding some elements of his prior belief and practice while finding new significances in and new relationships between many others. Because the old must be revalued and reordered when assimilating the new, discovery and invention in the sciences are usually intrinsically revolutionary. Therefore, they do demand just that flexibility and open-mindedness that characterize, or indeed define, the divergent thinker. Let us henceforth take for granted the need for these characteristics. Unless many scientists possessed them to a marked degree, there would be no scientific revolutions and very little scientific advance.

---

[3][Thomas Kuhn,] *The Structure of Scientific Revolutions* (Chicago, 1962). [Kuhn's note]

Yet flexibility is not enough, and what remains is not obviously 5
compatible with it. Drawing from various fragments of a project still
in progress, I must now emphasize that revolutions are but one of two
complementary aspects of scientific advance. Almost none of the research undertaken by even the greatest scientists is designed to be revolutionary, and very little of it has any such effect. On the contrary,
normal research, even the best of it, is a highly convergent activity
based firmly upon a settled consensus acquired from scientific education and reinforced by subsequent life in the profession. Typically, to
be sure, this convergent or consensus-bound research ultimately results in revolution. Then, traditional techniques and beliefs are abandoned and replaced by new ones. But revolutionary shifts of a scientific tradition are relatively rare, and extended periods of convergent
research are the necessary preliminary to them. As I shall indicate below, only investigations firmly rooted in the contemporary scientific
tradition are likely to break that tradition and give rise to a new one.
That is why I speak of an "essential tension" implicit in scientific
research. To do his job the scientist must undertake a complex set of
intellectual and manipulative commitments. Yet his claim to fame, if
he has the talent and good luck to gain one, may finally rest upon his
ability to abandon this net of commitments in favor of another of his
own invention. Very often the successful scientist must simultaneously display the characteristics of the traditionalist and of the
iconoclast.[4]

The multiple historical examples upon which any full documenta- 6
tion of these points must depend are prohibited by the time limitations of the conference. But another approach will introduce you to at
least part of what I have in mind—an examination of the nature of
education in the natural sciences. One of the working papers for this
conference . . . quotes Guilford's very apt description of scientific education as follows: "[It] has emphasized abilities in the areas of con-

---

[4]Strictly speaking, it is the professional group rather than the individual scientist that
must display both these characteristics simultaneously. In a fuller account of the ground
covered in this paper that distinction between individual and group characteristics would
be basic. Here I can only note that, though recognition of the distinction weakens the
conflict or tension referred to above, it does not eliminate it. Within the group some
individuals may be more traditionalistic, others more iconoclastic, and their contributions may differ accordingly. Yet education, institutional norms, and the nature of the
job to be done will inevitably combine to insure that all group members will, to a greater
or lesser extent, be pulled in both directions. [Kuhn's note] An *iconoclast* is not traditional, but likes to break with the past, often in very dramatic ways.

vergent thinking and evaluation, often at the expense of development in the area of divergent thinking. We have attempted to teach students how to arrive at 'correct' answers that our civilization has taught us are correct. . . . Outside the arts [and I should include most of the social sciences] we have generally discouraged the development of divergent-thinking abilities, unintentionally." That characterization seems to me eminently just, but I wonder whether it is equally just to deplore the product that results. Without defending plain bad teaching, and granting that in this country the trend to convergent thinking in all education may have proceeded entirely too far, we may nevertheless recognize that a rigorous training in convergent thought has been intrinsic to the sciences almost from their origin. I suggest that they could not have achieved their present state or status without it.

Let me try briefly to epitomize the nature of education in the natural sciences, ignoring the many significant yet minor differences between the various sciences and between the approaches of different educational institutions. The single most striking feature of this education is that, to an extent totally unknown in other creative fields, it is conducted entirely through textbooks. Typically, undergraduate *and* graduate students of chemistry, physics, astronomy, geology, or biology acquire the substance of their fields from books written especially for students. Until they are ready, or very nearly ready, to commence work on their own dissertations, they are neither asked to attempt trial research projects nor exposed to the immediate products of research done by others, that is, to the professional communications that scientists write for each other. There are no collections of "readings" in the natural sciences. Nor are science students encouraged to read the historical classics of their fields—works in which they might discover other ways of regarding the problems discussed in their textbooks, but in which they would also meet problems, concepts, and standards of solution that their future professions have long since discarded and replaced.

In contrast, the various textbooks that the student does encounter display different subject matters, rather than, as in many of the social sciences, exemplifying different approaches to a single problem field. Even books that compete for adoption in a single course differ mainly in level and in pedagogic detail, not in substance or conceptual structure. Last, but most important of all, is the characteristic technique of textbook presentation. Except in their occasional introductions, science textbooks do not describe the sorts of problems that the professional may be asked to solve and the variety of techniques available for their solution. Rather, these books exhibit concrete problem solutions that the profession has come to accept as paradigms,[5] and they then ask the student, either with a pencil and paper or in the laboratory, to solve for himself problems very closely related in both method and substance to those through which the textbook or the accompanying lecture has led him. Nothing could be better calculated to produce "mental sets" or *Einstellungen.*[6] Only in their most elementary courses do other academic fields offer as much as a partial parallel.

Even the most faintly liberal educational theory must view this   9
pedagogic technique as anathema. Students, we would all agree, must begin by learning a good deal of what is already known, but we also insist that education give them vastly more. They must, we say, learn to recognize and evaluate problems to which no unequivocal solution has yet been given; they must be supplied with an arsenal of techniques for approaching these future problems; and they must learn to judge the relevance of these techniques and to evaluate the possibly partial solutions which they can provide. In many respects these attitudes toward education seem to me entirely right, and yet we must recognize two things about them. First, education in the natural sciences seems to have been totally unaffected by their existence. It remains a dogmatic initiation in a pre-established tradition that the student is not equipped to evaluate. Second, at least in the period when it was followed by a term in an apprenticeship relation, this technique of exclusive exposure to a rigid tradition has been immensely productive of the most consequential sorts of innovations.

I shall shortly inquire about the pattern of scientific practice that   10
grows out of this educational initiation and will then attempt to say why that pattern proves quite so successful. But first, an historical excursion will reinforce what has just been said and prepare the way for what is to follow. I should like to suggest that the various fields of natural science have not always been characterized by rigid education in exclusive paradigms, but that each of them acquired something like that technique at precisely the point when the field began to make rapid and systematic progress. If one asks about the origin of our contemporary knowledge of chemical composition, of earthquakes, of biological reproduction, of motion through space, or of any other subject matter known to the natural sciences, one immediately encounters a

---

[5]*paradigms* Patterns or models of thought; the established views of the way something works or is.
[6]*Einstellungen* outlook (German).

characteristic pattern that I shall here illustrate with a single example.

Today, physics textbooks tell us that light exhibits some properties [11] of a wave and some of a particle: both textbook problems and research problems are designed accordingly. But both this view and these textbooks are products of an early twentieth-century revolution. (One characteristic of scientific revolutions is that they call for the rewriting of science textbooks.) For more than half a century before 1900, the books employed in scientific education had been equally unequivocal in stating that light was wave motion. Under those circumstances scientists worked on somewhat different problems and often embraced rather different sorts of solutions to them. The nineteenth-century textbook tradition does not, however, mark the beginning of our subject matter. Throughout the eighteenth century and into the early nineteenth, Newton's *Opticks*[7] and the other books from which men learned science taught almost all students that light was particles, and research guided by this tradition was again different from that which succeeded it. Ignoring a variety of subsidiary changes within these three successive traditions, we may therefore say that our views derive historically from Newton's views by way of two revolutions in optical thought, each of which replaced one tradition of convergent research with another. If we make appropriate allowances for changes in the locus[8] and materials of scientific education, we may say that each of these three traditions was embodied in the sort of education by exposure to unequivocal paradigms that I briefly epitomized above. Since Newton, education and research in physical optics have normally been highly convergent.

The history of theories of light does not, however, begin with New- [12] ton. If we ask about knowledge in the field before his time, we encounter a significantly different pattern—a pattern still familiar in the arts and in some social sciences, but one which has largely disappeared in the natural sciences. From remote antiquity until the end of the seventeenth century there was no single set of paradigms for the study of physical optics. Instead, many men advanced a large number of different views about the nature of light. Some of these views found few adherents, but a number of them gave rise to continuing schools of

---

[7]***Opticks (1704)*** By Sir Isaac Newton (1642–1727); one of the most important studies of light and color theory. The book began as a series of lectures in Trinity College, Cambridge. Newton developed here his theory that light was composed of tiny individual corpuscles, or particles.

[8]***locus*** place.

optical thought. Although the historian can note the emergence of new points of view as well as changes in the relative popularity of older ones, there was never anything resembling consensus. As a result, a new man entering the field was inevitably exposed to a variety of conflicting viewpoints; he was forced to examine the evidence for each, and there always was good evidence. The fact that he made a choice and conducted himself accordingly could not entirely prevent his awareness of other possibilities. This earlier mode of education was obviously more suited to produce a scientist without prejudice, alert to novel phenomena, and flexible in his approach to his field. On the other hand, one can scarcely escape the impression that, during the period characterized by this more liberal educational practice, physical optics made very little progress.[9]

The preconsensus (we might here call it the divergent) phase in the development of physical optics is, I believe, duplicated in the history of all other scientific specialties, excepting only those that were born by the subdivision and recombination of pre-existing disciplines. In some fields, like mathematics and astronomy, the first firm consensus is prehistoric. In others, like dynamics, geometric optics, and parts of physiology, the paradigms that produced a first consensus date from classical antiquity. Most other natural sciences, though their problems were often discussed in antiquity, did not achieve a first consensus until after the Renaissance. In physical optics, as we have seen, the first firm consensus dates only from the end of the seventeenth century; in electricity, chemistry, and the study of heat, it dates from the eighteenth; while in geology and the nontaxonomic[10] parts of biology no very real consensus developed until after the first third of the nineteenth century. This century appears to be characterized by the emergence of a first consensus in parts of a few of the social sciences.

In all the fields named above, important work was done before the achievement of the maturity produced by consensus. Neither the na-

13

14

---

[9] The history of physical optics before Newton has recently been well described by Vasco Ronchi in *Histoire de la lumière,* trans. J. Taton (Paris, 1956). His account does justice to the element I elaborate too little above. Many fundamental contributions to physical optics were made in the two millennia before Newton's work. Consensus is not prerequisite to a sort of progress in the natural sciences, any more than it is to progress in the social sciences or the arts. It is, however, prerequisite to the sort of progress that we now generally refer to when distinguishing the natural sciences from the arts and from most social sciences. [Kuhn's note]

[10]**nontaxonomic** unrelated to the classification of plants and animals.

ture nor the timing of the first consensus in these fields can be understood without a careful examination of both the intellectual and the manipulative techniques[11] developed before the existence of unique paradigms. But the transition to maturity is not less significant because individuals practiced science before it occurred. On the contrary, history strongly suggests that, though one can practice science—as one does philosophy or art or political science—without a firm consensus, this more flexible practice will not produce the pattern of rapid consequential scientific advance to which recent centuries have accustomed us. In that pattern, development occurs from one consensus to another, and alternate approaches are not ordinarily in competition. Except under quite special conditions, the practitioner of a mature science does not pause to examine divergent modes of explanation or experimentation.

I shall shortly ask how this can be so—how a firm orientation toward an apparently unique tradition can be compatible with the practice of the disciplines most noted for the persistent production of novel ideas and techniques. But it will help first to ask what the education that so successfully transmits such a tradition leaves to be done. What can a scientist working within a deeply rooted tradition and little trained in the perception of significant alternatives hope to do in his professional career? Once again limits of time force me to drastic simplification, but the following remarks will at least suggest a position that I am sure can be documented in detail. 15

In pure or basic science[12]—that somewhat ephemeral category of research undertaken by men whose most immediate goal is to increase understanding rather than control of nature—the characteristic problems are almost always repetitions, with minor modifications, of problems that have been undertaken and partially resolved before. For example, much of the research undertaken within a scientific tradition is an attempt to adjust existing theory or existing observation in order to bring the two into closer and closer agreement. The constant examination of atomic and molecular spectra during the years since the birth of wave mechanics, together with the design of theoretical approximations for the prediction of complex spectra, provides one important instance of this typical sort of work. Another was provided by 16

---

[11]***manipulative techniques*** practical testing, as opposed to theorizing.
[12]***pure or basic science*** The distinction, pure and applied, is equivalent to the distinction between theoretical and practical science.

the remarks about the eighteenth-century development of Newtonian dynamics[13] in the paper on measurement supplied to you in advance of the conference.[14] The attempt to make existing theory and observation conform more closely is not, of course, the only standard sort of research problem in the basic sciences. The development of chemical thermodynamics[15] or the continuing attempts to unravel organic structure illustrate another type—the extension of existing theory to areas that it is expected to cover but in which it has never before been tried. In addition, to mention a third common sort of research problem, many scientists constantly collect the concrete data (e.g., atomic weights, nuclear moments[16]) required for the application and extension of existing theory.

These are normal research projects in the basic sciences, and they 17 illustrate the sorts of work on which all scientists, even the greatest, spend most of their professional lives and on which many spend all. Clearly their pursuit is neither intended nor likely to produce fundamental discoveries or revolutionary changes in scientific theory. Only if the validity of the contemporary scientific tradition is assumed do these problems make much theoretical or any practical sense. The man who suspected the existence of a totally new type of phenomenon or who had basic doubts about the validity of existing theory would not think problems so closely modeled on textbook paradigms worth undertaking. It follows that the man who does undertake a problem of this sort—and that means all scientists at most times—aims to elucidate the scientific tradition in which he was raised rather than to change it. Furthermore, the fascination of his work lies in the difficulties of elucidation rather than in any surprises that the work is likely to produce. Under normal conditions the research scientist is not an innovator but a solver of puzzles, and the puzzles upon which he concentrates are just those which he believes can be both stated and solved within the existing scientific tradition.

Yet—and this is the point—the ultimate effect of this tradition- 18 bound work has invariably been to change the tradition. Again and

---

[13]**Newtonian dynamics** Newton's three laws of motion are: (1) An object stays at rest until an outside force moves it. (2) The change of motion is proportional to the force that moves it. (3) To every action there is an equal and opposite reaction.

[14]A revised version appeared in *Isis* 52 (1961): 161–93. [Kuhn's note]

[15]**chemical thermodynamics** laws determining motion, usually of gases, in relation to heat.

[16]**atomic weights, nuclear moments** Atomic weight of an element is the average of its isotopes, the average number of atoms in its molecule. Nuclear moment is the axis of the molecule, its center.

again the continuing attempt to elucidate a currently received tradition has at last produced one of those shifts in fundamental theory, in problem field,[17] and in scientific standards to which I previously referred as scientific revolutions. At least for the scientific community as a whole, work within a well-defined and deeply ingrained tradition seems more productive of tradition-shattering novelties than work in which no similarly convergent standards are involved. How can this be so? I think it is because no other sort of work is nearly so well suited to isolate for continuing and concentrated attention those loci of trouble or causes of crisis upon whose recognition the most fundamental advances in basic science depend.

As I have indicated in the first of my working papers, new theories and, to an increasing extent, novel discoveries in the mature sciences are not born *de novo*.[18] On the contrary, they emerge from old theories and within a matrix[19] of old beliefs about the phenomena that the world does *and does not* contain. Ordinarily such novelties are far too esoteric and recondite[20] to be noted by the man without a great deal of scientific training. And even the man with considerable training can seldom afford simply to go out and look for them, let us say by exploring those areas in which existing data and theory have failed to produce understanding. Even in a mature science there are always far too many such areas, areas in which no existing paradigms seem obviously to apply and for whose exploration few tools and standards are available. More likely than not the scientist who ventured into them, relying merely upon his receptivity to new phenomena and his flexibility to new patterns of organization, would get nowhere at all. He would rather return his science to its preconsensus or natural history phase.

Instead, the practitioner of a mature science, from the beginning of his doctoral research, continues to work in the regions for which the paradigms derived from his education and from the research of his contemporaries seem adequate. He tries, that is, to elucidate topographical detail on a map whose main outlines are available in advance, and he hopes—if he is wise enough to recognize the nature of his field—that he will some day undertake a problem in which the anticipated does

19

20

---

[17]***problem field*** theoretical questions.

[18]**de novo** over again; from the start.

[19]***matrix*** interrelated group of, in this case, beliefs; when one changes, all are altered.

[20]***esoteric and recondite*** designed for specially trained people and difficult to understand.

not occur, a problem that goes wrong in ways suggestive of a fundamental weakness in the paradigm itself. In the mature sciences the prelude to much discovery and to all novel theory is not ignorance, but the recognition that something has gone wrong with existing knowledge and beliefs.

What I have said so far may indicate that it is sufficient for the productive scientist to adopt existing theory as a lightly held tentative hypothesis, employ it *faute de mieux*[21] in order to get a start in his research, and then abandon it as soon as it leads him to a trouble spot, a point at which something has gone wrong. But though the ability to recognize trouble when confronted by it is surely a requisite for scientific advance, trouble must not be too easily recognized. The scientist requires a thoroughgoing commitment to the tradition with which, if he is fully successful, he will break. In part this commitment is demanded by the nature of the problems the scientist normally undertakes. These, as we have seen, are usually esoteric puzzles whose challenge lies less in the information disclosed by their solutions (all but its details are often known in advance) than in the difficulties of technique to be surmounted in providing any solution at all. Problems of this sort are undertaken only by men assured that there is a solution which ingenuity can disclose, and only current theory could possibly provide assurance of that sort. That theory alone gives meaning to most of the problems of normal research. To doubt it is often to doubt that the complex technical puzzles which constitute normal research have any solutions at all. Who, for example, would have developed the elaborate mathematical techniques required for the study of the effects of interplanetary attractions upon basic Keplerian orbits[22] if he had not assumed that Newtonian dynamics, applied to the planets then known, would explain the last details of astronomical observation? But without that assurance, how would Neptune have been discovered and the list of planets changed?

In addition, there are pressing practical reasons for commitment. Every research problem confronts the scientist with anomalies[23] whose sources he cannot quite identify. His theories and observations never quite agree; successive observations never yield quite the same

21

22

---

[21]**faute de mieux**   for want of something better.

[22]***Keplerian orbits***   Johannes Kepler (1571–1630) discovered that the planets move in elliptical, not circular orbits. He recognized the gravitational pull of the sun and planets and was noted for the care and exactitude of his measurements.

[23]***anomalies***   unaccountable variations from what is expected.

results; his experiments have both theoretical and phenomenological[24] by-products which it would take another research project to unravel. Each of these anomalies or incompletely understood phenomena could conceivably be the clue to a fundamental innovation in scientific theory or technique, but the man who pauses to examine them one by one never completes his first project. Reports of effective research repeatedly imply that all but the most striking and central discrepancies could be taken care of by current theory if only there were time to take them on. The men who make these reports find most discrepancies trivial or uninteresting, an evaluation that they can ordinarily base only upon their faith in current theory. Without that faith their work would be wasteful of time and talent.

Besides, lack of commitment too often results in the scientist's undertaking problems that he has little chance of solving. Pursuit of an anomaly is fruitful only if the anomaly is more than nontrivial. Having discovered it, the scientist's first efforts and those of his profession are to do what nuclear physicists are now doing. They strive to generalize the anomaly, to discover other and more revealing manifestations of the same effect, to give it structure by examining its complex interrelationships with phenomena they still feel they understand. Very few anomalies are susceptible to this sort of treatment. To be so they must be in explicit and unequivocal conflict with some structurally central tenet of current scientific belief. Therefore, their recognition and evaluation once again depend upon a firm commitment to the contemporary scientific tradition.

This central role of an elaborate and often esoteric tradition is what I have principally had in mind when speaking of the essential tension in scientific research. I do not doubt that the scientist must be, at least potentially, an innovator, that he must possess mental flexibility, and that he must be prepared to recognize troubles where they exist. That much of the popular stereotype is surely correct, and it is important accordingly to search for indices of the corresponding personality characteristics. But what is no part of our stereotype and what appears to need careful integration with it is the other face of this same coin. We are, I think, more likely fully to exploit our potential scientific talent if we recognize the extent to which the basic scientist must also be a firm traditionalist, or, if I am using your vocabulary at all correctly, a convergent thinker. Most important of all, we must seek to understand

---

[24]***phenomenological***   related to perceptible events.

how these two superficially discordant modes of problem solving can be reconciled both within the individual and within the group.

Everything said above needs both elaboration and documentation. Very likely some of it will change in the process. This paper is a report on work in progress. But, though I insist that much of it is tentative and all of it incomplete, I still hope that the paper has indicated why an educational system best described as an initiation into an unequivocal tradition should be thoroughly compatible with successful scientific work. And I hope, in addition, to have made plausible the historical thesis that no part of science has progressed very far or very rapidly before this convergent education and correspondingly convergent normal practice became possible. Finally, though it is beyond my competence to derive personality correlates from this view of scientific development, I hope to have made meaningful the view that the productive scientist must be a traditionalist who enjoys playing intricate games by pre-established rules in order to be a successful innovator who discovers new rules and new pieces with which to play them. 25

As first planned, my paper was to have ended at this point. But work on it, against the background supplied by the working papers distributed to conference participants, has suggested the need for a postscript. Let me therefore briefly try to eliminate a likely ground of misunderstanding and simultaneously suggest a problem that urgently needs a great deal of investigation. 26

Everything said above was intended to apply strictly only to basic science, an enterprise whose practitioners have ordinarily been relatively free to choose their own problems. Characteristically, as I have indicated, these problems have been selected in areas where paradigms were clearly applicable but where exciting puzzles remained about how to apply them and how to make nature conform to the results of the application. Clearly the inventor and applied scientist are not generally free to choose puzzles of this sort. The problems among which they may choose are likely to be largely determined by social, economic, or military circumstances external to the sciences. Often the decision to seek a cure for a virulent disease, a new source of household illumination, or an alloy able to withstand the intense heat of rocket engines must be made with little reference to the state of the relevant science. It is, I think, by no means clear that the personality characteristics requisite for pre-eminence in this more immediately practical sort of work are altogether the same as those required for a 27 great achievement in basic science. History indicates that only a few individuals, most of whom worked in readily demarcated areas, have achieved eminence in both.

I am by no means clear where this suggestion leads us. The troublesome distinctions between basic research,[25] applied research, and invention need far more investigation. Nevertheless, it seems likely, for example, that the applied scientist, to whose problems no scientific paradigm need be fully relevant, may profit by a far broader and less rigid education than that to which the pure scientist has characteristically been exposed. Certainly there are many episodes in the history of technology in which lack of more than the most rudimentary scientific education has proved to be an immense help. This group scarcely needs to be reminded that Edison's electric light[26] was produced in the face of unanimous scientific opinion that the arc light could not be "subdivided," and there are many other episodes of this sort.

This must not suggest, however, that mere differences in education will transform the applied scientist into a basic scientist or vice versa. One could at least argue that Edison's personality, ideal for the inventor and perhaps also for the "oddball" in applied science, barred him from fundamental achievements in the basic sciences. He himself expressed great scorn for scientists and thought of them as wooly-headed people to be hired when needed. But this did not prevent his occasionally arriving at the most sweeping and irresponsible scientific theories of his own. (The pattern recurs in the early history of electrical technology: both Tesla[27] and Gramme[28] advanced absurd cosmic schemes that they thought deserved to replace the current scientific knowledge of their day.) Episodes like this reinforce an impression that the per-

---

[25]***basic research*** Research designed to establish new theories. Other types of research attempt to put basic research to some practical use.

[26]***electric light*** Thomas Alva Edison (1847–1931) did not invent the electric light, but did the applied research that made it a practical commercial product, which it became in 1882.

[27]***Nikola Tesla (1856–1943)*** Yugoslavian inventor of carbon arc lighting, in which a huge electrical charge bridges a gap with a bright flash. He also invented alternating current. In later years he claimed to be able to communicate with distant planets and to be able to split the earth like an apple.

[28]***Zenobé-Theophile Gramme (1826–1901)*** A basically untrained French scientist and inventor who worked with direct and alternating current. He held some wild and ignorant views of the power of magnetism.

28

29

sonality requisites of the pure scientist and of the inventor may be quite different, perhaps with those of the applied scientist lying somewhere between.[29]

Is there a further conclusion to be drawn from all this? One speculative thought forces itself upon me. If I read the working papers correctly, they suggest that most of you are really in search of the *inventive* personality, a sort of person who does emphasize divergent thinking but whom the United States has already produced in abundance. In the process you may be ignoring certain of the essential requisites of the basic scientist, a rather different sort of person, to whose ranks America's contributions have as yet been notoriously sparse. Since most of you are, in fact, Americans, this correlation may not be entirely coincidental.

30

---

[29]For the attitude of scientists toward the technical possibility of the incandescent light see Francis A. Jones, *Thomas Alva Edison* (New York, 1908), pp. 99–100, and Harold C. Passer, *The Electrical Manufacturers, 1875–1900* (Cambridge, Mass., 1953), pp. 82–83. For Edison's attitude toward scientists see Passer, ibid., pp. 180–81. For a sample of Edison's theorizing in realms otherwise subject to scientific treatments see Dagobert D. Runes, ed., *The Diary and Sundry Observations of Thomas Alva Edison* (New York, 1948), pp. 205–44, passim. [Kuhn's note]

Q U E S T I O N S

1. What is divergent thinking? Give some examples from your own experience.
2. What is convergent thinking? Give some examples from your experience.
3. Assuming that Kuhn's audience was committed to the principles of divergent thinking before they heard his talk, do you feel that they would have changed their minds after hearing it? What are your reasons for thinking they would (or would not) have changed their minds?
4. Find all the signposts in the talk that explain where the argument is heading, what Kuhn is planning to do, and what he has done. How effective are these signposts for following his argument? Do you find them annoying or helpful? Are there any places where they are needed but not supplied?
5. Kuhn talks about reaching a consensus in science. What does he mean? See paragraphs 12–13.

WRITING ASSIGNMENTS

1. Kuhn is interested in the kind of personality that would be best suited to doing creative work in science. After listening to his talk, if you were a member of the audience responsible for selecting a potential scientist from a group of young people, what personality characteristics would you look for? What, in Kuhn's view, are the intellectual and personal characteristics of scientists that are most likely to ensure scientific discovery in the future?

2. Much of what Kuhn has to say about thinking relates directly to the way in which education in the sciences is conducted. The student is asked to master the basic paradigms of a branch of science—theories, models, patterns, examples—that are at hand. What are your views on the nature of scientific education? Based on your own experience, what is praiseworthy about it? What is not praiseworthy about it? Is science education much as Kuhn describes it?

3. What is it about the very nature of science that suits it best to convergent thinking? Consider the discovery of facts, laws, and principles that really work and that do not admit of much variance. Why would science resist divergent thought? What would actually constitute divergent thought in science? Why is consensus such a deterrent to divergence? *Should* it be a deterrent to divergence? What are the alternatives, if any, to such consensus?

4. In paragraph 3, Kuhn asserts that "these two modes of thought" (divergence and convergence) "are inevitably in conflict." Is this statement necessarily true? Find examples in any area of inquiry—science, politics, religion, education, or any other area that interests you—which help you decide just what the nature of the conflict (if there is one) actually is. If you find that there is no conflict, explain why there is none. If you find that there is conflict, explain why there is. Use Kuhn's rhetorical techniques of beginning with an introduction, dividing your topic in the body of the essay, and ending with a summary conclusion. Structure your essay like a talk and offer some of the same kinds of signposts that Kuhn uses.

5. If the principle of convergent thinking and the commitment to tradition and consensus were followed in education the way Kuhn says they should be followed in science, what would your educational experience have been like? Try to imagine what grade school would have been like and contrast that with what your actual experience was. Do the same thing regarding secondary school and college. Is divergent thinking more desirable or less desirable in education than in science? Is it more respected than convergent thinking? In your essay, try to give some examples from your own experience of when convergent thinking was most clearly expected of you and when divergent thinking was expected.

6. Look for examples of convergent and divergent thinking in your social life and write an essay based on your findings. Are most of your friends likely to be convergent or divergent in their thinking? Choose some specific persons and instances of their thinking. If possible, spend some time in observation of your friends (and yourself) to see which kind of thinking is more prevalent. How much tolerance do your friends have for divergent thinking? How much tolerance do older people seem to have for divergent thinking? What seem to be the most touchy issues with respect to divergent thinking? Make your essay into the shape of a talk like Kuhn's, using signposts, an introduction, a body, and a conclusion. Use the first person throughout.

PART FOUR

PHILOSOPHY ANCIENT AND MODERN

Plato · · · Aristotle
Bertrand Russell · · · John Dewey
Albert Camus

INTRODUCTION

PHILOSOPHY has no traceable beginnings and no imaginable endings. But for most Western thinkers, its roots reach down to the giants of the golden age of Athenian Greece: Socrates, his student Plato, and *his* student, Aristotle. Since their time, philosophy has developed innumerable schools, movements, and waves of influence. Every age, it seems, has had to evolve a number of philosophical systems to help characterize the problems of the day, put them into some intellectual perspective, and begin the clarification of thought that is essential to every reflective being. As Plato's teacher, Socrates, said, "The unexamined life is not worth living." Philosophers, by nature, are examiners of life. The result of their work is to help increase our understanding of why life is worth living and, by extension, how we can make our own lives more worthwhile.

The first selection in this part, Plato's "Allegory of the Cave," must rank as the premier document in ancient Greek philosophy. Its influence on later thought has been remarkable. Plato pictures us as being like people who live in a cave watching shadows on the wall before us. We think those shadows are real because we can see no other features of the real world. In fact, however, the shadows are the appearances of things, the sensory qualities—which are all that we can ever hope to apprehend. Plato tells us that there is something behind sensory qualities, some *reality* which, because we are limited by our senses, we cannot see or even imagine. Plato insists that the *real* can exist only in a pure spiritual realm. And since, in the Platonic scheme of things, we originally came from that realm, we have a dim memory of the real and interpret our sensory experience in accordance with our memory. Thus, there is a resemblance between the spiritual ideal and the sensory experiences we have; but the resemblance is merely as close as the shadows in the cave are to the people who cast them.

Aristotle differed with his master in that he attributed more value to the world of the senses. He thought that one could know the truth about many things—the nature of God, goodness, the soul—by proceeding through sensory avenues. For instance, it was possible for him, following Plato's lead, to see that physical love could lead one to an understanding of divine love and the nature of divine goodness. The world of experience for both philosophers was a guide to the ideal. But Aristotle insisted that new knowledge about the physical world could be gathered by scientific observation, which naturally placed a high value on sensory observation.

In *The Nichomachean Ethics,* Aristotle studies the nature of the good and insists that the good is not simply in a Platonic spiritual realm. It is attainable here on earth through our actions. His view is that we should pursue the ultimate good in this life, which he takes to be happiness. Yet, he cautions against a happiness that is merely self-indulgence, since that will satisfy a person only temporarily. The most profound, long-lasting happiness must include a commitment to "perfect virtue," because without virtue, all happiness is temporary, a sham. This examination of the nature of ethical behavior and the pursuit of happiness is one of the most influential such works in all philosophy.

Among modern philosophers, English Nobel Prize winner Bertrand Russell must be considered a major force. He is also a brilliant writer. His discussion of "A Free Man's Worship" is elegantly phrased and exquisitely worded. He warns us that we must be cautious as moderns to avoid worshiping mere power, whether it takes the form of political force, money, or influence. Rather, we must look within our own natures to discover the sources of human goodness. We are alone in the universe, perhaps; if so, we must recognize our own best natures. Out of that recognition comes a source of worship that befits a modern civilization.

John Dewey is a pragmatic philosopher. He believes that philosophy must be practical in its application and testing. His views are based on the concept that philosophy, like science, ought to have its theories tested by experiment. Those that are practical and workable should be saved; those that are not should be discarded. Because of these views and because of his conviction that philosophy can be as effective and influential in our lives as science, in the selection presented here he urges us to consider the need for a reconstruction of philosophy along scientific lines. In his meditation on Francis Bacon's aphorism "Knowledge is Power," he gives us some ideas about what he means.

Just as practical is Albert Camus, another Nobel Prize winner. A philosophical writer rather than a practicing philosopher, Camus was influential among the existentialists, philosophers who believe that actions define people. Existence (thoughts, deeds, expressed commitments) is what makes people what they are, not some vague "essential" nature. Camus wrote *The Myth of Sisyphus* during the dark early years of World War II when there was little reason to be joyful about human prospects. He was concerned with finding a reason to stay alive. People seemed to be doomed to repeating terrible forms of behavior, meaningless acts, even murderous wars. In the doomed figure of Sisyphus, who must push a rock to the top of a mountain only to have it roll back to its foot again—and to repeat this for eternity —Camus found a reason for being happy. For the existentialist, being alive, knowing the nature of one's fate—these are enough. Being conscious of what one is doing is cause enough for joy. Like Socrates, Camus tells us that it is the examined life that is worth living.

Philosophy is the process by which we examine life. By practicing it, we make life—our own lives—more valuable. We make life worth living because by practicing philosophy we are doing something that is unique to human beings: reflecting on our own nature. We know of nothing else in the universe that can do that. Being philosophical is both unique and essential to the human condition.

The rhetorical range of these essays is interesting, particularly since most philosophers confront the problems of addressing very abstract subject matter. Thus, it is no surprise perhaps that both Plato and Camus, an ancient and a modern thinker, rely on allegory. An allegory is an extended metaphor, developing a comparison between that which is described and that which is understood as its reference. Often the reference is not explicitly stated, although both Plato and Camus make their references clear.

Likewise, since the philosopher is concerned with understanding complex subjects, we should not be surprised to see that Bertrand Russell, for example, relies heavily on analysis, the separation of the totality of his subject into parts. He takes one element of his subject, discusses it thoroughly, then goes on to the next element. He also uses the device of the summary to remind us of what we have learned from time to time.

One surprise may come from our realization that some of these philosophers employ intense imagery and creative metaphor. But doing this is also part of their effort to make sure that they deal with the abstract nature of their subject. Imagery and metaphor make things more concrete. And while being philosophical may be a very abstract experience—and the highest calling of reflective humankind—the use of strictly abstract terminology is not absolutely necessary to the process of explaining a philosophical position. Careful rhetorical strategies, in terms of both organization and style, pay rich rewards when the mode of address is philosophical.

PLATO

The Allegory of the Cave

PLATO (428–347 B.C.) was born into an aristocratic Athenian family and educated according to the best precepts available. He eventually became a student of Socrates and later involved himself closely with Socrates' work and teaching. Plato was not only Socrates' finest student but was also the student who immortalized Socrates in his works. Most of Plato's works are philosophical essays, with Socrates as a character speaking in a dialogue with one or more students or listeners. Thus, Plato permits us the vision of Socrates written by one who knew him and listened carefully to what he said.

The times in which Plato lived were turbulent indeed. In 404 B.C. Athens was defeated by Sparta and was governed by tyrants. Political life in Athens was dangerous. Plato felt, however, that he could effect positive change in Athenian politics until, in 384 B.C., Socrates was tried unjustly for corrupting the youth of Athens and put to death. After that, Plato withdrew from public life and devoted himself to writing and to the Academy which he founded in an olive grove in Athens. The Academy endured for almost a thousand years, which tells us how greatly Plato's thought was valued.

From *The Republic*. Translated by Benjamin Jowett.

Although it is not easy to condense Plato's views, he may be said to have held the world of sense perception as inferior to the world of ideal entities that exist only in a pure spiritual realm. These ideals, or forms, had been perceived directly by everyone before birth, and then dimly remembered here on earth. But the memory, even dim as it is, makes it possible for people to understand what is perceived by the senses despite the fact that the senses are so unreliable and perceptions are so imperfect.

This view of reality has long been important to philosophers because it gives a philosophical basis to antimaterialistic thought. It values the spirit first and frees people from the tyranny of sensory perception and sensory reward. In the case of love, Plato held that Eros leads us to a reverence for the body and its pleasures; but the thrust of his teaching is that the body is a metaphor for spiritual delights. Plato assures us that the body is only a starting point and that it can eventually lead both to spiritual fulfillment and to the appreciation of true beauty.

"The Allegory of the Cave" is, on the one hand, a discussion of politics—the Republic *is a treatise on justice and the ideal government. On the other hand, it has long stood for a kind of demonstration of the fact that if our perceptions are what we must rely upon to know the truth about the world, then we actually know very little about it. We know what we perceive, but we have no way of knowing anything beyond that.*

This allegory has been persuasive for centuries and remains at the center of thought that attempts to counter the pleasures of the sensual life. Most religions aim for spiritual refinement and praise the qualities of the soul, which lies beyond perception. Thus, it comes as no surprise that Christianity and other religions have not only praised Plato but have developed systems of thought that bear a close resemblance to his. Later refinements of his thought, usually called Neo-Platonism, have been influential even into modern times.

PLATO'S RHETORIC

Two very important rhetorical techniques are at work in the following selection. The first and more obvious—at least on one level— is the reliance on the allegory, a story in which the characters and situations are meant to resemble people and situations in another context. It is a difficult technique to use well, although we have the example of Aesop's fables in which hares and tortoises represent people and their foibles. The advantage of the technique is that a complex and sometimes unpopular argument can be fought and won before the audience realizes that an argument is being fought. The disadvantage of the technique is that the terms of the allegory may only approximate the situation which it reflects; thus, the argument may fail to be convincing.

Another rhetorical technique Plato uses is the dialogue. In fact, it is a hallmark of Plato's work, since most of his writings are called dialogues. The Symposium, Apology, Phaedo, Crito, Meno, *and most of the famous works are all written in dialogue form. Usually Socrates is speaking to a student or a friend about highly abstract issues. Socrates asks questions which require simple answers. Slowly, the questioning proceeds to unravel the answers to the most complex of issues.*

This use of the question-and-answer dialogue is basically the Socratic method. Socrates analyzes the answer to each question, examines the implications of those answers, then asserts the truth. The method is functional in part because Plato's theory is that people do not learn things; they remember them. That is, since people came originally from heaven, where they knew the truth, they already possess that knowledge and must recover it by means of the dialogue. Socrates' method is ideally suited to that purpose.

Beyond these techniques, however, we must look at Plato's style. It is true that he is working with very difficult ideas, but the style of the work is so clear, simple, and direct that few people would have trouble understanding what is said at any given moment. Considering the influence this work has had on world thought and the reputation Plato had earned by the time he came to write the Republic, *it is remarkable that the style is so plain and so accessible. It is significant that such a great mind can express itself with such impressive clarity. Part of that capacity is due to Plato's respect for rhetoric and its proper uses.*

The Allegory of the Cave

SOCRATES,
GLAUCON. The
den, the
prisoners: the
light at a
distance;

And now, I said, let me show in a figure how far our 1
nature is enlightened or unenlightened:—Behold! human
beings living in an underground den, which has a mouth
open towards the light and reaching all along the den;
here they have been from their childhood, and have their
legs and necks chained so that they cannot move, and
can only see before them, being prevented by the chains
from turning round their heads. Above and behind them
a fire is blazing at a distance, and between the fire and
the prisoners there is a raised way; and you will see, if
you look, a low wall built along the way, like the screen
which marionette players have in front of them, over
which they show the puppets.

I see. 2

the low wall,
and the
moving figures
of which the
shadows are
seen on the
opposite wall
of the den.

And do you see, I said, men passing along the wall 3
carrying all sorts of vessels, and statues and figures of
animals made of wood and stone and various materials,
which appear over the wall? Some of them are talking,
others silent.

You have shown me a strange image, and they are 4
strange prisoners.

Like ourselves, I replied; and they see only their own 5
shadows, or the shadows of one another, which the fire
throws on the opposite wall of the cave?

True, he said; how could they see anything but the 6
shadows if they were never allowed to move their heads?

And of the objects which are being carried in like 7
manner they would only see the shadows?

Yes, he said. 8

And if they were able to converse with one another, 9
would they not suppose that they were naming what was
actually before them?

Very true. 10

And suppose further that the prison had an echo 11
which came from the other side, would they not be sure

The prisoners would mistake the shadows for realities.

to fancy when one of the passers-by spoke that the voice which they heard came from the passing shadow?

No question, he replied. 12

To them, I said, the truth would be literally nothing 13 but the shadows of the images.

That is certain. 14

And now look again, and see what will naturally fol- 15 low if the prisoners are released and disabused of their error. At first, when any of them is liberated and compelled suddenly to stand up and turn his neck round and walk and look towards the light, he will suffer sharp pains; the glare will distress him, and he will be unable to see the realities of which in his former state he had seen the shadows; and then conceive some one saying to him, that what he saw before was an illusion, but that now, when he is approaching nearer to being and his eye is turned towards more real existence, he has a clearer vision—what will be his reply? And you may further

And when released, they would still persist in maintaining the superior truth of the shadows.

imagine that his instructor is pointing to the objects as they pass and requiring him to name them,—will he not be perplexed? Will he not fancy that the shadows which he formerly saw are truer than the objects which are now shown to him?

Far truer. 16

And if he is compelled to look straight at the light, 17 will he not have a pain in his eyes which will make him turn away to take refuge in the objects of vision which he can see, and which he will conceive to be in reality clearer than the things which are now being shown to him?

True, he said. 18

When dragged upwards, they would be dazzled by excess of light.

And suppose once more, that he is reluctantly 19 dragged up a steep and rugged ascent, and held fast until he is forced into the presence of the sun himself, is he not likely to be pained and irritated? When he approaches the light his eyes will be dazzled, and he will not be able to see anything at all of what are now called realities.

Not all in a moment, he said. 20

He will require to grow accustomed to the sight of 21 the upper world. And first he will see the shadows best,

next the reflections of men and other objects in the water, and then the objects themselves; then he will gaze
upon the light of the moon and the stars and the span-
gled heaven; and he will see the sky and the stars by
night better than the sun or the light of the sun by day?

Certainly.

At length they will see the sun and understand his nature.

Last of all he will be able to see the sun, and not mere   23
reflections of him in the water, but he will see him in
his own proper place, and not in another; and he will
contemplate him as he is.

Certainly.   24

He will then proceed to argue that this is he who   25
gives the season and the years, and is the guardian of all
that is in the visible world, and in a certain way the
cause of all things which he and his fellows have been
accustomed to behold?

Clearly, he said, he would first see the sun and then   26
reason about him.

They would then pity their old companions of the den.

And when he remembered his old habitation, and the   27
wisdom of the den and his fellow prisoners, do you not
suppose that he would felicitate himself on the change,
and pity them?

Certainly, he would.   28

And if they were in the habit of conferring honors   29
among themselves on those who were quickest to observe the passing shadows and to remark which of them
went before, and which followed after, and which were
together; and who were therefore best able to draw conclusions as to the future, do you think that he would care
for such honors and glories, or envy the possessors of
them? Would he not say with Homer,

Better to be the poor servant of a poor master,

and to endure anything, rather than think as they do and
live after their manner?

Yes, he said, I think that he would rather suffer any-   30
thing than entertain these false notions and live in this
miserable manner.

Imagine once more, I said, such an one coming sud-   31
denly out of the sun to be replaced in his old situation;
would he not be certain to have his eyes full of darkness?

To be sure, he said. 32

And if there were a contest, and he had to compete 33
in measuring the shadows with the prisoners who had
never moved out of the den, while his sight was still
weak, and before his eyes had become steady (and the
time which would be needed to acquire this new habit of
sight might be very considerable), would he not be ridiculous? Men would say of him that up he went and down
he came without his eyes; and that it was better not even
to think of ascending; and if any one tried to loose another and lead him up to the light, let them only catch
the offender, and they would put him to death.

No question, he said. 34

This entire allegory, I said, you may now append, dear 35
Glaucon, to the previous argument; the prison house is
the world of sight, the light of the fire is the sun, and
you will not misapprehend me if you interpret the journey upwards to be the ascent of the soul into the intellectual world according to my poor belief, which, at your
desire, I have expressed—whether rightly or wrongly God
knows. But, whether true or false, my opinion is that in
the world of knowledge the idea of good appears last of
all, and is seen only with an effort; and, when seen, is
also inferred to be the universal author of all things beautiful and right, parent of light and of the lord of light in
this visible world, and the immediate source of reason
and truth in the intellectual; and that this is the power
upon which he who would act rationally either in public
or private life must have his eye fixed.

I agree, he said, as far as I am able to understand you. 36

Moreover, I said, you must not wonder that those 37
who attain to this beatific vision are unwilling to descend to human affairs; for their souls are ever hastening
into the upper world where they desire to dwell; which
desire of theirs is very natural, if our allegory may be
trusted.

Yes, very natural. 38

And is there anything surprising in one who passes 39
from divine contemplations to the evil state of man, mis-
behaving himself in a ridiculous manner; if, while his
eyes are blinking and before he has become accustomed

Marginal notes:

But when they returned to the den they would see much worse than those who had never left it.

The prison is the world of sight, the light of the fire is the sun.

Nothing extraordinary in the philosopher being unable to see in the dark.

to the surrounding darkness, he is compelled to fight in courts of law, or in other places, about the images or the shadows of images of justice, and is endeavoring to meet the conceptions of those who have never yet seen absolute justice?

Anything but surprising, he replied.   40

The eyes may be blinded in two ways, by excess or by defect of light.

Anyone who has common sense will remember that   41 the bewilderments of the eyes are of two kinds, and arise from two causes, either from coming out of the light or from going into the light, which is true of the mind's eye, quite as much as of the bodily eye; and he who remembers this when he sees anyone whose vision is perplexed and weak, will not be too ready to laugh; he will first ask whether that soul of man has come out of the brighter life, and is unable to see because unaccustomed to the dark, or having turned from darkness to the day is dazzled by excess of light. And he will count the one happy in his condition and state of being, and he will pity the other; or, if he have a mind to laugh at the soul which comes from below into the light, there will be more reason in this than in the laugh which greets him who returns from above out of the light into the den.

That, he said, is a very just distinction.   42

The conversion of the soul is the turning round the eye from darkness to light.

But then, if I am right, certain professors of education   43 must be wrong when they say that they can put a knowledge into the soul which was not there before, like sight into blind eyes.

They undoubtedly say this, he replied.   44

Whereas, our argument shows that the power and ca-   45 pacity of learning exists in the soul already; and that just as the eye was unable to turn from darkness to light without the whole body, so too the instrument of knowledge can only by the movement of the whole soul be turned from the world of becoming into that of being, and learn by degrees to endure the sight of being, and of the brightest and best of being, or in other words, of the good.

Very true.   46

And must there not be some art which will effect   47 conversion in the easiest and quickest manner; not implanting the faculty of sight, for that exists already, but has been turned in the wrong direction, and is looking away from the truth?

Yes, he said, such an art may be presumed.   48

The virtue of wisdom has a divine power which may be turned either towards good or towards evil.

And whereas the other so-called virtues of the soul   49
seem to be akin to bodily qualities, for even when they are not originally innate they can be implanted later by habit and exercise, the virtue of wisdom more than anything else contains a divine element which always remains, and by this conversion is rendered useful and profitable; or, on the other hand, hurtful and useless. Did you never observe the narrow intelligence flashing from the keen eye of a clever rogue—how eager he is, how clearly his paltry soul sees the way to his end; he is the reverse of blind, but his keen eyesight is forced into the service of evil, and he is mischievous in proportion to his cleverness?

Very true, he said.   50

But what if there had been a circumcision of such na-   51
tures in the days of their youth; and they had been severed from those sensual pleasures, such as eating and drinking, which, like leaden weights, were attached to them at their birth, and which drag them down and turn the vision of their souls upon the things that are below—if, I say, they had been released from these impediments and turned in the opposite direction, the very same faculty in them would have seen the truth as keenly as they see what their eyes are turned to now.

Very likely.   52

Neither the uneducated nor the overeducated will be good servants of the State.

Yes, I said; and there is another thing which is likely,   53
or rather a necessary inference from what has preceded, that neither the uneducated and uninformed of the truth, nor yet those who never make an end of their education, will be able ministers of State; not the former, because they have no single aim of duty which is the rule of all their actions, private as well as public; nor the latter, because they will not act at all except upon compulsion, fancying that they are already dwelling apart in the islands of the blessed.

Very true, he replied.   54

Then, I said, the business of us who are the founders   55
of the State will be to compel the best minds to attain

that knowledge which we have already shown to be the greatest of all—they must continue to ascend until they arrive at the good; but when they have ascended and seen enough we must not allow them to do as they do now.

What do you mean? 56

Men should ascend to the upper world, but they should also return to the lower.

I mean that they remain in the upper world: but this 57 must not be allowed; they must be made to descend again among the prisoners in the den, and partake of their labors and honors, whether they are worth having or not.

But is not this unjust? he said; ought we to give them 58 a worse life, when they might have a better?

You have again forgotten, my friend, I said, the inten- 59 tion of the legislator, who did not aim at making any one class in the State happy above the rest; the happiness was to be in the whole State, and he held the citizens together by persuasion and necessity, making them bene-factors of the State, and therefore benefactors of one an-other; to this end he created them, not to please them-selves, but to be his instruments in binding up the State.

True, he said, I had forgotten. 60

The duties of philosophers.

Observe, Glaucon, that there will be no injustice in 61 compelling our philosophers to have a care and provi-dence of others; we shall explain to them that in other States, men of their class are not obliged to share in the toils of politics: and this is reasonable, for they grow up at their own sweet will, and the government would rather not have them. Being self-taught, they cannot be expected to show any gratitude for a culture which they have never received. But we have brought you into the world to be rulers of the hive, kings of yourselves and of the other citizens, and have educated you far better and more perfectly than they have been educated, and you are better able to share in the double duty. Wherefore

Their obligations to their country will induce them to take part in her government.

each of you, when his turn comes, must go down to the general underground abode, and get the habit of seeing in the dark. When you have acquired the habit, you will see ten thousand times better than the inhabitants of the den, and you will know what the several images are, and what they represent, because you have seen the beautiful and just and good in their truth. And thus our State, which is also yours, will be a reality, and not a dream only, and will be administered in a spirit unlike that of other States, in which men fight with one another about shadows only and are distracted in the struggle for power, which in their eyes is a great good. Whereas the truth is that the State in which the rulers are most reluctant to govern is always the best and most quietly governed, and the State in which they are most eager, the worst.

Quite true, he replied. 62

And will our pupils, when they hear this, refuse to 63 take their turn at the toils of State, when they are allowed to spend the greater part of their time with one another in the heavenly light?

They will be willing but not anxious to rule.

Impossible, he answered; for they are just men, and 64 the commands which we impose upon them are just; there can be no doubt that every one of them will take office as a stern necessity, and not after the fashion of our present rulers of State.

The statesman must be provided with a better life than that of a ruler; and then he will not covet office.

Yes, my friend, I said; and there lies the point. You 65 must contrive for your future rulers another and a better life than that of a ruler, and then you may have a well-ordered State; for only in the State which offers this, will they rule who are truly rich, not in silver and gold, but in virtue and wisdom, which are the true blessings of life. Whereas if they go to the administration of public affairs, poor and hungering after their own private advantage, thinking that hence they are to snatch the chief good, order there can never be; for they will be fighting about office, and the civil and domestic broils which thus arise will be the ruin of the rulers themselves and of the whole State.

Most true, he replied. 66

And the only life which looks down upon the life of 67 political ambition is that of true philosophy. Do you know of any other?

Indeed, I do not, he said. 68

QUESTIONS

1. What does the situation seem to be in this dialogue? What would you say the relationship is between Socrates and Glaucon?
2. What is the allegory of the cave meant to represent?
3. Determine which of the following concepts seems most important in the dialogue: "truth," "justice," "happiness," "law." Is any of these concepts unimportant?
4. Socrates refers to "our philosophers" (para. 61 and elsewhere). What does he mean by that term?
5. How does the allegory relate to our concepts of sensory perception?
6. Are we made aware that Plato—rather than Socrates and Glaucon—is the author of this piece? What is the effect of Plato's presence (or lack of it)?

WRITING ASSIGNMENTS

1. Analyze the allegory of the cave for its strengths and weaknesses. Consider what it is meant to imply for people living in a world of the senses and what Plato implies lies behind that world. Consider the extent to which people are like (or unlike) the figures in the cave. Consider the extent to which the world we know is like the cave. Consider, too, the "revelations" implied in the allegory and its contemplation.
2. Socrates ends the dialogue by saying that after rulers of the state have served their term they must be able to look forward to a better life than that of being rulers. He and Glaucon agree that there is only one life that "looks down upon the life of political ambition"—"that of true philosophy." What is the life of true philosophy? Is it superior to that of being a ruler (or anything else)? How would you define its superiority? What would its qualities be? What would its concerns be? Would you be happy leading such a life?
3. In paragraph 43, Socrates refers to "professors of education." What do you think the nature of education was for Socrates and his pupils? Consider the questions of how education was conducted, who was educated, what the subjects of education must have been, and what the final purpose of education was. Inventory the passage for any references which might give some insight into the nature of education for Plato's contemporaries. If you wish, you may look up the subject of education in an encyclopedia or other resource, but be sure to relate your findings to this selection. Base your essay on the topic of definition.
4. In paragraph 61, Socrates outlines a program that would assure Athens of good rulers and good government. Clarify exactly what the program is, what its problems and benefits are, and how it would have to be put into action. Then decide whether or not the program would work. You may

consider whether or not it would work for our time, for Socrates' time, or both. If possible, use examples (hypothetical or real) to bolster your argument.

5. Socrates states unequivocally that Athens should compel the best and the most intelligent young men to be rulers of the state. Review his reasons for saying so; consider what his concept of the state is; then take a stand on the issue. Is it right to want to compel the best and most intelligent young people to become rulers? If so, would it be proper to compel those well suited for the professions of law, medicine, teaching, or religion to follow those respective callings? Would we not have an ideal society if everyone were forced to practice the calling for which they had the best aptitude?

ARISTOTLE

The Aim of Man

ARISTOTLE (384–322 B.C.) is the great inheritor of Plato's influence in philosophical thought. He was a student at the Academy of Plato in Athens from age seventeen to thirty-seven, and by all accounts he was Plato's most brilliant pupil. He did not agree with Plato on all issues, however, and seems to have broken with his master sometime around Plato's death (347 B.C.). In certain of his writings he is careful to disagree with the Platonists while insisting on his friendship with them. In The Nichomachean Ethics, for example, the most difficult section (omitted here) demonstrates that Plato is not correct in assuming that the good exists in some ideal form in a higher spiritual realm.

One interesting point concerning Aristotle's career is that when he became a teacher, his most distinguished student was Alexander the Great, the youthful ruler who spread Greek values and laws throughout the rest of the known world. Much speculation has centered on just what Aristotle might have taught Alexander about politics. The emphasis on statecraft and political goals in The Nichomachean Ethics suggests that he may have taught Alexander a great deal. A surviving fragment of a letter from Aristotle to Alexander suggests that

---

From The Nichomachean Ethics. Translated by Martin Ostwald.

he advised Alexander to become the leader of the Greeks and the master of the barbarians.

The Nichomachean Ethics *is a difficult document. Aristotle may have written it with an eye to tutoring his son, Nichomachus, but it is also a document meant to be read by those who have thought deeply about the ethical behavior of mankind. "The Aim of Man" treats of most of the basic issues in the entire document. It is difficult primarily because it is so thoroughly abstract. Abstract reason was thought to be the highest form of reason because it is independent of sensory experience and because only human beings can indulge in it. Aristotle, whose studies included works on plants, physics, animals, law, rhetoric, and logic, to name only some subjects, reminds us often of what we have in common with the animal and vegetable worlds. But because he values abstract thought so much, his reasoning tends to be highly abstract, demanding unusual attention from contemporary readers.*

Moreover, because he wrote so much on scientific subjects—and because he, unlike Plato, emphasized the role of sensory perception in scientific matters—he is careful to warn us that in abstract reasoning concerning the nature of mankind, we cannot expect the precision we take for granted in science. That warning is given to us several times in this selection, particularly when he tells us that certain branches of learning can be expected to have only limited precision. When studying humankind, we must keep in mind people's differences of background, education, habit, temperament, and other, similar factors. Such differences will impede the kinds of precision of definition and analysis taken for granted in other sciences.

Aristotle reveals an interesting Greek prejudice when he admits that the highest good for mankind is likely to be found in statecraft. What he tells us is that the well-ordered state—something that was the pride of the Greek way of life—is of such noble value that other values must take second place to it. Because our age is somewhat in agreement with this view, Aristotle seems to be peculiarly modern in this passage. Unlike the Christian theorists of the Middle Ages, the theorists of the Islamic insurgence, or the theorists of the Judaic Scriptures, Aristotle does not put divinity or godliness first. He is a practical man whose concerns are with the life that human beings know here on earth. When he considers the question, for instance, of whether a man can be thought of as happy before he has died (tragedy can always befall the happy man), he is thoroughly practical and does not point to happiness in heaven as any substitute for happiness on earth.

ARISTOTLE'S RHETORIC

Even though Aristotle is the author of the single most influential treatise on rhetoric, we do not see in this document as eloquent a style as might be expected, which has suggested to some that the manuscript was taken from lecture notes of a student. But, of course, he does use certain minor techniques that show us his awareness of rhetorical effect. For instance, he makes careful use of the aphorism, as in "One swallow does not make a spring" and as in the quotation, "Perfect justice is noblest, health is best, / But to gain one's heart's desire is pleasantest" (para. 21).

In terms of style, Aristotle is at a disadvantage—or perhaps it is we who are at a disadvantage!—because he addresses an audience of those who have thought very deeply on the issues of human behavior, so that his style is elevated and complex. Fortunately, nothing he says here is so complex as to be beyond the grasp of the careful reader, but we moderns expect to be provided with a good many concrete examples to help us understand abstract principles. Aristotle purposely avoids using them so as not to limit too sharply the truths he has to impart.

The most prominent rhetorical technique Aristotle uses is the topic of definition. His overall goal in this work is to define the aim of man. Thus, the first section of this work is entitled "Definition of the Good." In the "Primacy of Statecraft" he begins to qualify various types of good. Later, he considers the relationship of good and happiness (paras. 8–9) and the various views concerning happiness and its definition (paras 10–11). By then we are prepared for a "Functional Definition of Man's Highest Good" (paras. 12–18). He confirms his conclusions in the section entitled "Confirmation by Popular Beliefs" (paras. 19–22), using, in a sense, the topic of testimony. After happiness has been isolated as the ultimate good, paragraphs 23–32 are devoted to its causes; its effects; and the events that will affect it, such as luck and human decision. The final section (paras. 33–39) constitutes an examination of the soul (our most human element) and its relationship to virtue; he begins that section by repeating, for the third time, his definition of happiness: "Happiness is a certain activity of the soul in accordance with perfect virtue."

It could be said that, rhetorically, the body of the work is an exploration and definition of the highest good.

The Aim of Man

Definition of the Good

Every art and every "scientific investigation," as well as every action and "purposive choice," appears to aim at some good; hence the good has rightly been declared to be that at which all things aim. A difference is observable, to be sure, among the several ends: some of them are activities, while others are products over and above the activities that produce them. Wherever there are certain ends over and above the actions themselves, it is the nature of such products to be better than the activities.

As actions and arts and sciences are of many kinds, there must be a corresponding diversity of ends: health, for example, is the aim of medicine, ships of shipbuilding, victory of military strategy, and wealth of domestic economics. Where several such arts fall under some one faculty—as bridle-making and the other arts concerned with horses' equipment fall under horsemanship, while this in turn along with all other military matters falls under the head of strategy, and similarly in the case of other arts—the aim of the master art is always more choiceworthy than the aims of its subordinate arts, inasmuch as these are pursued for its sake. And this holds equally good whether the end in view is just the activity itself or something distinct from the activity, as in the case of the sciences above mentioned.

Primacy of Statecraft

If in all our conduct, then, there is some end that we wish on its own account, choosing everything else as a means to it; if, that is to say, we do not choose everything as a means to something else (for at that rate we should go on *ad infinitum*,[1] and our desire would be left empty and vain); then clearly this one end must be the good—even, indeed, the highest good. Will not a knowledge of it, then, have an important influence on our lives? Will it not better enable us to hit

---

[1] **ad infinitum** endlessly; to infinity.

the right mark, like archers who have a definite target to aim at? If so, we must try to comprehend, in outline at least, what that highest end is, and to which of the sciences or arts it belongs.

Evidently the art or science in question must be the most absolute and most authoritative of all. Statecraft answers best to this description; for it prescribes which of the sciences are to have a place in the state, and which of them are to be studied by the different classes of citizens, and up to what point; and we find that even the most highly esteemed of the arts are subordinated to it, e.g., military strategy, domestic economics, and oratory. So then, since statecraft employs all the other sciences, prescribing also what the citizens are to do and what they are to refrain from doing, its aim must embrace the aims of all the others; whence it follows that the aim of statecraft is man's proper good. Even supposing the chief good to be eventually the same for the individual as for the state, that of the state is evidently of greater and more fundamental importance both to attain and to preserve. The securing of even one individual's good is cause for rejoicing, but to secure the good of a nation or of a city-state[2] is nobler and more divine. This, then, is the aim of our present inquiry, which is in a sense the study of statecraft.

4

Two Observations
on the Study of Ethics

Our discussion will be adequate if we are content with as much precision as is appropriate to the subject matter; for the same degree of exactitude ought no more to be expected in all kinds of reasoning than in all kinds of handicraft. Excellence and justice, the things with which statecraft deals, involve so much disagreement and uncertainty that they come to be looked on as mere conventions, having no natural foundation. The good involves a similar uncertainty, inasmuch as good things often prove detrimental: there are examples of people destroyed by wealth, of others destroyed by courage. In such matters, then, and starting from such premises as we do, we must be content with a rough approximation to the truth; for when we are dealing with and starting out from what holds good only "as a general rule," the conclusions that we reach will have the same character. Let each of the views

5

---

[2]**city-state** Athens was an independent nation, a city-state *(polis)*. Greece consisted of a great many independent states, which often leagued together in confederations.

put forward be accepted in this spirit, for it is the mark of an educated mind to seek only so much exactness in each type of inquiry as may be allowed by the nature of the subject matter. It is equally wrong to accept probable reasoning from a mathematician and to demand strict demonstrations from an orator.

A man judges well and is called a good judge of the things about which he knows. If he has been educated in a particular subject he is a good judge of that subject; if his education has been well-rounded he is a good judge in general. Hence no very young man is qualified to attend lectures on statecraft; for he is inexperienced in the affairs of life, and these form the data and subject matter of statecraft. Moreover, so long as he tends to be swayed by his feelings he will listen vainly and without profit, for the purport of these [lectures] is not purely theoretical but practical. Nor does it make any difference whether his immaturity is a matter of years or of character: the defect is not a matter of time, but consists in the fact that his life and all his pursuits are under the control of his passions. Men of this sort, as is evident from the case of those we call incontinent,[3] do not turn their knowledge to any account in practice; but those whose desires and actions are controlled by reason will derive much profit from a knowledge of these matters.

So much, then, for our prefatory remarks about the student, the manner of inquiry, and the aim.

The Good as Happiness

To resume, then: since all knowledge and all purpose aims at some good, what is it that we declare to be the aim of statecraft; or, in other words, what is the highest of all realizable goods? As to its name there is pretty general agreement: the majority of men, as well as the cultured few, speak of it as happiness; and they would maintain that to live well and to do well are the same thing as to be happy. They differ, however, as to what happiness is, and the mass of mankind give a different account of it from philosophers. The former take it to be something palpable and obvious, like pleasure or wealth or fame; they differ, too, among themselves, nor is the same man always of one mind about it: when ill he identifies it with health, when poor with wealth; then growing aware of his ignorance about the whole matter

6

7

8

---

[3]*incontinent*   uncontrolled, in this case by reason.

he feels admiration for anyone who proclaims some grand ideal above his comprehension. And to add to the confusion, there have been some philosophers who held that besides the various particular good things there is an absolute good which is the cause of all particular goods. As it would hardly be worthwhile to examine all the opinions that have been entertained, we shall confine our attention to those that are most popular or that appear to have some rational foundation.

One point not to be overlooked is the difference between arguments that start from first principles[4] and arguments that lead up to first principles. Plato very wisely used to raise this question, and to ask whether the right way is from or toward first principles—as in the racecourse there is a difference between running from the judges to the boundary line and running back again. Granted that we must start with what is known, this may be interpreted in a double sense: as what is familiar to us or as what is intelligible in itself. Our own method, at any rate, must be to start with what is familiar to us. That is why a sound moral training is required before a man can listen intelligently to discussions about excellence and justice, and generally speaking, about statecraft. For in this field we must take as our "first principles" plain facts; if these are sufficiently evident we shall not insist upon the whys and wherefores. Such principles are in the possession of, or at any rate readily accessible to, the man with a sound moral training. As for the man who neither possesses nor can acquire them, let him hear the words of Hesiod:[5]

> Best is he who makes his own discoveries;
> Good is he who listens to the wise;
> But he who, knowing not, rejects another's wisdom
> Is a plain fool.

Conflicting Views of Happiness

Let us now resume our discussion from the point at which we digressed. What is happiness, or the chief good? If it is permissible to

---

[4]*first principles* Concepts such as goodness, truth, and justice. Arguments that lead to first principles usually begin with familiar, less abstract evidence.

[5]*Works and Days*, ll. 293–297. [Translator's note] Hesiod (eighth century B.C.) was a well-known Greek author. His *Works and Days* is notable for its portraits of everyday shepherd life and for its moralizing fables. His *Theogony* is a description of the creation, widely taken as accurate in his day.

judge from men's actual lives, we may say that the mass of them, being vulgarians, identify it with pleasure, which is the reason why they aim at nothing higher than a life of enjoyment. For there are three outstanding types of life: the one just mentioned, the political, and, thirdly, the contemplative. "The mass of men" reveal their utter slavishness by preferring a life fit only for cattle; yet their views have a certain plausibility from the fact that many of those in high places share the tastes of Sardanapalus.[6] Men of superior refinement and active disposition, on the other hand, identify happiness with honor, this being more or less the aim of a statesman's life. It is evidently too superficial, however, to be the good that we are seeking; for it appears to depend rather on him who bestows than on him who receives it, while we may suspect the chief good to be something peculiarly a man's own, which he is not easily deprived of. Besides, men seem to pursue honor primarily in order to assure themselves of their own merit; at any rate, apart from personal acquaintances, it is by those of sound judgment that they seek to be appreciated, and on the score of virtue. Clearly, then, they imply that virtue is superior to honor: and so, perhaps, we should regard this rather than honor as the end and aim of the statesman's life. Yet even about virtue there is a certain incompleteness; for it is supposed that a man may possess it while asleep or during lifelong inactivity, or even while suffering the greatest disasters and misfortunes; and surely no one would call such a man happy, unless for the sake of a paradox. But we need not further pursue this subject, which has been sufficiently treated of in current discussions. Thirdly, there is the contemplative life, which we shall examine at a later point.

As for the life of money-making, it is something unnatural. Wealth 11 is clearly not the good that we are seeking, for it is merely useful as a means to something else. Even the objects above mentioned come closer to possessing intrinsic goodness than wealth does, for they at least are cherished on their own account. But not even they, it seems, can be the chief good, although much labor has been lost in attempting to prove them so. With this observation we may close the present subject. . . .

---

[6]An ancient Assyrian king to whom is attributed the saying, "Eat, drink, and be merry: nothing else is worth a snap of the fingers." [Translator's note] Sardanapalus (d. 880 B.C.) was noted for his slothful and decadent life. When it was certain that he was to die—the walls of his city had been breached by an opposing army—he had his wives, animals, and possessions burned with him in his palace.

Functional Definition
of Man's Highest Good

Returning now to the good that we are seeking, let us inquire into its nature. Evidently it is different in different actions and arts: it is not the same thing in medicine as in strategy, and so on. What definition of good will apply to all the arts? Let us say it is that for the sake of which all else is done. In medicine this is health, in the art of war victory, in building it is a house, and in each of the arts something different, although in every case, wherever there is action and choice involved, it is a certain end; because it is always for the sake of a certain end that all else is done. If, then, there is one end and aim of all our actions, this will be the realizable good; if there are several such ends, these jointly will be our realizable goods. Thus in a roundabout way the discussion has been brought back to the same point as before; which we must now try to explain more clearly. 12

As there is evidently a plurality of ends, and as some of these are chosen only as means to ulterior ends (e.g., wealth, flutes, and instruments in general), it is clear that not all ends are final.[7] But the supreme good must of course be something final. Accordingly, if there is only one final end, this will be the good that we are seeking; and if there is more than one such end, the most complete and final of them will be this good. Now we call what is pursued as an end in itself more final than what is pursued as a means to something else; and what is never chosen as a means we call more final than what is chosen both as an end in itself and as a means; in fact, when a thing is chosen always as an end in itself and never as a means we call it absolutely final. Happiness seems, more than anything else, to answer to this description: for it is something we choose always for its own sake and never for the sake of something else; while honor, pleasure, reason, and all the virtues, though chosen partly for themselves (for we might choose any one of them without heeding the result), are chosen also for the sake of the happiness which we suppose they will bring us. Happiness, on the other hand, is never chosen for the sake of any of these, nor indeed as a means to anything else at all. 13

---

[7]**not all ends are final** By *ends* Aristotle means purposes. Some purposes are final—the most important; some are immediate—the less important. When a corporation contributes funds to Public Broadcasting, its immediate purpose may be to fund a worthwhile program. Its final purpose may be to benefit from the publicity gained from advertising.

We seem to arrive at the same conclusion if we start from the no- 14
tion of self-sufficiency; for the final good is admittedly self-sufficient.
To be self-sufficient we do not mean that an individual must live in
isolation. Parents, children, wife, as well as friends and fellow citizens
generally, are all permissible; for man is by nature political. To be
sure, some limit has to be set to such relationships, for if they are
extended to embrace ancestors, descendants, and friends of friends, we
should go on *ad infinitum*. But this point will be considered later on;
provisionally we may attribute self-sufficiency to that which taken by
itself makes life choiceworthy and lacking in nothing. Such a thing we
conceive happiness to be. Moreover, we regard happiness as the most
choiceworthy of all things; nor does this mean that it is merely one
good thing among others, for if that were the case it is plain that the
addition of even the least of those other goods would increase its de-
sirability; since the addition would create a larger amount of good, and
of two goods the greater is always to be preferred. Evidently, then,
happiness is something final and self-sufficient, and is the end and aim
of all that we do.

But perhaps it will be objected that to call happiness the supreme 15
good is a mere truism, and that a clearer account of it is still needed.
We can give this best, probably, if we ascertain the proper function of
man. Just as the excellence and good performance of a flute player, a
sculptor, or any kind of artist, and generally speaking of anyone who
has a function or business to perform, lies always in that function, so
man's good would seem to lie in the function of man, if he has one.
But can we suppose that while a carpenter and a cobbler each has a
function and mode of activity of his own, man qua man[8] has none, but
has been left by nature functionless? Surely it is more likely that as
his several members, eye and hand and foot, can be shown to have
each its own function, so man too must have a function over and
above the special functions of his various members. What will such a
function be? Not merely to live, of course: he shares that even with
plants, whereas we are seeking something peculiar to himself. We
must exclude, therefore, the life of nutrition and growth. Next comes
sentient[9] life, but this again is had in common with the horse, the ox,
and in fact all animals whatever. There remains only the "practical"[10]
life of his rational nature; and this has two aspects, one of which is

---

[8]***man qua man*** man as such, without reference to what he may be or do.
[9]***sentient*** knowing, aware, conscious.
[10]**"practical"** Aristotle refers to the actual practices which will define the ethical
nature of the individual.

rational in the sense that it obeys a "rational principle," the other in the sense that it possesses and exercises reason. To avoid ambiguity let us specify that by "rational" we mean the "exercise or activity," not the mere possession, of reason; for it is the former that would seem more properly entitled to the name. Thus we conclude that man's function is an activity of the soul in conformity with, or at any rate involving the use of, "rational principle."

An individual and a superior individual who belong to the same 16 class we regard as sharing the same function: a harpist and a good harpist, for instance, are essentially the same. This holds true of any class of individuals whatever; for superior excellence with respect to a function is nothing but an amplification of that selfsame function: e.g., the function of a harpist is to play the harp, while that of a good harpist is to play it well. This being so, if we take man's proper function to be a certain kind of life, viz. an activity and conduct of the soul that involves reason, and if it is the part of a good man to perform such activities well and nobly, and if a function is well performed when it is performed in accordance with its own proper excellence; we may conclude that the good of man is an activity of the soul in accordance with virtue, or, if there be more than one virtue, in accordance with the best and most perfect of them. And we must add, in a complete life. For one swallow does not make a spring, nor does one fine day; and similarly one day or brief period of happiness does not make a man happy and blessed.

So much, then, for a rough outline of the good: the proper proce- 17 dure being, we may suppose, to sketch an outline first and afterwards to fill in the details. When a good outline has been made, almost anyone presumably can expand it and fill it out; and time is a good inventor and collaborator in this work. It is in just such a way that progress has been made in the various "human techniques,"[11] for filling in the gaps is something anybody can do.

But in all this we must bear constantly in mind our previous warn- 18 ing: not to expect the same degree of precision in all fields, but only so much as belongs to a given subject matter and is appropriate to a particular "type of inquiry." Both the carpenter and the geometer investigate the right angle, but in different ways: the one wants only such an approximation to it as will serve his work; the other, being concerned with truth, seeks to determine its essence or essential attributes. And so in other subjects we must follow a like procedure, lest

---

[11]*"human techniques"* arts or skills; in a sense, technology.

we be so much taken up with side issues that we pass over the matter in hand. Similarly we ought not in all cases to demand the "reason why"; sometimes it is enough to point out the bare fact. This is true, for instance, in the case of "first principles"; for a bare fact must always be the ultimate starting point of any inquiry. First principles may be arrived at in a variety of ways: some by induction,[12] some by direct perception, some by a kind of habituation, and others in other ways. In each case we should try to apprehend them in whatever way is proper to them, and we should take care to define them clearly, because they will have a considerable influence upon the subsequent course of our inquiry. A good beginning is more than half of the whole inquiry, and once established clears up many of its difficulties.

Confirmation by Popular Beliefs

It is important to consider our ethical "first principle" not merely 19 as a conclusion drawn from certain premises, but also in its relation to popular opinion; for all data harmonize with a true principle, but with a false one they are soon found to be discordant. Now it has been customary to divide good things into three classes: external goods on the one hand, and on the other goods of the soul and goods of the body; and those of the soul we call good in the highest sense, and in the fullest degree. "Conscious actions," i.e., "active expressions of our nature," we take, of course, as belonging to the soul; and thus our account is confirmed by the doctrine referred to, which is of long standing and has been generally accepted by students of philosophy. . . .

We are in agreement also with those who identify happiness with 20 virtue or with some particular virtue; for our phrase "activity in accordance with virtue" is the same as what they call virtue. It makes quite a difference, however, whether we conceive the supreme good as the mere possession of virtue or as its employment—i.e., as a state of character or as its active expression in conduct. For a state of character may be present without yielding any good result, as in a man who is asleep or in some other way inactive; but this is not true of its active expression, which must show itself in action, indeed in good action. As at the Olympic games it is not merely the fairest and strongest that

---

[12]*induction* A process of reasoning based on careful observation and collection of details upon which theories are based. "A kind of habituation" may refer to a combination of intellectual approaches characteristic to an individual.

receive the victory wreath, but those who compete (since the victors will of course be found among the competitors), so in life too those who carry off the finest prizes are those who manifest their excellence in their deeds.

Moreover, the life of those active in virtue is intrinsically pleasant. 21 For besides the fact that pleasure is something belonging to the soul, each man takes pleasure in what he is said to love—the horse lover in horses, the lover of sights in public spectacles, and similarly the lover of justice in just acts, and more generally, the lover of virtue in virtuous acts. And while most men take pleasure in things which, as they are not truly pleasant by nature, create warring factions in the soul, the lovers of what is noble take pleasure in things that are truly pleasant in themselves. Virtuous actions are things of this kind; hence they are pleasant for such men, as well as pleasant intrinsically. The life of such men, therefore, requires no adventitious[13] pleasures, but finds its own pleasure within itself. This is further shown by the fact that a man who does not enjoy doing noble actions is not a good man at all: surely no one would call a man just who did not enjoy performing just actions, nor generous who did not enjoy performing generous actions, and so on. On this ground too, then, actions in conformity with virtue must be intrinsically pleasant. And certainly they are good as well as noble, and both in the highest degree, if the judgment of the good man is any criterion; for he will judge them as we have said. It follows, therefore, that happiness is at once the best and noblest and pleasantest of things, and that these attributes are not separable as the inscription at Delos[14] pretends:

> Perfect justice is noblest, health is best,
> But to gain one's heart's desire is pleasantest.

For our best activities possess all of these attributes; and it is in our best activities, or in the best one of them, that we say happiness consists.

Nevertheless, happiness plainly requires external goods as well; for 22 it is impossible, or at least not easy, to act nobly without the proper equipment. There are many actions that can only be performed through such instruments as friends, wealth, or political influence; and there are some things, again, the lack of which must mar felicity, such as good birth, fine children, and personal comeliness: for the man

---

[13]*adventitious* unnecessary; superfluous.

[14]*inscription at Delos* Delos is the island that once held the Athenian treasury. It was the birthplace of Apollo, with whom the inscription would be associated.

who is repulsive in appearance, or ill-born, or solitary and childless does not meet the requirements of a happy man, and still less does one who has worthless children and friends, or who has lost good ones by death. As we have said, then, happiness seems to require the addition of external prosperity, and this has led some to identify it with "good fortune," just as others have made the opposite mistake of identifying it with virtue.

Sources of Happiness

For the same reason there are many who wonder whether happiness is attained by learning, or by habituation or some other kind of training, or whether it comes by some divine dispensation,[15] or even by chance. Well, certainly if the gods do give any gifts to men we may reasonably suppose that happiness is god-given; indeed, of all human blessings it is the most likely to be so, inasmuch as it is the best of them all. While this question no doubt belongs more properly to another branch of inquiry, we remark here that even if happiness is not god-sent but comes as a result of virtue or some kind of learning or training, still it is evidently one of the most divine things in the world, because that which is the reward as well as the end and aim of virtuous conduct must evidently be of supreme excellence, something divine and most blessed. If this is the case, happiness must further be something that can be generally shared; for with the exception of those whose capacity for virtue has been stunted or maimed, everyone will have the ability, by study and diligence, to acquire it. And if it is better that happiness should be acquired in this way than by chance, we may reasonably suppose that it happens so; because everything in nature is arranged in the best way possible—just as in the case of man-made products, and of every kind of causation, especially the highest. It would be altogether wrong that what is greatest and noblest in the world should be left to the dispensation of chance. 23

Our present difficulty is cleared up by our previous definition of happiness, as a certain activity of the soul in accordance with virtue; whereas all other sorts of good are either necessary conditions of, or cooperative with and naturally useful instruments of this. Such a con- 24

---

[15]***divine dispensation*** A gift of the gods.

clusion, moreover, agrees with the proposition we laid down at the outset: that the end of statecraft is the best of all ends, and that the principal concern of statecraft is to make the citizens of a certain character—namely, good and disposed to perform noble actions.

Naturally, therefore, we do not call an ox or a horse or any other 25 brute happy, since none of them is able to participate in conduct of this kind. For the same reason a child is not happy, since at his age he too is incapable of such conduct. Or if we do call a child happy, it is in the sense of predicting for him a happy future. Happiness, as we have said, involves not only a completeness of virtue but also a complete lifetime for its fulfillment. Life brings many vicissitudes and chance happenings, and it may be that one who is now prosperous will suffer great misfortunes in his old age, as is told of Priam[16] in the Trojan legends; and a man who is thus buffeted by fortune and comes to a miserable end can scarcely be called happy.

Happiness and the
Vicissitudes of Fortune

Are we, then, to call no one happy while he lives? Must we, as 26 Solon[17] advises, wait to see his end? And if we accept this verdict, are we to interpret it as meaning that a man actually becomes happy only after he is dead? Would not this be downright absurd, especially for us who define happiness as a kind of vital activity? Or if we reject this interpretation, and suppose Solon to mean rather that it is only after death, when beyond the reach of further evil and calamity that a man can safely be said to have been happy during his life, there is still a possible objection that may be offered. For many hold that both good and evil may in a certain sense befall a dead man (just as they may befall a living man even when he is unconscious of them)—e.g., honors and disgraces, and the prosperity or misfortune of his children and the rest of his descendants. And this presents a further problem: suppose a man to have lived to a happy old age, and to have ended as he lived, there are still plenty of reverses that may befall his descendants—some

---

[16]***Priam*** King of Troy in Homer's *Iliad.* He suffered a terrible reversal of fortune when Troy was defeated by the Greeks.

[17]***Solon (630–560 B.C.)*** Greek lawgiver and one of Greece's earliest poets. He was one of the The Seven Sages of Athens.

of them will perhaps lead a good life and be dealt with by fortune as they deserve, others not. (It is clear, too, that a man's relationship to his descendants admits of various degrees.) It would be odd, then, if the dead man were to change along with the fortunes of his descendants, becoming happy and miserable by turns; although, to be sure, it would be equally odd if the fortunes of his descendants did not affect him at all, even for a brief time.

But let us go back to our earlier question,[18] which may perhaps 27 clear up the one we are raising at present. Suppose we agree that we must look to the end of a man's life, and only then call him happy, not because he then *is* happy but because we can only then know him to have been so: is it not paradoxical to have refused to call him happy during just the period when happiness was present to him? On the other hand, we are naturally loath to apply the term to living men, considering the vicissitudes to which they are liable. Happiness, we argue, must be something that endures without any essential change, whereas a living individual may experience many turns of fortune's wheel. Obviously if we judge by his changing fortunes we shall have to call the same man now happy now wretched, thereby regarding the happy man as a kind of chameleon and his happiness as built on no secure foundation; yet it surely cannot be right to regard a man's happiness as wholly dependent on his fortunes. True good and evil are not of this character; rather, as we have said, although good fortune is a necessary adjunct to a complete human life, it is virtuous activities that constitute happiness, and the opposite sort of activities that constitute its opposite.

The foregoing difficulty [that happiness can be judged of only in 28 retrospect] confirms, as a matter of fact, our theory. For none of man's functions is so permanent as his virtuous activities—indeed, many believe them to be more abiding even than a knowledge of the sciences; and of his virtuous activities those are the most abiding which are of highest worth, for it is with them that anyone blessed with supreme happiness is most fully and most continuously occupied, and hence never oblivious of. The happy man, then, will possess this attribute of permanence or stability about which we have been inquiring, and will keep it all his life; because at all times and in preference to everything else he will be engaged in virtuous action and contemplation, and he will bear the changes of fortune as nobly and in every respect as dec-

---

[18]I.e., whether we are to call no one happy while he still lives. [Translator's note]

orously as possible, inasmuch as he is truly good and "four-square beyond reproach."[19]

But the dispensations of fortune are many, some great, others 29 small. Small ones do not appreciably turn the scales of life, but a multitude of great ones, if they are of the nature of blessings, will make life happier; for they add to life a grace of their own, provided that a man makes noble and good use of them. If, however, they are of an evil kind, they will crush and maim happiness, in that they bring pain and thereby hinder many of our natural activities. Yet true nobility shines out even here, if a multitude of great misfortunes be borne with calmness—not, to be sure, with the calmness of insensibility, but of nobility and greatness of soul.

If, as we have declared, it is our activities that give life its charac- 30 ter, then no happy man can become miserable, inasmuch as he will never do what is hateful or base. For we hold that the truly good and wise man will bear with dignity whatever fortune sends, and will always make the best of his circumstances, as a good general makes the most effective use of the forces at his command, and a good shoemaker makes the best shoes out of the leather that is available, and so in the case of the other crafts. On this interpretation, the happy man can never become miserable—although of course he will not be blessed with happiness in the full sense of the word if he meets with such a fate as Priam's. At all events, he is not variable and always changing; for no ordinary misfortunes but only a multitude of great ones will dislodge him from his happy state, and should this occur he will not readily recover his happiness in a short time, but only, if at all, after a long period has run its course, during which he has achieved distinctions of a high order.

Is there any objection, then, to our defining a happy man as one 31 whose activities are an expression of complete virtue, and who at the same time enjoys a sufficiency of worldly goods, not just for some limited period, but for his entire lifetime? Or perhaps we had better add the proviso that he shall be destined to go on living in this manner, and die as he has lived; for, whereas the future is obscure to us, we conceive happiness to be an end, something altogether and in every respect final and complete. Granting all this, we may declare those living men to be "blessed with supreme happiness" in whom these

---

[19]A quotation from Simonides. [Translator's note] Simonides (556?–469 B.C.) was a Greek lyric poet who lived and wrote for a while in Athens. His works survive in a handful of fragments; this quote is from fragment 5.

conditions have been and are continuing to be fulfilled. Their blessedness, however, is of a human order.

So much for our discussion of this question.   32

Derivation of the Two Kinds
of Human Excellence

Since happiness is a certain activity of the soul in accordance with 33
perfect virtue, we must next examine the nature of virtue. Not only
will such an inquiry perhaps clarify the problem of happiness; it will
also be of vital concern to the true student of statecraft, whose aim is
to make his fellow citizens good and law-abiding. The Cretan and
Spartan lawgivers,[20] as well as such others as may have resembled
them, exemplify this aim. And clearly, if such an inquiry has to do
with statecraft, it will be in keeping with our original purpose to pursue it.

It goes without saying that the virtue we are to study is human 34
virtue, just as the good that we have been inquiring about is a human
good, and the happiness a human happiness. By human virtue we
mean virtue not of the body but of the soul, and by happiness too we
mean an activity of the soul. This being the case, it is no less evident
that the student of statecraft must have some knowledge of the soul,
than that a physician who is to heal the eye or the whole body must
have some knowledge of these organs; more so, indeed, in proportion
as statecraft is superior to and more honorable than medicine. Now all
physicians who are educated take much pains to know about the body.
Hence as students of statecraft, too, we must inquire into the nature
of the soul; but we must do so with reference to our own distinctive
aim and only to the extent that it requires, for to go into minuter
detail would be more laborious than is warranted by our subject
matter.

We may adopt here certain doctrines about the soul that have been 35
adequately stated in our public discourses:[21] as that the soul may be
distinguished into two parts, one of which is irrational while the other
possesses reason. Whether these two parts are actually distinct like the

---

[20]*Cretan and Spartan lawgivers*   Both Crete and Sparta were noted for their constitutions, based on the laws of Gortyn in Crete. These laws were aristocratic, not democratic as in Athens; they promoted a class system and a rigid code of personal behavior.

[21]*our public discourses*   Aristotle may be referring to speeches at which the public is welcome, as opposed to his lectures to students.

parts of the body or any other divisible thing, or are distinct only in a logical sense, like convex and concave in the circumference of a circle, is immaterial to our present inquiry.

Of the irrational part, again, one division is apparently of a vegetative nature and common to all living things: I mean that which is the cause of nutrition and growth. It is more reasonable to postulate a vital faculty of this sort, present in all things that take nourishment, even when in an embryo stage, and retained by the full-grown organism, than to assume a special nutritive faculty in the latter. Hence we may say that the excellence belonging to this part of the soul is common to all species, and not specifically human: a point that is further confirmed by the popular view that this part of the soul is most active during sleep. For it is during sleep that the distinction between good men and bad is least apparent; whence the saying that for half their lives the happy are no better off than the wretched. This, indeed, is natural enough, for sleep is an inactivity of the soul in those respects in which the soul is called good or bad. (It is true, however, that to a slight degree certain bodily movements penetrate to the soul; which is the reason why good men's dreams are superior to those of the average person.) But enough of this subject: let us dismiss the nutritive principle, since it has by nature no share in human excellence. 36

There seems to be a second part of the soul, which though irrational yet in some way partakes of reason. For while we praise the rational principle and the part of the soul that manifests it in the case of the continent and incontinent man alike, on the ground that it exhorts them rightly and urges them to do what is best; yet we find within these men another element different in nature from the rational element, and struggling against and resisting it. Just as ataxic limbs,[22] when we choose to move them to the right, turn on the contrary to the left, so it is with the soul: the impulses of the incontinent man run counter to his ruling part. The only difference is that in the case of the body we see what it is that goes astray, while in the soul we do not. Nevertheless the comparison will doubtless suffice to show that there is in the soul something besides the rational element, opposing and running counter to it. (In what sense the two elements are distinct is immaterial.) But this other element, as we have said, seems also to have some share in a rational principle: at any rate, in the continent man it submits to reason, while in the man who is at once temperate and courageous it is presumably all the more obedient; for 37

---

[22]***ataxic limbs***   Aristotle refers to a nervous disorder of the limbs.

in him it speaks on all matters harmoniously with the voice of reason.

Evidently, then, the irrational part of the soul is twofold. There is 38 the vegetative element, which has no share in reason, and there is the concupiscent,[23] or rather the appetitive element, which does in a sense partake of reason, in that it is amenable and obedient to it: i.e., it is rational in the sense that we speak of "having *logos* of" [paying heed to] father and friends, not in the sense of "having *logos* of" [having a rational understanding of] mathematical truths. That this irrational element is in some way amenable to reason is shown by our practice of giving admonishment, and by rebuke and exhortation generally. If on this account it is deemed more correct to regard this element as also possessing reason, then the rational part of the soul, in turn, will have two subdivisions: the one being rational in the strict sense as actually possessing reason, the other merely in the sense that a child obeys its father.

Virtue, too, is differentiated in accordance with this division of the 39 soul: for we call some of the virtues intellectual and others moral: wisdom, understanding, and sagacity being among the former, liberality and temperance among the latter. In speaking of a man's character we do not say that he is wise or intelligent, but that he is gentle or temperate; yet we praise the wise man too for the disposition he has developed within himself, and praiseworthy dispositions we call virtues.

---

[23]*concupiscent* sexual; Aristotle corrects himself to refer to the general nature of desire.

QUESTIONS

1. Define the following terms: "good," "virtue," "honor," "happiness," "truth," "soul," "body."
2. In the first paragraphs of the selection Aristotle talks about aims and ends. What does he mean by these terms?
3. Do you feel that the way Aristotle talks about the relationship of virtue to happiness is as important today as he argues it was in his day?
4. What is Aristotle's attitude toward most people?

5. What characteristics can we assume about the audience for whom Aristotle writes?
6. In what senses is the selection modern? In what senses is it antique or dated?

WRITING ASSIGNMENTS

1. In his section on the primacy of statecraft, Aristotle makes a number of assertions regarding the relationship of the happiness of the individual to the welfare (or happiness) of the state. Clarify as much as possible the relationship of the individual's happiness to that of the state. How can a state be happy? Is the term relevant to anything other than an individual? Does Aristotle think that the individual's interests should be subservient to the state's?
2. In paragraph 15, Aristotle talks about the function of man. Relying on that discussion (as well as on other aspects of the work), write your own version of "The Function of Man." Be sure to use "man" as a collective term for both men and women. Once you have clarified the function of man, establish the connection between function and happiness. Is it true that the best-functioning person will be the happiest person? Aristotle implies that it is not enough to be, say, honorable or noble, but that one must act honorably or nobly. Is this implication true?
3. Take Aristotle's definition that "Happiness is a certain activity of the soul in accordance with perfect virtue" and define it in terms that are clear, not only to you, but also to your peers. Each part of the definition must also be defined: "certain activity" (or lack of it), "soul" (which in modern terms may be "personality" or "psyche"), "in accordance with," "perfect virtue." You may rely on any parts of the selection that can be of help, but be sure to use the topic of definition to guide you through the selection. You certainly may disagree with Aristotle or amplify aspects of his definitions. In one sense, you will be defining "happiness" for yourself and your times.
4. In his "confirmation by popular beliefs" (para. 19 and following), Aristotle talks about the good. He mentions three classes of good, ranking them in order from lowest to highest: external goods, goods of the body, and goods of the soul. Using concrete examples, define each of these classes of good. Do you agree with Aristotle's ordering of these goods? Do you feel that your peers agree with his ordering of goods? Where possible, give examples to help establish the validity of your opinion. Finally, do you think that our society in general puts the same value on these three classes of good that Aristotle does? Again, use examples where possible in constructing a careful essay.
5. Analyze the following quotations from the selection, taking a stand on the

question of whether or not Aristotle is generally correct in his assertions about the aim of man:

"It is in our best activities, or in the best one of them, that we say happiness consists." (para. 21)

"A man who does not enjoy doing noble actions is not a good man at all." (para. 21)

"Even supposing the chief good to be eventually the same for the individual as for the state, that of the state is evidently of greater and more fundamental importance both to attain and to preserve." (para. 4)

"In life . . . those who carry off the finest prizes are those who manifest their excellence in their deeds." (para. 20)

"If, as we have declared, it is our activities that give life its character, then no happy man can become miserable, inasmuch as he will never do what is hateful or base." (para. 30)

BERTRAND RUSSELL

A Free Man's Worship

BERTRAND RUSSELL (1872–1970) was one of England's most distinguished modern analytic philosophers. His early career was largely devoted to the study of mathematics, and The Principles of Mathematics (1900) was his first major work. The most important of his mathematical works was his collaboration with Alfred North Whitehead at Cambridge University on Principia Mathematica, published in three volumes (1910–1913). Both he and Whitehead had to contribute money to its publication. It attempted to show that mathematics derives from logic and that nothing but the principles of pure logic need to be understood for mathematics to be understood.

Russell's social conscience was aroused by the brutal bloodshed of World War I. Because of his pacifist views, he suffered imprisonment, libelous attack, and—worst of all—the loss of his lectureship in Philosophy at Cambridge in 1916. His interests from that time forth expanded from mathematics. Among the books that he wrote were Our Knowledge of the External World (1920), Analysis of Mind (1921), Marriage and Morals (1929), Education and the Social Order (1932), History of Western Philosophy (1945), and Why I Am Not a

---

From *Mysticism and Logic*.

Christian *(1957). He lectured frequently in England and America and was invited to be a faculty member at the City College of New York, but a New York judge denied him a visa because of imputed sexual immorality—in one of his books he had proposed a scheme of temporary marriage for undergraduates! Nonetheless, he remained in the United States, lecturing at the Barnes Foundation in Merion, Pennsylvania until in 1944 Cambridge reappointed him to its faculty. By then he was so widely known as a philosopher and social critic that he was honored by people of many nations. In 1950 he was awarded the Nobel Prize for Literature in recognition of the breadth of his writings.*

Russell's "A Free Man's Worship" is typical of him only to the extent that it celebrates the indomitableness of the human spirit and encourages us to respect the most human aspects of our being.

The opening portrays a bleak, meaningless cosmos in which we are caught and entangled. There is nothing to qualify any action as good or bad, nothing to energize the spirit, nothing to make us aware of the value of living. It is, Russell says clearly, the world that the atheist scientist might portray for us. Yet, Russell does not suggest rejecting Mephistopheles' view (after all, Mephistopheles is a demon and thus speaks from another world); rather, he asks that we accept Mephistopheles' view. He suggests we accept the meaninglessness, the senselessness, the blindness of creation, and move on from there. He urges us to respect what humans alone understand: goodness. Power, he tells us, is everywhere: in nature as storm and change, in time as fate, in death as finality. But this power is senseless; it is by nature bad. Were we to be simple materialists, he suggests, we would be yielding to the force of blind, senseless matter. Instead, he asks that we live with fate, with nature, with the thought of death, and that we worship goodness. In this Russell agrees with both Plato and Aristotle, whose concern for the soul is uppermost and who found materialists to be only slightly above the animals.

Russell pleads for humankind's emancipation from the worship of power. He pleads with us to lose our selfishness. "To abandon the struggle for private happiness, to expel all eagerness of temporary desire, to burn with passion for eternal things—this is emancipation, and this is the free man's worship" (para. 19).

RUSSELL'S RHETORIC

In reading this piece, we must keep in mind the fact that Russell's Nobel Prize was for literature, not for mathematics or philosophy.

Thus it is no surprise that all Russell's rhetorical achievements in the piece are the products of his style. He uses very few of the common topics; he does not structure a persuasive argument; he does not divide the work neatly into beginning, middle, and end as a means of structuring the piece. Instead, he depends on summary and thorough analysis. He follows the implications of a thought almost casually, as if following a wandering stream.

Impressive rhetorical qualities are exhibited in Russell's handling of image and metaphor and in his allusions to pertinent literature. The image is a literary device that appeals to our senses; it makes us see, hear, touch, smell, and feel what it refers to. Consider the images from Mephistopheles' speech: "from black masses of cloud hot sheets of rain deluged the barely solid crust" (para. 3). Consider his description of the imagination: "in the golden sunset magic of lyrics, where beauty shines and glows" (para. 14). And consider his description of fate: "doom falls pitiless and dark" (para. 21). Russell has the capacity to make us feel at the emotional level the seriousness of what he wishes to communicate intellectually.

Even more impressive are Russell's metaphors. The metaphor is a figure of speech that suggests a comparison, such as that of man's life to a march: "The life of Man is a long march through the night, surrounded by invisible foes" (para. 20). Before long, we suddenly find that life is not only like a march but also like a war (where marches are most common). Russell tells us in another metaphor that "Of all the arts, Tragedy is the proudest, the most triumphant; for it builds its shining citadel in the very centre of the enemy's country, on the very summit of his highest mountain; from its impregnable watchtowers" (para. 16). He asserts that we can "build a temple for the worship of our own ideals" (para. 14) and that "there is a cavern of darkness to be traversed before that temple can be entered" (para. 15). By this metaphor he suggests simply that we must be willing to grant Mephistopheles his vision of a meaningless world of matter as a prelude to understanding the true force of the spirit that lives in each of us.

A Free Man's Worship

To Dr. Faustus[1] in his study Mephistopheles told the history of the Creation, saying: 1

"The endless praises of the choirs of angels had begun to grow wearisome; for, after all, did he not deserve their praise? Had he not given them endless joy? Would it not be more amusing to obtain undeserved praise, to be worshipped by beings whom he tortured? He smiled inwardly, and resolved that the great drama should be performed. 2

"For countless ages the hot nebula whirled aimlessly through space. At length it began to take shape, the central mass threw off planets, the planets cooled, boiling seas and burning mountains heaved and tossed, from black masses of cloud hot sheets of rain deluged the barely solid crust. And now the first germ of life grew in the depths of the ocean, and developed rapidly in the fructifying warmth into vast forest trees, huge ferns springing from the damp mould, sea monsters breeding, fighting, devouring, and passing away. And from the monsters, as the play unfolded itself, Man was born, with the power of thought, the knowledge of good and evil, and the cruel thirst for worship. And Man saw that all is passing in this mad, monstrous world, that all is struggling to snatch, at any cost, a few brief moments of life before Death's inexorable decree. And Man said: 'There is a hidden purpose, could we but fathom it, and the purpose is good; for we must reverence something, and in the visible world there is nothing worthy of reverence.' And Man stood aside from the struggle, resolving that God intended harmony to come out of chaos by human efforts. And when he followed the instincts which God had transmitted to him from his ancestry of beasts of prey, he called it Sin, and asked God to forgive him. But he doubted whether he could be justly forgiven, until he invented a divine Plan by which God's wrath was to have been appeased. And seeing the present was bad, he made it yet worse, that 3

---

[1]**Dr. Faustus** In this sentence Russell is referring to *Doctor Faustus* (1588) by Christopher Marlowe (1564–1593). Johann Wolfgang von Goethe (1749–1832) also wrote on the theme of Faustus's selling his soul to the Devil. Russell is offering, in what he calls "outline," a summary of Mephistopheles' appeal.

thereby the future might be better. And he gave God thanks for the strength that enabled him to forgo even the joys that were possible. And God smiled; and when he saw that Man had become perfect in renunciation and worship, he sent another sun through the sky, which crashed into Man's sun; and all returned again to nebula.

" 'Yes,' he murmured, 'it was a good play; I will have it performed again.' "

4

Such, in outline, but even more purposeless, more void of meaning, is the world which Science presents for our belief. Amid such a world, if anywhere, our ideals henceforward must find a home. That Man is the product of causes which had no prevision of the end they were achieving; that his origin, his growth, his hopes and fears, his loves and beliefs, are but the outcome of accidental collocations of atoms;[2] that no fire, no heroism, no intensity of thought and feeling, can preserve an individual life beyond the grave; that all the labours of the ages, all the devotion, all the inspiration, all the noonday brightness of human genius, are destined to extinction in the vast death of the solar system, and that the whole temple of Man's achievement must inevitably be buried beneath the debris of a universe in ruins—all these things, if not quite beyond dispute, are yet so nearly certain, that no philosophy which rejects them can hope to stand. Only within the scaffolding of these truths, only on the firm foundation of unyielding despair, can the soul's habitation henceforth be safely built.

5

How, in such an alien and inhuman world, can so powerless a creature as Man preserve his aspirations untarnished? A strange mystery it is that Nature, omnipotent but blind, in the revolutions of her secular hurryings through the abysses of space, has brought forth at last a child, subject still to her power, but gifted with sight, with knowledge of good and evil, with the capacity of judging all the works of his unthinking Mother. In spite of Death, the mark and seal of the parental control, Man is yet free, during his brief years, to examine, to criticise, to know, and in imagination to create. To him alone, in the world with which he is acquainted, this freedom belongs; and in this lies his superiority to the resistless forces that control his outward life.

6

The savage, like ourselves, feels the oppression of his impotence before the powers of Nature; but having in himself nothing that he respects more than Power, he is willing to prostrate himself before his gods, without inquiring whether they are worthy of his worship. Pathetic and very terrible is the long history of cruelty and torture, of

7

[2]***collocations of atoms*** groupings or arrangements of atoms.

degradation and human sacrifice, endured in the hope of placating the jealous gods: surely, the trembling believer thinks, when what is most precious has been freely given, their lust for blood must be appeased, and more will not be required. The religion of Moloch[3]—as such creeds may be generically called—is in essence the cringing submission of the slave, who dare not, even in his heart, allow the thought that his master deserves no adulation. Since the independence of ideals is not yet acknowledged, Power may be freely worshipped, and receive an unlimited respect, despite its wanton infliction of pain.

But gradually, as morality grows bolder, the claim of the ideal world begins to be felt; and worship, if it is not to cease, must be given to gods of another kind than those created by the savage. Some, though they feel the demands of the ideal, will still consciously reject them, still urging that naked Power is worthy of worship. Such is the attitude inculcated in God's answer to Job[4] out of the whirlwind: the divine power and knowledge are paraded, but of the divine goodness there is no hint. Such also is the attitude of those who, in our own day, base their morality upon the struggle for survival, maintaining that the survivors are necessarily the fittest. But others, not content with an answer so repugnant to the moral sense, will adopt the position which we have become accustomed to regard as specially religious, maintaining that, in some hidden manner, the world of fact is really harmonious with the world of ideals. Thus Man creates God, all-powerful and all-good, the mystic unity of what is and what should be.

8

But the world of fact, after all, is not good; and, in submitting our judgment to it, there is an element of slavishness from which our thoughts must be purged. For in all things it is well to exalt the dignity of Man, by freeing him as far as possible from the tyranny of nonhuman Power. When we have realised that Power is largely bad, that man, with his knowledge of good and evil, is but a helpless atom in a world which has no such knowledge, the choice is again presented to us: Shall we worship Force, or shall we worship Goodness? Shall our

9

---

[3]**Moloch** A pagan deity to which the sons of Judah sacrificed their children through a ritual of fire; see I Kings 11:7.

[4]**God's answer to Job** In the book of Job in the Bible, Satan asserts that he can tempt any of God's creatures to turn their backs on God. God insists that Job cannot be swayed. Satan tests Job, inflicting him with illness and destruction, but Job remains faithful. God explains to Job that he has suffered and come through the test. But Russell implies a criticism of the book of Job, in which suffering rather than love, and power rather than compassion, are stressed.

God exist and be evil, or shall he be recognised as the creation of our own conscience?

The answer to this question is very momentous, and affects profoundly our whole morality. The worship of Force, to which Carlyle[5] and Nietzsche and the creed of Militarism have accustomed us, is the result of failure to maintain our own ideals against a hostile universe: it is itself a prostrate submission to evil, a sacrifice of our best to Moloch. If strength indeed is to be respected, let us respect rather the strength of those who refuse that false "recognition of facts" which fails to recognise that facts are often bad. Let us admit that, in the world we know, there are many things that would be better otherwise, and that the ideals to which we do and must adhere are not realised in the realm of matter. Let us preserve our respect for truth, for beauty, for the ideal of perfection which life does not permit us to attain, though none of these things meet with the approval of the unconscious universe. If Power is bad, as it seems to be, let us reject it from our hearts. In this lies Man's true freedom: in determination to worship only the God created by our own love of the good, to respect only the heaven which inspires the insight of our best moments. In action, in desire, we must submit perpetually to the tyranny of outside forces; but in thought, in aspiration, we are free, free from our fellowmen, free from the petty planet on which our bodies impotently crawl, free even, while we live, from the tyranny of death. Let us learn, then, that energy of faith which enables us to live constantly in the vision of the good; and let us descend, in action, into the world of fact, with that vision always before us.

When first the opposition of fact and ideal grows fully visible, a spirit of fiery revolt, of fierce hatred of the gods, seems necessary to the assertion of freedom. To defy with Promethean constancy[6] a hos-

10

11

---

[5]*Thomas Carlyle (1795–1881)* Carlyle was an important historian, especially remembered for his studies of Frederick the Great, Oliver Cromwell, and the French Revolution. Russell is probably referring to his work on the French Revolution, which demonstrated the ways in which power could be used and misused. His *Sartor Resartus* (1832) inspired Friedrich Nietzsche (1844–1900) with its demonstration of the power of a strong personal will. Nietzsche's *The Will to Power* (1888) contains more than 1,000 aphorisms celebrating the independent will, the assertive and inspired person. Much of this philosophy of will power was misapplied to defend the actions of the Fascists in Europe before and during World War II.

[6]*Promethean constancy* Prometheus was a Titan of Greek mythology who gave fire to humankind. Zeus punished him by having him chained to a rock and having a giant bird constantly eat at his liver. Constancy is thus endurance, the will to prevail.

tile universe, to keep its evil always in view, always actively hated, to refuse no pain that the malice of Power can invent, appears to be the duty of all who will not bow before the inevitable. But indignation is still a bondage, for it compels our thoughts to be occupied with an evil world; and in the fierceness of desire from which rebellion springs there is a kind of self-assertion which it is necessary for the wise to overcome. Indignation is a submission of our thoughts, but not of our desires; the Stoic freedom[7] in which wisdom consists is found in the submission of our desires, but not of our thoughts. From the submission of our desires springs the virtue of resignation; from the freedom of our thoughts springs the whole world of art and philosophy, and the vision of beauty by which, at last, we half reconquer the reluctant world. But the vision of beauty is possible only to unfettered contemplation, to thoughts not weighted by the load of eager wishes; and thus Freedom comes only to those who no longer ask of life that it shall yield them any of those personal goods that are subject to the mutations of Time.

Although the necessity of renunciation is evidence of the existence of evil, yet Christianity, in preaching it, has shown a wisdom exceeding that of the Promethean philosophy of rebellion. It must be admitted that, of the things we desire, some, though they prove impossible, are yet real goods; others, however, as ardently longed for, do not form part of a fully purified ideal. The belief that what must be renounced is bad, though sometimes false, is far less often false than untamed passion supposes; and the creed of religion, by providing a reason for proving that it is never false, has been the means of purifying our hopes by the discovery of many austere truths. 12

But there is in resignation a further good element: even real goods, when they are unattainable, ought not to be fretfully desired. To every man comes, sooner or later, the great renunciation. For the young, there is nothing unattainable; a good thing desired with the whole force of a passionate will, and yet impossible, is to them not credible. Yet, by death, by illness, by poverty, or by the voice of duty, we must learn, each one of us, that the world was not made for us, and that, however beautiful may be the things we crave, Fate may nevertheless forbid them. It is the part of courage, when misfortune comes, to bear without repining the ruin of our hopes, to turn away our thoughts 13

---

[7]**Stoic freedom** This is a reference to the Stoic philosophy of acceptance of things as they come; it is also characterized by public service and good deeds. The Stoics flourished in the fourth and third centuries B.C. in Greece, but their influence also spread to Rome, where Seneca (4 B.C.–A.D. 65) wrote extensively on Stoicism.

from vain regrets. This degree of submission to Power is not only just and right: it is the very gate of wisdom.

But passive renunciation is not the whole of wisdom; for not by 14 renunciation alone can we build a temple for the worship of our own ideals. Haunting foreshadowings of the temple appear in the realm of imagination, in music, in architecture, in the untroubled kingdom of reason, and in the golden sunset magic of lyrics, where beauty shines and glows, remote from the touch of sorrow, remote from the fear of change, remote from the failures and disenchantments of the world of fact. In the contemplation of these things the vision of heaven will shape itself in our hearts, giving at once a touchstone to judge the world about us, and an inspiration by which to fashion to our needs whatever is not incapable of serving as a stone in the sacred temple.

Except for those rare spirits that are born without sin, there is a 15 cavern of darkness to be traversed before that temple can be entered. The gate of the cavern is despair, and its floor is paved with the gravestones of abandoned hopes. There Self must die; there the eagerness, the greed of untamed desire must be slain, for only so can the soul be freed from the empire of Fate. But out of the cavern the Gate of Renunciation leads again to the daylight of wisdom, by whose radiance a new insight, a new joy, a new tenderness, shine forth to gladden the pilgrim's heart.

When, without the bitterness of impotent rebellion, we have learnt 16 both to resign ourselves to the outward rule of Fate and to recognise that the nonhuman world is unworthy of our worship, it becomes possible at last so to transform and refashion the unconscious universe, so to transmute it in the crucible of imagination, that a new image of shining gold replaces the old idol of clay. In all the multiform facts of the world—in the visual shapes of trees and mountains and clouds, in the events of the life of man, even in the very omnipotence of Death— the insight of creative idealism can find the reflection of a beauty which its own thoughts first made. In this way mind asserts its subtle mastery over the thoughtless forces of Nature. The more evil the material with which it deals, the more thwarting to untrained desire, the greater is its achievement in inducing the reluctant rock to yield up its hidden treasures, the prouder its victory in compelling the opposing forces to swell the pageant of its triumph. Of all the arts, Tragedy is the proudest, the most triumphant; for it builds its shining citadel in the very centre of the enemy's country, on the very summit of his highest mountain; from its impregnable watchtowers, his camps and arsenals, his columns and forts, are all revealed; within its walls the free life continues, while the legions of Death and Pain and Despair, and all the servile captains of tyrant Fate, afford the burghers[8] of that dauntless city new spectacles of beauty. Happy those sacred ramparts, thrice happy the dwellers on that all-seeing eminence. Honour to those brave warriors who, through countless ages of warfare, have preserved for us the priceless heritage of liberty, and have kept undefiled by sacrilegious invaders the home of the unsubdued.

But the beauty of Tragedy does but make visible a quality which, 17 in more or less obvious shapes, is present always and everywhere in life. In the spectacle of Death, in the endurance of intolerable pain, and in the irrevocableness of a vanished past, there is a sacredness, an overpowering awe, a feeling of the vastness, the depth, the inexhaustible mystery of existence, in which, as by some strange marriage of pain, the sufferer is bound to the world by bonds of sorrow. In these moments of insight, we lose all eagerness of temporary desire, all struggling and striving for petty ends, all care for the little trivial things that, to a superficial view, make up the common life of day by day; we see, surrounding the narrow raft illumined by the flickering light of human comradeship, the dark ocean on whose rolling waves we toss for a brief hour; from the great night without, a chill blast breaks in upon our refuge; all the loneliness of humanity amid hostile forces is concentrated upon the individual soul, which must struggle alone, with what of courage it can command, against the whole weight of a universe that cares nothing for its hopes and fears. Victory, in this struggle with the powers of darkness, is the true baptism into the glorious company of heroes, the true initiation into the overmastering beauty of human existence. From that awful encounter of the soul with the outer world, enunciation,[9] wisdom, and charity are born; and with their birth a new life begins. To take into the inmost shrine of the soul the irresistible forces whose puppets we seem to be—Death and change, the irrevocableness of the past, and the powerlessness of man before the blind hurry of the universe from vanity to vanity—to feel these things and know them is to conquer them.

This is the reason why the Past has such magical power. The 18 beauty of its motionless and silent pictures is like the enchanted purity of late autumn, when the leaves, though one breath would make them fall, still glow against the sky in golden glory. The Past does not change or strive; like Duncan,[10] after life's fitful fever it sleeps well;

---

[8]***burghers*** The proper citizens of the town; the civic leaders.
[9]***enunciation*** A declaration or commitment to purpose.
[10]***Duncan*** A character in *Macbeth* (II.ii) by William Shakespeare (1564–1616), written about 1606. Duncan was the king murdered in his sleep by Macbeth.

what was eager and grasping, what was petty and transitory, has faded away, the things that were beautiful and eternal shine out of it like stars in the night. Its beauty, to a soul not worthy of it, is unendurable; but to a soul which has conquered Fate it is the key of religion.

The life of Man, viewed outwardly, is but a small thing in compar- 19 ison with the forces of Nature. The slave is doomed to worship Time and Fate and Death, because they are greater than anything he finds in himself, and because all his thoughts are of things which they devour. But, great as they are, to think of them greatly, to feel their passionless splendour, is greater still. And such thought makes us free men; we no longer bow before the inevitable in Oriental subjection,[11] but we absorb it, and make it a part of ourselves. To abandon the struggle for private happiness, to expel all eagerness of temporary desire, to burn with passion for eternal things—this is emancipation, and this is the free man's worship. And this liberation is effected by a contemplation of Fate; for Fate itself is subdued by the mind which leaves nothing to be purged by the purifying fire of Time.

United with his fellow-men by the strongest of all ties, the tie of a 20 common doom, the free man finds that a new vision is with him always, shedding over every daily task the light of love. The life of Man is a long march through the night, surrounded by invisible foes, tortured by weariness and pain, towards a goal that few can hope to reach, and where none may tarry long. One by one, as they march, our comrades vanish from our sight, seized by the silent orders of omnipotent Death. Very brief is the time in which we can help them, in which their happiness or misery is decided. Be it ours to shed sunshine on their path, to lighten their sorrows by the balm of sympathy, to give them the pure joy of a never-tiring affection, to strengthen failing courage, to instil faith in hours of despair. Let us not weigh in grudging scales their merits and demerits, but let us think only of their need— of the sorrows, the difficulties, perhaps the blindnesses, that make the misery of their lives; let us remember that they are fellow-sufferers in the same darkness, actors in the same tragedy with ourselves. And so, when their day is over, when their good and their evil have become eternal by the immortality of the past, be it ours to feel that, where they suffered, where they failed, no deed of ours was the cause; but wherever a spark of the divine fire kindled in their hearts, we were ready with encouragement, with sympathy, with brave words in which high courage glowed.

---

[11]**Oriental subjection**   The loss of self called for in many Eastern religions.

Brief and powerless is Man's life; on him and all his race the slow, 21
sure doom falls pitiless and dark. Blind to good and evil, reckless of
destruction, omnipotent matter rolls on its relentless way; for Man,
condemned today to lose his dearest, tomorrow himself to pass
through the gate of darkness, it remains only to cherish, ere yet the
blow falls, the lofty thoughts that ennoble his little day; disdaining
the coward terrors of the slave of Fate, to worship at the shrine that
his own hands have built; undismayed by the empire of chance, to
preserve a mind free from the wanton tyranny that rules his outward
life; proudly defiant of the irresistible forces that tolerate, for a moment, his knowledge and his condemnation, to sustain alone, a weary
but unyielding Atlas,[12] the world that his own ideals have fashioned
despite the trampling march of unconscious power.

---

[12]***Atlas*** A Greek mythic figure said to hold the pillars that separated heaven from the
earth.

QUESTIONS

1. What does Russell mean by power? What kinds of power can you find
   reference to?
2. Is it fair to say that Mephistopheles' description of creation agrees with
   science's description?
3. Why does Russell emphasize the fact that only humans understand the
   difference between good and evil?
4. Who did Russell expect to read this essay? What would their anxieties be?
   What would their attitudes toward belief be?
5. What does Russell seem to mean by the term "worship"? What does the
   savage's worship have in common with that of a "free man"?

WRITING ASSIGNMENTS

1. In the first five paragraphs, Russell paints a picture of the universe as a
   place of despair. On the one hand, it is the portrait of a demon; on the
   other, the portrait of modern science. Then he declares that "all these
   things, if not quite beyond dispute, are yet so nearly certain, that no philosophy which rejects them can hope to stand" (para. 5). Identify all the
   things Russell feels are nearly certain; then defend or attack this proposition that they are true beyond dispute.
2. In paragraph 10, Russell says, "If Power is bad, as it seems to be, let us
   reject it from our hearts. In this lies Man's true freedom: in determination

to worship only the God created by our own love of the good, to respect only the heaven which inspires the insight of our best moments." Establish exactly what is meant by these statements. Then establish your personal views on where true freedom lies. Point out what you can agree with Russell about and what you disagree on. Be sure to give your own arguments for your views. Decide for yourself what true freedom means for "Man."

3. Inventory the selection for the most interesting metaphors you can find. Find a dozen or so and list them. Establish exactly what they contribute to the power of this selection. What groupings do they fall into (military, natural, dramatic, etc.)? If there are a great many that are, say, military in nature, what does that fact mean for the force of Russell's argument? What moods are evoked by the metaphors? What emotions are meant to be aroused? Do you feel that any of the metaphors are overdone? Which metaphors are particularly effective? Do you think that the piece would be less interesting without them?

4. Assume that a group has declared that Russell is an atheist and that we should not read his work. Defend or attack the selection by siding with or against the "group." Is Russell being atheistic in this essay? What evidence will support or contradict such a view? If he were being atheistic, why would it be important not to read him? Or, why might it be very important to read him?

5. The title of this work is "A Free Man's Worship." What that actually is can be found in the definition in paragraph 19: "To abandon the struggle for private happiness, to expel all eagerness of temporary desire, to burn with passion for eternal things—this is emancipation, and this is the free man's worship." Begin your essay by clarifying each portion of this statement. Be sure to give examples where possible or to expand the statement enough so that someone who has not read this piece can understand what you mean. Then establish whether or not this really *is* a free man's worship. Why would it not be a slave's worship? What is freeing about it? Do you think that it represents emancipation in the same sense that Russell thinks it does?

JOHN DEWEY

Some Historical
Factors in Philosophical
Reconstruction

*J*OHN DEWEY *(1859–1952) was a prominent American philosopher and theoretician of education. He was born in Vermont and received a B.A. degree from the University of Vermont in 1879. He then studied at Johns Hopkins University, where he received a Ph.D. in philosophy in 1884. He taught philosophy at the University of Michigan, the University of Chicago, and then Columbia University until 1930. He spent the remaining twenty-two years of his life in lecturing and research. His central interests lay in the reform of education, particularly in the direction of making it more student centered and more useful for the daily lives of the mass of people.*

Dewey was one of a group of American philosophers—among whom was William James—who considered themselves pragmatists. Their philosophy was called pragmatism, and it focused on the questions of usefulness and practicality that could be tested only by experience. Accordingly, the ultimate values of any theories or ideas were to be tested by experience rather than by authority. As Dewey tells us in the selection included here, from his series of lectures— delivered in 1919 at the Imperial University in Japan and published

---

From *Reconstruction in Philosophy.*

as Reconstruction in Philosophy *(1920)—philosophy must be forward looking. Progress is forward, not backward. Because pragmatism seeks to test the validity of theories by practical experiment, it is progressive and forward looking. Philosophies which depend upon theories which must be adhered to because they have been pronounced dogmatically in the past must naturally be backward looking.*

Because pragmatism tests philosophical theories by experience, it is connected with experimental science. Dewey believed that the greatest progress in modern thought had occurred in science, and he felt that a truly modern philosophy—which is to say a "reconstructed" philosophy—would also have to be like science and submit to practical tests. Thus, pragmatism is a scientific philosophy, which is one reason why Dewey refers so frequently to science in this work and why he begins his discussion with an extensive summary of the thought of Francis Bacon. As he tells us, Bacon's age was the inheritor of two important changes. One of them was economic, a sudden, explosive financial growth in Europe created by the exploitation of the New World's riches. The other was intellectual, created by the first stirrings of scientific progress and the breakdown of the absolute hold on men's minds of medieval religious authority, a breakdown made possible by the rise of Protestantism.

Our own times, Dewey was certain, were no less in the throes of change. When he wrote the first of these lectures, in 1919, the world had seen one very massive breakdown in the old ways of aristocratic conservatism and class domination. After World War I aristocrats could no longer maintain power. The middle and lower classes grasped at the opportunities provided by economic change and educational developments after the war to begin to change their society. Moreover, the war itself had brought the developments of science to bear in fearful ways: aerial bombardment, murderous machine guns, and dynamite. Hence science had become one of the forces that had to be brought under control for the benefit of society. And philosophy, if it was to be of value in the modern age, had the responsibility of showing how to make such forces as economics, religion, and science more socially responsible.

When Dewey tells us that Bacon was correct in thinking that knowledge is power, he explains that there are several kinds of power. One kind is power over nature, which modern science has definitely provided. Science has controlled and exploited steam and electricity, two of the most extraordinary forces nature possesses. Any philosophy that ignores such achievements is not forward look-

*ing. But now a problem of philosophy is to be sure that science itself
is brought under control and put to the best service of humanity.
When Dewey wrote the Preface to the 1948 edition of his* Reconstruction in Philosophy *after World War II, he said he felt that controlling
science was much more important than it had been in 1919.*

DEWEY'S RHETORIC

*Dewey is a careful writer. He is generally, though not always,
clear when he expresses complex ideas. The general rhetorical form
he uses here might best be described as a meditation. He begins with
a reference to what he calls Francis Bacon's best-known aphorism:
"Knowledge is Power." This is the subject of his meditation throughout the rest of the piece; it is the focus of his attention, and nowhere
does he stray very far from it. The result of meditating so closely on
a given aphorism of this sort is that the work achieves a high degree
of unity. We may pause anywhere in the work and observe the connection with what is being said and the concept that knowledge is
power.*

*Dewey begins his meditation with a lengthy summary of Bacon's
thought, including what Dewey believes are its strengths and weaknesses (paras. 1–13). This constitutes almost half of the essay. He then
begins to examine our own time to see what it has in common with
Bacon's, focusing on what he thinks are new mental attitudes that
will affect contemporary social conditions.*

*He then focuses on the issues of science, relating science to the
highest pragmatic value—the relief of the human estate (para. 18)—
which he holds is the highest calling of science. It is by this standard
that he must measure its achievement. Any philosophy that will hold
science responsible to its calling will be part of the "reconstruction"
that Dewey demands. Dewey's final section discusses modern history, concentrating on the decay of authority and the construction of
the modern state as a product of the individual will and design; the
state is, in other words, a servant of the individual.*

*As he tells us, knowledge is power—power over nature, or per-
haps power over the minds of men. In two world wars Dewey saw
much misuse of power. His reconstructed philosophy would examine
the nature of that misuse and would put knowledge back into the
service of humankind.*

Some Historical Factors in Philosophical Reconstruction

Francis Bacon of the Elizabethan age is the great forerunner of the 1
spirit of modern life. Though slight in accomplishment, as a prophet
of new tendencies he is an outstanding figure of the world's intellectual life. Like many another prophet he suffers from confused inter-
mingling of old and new. What is most significant in him has been
rendered more or less familiar by the later course of events. But page
after page is filled with matter which belongs to the past from which
Bacon thought he had escaped. Caught between these two sources of
easy disparagement, Bacon hardly receives his due as the real founder
of modern thought, while he is praised for merits which scarcely belong to him, such as an alleged authorship of the specific methods of
induction pursued by science. What makes Bacon memorable is that
breezes blowing from a new world caught and filled his sails and
stirred him to adventure in new seas. He never himself discovered the
land of promise, but he proclaimed the new goal and by faith he described its features from afar.

The main traits of his thought put before our mind the larger fea- 2
tures of a new spirit which was at work in causing intellectual reconstruction. They may suggest the social and historical forces out of
which the new spirit was born. The best known aphorism of Bacon is
that Knowledge is Power. Judged by this pragmatic criterion, he condemned the great body of learning then extant as *not*-knowledge, as
pseudo- and pretentious-knowledge. For it did not give power. It was
otiose,[1] not operative. In his most extensive discussion he classified
the learning of his day under three heads, delicate, fantastic and contentious. Under delicate learning, he included the literary learning
which through the influence of the revival of ancient languages and
literatures occupied so important a place in the intellectual life of the
Renaissance. Bacon's condemnation is the more effective because he

---

[1] *otiose* wasteful; useless.

himself was a master of the classics and of all the graces and refinements which this literary study was intended to convey. In substance he anticipated most of the attacks which educational reformers since his time have made upon one-sided literary culture. It contributed not to power but to ornament and decoration. It was ostentatious and luxurious. By fantastic learning he meant the quasi-magical science that was so rife all over Europe in the sixteenth century—wild developments of alchemy, astrology, etc. Upon this he poured his greatest vials of wrath because the corruption of the good is the worst of evils. Delicate learning was idle and vain, but fantastic learning aped the form of true knowledge. It laid hold of the true principle and aim of knowledge—control of natural forces. But it neglected the conditions and methods by which alone such knowledge could be obtained, and thus deliberately led men astray.

For our purposes, however, what he says about contentious learning is the most important. For by this, he means the traditional science which had come down, in scanty and distorted measure to be sure, from antiquity through scholasticism.[2] It is called contentious both because of the logical method used and the end to which it was put. In a certain sense it aimed at power, but power over other men in the interest of some class or sect or person, not power over natural forces in the common interest of all. Bacon's conviction of the quarrelsome, self-displaying character of the scholarship which had come down from antiquity was of course not so much due to Greek science itself as to the degenerate heritage of scholasticism in the fourteenth century, when philosophy had fallen into the hands of disputatious theologians, full of hair-splitting argumentativeness and quirks and tricks by which to win victory over somebody else.

But Bacon also brought his charge against the Aristotelian method itself. In its rigorous forms it aimed at demonstration, and in its milder forms at persuasion. But both demonstration and persuasion aim at conquest of mind rather than of nature. Moreover they both assume that someone is already in possession of a truth or a belief, and that the only problem is to convince someone else, or to teach. In contrast, his new method had an exceedingly slight opinion of the amount of truth already existent, and a lively sense of the extent and importance of truths still to be attained. It would be a logic of discovery, not a

---

[2]*scholasticism* Academicism promoted by the medieval church and dominated by the thought of such religious philosophers as St. Augustine (354–430) and St. Thomas Aquinas (1225?–1274). It depended on argument, disputation, and logic for its force. It also built on the idealism of Plato and the logic *(organon)* of Aristotle.

logic of argumentation, proof and persuasion. To Bacon, the old logic even at its best was a logic for teaching the already known, and teaching meant indoctrination, discipling. It was an axiom of Aristotle that only that which was already known could be learned, that growth in knowledge consisted simply in bringing together a universal truth of reason and a particular truth of sense which had previously been noted separately. In any case, learning meant *growth* of knowledge, and growth belongs in the region of becoming, change, and hence is inferior to *possession* of knowledge in the syllogistic self-revolving manipulation of what was already known—demonstration.[3]

In contrast with this point of view, Bacon eloquently proclaimed the superiority of discovery of new facts and truths to demonstration of the old. Now there is only one road to discovery, and that is penetrating inquiry into the secrets of nature. Scientific principles and laws do not lie on the surface of nature. They are hidden, and must be wrested from nature by an active and elaborate technique of inquiry. Neither logical reasoning nor the passive accumulation of any number of observations—which the ancients called experience—suffices to lay hold of them. Active experimentation must force the apparent facts of nature into forms different to those in which they familiarly present themselves; and thus make them tell the truth about themselves, as torture may compel an unwilling witness to reveal what he has been concealing. Pure reasoning as a means of arriving at truth is like the spider who spins a web out of himself. The web is orderly and elaborate, but it is only a trap. The passive accumulation of experiences— the traditional empirical method—is like the ant who busily runs about and collects and piles up heaps of raw materials. True method, that which Bacon would usher in, is comparable to the operations of the bee who, like the ant, collects material from the external world, but unlike that industrious creature attacks and modifies the collected stuff in order to make it yield its hidden treasure. 5

Along with this contrast between subjugation of nature and subjection of other minds and the elevation of a method of discovery above a method of demonstration, went Bacon's sense of progress as the aim and test of genuine knowledge. According to his criticisms, the classic logic, even in its Aristotelian form, inevitably played into the hands of inert conservatism. For in accustoming the mind to think of truth as already known, it habituated men to fall back on the intellectual at- 6

---

[3]*syllogistic . . . demonstration* The syllogism is a sequence of logical deductions used to demonstrate the truth of a proposition. The syllogism originated with Aristotle and was a basic feature of much scholastic thought.

tainments of the past, and to accept them without critical scrutiny. Not merely the medieval but the renaissance mind tended to look back to antiquity as a Golden Age of Knowledge, the former relying upon sacred scriptures, the latter upon secular literatures. And while this attitude could not fairly be charged up against the classic logic, yet Bacon felt, and with justice, that any logic which identified the technique of knowing with demonstration of truths already possessed by the mind, blunts the spirit of investigation and confines the mind within the circle of traditional learning.

Such a logic could not avoid having for its salient[4] features defini- 7 tion of what is already known (or thought to be known), and its systematization according to recognized canons of orthodoxy. A logic of discovery on the other hand looks to the future. Received truth it regards critically as something to be tested by new experiences rather than as something to be dogmatically taught and obediently received. Its chief interest in even the most carefully tested ready-made knowledge is the use which may be made of it in further inquiries and discoveries. Old truth has its chief value in assisting the detection of new truth. Bacon's own appreciation of the nature of induction was highly defective. But his acute sense that science means invasion of the unknown, rather than repetition in logical form of the already known, makes him nevertheless the father of induction. Endless and persistent uncovering of facts and principles not known—such is the true spirit of induction. Continued progress in knowledge is the only sure way of protecting old knowledge from degeneration into dogmatic doctrines received on authority, or from imperceptible decay into superstition and old wives' tales.

Ever-renewed progress is to Bacon the test as well as the aim of 8 genuine logic. Where, Bacon constantly demands, where are the works, the fruits, of the older logic? What has it done to ameliorate[5] the evils of life, to rectify defects, to improve conditions? Where are the inventions that justify its claim to be in possession of truth? Beyond the victory of man over man in law courts, diplomacy and political administration, they are nil. One had to turn from admired "sciences" to despised arts to find works, fruits, consequences of value to human kind through power over natural forces. And progress in the arts was as yet intermittent, fitful, accidental. A true logic or technique of inquiry would make advance in the industrial, agricultural and medical arts continuous, cumulative and deliberately systematic.

---

[4]**salient** most important; primary.
[5]**ameliorate** make easier or better; improve.

If we take into account the supposed body of ready-made knowl-   9
edge upon which learned men rested in supine acquiescence and which
they recited in parrotlike chorus, we find it consists of two parts. One
of these parts is made up of the errors of our ancestors, musty with
antiquity and organized into pseudo-science through the use of the
classic logic. Such "truths" are in fact only the systematized mistakes
and prejudices of our ancestors. Many of them originated in accident;
many in class interest and bias, perpetuated by authority for this very
reason—a consideration which later actuated Locke's attack[6] upon the
doctrine of innate ideas. The other portion of accepted beliefs comes
from instinctive tendencies of the human mind that give it a dangerous bias until counteracted by a conscious and critical logic.

The mind of man spontaneously assumes greater simplicity, uni-   10
formity and unity among phenomena than actually exists. It follows
superficial analogies and jumps to conclusions; it overlooks the variety
of details and the existence of exceptions. Thus it weaves a web of
purely internal origin which it imposes upon nature. What had been
termed science in the past consisted of this humanly constructed and
imposed web. Men looked at the work of their own minds and thought
they were seeing realities in nature. They were worshipping, under
the name of science, the idols of their own making. So-called science
and philosophy consisted of these "anticipations" of nature. And the
worst thing that could be said about traditional logic was that instead
of saving man from this natural source of error, it had, through attributing to nature a false rationality of unity, simplicity and generality,
sanctioned these sources of delusion. The office of the new logic
would be to protect the mind against itself: to teach it to undergo a
patient and prolonged apprenticeship to fact in its infinite variety and
particularity: to obey nature intellectually in order to command it
practically. Such was the significance of the new logic—the new tool
or organon of learning, so named in express opposition to the organon
of Aristotle.[7]

Certain other important oppositions are implied. Aristotle thought   11
of reason as capable of solitary communion with rational truth. The
counterpart of his celebrated saying that man is a political animal, is

---

[6]***Locke's attack***   John Locke (1632–1704) was an English philosopher whose theories
focused on the knowledge we acquire from our experience; thus he attacked the idea that
people are born with any innate knowledge and held that knowledge is acquired only
through experience, in his *Essay Concerning Human Understanding* (1690).

[7]***the organon of Aristotle***   The writings that constituted his logic; literally, an *instrument* for thought.

that Intelligence, *Nous,* is neither animal, human nor political. It is divinely unique and self-enclosed. To Bacon, error had been produced and perpetuated by social influences, and truth must be discovered by social agencies organized for that purpose. Left to himself, the individual can do little or nothing; he is likely to become involved in his own self-spun web of misconceptions. The great need is the organization of cooperative research, whereby men attack nature collectively and the work of inquiry is carried on continuously from generation to generation. Bacon even aspired to the rather absurd notion of a method so perfected that differences in natural human ability might be discounted, and all be put on the same level in production of new facts and new truths. Yet this absurdity was only the negative side of his great positive prophecy of a combined and cooperative pursuit of science such as characterizes our own day. In view of the picture he draws in his New Atlantis[8] of a State organized for collective inquiry, we readily forgive him his exaggerations.

Power over nature was not to be individual but collective; the Empire, as he says, of Man over Nature, substituted for the Empire of Man over Man. Let us employ Bacon's own words with their variety of picturesque metaphor: "Men have entered into the desire of learning and knowledge, . . . seldom sincerely to give a true account of their gift of reason, to the benefit and use of men, but as if they sought in knowledge a couch whereon to rest a searching and wandering spirit; or a terrace for a wandering and variable mind to walk up and down with a fair prospect; or a tower for a proud mind to raise itself upon; or a fort or commanding ground for strife and contention; or a shop for profit and sale; and not a rich storehouse for the glory of the creator and the relief of man's estate." When William James called Pragmatism[9] a New Name for an Old Way of Thinking, I do not know that he was thinking expressly of Francis Bacon, but so far as concerns the spirit and atmosphere of the pursuit of knowledge, Bacon may be taken as the prophet of a pragmatic conception of knowledge. Many misconceptions of its spirit would be avoided if his emphasis upon the social factor in both the pursuit and the end of knowledge were carefully observed.

This somewhat overlong résumé of Bacon's ideas has not been gone

12

13

---

[8]***New Atlantis*** A political romance written by Bacon about 1605. It depicts an ideal society in which science works to benefit humanity.

[9]***Pragmatism*** Modern school of philosophy which tested its theories in practice. It attempted to be scientific. (Pragmatism is discussed in detail in the introduction to this selection, pp. 487–489.)

into as a matter of historic retrospect. The summary is rather meant to put before our minds an authentic document of the new philosophy which may bring into relief the social causes of intellectual revolution. Only a sketchy account can be here attempted, but it may be of some assistance even barely to remind you of the direction of that industrial, political and religious change upon which Europe was entering.

Upon the industrial side, it is impossible, I think, to exaggerate the influence of travel, exploration and new commerce which fostered a romantic sense of adventure into novelty; loosened the hold of traditional beliefs; created a lively sense of new worlds to be investigated and subdued; produced new methods of manufacture, commerce, banking and finance; and then reacted everywhere to stimulate invention, and to introduce positive observation and active experimentation into science. The Crusades,[10] the revival of the profane learning of antiquity[11] and even more perhaps, the contact with the advanced learning of the Mohammedans,[12] the increase of commerce with Asia and Africa, the introduction of the lens, compass and gunpowder, the finding and opening up of North and South America—most significantly called The New World—these are some of the obvious external facts. Contrast between peoples and races previously isolated is always, I think, most fruitful and influential for change when psychological and industrial changes coincide with and reinforce each other. Sometimes people undergo emotional change, what might almost be called a metaphysical change, through intercourse. The inner set of the mind, especially in religious matters, is altered. At other times, there is a lively exchange of goods, an adoption of foreign tools and devices, an imitation of alien habits of clothing, habitation and production of commodities. One of these changes is, so to speak, too internal and the other too external to bring about a profound intellectual development. But when the creation of a new mental attitude falls together with extensive material and economic changes, something significant happens.

14

---

[10]*The Crusades* European armies, motivated in part by religious zeal, attempted to reclaim Jerusalem and other holy lands from the Moslems during the tenth, eleventh, and twelfth centuries.

[11]*profane learning of antiquity* The Renaissance rediscovered the writings of Plato, Aristotle, and other ancients. These were considered *profane* because they were not Christian or religious in origin.

[12]*advanced learning of the Mohammedans* The Moslems had maintained academies and knew the works of Aristotle. They had also developed the sciences, particularly chemistry and mathematics.

This coincidence of two kinds of change was, I take it, character- 15
istic of the new contacts of the sixteenth and seventeenth centuries.
Clash of customs and traditional beliefs dispelled mental inertia and
sluggishness; it aroused a lively curiosity as to different and new ideas.
The actual adventure of travel and exploration purged the mind of fear
of the strange and unknown: as new territories geographically and
commercially speaking were opened up, the mind was opened up. New
contacts promoted the desire for still more contacts; the appetite for
novelty and discovery grew by what it fed upon. Conservative adherence to old beliefs and methods underwent a steady attrition with
every new voyage into new parts and every new report of foreign ways.
The mind became used to exploration and discovery. It found a delight
and interest in the revelations of the novel and the unusual which it
no longer took in what was old and customary. Moreover, the very act
of exploration, of expedition, the process of enterprising adventure into
the remote, yielded a peculiar joy and thrill.

This psychological change was essential to the birth of the new 16
point of view in science and philosophy. Yet alone it could hardly have
produced the new method of knowing. But positive changes in the
habits and purposes of life gave objective conformation and support to
the mental change. They also determined the channels in which the
new spirit found exercise. New-found wealth, the gold from the Amer-
icas and new articles of consumption and enjoyment, tended to wean
men from preoccupation with the metaphysical and theological, and
to turn their minds with newly awakened interest to the joys of nature
and this life. New material resources and new markets in America and
India undermined the old dependence upon household and manual
production for a local and limited market, and generated quantitative,
large-scale production by means of steam for foreign and expanding
markets. Capitalism, rapid transit, and production for exchange against
money[13] and for profit, instead of against goods and for consumption,
followed.

This cursory and superficial reminder of vast and complicated 17
events may suggest the mutual interdependence of the scientific revolution and the industrial revolution. Upon the one hand, modern industry *is* so much applied science. No amount of desire to make
money, or to enjoy new commodities, no amount of mere practical
energy and enterprise, would have effected the economic transforma-

---

[13]*production for exchange against money* Dewey means making objects for the
sake of producing wealth rather than satisfying one's immediate needs.

tion of the last few centuries and generations. Improvements in mathematical, physical, chemical and biological science were prerequisites. Businessmen through engineers of different sorts, have laid hold of the new insights gained by scientific men into the hidden energies of nature, and have turned them to account. The modern mine, factory, railway, steamship, telegraph, all of the appliances and equipment of production, and transportation, express scientific knowledge. They would continue unimpaired even if the ordinary pecuniary accompaniments of economic activity were radically altered. In short, through the intermediary of invention, Bacon's watchword that knowledge is power and his dream of continuous empire over natural forces by means of natural science have been actualized. The industrial revolution by steam and electricity is the reply to Bacon's prophecy.

On the other hand, it is equally true that the needs of modern industry have been tremendous stimuli to scientific investigation. The demands of progressive production and transportation have set new problems to inquiry; the processes used in industry have suggested new experimental appliances and operations in science; the wealth rolled up in business has to some extent been diverted to endowment of research. The uninterrupted and pervasive interaction of scientific discovery and industrial application has fructified both science and industry, and has brought home to the contemporary mind the fact that the gist of scientific knowledge is control of natural energies. These four facts, natural science, experimentation, control and progress have been inextricably bound up together. That up to the present the application of the newer methods and results has influenced the means of life rather than its ends; or, better put, that human aims have so far been affected in an accidental rather than in an intelligently directed way, signifies that so far the change has been technical rather than human and moral, that it has been economic rather than adequately social. Put in the language of Bacon, this means that while we have been reasonably successful in obtaining command of nature by means of science, our science is not yet such that this command is systematically and preeminently applied to the relief of human estate. Such applications occur and in great numbers, but they are incidental, sporadic and external. And this limitation defines the specific problem of philosophical reconstruction at the present time. For it emphasizes the larger social deficiencies that require intelligent diagnosis, and projection of aims and methods.

It is hardly necessary to remind you however that marked political changes have already followed upon the new science and its industrial applications, and that in so far some directions of social development have at least been marked out. The growth of the new technique of industry has everywhere been followed by the fall of feudal institutions,[14] in which the social pattern was formed in agricultural occupations and military pursuits. Wherever business in the modern sense has gone, the tendency has been to transfer power from land to financial capital, from the country to the city, from the farm to factory, from social titles based on personal allegiance, service and protection, to those based on control of labor and exchange of goods. The change in the political centre of gravity has resulted in emancipating the individual from bonds of class and custom and in producing a political organization which depends less upon superior authority and more upon voluntary choice. Modern states, in other words, are regarded less as divine, and more as human works than they used to be; less as necessary manifestations of some supreme and overruling principles, and more as contrivances of men and women to realize their own desires.

The contract theory[15] of the origin of the state is a theory whose   20
falsity may easily be demonstrated both philosophically and historically. Nevertheless this theory has had great currency and influence. In form, it stated that some time in the past men voluntarily got together and made a compact with one another to observe certain laws and to submit to certain authority and in that way brought the state and the relation of ruler and subject into existence. Like many things in philosophy, the theory, though worthless as a record of fact, is of great worth as a symptom of the direction of human desire. It testified to a growing belief that the state existed to satisfy human needs and could be shaped by human intention and volition. Aristotle's theory that the state exists by nature failed to satisfy the thought of the seventeenth century because it seemed by making the state a product of nature to remove its constitution beyond human choice. Equally significant was the assumption of the contract theory that individuals by

---

[14]*feudal institutions* Because of the breakdown of local government in the Middle Ages, groups of people banded into units, usually based upon the agricultural resources of the area. The peasants came under the "protection" of the landholder, and the region was under the "protection" of the local nobleman. Knights were on call as a military force to be used locally when needed. Feudal institutions died as strong central governments were reestablished in the Renaissance.

[15]*the contract theory* Jean Jacques Rousseau asserted that the origin of society involved a kind of contract between people to appoint a leader and establish laws they could abide by. (See "The Social Contract" in Part One, pp. 55–75.) Dewey thinks this is quite unlikely, but it is interesting to note that contracts were a standard ingredient in the feudal system.

their personal decisions expressing their personal wishes bring the state into existence. The rapidity with which the theory gained a hold all over western Europe showed the extent to which the bonds of customary institutions had relaxed their grip. It proved that men had been so liberated from absorption in larger groups that they were conscious of themselves as individuals having rights and claims on their own account, not simply as members of a class, guild or social grade.

Side by side with this political individualism went a religious and 21 moral individualism. The metaphysical doctrine[16] of the superiority of the species to the individual, of the permanent universal to the changing particular, was the philosophic support of political and ecclesiastical institutionalism. The universal church was the ground, end and limit of the individual's beliefs and acts in spiritual matters, just as the feudal hierarchical organization was the basis, law and fixed limit of his behavior in secular affairs. The northern barbarians[17] had never completely come under the sway of classic ideas and customs. That which was indigenous where life was primarily derived from Latin sources was borrowed and more or less externally imposed in Germanic Europe. Protestantism marked the formal breaking away from the domination of Roman ideas.[18] It effected liberation of individual conscience and worship from control by an organized institution claiming to be permanent and universal. It cannot truly be said that at the outset the new religious movement went far in promoting freedom of thought and criticism, or in denying the notion of some supreme authority to which individual intelligence was absolutely in bonds. Nor at first did it go far in furthering tolerance or respect for divergency of moral and religious convictions. But practically it did tend to disintegration of established institutions. By multiplying sects and churches it encouraged at least a negative toleration of the right of individuals to judge ultimate matters for themselves. In time, there developed a formulated belief in the sacredness of individual conscience and in the right to freedom of opinion, belief and worship.

It is unnecessary to point out how the spread of this conviction 22 increased political individualism, or how it accelerated the willingness of men to question received ideas in science and philosophy—to think and observe and experiment for themselves. Religious individualism

---

[16]***metaphysical doctrine*** In metaphysics the species naturally precedes the individual in importance for purposes of classification.

[17]***northern barbarians*** Germanic tribes. The term originated with the Greeks, who thought all foreigners spoke a language that sounded like *"bar-bar-bar-bar."*

[18]***Roman ideas*** The beliefs of the Roman Catholic church.

served to supply a much needed sanction to initiative and independence of thought in all spheres, even when religious movements officially were opposed to such freedom when carried beyond a limited point. The greatest influence of Protestantism was, however, in developing the idea of the personality of every human being as an end in himself. When human beings were regarded as capable of direct relationship with God, without the intermediary of any organization like the Church, and the drama of sin, redemption and salvation was something enacted within the innermost soul of individuals rather than in the species of which the individual was a subordinate part, a fatal blow was struck at all doctrines which taught the subordination of personality—a blow which had many political reverberations in promoting democracy. For when in religion the idea of the intrinsic worth of every soul as such was proclaimed, it was difficult to keep the idea from spilling over, so to say, into secular relationships.

The absurdity is obvious of trying in a few paragraphs to summarize movements in industry, politics and religion whose influence is still far from exhausted and about which hundreds and thousands of volumes have been written. But I shall count upon your forbearance to recall that these matters are alluded to only in order to suggest some of the forces that operated to mark out the channels in which new ideas ran. First, there is the transfer of interest from the eternal and universal to what is changing and specific, concrete—a movement that showed itself practically in carrying over of attention and thought from another world to this, from the supernaturalism characteristic of the Middle Ages to delight in natural science, natural activity and natural intercourse. Secondly, there is the gradual decay of the authority of fixed institutions and class distinctions and relations, and a growing belief in the power of individual minds, guided by methods of observation, experiment and reflection, to attain the truths needed for the guidance of life. The operations and results of natural inquiry gained in prestige and power at the expense of principles dictated from high authority. 23

Consequently principles and alleged truths are judged more and more by criteria of their origin in experience and their consequences of weal and woe in experience, and less by criteria of sublime origin from beyond everyday experience and independent of fruits in experience. It is no longer enough for a principle to be elevated, noble, universal and hallowed by time. It must present its birth certificate, it must show under just what conditions of human experience it was generated, and it must justify itself by its works, present and potential. Such is the inner meaning of the modern appeal to experience as an 24 ultimate criterion of value and validity. In the third place, great store is set upon the idea of progress. The future rather than the past dominates the imagination. The Golden Age[19] lies ahead of us not behind us. Everywhere new possibilities beckon and arouse courage and effort. The great French thinkers[20] of the later eighteenth century borrowed this idea from Bacon and developed it into the doctrine of the indefinite perfectibility of mankind on earth. Man is capable, if he will but exercise the required courage, intelligence and effort, of shaping his own fate. Physical conditions offer no insurmountable barriers. In the fourth place, the patient and experimental study of nature, bearing fruit in inventions which control nature and subdue her forces to social uses, is the method by which progress is made. Knowledge is power and knowledge is achieved by sending the mind to school to nature to learn her processes of change.

In this lecture . . . I can hardly close better than by reference to the new responsibilities imposed upon philosophy and the new opportunities opened to it. Upon the whole, the greatest effect of these changes up to date has been to substitute an Idealism based on epistemology, or the theory of knowledge, for the Idealism based on the metaphysics of classic antiquity. 25

Earlier modern philosophy (even though unconsciously to itself) had the problem of reconciling the traditional theory of the rational and ideal basis, stuff and end of the universe with the new interest in individual mind and the new confidence in its capacities. It was in a dilemma. On the one hand, it had no intention of losing itself in a materialism which subordinated man to physical existence and mind to matter—especially just at the moment when in actual affairs man and mind were beginning to achieve genuine rule over nature. On the other hand, the conception that the world as it stood was an embodiment of a fixed and comprehensive Mind or Reason was uncongenial to those whose main concern was with the deficiencies of the world and with an attempt to remedy them. The effect of the objective theological idealism that had developed out of classic metaphysical idealism was to make the mind submissive and acquiescent. The new individualism chafed under the restrictions imposed upon it by the no- 26

---

[19]**The Golden Age**   A persistent myth, ancient and modern, of a former wonderful age of perfection.

[20]**French thinkers**   The *Philosophes*, primarily Denis Diderot (1713–1784), editor of the first great encyclopedia, and Voltaire (1694–1778), an anticleric whose satires helped promote secularism in France.

tion of a universal reason which had once and for all shaped nature and destiny.

In breaking away from antique and medieval thought, accordingly, early modern thought continued the older tradition of a Reason that creates and constitutes the world, but combined it with the notion that this Reason operates through the human mind, individual or collective. This is the common note of idealism sounded by all the philosophies of the seventeenth and eighteenth centuries, whether belonging to the British school of Locke, Berkeley, and Hume[21] or the Continental school of Descartes.[22] In Kant[23] as everybody knows the two strains came together; and the theme of the formation of the knowable world by means of a thought that operated exclusively through the human knower became explicit. Idealism ceased to be metaphysical and cosmic in order to become epistemological and personal.

It is evident that this development represents merely a transitional stage. It tried, after all, to put the new wine in the old bottles. It did not achieve a free and unbiased formulation of the meaning of the power to direct nature's forces through knowledge—that is, purposeful, experimental action to reshape beliefs and institutions. The ancient tradition was still strong enough to project itself unconsciously into men's ways of thinking, and to hamper and compromise the expression of the really modern forces and aims. Essential philosophic reconstruction represents an attempt to state these causes and results in a way freed from incompatible inherited factors. It will regard intelligence not as the original shaper and final cause of things, but as the

27

28

---

[21]*British school of Locke, Berkeley, and Hume* These philosophers, John Locke (1632–1704), Bishop George Berkeley (1685–1753), and David Hume (1711–1776), concentrated on questions of the human understanding and reasoning capacities. They directed attention inward to the nature of thought and knowledge.

[22]*Continental school of Descartes* René Descartes (1596–1650) invented the phrase "I think, therefore I am" *(cogito ergo sum)*. Having found that one fact about which one cannot doubt, he built a philosophy that seemed coherent and workable. His *Discourse on the Method of Rightly Conducting the Reason* (1637) is his effort to provide a workable logic and method of inquiry into the nature of things. One unfortunate teaching of his work is the split between body and mind, belief in which dominated thought for centuries.

[23]*Immanuel Kant (1724–1804)* A German philosopher whose theories focused on the way we know things. Dewey is saying that a shift took place through Kant in which the universe was seen as a "creation" of the mind, but because all minds function similarly, a creation which can be known. The shift in philosophical thought was toward theories of how we know what we know.

purposeful energetic reshaper of those phases of nature and life that obstruct social well-being. It esteems the individual not as an exaggeratedly self-sufficient Ego which by some magic creates the world, but as the agent who is responsible through initiative, inventiveness and intelligently directed labor for re-creating the world, transforming it into an instrument and possession of intelligence.

The train of ideas represented by the Baconian Knowledge is Power 29 thus failed in getting an emancipated and independent expression. These became hopelessly entangled in standpoints and prepossessions that embodied a social, political and scientific tradition with which they were completely incompatible. The obscurity, the confusion of modern philosophy is the product of this attempt to combine two things which cannot possibly be combined either logically or morally. Philosophic reconstruction for the present is thus the endeavor to undo the entanglement and to permit the Baconian aspirations to come to a free and unhindered expression.

QUESTIONS

1. For whom was this work intended? What kind of audience would most respond to this essay today?
2. What kinds of power does Dewey discuss in this piece?
3. According to this selection, under what conditions does learning take place? What circumstances best benefit the expansion of the mind?
4. What are the three kinds of learning Bacon describes? Are you familiar with any of these kinds of learning?
5. Find a passage that you feel is not totally clear and try to explain it to someone. Does the discussion which follows the passage help clarify it for you?
6. What does "pragmatism" mean?

WRITING ASSIGNMENTS

1. In paragraph 15, Dewey says that travel and exploration in Bacon's time led to the expansion of human horizons. New contacts bred a desire for more new contacts, and thought itself was stimulated. In paragraph 14 he says that "Contrast between peoples and races previously isolated is always, I think, most fruitful and influential for change when psychological and industrial changes coincide with and reinforce each other." What is your experience with such contrast and change? Do you agree that these factors are mind-expanding and influential? If so, write an essay explaining

why so many people resist such changes. What is to be feared from them? What is to be gained from them?

2. Dewey describes an educational situation that he relates to Aristotle in which someone in the educational process is presumed to be in possession of the truth. Those who do not possess the truth are being educated in order to possess it. Write an essay on your experience in education. Have you been in (or are you still in) a situation that resembles the one described by Dewey? What are the implications of someone (or several people) possessing knowledge while others do not? How do those implications affect the learning experience? Have you been in a situation in which this is not true? Which situation is better for learning?

3. One of the interesting consequences for pragmatism is that moral values cannot be considered to be absolute. If they were, then the reconstructed philosophy would be backward looking rather than forward looking. Therefore, each moral situation has to be viewed as unique. It must be tested by experiment to see if it really works to produce happiness and to improve the estate of mankind. What are the benefits to society of such a philosophical view? What are the problems with that view? Consider such moral absolutes as "Thou shalt not lie" and "Thou shalt not kill." Do you think that most people today are pragmatic or traditional in their application of moral values? Make your essay take a clear stand on pragmatism and moral values.

4. In paragraphs 2 and 3, Dewey explores Bacon's three kinds of learning: the delicate, the fantastic, and the contentious. Begin an essay by defining these kinds of learning; then explore whether such kinds of learning still exist in your own educational environment. Are there studies which are only ornamental and not useful to your life? Are there people who adhere to superstitious beliefs as if they constituted genuine knowledge? Are there situations in which people are browbeaten into accepting a contentious "truth" as if it were their own? Do you think the learning environment is still seriously plagued with the kinds of learning that troubled Bacon?

5. Use Dewey's technique of meditation by meditating on the following "aphorism" abstracted from paragraph 23: "The authority of institutions has decayed, while the educated individual mind has developed the capacity to decide the truth for itself." Use whatever information you can inventory from the selection or from events or details outside it. You may interview friends or look for newspaper articles on the decay of authority. If you disagree with the aphorism, rewrite it in a negative form. Use Dewey's device of summarizing a historical situation; repeat the aphorism when necessary. But do not lose sight of it. Make it the subject of your essay.

ALBERT CAMUS

———◦≫◦———

The Myth of Sisyphus

*A*LBERT CAMUS *(1913–1960) was a French writer trained in philosophy. He was born in Algeria and educated at the University of Algiers. In the 1940s Algeria was French, and after it became independent in the late 1950s Camus was eventually able to maintain his French citizenship. His health was never very good, so that whereas his father died in World War I in 1914, Camus was prevented from serving in the French armed forces during World War II because of recurrent attacks of tuberculosis. Tuberculosis also prevented him from becoming a teacher of philosophy.*

After trying a number of jobs, Camus discovered that he was a proficient journalist. He worked in both Paris and Algeria during the German occupation of France, 1940–1944. He even wrote for the French Resistance underground paper, Combat. *It was during this time that he began to write philosophical fiction and commentary. His first novel,* The Stranger, *was written in 1940 and was published in 1942. Its theme was the absurd. It told the story of a strange man living in a moral wilderness, a man who was unable to see life as*

From *The Myth of Sisyphus.* Translated by Justin O'Brien.

meaningful in any genuine way. Camus's preoccupation with the absurd, his great theme in literature, was partly a product of his anxieties over World War II, following so soon after the massively destructive and absurd World War I. Such exercises in futility may have had an influence on the creation of such a figure as Camus's Sisyphus.

The Myth of Sisyphus (1942), a philosophical essay on suicide and the absurd, is among the best-known works of Camus. Others are his novels, The Plague *(1947) and* The Fall *(1956), which made him one of the most widely read writers of his time. Also a gifted playwright, he wrote* Caligula *(1945),* State of Siege *(1948), and* The Just Assassins *(1950).* The Rebel *(1951) is an extended essay on political dissent. Camus won the Nobel Prize for Literature in 1957. Perhaps it is a mere twist of irony—or an expression of fate congruent with his own philosophy—but Camus died in a car crash at the age of forty-six, in his literary prime.*

The Myth of Sisyphus is a meditation on the theme of suicide. Camus was faced with the view that life itself is without meaning. The traditional values had been weakened by war, lack of faith in authority, attacks on religion, and the worldwide economic depression that cast everything into doubt. Camus was searching through his own thoughts about suicide to see if he could come to a conclusion about life that would be positive. His question was: How does humankind live in an absurd world? He treats the ancient myth as an allegory for our own time.

Sisyphus, Camus explains, was assigned a repetitive task which would last through eternity as a punishment for his "rebellion" against the gods. Sisyphus loved life so much that he ignored the gods' command to remain underground in Hades. As a result, they gave him the task of pushing a rock up a mountain, and when he reached the top, it rolled back down the hill again. Then he had to push the rock up the hill again. In examining this myth, Camus found a parallel for man's condition in a world without meaning, a world whose values were self-created or at least community-created, a world in which many people do things as repetitive and as meaningless as what Sisyphus must do. It is Camus's insight into the awareness of Sisyphus during the process—his insight into the fact that Sisyphus knows what he is doing—that gives Camus courage. Like Sisyphus, Camus tells us, humans make their own fate, their own choices, and to that extent are in control of their own destinies. By defying the gods, Sisyphus made his choice and his fate.

CAMUS'S RHETORIC

The most important rhetorical device Camus uses is part of style: the allegory. Allegory is a narrative in which the principal characters or situations stand for other people or situations. It is a carefully extended metaphor. In the case of The Myth of Sisyphus *Camus tells us the classical myth, giving us some of the details as they appear in Homer and others as they appear in the works of other classical writers. Then he gives us his version of what Sisyphus is doing in the myth, hoping that we will eventually see how Sisyphus's situation is parallel to that of most people.*

In addition to his use of allegory, Camus is also adept at another classical form, the aphorism, or pithy statement. The aphorism is a saying that seems to contain wisdom, partly because it resembles all the wise old saws that have been passed down through the ages, such as "A penny saved is a penny earned" or "A setting hen never lays." Camus uses such aphoristic lines as "There is no fate that cannot be surmounted by scorn" (para. 6); "There is no sun without shadow" (para. 9); "One always finds one's burden again" (para. 10). There is a folksy quality to these aphorisms, but they also operate to make the entire tone of the passage seem wise and thoughtful.

One very interesting aspect of this selection is the mode of address Camus uses. He seems to have imagined a specific kind of audience, and he goes about addressing it in a manner suggesting unusual intimacy. He begins sentences with "As you have already grasped . . ." and "Again I fancy Sisyphus returning toward his rock," and begins the final paragraph with "I leave Sisyphus at the foot of the mountain!" The result is that we have the impression that we have overheard a one-sided conversation, pleasant and intimate.

The Myth of Sisyphus

The gods had condemned Sisyphus to ceaselessly rolling a rock to   1
the top of a mountain, whence the stone would fall back of its own
weight. They had thought with some reason that there is no more
dreadful punishment than futile and hopeless labor.

If one believes Homer,[1] Sisyphus was the wisest and most prudent   2
of mortals. According to another tradition, however, he was disposed
to practice the profession of highwayman. I see no contradiction in
this. Opinions differ as to the reasons why he became the futile laborer
of the underworld. To begin with, he is accused of a certain levity in
regard to the gods. He stole their secrets. Ægina,[2] the daughter of Æsopus, was carried off by Jupiter. The father was shocked by that disappearance and complained to Sisyphus. He, who knew of the abduction,
offered to tell about it on condition that Æsopus would give water to
the citadel of Corinth. To the celestial thunderbolts he preferred the
benediction of water. He was punished for this in the underworld. Homer tells us also that Sisyphus had put Death in chains. Pluto[3] could
not endure the sight of his deserted, silent empire. He dispatched the
god of war, who liberated Death from the hands of her conqueror.

It is said also that Sisyphus, being near to death, rashly wanted to   3
test his wife's love. He ordered her to cast his unburied body into the
middle of the public square. Sisyphus woke up in the underworld. And
there, annoyed by an obedience so contrary to human love, he obtained
from Pluto permission to return to earth in order to chastise his wife.
But when he had seen again the face of this world, enjoyed water and
sun, warm stones and the sea, he no longer wanted to go back to the
infernal darkness. Recalls, signs of anger, warnings were of no avail.
Many years more he lived facing the curve of the gulf, the sparkling
sea, and the smiles of earth. A decree of the gods was necessary.

---

[1]**Homer** This ancient Greek poet portrays Sisyphus in the *Iliad* (vi. 153 ff.).

[2]**Aegina** Jupiter seduced her in the form of a flame. When Aesopus bribed Sisyphus
with water and discovered who had taken his daughter, Jupiter hurled thunderbolts at
Aesopus and turned him back. Aegina seems to have perished in the storm.

[3]**Pluto** God of the underworld.

Mercury[4] came and seized the impudent man by the collar and, snatching him from his joys, led him forcibly back to the underworld, where his rock was ready for him.

You have already grasped that Sisyphus is the absurd hero. He *is*, as much through his passions as through his torture. His scorn of the gods, his hatred of death, and his passion for life won him that unspeakable penalty in which the whole being is exerted toward accomplishing nothing. This is the price that must be paid for the passions of this earth. Nothing is told us about Sisyphus in the underworld. Myths are made for the imagination to breathe life into them. As for this myth, one sees merely the whole effort of a body straining to raise the huge stone, to roll it and push it up a slope a hundred times over; one sees the face screwed up, the cheek tight against the stone, the shoulder bracing the clay-covered mass, the foot wedging it, the fresh start with arms outstretched, the wholly human security of two earth-clotted hands. At the very end of his long effort measured by skyless space and time without depth, the purpose is achieved. Then Sisyphus watches the stone rush down in a few moments toward that lower world whence he will have to push it up again toward the summit. He goes back down to the plain. 4

It is during that return, that pause, that Sisyphus interests me. A face that toils so close to stones is already stone itself! I see that man going back down with a heavy yet measured step toward the torment of which he will never know the end. That hour like a breathing space which returns as surely as his suffering, that is the hour of consciousness. At each of those moments when he leaves the heights and gradually sinks toward the lairs of the gods, he is superior to his fate. He is stronger than his rock. 5

If this myth is tragic, that is because its hero is conscious. Where would his torture be, indeed, if at every step the hope of succeeding upheld him? The workman of today works every day in his life at the same tasks, and this fate is no less absurd. But it is tragic only at the rare moments when it becomes conscious. Sisyphus, proletarian of the gods, powerless and rebellious, knows the whole extent of his wretched condition: it is what he thinks of during his descent. The lucidity that was to constitute his torture at the same time crowns his victory. There is no fate that cannot be surmounted by scorn. 6

---

[4]**Mercury** The messenger of the gods; also the Italian god of merchants, particularly grain dealers.

If the descent is thus sometimes performed in sorrow, it can also 7
take place in joy. This word is not too much. Again I fancy Sisyphus
returning toward his rock, and the sorrow was in the beginning. When
the images of earth cling too tightly to memory, when the call of happiness becomes too insistent, it happens that melancholy rises in
man's heart: this is the rock's victory, this is the rock itself. The
boundless grief is too heavy to bear. These are our nights of Gethsemane.[5] But crushing truths perish from being acknowledged. Thus,
Oedipus[6] at the outset obeys fate without knowing it. But from the
moment he knows, his tragedy begins. Yet at the same moment, blind
and desperate, he realizes that the only bond linking him to the world
is the cool hand of a girl. Then a tremendous remark rings out: "Despite so many ordeals, my advanced age and the nobility of my soul
make me conclude that all is well." Sophocles' Oedipus, like Dostoevsky's Kirilov,[7] thus gives the recipe for the absurd victory. Ancient
wisdom confirms modern heroism.

One does not discover the absurd without being tempted to write 8
a manual of happiness. "What! by such narrow ways—?" There is but
one world, however. Happiness and the absurd are two sons of the
same earth. They are inseparable. It would be a mistake to say that
happiness necessarily springs from the absurd discovery. It happens as
well that the feeling of the absurd springs from happiness. "I conclude
that all is well," says Oedipus, and that remark is sacred. It echoes in
the wild and limited universe of man. It teaches that all is not, has not
been, exhausted. It drives out of this world a god who had come into
it with dissatisfaction and a preference for futile sufferings. It makes
of fate a human matter, which must be settled among men.

All Sisyphus' silent joy is contained therein. His fate belongs to 9
him. His rock is his thing. Likewise, the absurd man, when he contemplates his torment, silences all the idols. In the universe suddenly restored to its silence, the myriad wondering little voices of the earth
rise up. Unconscious, secret calls, invitations from all the faces, they
are the necessary reverse and price of victory. There is no sun without

---

[5]**nights of Gethsemane**   This is a reference to Christ's discussions with his apostles
and agonizing prayer in the garden of Gethsemane on the evening before his crucifixion.

[6]**Oedipus**   In the play *Oedipus the King* by Sophocles (495–406 B.C.), Oedipus, who had
been told his fate and moved to another country to escape it, ironically moved to exactly
the place where his fate—to kill his father and marry his mother—was to be carried out.

[7]**Dostoevsky's Kirilov**   This is a reference to Alexey Nilitch Kirilov, a character in
the novel *The Possessed* (1871) by Russian novelist Fëdor Dostoevsky (1821–1881). Kirilov, an existentialist, kills himself. He is the subject of a chapter in *The Myth of
Sisyphus*.

shadow, and it is essential to know the night. The absurd man says yes and his effort will henceforth be unceasing. If there is a personal fate, there is no higher destiny, or at least there is but one which he concludes is inevitable and despicable. For the rest, he knows himself to be the master of his days. At that subtle moment when man glances backward over his life, Sisyphus returning toward his rock, in that slight pivoting he contemplates that series of unrelated actions which becomes his fate, created by him, combined under his memory's eye and soon sealed by his death. Thus, convinced of the wholly human origin of all that is human, a blind man eager to see who knows that the night has no end, he is still on the go. The rock is still rolling.

I leave Sisyphus at the foot of the mountain! One always finds 10
one's burden again. But Sisyphus teaches the higher fidelity that negates the gods and raises rocks. He too concludes that all is well. This universe henceforth without a master seems to him neither sterile nor futile. Each atom of that stone, each mineral flake of that night-filled mountain, in itself forms a world. The struggle itself toward the heights is enough to fill a man's heart. One must imagine Sisyphus happy.

QUESTIONS

1. What does Camus mean by "absurd"?
2. Why was Sisyphus condemned to roll the rock up the mountain repeatedly, forever?
3. What was Sisyphus's attitude toward the gods?
4. When is Camus's interest in Sisyphus most engaged? What part of Sisyphus's "journey" most impresses him?
5. What kind of gods seem to be portrayed in the myth?

WRITING ASSIGNMENTS

1. In paragraph 4, Camus speaks of a scorn for the gods that Sisyphus both feels and expresses. As clearly as possible, define what Camus means by such scorn, then explain what a modern equivalent for the scorn of the gods might be. Consider what the gods meant to Sisyphus, what their power was, and what they controlled. Then consider what, in modern life, would be their equivalent and what the consequences of scorning them might be.
2. What does Camus mean by stating that "One always finds one's burden again" (para. 10)? Consider this statement in regard to creating one's fate. What are the modern equivalents for the burden that Camus refers to?

3. Do you agree with Camus's final statement, "One must imagine Sisyphus happy"? What would Camus's reasons be for arriving at that conclusion? What reasons would there be for assuming that Camus is wrong? If you assume that Camus is wrong, what does that imply for your understanding of what Camus is trying to say in the entire essay? Why is it important that we accept Camus's view regarding the happiness of Sisyphus? Draft an essay that focuses on these questions.

4. Camus wrote this work as part of a long study of suicide. His efforts were directed, at an extremely dark time in history, toward finding reasons for avoiding suicide. What is there in the story of Sisyphus that makes suicide less an option for Camus? Why would it help Camus face life and struggle onward even in the face of the absurd? How does Camus make Sisyphus a symbol for mankind?

5. The gods imagined that there could be no more dreadful punishment than futile and hopeless labor. Is this belief true? Consider that the gods imagine a punishment that lasts for all eternity, and therefore "death" or annihilation are impossible punishments. Is it true, as Camus asserts in paragraph 6, that the workman of today suffers a fate similar to that of Sisyphus? Are most people condemned to repeating the same futile gestures again and again? Is the work most people do similar to, or different from, that of Sisyphus? Is their condition therefore similar to, or different from, that of Sisyphus?

6. Consider some of the statements Camus makes about fate. Inventory the essay for them. What, according to Camus, is fate? Be sure to look up the word in a good dictionary. Also, look up the words "tragedy" and "tragic." What is their connection with fate? Write an essay relying on the statements you have found which will clarify the nature of fate as Camus sees it. Be sure to consider such issues as what Camus means when he says that there is no fate that cannot be surmounted by scorn (para. 6). Also, consider the ways in which someone like Sisyphus—or even you—can be said to be fashioning his own fate.

PART FIVE

ARTS AND LETTERS

———❧———

George Santayana
Gyorgy Kepes ··· *Susanne K. Langer*
A. C. Bradley ··· *T. S. Eliot*

INTRODUCTION

ALL THE GREAT societies of the past have left evidence of a powerful interest in art, and it must be assumed that art is a major priority of civilization itself. Art is the expression of a society, in a sense its definition. The selections in this part are philosophical in tone. Some are written by noted philosophers, some by creative writers. All consider aspects of art that have been current in modern thought since the turn of the century. They reveal that in our time we have been struggling to clarify questions that still mystify us about the arts.

George Santayana was a noted philosopher whose works in aesthetics, the philosophy of art, were quite influential in the early years of this century. He is interested in the nature of beauty and the relationship of the philosophy of art to the philosophical concerns of ethics and morals. Since both aesthetics and ethics depend on questions of choice, they are related. Santayana interprets questions of choice interestingly: ethics is concerned with avoidance, with what not to do. Aesthetics has traditionally been concerned with preference—choosing that which is beautiful. Santayana believes that art and religion are products of the human imagination, and as such he thinks that they are to be especially valued. The connection between the contemplation of beauty and the contemplation of right action has, then, special relevance for him in all his thinking about art.

An eminent designer and teacher, Gyorgy Kepes believes that the arts have a significant function in our lives. Because our world is characterized by extraordinary industrial progress and because most of us live in cities, we have been torn away from our traditional foundations in nature. We no longer feel that we are part of a cycle of growth, as our forebears did. Kepes fears that we have lost our inner harmony and must somehow recover "the continuity between man and nature." The only way to do that, he believes, is through the artistic experience. Although Kepes believes that love is also a means by which we can restore the inner harmonies that are essential to happy living, he feels that art is more properly his subject. Specifically, it is the experience of the arts that restores us and makes us feel whole. He quotes the eighteenth-century German poet Novalis in urging us to understand the "fervent kinship with all things" through art.

The capacity of the arts to express and interpret emotions for us is at the center of Susanne K. Langer's "Expressiveness." Her contention is that there is a congruence between certain feelings or emotions and certain works of art. Furthermore, she holds that there is an important sense in which the arts can educate our emotional lives. This insight has special value for us, since education is aimed primarily at the rational mind. Education of the emotions is rarely if ever attempted in our schools—except, as Langer suggests, in our involvement with the arts. Her emphasis on expressiveness offers a fascinating insight into our relationship to the arts.

The last two selections in this part focus on literature, particularly on poetry. A. C. Bradley was one of the most important literary critics of the later nineteenth and early twentieth centuries. His work on Shakespeare pointed to directions that are yet to be fully explored. His work is still admired and still quite influential—a comment that can be made of very few critics of that time. In "Poetry for Poetry's Sake" Bradley examines the question of whether it is the subject, the substance, or the form of a poem that makes it great. In the process of wrestling with this question, Bradley analyzes the confusions of thought that abound on this issue. His clarity of mind—his capacity to treat each aspect of his thesis separately and with extraordinary precision—makes this essay unusual and striking. Bradley's wide reading in significant literature is evident in this piece and assures us that his observations about literature are based on a rich background and experience. By unraveling the question of what it means to consider poetry for its own sake, Bradley raises intriguing issues that remain central to any consideration of poetry.

T. S. Eliot's famous essay, "Tradition and the Individual Talent," pushes us toward a consideration of the role of history in poetry. Every major writer must find a place in the tradition of poetry, particularly the poetry of his or her own culture. Every writer is aware of the achievements of the past, and some writers are so acutely aware of those achievements that they see themselves as being in competition with the great writers of the past. But Eliot's contention is incisive. He contends that when a contemporary poet accomplishes a major achievement, the entire tradition itself is altered. Eliot implies, in other words, that the achievements of the present can affect those of the past. This is an extraordinary thesis, one which has affected literary critics profoundly for several decades. Eliot is himself a major modern poet, but he is, as well, among the most traditional poets of this century. The tensions he perceives in the relationship between tradition and talent are those he felt himself.

The rhetorical resources of these writers center on the topic of definition. Each realizes that one of the first requirements of clear exposition is the careful definition of key terms. Therefore, most of these writers isolate specific terms for careful study. That study usually turns out to be a study in definition.

But these writers are also gifted analysts. Their subject, arts and letters, is not a simple one to write about. Its inherent complexity is such that it cannot be dealt with head on. Rather, it must be treated point by point, with a careful discussion of each of several significant aspects of the key issues. The nature of beauty, the nature of poetry itself—these are subjects that can be elucidated only by the most carefully detailed considerations. Each writer brings special rhetorical skills to the task of thinking about art. They are skills that make an abstract and difficult task more tractable.

GEORGE SANTAYANA

The Nature of Beauty

GEORGE SANTAYANA (1863–1952) spent much of his life feeling like a displaced person. He was born in Madrid and died in Rome. He spent much of his childhood in Boston and went to Harvard University, where he began teaching in 1889. He was on the faculty of Harvard as professor of philosophy at the same time William James was there. When he secured an inheritance in 1912, he left teaching and spent the rest of his life in Europe, settling in a convent in Rome to reflect and write. His major works are the five-volume The Life of Reason (1906), Scepticism and Animal Faith (1923), and the four-volume Realms of Being (1927–1940).

Santayana was a noted philosopher whose thought had a significant impact on his century. Yet he never developed any school or group of followers, and he never attached himself to any of the several schools that flourished in his time. In some ways he was a rather practical thinker, assuming that the material world was the source on which the world of thought depends. He believed, however, that all that was worthwhile in human experience had developed from the imagination. And for this reason he particularly valued art and reli-

---

From *The Sense of Beauty.*

521

gion, although he was never in any sense committed to a specific religious view. Of art, he said simply that it is the most splendid creation of man's reason.

As an aesthetician, he wrote extensively on art, emphasizing the fact that because it deals with human values, it is related to the field of ethics, which deals with moral values. Much of the selection presented here is devoted to the question of values and to the connection between aesthetics and ethics. Because Santayana is interested in making a series of fine distinctions in this piece, each section is carefully reasoned and argued. Some sections are difficult and require patient examination.

Santayana thought that art was of immense significance in the life of humankind. In this selection he is deeply concerned with the concept of beauty, which occupied most thinkers about art during the late nineteenth century, when he wrote this work (1896). He sees beauty as a value with certain qualities which are essential to isolate. For example, he says that "Beauty is pleasure regarded as the quality of a thing" (para. 48). But, in the process of reaching the point that enables him to say this, he reveals the ramifications of all the ideas that go into such an apparently straightforward statement.

SANTAYANA'S RHETORIC

Santayana was often regarded as a remarkably graceful writer. He published several volumes of poetry, and his novel, The Last Puritan (1936), was exceptionally popular. Santayana's style is often remarkable. Sentences such as the following are noteworthy simply for their style: "The objects thus conceived and distinguished from our ideas of them, are at first compacted of all the impressions, feelings, and memories, which offer themselves for association and fall within the vortex of the amalgamating imagination" (para. 42). What this sentence says is that the imagination operates on our perception of things in order to give us our basic impression of them. The appropriateness of the image of the vortex is such that the concept becomes not only clearer but palpable and evident.

There is another achievement which makes this essay rhetorically significant, the handling of the common topic of definition. The entire work is a study of the nature of beauty, with its primary energy devoted to establishing a definition that satisfies the requirements set out in the opening paragraph: "A definition that should really define must be nothing less than the exposition of the origin, place, and

elements of beauty as an object of human experience." Santayana attempts to provide such a definition.

Along with the task of definition comes the task of establishing
the distinction between aesthetics and ethics, since both concern
themselves with values. The fact that aesthetics does concern itself
with values is the subject of paragraphs 1–8. Paragraphs 7–15 examine the rational aspects of preference, since beauty is that which is
preferred. In establishing the distinction between the moral and the
aesthetic, Santayana considers the difference between such things as
work and play. He then takes a number of qualities—disinterestedness (being valued in itself, not for what it can do), objectivity, and
universality—and examines them in turn. When he has completed his
examination of these issues, he is in a position to entitle the last
section of the work "The Definition of Beauty" (paras. 48–53).

As an extended definition, the work is remarkable. It demonstrates the fact that a full definition has to take into account many
problems which at first glance do not appear to be a part of the original issue. But Santayana persists, moves patiently, and shows us—if
not a satisfactory definition—at least what the materials of a definition must be.

------------<>------------

The Nature of Beauty

The Philosophy of Beauty
Is a Theory of Values

It would be easy to find a definition of beauty that should give in a   1
few words a telling paraphrase of the word. We know on excellent
authority that beauty is truth, that it is the expression of the ideal, the
symbol of divine perfection, and the sensible manifestation of the
good. A litany of these titles of honor might easily be compiled, and
repeated in praise of our divinity. Such phrases stimulate thought and
give us a momentary pleasure, but they hardly bring any permanent
enlightenment. A definition that should really define must be nothing
less than the exposition of the origin, place, and elements of beauty as
an object of human experience. We must learn from it, as far as pos-

sible, why, when, and how beauty appears, what conditions an object must fulfill to be beautiful, what elements of our nature make us sensible of beauty, and what the relation is between the constitution of the object and the excitement of our susceptibility. Nothing less will really define beauty or make us understand what esthetic appreciation is. The definition of beauty in this sense will be the task of this whole book, a task that can be only very imperfectly accomplished within its limits.

The historical titles of our subject may give us a hint towards the beginning of such a definition. Many writers of the last century called the philosophy of beauty *Criticism*, and the word is still retained as the title for the reasoned appreciation of works of art. We could hardly speak, however, of delight in nature as criticism. A sunset is not criticized; it is felt and enjoyed. The word "criticism," used on such an occasion, would emphasize too much the element of deliberate judgment and of comparison with standards. Beauty, although often so described, is seldom so perceived, and all the greatest excellences of nature and art are so far from being approved of by a rule that they themselves furnish the standard and ideal by which critics measure inferior effects.

This age of science and of nomenclature[1] has accordingly adopted a more learned word, *Esthetics*, that is, the theory of perception or of susceptibility. If criticism is too narrow a word, pointing exclusively to our more artificial judgments, esthetics seems to be too broad and to include within its sphere all pleasures and pains, if not all perceptions whatsoever. Kant[2] used it, as we know, for his theory of time and space as forms of all perception; and it has at times been narrowed into an equivalent for the philosophy of art.

If we combine, however, the etymological meaning of criticism with that of esthetics, we shall unite two essential qualities of the theory of beauty. Criticism implies judgment, and esthetics perception. To get the common ground, that of perceptions which are critical, or judgments which are perceptions, we must widen our notion of deliberate criticism so as to include those judgments of value which are instinctive and immediate, that is, to include pleasures and pains; and at the same time we must narrow our notion of esthetics so as to exclude all perceptions which are not appreciations, which do not find a value in their objects. We thus reach the sphere of critical or appre-

2

3

4

---

[1]*nomenclature* naming things; in this case, classification.

[2]*Immanuel Kant (1724–1804)* A German idealist philosopher who held that our perceptions of space and time are entirely limited by our senses.

ciative perception, which is, roughly speaking, what we mean to deal with. And retaining the word "esthetics," which is now current, we may therefore say that esthetics is concerned with the perception of values. The meaning and conditions of value are, then, what we must first consider.

Since the days of Descartes[3] it has been a conception familiar to philosophers that every visible event in nature might be explained by previous visible events, and that all the motions, for instance, of the tongue in speech, or of the hand in painting, might have merely physical causes. If consciousness is thus accessory to life and not essential to it, the race of man might have existed upon the earth and acquired all the arts necessary for its subsistence without possessing a single sensation, idea, or emotion. Natural selection might have secured the survival of those automata[4] which made useful reactions upon their environment. An instinct of self-preservation would have been developed, dangers would have been shunned without being feared, and injuries revenged without being felt.

In such a world there might have come to be the most perfect organization. There would have been what we should call the expression of the deepest interests and the apparent pursuit of conceived goods. For there would have been spontaneous and ingrained tendencies to avoid certain contingencies[5] and to produce others; all the dumb show[6] and evidence of thinking would have been patent to the observer. Yet there would surely have been no thinking, no expectation, and no conscious achievement in the whole process.

The onlooker might have feigned ends and objects of forethought, as we do in the case of the water that seeks its own level, or in that of the vacuum which nature abhors. But the particles of matter would have remained unconscious of their collocation,[7] and all nature would have been insensible of their changing arrangement. We only, the possible spectators of that process, by virtue of our own interests and habits, could see any progress or culmination in it. We should see culmination where the result attained satisfied our practical or esthetic demands, and progress wherever such a satisfaction was approached.

---

[3]*René Descartes (1596–1650)* French philosopher famous for the expression "I think, therefore I am" *(cogito ergo sum),* which he uses as a premise upon which to build his philosophy, tracing one cause-effect relationship after another.

[4]*automata* robots, unfeeling beings.

[5]*contingencies* developments.

[6]*dumb show* pantomime, pretense.

[7]*collocation* gathering, the nature of their organization.

But apart from ourselves, and our human bias, we can see in such a mechanical world no element of value whatever. In removing consciousness, we have removed the possibility of worth.

But it is not only in the absence of all consciousness that value 8
would be removed from the world; by a less violent abstraction from the totality of human experience, we might conceive beings of a purely intellectual cast, minds in which the transformations of nature were mirrored without any emotion. Every event would then be noted, its relations would be observed, its recurrence might even be expected; but all this would happen without a shadow of desire, of pleasure, or of regret. No event would be repulsive, no situation terrible. We might, in a word, have a world of idea without a world of will. In this case, as completely as if consciousness were absent altogether, all value and excellence would be gone. So that for the existence of good in any form it is not merely consciousness but emotional consciousness that is needed. Observation will not do, appreciation is required.

Preference Is Ultimately Irrational

We may therefore at once assert this axiom, important for all moral 9
philosophy and fatal to certain stubborn incoherences of thought, that there is no value apart from some appreciation of it, and no good apart from some preference of it before its absence or its opposite. In appreciation, in preference, lie the root and essence of all excellence. Or, as Spinoza[8] clearly expresses it, we desire nothing because it is good, but it is good only because we desire it.

It is true that in the absence of an instinctive reaction we can still 10
apply these epithets by an appeal to usage. We may agree that an action is bad or a building good, because we recognize in them a character which we have learned to designate by that adjective; but unless there is in us some trace of passionate reprobation or of sensible delight, there is no moral or esthetic judgment. It is all a question of propriety of speech, and of the empty titles of things. The verbal and mechanical proposition, that passes for judgment of worth, is the great cloak of ineptitude in these matters. Insensibility is very quick in the conventional use of words. If we appealed more often to actual feelings, our judgments would be more diverse, but they would be more

---

[8]***Baruch Spinoza (1632–1677)*** Dutch philosopher who wrote extensively on morals and on biblical criticism. His chief work is on ethics.

legitimate and instructive. Verbal judgments are often useful instruments of thought, but it is not by them that worth can ultimately be determined.

Values spring from the immediate and inexplicable reaction of vital [11] impulse, and from the irrational part of our nature. The rational part is by its essence relative; it leads us from data to conclusions, or from parts to wholes; it never furnishes the data with which it works. If any preference or precept were declared to be ultimate and primitive, it would thereby be declared to be irrational, since mediation, inference, and synthesis[9] are the essence of rationality. The idea of rationality is itself as arbitrary, as much dependent on the needs of a finite organization, as any other ideal. Only as ultimately securing tranquillity of mind, which the philosopher instinctively pursues, has it for him any necessity. In spite of the verbal propriety of saying that reason demands rationality, what really demands rationality, what makes it a good and indispensable thing and gives it all its authority, is not its own nature, but our need of it both in safe and economical action and in the pleasures of comprehension.

It is evident that beauty is a species of value, and what we have [12] said of value in general applies to this particular kind. A first approach to a definition of beauty has therefore been made by the exclusion of all intellectual judgments, all judgments of matter of fact or of relation. To substitute judgments of fact for judgments of value, is a sign of a pedantic and borrowed criticism. If we approach a work of art or nature scientifically, for the sake of its historical connections or proper classification, we do not approach it esthetically. The discovery of its date or of its author may be otherwise interesting; it only remotely affects our esthetic appreciation by adding to the direct effect certain associations. If the direct effect were absent, and the object in itself uninteresting, the circumstances would be immaterial. Molière's *Misanthrope*[10] says to the court poet who commends his sonnet as written in a quarter of an hour,

> *Voyons, monsieur, le temps ne fait rien à l'affaire,*

---

[9]*mediation, inference, and synthesis* The process of observing, drawing conclusions, and putting the conclusions to work.

[10]*Molière's* **Misanthrope** Molière was the stage name of Jean-Baptiste Poquelin (1622–1673), great French comic playwright and actor. In *The Misanthrope*, the puritanical title character despises and denounces the human weaknesses and vices of all the other characters, but is shown to be subject to them himself. The line means: "See here, sir, time has nothing to do with it." The point is that talent, not time, is what counts.

and so we might say to the critic that sinks into the archaeologist, show us the work, and let the date alone.

In an opposite direction the same substitution of facts for values 13 makes its appearance, whenever the reproduction of fact is made the sole standard of artistic excellence. Many half-trained observers condemn the work of some naïve or fanciful masters with a sneer, because, as they truly say, it is out of drawing. The implication is that to be correctly copied from a model is the prerequisite of all beauty. Correctness is, indeed, an element of effect and one which, in respect to familiar objects, is almost indispensable, because its absence would cause a disappointment and dissatisfaction incompatible with enjoyment. We learn to value truth more and more as our love and knowledge of nature increase. But fidelity is a merit only because it is in this way a factor in our pleasure. It stands on a level with all other ingredients of effect. When a man raises it to a solitary preeminence and becomes incapable of appreciating anything else, he betrays the decay of esthetic capacity. The scientific habit in him inhibits the artistic.

That facts have a value of their own, at once complicates and ex- 14 plains this question. We are naturally pleased by every perception, and recognition and surprise are particularly acute sensations. When we see a striking truth in any imitation we are therefore delighted, and this kind of pleasure is very legitimate, and enters into the best effects of all the representative arts. Truth and realism are therefore esthetically good, but they are not all sufficient, since the representation of everything is not equally pleasing and effective. The fact that resemblance is a source of satisfaction justifies the critic in demanding it, while the esthetic insufficiency of such veracity shows the different value of truth in science and in art. Science is the response to the demand for information, and in it we ask for the whole truth and nothing but the truth. Art is the response to the demand for entertainment, for the stimulation of our senses and imagination, and truth enters into it only as it subserves these ends.

Even the scientific value of truth is not, however, ultimate or ab- 15 solute. It rests partly on practical, partly on esthetic interests. As our ideas are gradually brought into conformity with the facts by the painful process of selection—for intuition runs equally into truth and into error, and can settle nothing if not controlled by experience—we gain vastly in our command over our environment. This is the fundamental value of natural science, and the fruit it is yielding in our day. We have no better vision of nature and life than some of our predecessors, but we have greater material resources. To know the truth about the composition and history of things is good for this reason. It is also good because of the enlarged horizon it gives us, because the spectacle of nature is a marvelous and fascinating one, full of a serious sadness and large peace, which gives us back our birthright as children of the planet and naturalizes us upon the earth. This is the poetic value of the scientific *Weltanschauung*.[11] From these two benefits, the practical and the imaginative, all the value of truth is derived.

Esthetic and moral judgments are accordingly to be classed together in contrast to judgments intellectual; they are both judgments of value, while intellectual judgments are judgments of fact. If the latter have any value, it is only derivative, and our whole intellectual life has its only justification in its connection with our pleasures and pains. 16

Contrast between Moral and Esthetic Values

The relation between esthetic and moral judgments, between the spheres of the beautiful and the good, is close, but the distinction between them is important. One factor of this distinction is that while esthetic judgments are mainly positive, that is, perceptions of good, moral judgments are mainly and fundamentally negative, or perceptions of evil. Another factor of the distinction is that whereas, in the perception of beauty, our judgment is necessarily intrinsic and based on the character of the immediate experience, and never consciously on the idea of an eventual utility in the object, judgments about moral worth, on the contrary, are always based, when they are positive, upon the consciousness of benefits probably involved. Both these distinctions need some elucidations. 17

Hedonistic ethics[12] have always had to struggle against the moral sense of mankind. Earnest minds, that feel the weight and dignity of life, rebel against the assertion that the aim of right conduct is enjoyment. Pleasure usually appears to them as a temptation, and they sometimes go so far as to make avoidance of it a virtue. The truth is that morality is not mainly concerned with the attainment of pleasure; it is rather concerned, in all its deeper and more authoritative maxims, with the prevention of suffering. There is something artificial in the 18

---

[11]**Weltanschauung** A German term meaning a comprehensive world view, especially from a distinct intellectual position.

[12]**Hedonistic ethics** A reference to the classical view of hedonists who predicated all their behavior on pleasurable sensations.

deliberate pursuit of pleasure; there is something absurd in the obligation to enjoy oneself. We feel no duty in that direction; we take to enjoyment naturally enough after the work of life is done, and the freedom and spontaneity of our pleasures are what is most essential to them.

The sad business of life is rather to escape certain dreadful evils to 19
which our nature exposes us—death, hunger, disease, weariness, isolation, and contempt. By the awful authority of these things which stand like specters behind every moral injunction, conscience in reality speaks, and a mind which they have duly impressed cannot but feel, by contrast, the hopeless triviality of the search for pleasure. It cannot but feel that a life abandoned to amusement and to changing impulses must run unawares into fatal dangers. The moment, however, that society emerges from the early pressure of the environment and is tolerably secure against primary evils, morality grows lax. The forms that life will further assume are not to be imposed by moral authority, but are determined by the genius of the race, the opportunities of the moment, and the tastes and resources of individual minds. The reign of duty gives place to the reign of freedom, and the law and the covenant to the dispensation of grace.[13]

The appreciation of beauty and its embodiment in the arts are ac- 20
tivities which belong to our holiday life, when we are redeemed for the moment from the shadow of evil and the slavery to fear, and are following the bent of our nature where it chooses to lead us. The values, then, with which we here deal are positive; they were negative in the sphere of morality. The ugly is hardly an exception, because it is not the cause of any real pain. In itself it is rather a source of amusement. If its suggestions are vitally repulsive, its presence becomes a real evil towards which we assume a practical and moral attitude. And, correspondingly, the pleasant is never, as we have seen, the object of a truly moral injunction.

Work and Play

We have here, then, an important element of the distinction be- 21
tween esthetic and moral values. It is the same that has been pointed

---

[13]***dispensation of grace*** According to some Christian thinkers, the Old Testament stressed following the law as the means to salvation, and the New Testament stressed God's free granting of grace to replace the demands of the law.

to in the famous contrast between work and play. These terms may be used in different senses and their importance in moral classification differs with the meaning attached to them. We may call everything play which is useless activity, exercise that springs from the physiological impulse to discharge the energy which the exigencies of life have not called out. Work will then be all action that is necessary or useful for life. Evidently if work and play are thus objectively distinguished as useful and useless action, work is a eulogistic[14] term and play a disparaging one. It would be better for us that all our energy should be turned to account, that none of it should be wasted in aimless motion. Play, in this sense, is a sign of imperfect adaptation. It is proper to childhood, when the body and mind are not yet fit to cope with the environment, but it is unseemly in manhood and pitiable in old age, because it marks an atrophy[15] of human nature, and a failure to take hold of the opportunities of life.

Play is thus essentially frivolous. Some persons, understanding the 22 term in this sense, have felt an aversion, which every liberal mind will share, to classifying social pleasures, art, and religion under the head of play, and by that epithet condemning them, as a certain school seems to do, to gradual extinction as the race approaches maturity. But if all the useless ornaments of our life are to be cut off in the process of adaptation, evolution would impoverish instead of enriching our nature. Perhaps that is the tendency of evolution, and our barbarous ancestors amid their toils and wars, with their flaming passions and mythologies, lived better lives than are reserved to our well-adapted descendants.

We may be allowed to hope, however, that some imagination 23 may survive parasitically even in the most serviceable brain. Whatever course history may take—and we are not here concerned with prophecy—the question of what is desirable is not affected. To condemn spontaneous and delightful occupations because they are useless for self-preservation shows an uncritical prizing of life irrespective of its content. For such a system the worthiest function of the universe should be to establish perpetual motion. Uselessness is a fatal accusation to bring against any act which is done for its presumed utility, but those which are done for their own sake are their own justification.

At the same time there is an undeniable propriety in calling all the 24

---

[14]***eulogistic*** Full of praise. Santayana says that work would be considered good, play bad.
[15]***atrophy*** withering away.

liberal and imaginative activities of man play, because they are spontaneous, and not carried on under pressure of external necessity or danger. Their utility for self-preservation may be very indirect and accidental, but they are not worthless for that reason. On the contrary, we may measure the degree of happiness and civilization which any race has attained by the proportion of its energy which is devoted to free and generous pursuits, to the adornment of life and the culture of the imagination. For it is in the spontaneous play of his faculties that man finds himself and his happiness. Slavery is the most degrading condition of which he is capable, and he is as often a slave to the niggardliness of the earth and the inclemency of heaven, as to a master or an institution. He is a slave when all his energy is spent in avoiding suffering and death, when all his action is imposed from without, and no breath or strength is left him for free enjoyment.

Work and play here take on a different meaning, and become equivalent to servitude and freedom. The change consists in the subjective point of view from which the distinction is now made. We no longer mean by work all that is done usefully, but only what is done unwillingly and by the spur of necessity. By play we are designating, no longer what is done fruitlessly, but whatever is done spontaneously and for its own sake, whether it have or not an ulterior utility. Play, in this sense, may be our most useful occupation. So far would a gradual adaptation to the environment be from making this play obsolete, that it would tend to abolish work, and to make play universal. For with the elimination of all the conflicts and errors of instinct, the race would do spontaneously whatever conduced to its welfare and we should live safely and prosperously without external stimulus or restraint. . . .

In this second and subjective sense, then, work is the disparaging term and play the eulogistic one. All who feel the dignity and importance of the things of the imagination, need not hesitate to adopt the classification which designates them as play. We point out thereby, not that they have no value, but that their value is intrinsic, that in them is one of the sources of all worth. Evidently all values must be ultimately intrinsic. The useful is good because of the excellence of its consequences; but these must somewhere cease to be merely useful in their turn, or only excellent as means; somewhere we must reach the good that is good in itself and for its own sake, else the whole process is futile, and the utility of our first object illusory. We here reach the second factor in our distinction, between esthetic and moral values, which regards their immediacy. . . .

Esthetic and Physical Pleasure

We have now separated with some care intellectual and moral judg- 27 ments from the sphere of our subject, and found that we are to deal only with perceptions of value, and with these only when they are positive and immediate. But even with these distinctions the most remarkable characteristic of the sense of beauty remains undefined. All pleasures are intrinsic and positive values, but all pleasures are not perceptions of beauty. Pleasure is indeed the essence of that perception, but there is evidently in this particular pleasure a complication which is not present in others and which is the basis of the distinction made by consciousness and language between it and the rest. It will be instructive to notice the degrees of this difference.

The bodily pleasures are those least resembling perceptions of 28 beauty. By bodily pleasures we mean, of course, more than pleasures with a bodily seat; for that class would include them all, as well as all forms and elements of consciousness. Esthetic pleasures have physical conditions, they depend on the activity of the eye and the ear, of the memory and the other ideational functions[16] of the brain. But we do not connect those pleasures with their seats except in physiological studies; the ideas with which esthetic pleasures are associated are not the ideas of their bodily causes. The pleasures we call physical, and regard as low, on the contrary, are those which call our attention to some part of our own body, and which make no object so conspicuous to us as the organ in which they arise.

There is here, then, a very marked distinction between physical 29 and esthetic pleasure; the organs of the latter must be transparent, they must not intercept our attention, but carry it directly to some external object. The greater dignity and range of esthetic pleasure is thus made very intelligible. The soul is glad, as it were, to forget its connection with the body and to fancy that it can travel over the world with the liberty with which it changes the objects of its thought. The mind passes from China to Peru without any conscious change in the local tensions of the body. This illusion of disembodiment is very exhilarating, while immersion in the flesh and confinement to some organ gives a tone of grossness and selfishness to our consciousness. The generally meaner associations of physical pleasures also help to explain their comparative crudity.

---

[16]*ideational functions* Capacities of the mind to imagine and to conceive ideas.

The Differentia of Esthetic Pleasure
Not Its Disinterestedness

The distinction between pleasure and the sense of beauty has 30
sometimes been said to consist in the unselfishness of esthetic satisfaction. In other pleasures, it is said, we gratify our senses and passion;
in the contemplation of beauty we are raised above ourselves, the passions are silenced and we are happy in the recognition of a good that
we do not seek to possess. The painter does not look at a spring of
water with the eyes of a thirsty man, nor at a beautiful woman with
those of a satyr.[17] The difference lies, it is urged, in the impersonality
of the enjoyment. But this distinction is one of intensity and delicacy,
not of nature, and it seems satisfactory only to the least esthetic
minds.

In the second place, the supposed disinterestedness of esthetic de- 31
lights is not truly fundamental. Appreciation of a picture is not identical with the desire to buy it, but it is, or ought to be, closely related
and preliminary to that desire. The beauties of nature and of the plastic arts are not consumed by being enjoyed; they retain all the efficacy
to impress a second beholder. But this circumstance is accidental, and
those esthetic objects which depend upon change and are exhausted in
time, as are all performances, are things the enjoyment of which is an
object of rivalry and is coveted as much as any other pleasure. And
even plastic beauties can often not be enjoyed except by a few, on
account of the necessity of travel or other difficulties of access, and
then this esthetic enjoyment is as selfishly pursued as the rest.

The truth which the theory is trying to state seems rather to be 32
that when we seek esthetic pleasures we have no further pleasure in
mind; that we do not mix up the satisfactions of vanity and proprie-
torship with the delight of contemplation. This is true, but it is true
at bottom of all pursuits and enjoyments. Every real pleasure is in one
sense disinterested. It is not sought with ulterior motives, and what
fills the mind is no calculation, but the image of an object or event,
suffused with emotion. A sophisticated consciousness may often take
the idea of self as the touchstone of its inclinations; but this self, for
the gratification and aggrandizement of which a man may live, is itself
only a complex of aims and memories, which once had their direct
objects, in which he had taken a spontaneous and unselfish interest.
The gratifications which, merged together, make the selfishness are

---

[17]*satyr*   Classical figure, half man, half goat; usually a symbol of lust.

each of them ingenuous,[18] and no more selfish than the most altruistic, impersonal emotion. The content of selfishness is a mass of unselfishness. There is no reference to the nominal essence called oneself either in one's appetites or in one's natural affections; yet a man absorbed in his meat and drink, in his houses and lands, in his children and dogs, is called selfish because these interests, although natural and instinctive in him, are not shared by others. The unselfish man is he whose nature has a more universal direction, whose interests are more widely diffused.

But as impersonal thoughts are such only in their object, not in   33
their subject or agent, since all thoughts are the thoughts of somebody: so also unselfish interests have to be somebody's interests. If we were not interested in beauty, if it were of no concern to our happiness whether things were beautiful or ugly, we should manifest not the maximum, but the total absence of esthetic faculty. The disinterestedness of this pleasure is, therefore, that of all primitive and intuitive satisfactions, which are in no way conditioned by a reference to an artificial general concept, like that of the self, all the potency of which must itself be derived from the independent energy of its component elements. I care about myself because "myself" is a name for the things I have at heart. To set up the verbal figment of personality and make it an object of concern apart from the interests which were its content and substance, turns the moralist, into a pedant, and ethics into a superstition. The self which is the object of *amour propre*[19] is an idol of the tribe, and needs to be disintegrated into the primitive objective interests that underlie it before the cultus of it can be justified by reason.

The Differentia of Esthetic Pleasure
Not Its Universality

The supposed disinterestedness of our love of beauty passes into   34
another characteristic of it often regarded as essential—its universality. The pleasures of the senses have, it is said, no dogmatism in them; that anything gives me pleasure involves no assertion about its capac-

---

[18]*ingenuous* Innocent. *Altruistic* means unselfish.

[19]**amour propre** French term meaning self-esteem; self-conceit. The reference to "an idol of the tribe" is from Francis Bacon's "The Four Idols." The term means an intellectual prejudice common to all people. (See pages 327–343.) *Cultus* is a general acceptance or belief.

ity to give pleasure to another. But when I judge a thing to be beautiful, my judgment means that the thing is beautiful in itself, or (what
is the same thing more critically expressed) that it should seem so to
everybody. The claim to universality is, according to this doctrine, the
essence of the esthetic; what makes the perception of beauty a judgment rather than a sensation. All esthetic precepts would be impossible, and all criticism arbitrary and subjective, unless we admit a paradoxical universality in our judgment, the philosophical implications
of which we may then go on to develop. But we are fortunately not
required to enter the labyrinth into which this method leads; there is
a much simpler and clearer way of studying such questions, which is
to challenge and analyze the assertion before us and seek its basis in
human nature. Before this is done, we should run the risk of expanding
a natural misconception or inaccuracy of thought into an inveterate
and pernicious prejudice by making it the center of an elaborate construction.

That the claim of universality is such a natural inaccuracy will not 35
be hard to show. There is notoriously no great agreement upon esthetic matters; and such agreement as there is, is based upon similarity of origin, nature, and circumstance among men, a similarity which,
where it exists, tends to bring about identity in all judgments and feelings. It is unmeaning to say that what is beautiful to one man *ought*
to be beautiful to another. If their senses are the same, their associations and dispositions similar, then the same thing will certainly be
beautiful to both. If their natures are different, the form which to one
will be entrancing will be to another even invisible, because his clas-
sifications and discriminations in perception will be different, and he
may see a hideous detached fragment or a shapeless aggregate of
things, in what to another is a perfect whole—so entirely are the unities of objects unities of function and use. It is absurd to say that what
is invisible to a given being *ought* to seem beautiful to him. Evidently
this obligation of recognizing the same qualities is conditioned by the
possession of the same faculties. But no two men have exactly the
same faculties, nor can things have for any two exactly the same
values.

What is loosely expressed by saying that anyone ought to see this 36
or that beauty is that he would see it if his disposition, training, or
attention were what our ideal demands for him; and our ideal of what
any one should be has complex but discoverable sources. We take, for
instance, a certain pleasure in having our own judgments supported by
those of others; we are intolerant, if not of the existence of a nature
different from our own, at least of its expression in words and judg-

ments. We are confirmed or made happy in our doubtful opinions by seeing them accepted universally. We are unable to find the basis of our taste in our own experience and therefore refuse to look for it there. If we were sure of our ground, we should be willing to acquiesce in the naturally different feelings and ways of others, as a man who is conscious of speaking his language with the accent of the capital confesses its arbitrariness with gaiety, and is pleased and interested in the variations of it he observes in provincials; but the provincial is always zealous to show that he has reason and ancient authority to justify his oddities. So people who have no sensations, and do not know why they judge, are always trying to show that they judge by universal reason.

Thus the frailty and superficiality of our own judgments cannot 37 brook[20] contradiction. We abhor another man's doubt when we cannot tell him why we ourselves believe. Our ideal of other men tends therefore to include the agreement of their judgments with our own; and although we might acknowledge the fatuity of this demand in regard to natures very different from the human, we may be unreasonable enough to require that all races should admire the same style of architecture, and all ages the same poets.

The great actual unity of human taste within the range of conventional history helps the pretension. But in principle it is untenable. 38 Nothing has less to do with the real merit of a work of imagination than the capacity of all men to appreciate it; the true test is the degree and kind of satisfaction it can give to him who appreciates it most. The symphony would lose nothing if half mankind had always been deaf, as nine-tenths of them actually are to the intricacies of its harmonies; but it would have lost much if no Beethoven[21] had existed. And more: incapacity to appreciate certain types of beauty may be the condition *sine qua non*[22] for the appreciation of another kind; the greatest capacity both for enjoyment and creation is highly specialized and exclusive, and hence the greatest ages of art have often been strangely intolerant.

The invectives of one school against another, perverse as they are 39 philosophically, are artistically often signs of health, because they indicate a vital appreciation of certain kinds of beauty, a love of them that has grown into a jealous passion. The architects that have pieced

---

[20]**brook**   tolerate or permit.

[21]***Ludwig van Beethoven (1770–1827)*** Great German Romantic composer whose symphonies helped expand and define the form. He himself grew deaf in his late years.

[22]**sine qua non** A Latin term meaning the indispensable condition (lit., "without which nothing").

out the imperfections of ancient buildings with their own thoughts, like Charles V[23] when he raised his massive palace beside the Alhambra, may be condemned from a certain point of view. They marred much by their interference; but they showed a splendid confidence in their own intuitions, a proud assertion of their own taste, which is the greatest evidence of esthetic sincerity. On the contrary, our own gropings, eclecticism,[24] and archaeology are the symptoms of impotence. If we were less learned and less just, we might be more efficient. If our appreciation were less general, it might be more real, and if we trained our imagination into exclusiveness, it might attain to character.

The Differentia of Esthetic Pleasure: Its Objectification

There is, however, something more in the claim to universality in esthetic judgments than the desire to generalize our own opinions. There is the expression of a curious but well-known psychological phenomenon, namely, the transformation of an element of sensation into the quality of a thing. If we say that other men should see the beauties we see, it is because we think those beauties *are in the object*, like its color, proportion, or size. Our judgment appears to us merely the perception and discovery of an external existence, of the real excellence that is without. But this notion is radically absurd and contradictory. Beauty, as we have seen, is a value; it cannot be conceived as an independent existence which affects our senses and which we consequently perceive. It exists in perception, and cannot exist otherwise. A beauty not perceived is a pleasure not felt, and a contradiction. But modern philosophy has taught us to say the same thing of every element of the perceived world; all are sensations; and their grouping into objects imagined to be permanent and external is the work of certain habits of our intelligence. We should be incapable of surveying or retaining the diffused experiences of life, unless we organized and classified them, and out of the chaos of impressions framed the world of conventional and recognizable objects.

How this is done is explained by the current theories of perception. 41

---

[23]*Charles V (1500–1558)* Holy Roman Emperor from 1519 to 1556, and also, as Charles I, king of Spain from 1516 to 1556. He defaced the Alhambra, an Islamic palace and fortress built in Granada, Spain, between 1248 and 1356, and built his own square palace next to it in a radically different style.

[24]*eclecticism* Habit of joining together many different styles.

External objects usually affect various senses at once, the impressions of which are thereby associated. Repeated experiences of one object are also associated on account of their similarity; hence a double tendency to merge and unify into a single percept, to which a name is attached, the group of those memories and reactions which in fact had one external thing for their cause. But this percept, once formed, is clearly different from those particular experiences out of which it grew. It is permanent, they are variable. They are but partial views and glimpses of it. The constituted notion therefore comes to be the reality, and the materials of it merely the appearance. The distinction between substance and quality, reality and appearance, matter and mind, has no other origin.

The objects thus conceived and distinguished from our ideas of   42
them, are at first compacted of all the impressions, feelings, and memories, which offer themselves for association and fall within the vortex[25] of the amalgamating imagination. Every sensation we get from a thing is originally treated as one of its qualities. Experiment, however, and the practical need of a simpler conception of the structure of objects lead us gradually to reduce the qualities of the object to a minimum, and to regard most perceptions as an effect of those few qualities upon us. These few primary qualities, like extension which we persist in treating as independently real and as the quality of a substance, are those which suffice to explain the order of our experiences. All the rest, like color, are relegated to the subjective sphere, as merely effects upon our minds, and apparent or secondary qualities of the object.

But this distinction has only a practical justification. Convenience   43
and economy of thought alone determine what combination of our sensations we shall continue to objectify and treat as the cause of the rest. The right and tendency to be objective is equal in all, since they are all prior to the artifice of thought by which we separate the concept from its materials, the thing from our experiences.

The qualities which we now conceive to belong to real objects are   44
for the most part images of sight and touch. One of the first classes of effects to be treated as secondary were naturally pleasures and pains, since it could commonly conduce very little to intelligent and successful action to conceive our pleasures and pains as resident in objects. But emotions are essentially capable of objectification, as well as impressions of sense; and one may well believe that a primitive and

---

[25]**vortex** a rushing swirl, as is made by the water one lets out of a tub.

inexperienced consciousness would rather people the world with ghosts of its own terrors and passions than with projections of those luminous and mathematical concepts which as yet it could hardly have formed.

This animistic[26] and mythological habit of thought still holds its 45 own at the confines of knowledge, where mechanical explanations are not found. In ourselves, where nearness makes observation difficult, in the intricate chaos of animal and human life, we still appeal to the efficacy of will and ideas, as also in the remote night of cosmic and religious problems. But in all the intermediate realm of vulgar day, where mechanical science has made progress, the inclusion of emotional or passionate elements in the concept of the reality would be now an extravagance. Here our idea of things is composed exclusively of perceptual elements, of the ideas of form and of motion.

The beauty of objects, however, forms an exception to this rule. 46 Beauty is an emotional element, a pleasure of ours, which nevertheless we regard as a quality of things. But we are now prepared to understand the nature of this exception. It is the survival of a tendency originally universal to make every effect of a thing upon us a constituent of its conceived nature. The scientific idea of a thing is a great abstraction from the mass of perceptions and reactions which that thing produces; the esthetic idea is less abstract, since it retains the emotional reaction, the pleasure of the perception, as an integral part of the conceived thing.

Nor is it hard to find the ground of this survival in the sense of 47 beauty of an objectification of feeling elsewhere extinct. Most of the pleasures which objects cause are easily distinguished and separated from the perception of the object: the object has to be applied to a particular organ, like the palate, or swallowed like wine, or used and operated upon in some way before the pleasure arises. The cohesion is therefore slight between the pleasure and the other associated elements of sense; the pleasure is separated in time from the perception, or it is localized in a different organ, and consequently is at once recognized as an effect and not as a quality of the object. But when the process of perception itself is pleasant, as it may easily be, when the intellectual operation, by which the elements of sense are associated and projected, and the concept of the form and substance of the thing produced, is naturally delightful, then we have a pleasure intimately

---

[26]*animistic* Assuming that objects have souls or spirits. A characteristic of many religions, ancient and modern.

bound up in the thing, inseparable from its character and constitution, the seat of which in us is the same as the seat of the perception. We naturally fail, under these circumstances, to separate the pleasure from the other objectified feelings. It becomes, like them, a quality of the object, which we distinguish from pleasures not so incorporated in the perception of things, by giving it the name of beauty.

The Definition of Beauty

We have now reached our definition of beauty, which, in the terms of our successive analysis and narrowing of the conception, is value positive, intrinsic, and objectified. Or, in less technical language, Beauty is pleasure regarded as the quality of a thing.   48

This definition is intended to sum up a variety of distinctions and identifications which should perhaps be here more explicitly set down. Beauty is a value, that is, it is not a perception of a matter of fact or of a relation: it is an emotion, an affection of our volitional and appreciative nature. An object cannot be beautiful if it can give pleasure to nobody: a beauty to which all men were forever indifferent is a contradiction in terms.   49

In the second place, this value is positive, it is the sense of the presence of something good, or (in the case of ugliness) of its absence. It is never the perception of a positive evil, it is never a negative value. That we are endowed with the sense of beauty is a pure gain which brings no evil with it. When the ugly ceases to be amusing or merely uninteresting and becomes disgusting, it becomes indeed a positive evil: but a moral and practical, not an esthetic, one. In esthetics that saying is true—often so disingenuous[27] in ethics—that evil is nothing but the absence of good: for even the tedium and vulgarity of an existence without beauty is not itself ugly so much as lamentable and degrading. The absence of esthetic goods is a moral evil: the esthetic evil is merely relative, and means less of esthetic good than was expected at the place and time. No form in itself gives pain, although some forms give pain by causing a shock of surprise even when they are really beautiful: as if a mother found a fine bull pup in her child's cradle, when her pain would not be esthetic in its nature.   50

Further, this pleasure must not be in the consequence of the utility of the object or event, but in its immediate perception; in other words,   51

---

[27]**disingenuous** insincere, not frank; willfully ignoring the truth.

beauty is an ultimate good, something that gives satisfaction to a natural function, to some fundamental need or capacity of our minds. Beauty is therefore a positive value that is intrinsic; it is a pleasure. These two circumstances sufficiently separate the sphere of esthetics from that of ethics. Moral values are generally negative, and always remote. Morality has to do with the avoidance of evil and the pursuit of good: esthetics only with enjoyment.

Finally, the pleasures of sense are distinguished from the perception of beauty, as sensation in general is distinguished from perception; by the objectification of the elements and their appearance as qualities rather of things than of consciousness. The passage from sensation to perception is gradual, and the path may be sometimes retraced: so it is with beauty and the pleasures of sensation. There is no sharp line between them, but it depends upon the degree of objectivity my feeling has attained at the moment whether I say "It pleases me," or "It is beautiful." If I am self-conscious and critical, I shall probably use one phrase; if I am impulsive and susceptible, the other. The more remote, interwoven, and inextricable the pleasure is, the more objective it will appear; and the union of two pleasures often makes one beauty. In Shakespeare's LIVth sonnet are these words: 52

> O how much more doth beauty beauteous seem
> By that sweet ornament which truth doth give!
> The rose looks fair, but fairer we it deem
> For that sweet odor which doth in it live.
> The canker-blooms have full as deep a dye
> As the perfumèd tincture of the roses,
> Hang on such thorns, and play as wantonly
> When summer's breath their maskèd buds discloses.
> But, for their beauty only is their show,
> They live unwooed and unrespected fade;
> Die to themselves. Sweet roses do not so:
> Of their sweet deaths are sweetest odors made.

One added ornament, we see, turns the deep dye, which was but show and mere sensation before, into an element of beauty and reality; and as truth is here the cooperation of perceptions, so beauty is the cooperation of pleasures. If color, form, and motion are hardly beautiful without the sweetness of the odor, how much more necessary would they be for the sweetness itself to become a beauty! If we had the perfume in a flask, no one would think of calling it beautiful: it would give us too detached and controllable a sensation. There would be no object in which it could be easily incorporated. But let it float from the garden, and it will add another sensuous charm to objects 53 simultaneously recognized, and help to make them beautiful. Thus beauty is constituted by the objectification of pleasure. It is pleasure objectified.

QUESTIONS

1. What does Santayana mean by the word "values"? What is a value in his terms?
2. What is the relationship of beauty to truth?
3. How are values perceived? Are values rational or emotional in nature?
4. Santayana says that "Beauty is a species of value" (para. 12). What does he seem to mean by this statement?
5. What is the scientific habit and what is its relation to truth?
6. What are the proper concerns of morality? Are they like or unlike the concerns of aesthetics?

WRITING ASSIGNMENTS

1. Santayana says that there is no value unless there is some appreciation of it (para. 9). Is this assertion true? Explain what leads Santayana to make this statement, then examine the strengths and weaknesses of his position. Consider the question of defining what a value is and what appreciation is.
2. Santayana has a great deal to say about the scientific attitude. Inventory the essay for his references to science, facts, and truth. What are his views on the usefulness of science? Refer to his comments on the "scientific habit" in paragraph 13 and to his comments on truth in subsequent paragraphs. How does the scientific attitude differ from the aesthetic attitude?
3. One comment Santayana makes is that "those [things] done for their own sake are their own justification" (para. 23). What do you do for its own sake? Is it its own justification? Is it related to the practice of science or of art? Do you think that your own experience supports Santayana's opinion or contradicts it? Make your essay support or oppose his views.
4. In paragraph 31, Santayana raises a touchy question: Should one dismiss all thoughts of ownership when appreciating a great painting? Is it really inappropriate to want to own a Picasso or a Rembrandt or any painting that one admires? Is, in fact, the admiration of beauty in general genuine only when questions of ownership or possession are dismissed from consideration? Or is it possible that the most intense and genuine appreciation of great art is almost always accompanied by desires of ownership and possession? If possible, answer these questions in an essay that refers to specific works of art, specific observations, and specific personal experiences.

5. In paragraph 37, Santayana talks about the fact that we like people to agree with our judgments: "Our ideal of other men tends therefore to include the agreement of their judgments with our own." Is this assertion generally true? Examine yourself and your friends in this regard. Do you find that most of your friends agree in judging the values of, say, popular or classical music, art, literature, and architecture? About which art form do you find the most heated disagreement? About which art form do you find the most intense agreement? You may choose a specific friend with whom to match your own interests and appreciation.

6. Beauty is one of the most difficult terms to define. You will notice that Santayana mentions few works of art, nor does he point to anything that is specifically beautiful (except for a sunset). As a result, his discussion is generally abstract. Offer your own definition of "the nature of beauty." In doing so, use any materials you find useful from Santayana's argument but try to make your definition clear, specific, concrete, and intelligible. Use the topic of definition as carefully as possible.

GYORGY KEPES

———❧———

Comments on Art

GYORGY KEPES *(b. 1906) has done distinguished work at the Massachusetts Institute of Technology that marks him as among a handful of thinkers who have been able to bridge the span between the arts and technology. Kepes was born in Hungary where he was educated in Budapest's Royal Academy of Fine Arts. He came to America in 1937 to head the Light and Color Department at the Institute of Design in Chicago. He has been a designer whose works have been exhibited widely in such museums as the Museum of Modern Art in New York City, the Institute of Contemporary Arts in Boston, Massachusetts, as well as in museums in Copenhagen, Amsterdam, and Rome, to name only a few.*

Kepes has been instrumental in fashioning the humanities program at MIT. Through his writings he has made an effort to demonstrate the integrity of the arts with nature, technology, and humankind. His books, Language of Vision *(1944) and* The New Landscape *(1956), have been influential in the struggle to demonstrate the significance of the arts in our lives.*

The selection that follows is an argumentative work that stresses the importance of the arts in helping us organize our inner harmonies. Kepes begins by comparing modern men and women to children who have lost their parents. He tells us that the rapid growth of technology combined with science's control over nature—and its subsequent distortion of nature—has ripped us from the emotional and cultural moorings that stabilized people for generations before us. Therefore, our task as modern people is to refashion for ourselves some form of inner harmony that will keep us emotionally and intellectually intact.

Kepes thinks that there are several guides to producing such a harmony. One of them is love, which he conceives as being both human and divine. Another is art and the artistic experience. His reasoning concerning art is quite careful, if rather brief. It centers on the capacity of the arts to organize our emotional experience and thus to put our inner lives into some significant order and harmony. He complains that as persons we have lost our capacity to see the world as a unified whole; instead, we see only a part of experience here, another part there. We cannot grasp the completeness of experience. Art is a guide to learning how we can do that.

Moreover, Kepes is concerned with our attitude toward nature. He complains—as have many philosophical thinkers since the early nineteenth century—that we have lost touch with nature and that the world of visual and emotional experience we have substituted for it is ugly and demoralizing. Kepes refers again and again to "the continuity between man and nature." We have lost that sense of continuity, and we need to restore it. That has become, he tells us, the task of humankind.

KEPES'S RHETORIC

Kepes presents an argument concerning the problems that we face in the contemporary world. He aims to convince us that since we have lost the sense of continuity that once existed between nature and us, we ourselves are essentially lost. Our guides to finding ourselves lie in two areas, love—which is not his primary subject in this essay—and the experience of the arts. The argument picks up the thread of the arts, explaining the nature of the artistic experience and its importance to us.

An important rhetorical device that Kepes uses is apparent in the first paragraph—the use of the topic of comparison—where he compares humankind to a lost child and then, in an extended analogy, shows why the comparison is appropriate. That the analogy is effective is clear; its effectiveness is a result of his immediate comparison of the abstract concept of the human situation to that of the very concrete image of the lost child. We 'must reconstruct our world through our own efforts. We are worse off than a lost child, because we have no parents to find; we are alone.

Another rhetorical device Kepes relies upon is the topic of testimony. Kepes frequently pauses to quote a noted authority on the subject of the ways in which the arts affect our lives, including Friedrich Nietzsche, William Butler Yeats, Alfred North Whitehead, William Morris, the poet Novalis, and others. Thus, he brings into his argument the testimony of important witnesses who obviously agree with his views. Doing this naturally strengthens and deepens the argument. The concerns of the authorities he quotes are not exactly the same as his; yet, his discussion is enriched by the use he makes of the quotations.

We are left with the impression that Kepes feels very deeply about the importance of the arts in our lives. He envisions us as engaged in a campaign to reform our environment and to bring ourselves closer to achieving the inner harmony that can make us at peace with ourselves and our world. Such a task is monumental. Simply getting it under way would be a great achievement.

Comments on Art

The present human situation resembles that of a lost child. The order, and thus the surety of existence, seem to be lost. Industrial civilization has torn us out of the relatedness that people knew in a smaller world. The forces of nature that were brought by gradual domestication into a human scale have again become alien forces: now they approach us menacingly along the avenues opened by science and technology. In this complex, changing world, we feel alone. We feel that we have lost parental guidance. Old mores, feelings and concepts which were both guides and shelter in a smaller and calmer world, have been swept away in the turmoil of new dynamic conditions. Like a lost child, we try to cope with the apparently hostile, new scale of things, without a measure to make them perceivable. We are even worse off than a lost child, for we have no hope of finding the parents, the old interpreters, because the world is on the move and this movement is not reversible. Our dominant reaction is fear—a fear which keeps us from accepting the challenge of our wider and potentially richer world. Insecure and afraid, we freeze our feelings and ideas, and we do not know how to take action to eliminate the basis of our fears.

No longer secure in our relationship to the world around us, we   2 lose our ability to live a free and complete life. Our self-confidence is gone; we are unable to respond with courageous acceptance to the challenges that face us. Instead of using all that we have—eye, heart, brain—mobilizing all our faculties and capacities in a common focus, we react with frantic one-sided intensity. One aspect of ourself lives at the expense of the other. Our thoughts disregard and discredit our emotions, push them into the background, and thus lose contact with the energy and richness the emotions may provide. Our feelings are thereby frustrated and go underground or into dangerous blind alleys. Our sensibilities are also frozen. We are incapable of absorbing the new landscape, with its wealth of new sensations; therefore we cannot reinforce ourselves with the joys of light, color and forms, the rhythm of sound and movement essential to healthy growth. The inner wholeness, the essential key to a healthy act is gone. Nietzsche[1] once commented on literature: "What is the characteristic of all literary decadence? It is that life no longer resides in the whole. The word gets the upper hand and jumps out of the sentence. The sentence stretches too far and obscures the meaning of the page. The page acquires life at the expense of the whole. The whole is no longer a whole." His comment is bitterly true for our contemporary life. Confused and cornered by the impact of the complex world, we have lost the ability to perceive the world as a connected whole and to react to it with healthy openness. The part has taken over the upper hand. With dazzling pace we shift focus from one aspect of our inner or outer horizon to another. Without an ability to live with undivided inner loyalties and without finding a sense of loyalty to the complete horizon of our contemporary scene, we gradually diminish our strength.

---

[1]*Friedrich Nietzsche (1844–1900)* German philosopher. His observation is about literature in a period of decline (decadence). His own period, the latter part of the nineteenth century, was sometimes styled as a decadent period. Yet the decadent period in modern literature, the 1880s and 1890s in Britain and France, produced much great writing. (See pages 209–211 for more on Nietzsche.)

The Tasks We Face

We have then two interdependent tasks in front of us. We have to span the gap between man and his newly won possessions, knowledge and power; to build a foundation safe and broad enough to hold our common physical life securely on a twentieth-century standard, and we have to build bridges within ourselves and reach an inner oneness, a union of our sensory, emotional and rational aspects of life. 3

What inner guide do we have to meet these tasks? To realize completeness, we have to have some inner models, some concrete vital experiences of order, harmony and self-realization. We have to have some inner seeds which contain patterns of "wholeness." As the perfectly patterned group of atoms, a small fraction of a cell, radiate orderly patterns and become the guide and guardian of the development of the organism, so we have to have in more complex dimensions guides and guardians. 4

Love is the closest to this inner model. Love in a personal or in a deep religious sense translates every experience to an embrace so that we project our basic sense of belonging to everything and everybody we may encounter. In love, or with a deep love, the world becomes a friendly world; the cloudy day becomes a sunny day and faces become the faces of friends. A strongly felt loyalty to somebody or a deeply felt loyalty to men generates a growing chain of loyalties to everything we encounter. 5

There is another inner model which parallels the role of love. Artistic experience in making or reliving an artistic form can also serve as an inner guide and guardian. 6

The Artistic Experience

What is the nature of an artistic experience? First of all it is an orderer. As common perception gathers a number of sense impressions into a *gestalt*,[2] a pattern-vision, this heightened perception of artistic vision collates sense impressions into vision of the high patterning of works of art, with their harmony, balance, melodic sequence and rhythm. The uncomplicated symmetry of prehistoric tools; the intri- 7

---

[2] **gestalt** German term for perceptible form, a basic pattern.

cate axial inversions of neolithic ornaments;[3] the rhythmic variations of Peruvian fabrics; the orderly pulsation of the mosaic of San Vitale;[4] and the convincing unity of shapes and colors in the paintings of Piero della Francesca,[5] Sesshu, Bellini, Juan Gris or Mondrian; all these visual syntheses document convincingly man's supreme ability to focus and unify the diffused variety of the changing, seen world. Our sensibilities need to be sustained with the joy of felt order. As a basic aspect of the human organism, the artistic form is a significant organizer of life, enabling us to deal with the environment and directing and controlling our development. Artistic images order our thoughts and feelings as the genetic material orders the composition, growth and reproduction of our bodies. The artistic images we share encode our common culture; our private images encode our inner, unique world, impressing on us both the richness of the sensed and the order of the understood.

But there is another still deeper role of the artistic experience. We 8 respond to the forms and images of artists because their harmonies, rhythms, colors, and shapes touch us not just on one level of our being or another, but, as Yeats[6] has put it: they "could not move us at all, if our thought did not rush out to the edge of our flesh and it is so with all good art, whether the victory of Samothrace which reminds the soles of our feet of swiftness, or the Odyssey that would send us out under the salt wind, or the young horsemen on the Parthenon that seem happier than our boyhood ever was, and in boyhood's way."

And between the pulsating life of our sensation and the intense 9 richness of our emotion up to their final symbolic focus there is a continuous analogue. In this aspect of many-layered, analogous experience, participation in a work of art often supplies us with deep ties with the world around us. The physical base outside us which stimulated us and our sensations within are bridged. Our sensations, feel-

---

[3]**neolithic ornaments** Stone Age decoration carved in complex swirls.

[4]**San Vitale** A church in Ravenna, Italy, whose ninth- and tenth-century mosaics are among the most beautiful in the world.

[5]**Piero della Francesca (1418–1492)** della Francesca and Giovanni Bellini (1430–1516) are Italian Renaissance painters; Sesshu (1420–1506) is a classic Japanese artist; Juan Gris (1887–1927) and Piet Mondrian (1874–1944) are modern painters. All are noted for their powerful sense of design.

[6]**William Butler Yeats (1865–1939)** Ireland's greatest modern poet. He refers to the Winged Victory of Samothrace, a Greek sculpture; Homer's Odyssey, a Greek epic; and the Parthenon, the Greek temple that stands above Athens. The young horsemen are part of the bas-relief procession on the Parthenon frieze. All these allude to the great Greek sense of harmony in design and art.

ings, and thoughts march in a unison of completeness. Whitehead[7] described religion as "world loyalty," and in a certain sense artistic experience leads us to such world loyalty. It gives us what one may express with a paradox, our vertical horizon, our depth horizon. For no level of human response is neglected in an optimum form of an artistic statement. Sensations, the emotional and rational illumination are spanned in a living, unbroken, complete spectrum. Through experiencing it we are bound with deep loyalties to our total horizon.

The Decay of the Artistic Experience

In a climate of chaos and frustration these basic keys to a richer life in art have also come close to disappearing. 10

The industrial world sprang up without regarding our human need to find what Walt Whitman[8] called the "primal sanities of nature." Our technical wonders have not provided us with the wide visions of harmony and order but, increasing without plan, have jumbled the basic wealth of the mechanical era into a dazzling kaleidoscopic pattern which shocks and numbs our sensibilities. 11

The modern metropolis, a giant focus of our unsettled world, spreads out upon the land in widening rings of visual disorder. At its core, bludgeoning us with their vulgar images, massive structures blot out open space; industrial areas beyond are dumped with factory buildings and dingy barracks where we house our poor; the residential fringes are dotted with characterless cottages repeated endlessly. Everywhere, smoke and dirt screen out the sun; and our containers, advertisements, commercial entertainment, films, our home furnishings and clothes, our gestures and facial expressions mount up to grotesque, formless aggregates lacking sincerity, scale, and cleanliness. 12

This is the world we continue to reproduce, and this is the world that shapes our vision. Our distorted surroundings, by distorting us, have robbed us of the power to make our experience rich and coherent. When visual responses are warped visual creativeness is impaired. 13

The starvation of the eye has paralleled the decline of the rhythmic joy in work. For the workers, unable to sense the total process of making, have been deprived of their power to organize their work rhyth- 14

---

[7]*Alfred North Whitehead (1861–1947)* English philosopher. (See the introduction to his essay on pages 391–393.)

[8]*Walt Whitman (1819–1892)* American poet whose *Leaves of Grass* (1855) was itself a call to the reintegration of the individual into more humane patterns of life.

mically and have lost the "joy in labor" that is the elementary sap of every creative act, and that William Morris[9] called their only birthright.

Because of these failings, the man of our time has come close to losing two of his important resources: the outer richness of the environment, and the inner richness of sensed unity derived from rhythmically articulated work.

But still more fatal, the creative vision has lost not only the basic nourishment of our sensations, but it has lost its broadest background—its relatedness to the complete natural world. The artist, like his fellow man, has gradually become closed in within a limited world. When scientific insights, with their magnificent constructs, encompassed and unified vistas of nature on a never dreamt of scale, the artist remained only an outsider hardly able to follow the outlines of the new wonderful spans of unity. While the scientists with uncompromising courage linked the old models of the planetary system with the new models of the smallest unit, the atom, and fused time and space and mass with energy in a consistent and legible construct, the artist timidly reduced his vistas to the narrow ranges of reacting to personal hurts.

Art and the Nature of Man

Our great task is to bring man in scale again with the entire horizon of nature, so that he can sense it in all its wealth and promises, harmonies and mysteries. In ignorance and pride and by insecurity, we have severed ourselves from our broader background. We have to re-establish our bonds and recognize our loyalties on this all-inclusive level. Eastern philosophy and art had an age-old awareness that men lived most fully by opening themselves to the universal rhythm of nature. With deep insights, Eastern philosophers and artists responded to inner and outer correspondences and reached stages of wonderful tranquillity. The artists of our century, groping for self-realization, for an inner freedom, for the true ecstasy of spontaneity, jealously followed the expressive intensity and spontaneity of oriental art. But they did so without recognizing that the freedom of oriental art grew from

[9]*William Morris (1834–1896)* An English craftsman, artist, and poet whose socialist views led him to help educate working people and try to help them gain a more integrated view of their lives through art. He was opposed to mass production and promoted a return to the older crafts.

its recognition of the continuity between man and nature. Our artists borrowed the exterior appearances and techniques of Eastern art, their calligraphic[10] fluency with the uninhibited traceries of lines, their moods of nature feelings; our architects borrowed the attitudes of blending the man-created shelter into its broadest natural abode.

If one were to write a synoptic history[11] of the last eighty years of 18 artistic transformations, the dominant thread would, I am sure, be the assimilation of Eastern dreams and vision. Underlying this assimilation is an important truth: artistic sensibility, the seismograph[12] of every creative act, has registered the main need of our time. It has sensed the urgent need to form a new sense of wholeness by accepting the deep continuities between man and nature.

"No one will fathom nature who possesses no sense of nature, no 19 inward organ for creating and dividing nature, who does not, as though spontaneously, recognize and distinguish nature everywhere, who does not with inborn creative joy, a rich and fervent kinship with all things, mingle with all of nature's creatures through the medium of feeling, who does not feel his way into them," wrote the German poet Novalis[13] at the beginning of the nineteenth century.

At the end of the century Charles S. Peirce[14] expressed the same 20 idea but with different emphasis: "That every scientific explanation of natural phenomenon is a hypothesis that there is something in nature to which the human reason is analogous; and that it really is so all the successes of science in its applications to human convenience are witnesses."

This has to be restated once more only with a yet still different 21 emphasis: Novalis's "fervent kinship with all things" can only be reached by being able to face these things in the natural world as it is given to us. But the world of nature known to our fathers is changed beyond recognition. Science has opened up new resources for new sights and sounds, new tastes and textures. To accept the essential

---

[10]*calligraphic* This term refers to handwriting as an art.

[11]*synoptic history* A general or summary view of history as a whole.

[12]*seismograph* Device for measuring earth tremors. Kepes is using a metaphor, implying that every creative act is like an earthquake.

[13]*Novalis (1722–1801)* German Romantic poet; his real name was Friedrich Leopold von Hardenberg. His "Hymn to the Night" was a religious and mystical poem written after the death of Sophie, the woman he was to marry. He was a poet of considerable power, and his works were very influential after his death.

[14]*Charles S. Peirce (1839–1914)* An American physicist and logician. His practice of symbolic logic became generally accepted in both logic and mathematics. He is also known for coining the term "pragmatism" as the description of a philosophical view.

continuity between man and nature, we have to accept nature in its new dimensions. And our artists will live up to their great historical challenge if they can embrace these new dimensions and make them their own.

QUESTIONS

1. What does Kepes mean by "artistic experience"? Does he mean creating works of art, appreciating them, or both?
2. In paragraphs 4, 5, and 6, Kepes talks about love as an inner loyalty. What does he mean by this idea?
3. Which quotations that Kepes uses from authorities on art seem most effective to you? Which quotations seem least effective?
4. Kepes begins a section of his essay with the subtitle "The Tasks We Face." What are those tasks?
5. How can the arts, according to Kepes, hope to help us with the tasks that lie ahead?

WRITING ASSIGNMENTS

1. Offer a critique of the analogy that opens the work in which Kepes compares modern people to a child who is lost. Examine this paragraph in detail, asking whether or not the analogy really holds for "the human situation" or whether it is forced. Are there aspects of the analogy that Kepes has perhaps ignored? Is it even more effective than he realized?
2. Inventory the essay for Kepes's references to nature. He constantly tells us that there has been a loss of "continuity between man and nature." What does he seem to mean by this claim? What kind of continuity seems to have existed in the past? What has caused us to lose this continuity? What can we do to recover it? Do you feel that the human situation is hopeful?
3. Kepes praises the arts for their capacity to order experience: "Our sensibilities need to be sustained with the joy of felt order. As a basic aspect of the human organism, the artistic form is a significant organizer of life, enabling us to deal with the environment and directing and controlling our development" (para. 7). Using references to any of the arts, comment on how Kepes's argument is sustained by looking at (or listening to) works of art. If you have experience with creating works of art, explain how those experiences support his views. If possible, attempt to use Kepes's approach to the topic of testimony by quoting other writers on art—either from this book or another source. How do the arts order our experience?
4. Kepes makes a sharp attack on the "vulgar" environment that has been created by modern industry and technology. With reference to an urban

landscape of your own choosing (you may refer to photographs, if necessary), defend or attack his views. He accuses the "modern metropolis" of "visual disorder." He says that we are "bludgeoned" with vulgar images (para. 12). He proceeds to say that this world shapes our vision and distorts us. Are these observations true? Take a stand on the issue, being as concrete as you can be. If you have found some authorities to quote, be sure to do so. Make your argument effective and precise.

5. Which of the arts is for you the most important organizer of your own experience? In answering this question, you may refer to specific works that have impressed you deeply, recalling the circumstances in which you first beheld them, and as you now behold them. Do you feel that this art has helped you to grow and develop? Has it helped to establish a continuity between you and nature? Why has it been important to you? Do others share your views?

SUSANNE K. LANGER

Expressiveness

SUSANNE K. LANGER (b. 1895) developed a youthful interest in philosophy. She was born in New York and attended Radcliffe College of Harvard University, where she studied with Alfred North Whitehead and a number of other distinguished philosophers. She stayed on as a tutor at Harvard University from 1927 to 1942. Thereafter, she taught at the University of Delaware, Columbia University, and from 1954 to the end of her teaching career at Connecticut College. Her career as a teacher has been distinguished, and her influence as a philosopher in the area of the arts has been widespread. Her Philosophy in a New Key: A Study in the Symbolism of Reason, Rite, and Art (1942) is probably her most widely read book. It deals carefully with certain implications of language and other kinds of symbols by which we shape our lives.

In Problems of Art (1957), from which the following selection is taken, she continues her interest in symbolism but concerns herself, too, with questions of creativity, abstraction, and the relation of emotion to the arts. "Expressiveness" is important because it at-

---

From Problems of Art.

tempts to establish the ways in which a work of art will express emotion. Her major assertion is, as it is in **Philosophy in a New Key,** that
the arts are somehow congruent with our emotions, that they express
those emotions. This view is extraordinarily complex, but it has also
been unusually influential. Her idea is that works of art are by nature
ineffable, that is, they cannot be reduced to language or discourse.
They simply are. Emotions are also not reducible to language: Who
can "translate" disappointment into words! In music, as Langer has
shown in another essay, we have become accustomed to a composer
using a specific musical passage to suggest a specific range of emotions. Agitated strings and horns will suggest emotional agitation to
a listener. All that is rather oversimple, perhaps, but for many aestheticians, her view has the seeds of truth.

Essentially, Langer is interested in the ways in which the arts extend our capacities of understanding beyond language. She tells us
that "it is by virtue of language that we can think, remember, imagine" (para. 19). But she also tells us that language has limits (para.
20) and that many human experiences are beyond the reach of language to describe. The arts reach into these areas because they are
areas dominated by feeling.

One of the points she has made in her work in aesthetics is that
it is by virtue of studying and responding to works of art that we
educate our feelings. Most of us spend a good deal of time mastering
facts, learning processes, and performing rational exercises. But we
spend little time developing our emotional capacities. These are best
"educated" by the arts because the arts are products of emotional
understanding—they are, she says, congruent with feeling—and they
are therefore capable of extending our feelings. Thus, they can educate our emotions. The subject of "Expressiveness" is the issue of art's
capacity to express and interpret emotion.

LANGER'S RHETORIC

This work is, like most philosophical essays, a closely reasoned
one. Langer has an argument which takes a complex form. The process of presenting the argument that the arts express emotion and that
we can learn from that expressiveness demands careful analysis of a
variety of implications. Analysis, taking the argument point by
point, is the principle that guides her rhetorical strategy.

The topic of definition is the most important device she uses in *her argument, since she must make clear precisely what she is talking about to enable us to grasp the importance of her position. The most difficult of all definitions in a work of this sort is the definition of art. But Langer aims directly at providing a definition that will work within her theory regarding expressiveness: "A work of art is an expressive form created for our perception through sense or imagination, and what it expresses is human feeling" (para. 5). This definition, like most definitions, presents problems.*

Langer recognizes these problems and organizes the remainder of the work around the simplest approach to solving them. She tells us at the end of paragraph 5, "In stating what a work of art is, I have just used the words 'form,' 'expressive,' and 'created'; these are key words. One at a time, they will keep us engaged." The rest of this piece considers the implications of each of these terms in order. Paragraphs 6–17 treat of the questions relating to form, offering a complex definition of the term. Paragraphs 18–25 clarify the nature of expressiveness. The remainder of the piece examines the term "created," although this concept receives vastly less emphasis than do the first two.

In conducting her argument and in making the points she wishes to make about the relationship of the arts to expression, Langer's most reliable rhetorical strategy is that of attempting definitions. Once the terms of her definition of art are defined, we are in a position to accept or reject it. If we accept it, then we accept, too, her basic contention that the arts have in common one thing—the fact that they express emotions and feelings.

Expressiveness

When we talk about "Art" with a capital "A"—that is, about any 1 or all of the arts: painting, sculpture, architecture, the potter's and goldsmith's and other designers' arts, music, dance, poetry, and prose fiction, drama and film—it is a constant temptation to say things about "Art" in this general sense that are true only in one special domain, or to assume that what holds for one art must hold for another.

For instance, the fact that music is made for performance, for presentation to the ear, and is simply not the same thing when it is given only to the tonal imagination of a reader silently perusing the score, has made some estheticians pass straight to the conclusion that literature, too, must be physically heard to be fully experienced, because words are originally spoken, not written; an obvious parallel, but a careless and, I think, invalid one. It is dangerous to set up principles by analogy, and generalize from a single consideration.

But it is natural, and safe enough, to ask analogous questions: 2
"What is the function of sound in music? What is the function of sound in poetry? What is the function of sound in prose composition? What is the function of sound in drama?" The answers may be quite heterogeneous; and that is itself an important fact, a guide to something more than a simple and sweeping theory. Such findings guide us to exact relations and abstract, variously exemplified basic principles.

At present, however, we are dealing with principles that have 3
proven to be the same in all the arts, when each kind of art—plastic, musical, balletic, poetic, and each major mode, such as literary and dramatic writing, or painting, sculpturing, building plastic shapes—has been studied in its own terms. Such candid study is more rewarding than the usual passionate declaration that all the arts are alike, only their materials differ, their principles are all the same, their techniques all analogous, etc. That is not only unsafe, but untrue. It is in pursuing the differences among them that one arrives, finally, at a point where no more differences appear; then one has found, not postulated, their unity. At that deep level there is only one concept exemplified in all the different arts, and that is the concept of Art.

The principles that obtain wholly and fundamentally in every kind 4
of art are few, but decisive; they determine what is art, and what is not. Expressiveness, in one definite and appropriate sense, is the same in all art works of any kind. What is created is not the same in any two distinct arts—this is, in fact, what makes them distinct—but the principle of creation is the same. And "living form" means the same in all of them.

A work of art is an expressive form created for our perception 5
through sense or imagination, and what it expresses is human feeling. The word "feeling" must be taken here in its broadest sense, meaning *everything that can be felt*, from physical sensation, pain and comfort, excitement and repose, to the most complex emotions, intellectual tensions, or the steady feeling-tones of a conscious human life. In stating what a work of art is, I have just used the words "form," "ex-

pressive," and "created"; these are key words. One at a time, they will keep us engaged.

Let us consider first what is meant, in this context, by a *form*. The word has many meanings, all equally legitimate for various purposes; even in connection with art it has several. It may, for instance—and often does—denote the familiar, characteristic structures known as the sonnet form, the sestina, or the ballad form in poetry, the sonata form, the madrigal, or the symphony in music, the contre-dance[1] or the classical ballet in choreography, and so on. This is not what I mean; or rather, it is only a very small part of what I mean. There is another sense in which artists speak of "form" when they say, for instance, "form follows function," or declare that the one quality shared by all good works of art is "significant form," or entitle a book *The Problem of Form in Painting and Sculpture* or *The Life of Forms in Art,* or *Search for Form.* They are using "form" in a wider sense, which on the one hand is close to the commonest, popular meaning, namely just the *shape* of a thing, and on the other hand to the quite unpopular meaning it has in science and philosophy, where it designates something more abstract; "form" in its most abstract sense means structure, articulation, a whole resulting from the relation of mutually dependent factors, or more precisely, the way that whole is put together.

The abstract sense, which is sometimes called "logical form," is involved in the notion of expression, at least the kind of expression that characterizes art. That is why artists, when they speak of achieving "form," use the word with something of an abstract connotation, even when they are talking about a visible and tangible art object in which that form is embodied.

The more recondite[2] concept of form is derived, of course, from the naive one, that is, material shape. Perhaps the easiest way to grasp the idea of "logical form" is to trace its derivation.

Let us consider the most obvious sort of form, the shape of an object, say a lampshade. In any department store you will find a wide choice of lampshades, mostly monstrosities, and what is monstrous is usually their shape. You select the least offensive one, maybe even a good one, but realize that the color, say violet, will not fit into your room; so you look about for another shade of the same shape but a

6

7

8

9

---

[1]*contre–dance* A formal, composed dance involving two lines of dancers; originally an English country dance.
[2]*recondite* learned and obscure.

different color, perhaps green. In recognizing this same shape in another object, possibly of another material as well as another color, you have quite naturally and easily abstracted the concept of this shape from your actual impression of the first lampshade. Presently it may occur to you that this shade is too big for your lamp; you ask whether they have *this same shade* (meaning another one of this shape) in a smaller size. The clerk understands you.

But what is *the same* in the big violet shade and the little green 10 one? Nothing but the interrelations among their respective various dimensions. They are not "the same" even in their spatial properties, for none of their actual measures are alike; but their shapes are congruent. Their respective spatial factors are put together in the same way, so they exemplify the same form.

It is really astounding what complicated abstractions we make in 11 our ordinary dealing with forms—that is to say, through what twists and transformations we recognize the same logical form. Consider the similarity of your two hands. Put one on the table, palm down, superimpose the other, palm down, as you may have superimposed cut-out geometric shapes in school—they are not alike at all. But their shapes are *exact opposites*. Their respective shapes fit the same description, provided that the description is modified by a principle of application whereby the measures are read one way for one hand and the other way for the other—like a timetable in which the list of stations is marked: "Eastbound, read down; Westbound, read up."

As the two hands exemplify the same form with a principle of reversal understood, so the list of stations describes two ways of moving, 12 indicated by the advice to "read down" for one and "read up" for the other. We can all abstract the common element in these two respective trips, which is called the *route*. With a return ticket we may return only by the same route. The same principle relates a mold to the form of the thing that is cast in it, and establishes their formal correspondence, or common logical form.

So far we have considered only objects—lampshades, hands, or regions of the earth—as having forms. These have fixed shapes; their 13 parts remain in fairly stable relations to each other. But there are also substances that have no definite shapes, such as gases, mists, and water, which take the shape of any bounded space that contains them. The interesting thing about such amorphous fluids[3] is that when they

---

[3]*amorphous fluids* Fluids without a shape of their own.

are put into violent motion they do exhibit visible forms, not bounded by any container. Think of the momentary efflorescence of a bursting rocket, the mushroom cloud of an atomic bomb, the funnel of water or dust screwing upward in a whirlwind. The instant the motion stops, or even slows beyond a certain degree, those shapes collapse and the apparent "thing" disappears. They are not shapes of things at all, but forms of motions, or dynamic forms.

Some dynamic forms, however, have more permanent manifesta- 14 tions, because the stuff that moves and makes them visible is constantly replenished. A waterfall seems to hang from the cliff, waving streamers of foam. Actually, of course, nothing stays there in midair; the water is always passing; but there is more and more water taking the same paths, so we have a lasting shape made and maintained by its passage—a permanent dynamic form. A quiet river, too, has dynamic form; if it stopped flowing it would either go dry or become a lake. Some twenty-five hundred years ago, Heracleitos[4] was struck by the fact that you cannot step twice into the same river at the same place—at least, if the river means the water, not its dynamic form, the flow.

When a river ceases to flow because the water is deflected or dried 15 up, there remains the river bed, sometimes cut deeply in solid stone. That bed is shaped by the flow, and records as graven lines the currents that have ceased to exist. Its shape is static, but it *expresses* the dynamic form of the river. Again, we have two congruent forms, like a cast and its mold, but this time the congruence is more remarkable because it holds between a dynamic form and a static one. That relation is important; we shall be dealing with it again when we come to consider the meaning of "living form" in art.

The congruence of two given perceptible forms is not always evi- 16 dent upon simple inspection. The common *logical* form they both exhibit may become apparent only when you know the principle whereby to relate them, as you compare the shapes of your hands not by direct correspondence, but by correspondence of opposite parts. Where the two exemplifications of the single logical form are unlike in most other respects one needs a rule for matching up the relevant factors of one with the relevant factors of the other; that is to say, a

---

[4]*Heracleitos (540?–475 B.C.)* A Greek philosopher who believed that the basis of all matter was fire. He also believed that everything was a result of the clash of opposite forces.

rule of translation, whereby one instance of the logical form is shown to correspond formally to the other.

The logical form itself is not another thing, but an abstract con- 17 cept, or better an *abstractable* concept. We usually don't abstract it deliberately, but only use it, as we use our vocal cords in speech without first learning all about their operation and then applying our knowledge. Most people perceive intuitively the similarity of their two hands without thinking of them as conversely related; they can guess at the shape of the hollow inside a wooden shoe from the shape of a human foot, without any abstract study of topology.[5] But the first time they see a map in the Mercator projection[6]—with parallel lines of longitude, not meeting at the poles—they find it hard to believe that this corresponds logically to the circular map they used in school, where the meridians bulged apart toward the equator and met at both poles. The visible shapes of the continents are different on the two maps, and it takes abstract thinking to match up the two representations of the same earth. If, however, they have grown up with both maps, they will probably see the geographical relationships either way with equal ease, because these relationships are not *copied* by either map, but *expressed*, and expressed equally well by both; for the two maps are different *projections* of the same logical form, which the spherical earth exhibits in still another—that is, a spherical—projection.

An expressive form is any perceptible or imaginable whole that ex- 18 hibits relationships of parts, or points, or even qualities or aspects within the whole, so that it may be taken to represent some other whole whose elements have analogous relations. The reason for using such a form as a symbol is usually that the thing it represents is not perceivable or readily imaginable. We cannot see the earth as an object. We let a map or a little globe express the relationships of places on the earth, and think about the earth by means of it. The understanding of one thing through another seems to be a deeply intuitive process in the human brain; it is so natural that we often have difficulty in distinguishing the symbolic expressive form from what it conveys. The symbol seems to be the thing itself, or contain it, or be contained in it. A child interested in a globe will not say, "This means the earth,"

---

[5]*topology*   The study or mapping of surfaces.

[6]*Mercator projection*   A flattened map of the earth. Gerardus Mercator (1512–1594), Flemish mapmaker, published his first Mercator projection in 1568, with longitudes and latitudes at right angles.

but "Look, this is the earth." A similar identification of symbol and meaning underlies the widespread conception of holy names, of the physical efficacy of rites, and many other primitive but culturally persistent phenomena. It has a bearing on our perception of artistic import; that is why I mention it here.

The most astounding and developed symbolic device humanity has 19 evolved is language. By means of language we can conceive the intangible, incorporeal things we call our *ideas*, and the equally inostensible[7] elements of our perceptual world that we call *facts*. It is by virtue of language that we can think, remember, imagine, and finally conceive a universe of facts. We can describe things and represent their relations, express rules of their interactions, speculate and predict and carry on a long symbolizing process known as reasoning. And above all, we can communicate, by producing a serried array of audible or visible words, in a pattern commonly known, and readily understood to reflect our multifarious concepts and percepts and their interconnections. This use of language is *discourse*; and the pattern of discourse is known as *discursive form*. It is a highly versatile, amazingly powerful pattern. It has impressed itself on our tacit thinking, so that we call all systematic reflection "discursive thought." It has made, far more than most people know, the very frame of our sensory experience—the frame of objective facts in which we carry on the practical business of life.

Yet even the discursive pattern has its limits of usefulness. An ex- 20 pressive form can express any complex of conceptions that, via some rule of projection, appears congruent with it, that is, appears to be of that form. Whatever there is in experience that will not take the impress—directly or indirectly—of discursive form, is not discursively communicable or, in the strictest sense, logically thinkable. It is unspeakable, ineffable;[8] according to practically all serious philosophical theories today, it is unknowable.

Yet there is a great deal of experience that is knowable, not only as 21 immediate, formless, meaningless impact, but as one aspect of the intricate web of life, yet defies discursive formulation, and therefore ver-

---

[7]***inostensible*** Not apparent or evident. Langer implies here that the world of perceived "facts" is no more tangible than the world of ideas because all perceptions are filtered through the mind, which creates ideas of things.

[8]***ineffable*** Literally, unspeakable; thus unknowable, because anything that cannot be expressed through language cannot be known.

bal expression: that is what we sometimes call the *subjective aspect* of experience, the direct feeling of it—what it is like to be waking and moving, to be drowsy, slowing down, or to be sociable, or to feel self-sufficient but alone; what it feels like to pursue an elusive thought or to have a big idea. All such directly felt experiences usually have no names—they are named, if at all, for the outward conditions that normally accompany their occurrence. Only the most striking ones have names like "anger," "hate," "love," "fear," and are collectively called "emotion." But we feel many things that never develop into any designable emotion. The ways we are moved are as various as the lights in a forest; and they may intersect, sometimes without cancelling each other, take shape and dissolve, conflict, explode into passion, or be transfigured. All these inseparable elements of subjective reality compose what we call the "inward life" of human beings. The usual factoring of that life-stream into mental, emotional, and sensory units is an arbitrary scheme of simplification that makes scientific treatment possible to a considerable extent; but we may already be close to the limit of its usefulness, that is, close to the point where its simplicity becomes an obstacle to further questioning and discovery instead of the revealing, ever-suitable logical projection it was expected to be.

Whatever resists projection into the discursive form of language is, 22 indeed, hard to hold in conception, and perhaps impossible to communicate, in the proper and strict sense of the word "communicate." But fortunately our logical intuition, or form-perception, is really much more powerful than we commonly believe, and our knowledge—genuine knowledge, understanding—is considerably wider than our discourse. Even in the use of language, if we want to name something that is too new to have a name (for example, a newly invented gadget or a newly discovered creature), or want to express a relationship for which there is no verb or other connective word, we resort to metaphor; we mention it or describe it as something else, something analogous. The principle of metaphor is simply the principle of saying one thing and meaning another, and expecting to be understood to mean the other. A metaphor is not language, it is an idea expressed by language, an idea that in its turn functions as a symbol to express something. It is not discursive and therefore does not really make a statement of the idea it conveys; but it formulates a new conception for our direct imaginative grasp.

Sometimes our comprehension of a total experience is mediated by 23 a metaphorical symbol because the experience is new, and language has words and phrases only for familiar notions. Then an extension of language will gradually follow the wordless insight, and discursive expression will supersede the nondiscursive pristine symbol. This is, I think, the normal advance of human thought and language in that whole realm of knowledge where discourse is possible at all.

But the symbolic presentation of subjective reality for contempla- 24 tion is not only tentatively beyond the reach of language—that is, not merely beyond the words we have; it is impossible in the essential frame of language. That is why those semanticists[9] who recognize only discourse as a symbolic form must regard the whole life of feeling as formless, chaotic, capable only of symptomatic expression, typified in exclamations like "Ah!" "Ouch!" "My sainted aunt!" They usually do believe that art is an expression of feeling, but that "expression" in art is of this sort, indicating that the speaker has an emotion, a pain, or other personal experience, perhaps also giving us a clue to the general kind of experience it is—pleasant or unpleasant, violent or mild—but not setting that piece of inward life objectively before us so we may understand its intricacy, its rhythms and shifts of total appearance. The differences in feeling-tones or other elements of subjective experience are regarded as differences in quality, which must be felt to be appreciated. Furthermore, since we have no intellectual access to pure subjectivity, the only way to study it is to study the symptoms of the person who is having subjective experiences. This leads to physiological psychology—a very important and interesting field. But it tells us nothing about the phenomena of subjective life, and sometimes simplifies the problem by saying they don't exist.

Now, I believe the expression of feeling in a work of art—the func- 25 tion that makes the work an expressive form—is not symptomatic at all. An artist working on a tragedy need not be in personal despair or violent upheaval; nobody, indeed, could work in such a state of mind. His mind would be occupied with the causes of his emotional upset. Self-expression does not require composition and lucidity; a screaming baby gives his feeling far more release than any musician, but we don't go into a concert hall to hear a baby scream; in fact, if that baby is brought in we are likely to go out. We don't want self-expression.

A work of art presents feeling (in the broad sense I mentioned be- 26 fore, as everything that can be felt) for our contemplation, making it visible or audible or in some way perceivable through a symbol, not

---

[9]*semanticists* Those concerned with the meaning of words; in this case, Langer refers to those who treat words as coherent symbols of meaning and think of feelings as simply reactions to (symptoms of) a stimulus.

inferable from[10] a symptom. Artistic form is congruent with the dynamic forms of our direct sensuous, mental, and emotional life; works of art are projections of "felt life," as Henry James[11] called it, into spatial, temporal, and poetic structures. They are images of feeling, that formulate it for our cognition. What is artistically good is whatever articulates and presents feeling to our understanding.

Artistic forms are more complex than any other symbolic forms we   27 know. They are, indeed, not abstractable from the works that exhibit them. We may abstract a shape from an object that has this shape, by disregarding color, weight and texture, even size; but to the total effect that is an artistic form, the color matters, the thickness of lines matters, and the appearance of texture and weight. A given triangle is the same in any position, but to an artistic form its location, balance, and surroundings are not indifferent. Form, in the sense in which we artists speak of "significant form" or "expressive form," is not an abstracted structure, but an apparition; and the vital processes of sense and emotion that a good work of art expresses seem to the beholder to be directly contained in it, not symbolized but really presented. The congruence is so striking that symbol and meaning appear as one reality. Actually, as one psychologist who is also a musician has written, "Music sounds as feelings feel." And likewise, in good painting, sculpture, or building, balanced shapes and colors, lines and masses look as emotions, vital tensions and their resolutions feel.

An artist, then, expresses feeling, but not in the way a politician   28 blows off steam or a baby laughs and cries. He formulates that elusive aspect of reality that is commonly taken to be amorphous and chaotic; that is, he objectifies the subjective realm. What he expresses is, therefore, not his own actual feelings, but what he knows about human feeling. Once he is in possession of a rich symbolism, that knowledge may actually exceed his entire personal experience. A work of art expresses a conception of life, emotion, inward reality. But it is neither a confessional nor a frozen tantrum; it is a developed metaphor, a nondiscursive symbol that articulates what is verbally ineffable—the logic of consciousness itself.

---

[10]*inferable from*   able to be rendered understandable from.

[11]*Henry James (1843–1916).*   One of America's greatest novelists; brother of the philosopher William James. "Felt life" was James's term for a deeply understood experience, particularly of the sort that developed into his own works.

QUESTIONS

1. What is Susanne Langer's definition of "art"?
2. Why does Langer tell us that it is "dangerous to set up principles by analogy" (para. 1)?
3. What does Langer mean by "feeling" (para. 5)?
4. Is Langer's use of the analogy of the lampshade "dangerous" (paras. 9–10)? Is it effective in her argument?
5. What does it mean to say that "Music sounds as feelings feel" (para. 27)?

WRITING ASSIGNMENTS

1. In paragraph 25, Langer says, "Now, I believe the expression of feeling in a work of art—the function that makes the work an expressive form—is not symptomatic at all." Clarify precisely what she means by this statement. Use her rhetorical method of relying on the topic of definition. The key terms to define are "expression of feeling," "expressive form," and "symptomatic." You may wish to quote from statements Langer makes on the question.
2. At one point Langer asserts that things which are not discursive, that is, not susceptible to discursive treatment, are not knowable. In essence, she is saying that language is essential for thinking and for knowing things. Is this assertion true? Is it possible for someone to know something that is not determined by language? If it is not possible, what are the implications for someone who is deficient in mastering language? To what extent is knowledge dependent on a mastery of language and discourse? Construct an essay that answers these questions.
3. One of the important points Langer makes at the end of this piece has to do with what feelings an artist expresses in a work of art. She discusses the question of whether a work of art is symptomatic; by that she means whether a given work expresses a feeling that the artist happens to have while he or she is creating. Her opinion is that the artist does not express feeling in this way. She says that the artist expresses what is serious about feelings, not his own feelings (para. 28). Do you feel that this assertion is true? Argue for this position using what you know about your own efforts to create works of art. But be sure, too, that you consult other people who make works of art for their views. It would help to ask anyone who is seriously interested in art what they think about this question. See paragraph 24.

4. In essence, this piece is an extended definition of art with separate definitions of several key terms. If possible, construct your own definition of art and use the technique Langer uses to develop a complete essay that clarifies the nature of that definition. If you find it impossible to construct your own definition, use someone else's definition. You may select one of the following definitions to work from:

> Art is the exercise of objectifying the depth of understanding of the human condition.

> A work of art is the most natural response the artist can give to the circumstances of his life.

> The work of art is by nature a symbolic interpretation of an artist's experience.

5. In paragraph 25, Langer asserts that we do not want self-expression in art. This statement may seem to be a contradiction in terms, since art is often represented to us as a useful means of self-expression. Is Langer's assertion correct? Analyze her statements on this subject, using her rhetorical strategies of definition. What exactly is self-expression, and how might it relate to art?

A. C. BRADLEY

Poetry for Poetry's Sake

ANDREW CECIL BRADLEY (1851–1935) was among the most distinguished English critics of literature in the generation that flourished before World War I. His Shakespearean Tragedy (1904) has been rightly regarded as the single most influential book on Shakespeare in modern times. His career at Oxford University was long and varied, marked by a sustained influence on a considerable number of English literary figures.

In the selection presented here Bradley is reacting to a trend in art criticism which was taking to task the concept that art served only itself. The "art-for-art's-sake" movement was an attempt to separate artistic matters from subsidiary concerns such as morality, social concerns, nationalism, even personal biography. It was clear that art could be made to serve the needs of many important interests, and the "art-for-art's-sake" critics feared that art would become a servant of such interests instead of being a master of its own destiny. That fear made certain critics claim too much for art, and thus the controversy grew. It continues even today.

A. C. Bradley picks up the controversy again, but in terms of po-

---

From *Oxford Lectures on Poetry*.

etry rather than of painting or the other arts. He notes that the controversy focuses on an antithesis: the antithesis between subject and form, matter and treatment, and substance and handling. What makes a poem great? Is it the greatness of the subject? Or is the subject irrelevant? Is it the depth of the substance? Is it the greatness of the form? As he discusses the problems inherent in both positions, Bradley reveals a remarkable range of literary reference—from the Greeks to the writers of 1909—something that his audience of Oxford students naturally relished. What this range reveals is the scope of vision that Bradley brings to any basic literary question.

It may be that we can more naturally regard this work as a philosophical rather than a purely literary one, since it deals with issues that aestheticians normally wrestle with: the nature of form, the nature of poetic experience, and the nature of meaning. Bradley's discussion is very cautious. He spells out each aspect of the issue as he goes, preparing us carefully for his observations and his conclusions.

In the final analysis, he concludes that there is a controversy because both sides of the argument claim too much. They claim too singular a force for subject, substance, or form. Bradley concludes— as modern literary critics insist—that subject and form are one, that although we can talk about them as being distinct, they are interdependent and inseparable.

BRADLEY'S RHETORIC

Bradley offers us an analysis of a term and the concepts that lie behind it. His method is basically expository: he begins by telling us what he is going to do in the remainder of the essay. "I propose to state briefly what I understand by 'Poetry for poetry's sake,' and then, after guarding against one or two misapprehensions of the formula, to consider more fully a single problem connected with it." This is precisely what he does, and what he means by "consider more fully a . . . problem" is to submit the problem to the most rigorous scrutiny possible.

He then connects life and poetry (para. 4), because if poetry is to be considered for its own sake, it must be considered as something apart from the life it describes. Bradley next shifts the focus to the question of form for its own sake (para. 5), which leads to the central controversy. In a classic move associated with legal rhetoric, he raises the question: Is there an antithesis between subject and form? Then, after considering that question in paragraphs 6–12, he raises *the next logical question: What kind of antithesis is it? Is it valid? Then, in classic fashion, he takes the important terms* subject *(paras. 9–10),* substance *(paras. 11–16), and* form *(paras. 17–22) in turn, giving them meticulous scrutiny.*

He finally gets to the question of what poetry means, but not until he has virtually ended the essay (para. 25). There we realize that Bradley has used an interesting strategy. He has examined a subject in great detail only to bring us to an interesting point—being prepared to ask a very serious question—"What does poetry mean?" His answer to this question is rather poetical in itself, and it may not satisfy the dictionary writer. Yet, it is not by itself all-important. What is important is the fact that as readers we have come a great distance and can see the significance of the question in a way that we would not have been able to do without Bradley's examination of the issues.

————————❦————————

Poetry for Poetry's Sake

The words "Poetry for poetry's sake" recall the famous phrase "Art   1
for Art." It is far from my purpose to examine the possible meanings
of that phrase, or all the questions it involves. I propose to state briefly
what I understand by "Poetry for poetry's sake," and then, after guarding against one or two misapprehensions of the formula, to consider
more fully a single problem connected with it. And I must premise,
without attempting to justify them, certain explanations. We are to
consider poetry in its essence, and apart from the flaws which in most
poems accompany their poetry. We are to include in the idea of poetry
the metrical form, and not to regard this as a mere accident or a mere
vehicle. And, finally, poetry being poems, we are to think of a poem
as it actually exists; and, without aiming here at accuracy, we may say
that an actual poem is the succession of experiences—sounds, images,
thoughts, emotions—through which we pass when we are reading as
poetically as we can. Of course this imaginative experience—if I may
use the phrase for brevity—differs with every reader and every time of
reading: a poem exists in innumerable degrees. But that insurmountable fact lies in the nature of things and does not concern us now.

What then does the formula "Poetry for poetry's sake" tell us about   2 this experience? It says, as I understand it, these things. First, this experience is an end in itself, is worth having on its own account, has an intrinsic value. Next, its *poetic* value is this intrinsic worth alone. Poetry may have also an ulterior value as a means to culture or religion; because it conveys instructions, or softens the passions, or furthers a good cause; because it brings the poet fame or money or a quiet conscience. So much the better: let it be valued for these reasons too. But its ulterior worth neither is nor can directly determine its poetic worth as a satisfying imaginative experience; and this is to be judged entirely from within. And to these two positions the formula would add, though not of necessity, a third. The consideration of ulterior ends, whether by the poet in the act of composing or by the reader in the act of experiencing, tends to lower poetic value. It does so because it tends to change the nature of poetry by taking it out of its own atmosphere. For its nature is to be not a part, nor yet a copy, of the real world (as we commonly understand that phrase), but to be a world by itself, independent, complete, autonomous; and to possess it fully you must enter the world, conform to its laws, and ignore for the time the beliefs, aims, and particular conditions which belong to you in the other world of reality.

Of the more serious misapprehensions to which these statements may give rise I will glance only at one or two. The offensive consequences often drawn from the formula "Art for Art" will be found to attach not to the doctrine that Art is an end in itself, but to the doctrine that Art is the whole or supreme end of human life. And as this latter doctrine, which seems to me absurd, is in any case quite different from the former, its consequences fall outside my subject. The formula "Poetry is an end in itself" has nothing to say on the various questions of moral judgment which arise from the fact that poetry has its place in a many-sided life. For anything it says, the intrinsic value of poetry might be so small, and its ulterior effects so mischievous, that it had better not exist. The formula only tells us that we must not place in antithesis poetry and human good, for poetry is one kind of human good; and that we must not determine the intrinsic value of this kind of good by direct reference to another. If we do, we shall find ourselves maintaining what we did not expect. If poetic value lies in the stimulation of religious feelings, *Lead, Kindly Light*[1] is no better

3

---

[1]**Lead, Kindly Light**   a sentimental religious poem by John Henry Cardinal Newman (1801–1890).

a poem than many a tasteless version of a Psalm: if in the excitement of patriotism, why is *Scots, Wha Hae*[2] superior to *We Don't Want to Fight?* if in the mitigation of the passions, the Odes of Sappho[3] will win but little praise: if in instruction, Armstrong's *Art of Preserving Health*[4] should win much.

Again, our formula may be accused of cutting poetry away from its connection with life. And this accusation raises so huge a problem that I must ask leave to be dogmatic as well as brief. There is plenty of connection between life and poetry, but it is, so to say, a connection underground. The two may be called different forms of the same thing: one of them having (in the usual sense) reality, but seldom fully satisfying imagination; while the other offers something which satisfies imagination but has not fully "reality." They are parallel developments which nowhere meet, or, if I may use loosely a word which will be serviceable later, they are analogous. Hence we understand one by help of the other, and even, in a sense, care for one because of the other; but hence also, poetry neither is life, nor, strictly speaking, a copy of it. They differ not only because one has more mass and the other a more perfect shape, but because they have different *kinds* of existence. The one touches us as beings occupying a given position in space and time, and having feelings, desires, and purposes due to that position: it appeals to imagination, but appeals to much besides. What meets us in poetry has not a position in the same series of time and space, or, if it has or had such a position, it is taken apart from much that belonged to it there; and therefore it makes no direct appeal to those feelings, desires, and purposes, but speaks only to contemplative imagination—imagination the reverse of empty or emotionless, imagination saturated with the results of "real" experience, but still contemplative. Thus, no doubt, one main reason why poetry has poetic value for us is that it presents to us in its own way something which we meet in another form in nature or life; and yet the test of its poetic value for us lies simply in the question whether it satisfies our imagination; the rest of us, our knowledge or conscience, for example, judging it only so far as they appear transmuted in our imagination. So also

4

---

[2]*Scots, Wha Hae* A poem by Scots poet Robert Burns (1759–1796), dramatizing Robert Bruce's address to his army to encourage them to fight; Bradley contrasts it with a popular but undistinguished poem.

[3]*Sappho* Seventh century B.C. Greek lyric poet; she lived in Lesbos.

[4]**Art of Preserving Health** an early "home-medical" how-to book.

Shakespeare's knowledge or his moral insight,[5] Milton's greatness of soul, Shelley's "hate of hate" and "love of love," and that desire to help men or make them happier which may have influenced a poet in hours of meditation—all these have, as such, no poetical worth: they have that worth only when, passing through the unity of the poet's being, they reappear as qualities of imagination, and then are indeed mighty powers in the world of poetry.

I come to a third misapprehension, and so to my main subject. This   5 formula, it is said, empties poetry of its meaning: it is really a doctrine of form for form's sake. "It is of no consequence what a poet says, so long as he says the thing well. The *what* is poetically indifferent: it is the *how* that counts. Matter, subject, content, substance, determines nothing; there is no subject with which poetry may not deal: the form, the treatment, is everything. Nay, more: not only is the matter indifferent, but it is the secret of Art to 'eradicate the matter by means of the form,' "—phrases and statements like these meet us everywhere in current criticism of literature and the other arts. They are the stock-in-trade of writers who understand of them little more than the fact that somehow or other they are not "bourgeois." But we find them also seriously used by writers whom we must respect, whether they are anonymous or not; something like one or another of them might be quoted, for example, from Professor Saintsbury,[6] the late R. A. M. Stevenson, Schiller, Goethe[7] himself; and they are the watchwords of a school in the one country where esthetics has flourished. They come, as a rule, from men who either practice one of the arts, or, from study of it, are interested in its methods. The general reader—a being so general that I may say what I will of him—is outraged by them. He feels that he is being robbed of almost all that he cares for in a work of art.

---

[5]*Shakespeare's knowledge or his moral insight* Bradley refers to qualities normally praised in or related to the work of three important English poets from three important periods in English poetry. William Shakespeare (1564–1616) was an Elizabethan playwright; John Milton (1608–1674) was a seventeenth-century poet; Percy Bysshe Shelley (1792–1822) was a Romantic poet. Bradley's point is simply that the imaginative qualities of the work, not the personal qualities we associate with the writer, are what count.

[6]*George Saintsbury (1845–1933)* A contemporary British historical critic toward whom Bradley had feelings of rivalry.

[7]*Johann Wolfgang von Goethe (1749–1832)* A German Romantic playwright and poet, as was Johann Christoph Friedrich von Schiller (1759–1805). Both Schiller and Goethe had written criticism of the sort Bradley discusses, and both are of the country "where esthetics has flourished."

"You are asking me," he says, "to look at the Dresden Madonna[8] as if it were a Persian rug. You are telling me that the poetic value of *Hamlet* lies solely in its style and versification, and that my interest in the man and his fate is only an intellectual or moral interest. You allege that, if I want to enjoy the poetry of *Crossing the Bar*, I must not mind what Tennyson[9] says there, but must consider solely his way of saying it. But in that case I can care no more for a poem than I do for a set of nonsense verses; and I do not believe that the authors of *Hamlet* and *Crossing the Bar* regarded their poems thus."

These antitheses of subject, matter, substance on the one side, form, treatment, handling on the other, are the field through which I especially want, in this lecture, to indicate a way. It is a field of battle; and the battle is waged for no trivial cause; but the cries of the combatants are terribly ambiguous. Those phrases of the so-called formalist[10] may each mean five or six different things. Taken in one sense they seem to me chiefly true; taken as the general reader not unnaturally takes them, they seem to me false and mischievous. It would be absurd to pretend that I can end in a few minutes a controversy which concerns the ultimate nature of Art, and leads perhaps to problems not yet soluble; but we can at least draw some plain distinctions which, in this controversy, are too often confused.

In the first place, then, let us take "subject" in one particular sense; let us understand by it that which we have in view when, looking at the title of an unread poem, we say that the poet has chosen this or that for his subject. The subject, in this sense, so far as I can discover, is generally something, real or imaginary, as it exists in the minds of fairly cultivated people. The subject of *Paradise Lost*[11] would be the

6

7

---

[8]***Dresden Madonna*** One of the most famous madonnas of Raphael (1483–1520), usually called the Sistine Madonna or Madonna di San Sisto, it shows the Madonna and Child adored by Pope Sixtus.

[9]***Alfred, Lord Tennyson (1809–1892)*** Tennyson was poet laureate of England from 1850 until his death and among the most popular poets of the nineteenth century. "Crossing the Bar" (1889) is a statement of faith in a life after death and appears by his request at the end of all collections of his poetry.

[10]***so-called formalist*** Bradley refers to a school of criticism in which only formal matters are considered; matters that relate to the terms *subject, matter,* and *substance* are among those considered by the formalist critics, and Bradley himself is being something of a formalist.

[11]**Paradise Lost** The great epic poem by John Milton. It has as its core the story of Adam and Eve, the fall of mankind, and as its stated purpose "to justify the ways of God to man." Bradley is demonstrating how difficult it is to talk about the "subject" of a poem that is as vast and complex as *Paradise Lost*.

story of the Fall as that story exists in the general imagination of a Bible-reading people. The subject of Shelley's stanzas *To a Skylark*[12] would be the ideas which arise in the mind of an educated person when, without knowing the poem, he hears the word "skylark." If the title of a poem conveys little or nothing to us, the "subject" appears to be either what we should gather by investigating the title in a dictionary or other book of the kind, or else such a brief suggestion as might be offered by a person who had read the poem, and who said, for example, that the subject of *The Ancient Mariner*[13] was a sailor who killed an albatross and suffered for his deed.

Now the subject, in this sense (and I intend to use the word in no 8 other), is not, as such, inside the poem, but outside it. The contents of the stanzas *To a Skylark* are not the ideas suggested by the word "skylark" to the average man; they belong to Shelley just as much as the language does. The subject, therefore, is not the matter *of* the poem at all; and its opposite is not the *form* of the poem, but the whole poem. The subject is one thing; the poem, matter and form alike, another thing. This being so, it is surely obvious that the poetic value cannot lie in the subject, but lies entirely in its opposite, the poem. How can the subject determine the value when on one and the same subject poems may be written of all degrees of merit and demerit; or when a perfect poem may be composed on a subject so slight as a pet sparrow,[14] and, if Macaulay[15] may be trusted, a nearly worthless poem on a subject so stupendous as the omnipresence of the Deity? The "formalist" is here perfectly right. Nor is he insisting on something unimportant. He is fighting against our tendency to take the work of art as a mere copy or reminder of something already in our heads, or at the best as a suggestion of some idea as little removed as possible from the familiar. The sightseer who promenades a picture-gallery, remark-

---

[12]**To a Skylark**   Poem by Percy Bysshe Shelley. It begins, "Hail to thee, blithe Spirit!" Its subject, however, is not a skylark, but rather the vastly complex responses of the poet when contemplating himself in relation to the skylark.

[13]**Rime of the Ancient Mariner**   Poem by Samuel Taylor Coleridge (1772–1834). The lament of the mariner cursed for killing an innocent albatross was well known to Bradley's audience. His summary is purposely ironic.

[14]*a pet sparrow*   The Roman poet Gaius Valerius Catullus (84?–54 B.C.) wrote two poems about his mistress Lesbia's pet sparrow. Greek poets before him had written on similar subjects.

[15]**Thomas Babington Macaulay (1800–1859)**   English politician and historian. Bradley is referring to his attack, in the *Edinburgh Review* (April 1830), of the work of a minor English poet, Robert Montgomery (1807–1855).

ing that this portrait is so like his cousin, or that landscape the very image of his birthplace, or who, after satisfying himself that one picture is about Elijah,[16] passes on rejoicing to discover the subject, and nothing but the subject, of the next—what is he but an extreme example of this tendency? Well, but the very same tendency vitiates[17] much of our criticism, much criticism of Shakespeare, for example, which, with all its cleverness and partial truth, still shows that the critic never passed from his own mind into Shakespeare's; and it may be traced even in so fine a critic as Coleridge,[18] as when he dwarfs the sublime struggle of Hamlet into the image of his own unhappy weakness. Hazlitt[19] by no means escaped its influence. Only the third of that great trio, Lamb,[20] appears almost always to have rendered the conception of the composer.

Again, it is surely true that we cannot determine beforehand what 9 subjects are fit for Art, or name any subject on which a good poem might not possibly be written. To divide subjects into two groups, the beautiful or elevating, and the ugly or vicious, and to judge poems according as their subjects belong to one of these groups or the other, is to fall into the same pit, to confuse with our preconceptions the meaning of the poet. What the thing is in the poem he is to be judged by, not by the thing as it was before he touched it; and how can we venture to say beforehand that he cannot make a true poem out of something which to us was merely alluring or dull or revolting? The question whether, having done so, he ought to publish his poem; whether the thing in the poet's work will not be still confused by the incompetent Puritan or the incompetent sensualist with the thing in *his* mind, does not touch this point; it is a further question, one of ethics, not of art. No doubt the upholders of "Art for Art's sake" will generally be in favor of the courageous course, of refusing to sacrifice the better or stronger part of the public to the weaker or worse; but

---

[16]*Elijah* An Old Testament prophet of the ninth century B.C. (See I Kings 17–19 and II Kings 2:1–11.)

[17]*vitiates* saps the life from.

[18]*Samuel Taylor Coleridge* English Romantic poet. Coleridge's lectures in England and America, as well as his critical essays, helped make Shakespeare's work popular again and influenced modern critical attitudes toward Shakespeare.

[19]*William Hazlitt (1778–1830)* Hazlitt wrote extensively on Shakespeare's critics, helping build a new modern appreciation of his work.

[20]*Charles Lamb (1775–1830)* With his sister Mary (1764–1847), Lamb wrote *Tales from Shakespeare,* popular prose retellings of the plays. All these Shakespearean interpreters are Bradley's immediate critical forebears in his work on Shakespeare.

their maxim in no way binds them to this view. Rossetti[21] suppressed one of the best of his sonnets, a sonnet chosen for admiration by Tennyson, himself extremely sensitive about the moral effect of poetry; suppressed it, I believe, because it was called fleshly. One may regret Rossetti's judgment and at the same time respect his scrupulousness; but in any case he judged in his capacity of citizen, not in his capacity of artist.

So far then the "formalist" appears to be right. But he goes too far, I think, if he maintains that the subject is indifferent and that all subjects are the same to poetry. And he does not prove his point by observing that a good poem might be written on a pin's head, and a bad one on the Fall of Man. That truth shows that the subject *settles* nothing, but not that it counts for nothing. The Fall of Man is really a more favorable subject than a pin's head. The Fall of Man, that is to say, offers opportunities of poetic effects wider in range and more penetrating in appeal. And the fact is that such a subject, as it exists in the general imagination, has some esthetic value before the poet touches it. It is, as you may choose to call it, an inchoate[22] poem or the debris of a poem. It is not an abstract idea or a bare isolated fact, but an assemblage of figures, scenes, actions, and events, which already appeal to emotional imagination; and it is already in some degree organized and formed. In spite of this a bad poet would make a bad poem on it; but then we should say he was unworthy of the subject. And we should not say this if he wrote a bad poem on a pin's head. Conversely, a good poem on a pin's head would almost certainly transform its subject far more than a good poem on the Fall of Man. It might revolutionize its subject so completely that we should say, "The subject may be a pin's head, but the substance of the poem has very little to do with it."

This brings us to another and a different antithesis. Those figures, scenes, events, that form part of the subject called the Fall of Man, are not the substance of *Paradise Lost*; but in *Paradise Lost* there are figures, scenes, and events resembling them in some degree. These, with much more of the same kind, may be described as its substance, and may then be contrasted with the measured language of the poem, which will be called its form. Subject is the opposite not of form but

---

[21]***Dante Gabriel Rossetti (1828–1882)*** English Pre-Raphaelite poet and painter, member of the Pre-Raphaelite Brotherhood, a group that attempted to recover an innocence of vision untainted by the overdone academic realism and spiritual emptiness of the modern work they disliked.

[22]***inchoate*** Not fully formulated and therefore inexpressible in words.

of the whole poem. Substance is within the poem, and its opposite, form, is also within the poem. I am not criticizing this antithesis at present, but evidently it is quite different from the other. It is practically the distinction used in the old-fashioned criticism of epic and drama, and it flows down, not unsullied, from Aristotle.[23] Addison,[24] for example, in examining *Paradise Lost* considers in order the fable, the characters, and the sentiments; these will be the substance: then he considers the language, that is, the style and numbers;[25] this will be the form. In like manner, the substance or meaning of a lyric may be distinguished from the form.

Now I believe it will be found that a large part of the controversy 12 we are dealing with arises from a confusion between these two distinctions of substance and form, and of subject and poem. The extreme formalist lays his whole weight on the form because he thinks its opposite is the mere subject. The general reader is angry, but makes the same mistake, and gives to the subject praises that rightly belong to the substance.[26] I will give an example of what I mean. I can only explain the following words of a good critic[27] by supposing that for the moment he has fallen into this confusion: "The mere matter of all poetry—to wit, the appearances of nature and the thoughts and feelings of men—being unalterable, it follows that the difference between poet and poet will depend upon the manner of each in applying language, meter, rhyme, cadence, and what not, to this invariable material." What has become here of the substance of *Paradise Lost*—the story, scenery, characters, sentiments as they are in the poem? They have vanished clean away. Nothing is left but the form on one side, and on the other not even the subject, but a supposed invariable material, the appearances of nature and the thoughts and feelings of men. Is it surprising that the whole value should then be found in the form?

So far we have assumed that this antithesis of substance and form 13

---

[23]*Aristotle (384–322 B.C.)* The reference is to his *Poetics*, which defines the genre of the tragic play. By "old-fashioned criticism" Bradley means the criticism that categorizes and classifies in an effort to establish the genre of, say, epic or drama.

[24]*Joseph Addison (1672–1719)* English essayist. The reference is to his five-part essay in his publication called *The Spectator*.

[25]*numbers* This term refers to the metrical qualities of a poem.

[26]What is here called "substance" is what people generally mean when they use the word "subject" and insist on the value of the subject. I am not arguing against this usage, or in favor of the usage which I have adopted for the sake of clearness. It does not matter which we employ, so long as we and others know what we mean. (I use "substance" and "content" indifferently.) [Bradley's note]

[27]George Saintsbury. [Bradley's note]

is valid, and that it always has one meaning. In reality it has several, but we will leave it in its present shape, and pass to the question of its validity. And this question we are compelled to raise, because we have to deal with the two contentions that the poetic value lies wholly or mainly in the substance, and that it lies wholly or mainly in the form. Now these contentions, whether false or true, may seem at least to be clear; but we shall find, I think, that they are both of them false, or both of them nonsense: false if they concern anything outside the poem, nonsense if they apply to something in it. For what do they evidently imply? They imply that there are in a poem two parts, factors, or components, a substance and a form; and that you can conceive them distinctly and separately, so that when you are speaking of the one you are not speaking of the other. Otherwise how can you ask the question, In which of them does the value lie? But really in a poem, apart from defects, there are no such factors or components; and therefore it is strictly nonsense to ask in which of them the value lies. And on the other hand, if the substance and the form referred to are not in the poem, then both the contentions are false, for its poetic value lies in itself.

What I mean is neither new nor mysterious; and it will be clear, I 14 believe, to anyone who reads poetry poetically and who closely examines his experience. When you are reading a poem, I would ask—not analyzing it, and much less criticizing it, but allowing it, as it proceeds, to make its full impression on you through the exertion of your re-creating imagination—do you then apprehend and enjoy as one thing a certain meaning or substance, and as another thing certain articulate sounds, and do you somehow compound these two? Surely you do not, any more than you apprehend apart, when you see someone smile, those lines in the face which express a feeling, and the feeling that the lines express. Just as there the lines and their meaning are to you one thing, not two, so in poetry the meaning and the sounds are one: there is, if I may put it so, a resonant meaning, or a meaning resonance. If you read the line, "The sun is warm, the sky is clear,"[28] you do not experience separately the image of a warm sun and clear sky, on the one side, and certain unintelligible rhythmical sounds on the other; nor yet do you experience them together, side by side; but you experience the one *in* the other. And in like manner when you are really reading *Hamlet*, the action and the characters are not some-

---

[28]Shelley, "Lines Written in Dejection—December 1818, Near the Bay of Naples." [Bradley's note]

thing which you conceive apart from the words; you apprehend them from point to point *in* the words, and the words as expressions of them. Afterwards, no doubt, when you are out of the poetic experience but remember it, you may by analysis decompose this unity, and attend to a substance more or less isolated, and a form more or less isolated. But these are things in your analytic head, not in the poem, which is *poetic* experience. And if you want to have the poem again, you cannot find it by adding together these two products of decomposition; you can only find it by passing back into poetic experience. And then what you recover is no aggregate of factors, it is a unity in which you can no more separate a substance and a form than you can separate living blood and the life in the blood. This unity has, if you like, various "aspects" or "sides," but they are not factors or parts; if you try to examine one, you find it is also the other. Call them substance and form if you please, but these are not the reciprocally exclusive substance and form to which the two contentions *must* refer. They do not "agree," for they are not apart: they are one thing from different points of view, and in that sense identical. And this identity of content and form, you will say, is no accident; it is of the essence of poetry insofar as it is poetry, and of all art insofar as it is art. Just as there is in music not sound on one side and a meaning on the other, but expressive sound, and if you ask what is the meaning you can only answer by pointing to the sounds; just as in painting there is not a meaning *plus* paint, but a meaning *in* paint, or significant paint, and no man can really express the meaning in any other way than in paint and in *this* paint; so in a poem the true content and the true form neither exist nor can be imagined apart. When then you are asked whether the value of a poem lies in a substance got by decomposing the poem, and present, as such, only in reflective analysis, or whether the value lies in a form arrived at and existing in the same way, you will answer, "It lies neither in one, nor in the other, nor in any addition of them, but in the poem, where they are not."

We have then, first, an antithesis of subject and poem. This is clear 15 and valid; and the question in which of them does the value lie is intelligible; and its answer is, *In the poem*. We have next a distinction of substance and form. If the substance means ideas, images, and the like taken alone, and the form means the measured language taken by itself, this is a possible distinction, but it is a distinction of things not in the poem, and the value lies *in neither of them*. If substance and form mean anything *in* the poem, then each is involved in the other, and the question in which of them the value lies has no sense. No doubt you may say, speaking loosely, that in this poet or poem the aspect of substance is the more noticeable, and in that the aspect of form; and you may pursue interesting discussions on this basis, though no principle or ultimate question of value is touched by them. And apart from that question, of course, I am not denying the usefulness and necessity of the distinction. We cannot dispense with it. To consider separately the action or the characters of a play, and separately its style or versification, is both legitimate and valuable, so long as we remember what we are doing. But the true critic in speaking of these apart does not really think of them apart; the whole, the poetic experience, of which they are but aspects, is always in his mind; and he is always aiming at a richer, truer, more intense repetition of that experience. On the other hand, when the question of principle, of poetic value, is raised, these aspects *must* fall apart into components, separately inconceivable; and then there arise two heresies, equally false, that the value lies in one of two things, both of which are outside the poem, and therefore where its value cannot lie.

On the heresy of the separable substance a few additional words 16 will suffice. This heresy is seldom formulated, but perhaps some unconscious holder of it may object: "Surely the action and the characters of *Hamlet* are in the play; and surely I can retain these, though I have forgotten all the words. I admit that I do not possess the whole poem, but I possess a part, and the most important part." And I would answer: "If we are not concerned with any question of principle, I accept all that you say except the last words, which do raise such a question. Speaking loosely, I agree that the action and characters, as you perhaps conceive them, together with a great deal more, are in the poem. Even then, however, you must not claim to possess all of this kind that is in the poem; for in forgetting the words you must have lost innumerable details of the action and the characters. And, when the question of value is raised, I must insist that the action and characters, as you conceive them, are not in *Hamlet* at all. If they are, point them out. You cannot do it. What you find at any moment of that succession of experiences called *Hamlet* is words. In these words, to speak loosely again, the action and characters (more of them than you can conceive apart) are focused; but your experience is not a combination of them, as ideas, on the one side, with certain sounds on the other; it is an experience of something in which the two are indissolubly fused. If you deny this, to be sure I can make no answer, or can only answer that I have reason to believe that you cannot read poetically, or else are misinterpreting your experience. But if you do not deny this, then you will admit that the action and characters of the poem, as you separately imagine them, are no part of it, but a product of it in your reflective imagination, a faint analogue of one aspect of it taken in detachment from the whole. Well, I do not dispute, I would even insist, that, in the case of so long a poem as *Hamlet*, it may be necessary from time to time to interrupt the poetic experience, in order to enrich it by forming such a product and dwelling on it. Nor, in a wide sense of 'poetic,' do I question the poetic value of this product, as you think of it apart from the poem. It resembles our recollections of the heroes of history or legend, who move about in our imaginations, 'forms more real than living man,' and are worth much to us though we do not remember anything they said. Our ideas and images of the 'substance' of a poem have this poetic value, and more, if they are at all adequate. But they cannot determine the poetic value of the poem, for (not to speak of the competing claims of the 'form') nothing that is outside the poem can do that, and they, as such, are outside it."[29]

Let us turn to the so-called form—style and versification. There is no such thing as mere form in poetry. All form is expression. Style may have indeed a certain esthetic worth in partial abstraction from the particular matter it conveys, as in a well-built sentence you may take pleasure in the build almost apart from the meaning. Even so, style is expressive—presents to sense, for example, the order, ease, and rapidity with which ideas move in the writer's mind—but it is not expressive of the meaning of that particular sentence. And it is possible, interrupting poetic experience, to decompose it and abstract for comparatively separate consideration this nearly formal element of style. But the esthetic value of style so taken is not considerable;[30] you could not read with pleasure for an hour a composition which had no other merit. And in poetic experience you never apprehend this value by itself; the style is here expressive also of a particular meaning, or rather is one aspect of that unity whose other aspect is meaning. So that what you apprehend may be called indifferently an expressed

17

---

[29]These remarks will hold good, *mutatis mutandis* [if the proper changes are made], if by "substance" is understood the "moral" or the "idea" of a poem, although perhaps in one instance out of five thousand this may be found in so many words in the poem. [Bradley's note]

[30]On the other hand, the absence, or worse than absence, of style, in this sense, is a serious matter. [Bradley's note]

meaning or a significant form. Perhaps on this point I may in Oxford appeal to authority, that of Matthew Arnold[31] and Walter Pater,[32] the latter at any rate an authority whom the formalist will not despise. What is the gist of Pater's teaching about style, if it is not that in the end the one virtue of style is truth or adequacy; that the word, phrase, sentence, should express perfectly the writer's perception, feeling, image, or thought; so that, as we read a descriptive phrase of Keats's,[33] we exclaim, "That is the thing itself"; so that, to quote Arnold, the words are "symbols equivalent with the thing symbolized," or, in our technical language, a form identical with its content. Hence in true poetry it is, in strictness, impossible to express the meaning in any but its own words, or to change the words without changing the meaning. A translation of such poetry is not really the old meaning in a fresh dress; it is a new product, something like the poem, though, if one chooses to say so, more like it in the aspect of meaning than in the aspect of form.

No one who understands poetry, it seems to me, would dispute 18 this, were it not that, falling away from his experience, or misled by theory, he takes the word "meaning" in a sense almost ludicrously inapplicable to poetry. People say, for instance, "steed" and "horse" have the same meaning; and in bad poetry they have, but not in poetry that *is* poetry.

> "Bring forth the horse!" The horse was brought:
> In truth he was a noble steed!

says Byron[34] in *Mazeppa*. If the two words mean the same here, transpose them:

---

[31]***Matthew Arnold (1822–1888)*** Important English poet. He was elected poetry professor at Oxford in 1857, and is the author of "The Scholar Gypsy" (1853) and "Dover Beach" (1867), both of which express fear and criticism of contemporary industrialism. In *Culture and Anarchy* (1869) Arnold wrote extensively about the tastes of the public and the problems of a modern society that tended not to value excellence of style or purity of thought and feeling.

[32]***Walter Pater (1839–1894)*** *Studies in the History of the Renaissance* (1873) made Pater one of the most influential art critics of the Victorian period. He was above all an art-for-art's-sake critic—quite unlike Arnold. Yet, like Arnold, he was a gifted stylist.

[33]***a descriptive phrase of Keats's*** John Keats (1795–1821) was noted for intense and emotional descriptive passages in his poems. He often appealed to more than one sense in his images.

[34]***George Gordon, Lord Byron (1788–1824)*** The most famous of the English Romantic poets. *Mazeppa, a Tale of the Russian Ukraine* (1819) was a typical exotic adventure tale of the sort prized by Byron's international readership.

> "Bring forth the steed!" The steed was brought:
> In truth he was a noble horse!

and ask again if they mean the same. Or let me take a line certainly very free from "poetic diction":[35]

> To be or not to be, that is the question.

You may say that this means the same as "What is just now occupying my attention is the comparative disadvantages of continuing to live or putting an end to myself." And for practical purposes—the purpose, for example, of a coroner—it does. But as the second version altogether misrepresents the speaker at that moment of his existence, while the first does represent him, how can they for any but a practical or logical purpose be said to have the same sense? Hamlet was well able to "unpack his heart with words,"[36] but he will not unpack it with our paraphrases.

These considerations apply equally to versification. If I take the famous line which describes how the souls of the dead stood waiting by the river, imploring a passage from Charon: ₁₉

> Tendebantque manus ripae ulterioris amore,[37]

and if I translate it, "and were stretching forth their hands in longing for the further bank," the charm of the original has fled. Why has it fled? Partly (but we have dealt with that) because I have substituted for five words, and those the words of Virgil, twelve words, and those my own. In some measure because I have turned into rhythmless prose a line of verse which, as mere sound, has unusual beauty. But much more because in doing so I have also changed the *meaning* of Virgil's line. What that meaning is *I* cannot say: Virgil has said it. But I can see this much, that the translation conveys a far less vivid picture of the outstretched hands and of their remaining outstretched, and a far less poignant sense of the distance of the shore and the longing of the souls. And it does so partly because this picture and this sense are

---

[35]***poetic diction*** "Steed" rather than "horse" is an example of the high-flown poetic diction Bradley considers undesirable. He equates it with a falsification of style. Byron and other Romantics fought against any unnatural poetic diction, and Byron, in particular, often ridiculed it.

[36]***"unpack [his] heart with words"*** In one of his soliloquies, Hamlet chastises himself for needing to do this, and so for delaying the vengeance he feels he must take on his father's murderer (Hamlet II.ii:561).

[37]The line is from Virgil's *Aeneid* (vi.314). In classical mythology, Charon is the ferryman who brought the recently dead to Hades.

conveyed not only by the obvious meaning of the words, but through the long-drawn sound of "tendebantque," through the time occupied by the five syllables and therefore by the idea of "ulterioris," and through the identity of the long sound "or" in the penultimate syllables[38] of "ulterioris amore"—all this, and much more, apprehended not in this analytical fashion, nor as *added* to the beauty of mere sound and to the obvious meaning, but in unity with them and so as expressive of the poetic meaning of the whole.

It is always so in fine poetry. The value of versification, when it is 20 indissolubly fused with meaning, can hardly be exaggerated. The gift for feeling it, even more perhaps than the gift for feeling the value of style, is the *specific* gift for poetry, as distinguished from other arts. But versification, taken, as far as possible, all by itself, has a very different worth. Some esthetic worth it has; how much, you may experience by reading poetry in a language of which you do not understand a syllable. The pleasure is quite appreciable, but it is not great; nor in actual poetic experience do you meet with it, as such, at all. For, I repeat, it is not *added* to the pleasure of the meaning when you read poetry that you do understand: by some mystery the music is then the music *of* the meaning, and the two are one. However fond of versification you might be, you would tire very soon of reading verses in Chinese; and before long of reading Virgil and Dante[39] if you were ignorant of their languages. But take the music as it is *in* the poem, and there is a marvelous change. Now

> It gives a very echo to the seat
> Where Love is throned,[40]

or "carries far into your heart," almost like music itself, the sound

> Of old, unhappy, far-off things
> And battles long ago.[41]

What then is to be said of the following sentence of the critic 21 quoted before:[42] "But when anyone who knows what poetry is reads—

---

[38]*penultimate syllables*   next-to-last syllables.
[39]*Virgil (70–19 B.C.) and Dante (1265–1321)*   Great epic poets.
[40]*Twelfth Night*, II.iv. [Bradley's note] Shakespeare's comedy.
[41]Wordsworth, "The Solitary Reaper." [Bradley's note]
[42]Saintsbury, *History of English Prosody*, iii. pp. 71–74. [Bradley's note]

> Our noisy years seem moments in the being
> Of the eternal silence,[43]

he sees that, quite independently of the meaning, . . . there is one note added to the articulate music of the world—a note that never will leave off resounding till the eternal silence itself gulfs it"? I must think that the writer is deceiving himself. For I could quite understand his enthusiasm, if it were an enthusiasm for the music of the meaning; but as for the music, "quite independently of the meaning," so far as I can hear it thus (and I doubt if any one who knows English can quite do so), I find it gives some pleasure, but only a trifling pleasure. And indeed I venture to doubt whether, considered as mere sound, the words are at all exceptionally beautiful, as Virgil's line certainly is. . . .

Pure poetry is not the decoration of a preconceived and clearly de- 22 fined matter: it springs from the creative impulse of a vague imaginative mass pressing for development and definition. If the poet already knew exactly what he meant to say, why should he write the poem? The poem would in fact already be written. For only its completion can reveal, even to him, exactly what he wanted. When he began and while he was at work, he did not possess his meaning; it possessed him. It was not a fully formed soul asking for a body: it was an inchoate soul in the inchoate body of perhaps two or three vague ideas and a few scattered phrases. The growing of this body into its full stature and perfect shape was the same thing as the gradual self-definition of the meaning. And this is the reason why such poems strike us as creations, not manufactures, and have the magical effect which mere decoration cannot produce. This is also the reason why, if we insist on asking for the meaning of such a poem, we can only be answered, "It means itself."

And so at last I may explain why I have troubled myself and you 23 with what may seem an arid controversy about mere words. It is not so. These heresies which would make poetry a compound of two factors—a matter common to it with the merest prose, *plus* a poetic form, as the one heresy says: a poetical substance *plus* a negligible form, as the other says—are not only untrue, they are injurious to the dignity of poetry. In an age already inclined to shrink from those higher realms where poetry touches religion and philosophy, the formalist heresy en-

---

[43]Wordsworth, "Ode on the Intimations of Immortality." [Bradley's note]

courages men to taste poetry as they would a fine wine, which has indeed an esthetic value, but a small one. And then the natural man, finding an empty form, hurls into it the matter of cheap pathos, rancid sentiment, vulgar humor, bare lust, ravenous vanity—everything which, in Schiller's phrase,[44] the form should extirpate, but which no mere form can extirpate. And the other heresy—which is indeed rather a practice than a creed—encourages us in the habit so dear to us of putting our own thoughts or fancies into the place of the poet's creation. What he meant by *Hamlet,* or the *Ode to a Nightingale,* or *Abt Vogler,*[45] we say, is this or that which we knew already; and so we lose what he had to tell us. But he meant what he said, and said what he meant.

Poetry in this matter is not, as good critics of painting and music 24 often affirm, different from the other arts; in all of them the content is one thing with the form. What Beethoven[46] meant by his symphony, or Turner[47] by his picture, was not something which you can name, but the picture and the symphony. Meaning they have, but *what* meaning can be said in no language but their own: and we know this, though some strange delusion makes us think the meaning has less worth because we cannot put it into words. Well, it is just the same with poetry. But because poetry is words, we vainly fancy that some other words than its own will express its meaning. And they will do so no more—or, if you like to speak loosely, only a little more—than words will express the meaning of the Dresden Madonna. Something a little like it they may indeed express. And we may find analogues of the meaning of poetry outside it, which may help us to appropriate it. The other arts, the best ideas of philosophy or religion, much that nature and life offer us or force upon us, are akin to it. But they are only akin. Nor is it the expression of them. Poetry does not present to imagination our highest knowledge or belief, and much less our dreams and opinions; but it, content and form in unity, embodies in its own irreplaceable way something which embodies itself also in other irreplaceable ways, such as philosophy or religion. And just as each of these gives a satisfaction which the other cannot possibly give, so we find in

---

[44]Not that to Schiller "form" meant mere style and versification. [Bradley's note] *Extirpate* means to root out, remove completely.

[45]**Abt Vogler** A poem by the English poet Robert Browning (1812–1899).

[46]*Ludwig van Beethoven (1770–1827)* German composer.

[47]*Joseph Mallord William Turner (1775–1851)* One of the most popular English painters.

poetry, which cannot satisfy the needs they meet, that which by their natures they cannot afford us. But we shall not find it fully if we look for something else.

And now, when all is said, the question will still recur, though now 25 in quite another sense, What does poetry mean? This unique expression, which cannot be replaced by any other, still seems to be trying to express something beyond itself. And this, we feel, is also what the other arts, and religion, and philosophy are trying to express: and that is what impels us to seek in vain to translate the one into the other. About the best poetry, and not only the best, there floats an atmosphere of infinite suggestion. The poet speaks to us of one thing, but in this one thing there seems to lurk the secret of all. He said what he meant, but his meaning seems to beckon away beyond itself, or rather to expand into something boundless which is only focused in it; something also which, we feel, would satisfy not only the imagination, but the whole of us; that something within us, and without, which everywhere

> makes us seem
> To patch up fragments of a dream,
> Part of which comes true, and part
> Beats and trembles in the heart.[48]

Those who are susceptible to this effect of poetry find it not only, perhaps not most, in the ideals which she has sometimes described, but in a child's song by Christina Rossetti[49] about a mere crown of wind-flowers, and in tragedies like *Lear*,[50] where the sun seems to have set forever. They hear this spirit murmuring its undertone through the *Aeneid*, and catch its voice in the song of Keats's nightingale, and its light upon the figures on the Urn,[51] and it pierces them

---

[48]Shelley, "Is it that in some brighter sphere?" [Bradley's note]

[49]*Christina Rossetti (1830–1894)* English poet of generally religious lyrics; sister of Dante Gabriel Rossetti (see note 21).

[50]**King Lear** Tragedy by William Shakespeare. This was so dark a play that eighteenth-century interpreters rewrote it with a happier ending. In Shakespeare's play, not only does Lear die, but his innocent daughter Cordelia, the only one who has not betrayed him, dies as well.

[51]*the Urn* John Keats (1795–1821) wrote "Ode on a Grecian Urn" (1820), a poem that describes ancients in a procession to a sacrifice as portrayed on the side of an urn. Keats was moved deeply by the permanence with which they had been captured in the artistry of the urn. His "Ode to a Nightingale" (1819) is a celebration of the permanence of the song of the nightingale in contrast to Keats's own impermanence: He knew he was dying of tuberculosis.

no less in Shelley's hopeless lament, *O world, O life, O time,*[52] than in the rapturous ecstasy of his *Life of Life.* This all-embracing perfection cannot be expressed in poetic words or words of any kind, nor yet in music or in color, but the suggestion of it is in much poetry, if not all, and poetry has in this suggestion, this "meaning," a great part of its value. We do it wrong, and we defeat our own purposes when we try to bend it to them:

> We do it wrong, being so majestical,
> To offer it the show of violence;
> For it is as the air invulnerable,
> And our vain blows malicious mockery.[53]

It is a spirit. It comes we know not whence. It will not speak at our bidding, nor answer in our language. It is not our servant; it is our master.

QUESTIONS

1. Bradley delivered this piece as a lecture. What assumptions can you make about the audience that heard him?
2. What is the subject of a poem? What is its form?
3. What does Bradley mean by the title, "Poetry for Poetry's Sake"? How can poetry ever be for its own sake?
4. Judging from this work, what do formalists seem to believe about poetry? Are their views defensible?
5. What are Bradley's views about the "imaginative experience" of poetry? Would it be the same for most readers?

WRITING ASSIGNMENTS

1. In paragraphs 7, 8, and 9, Bradley essentially "proves" the truth of the formalist position. Yet, he eventually moves away from it. Why? Analyze the formalist argument, establishing what you think is accurate and defensible

---

[52]**O world, O life, O time** English poet Percy Bysshe Shelley wrote this lament in 1821, near the end of his life, shortly before his accidental drowning at age thirty. *Life of Life* is a hymn to the sun, sung by spirits in Shelley's lyrical drama *Prometheus Unbound* (II.ii. 48–71), written in 1818.

[53]From Shakespeare's *Hamlet* (I.i. 143–146). The lines are delivered by Marcellus and refer to the Ghost of Hamlet's father.

about it. Then show what the shortcomings of the position are and try to explain why Bradley moved away from it.

2. In paragraph 16 and elsewhere, Bradley discusses Shakespeare's *Hamlet*. If you have read the play, inventory this selection for references to *Hamlet* and explain why it is a good (or bad) choice for Bradley's discussion. Does the character Hamlet have anything in common with Bradley? Is there anything analogous between Hamlet's search and Bradley's? Are there any curious connections between Bradley's comments on *Hamlet* and the rest of the argument of the essay?

3. After having seen a play, film, or television production, what do you take away with you? You cannot remember all the words of it so the problem is, what stays with you? Is it the substance of the work? Is it an aspect of the form? Or is it an impression? If so, what kind of impression? Answer these questions with reference to a specific work you have recently seen.

4. On the basis of reading this work, and referring to specific statements in it, defend or attack the view that poetry should be for its own sake. This means that poetry should not serve any purposes but the purposes of what the artist conceives to be the work itself. It should not "serve" society, the nation, religion, science, or any end other than an aesthetic one. Find as much evidence as you can for or against this view. Rely on this selection, on other reading you have done, and on your own reasoning.

5. Assume that you cannot do as Bradley has done, that is, defend subject, substance, and form. Assume that you must defend one factor as being the most important one in evaluating a work of art. Which will you defend? Why? In the process of arguing, be sure to define carefully each key term in your early statements. Leave yourself room to analyze thoroughly all relevant aspects of your key terms.

6. Attempt to answer the question Bradley raises in paragraph 25: "What does poetry mean?" Try to analyze the complexities that reside in the concept of "mean." Analyze Bradley's views on the way in which a poem can mean; be sure to include, as well, any relevant arguments relating to the way other works of art "mean." Does a poem have to be translated into different words in order to mean something? Why would anyone worry about whether a poem means something or not?

T. S. ELIOT

————◈————

Tradition and
the Individual Talent

THOMAS STEARNS ELIOT (1888–1965) is generally regarded as one
of the most important twentieth-century American poets. His
achievements in poetry were accompanied by a large body of literary
criticism and several verse plays. His poetry became so influential
that it was almost impossible for an American poet of the 1950s and
1960s to avoid working in his shadow. "The Love Song of J. Alfred
Prufrock" (1917), The Waste Land (1922), and "The Hollow Men"
(1925) constituted in themselves a modernist movement in poetry,
introducing Eliot's particular approach to style: using traditional
rhythms, abrupt shifts, and sudden parodies, sometimes resembling
the collage. Four Quartets (1943) was a major work, four religious
poems establishing Eliot as the only major religious poet of his age.
In 1948 Eliot received the Nobel Prize for Literature.

Eliot's career in business brought him from a clerkship in a Lloyds
bank in London, where he lived most of his adult life—despite having New England roots and having been born in Missouri—to a direc-
torship in the English publishing firm of Faber and Faber. He became
a British citizen in 1927. He also was an editor of the literary journals
The Criterion (of which he was a co-founder) and The Egoist. His
plays include Murder in the Cathedral (1935), The Cocktail Party
(1949), and The Confidential Clerk (1954). His work as a playwright

met with considerable success, although it was by no means as influential as his poetry.

"Tradition and the Individual Talent" (1919) was one of Eliot's
major critical documents. But it was only one part of a large and very
important body of critical statements included in such works as The
Sacred Wood (1920), Selected Essays: 1917–1932 (1932), The Use of
Poetry and the Use of Criticism (1933), and After Strange Gods: A
Primer of Modern Heresy (1934). The last of these attempted to apply
some of the theories expressed in "Tradition and the Individual Talent" to cultural matters.

"Tradition and the Individual Talent" argues for a poetry which is
impersonal, or which at least avoids the expression of personal emotion. The poet's mind is seen as a kind of catalyst, separate from the
emotions the poems portray. Eliot implies that many poets are so ordinary in their own lives that it is unreasonable to ask that their work
express their own emotions. He suffered a good many personal agon-
ies—such as the institutionalization of his first wife—which he kept
much to himself.

The essay also argues a fascinating point: that the creation of a
major work of poetry alters the history of poetry. The tradition to
which Eliot refers is the canon of great poetry which one perceives in
reviewing its history. In a sense, he says that every poet writes with
an awareness of the great poets of the past, hoping to be worthy of
being one of their number. But he also says that it is possible to be
part of the steady flow of history, past and present, which is the
history of poetry. And, finally, he claims that it is possible for the
present to affect the past. The contemporary poet can, in other
words, affect the history of poetry.

ELIOT'S RHETORIC

Eliot's rhetorical devices include the familiar use of analysis, particularly through the device of definition. The opening paragraph, for
instance, begins with an examination of what is generally meant by
the term "tradition." His conclusion is that it is used in a vaguely
disapproving way, as if it were a problem for a poet rather than the
poet's major resource. In paragraph 2 he points out that we often most
value the work of a poet who breaks with tradition, since this implies
novelty, which we tend to value highly. In paragraph 3 he brings us
to the awareness that tradition in literature is not inherited; it is
earned by the labor of the poet. And he tells us that it may be the

things a modern poet has in common with Virgil, Dante, and Shakespeare that will make the poet valuable to us.

Eliot is a cautious writer. He moves carefully from point to point, considering in a given paragraph a single issue that demands his complete attention. He also tends to weight the end of each paragraph with its most important and definitive statement. Thus, it is useful to read Eliot knowing that he feels that the end of a paragraph has the most important rhetorical force for the reader.

One of Eliot's most interesting stylistic capacities is his ability to produce a memorable sentence or phrase. This essay has a number of statements that are often taken by themselves as if they were aphorisms. The aphorism, as we know, has special powers because we naturally want to accept its wisdom. Consider just a few:

> Every nation, every race, has not only its own creative, but its own critical turn of mind. (para. 2)

> The progress of the artist is a continual self-sacrifice, a continual extinction of personality. (para. 9)

> Poetry is not a turning loose of emotion, but an escape from emotion. (para. 17)

The use of the aphorism, or of a statement that is designed to be compressed and emphatic like an aphorism, is a great resource in writing. It conveys to the reader a sense of wisdom, and it permits the reader to absorb a considerable understanding from a very brief expression. There is, as it were, an impressive intellectual economy in the aphorism, and that translates into a remarkable rhetorical advantage.

Tradition and
the Individual Talent

In English writing we seldom speak of tradition, though we occa- 1
sionally apply its name in deploring its absence. We cannot refer to
"the tradition" or to "a tradition"; at most, we employ the adjective in
saying that the poetry of So-and-so is "traditional" or even "too traditional." Seldom, perhaps, does the word appear except in a phrase of
censure. If otherwise, it is vaguely approbative,[1] with the implication,
as to the work approved, of some pleasing archaeological reconstruction. You can hardly make the word agreeable to English ears without
this comfortable reference to the reassuring science of archaeology.

Certainly the word is not likely to appear in our appreciations of 2
living or dead writers. Every nation, every race, has not only its own
creative, but its own critical turn of mind; and is even more oblivious
of the shortcomings and limitations of its critical habits than of those
of its creative genius. We know, or think we know, from the enormous
mass of critical writing that has appeared in the French language the
critical method or habit of the French; we only conclude (we are such
unconscious people) that the French are "more critical" than we, and
sometimes even plume ourselves a little with the fact, as if the French
were the less spontaneous. Perhaps they are; but we might remind
ourselves that criticism is as inevitable as breathing, and that we
should be none the worse for articulating what passes in our minds
when we read a book and feel an emotion about it, for criticizing our
own minds in their work of criticism. One of the facts that might
come to light in this process is our tendency to insist, when we praise
a poet, upon those aspects of his work in which he least resembles
anyone else. In these aspects or parts of his work we pretend to find
what is individual, what is the peculiar essence of the man. We dwell
with satisfaction upon the poet's difference from his predecessors, especially his immediate predecessors; we endeavour to find something
that can be isolated in order to be enjoyed. Whereas if we approach a
poet without his prejudice we shall often find that not only the best,

---

[1]**approbative** approving; used in a good sense.

but the most individual parts of his work may be those in which the dead poets, his ancestors, assert their immortality most vigorously. And I do not mean the impressionable period of adolescence, but the period of full maturity.

Yet if the only form of tradition, of handing down, consisted in 3 following the ways of the immediate generation before us in a blind or timid adherence to its successes, "tradition" should positively be discouraged. We have seen many such simple currents soon lost in the sand; and novelty is better than repetition. Tradition is a matter of much wider significance. It cannot be inherited, and if you want it you must obtain it by great labour. It involves, in the first place, the historical sense, which we may call nearly indispensable to any one who would continue to be a poet beyond his twenty-fifth year; and the historical sense involves a perception, not only of the pastness of the past, but of its presence; the historical sense compels a man to write not merely with his own generation in his bones, but with a feeling that the whole of the literature of Europe from Homer and within it the whole of the literature of his own country has a simultaneous existence and composes a simultaneous order. This historical sense, which is a sense of the timeless as well as of the temporal and of the timeless and of the temporal together, is what makes a writer traditional. And it is at the same time what makes a writer most acutely conscious of his place in time, of his own contemporaneity.

No poet, no artist of any art, has his complete meaning alone. His 4 significance, his appreciation is the appreciation of his relation to the dead poets and artists. You cannot value him alone; you must set him, for contrast and comparison, among the dead. I mean this as a principle of aesthetic, not merely historical, criticism. The necessity that he shall conform, that he shall cohere, is not onesided; what happens when a new work of art is created is something that happens simultaneously to all the works of art which preceded it. The existing monuments form an ideal order among themselves, which is modified by the introduction of the new (the really new) work of art among them. The existing order is complete before the new work arrives; for order to persist after the supervention[2] of novelty, the *whole* existing order must be, if ever so slightly, altered; and so the relations, proportions, values of each work of art toward the whole are readjusted; and this is conformity between the old and the new. Whoever has approved this idea of order, of the form of European, of English literature will

---

[2]**supervention** coming unexpectedly; an addition.

not find it preposterous that the past should be altered by the present as much as the present is directed by the past. And the poet who is aware of this will be aware of great difficulties and responsibilities.

In a peculiar sense he will be aware also that he must inevitably be   5 judged by the standards of the past. I say judged, not amputated, by them; not judged to be as good as, or worse or better than, the dead; and certainly not judged by the canons of dead critics. It is a judgment, a comparison, in which two things are measured by each other. To conform merely would be for the new work not really to conform at all; it would not be new, and would therefore not be a work of art. And we do not quite say that the new is more valuable because it fits in; but its fitting in is a test of its value—a test, it is true, which can only be slowly and cautiously applied, for we are none of us infallible judges of conformity. We say: it appears to conform, and is perhaps individual, or it appears individual, and may conform; but we are hardly likely to find that it is one and not the other.

To proceed to a more intelligible exposition of the relation of the   6 poet to the past: he can neither take the past as a lump, an indiscriminate bolus,[3] nor can he form himself wholly on one or two private admirations, nor can he form himself wholly upon one preferred period. The first course is inadmissible, the second is an important experience of youth, and the third is a pleasant and highly desirable supplement. The poet must be very conscious of the main current, which does not at all flow invariably through the most distinguished reputations. He must be quite aware of the obvious fact that art never improves, but that the material of art is never quite the same. He must be aware that the mind of Europe—the mind of his own country—a mind which he learns in time to be much more important than his own private mind—is a mind which changes, and that this change is a development which abandons nothing *en route*, which does not superannuate[4] either Shakespeare, or Homer, or the rock drawing of the Magdalenian draughtsmen.[5] That this development, refinement perhaps, complication certainly, is not, from the point of view of the artist, any improvement. Perhaps not even an improvement from the point of view of the psychologist or not to the extent which we imag-

---

[3]***bolus*** A large pill or mass of chewed food. Eliot means we cannot take the past without examination, as if it were medication or a predigested lump urged upon us. We must understand it because it is a part of us.

[4]***superannuate*** make obsolete.

[5]***Magdalenian draughtsmen*** prehistoric artists who painted walls of caves discovered near the village of La Madeleine, France.

ine; perhaps only in the end based upon a complication in economics and machinery. But the difference between the present and the past is that the conscious present is an awareness of the past in a way and to an extent which the past's awareness of itself cannot show.

Someone said: "The dead writers are remote from us because we 7 *know* so much more than they did." Precisely, and they are that which we know.

I am alive to a usual objection to what is clearly part of my pro- 8 gramme for the *métier* of poetry.[6] The objection is that the doctrine requires a ridiculous amount of erudition (pedantry), a claim which can be rejected by appeal to the lives of poets in any pantheon.[7] It will even be affirmed that much learning deadens or perverts poetic sensibility. While, however, we persist in believing that a poet ought to know as much as will not encroach upon his necessary receptivity and necessary laziness, it is not desirable to confine knowledge to whatever can be put into a useful shape for examinations, drawing-rooms, or the still more pretentious modes of publicity. Some can absorb knowledge, the more tardy must sweat for it. Shakespeare acquired more essential history from Plutarch[8] than most men could from the whole British Museum. What is to be insisted upon is that the poet must develop or procure the consciousness of the past and that he should continue to develop this consciousness throughout his career.

What happens is a continual surrender of himself as he is at the 9 moment to something which is more valuable. The progress of an artist is a continual self-sacrifice, a continual extinction of personality.

There remains to define this process of depersonalization[9] and its 10 relation to the sense of tradition. It is in this depersonalization that art may be said to approach the condition of science. I, therefore, invite you to consider, as a suggestive analogy, the action which takes place when a bit of finely filiated platinum[10] is introduced into a chamber containing oxygen and sulphur dioxide.

---

[6]**métier** *of poetry*   the practice or vocation of poetry.

[7]**pantheon**   Grouping of gods. The word refers to the place where all *(pan)* the gods *(theoi)* dwell. Here it means the most immortal or long-lived of poets.

[8]**Plutarch (46?–120 A.D.)**   Greek biographer of some of Shakespeare's heroes, such as Julius Caesar, Antony, and Cleopatra. His *Parallel Lives* is a chief source of Roman history. The British Museum holds historical monuments (such as the Rosetta Stone) but does not vivify or explain them.

[9]**depersonalization**   The avoidance of limited, personal involvement; transcending personal limits.

[10]**filiated platinum**   thin platinum wire.

Honest criticism and sensitive appreciation are directed not upon 11
the poet but upon the poetry. If we attend to the confused cries of the
newspaper critics and the *susurrus*[11] of popular repetition that follows,
we shall hear the names of poets in great numbers; if we seek not Blue-
book knowledge[12] but the enjoyment of poetry, and ask for a poem, we
shall seldom find it. I have tried to point out the importance of the
relation of the poem to other poems by other authors, and suggested
the conception of poetry as a living whole of all the poetry that has
ever been written. The other aspect of this Impersonal theory of poetry
is the relation of the poem to its author. And I hinted, by an analogy,
that the mind of the mature poet differs from that of the immature
one not precisely in any valuation of "personality," not being necessarily more interesting, or having "more to say," but rather by being a
more finely perfected medium in which special, or very varied, feelings
are at liberty to enter into new combinations.

The analogy was that of the catalyst.[13] When the two gases previ- 12
ously mentioned are mixed in the presence of a filament of platinum,
they form sulphurous acid. This combination takes place only if the
platinum is present; nevertheless the newly formed acid contains no
trace of platinum, and the platinum itself is apparently unaffected; has
remained inert, neutral, and unchanged. The mind of the poet is the
shred of platinum. It may partly or exclusively operate upon the experience of the man himself; but, the more perfect the artist, the more
completely separate in him will be the man who suffers and the mind
which creates; the more perfectly will the mind digest and transmute
the passions which are its material.

The experience, you will notice, the elements which enter the pres- 13
ence of the transforming catalyst, are of two kinds: emotions and feelings. The effect of a work of art upon the person who enjoys it is an
experience different in kind from any experience not of art. It may be
formed out of one emotion, or may be a combination of several; and
various feelings, inhering for the writer in particular words or phrases
or images, may be added to compose the final result. Or great poetry
may be made without the direct use of any emotion whatever: com-

---

[11]**susurrus** murmuring or rustling sound.

[12]**Blue-book knowledge** Knowledge of the kind useful in an examination.

[13]**catalyst** A chemical substance whose presence causes a reaction, but which itself
remains inert and uninvolved in the reaction.

posed out of feelings solely. Canto XV of the *Inferno* (Brunetto Latini)[14] is a working up of the emotion evident in the situation; but the effect, though single as that of any work of art, is obtained by considerable complexity of detail. The last quatrain gives an image, a feeling attaching to an image, which "came," which did not develop simply out of what precedes, but which was probably in suspension in the poet's mind until the proper combination arrived for it to add itself to. The poet's mind is in fact a receptacle for seizing and storing up numberless feelings, phrases, images, which remain there until all the particles which can unite to form a new compound are present together.

If you compare several representative passages of the greatest poetry you see how great is the variety of types of combination, and also how completely any semi-ethical criterion of "sublimity" misses the mark. For it is not the "greatness," the intensity, of the emotions, the components, but the intensity of the artistic process, the pressure, so to speak, under which the fusion takes place, that counts. The episode of Paolo and Francesca[15] employs a definite emotion, but the intensity of the poetry is something quite different from whatever intensity in the supposed experience it may give the impression of. It is no more intense, furthermore, than Canto XXVI, the voyage of Ulysses,[16] which has not the direct dependence upon an emotion. Great variety is possible in the process of transmutation of emotion: the murder of Agamemnon, or the agony of Othello,[17] gives an artistic effect apparently closer to a possible original than the scenes from Dante. In the *Agamemnon*, the artistic emotion approximates to the emotion of an actual spectator; in *Othello* to the emotion of the protagonist[18] himself. But the difference between art and the event is always absolute; the

14

---

[14]***Brunetto Latini (ca. 1210–1294)*** In one of the most touching sections of the *Divine Comedy* by Dante Alighieri (1265–1321), the poet meets his former mentor and is moved to see him in hell (*Inferno*, Canto XV). Dante puts Latini in the seventh circle of hell, in the zone where sodomites are punished. This surprised Dante's contemporaries and later commentators, for Latini vehemently denounced this crime in his own work. The last quatrain, to which Eliot refers, presents a startling image of Latini turning and running "like one of those who race across the fields to win the green cloth at Verona."

[15]***Paolo and Francesca*** Illicit lovers forever joined together in Canto V of Dante's *Inferno*, the first of the three parts of the *Divine Comedy*.

[16]***Ulysses*** Hero of Homer's *Odyssey* who appears as a restless old man in the *Inferno*.

[17]***Agamemnon and Othello*** Tragic heroes of *Agamemnon* by Aeschylus (525?–456 B.C.) and *Othello* by William Shakespeare (1564–1616).

[18]***protagonist*** main character; hero.

combination which is the murder of Agamemnon is probably as complex as that which is the voyage of Ulysses. In either case there has been a fusion of elements. The ode of Keats[19] contains a number of feelings which have nothing particular to do with the nightingale, but which the nightingale, partly, perhaps, because of its attractive name, and partly because of its reputation, served to bring together.

The point of view which I am struggling to attack is perhaps related to the metaphysical theory of the substantial unity of the soul:[20] for my meaning is, that the poet has, not a "personality" to express, but a particular medium, which is only a medium and not a personality, in which impressions and experiences combine in peculiar and unexpected ways. Impressions and experiences which are important for the man may take no place in the poetry, and those which become important in the poetry may play quite a negligible part in the man, the personality.   15

I will quote a passage which is unfamiliar enough to be regarded with fresh attention in the light—or darkness—of these observations: 16

> And now methinks I could e'en chide myself
> For doating on her beauty, though her death
> Shall be revenged after no common action.
> Does the silkworm expend her yellow labours
> For thee? For thee does she undo herself?
> Are lordships sold to maintain ladyships
> For the poor benefit of a bewildering minute?
> Why does yon fellow falsify highways,
> And put his life between the judge's lips,
> To refine such a thing—keeps horse and men
> To beat their valours for her? . . .[21]

In this passage (as is evident if it is taken in its context) there is a combination of positive and negative emotions: an intensely strong attraction toward beauty and an equally intense fascination by the ugliness which is contrasted with it and which destroys it. This balance of contrasted emotion is in the dramatic situation to which the speech

---

[19]***John Keats (1795–1821)*** English romantic poet who wrote "Ode to a Nightingale" and other odes which are among the finest poems in this form in English.

[20]**substantial unity of the soul** Theory that the soul is one with God and free of the quirks and accidents of personality.

[21]The lines are from *The Revenger's Tragedy* (1607) by English playwright Cyril Tourneur (1580–1626). Eliot had a special interest in Jacobean drama, a term applied to characteristics of the reign of King James I (1603–1625). "Jacobean" is derived from *Jacobus*, the Latin name for James.

is pertinent, but that situation alone is inadequate to it. This is, so to speak, the structural emotion, provided by the drama. But the whole effect, the dominant tone, is due to the fact that a number of floating feelings, having an affinity to this emotion by no means superficially evident, have combined with it to give us a new art emotion.

It is not in his personal emotions, the emotions provoked by partic-   17 ular events in his life, that the poet is in any way remarkable or interesting. His particular emotions may be simple, or crude, or flat. The emotion in his poetry will be a very complex thing, but not with the complexity of the emotions of people who have very complex or unusual emotions in life. One error, in fact, of eccentricity in poetry is to seek for new human emotions to express; and in this search for novelty in the wrong place it discovers the perverse. The business of the poet is not to find new emotions, but to use the ordinary ones and, in working them up into poetry, to express feelings which are not in actual emotions at all. And emotions which he has never experienced will serve his turn as well as those familiar to him. Consequently, we must believe that "emotion recollected in tranquillity"[22] is an inexact formula. For it is neither emotion, nor recollection, nor, without distortion of meaning, tranquillity. It is a concentration, and a new thing resulting from the concentration, of a very great number of experiences which to the practical and active person would not seem to be experiences at all; it is a concentration which does not happen consciously or of deliberation. These experiences are not "recollected," and they finally unite in an atmosphere which is "tranquil" only in that it is a passive attending upon the event. Of course this is not quite the whole story. There is a great deal, in the writing of poetry, which must be conscious and deliberate. In fact, the bad poet is usually unconscious where he ought to be conscious, and conscious where he ought to be unconscious. Both errors tend to make him "personal." Poetry is not a turning loose of emotion, but an escape from emotion; it is not the expression of personality, but an escape from personality. But, of course, only those who have personality and emotions know what it means to want to escape from these things.

ὁ δὲ νοῦς ἴσως Θειότερόν τι χαὶ ἀπαθές ἐστιν.[23]

---

[22]**tranquillity**   The English romantic poet William Wordsworth (1770–1850) said in "Preface" to the *Lyrical Ballads* (1800) that poetry "takes its origin from emotion recollected in tranquillity." Eliot quarrels with this view.

[23]The line is from *On the Soul* by Aristotle (384–322 B.C.): "The mind is doubtless something more divine and unimpressionable.

This essay proposes to halt at the frontier of metaphysics or mys- 18
ticism, and confine itself to such practical conclusions as can be applied by the responsible person interested in poetry. To divert interest
from the poet to the poetry is a laudable aim: for it would conduce to
a juster estimation of actual poetry, good and bad. There are many
people who appreciate the expression of sincere emotion in verse, and
there is a smaller number of people who can appreciate technical excellence. But very few know when there is an expression of *significant*
emotion, emotion which has its life in the poem and not in the history
of the poet. The emotion of art is impersonal. And the poet cannot
reach this impersonality without surrendering himself wholly to the
work to be done. And he is not likely to know what is to be done
unless he lives in what is not merely the present, but the present moment of the past, unless he is conscious, not of what is dead, but of
what is already living.

QUESTIONS

1. What does T. S. Eliot seem to mean by "tradition"? Does he use the term
   approvingly or disapprovingly? Do you agree with his use of the term?
2. According to Eliot, what should the relationship of the poetry of the present be to the poetry of the past?
3. What analogy does Eliot call our attention to in paragraphs 10, 11, and 12?
4. What are Eliot's views on the personal emotions of the poet?
5. Eliot uses the term "depersonalization" (para. 10). What is meant by that
   term?
6. To whom does Eliot seem to be speaking?

WRITING ASSIGNMENTS

1. Establish clearly what tradition and individual talent are for a poet (or any
   other kind of artist). Using the topic of comparison, explain what distin-
   guishes "tradition" and "individual talent" and what makes them independent of one another. At the same time, establish any important comparisons that seem to be helpful in making these concepts clearer. If you feel
   that one is more important than the other to the artist, explain why. Be
   sure to clarify any points of agreement or disagreement in your thinking
   with that of Eliot.
2. In paragraph 5, Eliot says that poetry must be judged "inevitably . . . by
   the standards of the past" (para. 5). Is this assertion true? What does the
   idea that a poem should be judged by the standards of the past mean? Is it

possible to judge any poetry without resorting to the standards of the past? Why would it be important for a poet to consider this point at all? Make a clear case in your essay.

3. Eliot says that "what is to be insisted upon is that the poet must develop . . . consciousness of the past" (para. 8). Is there evidence in the work that Eliot has developed a consciousness of the past? Inventory the essay for such evidence and examine its implications for his theories as carefully as possible.

4. One of Eliot's chief arguments in this work is that a poet should attempt to be impersonal in writing poems. Find the chief statements Eliot makes regarding this viewpoint; then, in the process of analyzing those statements and making Eliot's point as clear as possible, take a stand on this viewpoint. Do you agree or disagree with it? Try to deal with the meaning of such declarative statements as, "The emotion of art is impersonal" (para. 18). You may find it particularly effective to refer to a poem of your own choosing when working with this question.

5. A major idea Eliot develops in this work relates to the question of developing a historical sense (para. 3). Take a stand on the truth of Eliot's statement that "the past should be altered by the present as much as the present is directed by the past" (para. 4). Eliot is speaking about poetry, of course, but you may wish to expand the scope of the statement. Is it really possible to alter the past by the present? If not, what would permit Eliot to think so? What are the implications of this idea?

6. Inventory the essay for Eliot's comments on emotions and poetry. Are there many such references? Are they coherent with one another? What is Eliot's basic position regarding the relationship between poetry and emotions? Take into account such a statement as, "Poetry is not a turning loose of emotion, but an escape from emotion" (para. 17). Are you in agreement with Eliot's overall views?

Acknowledgments (continued from page iv)

Lincoln Barnett. "Einstein's Relativity." Chapters 2, 3, 4, and 8 of *The Universe and Dr. Einstein*, rev. ed., by Lincoln Barnett. Copyright 1948 by Harper & Brothers. Copyright 1950, 1957 by Lincoln Barnett. By permission of William Morrow & Company.

A. C. Bradley. "Poetry for Poetry's Sake." From *Oxford Lectures on Poetry* by A. C. Bradley (1909). Reprinted by permission of Macmillan, London and Basingstoke.

Albert Camus. "The Myth of Sisyphus." From *The Myth of Sisyphus and Other Essays*, by Albert Camus, translated by Justin O'Brien. Copyright © 1955 by Alfred A. Knopf, Inc. Reprinted by permission of the publisher.

John Dewey. "Some Historical Factors in Philosophical Reconstruction." From *Reconstruction in Philosophy* by John Dewey. Copyright © 1948 by Beacon Press. Reprinted by permission of the publisher.

T. S. Eliot. "Tradition and the Individual Talent." From *Selected Essays* by T. S. Eliot, copyright 1932, 1936, 1950 by Harcourt Brace Jovanovich, Inc.; renewed 1960, 1964 by T. S. Eliot, 1978 by Esme Valerie Eliot. Reprinted by permission of the publisher and Faber and Faber Ltd.

Sigmund Freud. "Infantile Sexuality." From *The Basic Writings of Sigmund Freud*, translated and edited by Dr. A. A. Brill. Copyright 1938, copyright © renewed 1965 by Gioia B. Bernheim and Edmund R. Brill. Reprinted by permission. Originally from *Three Essays on the Theory of Sexuality* (1905).

Carl Jung. "The Mother Archetype." From *The Collected Works of C. G. Jung*, trans. R. F. C. Hull, Bollingen Series XX, Vol. 9, I: *The Archetypes and the Collective Unconscious*. Copyright © 1959, 1969 by Princeton University Press. Reprinted by permission of Princeton University Press.

Gyorgy Kepes. "Comments on Art." From *New Knowledge in Human Values* edited by Abraham H. Maslow. Copyright © 1959 by Research Society for Creative Altruism. Reprinted by permission of Harper & Row, Publishers, Inc.

Martin Luther King, Jr. "Letter from Birmingham Jail" (April 16, 1963). From *Why We Can't Wait* by Martin Luther King, Jr. Copyright © 1963 by Martin Luther King, Jr. Reprinted by permission of Harper & Row, Publishers, Inc.

Thomas S. Kuhn. "The Essential Tension: Tradition and Innovation in Scientific Research." From *The Third (1959) University of Utah Research Conference on the Identification of Scientific Talent* (1959). Permission granted by University of Utah Press.

Susanne K. Langer. "Expressiveness." From *Problems of Art*. Copyright © 1957 Susanne K. Langer. Reprinted with the permission of Charles Scribner's Sons.

Niccolò Machiavelli. "The Qualities of the Prince." Excerpt from "The Prince," from *The Portable Machiavelli*, edited and translated by Peter Bondanella and Mark Musa. Copyright © 1979 by Peter Bondanella and Mark Musa. Reprinted by permission of Viking Penguin Inc.

Friedrich Nietzsche. "Apollonianism and Dionysianism." Excerpts from *The Birth of Tragedy and the Genealogy of Morals* by Friedrich Nietzsche, translated by Francis Golffing. Copyright © 1956 by Doubleday & Company. Reprinted by permission of the publisher.

Jean Jacques Rousseau. "The Origin of Civil Society." From *Social Contract: Essays by Locke, Hume, and Rousseau* edited by Sir Ernest Barker (1947). Reprinted by permission of Oxford University Press.

Bertrand Russell. "A Free Man's Worship." From *Mysticism and Logic* by Bertrand Russell. Reprinted by permission of George Allen & Unwin (Publishers) Ltd.

B. F. Skinner. "What Is Man?" From *Beyond Freedom and Dignity*, by B. F. Skinner. Copyright © 1971 by B. F. Skinner. Reprinted by permission of Alfred A. Knopf, Inc.

Alfred North Whitehead. "Religion and Science." Reprinted with permission of Macmillan Publishing Co., Inc. from *Science and the Modern World* by Alfred North Whitehead. Copyright 1925 by Macmillan Publishing Co., Inc., renewed 1953 by Evelyn Whitehead.

SUGGESTIONS FOR
FURTHER READING

———••◦◦◦••———

MACHIAVELLI

Anglo, Sydney. *Machiavelli: A Dissection.* New York: Harcourt, Brace, and World, 1970.

Bondanella, Peter. *Machiavelli and the Art of Renaissance History.* Detroit: Wayne State University Press, 1973.

Butterfield, Herbert. *The Structure of Machiavelli.* New York: Collins Books, 1962.

Jay, Anthony. *Management and Machiavelli: An Inquiry into the Politics of Corporate Life.* New York: Holt, Rinehart and Winston, 1968.

Jensen, De Lamar. *Machiavelli: Cynic, Patriot or Political Scientist?* Boston: D. C. Heath, 1960.

*Machiavelli, Niccolò. *The Viking Portable Machiavelli.* Edited and translated by Peter Bondanella and Mark Musa. New York: Viking Penguin, 1979.

---

*Starred entries throughout bibliographies indicate paperbacks or other inexpensive editions of the major works of these authors.

Olschki, Leonard. *Machiavelli the Scientist.* Berkeley, California: The Gallick Press, 1945.

Pocock, John. *The Machiavellian Moment.* Princeton, N. J.: Princeton University Press, 1974.

Parel, Anthony, ed. *The Political Calculus: Essays on Machiavelli's Philosophy.* Toronto: University of Toronto Press, 1972.

Ridofi, Roberto. *The Life of Machiavelli.* Translated by Cecil Grayson. Chicago: University of Chicago Press, 1963.

ROUSSEAU

Blanchard, William. *Rousseau and the Spirit of Revolt.* Ann Arbor: University of Michigan Press, 1967.

Broome, Jack Howard. *Rousseau: A Study of His Thought.* New York: Barnes and Noble, 1963.

Cassirer, Ernst. *The Question of Jean Jacques Rousseau.* Translated and edited by Peter Gay. New York: Columbia University Press, 1954.

Chapman, John William. *Rousseau—Totalitarian or Liberal?* New York: Columbia University Press, 1956.

Dobinson, Charles Henry. *Jean Jacques Rousseau: His Thought and Its Relevance Today.* London: Methuen, 1969.

Huizinga, Jacob Herman. *Rousseau: The Self-Made Spirit.* New York: Grossman, 1976.

Masters, Roger. *The Political Philosophy of Rousseau.* Princeton, N. J.: Princeton University Press, 1968.

Murry, John Middleton. *Heroes of Thought.* New York: J. Messner Inc., 1938.

Perkins, Merle. *Jean Jacques Rousseau on the Individual and Society.* Lexington: The University Press of Kentucky, 1974.

*Rousseau, Jean Jacques. *The Annotated Social Contract.* Edited by Charles M. Sherover. New York: New American Library.

*Rousseau, Jean Jacques. *Confessions.* Translated by John M. Cohen. Baltimore: Penguin, 1953.

JEFFERSON

Becker, Carl L. *The Declaration of Independence: A Study in the History of Political Ideas.* Rev. ed. New York: Alfred A. Knopf, 1966.

Brodie, Fawn M. *Thomas Jefferson: An Intimate History.* New York: W. W. Norton, 1974.

*Jefferson, Thomas. *The Life and Selected Writings of Thomas Jefferson.* Edited by Adrienne Koch and William Peden. New York: Modern Library, 1944.

*Jefferson, Thomas. *The Viking Portable Thomas Jefferson.* Edited by Merrill D. Peterson. New York: Viking Penguin, 1977.

Malone, Dumas. *Jefferson and His Time.* 6 vols. Boston: Little, Brown, 1948–1981.

Wills, Garry. *Inventing America: Jefferson's Declaration of Independence.* Garden City, N. Y.: Doubleday, 1978.

WOLLSTONECRAFT

Flexner, Eleanor. *Mary Wollstonecraft: A Biography.* New York: Coward, McCann and Geoghegan, 1972.

George, Margaret. *One Woman's Situation: A Study of Mary Wollstonecraft.* Urbana: University of Illinois Press, 1970.

Nixon, Edna. *Mary Wollstonecraft: Her Life and Times.* London: J. M. Dent, 1971.

Tims, Margaret. *Mary Wollstonecraft: A Social Pioneer.* London: Millington, 1976.

Sunstein, Emily. *A Different Face: The Life of Mary Wollstonecraft.* New York: Harper and Row, 1975.

Wardle, Ralph, ed. *Collected Letters of Mary Wollstonecraft.* Ithaca, New York: Cornell University Press, 1979.

*Wollstonecraft, Mary. *A Vindication of the Rights of Woman.* Edited by Miriam Kramick. New York: Viking Penguin, 1978.

MARX

Avineri, Schlomo. *The Social and Political Thought of Karl Marx.* London: Cambridge University Press, 1968.

Dupre, Louis. *The Philosophical Foundations of Marxism.* New York: Harcourt, Brace and World, 1966.

Fetscher, Irving. *Marx and Marxism.* New York: Herder and Herder, 1971.

Lichtheim, George. *Marxism: An Historical and Critical Study.* New York: Praeger, 1961.

Lukacs, Gyorgy. *History and Class Consciousness: Studies in Marxist Dialectics.* Cambridge, Mass.: MIT Press, 1971.

*Marx, Karl. *Capital.* 3 vols. New York: International Publishers, 1976.

*Marx, Karl. *The Communist Manifesto.* Edited by A. J. Taylor. Baltimore: Penguin, 1968.

Meszaros, Istvan. *Marx's Theory of Alienation.* New York: Harper and Row, 1972.

Ollman, Bertell. *Alienation: Marx's Conception of Man in Capitalist Society.* New York: Cambridge University Press, 1976.

Rubel, M., and M. Mamale. *Marx without Myth: A Chronological Study of His Life and Work.* New York: Harper and Row, 1975.

Tucker, Robert C. *The Marxian Revolutionary Idea.* New York: W. W. Norton, 1968.

THOREAU

Bridgeman, Richard. *Dark Thoreau.* Lincoln: University of Nebraska Press, 1982.

Edel, Leon. *Henry D. Thoreau.* Minneapolis: University of Minnesota Press, 1970.

Harding, Walter Roy. *The Days of Henry Thoreau.* New York: Alfred A. Knopf, 1966.

Howarth, William. *The Book of Concord: Thoreau's Life as a Writer.* New York: Viking Press, 1982.

Longstreth, Thomas. *Henry Thoreau: American Rebel.* New York: Dodd, Mead, 1963.

Mathiessen, F. O. *American Renaissance: Art and Expression in the Age of Emerson and Whitman.* New York: Oxford University Press, 1960.

Moller, Mary Elkins. *Thoreau in the Human Community.* Amherst: University of Massachusetts Press, 1980.

Meyer, Michael. *Several More Lives to Live: Thoreau's Political Reputation in America.* Westport, Conn.: Greenwood Press, 1977.

*Thoreau, Henry D. *The Viking Portable Thoreau.* Edited by Carl Bode. New York: Viking Penguin, 1977.

*Thoreau, Henry D. *Walden and Other Writings.* Edited by Joseph Wood Krutch. New York: Bantam, 1971.

DOUGLASS

Bontemps, Arna. *Free at Last: The Life of Frederick Douglass.* New York: Dodd, Mead, 1971.

Douglass, Frederick. *The Frederick Douglass Papers, Series One: Speeches, Debates, and Interviews, Volume I: 1841–1846.* Edited by John W. Blassingame, et al. New Haven, Conn.: Yale University Press, 1979.

Douglass, Frederick. *Frederick Douglass on Women's Rights.* Edited by Philip S. Foner. Westport, Conn.: Greenwood Press, 1976.

Douglass, Frederick. *The Life and Writings of Frederick Douglass.* Edited by Philip S. Foner. 5 vols. New York: International Publishers, 1950–1975.

*Douglass, Frederick. *Narrative of the Life of Frederick Douglass, an American Slave.* Edited by Benjamin Quarles. Cambridge, Mass.: Harvard University Press, 1960.

Foner, Philip S. *Frederick Douglass.* New York: Citadel, 1964.

Huggins, Nathan Irvin. *Slave and Citizen: The Life of Frederick Douglass.* Boston: Little, Brown, 1980.

Inge, Thomas, et al., eds. *Black American Writers: Bibliographical Essays*, Vol. I. London: Macmillan, 1978.

Preston, Dickson J. *Young Frederick Douglass: The Maryland Years.* Baltimore: Johns Hopkins University Press, 1980.

Quarles, Benjamin. *Frederick Douglass.* Washington, D.C.: Associated Publishers, 1948.

Walker, Peter F. *Moral Choices: Memory, Desire, and Imagination in Nineteenth-Century American Abolition.* Baton Rouge: Louisiana State University Press, 1978.

Washington, Booker T. *Frederick Douglass.* Philadelphia: Jacobs, 1907.

KING

*King, Martin Luther, Jr. *Strength to Love.* Philadelphia: Fortress Press, 1981.

*King, Martin Luther, Jr. *Where Do We Go from Here: Chaos or Community?* Boston: Beacon Press, 1968.

*King, Martin Luther, Jr. *Why We Can't Wait.* New York: New American Library, 1965.

Lewis, David. *King: A Critical Biography.* New York: Praeger, 1970.

Lyght, Ernest Shaw. *The Religious and Philosophical Foundations in the Thought of Martin Luther King.* New York: Vantage Press, 1972.

Oates, Stephen B. *Let the Trumpet Sound: The Life of Martin Luther King, Jr.* New York: Harper and Row, 1982.

Ramachandram, G., and T. K. Mahadevan. *Nonviolence after Gandhi: A Study of Martin Luther King.* New Delhi: Gandhi Peace Foundation, 1968.

Walton, Hanes. *The Political Philosophy of Martin Luther King.* Westport, Conn.: Greenwich Publishing Corp., 1971.

NIETZSCHE

Danto, Arthur C. *Nietzsche as Philosopher.* New York: Macmillan, 1965.

Heller, Otto. *Prophets of Dissent.* New York: Alfred A. Knopf, 1918.

Hollingdale, R. J. *Nietzsche: The Man and His Philosophy.* Baton Rouge: Louisiana State University Press, 1965.

Jaspers, Karl. *Nietzsche and Christianity.* Translated by E. B. Ashton. Chicago: H. Regnery Co., 1961.

Kaufmann, Walter A. *Nietzsche: Philosopher, Psychologist, Antichrist.* Princeton, N. J.: Princeton University Press, 1950.

*Nietzsche, Friedrich. *The Viking Portable Nietzsche.* Edited by Walter A. Kaufmann. New York: Viking Penguin, 1977.

Pfeffer, Rose. *Nietzsche: Disciple of Dionysus.* Lewisburg, Pa.: Bucknell University Press, 1972.

Salter, William. *Nietzsche the Thinker.* London: Cecil, Palmer, and Hayward, 1917.

Wilcox, John. *Truth and Value in Nietzsche.* Ann Arbor: University of Michigan Press, 1974.

JAMES

Allen, Gay Wilson. *William James: A Biography.* New York: Viking Press, 1967.

Brennan, Bernard P. *The Ethics of William James.* New York: Bookman Associates, 1961.

Ducasse, C. J. *A Philosophical Scrutiny of Religion.* New York: Ronald Press Co., 1953.

Hardwick, Elizabeth, ed. *The Selected Letters of William James.* New York: Farrar, Straus and Cudahy, 1961.

*James, William. *Pragmatism.* Edited by Ralph B. Perry. New York: New American Library, 1965.

*James, William. *Varieties of Religious Experience.* Edited by Martin E. Marty. New York: Viking Penguin, 1982.

Morris, Lloyd R. *William James: The Message of a Modern Mind.* New York: Charles Scribner's Sons, 1950.

Perry, Ralph Barton. *The Thought and Character of William James.* 2 vols. Boston: Little, Brown, 1935.

FREUD

Arlow, Jacob. *The Legacy of Sigmund Freud.* New York: International Universities Press, 1956.

Balogh, Penelope. *Freud: A Biographical Introduction.* New York: Charles Scribner's Sons, 1972.

Clark, Ronald William. *Freud: The Man and the Cause.* London: Cape, 1980.

Fine, Reuben. *Freud: A Critical Reevaluation of His Theories.* New York: McKay, 1962.

Freeman, Lucy. *Freud Rediscovered.* New York: Arbor House, 1980.

*Freud, Sigmund. *General Selection from the Works of Sigmund Freud.* Garden City, N. Y.: Doubleday, 1957.

*Freud, Sigmund. *New Introductory Lectures in Psychoanalysis.* Edited by James Strachey. New York: W. W. Norton, 1965.

*Freud, Sigmund. *Outline of Psychoanalysis.* Edited by James Strachey. New York: W. W. Norton, 1970.

*Freud, Sigmund. *The Psychopathology of Everyday Life.* Edited by James Strachey. New York: W. W. Norton, 1971.

*Freud, Sigmund. *Three Contributions to the Theory of Sex.* Translated by A. A. Brill. New York: E. P. Dutton, 1962.

Fromm, Erich. *The Crisis of Psychoanalysis.* New York: Holt, Rinehart and Winston, 1970.

Jones, Ernest. *The Life and Work of Sigmund Freud.* Edited by Lionel Trilling and Steven Marcus. New York: Basic Books, 1961.

Reiff, Philip. *Freud: The Mind of the Moralist.* Garden City, N. Y.: Doubleday, 1961.

Rosenfeld, Israel. *Freud: Character and Consciousness.* New York: University Books, 1970.

Stoodley, Bartlett. *The Concepts of Sigmund Freud.* Glencoe, Ill.: Free Press, 1959.

J U N G

Fordheim, Frieda. *An Introduction to Jung's Psychology.* Baltimore: Penguin, 1954.

Hall, Calvin Springer. *A Primer of Jungian Psychology.* New York: New American Library, 1973.

Hannah, Barbara. *Jung: His Life and Work.* New York: Putnam, 1976.

*Jung, Carl. *Man and His Symbols.* New York: Dell, 1968.

*Jung, Carl. *Memories, Dreams, Reflections.* New York: Random House, 1965.

*Jung, Carl. *The Viking Portable Jung.* Edited by Joseph Campbell. New York: Viking Penguin, 1976.

Moreno, Artorio. *Jung, God, and Modern Man.* Notre Dame, Ind.: University of Notre Dame Press, 1970.

Prograff, Ira. *Jung's Psychology and Its Social Meaning.* New York: Julian Press, 1953.

Sanford, John. *The Invisible Partners: How the Male and Female in Each of Us Affects Our Relationships.* New York: Paulist Press, 1980.

Ulanov, Ann Bedford. *The Feminine in Jungian Psychology and in Christian Theology.* Evanston, Ill.: Northwestern University Press, 1971.

S K I N N E R

Hull, Clark Leonard. *Principles of Behavior: An Introduction to Behavior Theory.* New York: D. Appleton–Century Co., 1943.

McLeish, John. *The Science of Behavior.* London: Barrie and Rockliff, 1963.

*Skinner, B. F. *About Behaviorism.* New York: Random House, 1976.

*Skinner, B. F. *Beyond Freedom and Dignity.* New York: Bantam, 1972.

*Skinner, B. F. *Walden Two Revisited.* New York: Macmillan, 1976.

Staats, Arthur. *Social Behaviorism.* Homewood, Ill.: Dorsey, 1975.

Tilney, Frederick. *The Structural Basis of Behaviorism.* Philadelphia: J. B. Lippincott Co., 1930.

BACON

*Bacon, Francis. *Francis Bacon: A Selection of His Works*. Edited by Sidney Warhaft. Indianapolis: Odyssey Press, 1965.

*Bacon, Francis. *New Organon and Related Writings*. Edited by H. Fulton Anderson. Indianapolis: Bobbs-Merrill, 1960.

Eiseley, Loren. *Francis Bacon and the Modern Dilemma*. Lincoln: University of Nebraska Press, 1962.

Epstein, Joel. *Francis Bacon: A Political Biography*. Athens: Ohio University Press, 1977.

Farrington, Benjamin. *The Philosophy of Francis Bacon*. Liverpool: University Press, 1964.

Rossi, Paolo. *Francis Bacon: From Magic to Science*. Translated by Sacha Rabinovitch. Chicago: University of Chicago Press, 1968.

Stephens, James. *Francis Bacon and the Style of Science*. Chicago: University of Chicago Press, 1975.

Vickers, Brian. *Essential Articles for the Study of Francis Bacon*. Hamden, Conn.: Archon Books, 1968.

Wallace, Karl. *Francis Bacon on Communication and Rhetoric*. Chapel Hill: University of North Carolina Press, 1943.

DARWIN

Appleman, Philip, ed. *Darwin*. New York: W. W. Norton, 1970.

Bannister, Robert. *Social Darwinism: Science and Myth in Anglo-American Social Thought*. Philadelphia: Temple University Press, 1979.

*Darwin, Charles. *The Autobiography of Charles Darwin*. Edited by Nora Barlow. New York: W. W. Norton, 1969.

*Darwin, Charles. *On the Origin of Species*. Edited by J. W. Burrow. Baltimore: Penguin, 1968.

*Darwin, Charles. *The Descent of Man and Selection in Relation to Sex*. Princeton, N. J.: Princeton University Press, 1981.

Eiseley, Loren. *Darwin's Century: Evolution and the Men Who Discovered It*. Garden City, N. Y.: Doubleday, 1958.

Himmelfarb, Gertrude. *Darwin and the Darwinian Revolution*. Garden City, N. Y.: Doubleday, 1962.

Irvine, William. *Apes, Angels, and Victorians*. New York: McGraw-Hill, 1955.

Miller, Jonathan. *Darwin for Beginners*. New York: Pantheon, 1982.

Russett, Cynthia. *Darwin in America*. San Francisco: W. H. Freeman, 1976.

EINSTEIN

Barnett, Lincoln. *The Universe and Dr. Einstein*. Rev. ed. New York: William Morrow, 1972.

Bernstein, Jeremy. *Einstein*. New York: Viking, 1973.

Clark, Ronald W. *Einstein: The Life and Times*. New York: World, 1971.

*Einstein, Albert. *Einstein on Peace*. Edited by Otto Nathan and Heinz Norden. New York: Schocken, 1968.

*Einstein, Albert. *The Meaning of Relativity*. 5th ed. Princeton, N. J.: Princeton University Press, 1956.

Favor, Lewis. *Einstein and the Generations of Science*. New York: Basic Books, 1974.

Hoffman, Banesh. *Albert Einstein: Creator and Rebel*. New York: New American Library, 1972.

Infeld, Leopold. *Albert Einstein: His Work and Its Influence on Our World*. New York: Charles Scribner's Sons, 1950.

Jammer, Max. *The Conceptual Development of Quantum Mechanics*. New York: McGraw-Hill, 1966.

Pais, Abraham. *"Subtle is the Lord . . . ": The Science and the Life of Albert Einstein*. New York: Oxford University Press, 1982.

Schilpp, Paul, ed. *Albert Einstein: Philosopher-Scientist*. LaSalle, Ill.: Open Court, 1969–1970.

Schwartz, Joe. *Einstein for Beginners*. New York: Pantheon, 1979.

Whitrow, Gerald, ed. *Einstein: The Man and His Achievement*. New York: Dover, 1973.

WHITEHEAD

Cobb, John B., Jr. *A Christian Natural Theology Based on the Thought of Alfred North Whitehead*. Philadelphia: Westminster Press, 1965.

Johnson, A. H. *Whitehead's Philosophy of Civilization*. Boston: Beacon Press, 1958.

Lawrence, Nathaniel. *Alfred North Whitehead: A Primer of His Philosophy*. New York: Twayne, 1974.

LeClerc, Ivor. *The Relevance of Whitehead.* New York: Macmillan, 1961.

Lowe, Victor. *Understanding Whitehead.* Baltimore: Johns Hopkins University Press, 1962.

Mack, Robert. *The Appeal to Immediate Experience: Philosophic Method in Bradley, Whitehead, and Dewey.* New York: King's Crown Press, 1945.

Overman, Richard. *Evolution and the Christian Doctrine of Creation: A Whiteheadian Interpretation.* Philadelphia: Washington Press, 1967.

Pittenger, William. *Alfred North Whitehead.* Richmond, Virginia: John Knox Press, 1969.

Schilpp, Paul A., ed. *The Philosophy of Alfred North Whitehead.* 2nd ed. Evanston, Ill.: Northwestern University Press, 1951.

Sherburne, Donald, ed. *A Key to Whitehead's "Process and Reality."* Chicago: University of Chicago Press, 1961.

*Whitehead, Alfred N. *Adventures of Ideas.* New York: Free Press, 1967.

*Whitehead, Alfred N. *Process and Reality.* Corrected edition. New York: Free Press, 1967.

*Whitehead, Alfred N. *Science and the Modern World.* New York: Free Press, 1967.

KUHN

Gutting, Gary, ed. *Paradigms and Revolutions: Appraisals and Applications of Thomas Kuhn's Philosophy of Science.* Notre Dame, Ind.: University of Notre Dame Press, 1980.

*Kuhn, Thomas. *The Copernican Revolution: Planetary Astronomy in the Development of Western Thought.* Cambridge, Mass.: Harvard University Press, 1957.

*Kuhn, Thomas. *The Essential Tension: Selected Studies in Scientific Tradition.* Chicago: University of Chicago Press, 1979.

*Kuhn, Thomas. *The Structure of Scientific Revolutions.* 2nd ed. Chicago: University of Chicago Press, 1970.

PLATO

Barrow, Robin. *Plato, Utilitarianism, and Education.* London: Routledge and Kegan Paul, 1975.

Brumbaugh, Robert Sherrick. *Plato for the Modern Age*. New York: Crowell–Collier, 1962.

Clegg, Jerry. *The Structure of Plato's Philosophy*. Lewisburg, Pa.: Bucknell University Press, 1976.

Cornford, Francis MacDonald. *Before and after Socrates*. Cambridge: University Press, 1958.

Fox, Adam. *Plato for Pleasure*. London: Westhouse, 1945.

Grube, Georges. *Plato's Thought*. Boston: Beacon Press, 1958.

Gulley, Norman. *Plato's Theory of Knowledge*. New York: Barnes and Noble, 1962.

*Plato. *The Dialogues of Plato*. Edited by Justin D. Kaplan. New York: Washington Square Press, 1982.

*Plato. *The Viking Portable Plato*. Edited by Scott Buchanan. New York: Viking Penguin, 1977.

Rankin, H. D. *Plato and the Individual*. New York: Barnes and Noble, 1964.

Taylor, Alfred. *Plato: The Man and His Work*. London: Methuen, 1960.

Vlastos, Gregory. *Plato's Universe*. Seattle: University of Washington Press, 1975.

ARISTOTLE

Adler, Mortimer. *Aristotle for Everybody: Difficult Thought Made Easy*. New York: Macmillan, 1978.

*Aristotle. *The Nichomachean Ethics*. Translated by Martin Ostwald. Indianapolis: Bobbs-Merrill, 1962.

*Aristotle. *The Pocket Aristotle*. Edited by Justin D. Kaplan. New York: Washington Square Press, 1982.

*Aristotle. *Poetics*. Edited by G. M. Kirkwood. New York: W. W. Norton, 1982.

*Aristotle. *Politics*. Rev. ed. New York: Viking Penguin, 1982.

Cherniss, Harold. *Aristotle's Criticism of Plato and the Academy*. Baltimore: Johns Hopkins University Press, 1944.

Davidson, Thomas. *Aristotle and Ancient Educational Ideals*. New York: Franklin, 1969.

Ferguson, John. *Aristotle*. New York: Twayne, 1972.

Hardie, William. *Aristotle's Ethical Theory.* New York: Oxford University Press, 1980.

Lloyd, Geoffrey. *Aristotle: The Growth and Structure of His Thought.* London: Cambridge University Press, 1968.

Lear, Jonathan. *Aristotle and Logical Theory.* Cambridge: University Press, 1980.

Oates, Whitney. *Aristotle and the Problem of Value.* Princeton, N. J.: Princeton University Press, 1963.

Veatch, Henry. *Aristotle: A Contemporary Appreciation.* Bloomington: Indiana University Press, 1974.

R U S S E L L

Ayer, Alfred. *Bertrand Russell.* New York: Viking, 1972.

Booth, Wayne. *Modern Dogma and the Rhetoric of Assent.* Notre Dame, Ind.: University of Notre Dame Press, 1974.

Clark, Ronald William. *Bertrand Russell and His World.* New York: Thames and Hudson, 1981.

Dorward, Alan. *Bertrand Russell: A Short Guide to His Philosophy.* New York: Longmans, Green, 1951.

Gottschalk, Herbert. *Bertrand Russell: A Life.* New York: Roy, 1965.

Lewis, John. *Bertrand Russell: Philosopher and Humanist.* London: Laurence and Wishart, 1968.

Pears, David. *Bertrand Russell and the British Tradition in Philosophy.* London: Collins, 1967.

*Russell, Bertrand. *The Basic Writings of Bertrand Russell.* Edited by Robert E. Egner and Lester E. Dennon. New York: Simon and Schuster, 1967.

*Russell, Bertrand. *Philosophical Essays.* New York: Simon and Schuster, 1968.

*Russell, Bertrand. *Problems of Philosophy.* New York: Oxford University Press, 1959.

*Russell, Bertrand. *Why I Am Not a Christian, and Other Essays on Religion and Related Subjects.* New York: Simon and Schuster, 1967.

Schoenman, Ralph, ed. *Bertrand Russell: Philosopher of the Century.* London: Allen and Unwin, 1967.

DEWEY

Blewitt, John. *John Dewey: His Thought and Influence.* New York: Fordham University Press, 1960.

Cambell, Harry. *John Dewey.* New York: Twayne, 1971.

*Dewey, John. *The Child and the Curriculum, and the School and Society.* 2nd ed. Chicago: University of Chicago Press, 1956.

*Dewey, John. *John Dewey on Education.* Edited by Reginald D. Archambault. Chicago: University of Chicago Press, 1974.

*Dewey, John. *Reconstruction in Philosophy.* Boston: Beacon Press, 1957.

Frankena, William. *Three Philosophies of Education: Aristotle, Kant, Dewey.* Chicago: Scott Foresman, 1965.

Handlin, Oscar. *John Dewey's Challenge to Education.* New York: Harper and Row, 1959.

Howlett, Charles. *Troubled Philosopher: John Dewey and the Struggle for World Peace.* Port Washington, N. Y.: Kennikat Press, 1977.

Levitt, Morton. *Freud and Dewey on the Nature of Man.* New York: Philosophical Library, 1960.

Mack, Robert. *The Appeal to Immediate Experience: Philosophic Method in Bradley, Whitehead, and Dewey.* New York: King's Crown Press, 1945.

McNitt, Harold. *John Dewey's Democratic Liberalism.* Ann Arbor, Mich.: University Microfilms, 1957.

Parkins, Ivan. *John Dewey: Freedom as Intellectual Participation.* Chicago: University of Chicago Press, 1955.

CAMUS

Braun, Lev. *Witness of Decline: Albert Camus, Moralist of the Absurd.* Rutherford: Fairleigh Dickinson University Press, 1974.

Brée, Germaine. *Camus: A Collection of Critical Essays.* Rev. ed. New Brunswick, N. J.: Rutgers University Press, 1972.

*Camus, Albert. *The Fall.* Translated by Justin O'Brien. New York: Random House, 1963.

*Camus, Albert. *The Myth of Sisyphus and Other Essays.* Translated by Justin O'Brien. New York: Random House, 1959.

*Camus, Albert. *The Plague.* Translated by Stuart Gilbert. New York: Random House, 1972.

*Camus, Albert. *The Stranger*. Translated by Stuart Gilbert. New York: Random House, 1954.

Cruickshank, John. *Albert Camus and the Literature of Revolt*. New York: Oxford University Press, 1959.

Hanna, Thomas. *The Thought and Art of Albert Camus*. Chicago: H. Regnery, 1958.

Lazare, Donald. *The Unique Creation of Albert Camus*. New Haven, Conn.: Yale University Press, 1973.

McCarthy, Patrick. *Camus*. New York: Random House, 1982.

Onimus, Jean. *Albert Camus and Christianity*. Translated by Emmett Parker. University: University of Alabama Press, 1970.

Proix, Robert, ed. *Albert Camus and the Men of Stone*. Translated by Gregory Davis. San Francisco: Greenwood Press, 1971.

Thody, Philip. *Albert Camus: A Study of His Work*. New York: Grove Press, 1959.

Viallaneix, Paul. *The First Camus: An Introductory Essay*. Translated by Ellen Kennedy. New York: Alfred A. Knopf, 1976.

SANTAYANA

Arnett, Willard Eugene. *Santayana and the Sense of Beauty*. Bloomington: Indiana University Press, 1968.

Ashmore, Jerome. *Santayana, Art, and Aesthetics*. Cleveland: Press of Western Reserve University, 1966.

Butler, Richard. *The Life and Works of George Santayana*. Chicago: H. Regnery, 1960.

Kirkwood, Mossie May. *Santayana: Saint of the Imagination*. Toronto: University of Toronto Press, 1961.

Munitz, Milton Karl. *The Moral Philosophy of Santayana*. New York: Columbia University Press, 1939.

Munson, Thomas. *The Essential Wisdom of George Santayana*. New York: Columbia University Press, 1962.

*Santayana, George. *The Life of Reason*. 4 vols. New York: Dover, 1980–1982.

*Santayana, George. *Selected Critical Writings*. Edited by Norman Henfrey. New York: Cambridge University Press, 1968.

*Santayana, George. *The Sense of Beauty*. New York: Dover, 1955.

Schilpp, Paul Arthur, ed. *The Philosophy of George Santayana*. Evanston, Ill.: Northwestern University, 1940.

KEPES

Kepes, Gyorgy. *Language of Vision.* Rev. ed. Chicago: P. Theobald, 1961.

Kepes, Gyorgy. *The New Landscape in Art and Science.* Chicago: P. Theobald, 1956.

Kepes, Gyorgy, ed. *The Visual Arts Today.* Middletown, Conn.: Wesleyan University Press, 1960.

LANGER

*Langer, Susanne K. *Feeling and Form.* New York: Charles Scribner's Sons, 1953.

*Langer, Susanne K. *Mind: An Essay on Human Feeling.* 3 vols. Baltimore: Johns Hopkins University Press, 1967, 1973, 1982.

Langer, Susanne K. *Philosophical Sketches.* Baltimore: Johns Hopkins University Press, 1962.

*Langer, Susanne K. *Philosophy in a New Key.* 3rd ed. Cambridge, Mass.: Harvard University Press, 1957.

*Langer, Susanne K. *Problems of Art.* New York: Charles Scribner's Sons, 1957.

BRADLEY

Bradley, A. C. *Oxford Lectures on Poetry.* New York: St. Martin's, 1955.

*Bradley, A. C. *Shakespearean Tragedy.* New York: Fawcett, 1977.

ELIOT

Brombert, Victor. *The Criticism of T. S. Eliot.* New Haven, Conn.: Yale University Press, 1949.

Eliot, T. S. *Collected Poems, 1909–1962.* New York: Harcourt, Brace and World, 1963.

Eliot, T. S. *The Complete Plays.* New York: Harcourt, Brace and World, 1967.

*Eliot, T. S. *On Poetry and Poets.* New York: Farrar, Straus and Cudahy, 1957.

*Eliot, T. S. *Selected Poems.* New York: Harcourt, Brace and World, 1967.

Eliot, T. S. *Selected Prose of T. S. Eliot.* Edited by Frank Kermode. New York: Harcourt Brace Jovanovich, 1975.

Freed, Lewis. *T. S. Eliot: The Critic as Philosopher.* West Lafayette, Ind.: Purdue University Press, 1979.

Frye, Northrop. *T. S. Eliot: An Introduction.* Chicago: University of Chicago Press, 1981.

Kirk, Russell. *Eliot and His Age.* New York: Random House, 1971.

Lucy, Sean. *T. S. Eliot and the Idea of Tradition.* London: Cohen and West, 1960.

Nuttall, Anthony. *A Common Sky: Philosophy and the Literary Imagination.* Berkeley: University of California Press, 1974.

Unger, Leonard. *The Man in the Name: Essays on the Experience of Poetry.* Minneapolis: University of Minnesota Press, 1956.

INDEX OF
RHETORICAL TERMS

————⟨∞⟩————

abstract reasoning, 14, 432
allegory, 432, 436–437, 509
allusion, 91, 137–138, 182, 279,
    475
analogy, 58, 548–549. *See also*
    topic of comparison
analysis, 58, 183, 257, 432, 475,
    518, 560, 576, 600
anaphora, 81
anecdote, 90
annotations, 2–6
antagonist, 109
antithesis, 40–41, 135, 576. *See*
    also topic of comparison
aphorism, 41, 91, 451, 489, 509,
    601. *See also* topic of
    testimony
argument, 29–31, 40, 90, 491n,
    547–548, 560
artifact, 211
asking questions, 10–12
audience, 81, 90, 136, 138, 182,
    257, 411, 451, 509

authorities. *See* reference to
    authorities

balance, 80–81, 165, 328
beginning. *See* introduction
body, 27, 231, 410
brevity, 40, 90

cause and effect, 81, 451. *See*
    also topic of relationship
character sketch, 136
chronological narrative. *See*
    narrative
classification, 488–489
comparison and contrast, 108,
    109, 138, 210, 347, 392, 411,
    548. *See also* topic of
    comparison
complaint, 109
conclusion, 27–28, 231, 257,
    410–411

concrete reasoning, 15, 183
connotation, 137

deduction, 330n
definition, 8, 59, 109, 211, 329,
   347, 392, 451, 522–523, 560–
   561, 600. *See also* topic of
   definition
demonstration, 347
dialogue, 437

effect. *See* cause and effect
encomium, 29, 136
end. *See* conclusion; summary
enumeration, 81, 109, 328–329,
   369, 561
episodical observation. *See*
   anecdote
epistle. *See* letter
essay, 26–34
evidence, 15–17, 257, 347, 369
example, 15, 19, 81, 90–91, 329,
   347, 392, 411
experience, 29, 40
exposition, 29, 278, 369, 576
extended definition, 523

facts, 16
figurative language, 8–9, 137,
   475
first person, 165, 410
folk aphorism. *See* aphorism
funeral oration, 136

historical perspective, 369
hypothesis, 328, 347

illustration. *See* example
imagery, 8, 90, 432, 475
imaginary examples, 347, 369
induction, 328, 330n, 347, 460n
inference, 231

introduction, 27, 329, 410
inventory, 7–10
irony, 8–9, 137

key terms, 8, 18, 80, 518, 561

lecture, 230, 451
letter, 182
list. *See* enumeration
literary allusion. *See* allusion
logic, 58, 183, 327, 491n

meditation, 489, 508
memorable phrase, 257, 601
metaphor, 8–9, 91, 137, 295,
   432, 475, 509
middle. *See* body
myth, 279, 508–509

narrative, 28–29, 165

observation, 328, 347
opposition. *See* antithesis
organization, 26–31, 328
organon, 327, 491n

parable, 136
paradigm, 416n
paradox, 59, 411
parallelism, 80–81
past time, 369. *See also* topic of
   relationship
periodic sentence, 80–81
points. *See* enumeration
process, 347
process of evidence and
   inference, 257. *See also*
   evidence; inference
pun, 95n

questions, 10–12, 437, 576–577.
   See also rhetorical questions
quotation, 15, 91, 549. *See also*
   topic of testimony

readers. *See* audience
reasoning, 16–17, 183, 329, 560.
   See also deduction;
   induction; logic
reference to authorities, 16, 59,
   231, 549. *See also* topic of
   testimony
rhetoric, 451
rhetorical question, 59, 294–295

sequence of events, 165
signpost, 329, 410
simile, 8, 137, 156n
Socratic method, 437
speech. *See* funeral oration;
   lecture; talk
structure, 26–28, 165, 231
style, 90, 108–109, 137, 165,
   437, 475, 522
subject, 12–13

summary, 6–7, 109, 329, 475,
   489
syllogism, 429n
symbol, 8–9, 137–138, 278

talk, 410
theory, 257, 293, 346, 369
thesis, 13–14, 347, 410
tone, 183
topic of circumstance, 22–24
topic of comparison, 20, 41. *See
   also* analogy; antithesis;
   comparison and contrast
topic of definition, 18–19, 517–
   518. *See also* definition
topic of relationship, 21–22, 392.
   See also cause and effect; past
   time
topic of testimony, 24–26, 230–
   231, 347, 451. *See also*
   aphorism; quotation;
   reference to authorities
trope, 150n

wordiness, 90

To the Student

We regularly revise the books we publish in order to make them better. To do this well we need to know what instructors and students think of the previous edition. At some point your instructor will be asked to comment on *A World of Ideas*; now we would like to hear from you.

Please take a few minutes to complete this questionnaire and send it to Bedford Books of St. Martin's Press, 165 Marlborough Street, Boston, Massachusetts 02116. We promise to listen to what you have to say. Thanks.

School _____

School Location (city, state) _____

Course title _____

Instructor's name _____

Please rate the selections.

	DEFINITELY KEEP	*KEEP*	*DROP*	*NOT ASSIGNED*
Machiavelli, *The Qualities of the Prince*	___	___	___	___
Rousseau, *The Origin of Civil Society*	___	___	___	___
Jefferson, *The Declaration of Independence*	___	___	___	___
Wollstonecraft, *Pernicious Effects Which Arise from the Unnatural Distinctions Established in Society*	___	___	___	___
Marx, *The Communist Manifesto*	___	___	___	___

	DEFINITELY KEEP	KEEP	DROP	NOT ASSIGNED
Thoreau, *A Plea for Captain John Brown*	——	——	——	——
Douglass, from *The Narrative of the Life of Frederick Douglass*	——	——	——	——
King, *Letter from Birmingham Jail*	——	——	——	——
Nietzsche, *Apollonianism and Dionysianism*	——	——	——	——
James, *The Reality of the Unseen*	——	——	——	——
Freud, *Infantile Sexuality*	——	——	——	——
Jung, *The Mother Archetype*	——	——	——	——
Skinner, *What Is Man?*	——	——	——	——
Bacon, *The Four Idols*	——	——	——	——
Darwin, *Natural Selection*	——	——	——	——
Barnett, *Einstein's Relativity*	——	——	——	——
Whitehead, *Religion and Science*	——	——	——	——
Kuhn, *The Essential Tension*	——	——	——	——
Plato, *The Allegory of the Cave*	——	——	——	——
Aristotle, *The Aim of Man*	——	——	——	——
Russell, *A Free Man's Worship*	——	——	——	——

	DEFINITELY KEEP	KEEP	DROP	NOT ASSIGNED
Dewey, *Some Historical Factors in Philosophical Reconstruction*	___	___	___	___
Camus, *The Myth of Sisyphus*	___	___	___	___
Santayana, *The Nature of Beauty*	___	___	___	___
Kepes, *Comments on Art*	___	___	___	___
Langer, *Expressiveness*	___	___	___	___
Bradley, *Poetry for Poetry's Sake*	___	___	___	___
Eliot, *Tradition and the Individual Talent*	___	___	___	___

Did you find the introductions to each writer helpful? How can we improve them? _____

_____

_____

_____

_____

_____

_____

_____

Did your instructor assign the general introduction to the text? If so, did you find it useful? _____

_____

_____

_____

_____

_____

_____

Any general comments or suggestions? _____

_____

_____

_____

_____

_____

_____

_____

Name _____

Mailing Address _____

Date _____